CAMBRIDGE READINGS IN
THE LITERATURE OF MUSIC

General Editors: John Stevens and Peter le Huray

Greek Musical Writings 1

CAMBRIDGE READINGS IN
THE LITERATURE OF MUSIC

Cambridge Readings in the Literature of Music is a series of source materials (original documents in English translation) for students of the history of music. Many of the quotations in the volumes will be substantial, and introductory material will place the passages in context. The period covered will be from antiquity to the present day, with particular emphasis on the nineteenth and twentieth centuries. The series is part of *Cambridge Studies in Music*.

Already published:
Peter le Huray and James Day, *Music and Aesthetics in the Eighteenth and Early-Nineteenth Centuries*

Forthcoming volumes include:

John Stevens, *The Middle Ages*
Bojan Bujić, *1850–1910*
Ian Bent, *Music, Theory and Education 1750–1900*
Ian Bent, *Nineteenth-Century Music Analysis*

Greek Musical Writings

Volume 1
The Musician and his Art

Edited by
Andrew Barker

Lecturer in Philosophy
University of Warwick

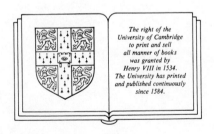

The right of the
University of Cambridge
to print and sell
all manner of books
was granted by
Henry VIII in 1534.
The University has printed
and published continuously
since 1584.

Cambridge University Press

Cambridge
London   New York   New Rochelle
Melbourne   Sydney

Published by the Press Syndicate of the University of Cambridge
The Pitt Building, Trumpington Street, Cambridge CB2 1RP
32 East 57th Street, New York, NY 10022, USA
296 Beaconsfield Parade, Middle Park, Melbourne 3206, Australia

First published 1984

Printed in Great Britain at The Pitman Press, Bath

Library of Congress catalogue card number: 83-20924

British Library Cataloguing in Publication Data
Greek musical writings – (Cambridge readings
in the literature of music)
Vol. 1: The musician and his art
1. Music – Greece   2. Music – Theory
I. Barker, Andrew
781   MT6

ISBN 0 521 23593 6

Contents

Illustrations

The author and publisher are grateful to the following for permission to reproduce illustrations: the Museum, Heraklion (3); the Ethnic Archaeological Museum, Athens (4); the Staatliches Museum Schwerin (8); the Museum of Fine Arts, Boston (10); the Trustees of the British Museum (11, 13, 15); The Staatliche Antikensammlungen und Glyptothek München (14); the Soprintendenza Archeologica dell puglia (16, 18); the Muzeo nazionale, Taranto (17, 19).

Authors and passages quoted

Acknowledgements

Very many scholars have contributed to my work on these books, either through their published writings or through conversation and correspond-ence. I cannot mention them all individually, but I have two particular debts to acknowledge. Though Greek music was not his speciality, it was G. E. L. Owen who first sparked off my interest in the subject, and encouraged my early investigations. His death is a loss to all classicists, not only students of philosophy. Professor R. P. Winnington-Ingram is in this field indisputably the master of those who know. His published work has been a source of insight and illumination, and he has been an unfailingly tolerant and generous correspondent. In the second of these volumes, even more than in the first, I owe to him a major part of such understanding of the material as I have: my misunderstandings should not be laid at his door.

I am grateful to the University of Warwick for the period of sabbatical leave during which much of the preliminary spade-work was done. I should like to thank Marie Sadler for the care with which she helped to sift some of the Hellenistic sources, and Melanie Cable-Alexander and Simon Whittaker for their work on the drawings. The staff of Cambridge University Press have dealt with my difficult typescript with sympathy and skill. My thanks are due especially to Rosemary Dooley and Susan Moore for their patience and resourcefulness in guiding me through the mysteries involved in preparing a book for publication.

During the years in which these volumes and their offshoots have been developing, my efforts have been encouraged and my preoccupation cheer-fully tolerated by my family, and especially by my wife, Jill. The books are dedicated to her with love and gratitude.

Texts and abbreviations

On the editions used as a basis for the translations see pp. 3–4 below. It has seemed unnecessary to give a list of the works and editions of the majority of Greek writers cited in the notes. Names of authors, and titles of both ancient and modern works, are abbreviated in ways that are standard or otherwise self-explanatory. An exception may usefully be made in the case of the technical writings of the Greek musicologists: I have mentioned below all those to which my commentary refers, explaining the system of reference I have adopted in each case. An asterisk against the name of a work indicates that a translation of it, in whole or in part, will appear in the second volume. These titles are followed by a list of other abbreviations that might require explanation.

Anon. Bell.	*Anonyma de Musica Scripta Bellermania* ed. D. Najock, Leipzig 1975. Cited by section number.
*Arist. Quint.	Aristides Quintilianus, *De Musica* ed. R. P. Winnington-Ingram, Leipzig 1963. Cited by Winnington-Ingram's page and line numbers.
*Aristox. *El. Harm.*	Aristoxenus, *Elementa Harmonica* ed. R. da Rios, Rome 1954. Cited by Meibom's page and line numbers.
Bacch.	Bacchius, *Eisagoge*, in C. von Jan, *Musici Scriptores Graeci*, Leipzig 1895. Cited by Jan's page and line numbers.
Cleonides	Cleonides, *Eisagoge*, in Jan op. cit. Cited by Jan's page and line numbers.
Gaudentius	Gaudentius, *Eisagoge*, in Jan op. cit. Cited by Jan's page and line numbers.
*Nicom.	Nicomachus, *Encheiridion* and *Excerpta ex Nicomacho*, in Jan op. cit. Cited by Jan's page and line numbers.
Philodemus	Philodemus, *De Musica* ed. J. Kemke, Leipzig 1884. Cited by Kemke's page and line numbers, sometimes also by fragment numbers.
Pollux	Pollux, *Onomastikon* ed. E. Bethe, Leipzig 1900. Cited by book and section numbers.
*Porph. *Comm.*	Porphyry, *Commentary on Ptolemy's Harmonics* ed. I. Düring, Göteborg 1932. Cited by Düring's page and line numbers.

*Ptol. *Harm.**	Ptolemy, *Harmonics* ed. I. Düring, Göteborg 1930. Cited by Düring's page and line numbers.
Theon Smyrn.	Theon Smyrnaeus, *De Musica* ed. E. Hiller, Leipzig 1878. Cited by Hiller's page and line numbers.
Sect. Can.	(Euclid) *Sectio Canonis*, in Jan op. cit. Cited by Jan's page and line numbers.
d	ditone.
DK	H. Diels and W. Kranz, *Die Fragmente der Vorsokratiker*, 8th edition, Berlin 1956–59.
Jacoby	F. Jacoby, *Fragmente der griechischen Historiker*, Berlin 1923.
Kock	T. Kock, *Comicorum Atticorum Fragmenta*, Leipzig 1880–8.
Lasserre	*Plutarque de la Musique* ed. F. Lasserre, Olten and Lausanne 1954.
Lobel–Page	*Poetarum Lesbiorum Fragmenta* eds. E. Lobel and D. Page, Oxford 1955.
LSJ	*A Greek–English Lexicon* compiled by H. G. Liddell and R. Scott, revised by H. S. Jones, Oxford 1968.
P.M.G.	*Poetae Melici Graeci* ed. D. Page, Oxford 1962.
q	quarter-tone.
s	semitone.
t	tone.
W. and R.	*Plutarque: de la Musique*, eds. H. Weil and T. Reinach, Paris 1900.

+ (when it follows a letter representing a note of the modern scale) indicates that the note is raised by a quarter-tone.

$\frac{1}{4}$, $\frac{1}{8}$, etc. in lists of musical intervals indicate fractions of a tone.

Bold numerals are used to number the passages quoted in this volume. In the notes and Appendices, references to passages by number are usually followed by the names of author and work, and a more precise indication of the portion of the text to which reference is being made. Thus, for example, passage **27** is the whole of Pindar's twelfth Pythian Ode: line 13 of the Ode would be referred to in the form **27** Pindar, *Pyth.* 12.13.

Transliteration of Greek words

Certain Greek words are spelled differently in different dialects, or at the whim of individual authors. In transliterating them I have normally retained the form given in the manuscripts. Note especially that '*ss*' is interchangeable with '*tt*' (so that e.g. '*glōssa*' = '*glōtta*'), and the prefix '*xyn-*' is equivalent to '*syn-*' (so that e.g. '*xynaulia*' = '*synaulia*'). A long '*a*' sometimes replaces '*ē*'. Greek has different letters for short and long '*e*' and short and long '*o*': except in proper names I have indicated the long forms by a line over the vowel. The Greek upsilon is usually represented by '*y*', but in diphthongs and occasionally elsewhere by '*u*'. Proper names are generally given in 'Latinised' form (e.g. 'Thucydides' rather than 'Thoukydides'): in particular, the letter '*c*' is used here for the Greek kappa, whereas in transliterating words other than proper names I have used '*k*'. The letter chi always appears as '*ch*'.

Introduction

There can be no doubt of the importance of music in the life of the ancient Greeks: it pervaded every aspect of their private and social existence. The sophistication of their own attitudes to it, and the towering stature of the poetry and drama for which it was often the vehicle have enticed many Hellenists and musicians into the attempt to recapture its forms and characters. But though the centuries have seen the spilling of much scholarly ink, and many imaginative musical reconstructions, we are still far from achieving an adequate understanding.

I do not believe, however, that our resources are yet exhausted. Both the study of archaeological material, especially vase paintings, and the science of comparative ethnomusicology, may in the future bear further fruits, the more so if they are pursued by competent practical musicians. Our most valuable source of information, however, and that against which all hypotheses based on other evidence must in the end be tested, remains the literary material, the writings of the Greeks themselves. We can have no other reliable guide to the structures and genres of musical composition, and it is here that we shall find expressions of the emotions and ideas with which the Greeks approached their music, reflecting their conceptions of its significance, its roles in social and moral life and in the play of the passions, its relation to the other arts and sciences, and the canons of judgement by which it is to be assessed.

The task of the present volume and its sequel is to make a collection of these writings more accessible to English-speaking readers. All the translations are new. A few of the texts have not previously been translated; and while English versions of the majority of passages in this volume do exist, they are not in the main specifically designed for musical purposes. Not infrequently they misrepresent or gloss over details which the historian of music needs to have made as precise as possible. Many of the excerpts collected here are by no means inaccessible elsewhere, but consist of scattered remarks embedded in works whose principal theme is not music, and need to be laboriously tracked down: it may at least be a convenience to have some of them gathered together.

The writings that have come down to us fall broadly into three major categories. First, there are those that describe or evoke features of the practical activities of music-making and composition. These include passages taken from the poets and dramatists, who were of course their own composers, more or less casual remarks made by historians and essayists of every description, and the deliberate attempts at analysis and historical reconstruction made by scholars and compilers of later antiquity. Secondly there are those that attempt a more reflective and broadly-based investigation of the social, psychological and moral functions of music, particularly in the context of education. Here the principal authors are the philosophers, together with various other social commentators and critics: the comic dramatist Aristophanes is a good example. Their discussions, and particularly their vivid attacks on contemporary attitudes and practices, not only offer intriguing and sophisticated hypotheses about the matters in hand, but also dispense, in passing, a rich collection of facts about the phenomena they criticise. Finally there are the technical works of the ancient harmonic and acoustic theorists, who deliberately set out to describe, analyse and reduce to order the data presented in musical practice. Their writings are plainly of very great value, though they pose endless problems of interpretation. But we must be wary of relying on them uncritically as giving us representations, however abstract, of any actual music. The science of harmonics, within two different and rival traditions, rapidly became an autonomous field of intellectual enquiry, and tended to detach itself from any substantial contact with the facts of contemporary performance.

Of these categories of writing, the first and second are the subject of the present volume, the third being reserved for its successor. As a result, certain versatile authors (notably Plato and Aristotle) will be represented in both. But the categories inevitably overlap. Material in one volume will need interpretation in the light of discussions in the other: and because I thought it best to present certain passages and some whole treatises in their complete state, a few short discussions of harmonic theory appear, anomalously, in the first volume, while a substantial essay on music in education, for instance, will be found with the rest of Aristides Quintilianus in Volume 2. I have done my best to make these passages comprehensible where they occur, through brief discussions in the footnotes.

There could be no question of collecting all the references to music in the writings of Greek antiquity, or even a high proportion of them. The process of selection is inevitably based to some extent on the compiler's own tastes and interests. I have allowed little space, for example, to the historians of the fifth century or the orators of the fourth, preferring to give adequate representation to the poet-composers themselves, and to the philosophers. I have concentrated on material relevant to the study of the period from the time of Homer to the end of the fourth century: music of the Hellenistic and Roman periods falls, for the most part, outside the scope of these books. The choice is not arbitrary. Modern opinion has rightly treated the earlier period as containing the highest achievements of Greek civilisation, and the Greeks of later antiquity themselves unanimously looked to it for the wonderful and truly Greek music that their own age had lost. When Greek authors of Roman times write seriously about music, it is the music of a much earlier phase of their culture that they have in mind, usually that of the sixth and fifth centuries. Hence the two authors quoted at length in the present volume who belong to the first centuries of our own era (pseudo-Plutarch and

Athenaeus) are not out of place. They are concerned with the music of their own day hardly at all, but are trying to review such evidence as they had concerning musical practices and theories that were current centuries earlier. When they speak of 'modern music', it is to Timotheus and his associates in the fifth century or the Theban auletes of the fourth that they are most likely to be referring.

Two further features of this volume call for some explanation. First, there are two chapters (Chapters 4 and 7) which are independent essays, rather than collections of source material. They attempt to sketch the principal developments in musical practice during two crucial phases, drawing on a variety of sources, some of which are quoted elsewhere in the book (particularly in Chapters 8, 10, 15 and 16). The purpose of this anomalous treatment was to maintain a more or less continuous chronological flow through the bulk of the volume. Our evidence for the phases of music in question is largely embedded in works of a different period, intertwined with passages concerning other times and other matters: the alternatives to the policy I have adopted were either to dismember such treatises as those of ps.-Plutarch and Athenaeus, relocating each fragment in a chapter devoted to the period to which it relates, or else to abandon all hope of preserving chronological sequence. The former could hardly have been achieved without loss of both content and context: the latter would make the reader's task unnecessarily difficult.

Secondly, I have tried to allow the Greek authors to speak, as far as possible, for themselves. This statement may seem perverse, considering the proliferation of footnotes with which some of the passages are festooned. The notes, however, seek to make what the authors say accessible, rather than to add substantially to its content. They try to interpret for English-speaking students points that hang directly on features of the Greek language, or on unfamiliar aspects of Greek cultural practice. They also attempt to elucidate obscure features of what one Greek author says by reference to remarks made by others, whether the latter are represented in this collection or not: in this way they offer a modest guide to the Greek literature as a whole. It seemed inappropriate, however, in a book of this nature, to provide an extensive guide to modern studies on the subject, or to expound and adjudicate in modern controversies. It has of course been necessary on occasion to broach controversial issues: where these demanded treatment at length, they have been relegated to appendices. On such matters I have outlined my own views, and referred briefly to other interpretations: these abbreviated discussions should not be mistaken for full scholarly analyses of the matters in question, nor should the references to modern authors be mistaken for attempts at constructing a complete bibliography.

In preparing the translations I have of course consulted various scholarly editions of the texts. But in order to make it possible for readers with some knowledge of Greek to refer readily to the versions of the texts that I have translated, I have treated as the basis for the translations the editions that are most easily to be found, mentioning in the footnotes the points at which I have preferred a different reading. For the Aristotelian *Problems*, Theophrastus, Strabo, ps.-Plutarch and Athenaeus I have used the Loeb editions, for Pollux the Teubner edition, for the Hibeh musical papyrus the text printed by Grenfell and Hunt (see Ch. 12 n. 1), for Sappho the text in Lobel–Page, and for Timotheus that in *P.M.G.* All the other translations are based on the Oxford Classical Texts.

Any understanding of the texts requires a familiarity with the general nature of the musical instruments that the Greeks employed. Some points of detail are discussed in footnotes to relevant pieces of text, but it seems appropriate, as a preliminary, to offer a rough sketch of the main types, if only to clear up a few pervasive misconceptions.

The principal stringed instruments are designated by the names *phorminx*, *kithara*, *lyra* and *barbitos*. I shall follow the practice of the late Greek commentators and most modern scholars, and use these words to refer to instruments of four fairly distinct types, though many Greek literary writers employed them quite indiscriminately (see Ch. 1 n. 19, with the references given there).

All four instruments consisted of a sound-box, to which two arms were attached, the arms being joined by a crossbar near the end furthest from the sound-box (Fig. 1). The strings were usually made of twisted gut: they were of equal length, differing only in thickness and tension, and ran from an attachment at the bottom of the box, over a bridge, and up to the crossbar, to which they were fixed by strips of raw leather (*kollopes*). The *kollopes* were twisted on the bar to adjust tension. The instruments were held by their performers in any of a number of positions, but always to the left side of the body, commonly supported by a cloth band running from the base of the instrument's outer arm to the player's left wrist. They were usually played with a large plectrum, held in the player's right hand: the fingers of the left hand were also employed, both to pick out melodic figures, and to damp strings that were not required to sound when the plectrum was swept across the whole set. The earliest instruments of the Archaic period had three or four strings, though pictures from Minoan times in Crete, centuries before, show examples with seven. Seven became the norm from the seventh century, but professional performers in the sixth and especially the fifth centuries added more: we hear of instruments with as many as twelve, but these were reckoned scandalous by conservatives and were always exceptional. Ordinary instruments continued to have seven or eight.

The technique required to support the instrument in the proper position, while leaving the fingers of the left hand free to damp and pluck, is not altogether simple, particularly with an instrument as large as the concert *kithara*. What is involved can be seen in outline in Figs. 9 and 10. My own experiments suggest that the lower corner of the *kithara* must be trapped against the player's body by his left elbow: the tension of the cloth band,

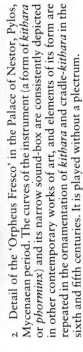

2 Detail of the 'Orpheus Fresco' in the Palace of Nestor, Pylos, Mycenaean period. The curves of the instrument (a form of *kithara* or *phorminx*) and its narrow sound-box are consistently depicted in other contemporary works of art, and elements of its form are repeated in the ornamentation of *kithara* and cradle-*kithara* in the sixth and fifth centuries. It is played without a plectrum.

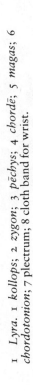

1 *Lyra*. 1 *kollops*; 2 *zygon*; 3 *pēchys*; 4 *chordē*; 5 *magas*; 6 *chordotonion*; 7 plectrum; 8 cloth band for wrist.

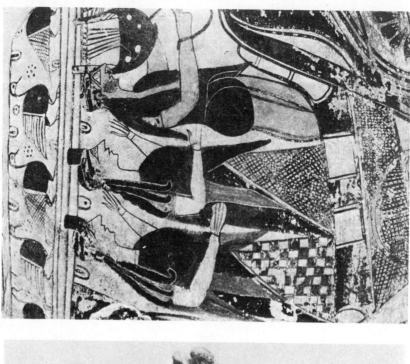

4 A procession of singers, representing Apollo and the Muses. The instrument has the simple shape of the old *phorminx*, but seven strings, and is played with a plectrum. From Melos, third

3 Bronze statuette of a musician with four-stringed *phorminx*, probably a minstrel of the kind described by Homer. From Crete, late eighth century.

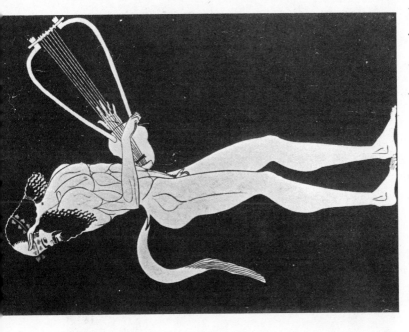

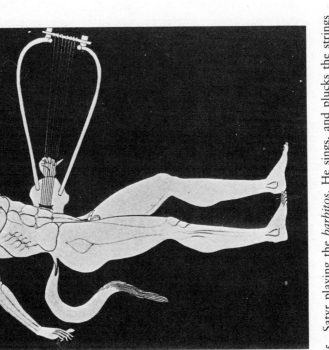

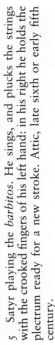

6 The satyr has swept the plectrum across the strings, damping some with the fingers of the left hand. From the same vase as Fig. 5.

5 Satyr playing the *barbitos*. He sings, and plucks the strings with the crooked fingers of his left hand: in his right he holds the plectrum ready for a new stroke. Attic, late sixth or early fifth century.

8 Music lesson with tortoiseshell *lyrai*. The young pupil is the legendary musician Linus, but the scene is drawn from the common educational practices of the fifth century. An elaborate cradle-*kithara* hangs behind the players. Attic, about 475 B.C.

7 Eros with tortoiseshell *lyra*. In his right hand he holds an *aulos*-case, showing the places for two pipes and the separate compartment for *holmoi* and reeds. Attic, late sixth or early fifth century.

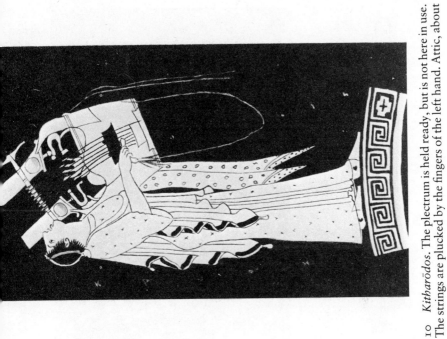

9 *Kitharōdos*, with concert *kithara* of the fully developed type. The upturned head of the singer is characteristic. The plectrum has just been swept across the strings, some of which are damped by the fingers of the left hand, which also supports the instrument by means of a cloth band round the wrist. Attic, late sixth or early fifth century.

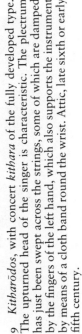

10 *Kitharōdos*. The plectrum is held ready, but is not here in use. The strings are plucked by the fingers of the left hand. Attic, about 480 B.C.

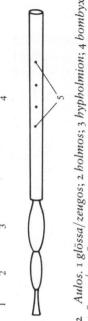

12 Aulos. 1 glōssa/zeugos; 2 holmos; 3 hypholmion; 4 bombyx; 5 trēmata/trypēmata.

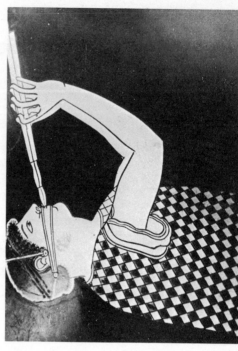

13 Aulete dressed for competition. He wears the *phorbeia* to support his cheeks. *Holmos* and *hypholmion* are clearly shown: the reed is entirely inside the player's mouth. Attic, about 480 B.C.

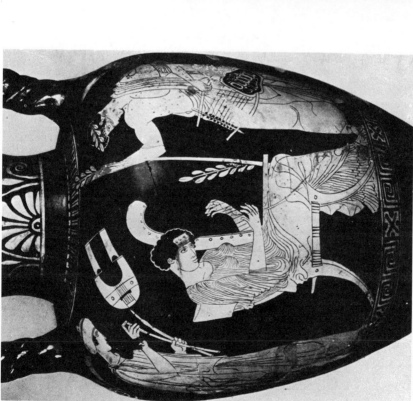

11 A Muse plays one of the commoner types of harp, plucking with the fingers of both hands. Behind her, another fits a new reed to one of her *auloi*. Musaeus holds an eight-stringed tortoiseshell

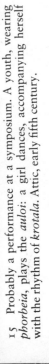

15 Probably a performance at a symposium. A youth, wearing *phorbeia*, plays the *auloi*: a girl dances, accompanying herself with the rhythm of *krotala*. Attic, early fifth century.

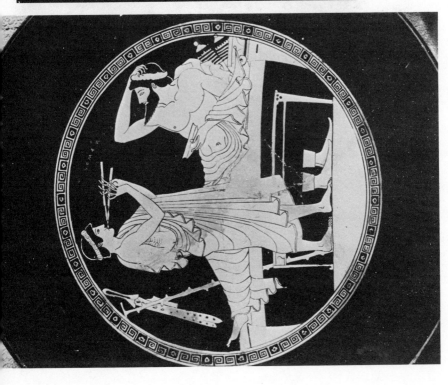

14 Symposium scene. A youth plays the *auloi*, without *phorbeia*, while reclining guest sings. A case for *auloi* hangs on the wall. Attic, about 480 B.C.

16 Performance for a symposium, closely similar to that described by Xenophon. Girls perform acrobatic dances, accompanied by *auloi* and *krotala*. Attic, about 440 B.C.

17 Maenads playing *auloi* and dancing before Dionysus. Italian, late fifth century.

19 Dancers at the Tarentine festival of the Carneia. Italian, late fifth century.

18 Maenads dancing and playing the *tympanon*. Italian, late fifth century.

which needs to be carefully adjusted, is used to pull the instrument towards
the body, and also to steady the sound-box against the player's left forearm.
The arm must then be held still. The left hand can move a little from the
wrist, but most of its work must be done by independent movements of the
fingers alone. It may be the restrictions imposed by this technique that
explain why the strings of Greek instruments in this family are always set
closely together, within the span of a hand: those of some early Middle
Eastern lyres are placed much further apart.

Of the four types, what I shall call the *phorminx* (Figs. 3 and 4) belongs
principally to the Homeric bards and their immediate successors. The name
survived, applied to more developed forms, but professionals abandoned the
instrument at quite an early date, though it never entirely disappeared. Its
most direct descendant in terms of shape and structure seems to be the
so-called cradle-*kithara* (Figs. 8 and 11), of which an ancestor existed in
Mycenaean times (Fig. 2). This style of instrument, in a number of variants,
was redeveloped in the seventh century and continued in use down to the
fifth at least, but from the sixth century, if not earlier, what we may call the
kithara proper, or concert *kithara* (Figs. 9 and 10), was almost always preferred for the purpose of public performance. Apart from its strings and
kollopes, this instrument, like the *phorminx* and the cradle-*kithara*, was
wooden throughout: it was quite large, often a metre or more in height, solid
in construction, and capable of producing a substantial volume of sound.
The *lyra* (Figs. 7, 8 and 11) is well known. Its sound-box was made from a
tortoiseshell, or sometimes from wood carved and painted to represent tortoiseshell, its opening being covered with a membrane of thin hide. Its arms
were usually wooden, but sometimes made from an animal's horns. (Its
construction is described in detail in **21** *Hymn to Hermes*.) It was a light
instrument, soft in timbre, used mainly for private, small-scale music-
making, and in the system of general education that was intended to instil
the cultural awareness proper to a citizen, rather than any professional
expertise. Finally, the *barbitos* or *barbiton* (Figs. 5 and 6) may be conceived
of as an elongated and reshaped *lyra*. Its sound-box remained small, but its
much longer arms gave it a deeper pitch and a fuller sound. It was associated
especially with the revelries dedicated to Dionysus, and in vase paintings its
players are usually satyrs, or men dressed as satyrs. The *kithara* appears
sometimes as a solo instrument in its own right, and *kitharai* and *lyrai* were
also used in purely instrumental performances in conjunction with wind
instruments. But the principal role of all four types was in the accompaniment of the human voice.

The most important wind instrument was the *aulos* (Fig. 12), whose name
is commonly but quite misleadingly translated 'flute'. It was in fact a reed
instrument, usually, if not always, equipped with a 'double reed' comparable
to that of the modern oboe. 'Single' or 'beating' reeds of the clarinet type
may have been known in our period, but the evidence is inconclusive. (On the
mouthpiece of this instrument see particularly **163** Theophrastus, *Hist.*

Plant. IV.11.1–7.) Of more modern instruments the one that resembles the *aulos* most closely is probably the shawm. Like all such instruments, its performance required considerable muscular effort: Greek auletes commonly wore a strap called the *phorbeia* to support the muscles of their cheeks.

The *aulos* is mentioned by Homer, but it seems to have become fully established in Greece during the seventh century. (Most Greek writers trace its origins to Phrygia.) In outline, it consisted of a reed fitted to a bulbous section of tube called the *holmos*, below which came a second, short section known as the *hypholmion*, this in turn being attached to the main pipe. The bore of this pipe was usually cylindrical, and would therefore have produced notes of a deeper pitch than a conical bore of similar length. It had finger-holes, often (but not always) drilled into the side of the pipe, rather than the top. The earliest *auloi* had four such holes, one for each finger, since each *aulos* was fingered with one hand, and the thumb was generally used only to support the instrument. (Thumb-holes do exist on some surviving pipes.) Perhaps in the later sixth century, and certainly in the fifth and fourth, devices for opening and closing extra finger-holes were developed: these took the form of metal collars that could be rotated by a movement of the finger. By the fifth century, possibly earlier, the principle of the 'speaker hole' was also known and employed, to give easier access to the upper harmonics (see **25** Strabo 9.3.10 and especially **187** ps.-Plut. 1138b). The pipes of these instruments were made from a wide variety of materials, usually wood, sometimes bone or horn, occasionally reed, metal, or even pottery.

Auloi were almost always played in pairs, each *aulos* being a self-contained, separate instrument (Figs. 12–17). Their mouthpieces were held side by side in the player's mouth. Sometimes the two pipes were of equal size, sometimes not: in the latter case the left-hand *aulos* seems always to have been the larger. The purpose of this practice is a matter of dispute, and probably it had no single, invariable function. It is likely that one pipe sometimes supplied the melody of the other with a 'moving drone' accompaniment; but there are indications that both might have had fully melodic parts to play.

Very many varieties of *auloi* are distinguished by our sources, though we cannot now be sure of the precise character of all of them. (See particularly the discussions in Athenaeus, 188–9.) In general, the music of the *aulos* was dramatic and emotional: it was versatile in mood and effect, capable of blaring vigour, plangent lamentation or sensual suggestiveness, and was used to create vivid and diverse forms of 'representation'. *Auloi* had notable roles in solo concert performance, in the drama, and in the flamboyant and ecstatic dancing of the cults of Dionysus and Cybele (Figs. 14–17), but there were in fact few niches in Greek culture where they did not have some part to play. Their range extended from the accompaniment of athletic events, through dancing of all sorts, to the often lascivious entertainments of drunken dinner-parties (Figs. 14–16). It was their emotional effectiveness that was their outstanding characteristic, endearing them to their performers and to the bulk of the public, but earning them the vigorous disapproval of such conservative moralisers and social theorists as Plato.

Of the other melodic instruments used by the Greeks, the one most commonly mentioned is the *syrinx* or 'Pan-pipe'. It had little or no place in serious 'art' music (i.e., in the Greek context, the music of the elaborate religious festivals and competitions), and was largely confined to pastoral or 'folk' settings. Its general structure is too well known to need discussion here (but see further 121–8 with notes, and 175 ps.-Ar. *Probs.* XIX.23). It was probably from the *syrinx* that the principle of the organ was originally derived (see the discussion of the *hydraulis*, the 'water-organ', in 188 Ath. 174a ff). This form of the *syrinx* is properly called the 'many-reeded' (*polykalamos*) *syrinx*: a single-pipe (*monokalamos*) *syrinx* was also used, in similar contexts. It had finger-holes like the *aulos*, but was blown, like the Pan-pipe, across the open end of the tube, without a mouthpiece of any sort. Whether the Greeks had anything comparable to a true flute is uncertain: see 188 Ath. 174b and 175e ff, with notes, on the subject of the *monaulos* and the *phōtinx*. The only other wind instrument of any significance was the *salpinx*, a kind of trumpet: it was an instrument of martial summons, or used to give signals at the games, very seldom considered as a means of creating music.

As to stringed instruments, various other types were known. Fifth-century vase paintings show a number of forms of harp (one form is shown in Fig. 11), and harps are mentioned by our literary sources in a number of contexts. The generic term for a harp is *psaltērion*, literally 'plucked instrument', and as this designation suggests they were usually plucked with the fingers of both hands, not struck with a plectrum. At times they may have been quite widespread, but they were always treated as essentially foreign. Our sources often speak also of 'many-stringed' instruments as a general class, and it is harps that they usually seem to have in mind. But difficulties arise as soon as we try to identify the special types of harp to which the plethora of more specific names refer, names such as *trigōnos*, *pēktis*, *magadis*, *sambykē*. With the possible exception of *trigōnos*, we have no clear and unambiguous description of any of these instruments, and cannot readily match the names to the types shown in the surviving pictures. Though all of them are called 'many-stringed' by at least some sources, others appear to contradict this description: it is possible, for instance, that the *sambykē* was not a harp at all (see 196 Ath. 633f ff). In any case it seems likely that the sources are not using the names consistently: some of our later authorities patently fail to understand them.

Necked instruments, comparable to the guitar or lute, also existed, though they were not common and our literary and iconographical evidence is slight. The usual word for such an instrument is *pandoura*: see 188 Ath. 183f. Neither it nor the more pervasive harps attained a substantial stature in Greek music-making: with a few local and temporary exceptions (e.g. 196

Ath. 635a–b) they seem to have been largely confined to private and domestic entertainments. Peculiar new importations from abroad sometimes had a short-lived public vogue as curiosities, as did inventions such as the *epigoneion* (perhaps a sort of zither: see **188** Ath. 183c–d) and the extraordinary contrivance known as the *tripous* (**196** Ath. 637b–f): but the *kithara* and the *aulos* remained unchallenged, to the end of our period, as the only serious instruments of public music.

As well as melodic instruments, percussion was widely employed. Its main role, naturally enough, was as an accompaniment to dancing, and it attained a special prominence in the wilder and more ecstatic rituals of the mystery cults, especially the predominantly female cult of Cybele. There, and hardly less in the revels of Dionysus, it was as essential an ingredient as the *aulos*. References to cymbals (*kymbala*) and small hand-drums or tambourines (*tympana*, Fig. 18) are common, but the instruments mentioned and depicted most often are *krotala* or *krembala*, hand-held clappers comparable to castanets, but substantially larger (Figs. 15 and 16). They were usually wooden, sometimes metal: shells or pieces of pottery could serve the same purpose. They appear as accompaniments to dance of all sorts, public and private, not only in cult; but there are suggestions in some authors (e.g. **140** Aristoph. *Frogs* 1304–7) that they went with a type of music that was orgiastic and unseemly, not elevated and dignified. They are natural associates of Dionysus and the *aulos*, rather than Apollo and the *kithara*.

CHAPTER I

Homer

Though the *Iliad* and the *Odyssey* are the earliest works of Greek literature that we possess, they preserve the memory of a civilisation and a tradition of epic poetry that is more than five hundred years older. Versions of these heroic tales had been told at the courts of Mycenaean kings, and reflected the social forms and ideals of their time: but they survived on the lips of story-tellers and minstrels through the centuries of darkness and confusion that followed the downfall of their culture. No doubt they underwent various changes during this long period, each minstrel presenting the material afresh, to suit his own vision and the sensibilities of his audience: but the formulaic techniques of oral poetry, together with an enduring nostalgia for the golden age that the epics described, probably ensured that these changes were not great, and that they appeared more as additions of descriptive detail and minor narrative episodes than as modifications of real substance. In the new prosperity of the eighth century, or just possibly the ninth, the poet or poets known to us as Homer created, from these materials of traditional theme, metre and language, the two great epics in a form very close to that in which we now have them. Of Homer himself we know nothing at all: the stories told about him in later antiquity are the merest fictions.

The earlier poems were composed and transmitted by word of mouth. They were designed originally for performance in a king's hall over the wine, in the manner that Homer himself describes. They were chanted by a professional minstrel, accompanying himself on the stringed instrument which Homer calls the *phorminx*. The same method of performance probably survived into Homer's own time, though the great courts had gone: we know that musical renderings of epics were used and elaborated in the seventh century by Terpander and Archilochus, and Hesiod certainly sang, even if not all his works were performed in that way. But the context of performance had changed, and a new method of presentation had also grown up alongside the old. Homer's poems were not designed as after-dinner entertainments, but as pieces for performance in the great public festivals that took place in various Greek centres from the eighth century onwards, being recited in their entirety in the quadrennial festival at Delos, and later (from the middle of the sixth century) at the Panathenaea in Athens. (It was probably at this time that a canonical text was firmly established and written down, though writing had certainly played a part in their earlier transmission, and quite possibly even in their composition.)

The fact that they were recited indicates the major change in the form of epic performance. The reciters were called *rhapsōdoi*: their performances were spoken, not sung, and they used no instruments. They were not, like the minstrels Homer describes, poets or composers themselves: they recited other people's work, especially epic, and the festivals, great and small, were their main forum, perhaps their only one. (Such festivals included occasional events, such as the funeral games of a king mentioned at 15 Hesiod, *W.D.* 650 ff, and many minor but regular local celebrations, as well as the famous gatherings that attracted performers from all over the Greek world.) This method of presenting Homer retained its popularity throughout antiquity. But whether or not the line of continuity with the Mycenaean minstrels had been broken, a musical method of performing epic certainly existed, as we have seen, n the seventh century, and persisted alongside the rhapsodic style. The two methods were in fact scarcely rivals, since musical performances, by contrast with those of the *rhapsōdoi*, attempted only relatively short passages, and must have been conceived and appreciated in a very different way. In the hands of Terpander and Archilochus, and their successors, musical performances of Homeric excerpts were transformed from bardic chantings into fully melodic pieces for a solo singer, accompanying himself on the *kithara*, and they made a major contribution to the development of what later authors call the kitharodic *nomos* (see particularly Ch. 15, Appendix A). By the sixth century this kitharodic style had become a sophisticated and technically elaborate musical vehicle of dramatic expression.

Homer's exalted status in later Greek culture was not founded only on his role as the favourite author of works for public performance: his poems were also learned by ordinary citizens as a normal and essential part of their general education. It would be hard to exaggerate their influence in establishing and perpetuating the framework of self-image and ideal that underpinned the special character of Greek society. They were the touchstone of all good poetry and drama; but more importantly they were for centuries the basis of every civilised person's conception of a man's stature in the order of things, of the values by which he should live, and of his relation to the gods and the forces of nature.

(1) Iliad

> Whether it took a religious or a secular form, music was, for the Greeks, primarily an accompaniment and an expression of joy. Hence it is not surprising that the *Iliad*, a story of war, pain, doom and hardship, has few allusions to music, and of these the most significant occur in passages not directly concerned with themes of battle. There are some minor exceptions. Agamemnon hears the Trojans playing *auloi* and *syringes* at night by their campfires (II.11–13). The *salpinx* has a mention (XVIII.219), but it is an instrument of military summons, not of music. More importantly, there are two references to the 'paean', illustrating two of the main senses of this versatile word. *Paiōn* is a title of Apollo, and means 'Healer' (cf. e.g. 100 Eurip. *Ion* 125–7): as in 1 below, a paean may be a prayer for healing or deliverance (cf. e.g. 101 Eurip. *Heracles* 820–1, 102 Soph. *O.T.* 4–5). It may also be a song of victory, when deliverance has come: this is its role in 2. (Cf. e.g. 75 Soph. *Trach.* 205–21, 76 Eurip. *Heracles* 674–96.) Tragedy offers a number of variants on these main senses: see particularly 103–9, and cf. also 20 *Hymn to Apollo* 516–19, Plato, *Symp.* 177a.

I   *Iliad* 1.472–3

> The Greek army has been smitten with a plague for an offence against Apollo. The wrong has been righted, and the priest Chryses petitions Apollo to end the plague. His prayer is followed by sacrifice, and then by a hearty meal.

And all day long the young Achaeans sought to please the god with song and dance,[1] singing a beautiful paean, celebrating far-working Apollo in song;[2] and he heard it and was delighted in his heart.

[1] The word *molpē* usually designates the combined activity of singing and dancing, though the emphasis is on song: it is sometimes linked with an additional word meaning 'dance', as at 9 *Od.* 1.152.

[2] 'Celebrating in song' translates *melpontes*, from the verb cognate with *molpē*.

2   *Iliad* XXII.391–4

From Achilles' speech to the Greeks, after he has killed Hector.

'Come now, Achaean warriors, let us go to the hollow ships, carrying this corpse and singing a paean: we have won great glory: we have killed magnificent Hector, whom the Trojans used to acclaim like a god in their city.'[3]

> Despite its close connections with joyfulness, music also had a place in lamentation, though it is music of a very specialised kind. The later books of the *Iliad* have a number of brief references to the practices involved in mourning, and one major set piece, at the end of the whole work.

3   *Iliad* XXIV.719–76 (excerpts)

The Trojans' lament for Hector.

When they had brought him into the splendid palace, they laid him on a bed, worked with the auger, and beside it they placed singers to be leaders[4] of the laments. They sang a melancholy dirge, and the women wailed in answer. White-armed Andromache led the women's lament,[5] cradling in her hands the head of man-killing Hector: 'Husband, you are dead before your time . . .'[6]

[746]   Thus she spoke, weeping, and the women wailed in answer. Next, Hecabe led them in the loud lament: 'Hector, of all my children much the dearest to my heart . . .'

[760]   Thus she spoke, weeping, and aroused uncontrollable cries. Then, thirdly, Helen led them in the lament: 'Hector, dearest to my heart of all my husband's brothers . . .'

[776]   Thus she spoke, weeping, and the countless people groaned in answer.

---

[3]   The last two sentences are probably intended to represent the words of the paean.
[4]   *Exarchoi.* These laments, of which there are good later examples in fifth-century tragedy, were antiphonal, the leader (*exarchos*) uttering a phrase or sometimes an extended song of lamentation, the other mourners responding with exclamations or sentences of grief. The latter element is expressed here by 'the women wailed in answer': in Homer much the larger part is given to the leader. The *Iliad* contains several other instances: see XVIII.50 ff, 316, XXIII.17. For some examples in tragedy see 41 Aesch. *Persae* 1038 ff, 42 Eurip. *Helen* 164 ff, 44 *Phoen.* 1033 ff, 51 *I.T.* 179 ff, cf. Aesch. *Suppl.* 71–8, 1022 ff, Eurip. *Suppl.* 798 ff. A similar relation between leader and chorus exists in many other forms of song and dance. See e.g. 7 *Il.* XVIII.605–6, 19 and 20 *Hymn to Apollo* 182–206, 513–23, 65 Eurip. *Bacch.* 151 ff, 85 *Heracles* 760 ff, cf. Sappho, frs. 111, 140 (Lobel–Page), Aesch. *Eum.* 1035 ff.
[5]   That is, she acted as first *exarchos* for the women. This seems to record a separate stage in the mourning, since the *exarchoi* mentioned previously are men, and their description as *aoidoi*, 'singers', strongly suggests that they are professionals, or at least accredited experts, not simply members of the family. (*Aoidos* is the regular word for a 'minstrel' or professional singer throughout Homer.) For professional mourners in fifth century literature see e.g. 37 Aesch. *Persae* 935–40, 38 *Choeph.* 423 ff.
[6]   Andromache's lament is a substantial piece, taking up the next 21 lines. Hecabe has 12 lines, and Helen 14.

But the principal references to music deal with occasions proper to peacetime, or at least not specific to war. Book IX contains our earliest clear mention of purely private music-making.

4   *Iliad* IX.182–94

Ajax and Odysseus have been sent to try to persuade Achilles to abandon his quarrel with Agamemnon.

The two of them walked along the shore of the loud-roaring sea, praying fervently to the god who holds and shakes the earth [i.e. Poseidon] that it would be easy to win over the proud heart of Achilles. When they came to the tents and ships of the Myrmidons, they found him beguiling his heart with the clear-sounding *phorminx*. It was beautiful and skilfully decorated, and the crossbar on it was silver: Achilles had chosen it from the spoils when he sacked the city of Eëtion.[7] With it he was giving delight to his heart, and singing the famous deeds of men. [190] Patroclus was sitting alone in silence opposite him, waiting for Achilles to finish his singing.[8] The two men came forward, Odysseus in the lead, and stood in front of Achilles; and he jumped up in surprise, with his *phorminx* in his hand, from the seat where he had been sitting.

> In three passages the musical content has nothing whatever to do with war. The story of Thamyris is a legend with a moral, mentioned quite casually in passing. The allusion to the dances of Artemis, and above all the scenes of singing and dancing depicted on Achilles' shield, are deliberate evocations of the joys of peace, setting off the grim ugliness of war.

5   *Iliad* II.594–600

From the 'Catalogue of Ships'.

There were the men of Pteleos and Helos, and of Dorion, where the Muses met Thamyris the Thracian and put a stop to his singing, as he was going from the home of Oechalian Eurytus in Oechalia. For he had boasted that he would be victorious even if the Muses themselves, daughters of aegis-bearing Zeus, were singing. In their fury they struck him blind: they took away his divine gift of song, and made him forget his kitharist's skill.[9]

---

7   The *phorminx* described here is no ordinary household instrument, though it is small enough to be picked up comfortably, as the last lines of the quotation show. It is a rich and elaborate piece of workmanship, a valuable prize among the spoils of war. The city of Eëtion, Andromache's father, was in Cilicia, in southern Asia Minor; but this does not mean that the instrument is not properly speaking 'Greek' (cf. e.g. N. G. L. Hammond, *A History of Greece* 64–5).

8   For other examples of purely private singing in Homer see *Od.* v.61, x.221, 227, 254.

9   Thamyris the Thracian is an important figure in the mythology of early Greek music. He was a singer and kitharist of high repute: Plato mentions him in the same breath as Orpheus (**148** *Ion* 533b, *Rep.* 620a). (The word 'kitharist', *kitharistēs*, refers to a player on any stringed instrument of the *kithara* and *lyra* families. From the sixth

6   *Iliad* XVI.179–83

> Part of a description of the troops under Achilles' command.

The second company was led by warlike Eudorus, a love-child of Polymele, beautiful in the dance, daughter of Phylas. She was loved by Hermes, great slayer of Argus, whose eyes caught sight of her among the girls singing and dancing[10] in the chorus of Artemis, the huntress with the golden distaff.

7   *Iliad* XVIII.490–606 (excerpts)

> Hephaestus, the god of fire and of metal-working, makes a wonderful set of arms for Achilles. It includes a shield, decorated with pictures showing people engaged in a profusion of activities, drawn from many aspects of Greek life. It is described in detail at lines 478–608: its references to music appear in the following excerpts. The central idea is used again in the Hesiodic *Shield of Heracles*, one scene of which (17) is an interesting variant on Homer's depiction of a wedding.

[490–6]   On the shield he made two cities of mortal men. In one of them weddings and banquets were in progress: they were leading the brides from their houses through the town with blazing torches, and a loud wedding-song rose up.[11] Young men whirled in the dance, while among them *auloi* and *phorminges* gave out their cry; and the women stood in their doorways admiring the sight.
[523–6]

> Cattle rustlers are depicted, lying in wait for a herd.

Two scouts were posted at a distance from the group, to watch till they could see the sheep and crook-horned cattle. These soon appeared, and two

century it is sometimes reserved for one who plays without singing, while a *kithar-ōdos* is always a singer who accompanies himself on such an instrument. But in earlier Greek, and often later too, calling someone a kitharist need not imply that he does not sing.) He was said to have composed a lay on the theme of the war between the Titans and the gods (187 ps.-Plut. 1132b-c). For another version of the present story see Eurip. *Rhesus* 915–25. The warning against *hybris* provided by stories of those who challenged the gods is a favourite subject of Greek legend: for another well-known musical example see the tale of Marsyas and Apollo, e.g. Hdt. 7.26, Xen. *Anab.* 1.2.8, cf. Plato, *Euthyd.* 285c-d. The competitive aspect of musical perform-ance, which these stories presuppose, was a well-established element of Greek prac-tice from very ancient times. For an early historical example see 15 Hesiod, *W.D.* 650–62.

10   *Melpomenēisi*, again from the verb cognate with *molpē*. For dances of girls in cele-bration of Artemis and Apollo, see 18 *Hymn to Apollo* 154 ff and notes.

11   The *hymenaios*, hymn to Hymen, god of marriage. Greek weddings typically in-volved music at four stages: at the wedding feast, during the procession taking the bride to the groom's house, outside the bridal chamber after the bride had entered, and again in the same place the next morning. (See T. B. L. Webster, *The Greek Chorus* 73 ff, with his discussion of Sappho's wedding songs; cf. 23(a) Sappho fr. 44.) Here we have the procession: 11 *Od.* XXIII.129–49 gives a description of the music of a (pretended) wedding feast. Cf. *Il.*XXIV. 62–3.

herdsmen followed them, enjoying themselves on their *syringes*: they had no thought of a trap.
[567–72]

Grape-picking.

Girls and cheerful boys were carrying the honey-sweet fruit in woven baskets, and in the midst of them a boy played lovely music on his clear-sounding *phorminx*, and sang the beautiful Linus song[12] in a piping voice. The others followed him, stamping in unison, skipping on their feet with singing and joyful shouts.
[590–606]   The illustrious lame god next decorated it with a dancing-ground,[13] like the one that Daedalus designed in broad Cnossos for beautiful-haired Ariadne. In it young men and marriageable[14] maidens were dancing, holding one another's hands by the wrist.[15] The girls wore light linen, the men well-woven tunics faintly glossy with olive oil: the girls had beautiful garlands, and the men had golden daggers hanging from silver belts. At one time they would run round swiftly on skilful feet, just as when a potter sits and spins his wheel with his hands to try it out, to see if it runs smoothly. At another time they would run in lines towards one another. A

---

12   Linus: a legendary musician (cf. 187 ps.-Plut. 1132a). According to the commonest tradition, his untimely death provoked universal mourning, commemorated in the Linus song or *linōidia*. (For a reconstruction of the song see *P.M.G.* 880. See also Paus. I.43.7, IX.29.6.) The exclamation *'ai Linon'* ('alas for Linus') became a cry used in mourning of every kind: it seems also to have been transformed into a noun, *ailinos*, meaning 'lament', and an adjective meaning 'unhappy'. (Cf. Aesch. *Ag.* 121, Soph. *Ajax* 627, Eurip. *Orestes* 1395–7, 42 *Helen* 171.) According to Herodotus (II.79), versions of the story and the song existed throughout the world: he mentions an Egyptian example. The song is evidently not merely a lament for a musician. The present reference suggests that it was associated with the harvest, and it may well have been a song for a personification of the cycle of nature, fruitful in its death and renewable through the seed. This would explain the ubiquitousness of forms which Herodotus recognises as resembling it: cf. 188 and 189 Ath. 174f–175a, 619f–620a, Pollux IV.54–5. Athenaeus uses Eurip. *Heracles* 348 to show that it could be sung on cheerful occasions (189 619c); and the harvest has an appropriately double-sided significance. Diog. Laert. VIII.1.25 quotes the following lines of Hesiod: 'Ourania bore Linus, a most lovely son, whom all mortals that are singers and kitharists bewail at feasts and dances, beginning and ending with an invocation of Linus.' There seem to be links between the Linus story and the cult of Adonis: see Paus. IX.29.8 on Sappho's Linus and Adonis songs.
13   *Choros*: the word may mean a group of singers or dancers, or their performance, or (as at 10 *Od.* VIII.260) the place where they perform. It is usually thought that it has this last sense here, but possibly the reference is to the performers. In that case Daedalus must be construed as chorus-trainer rather than architect (*askein*, the verb here translated 'design', can mean 'train', but does not seem to have this sense elsewhere in Homer). If that is correct, the dance described is a Cretan dance: Ath. 181a–d evidently takes it as such. (The passage also gives information on Cretan dances generally: cf. also the lines credited to Sappho on the subject, Inc. Auct. fr. 16 in Lobel–Page. Cretan dances of the Minoan period are discussed in Webster, *The Greek Chorus* 4–5.)
14   *Alphesiboiai*, 'bringing in oxen', i.e. worth many gifts as a bride-price.
15   The position of hands in the round dance is indicated in the same terms at 19 *Hymn to Apollo* 196.

great crowd stood round the lovely dance in delight; and two tumblers, leaders of the dance, whirled in the midst of them.[16]

> Musical prowess, though recognised as a genuine skill (XIII.730–1, and many passages of the *Odyssey*), is one that may conflict with the character expected of a warrior. Paris in particular is represented as a little too elegant and sophisticated for war: Hector rebukes him by saying that his *kitharis* (see n. 19 below) and the gifts of Aphrodite will not help him (III.54), and when he has been magically rescued from battle, and is described as looking as if he were going to a dance, or as if he had just stopped dancing and sat down (III.393–4), this is not altogether a compliment. Priam insults his remaining sons by calling them 'liars, dancers, champions at beating the dance floor' (XXIV.261). (For some later reflections on this theme see e.g. 151 Plato, *Rep.* 410c ff, cf. *Symp.* 179d.) The true place of music, in the world of the heroes, is at the relaxation of a banquet, and it is here that we find it richly depicted in the *Odyssey*. One short passage of the *Iliad* gives a foretaste.

8   *Iliad* 1.601–4

Part of a description of a banquet of the gods.

Thus they feasted all day until sunset, and none of them lacked appetite for the feast that they shared, or for the music of the splendid *phorminx* that Apollo played, or for that of the Muses, who sang, answering one another[17] with their beautiful voices.

(2) Odyssey

> The atmosphere of the *Odyssey* is lighter and less oppressive than that of the *Iliad*, even though the echoes of war and suffering continue to reverberate. Feasting and merry-making are part of its fabric, and it is there that music is most at home, in the lays of minstrels and in festive song and dance. A few musical references fall outside this framework: Calypso (V.61) and Circe (X.221, 227, 254) sing while they work at their looms; Nausicaa and her serving-girls play a musical ball-game (VI.99–109); and the magical powers of music are vividly evoked by the singing of the Sirens (14 XII.36 ff.). Two of the poem's banquets are particularly rich in musical allusions. The first is one of the regular parties indulged in by the rabble of

---

16   'Leaders of the dance', *molpēs exarchontes*, are parallel to the *exarchoi* of the lament (see 3 *Il.* XXIV.719 ff). Such acrobatic dance-leaders are sometimes represented on archaic Greek vases. The last lines, from 'in delight', recur in our texts of *Od.* IV.17 ff, in a description of a banquet given by Menelaus. There, after 'in delight', there occurs the sentence 'With them sang and danced (*emelpeto*) an inspired singer, playing the *phorminx.*' These words also occurred at one time in texts of the present passage, but were excised by the ancient editors. The excision may be a mistake. Some ancient authorities believed that the whole *Odyssey* passage was out of place. On the controversy, including the question who counted as 'leader' of a dance, see Ath. 180b–182a, which also contains useful information about dancing in general.

17   *Ameibomenai.* The reference may be to a form of antiphonal singing, perhaps an ancestor of the practice mentioned at 21 *Hymn to Hermes* 55–6. But they may be simply 'answering' the sound of Apollo's instrument: cf. 19 *Hymn to Apollo* 189.

Penelope's suitors at Odysseus' home in Ithaca: the second is the entertainment of Odysseus by Alcinous, king of the Phaeacians, a people of fairy-tale charm and delightfulness, if slightly effete by heroic standards.

9   *Odyssey* I.150–424 (excerpts)

[150–5] But when the suitors had eaten and drunk their fill, their thoughts turned to other matters, to singing and dancing;[18] for they are the ornaments of a feast. A herald placed in the hands of Phemius a most beautiful *kitharis*: he had been forced by the suitors to be their singer. So he played the *phorminx* and set out on his beautiful song.[19]

> The song is not immediately described: a conversation between Telemachus and Athena intervenes. The scene is picked up again at line 325.

[325–31] The renowned singer was singing to them, while they sat in silence and listened. He sang the dreadful homecoming of the Achaeans from Troy, laid upon them by Pallas Athena. Wise Penelope, daughter of Icarius, recognised the divine song from the upper room, and came down the steep staircase of her house. She was not alone: two servants came behind her . . .

---

[18]   *Molpē* and *orchēstys*: here *molpē* picks out only the element of song, since *orchēstys* plainly means 'dance'. Here the suitors are not sitting quietly listening to the minstrel, but are joining in with communal song and dance: contrast 325–6.

[19]   Homer never uses the form *kithara*: *kitharis* can be an instrument (as here, and probably at 10 *Od.* VIII.248), or the activity of playing on it (*Il.* III.54, XIII.731). Although according to later classifiers *kithara*, *lyra*, and *phorminx* are distinct instruments, many passages in early poetry show no tendency to differentiate them. The word *lyra* does not occur in Homer, and it seems likely that the only instrument in general use in the period when Homer was writing was of the kind that later retained the Homeric name *phorminx*. Mycenaean civilisation knew a number of types, but Homer projects back into the heroic past the one variety with which he was himself familiar. When the tortoiseshell *lyra* and the reshaped concert *kithara* became widespread, Homer's words *kitharis* (later *kithara*) and *phorminx*, together with the new term *lyra*, seem at first to have been used of them all interchangeably. Ps.-Plutarch says (187 1133c) that the form of the *kithara* became established in the time of Cepion, a pupil of Terpander, that is, not before the mid-seventh century. Vase paintings tend to confirm this. The word *lyra* first occurs in Archilochus (fr. 51.47 Diehl), and we have a full description of the tortoiseshell instrument in 21 *Hymn to Hermes*, where all three names are indiscriminately applied to it. (The next plain reference seems to be Sappho fr. 58.12: there is also a sixth-century vase depicting this sort of instrument labelled with the word *lyra*, Besseler and Schneider Pl.21.) Pindar attributes the invention of its variant, the *barbitos*, to Terpander (see 196 Ath. 635d). But *phorminx* is still the regular word for the professional musician's instrument and the instrument of Apollo in Pindar, with *lyra* used occasionally (not *kithara*). All three appear in fifth-century tragedy, apparently interchangeably, though *phorminx* may by now be a conscious archaism. In the fourth century a clear classification with appropriate terminology was developed (see e.g. 161 Ar. *Pol.* 1341a), but literature commonly neglects these technicalities even after that date.

In the present passage the noun *phorminx* does not appear, only the verb *phormizein*: but there are many clear cases where the three nouns refer to the same instrument. The most striking examples are in 21–2 *Hymn to Hermes* (17, 64, 422, 499): see also 19 *Hymn to Apollo* 184, 188.

'Set out on' translates *aneballeto*, from the verb cognate with the noun *anabolē* or *ambolē*, a 'prelude'. See notes to 22 *Hymn to Hermes* 426 and 26 Pindar, *Pyth.* I.4.

[336–52]   Then she wept, and said to the inspired singer: 'Phemius, you know many other themes to soothe men, the deeds of men and gods which singers celebrate. Sit here and sing one of them, and let these people drink their wine in silence. But stop this song of misery, which always[20] wears down my heart within my breast; for inconsolable grief has come to me above all. I lament continually, remembering my noble husband, whose fame runs through broad Greece and the heart of Argos.'

But wise Telemachus answered her: 'Mother, why do you grudge the trusty singer the right to give delight in whatever way his mind urges him? Singers are not to blame: the cause is Zeus, who gives as he wishes to each of us toiling people. We should not be angry with Phemius for singing the evil fate of the Greeks; for people always praise more highly the song that has come most recently to their ears.'[21]

After sending Penelope back to her room, Telemachus speaks to the suitors.

[368–71]   'Suitors of my mother, you are insolent beyond bearing. Let us now enjoy our meal, and let there be no shouting, for it is fine to listen to a singer as good as this one, whose voice is the equal of the gods.'

But Telemachus' suggestion seems to meet with little success. After some conversation the narrative continues:

[421–4]   Then they turned to the delights of dancing and lovely song, and so they continued until evening. Dark night came upon them as they were merry-making still, and then each of them went home to bed.[22]

10   *Odyssey* VIII.40 – IX.11 (excerpts)

Alcinous, king of the Phaeacians, has given orders for the provision of a ship to take Odysseus home. He continues:

[40–7]   'Those are my orders to the young men. You others, sceptre-bearing kings, come to my fine palace, so that we may entertain our visitor in the house. Let no one refuse: and call the inspired singer Demodocus, for a god has given him in abundance the gift of song, to delight us with whatever theme his heart arouses him to sing.'

With these words he led the way, and the sceptre-bearing kings followed. A herald went to find the inspired singer.

20   The song is evidently a familiar one, not newly made for the occasion. But see 351–2 and 10 *Od.* VIII.491 with n. 31.
21   Cf. Pindar, *Ol.* 9.48–9: 'Praise old wine, but the flowers of new hymns.' A fourth-century source, however, takes it as obvious that we enjoy familiar songs more than new ones (**164** ps.-Ar. *Probs.* XIX.5). But he is writing in a time when melodic invention had become a much more important part of music. Homer and even Pindar are more concerned with the merits of new themes and words, the writer of the Problem with the delights of well-known melodies. See also Plato's remarks on the present passage, **152** *Rep.* 424b–c.
22   All Homer's feasts are daytime affairs, ending at nightfall. Cf. *Il.* 1.472–4, 601–4, *Od.* XVII.605–6, XVIII.304–5.

[62–75]   Then the herald came in, leading the trusty singer, whom the Muse loved, though she gave him both good and evil: she had robbed him of his sight, but gave him sweet song. Pontonous placed a silver-studded seat in the midst of the banqueters, against a great pillar. From a peg the herald hung the clear-sounding *phorminx* above Demodocus' head, and showed him how to reach it with his hands. Beside him he placed a basket and a beautiful table, and a cup of wine, for him to drink when his heart desired. Then they laid their hands to the good things that were set ready before them.

But when they had eaten and drunk their fill, the Muse roused the singer to sing the praises of men, a lay whose fame at that time reached to the broad heaven, the quarrel between Odysseus and Achilles, son of Peleus . . .

[83–107]   That is what the renowned singer sang. But Odysseus took a large crimson cloth in his strong hands, and pulled it down over his head to cover his handsome face, for he was ashamed to let tears pour from his eyes in front of the Phaeacians. So whenever the inspired singer paused in his singing, Odysseus would wipe away the tears and take the cloth from his head, and picking up a two-handled cup he would pour libations to the gods. But as soon as he began again, and the leaders of the Phaeacians urged him to sing, since they delighted in his lays,[23] Odysseus again would cover his head and lament. He succeeded in hiding his weeping from the others, except Alcinous, who was sitting near him, and realised what was happening, for he heard his deep[24] groans. At once he addressed the Phaeacians, lovers of the oar.

'Listen, leaders and counsellors of the Phaeacians. We have now had our fill of the feast that we have shared, and of the *phorminx*, yoke-fellow of the abundant feast.[25] Now let us go outside and try our hands at all kinds of sports, so that our guest may tell his friends, when he reaches home, how much we excel all others in boxing and wrestling and jumping and running.'

With these words he led the way, and the others followed. The herald hung the clear-sounding *phorminx* on its peg, and taking Demodocus by the hand he led him out of the house.

> The games are contested. Odysseus shows his mettle with the discus, and challenges all comers at any sport they choose, apart from running. Alcinous makes a courteous reply, and goes on:

[246–67]   'We are not outstanding at boxing or wrestling, but we run swiftly, and are champion sailors; and we continually delight in feasting and the *kitharis* and dances [see n. 19 above], in abundant changes of clothes, hot baths, and beds. Come now, those of you who are the best dancers[26] of the

---

23   *Epeessin*, dative plural of *epos*, lit. 'word': the term came to have the special sense 'epic poem', one written in the dactylic hexameters of Homer and the ancient bards.

24   *Bary*, lit. 'heavy'. It is the regular word for 'deep in pitch', but here probably means 'heavy' in the sense 'sad'.

25   Cf. e.g. 9 *Od.* 1.152, XIII.7–9, XXI.429–30.

26   'Dancers', *bētarmones*, a word found only in Homer and in late Greek: *bētarmos* is used to mean 'dance' by Apollonius Rhodius as a deliberate Homericism (1.1135). The word seems to be compounded out of the verbs *bainein*, 'to go' or 'to step', and

Phaeacians, dance,[27] so that our guest may tell his friends, when he reaches home, how much we excel all others at seamanship and running and dancing and song.[28] Let someone go quickly and bring Demodocus his clear-sounding *phorminx*. It is lying somewhere in the house.'

So spoke godlike Alcinous; and the herald jumped up to fetch the hollow *phorminx* from the king's house. Then nine stewards stood up, officials of the people, who used to organise everything properly at the games: they smoothed the dancing-place [*choros*: see n. 13 above], and cleared a fine, wide arena. The herald came up, bringing Demodocus his clear-sounding *phorminx*, and he walked into the middle. Around him stood young men in the first bloom of youth, skilled dancers, and they beat the sacred dance-ground with their feet. Odysseus watched the twinkling of their feet, and was astonished.

Then Demodocus, as he played the *phorminx*, set off [*aneballeto*: see n. 19 above] to sing beautifully about the love of Ares and fine-wreathed Aphrodite.

The story is related.

[367–84]   That is what the illustrious singer sang, and Odysseus was delighted in his heart as he heard it: so too were the others, the Phaeacians of the long oars, famous seafarers.

Then Alcinous commanded Halios and Laodamas to dance alone, since no one could compete with them.[29] So they took in their hands a fine purple ball[30] which the clever Polybus had made; and one of them would bend over backwards and throw it up towards the shadowy clouds, while the other, leaping upwards from the ground, caught it with ease before touching the ground with his feet. After testing their skill with high throws of the ball, they danced on the fertile earth, rapidly passing the ball to and fro between them, while the other young men stood around the arena beating time, and a great sound went up. Then noble Odysseus spoke to Alcinous.

'Lord Alcinous, most renowned among all the people, you promised that your dancers [*bētarmones*: see n. 26 above] were the best, and your promise is fulfilled. I am filled with wonder as I watch.'

arariskein, 'to join' or 'to fit together'. (This verb is etymologically related to *harmozein, harmonia*.) The sense of the term is therefore 'step-joiners': it is probably used to indicate the craftsmanlike skill of these experts.

27   *Paisate*, lit. 'play' (like a child).

28   Notice the ironic echo of Alcinous' previous advertisement of his people's attainments (100–3), before Odysseus had displayed his own physical prowess. Charming though the Phaeacians are, they are rather a soft-living people. On the slightly unmanly connotations of dancing, in some contexts, see *Il.* III.54, 393–4, XXIV.261, and perhaps *Od.* VI.64–5. But contrast the special character of one kind of dance: 'I know how to sing and dance (*melpesthai*) to terrible Ares, at close quarters', says Hector to Ajax (*Il.* VII.241), where he means no more than 'I am good at hand-to-hand fighting', but the direct reference is plainly to the war dance.

29   This means no more than 'they were the best', but the form of expression reflects again the pervasive competitiveness of much Greek musical practice.

30   Cf. Nausicaa's musical ball-game, *Od.* VI.99–101.

Odysseus is given presents and a warm bath, after which he goes to join the Phaeacians at dinner.

[469–99]   He sat down on a seat beside King Alcinous. They were already serving the portions and mixing the wine. Then the herald came in, leading the trusty singer Demodocus, honoured by the people. He sat him in the midst of the banqueters, against a great pillar. Then subtle Odysseus spoke to the herald, after carving a slice from the back of a white-tusked boar – more than half was left, and there was rich fat on both sides. 'Here, herald, take this to Demodocus for him to eat, with a greeting from me, sad though I am. For singers are given honour and respect by all people on the earth, since the Muse has taught them their songs, and she loves the race of singers.'

So he spoke, and the herald took it in his hands and gave it to the noble Demodocus. He accepted it with pleasure in his heart. Then they laid their hands to the good things that were set before them. But when they had eaten and drunk their fill, subtle Odysseus spoke to Demodocus.

'Demodocus, of all men I praise you most highly. It was either the Muse, the child of Zeus, who taught you, or Apollo [cf. 13 *Od.* XXII.347–8]. You sing the sufferings of the Achaeans extraordinarily well, all that they did and suffered and laboured, almost as though you had been there yourself, or had heard it from a witness.[31] But now change your theme, and sing the making of the wooden horse, which Epeius made with Athena's help, the crafty device which noble Odysseus brought that day to the citadel, after filling it with men who then sacked Troy. If you can narrate all that in the proper way, I shall not hesitate in saying to all men how generously the god has endowed you with divine song.'

So he spoke; and Demodocus, having begun by invoking the god,[32] revealed the song.

Odysseus is again greatly affected by Demodocus' singing, and is pressed by Alcinous to reveal his true identity. At the beginning of the next book he begins his story.

[IX.1–11]   Subtle Odysseus answered the king: 'Lord Alcinous, most renowned among all the people, it is a fine thing to listen to a singer such as this one, whose voice is the equal of the gods'. For myself, I would say that no accomplishment is more delightful than when good cheer reigns throughout the people, and banqueters sit next to one another in a house listening to a singer, while beside them are tables covered with bread and meat, and a

---

31   The implication appears to be that Demodocus had composed the words of the song himself: yet we are told earlier (line 74) that it was a song popular throughout the world at that time. The apparent conflict may reflect bardic practice: the *theme* is now universally popular, and the main elements of the story, together, perhaps, with many linguistic formulae, were shared by all singers; but given that material, what the singer made of it was his own. Cf. 9 *Od.* 1.341 and 351–2 with notes.

32   A common practice in musical performance: see e.g. 16 Hesiod, *Theog.* 34, 43 ff, Pindar, *Nem.* 2.1–3. Cf. also the introduction to the *Homeric Hymns* given below.

wine-server draws wine from the mixing-bowl and carries it round to pour into the cups. This, I think, is the finest thing of all.'

> A passage of Book XXIII represents the sounds of a celebration of a special kind. After the suitors have been killed, Odysseus gives orders for music and dancing, to give the impression that a wedding feast is going on, so misleading passers-by about the real state of affairs.

11   *Odyssey* XXIII.129–49

Subtle Odysseus answered him with these words. 'I will tell you what seems the best thing to me. First wash yourselves and put on your tunics, and tell the serving-women in the house to get dressed. Then let the inspired singer, holding his clear-sounding *phorminx*, lead us in a playful dance, so that if someone hears it from outside – anyone passing by, or anyone who lives near – he will think it is a wedding. This will prevent any rumour of the killing of the suitors reaching the town until we can get away into our fields with their many trees. After that we shall see what good luck Olympian Zeus will give us.'

So he spoke, and they heard his words and obeyed them. First they washed themselves and dressed in their tunics, and the women put on their finery. Then the inspired singer took up his hollow *phorminx*, and a longing arose within them for sweet song and the splendid dance. The great house resounded to the feet of the merrily dancing men and the beautifully dressed women. People hearing them from outside all said 'Aha! So someone has married the much-courted queen!'

> One of the special techniques of the minstrels depicted in the passages above, and something of the ways in which their skills were generally regarded, are sketched in the following pair of passages from Books XXI and XXII.

12   *Odyssey* XXI.404–11

That is what the suitors said, while subtle Odysseus had been weighing the great bow in his hands and looking at it all over. Then, just as a man who understands the *phorminx* and song easily stretches a string round a new *kollops*,[33] tying the well-twisted sheep-gut at both ends,[34] so Odysseus strung the great bow without difficulty. Then, taking it in his right hand, he tested the string, and it sang out beautifully like the voice of a swallow.

[33] The *kollops* was the device, fitted to the crossbar of the instrument, to which the string was attached, and by means of which its tension was adjusted. In the early period it consisted of a strip of raw hide, which could be moved or twisted on the crossbar to increase tension. Pegs were a later invention. See Sachs, *The History of Musical Instruments*, 130.

[34] For the use of sheep-gut as the strings of instruments see **21** *Hymn to Hermes* 51. They were twisted, and in some late authors there occurs a special designation, *chordostrophos*, for the man whose job it was to twist strings. See Dio Chrys. VIII.4, Ptol. *Tetr.* 180, and cf. Aelian, *N.A.* XVII.6.

13   *Odyssey* XXII.330–53

> From the description of the fight in the hall, when Odysseus kills the suitors.

Phemius the singer, son of Terpios, whom the suitors had forced to sing for them, had so far escaped black death. He was sitting with his clear-sounding *phorminx* in his hands close to the stairway-door; and he was in two minds, whether to slip out of the hall to sit at the strongly built altar of great Zeus of the Household, where Laertes and Odysseus had burned many ox-thighs in sacrifice, or to run forward and pray for mercy at the knees of Odysseus. After pondering it, he decided that it was better to clasp the knees of Odysseus, son of Laertes. So he put down his hollow *phorminx* on the ground between a mixing-bowl and a silver-studded chair; and he ran forward and clasped Odysseus' knees, pleading with him, with these winged words.

'I beseech you, Odysseus. Respect me and have mercy. It will bring harm to you later, if you kill a singer, one who sings for gods and men. I am self-taught, and a god has breathed all kinds of melodies into my mind.[35] I could sing beside you as though to a god. So do not be eager to cut my throat. Telemachus, your dear son, could tell you that I did not come to your house voluntarily or for payment,[36] to sing for the suitors at their banquets, but a large number of people overpowered me and brought me here forcibly.'

> The persuasive and magical powers of music are often mentioned by later Greek writers, and analysed for their own purposes by the philosophers. The prototypes of the singers of magical enchantments are the Sirens, who lure men to their doom with their entrancing voices.

14   *Odyssey* XII.36–200 (excerpts)

> Odysseus is on the point of leaving Circe's island. Circe warns him of the dangers he will next encounter.

[36–54]   Then noble Circe spoke to me. 'All these things are now accomplished. Now listen to the things I tell you, and the god himself will keep you in mind of them. You will come first to the Sirens, who enchant everyone who comes near them. If anyone approaches them without knowing, and hears the voice[37] of the Sirens, for him there will be no wife and little children standing by to gladden his homecoming, but the Sirens enchant him with their clear song. They sit in a meadow, and around them is a great heap of the bones of rotting corpses, their skin withering upon them. Hurry your ship past them: knead some honey-sweet beeswax and put it in your companions'

---

[35] The two claims are thought of as being perfectly compatible. See Dodds, *The Greeks and the Irrational*, 10.

[36] Implying that it would be quite usual for a minstrel to offer himself for hire in a princely house.

[37] *Phthongos*: any sound, not necessarily that of the voice. Later the word is used by technical writers to mean a musical note.

ears, so that none of them can hear. But if you yourself want to hear, let them bind you hand and foot, upright against the mast in your swift ship, with the ropes lashed to the mast itself, so that you may hear and delight in the voice of the two Sirens. And if you plead with your comrades and urge them to release you, they must bind you with more ropes still.'

[181–200]   The ship is now approaching the Sirens' island.

But when we had come within shouting distance of the shore, as we sped along, the Sirens did not fail to notice that a swift ship was coming near, and they began[38] their clear song.

'Come hither, renowned Odysseus, great glory of the Achaeans. Stop your ship, so that you may hear our voice. No one has ever sailed by this place in a black ship until he has heard the honey-speaking voice that comes from our mouths; and he receives both delight and new knowledge before he goes on. For we know all the sufferings endured by the Greeks and Trojans in broad Troy at the will of the gods, and we know everything that happens upon the fruitful earth.'

So they spoke, sending forth their beautiful voice. My heart longed to listen, and with nods and frowns I urged my comrades to release me. But they leaned forward and rowed on. Perimedes and Eurylochus jumped up and bound me still tighter with more ropes. But when we had passed them by, and we could no longer hear the voice and the song of the Sirens, my trusty companions at once took out the wax with which I had blocked their ears, and loosed me from my bonds.

---

[38]   *Entynon*, lit. 'prepared', 'made ready', as of setting out a meal, harnessing a chariot, etc.

CHAPTER 2

Hesiod

Hesiod's dates cannot be established with certainty, any more than can Homer's: somewhere in the eighth century is probably a reasonable guess. But while Homer as an individual is wholly unknown to us, we do know something of Hesiod's life, since his own writings, and particularly certain passages of the *Works and Days*, offer substantial information. He was a Boeotian farmer, and his attitudes were clearly shaped by the unheroic, unromantic, laborious life that such people led. Though the patterns of his verse are Homeric, their import is not: the task of his poetry is to express a moral position, together with its practical implications and its origins in the divine and human order. This task is addressed directly: the poems are didactic, and any narrative elements that occur are incidental. They present a view of the world based not upon tales of the heroes, but on the experience of ordinary working people.

We know a good deal more of Hesiod the practical farmer than of Hesiod the poet and musician. But though the later tales of his musical activities, including the story of his contest with Homer, are certainly fabrications, we know from his own works that he sang as a public performer, and on at least one occasion carried off the prize. The occasion recorded was admittedly a minor event, the funeral games of Amphidamas, king of Chalcis, and Hesiod does not tell us why he was there. It is at least possible, however, that though his presence in Chalcis at the right time was accidental, the journey he was engaged in – the only time he had crossed the sea, so he says – was undertaken in order to compete at some other festival. The competitive element in musical performance, both at regular religious celebrations and at such gatherings as funerals, was an essential part of the Greek scheme of things from earliest times.

Not everything that has come down to us under Hesiod's name is genuine. But *Works and Days* is certainly his, and despite some scholarly doubts there is no adequate reason to deny his authorship of the *Theogony*, from which our second passage is taken. The *Shield of Heracles*, part of which follows, is another matter: it is certainly later, and in both its style and its theme it is an uneasy combination of the Hesiodic and the Homeric manner. It may tentatively be placed in the seventh century.

15   *Works and Days 650–62*

I have never sailed by ship on the wide sea, except to Euboea from Aulis, where once the Greeks were held up by a storm, after gathering a great army to go from holy Greece to Troy, land of beautiful women. From there I went on to Chalcis, to the games of wise-minded Amphidamas; and the sons of the great-hearted king set up many prizes, which they had announced beforehand. There, I tell you, I won the victory with a hymn,[1] and carried off

---

[1]   A hymn, *hymnos*, is primarily a song of praise, addressed to a god or a hero (e.g. Plato, *Rep.* 607a, *Symp.* 177a). The 'Homeric Hymns' belong, with some qualifications, to this genre (see introduction to ch. 3). It seems likely that Hesiod is telling us

a tripod with handles as my prize. This I dedicated to the Heliconian Muses, in the place where they first set me on the road of clear-sounding song [see **16** *Theog.* 22 ff]. That is all my experience of ships with their many pegs: but even so I shall explain to you the mind of aegis-bearing Zeus, for the Muses taught me to sing most marvellous song.[2]

16   *Theogony* 1–104

Let us begin our song from the Heliconian Muses, who live on the great and holy mountain of Helicon, and dance with their tender feet around the violet-coloured spring and the altar of the mighty son of Cronos. When they have washed their soft bodies in Permessus, or in the Spring of the Horse, or in sacred Olmeius, they begin to make their beautiful, lovely dances on the top of Helicon, stepping strongly with their feet. From there they fly up, covered in a thick mist, [10] and go about in the night, singing with most beautiful voices, hymning [see n. 1 above] Zeus the aegis-bearer and noble Argive Hera who walks on golden sandals, and grey-eyed Athena, daughter of aegis-bearing Zeus, and Phoebus Apollo and Artemis who delights in arrows, and Poseidon who holds and shakes the earth, and revered Themis, and Aphrodite with her curling glances,[3] and golden-wreathed Hebe and beautiful Dione, and Leto and Iapetus and Cronos the subtle counsellor, and Eos and great Helios and bright Selene, [20] and Earth and great Oceanus and black Night, and the holy race of all the other everlasting immortals.

It was the Muses who once taught Hesiod beautiful song, while he was shepherding his lambs under holy Helicon. The first word spoken to me by the goddesses, the Olympian Muses, daughters of aegis-bearing Zeus, was this:

'Shepherds of the wild, shameful creatures, nothing but bellies, we know how to speak many false things as if they were true, and we know, when we wish, how to utter true things as well.'

So spoke the ready-voiced daughters of great Zeus. [30] And they picked and gave me a rod, a shoot of flourishing laurel, a wonderful thing; and they breathed into me a heavenly voice, so that I might celebrate things to come and things past. They commanded me to hymn the race of blessed everlasting gods, and always to sing of themselves, the Muses, both first and last. But why should I tell all this about oak or rock?[4]

that he won a victory in the competition for singing a *hymnos* in this sense, not just for singing generally. But the word can be used quite loosely, to mean song of any kind (cf. e.g. **93** Eurip. *Ion* 881–6); and its primary sense is often extended or distorted in later literature, particularly in tragedy. See e.g. **95–9**.

[2]   'Song' translates *hymnos*, which must here have its more general sense. Note that the Muses not only give the power of song, but inspire the poet with knowledge, insight into the mind of Zeus. Such claims continued to be taken seriously, and became a subject for philosophical investigation: see e.g. **148** Plato, *Ion* 533b ff.

[3]   *Helikoblepharon*, which I have rendered literally: commonly translated 'swift-glancing'. The word suggests liveliness and flirtatiousness.

[4]   Proverbial for 'Why talk about what is not to the point?'

Come then, let us begin from the Muses, whose hymns delight the great heart of Zeus their father in Olympus, speaking of what is, what will be, and what has been, agreeing[5] with their voices. Their sweet sound flows tireless [40] from their mouths, and the home of their father, Zeus the loud thunderer, rejoices at the goddesses' lily-like voice[6] as it is scattered. The peaks of snowy Olympus and the homes of the gods resound. Uttering their immortal voice they praise first in song the revered race of gods from the beginning, the gods whose parents were Earth and broad Heaven, and the gods who were born from them, givers of good gifts. Next, as they begin and as they end their song,[7] they hymn Zeus, father of gods and men, saying how much he is the greatest and strongest of the gods. [50] And then they hymn the race of men and strong Giants, and delight the heart of Zeus in Olympus, they, the Olympian Muses, daughters of aegis-bearing Zeus.

It was Memory, who rules the hills of Eleuther, who bore them of her union with the father, the son of Cronos, as a way of forgetting evils and an intermission of sufferings.[8] Nine times, at night, wise Zeus mingled with her, going into her holy bed far away from the immortal gods. But when a year had passed, and the season came round as the months waned, and many days were accomplished, [60] she bore nine daughters, all of like mind, the concern of whose hearts is song, and whose spirit is free of care, a little way from the highest peak of snowy Olympus. There are their gleaming dance-places[9] and their beautiful homes. With them the Graces and Desire live in joyous festivities. And uttering through their mouths a lovely voice, they sing in praise of the customs[10] of all and the noble practices of the immortals, uttering a most lovely sound. Then they went to Olympus, rejoicing in their beautiful voice, with undying song and dance:[11] the dark earth rang about them [70] as they sang their hymn, and a lovely clamour rose from beneath their feet as they went to their father. He it is that reigns in heaven, holding the lightning

---

5   *Homēreusai*: not a technical term of music, but here suggesting 'singing in perfect unison'.

6   The same simile, indicating delicacy of sound, occurs at Hom. *Il.* III.152, where the subjects are cicadas.

7   The invocation of a god at beginning and end forms a common pattern in Greek poetry. Hesiod has already been instructed in a comparable practice, that of putting the Muses both first and last in his compositions (line 34).

8   Greek literature often expresses this conception of the function of music: it is emphasised again at 98–103 below. It is probably one source of the idea that music has the 'magical' power to cure even bodily ills (e.g. Theophrastus quoted at 192 Ath. 624a–b) as well as ministering to the soul. For a vigorous denial that music has any power to cure human evils, see 117 Eurip. *Medea* 190–203.

9   *Choros* here refers to the place where dances are held, not to the dance itself or the performers. Cf. 7 Hom. *Il.* XVIII. 590. See also *Od.* XII.4 and 318 for passages closely comparable to the present one.

10   *Nomoi.* There are contexts in which this word has a special musical sense (see particularly Ch. 15, Appendix A), but here it must mean 'customs' or 'laws' quite generally, as its conjunction with the 'habits' or 'practices' of the gods makes clear.

11   *Molpē*, here as usually, refers to a combination of song and dance. The word's emphasis is always on the singing, and sometimes no element of dancing is implied: but here, as line 70 shows, the Muses dance in procession as they go to Olympus.

and the glittering thunderbolt, having conquered his father Cronos by his strength. And he distributed everything fairly to each of the immortals and announced their prerogatives.

Of these things, then, the Muses sang, the Muses who live on Olympus, the nine daughters begotten by great Zeus – Clio, Euterpe, Thalia, Melpomene, Terpsichore, Erato, Polhymnia, Ourania and Calliope: she is the most eminent of them all, [80] for she ministers to revered kings. Any of the god-nourished kings whom the daughters of great Zeus honour, and look upon at his birth, upon his tongue they put a sweet dew, and from his mouth flow gentle words. All the people look to him as he apportions judgements with righteous justice; and with sure speech he quickly puts an end, with understanding, to even a great quarrel. That is why kings are wise-minded, for when the people in their assemblies fall into error, they turn things to right again [90] with ease, persuading the people with soft words.[12] As he goes through an assembly[13] they greet him with gentle reverence, like a god, and he is pre-eminent among the company. Such is the sacred gift of the Muses to men. For it is through the Muses and far-shooting Apollo that there are singers and players of the *kithara*[14] upon the earth, and through Zeus that there are kings. He whom the Muses love is happy, for a sweet voice flows from his mouth. For if someone has grief in his new-troubled spirit, and is in fear, distressed in his heart, still, when a singer, [100] a servant of the Muses, hymns the glories of men of the past and of the blessed gods who live on Olympus, at once he forgets his miseries and remembers his troubles no more: the gifts of the goddesses swiftly turn him another way.

Hail, children of Zeus! Give me a lovely song.

17   The Hesiodic *Shield of Heracles* 270–85

Nearby was a city of men with fine towers, and seven golden gates, fitted to their lintels, enclosed it. The men were enjoying themselves in revelries and dances. Some were bringing a bride to her husband on a cart with good wheels, and the wedding song rose loud, while the glitter of blazing torches in the hands of the maidservants whirled round far away. These maidens went in front, delighting in the revelry, and companies of playful dancers followed them. The men sent out a song from their tender mouths, accompanied by shrill *syringes*, and the sound broke about them;[15] while the

---

[12] The power of music is akin to that of persuasion: it has the same divine capacity to alter people's thoughts and emotions. Hence the two are traced here to the same source. The idea is vividly illustrated in the legend of Orpheus, and in the way this legend was applied to common experience: cf. e.g. **119** Eurip. *I.A.* 1211–15. It is taken up and elaborated in abstract detail by the philosophers, particularly those in the tradition of Plato.

[13] *Agōn*: in Homer any kind of assembly. Later, specifically the gathering of people to see the games, and hence the games themselves or any kind of contest.

[14] *Kitharistai*: but see **9** *Od.* 1.155 with n. 19.

[15] The word translated 'sound' can mean 'echo'. The metaphor of a sound breaking is a common one, suggesting its dispersal in all directions.

girls led the lovely dance with the music of *phorminges*. On either side young men sported to the sound of the *aulos*, some playing games with dance and song, some going forward laughing, each to the music of an aulete.[16] Festivities and dances and revels filled the whole city.[17]

16 An aulete (*aulētēr*, later *aulētēs*) is a male player of the *aulos*. (There is also a form *aulētris*, indicating a female player.) The scene depicted is a little unclear, but the poet seems to be contrasting the communal dances of some of the young men with others who 'go forward' individually, each with his own aulete.

17 The passage as a whole is taken from a description of the decorations on Heracles' shield, and is closely modelled on Homer's account of the shield of Achilles at 7 *Il.* XVIII.490 ff.

CHAPTER 3

The Homeric Hymns

The so-called Homeric Hymns are not by the author of the *Iliad* and the *Odyssey*, and they are of various dates. Of the ones quoted here the *Hymn to Apollo* is the earliest, and may go back at least in part to the eighth century: the *Hymn to Hermes* may be as late as the beginning of the sixth.

Something of the context of the performance of such pieces may be gathered from the *Hymn to Apollo*. There is no reason to doubt that it means what it says, and that at least the Delian part was performed as an element in the regular festival of Apollo at Delos, which included the famous dances of Delian maidens. It bears plainly the marks of a competition-piece: the two functions were regularly combined. The great competitive festivals were religious occasions, and many major religious ceremonials contained elements of competition.[1] It might be supposed that the recitation of a poem like the *Hymn to Hermes* must have been less directly linked with a religious context: but such a judgement depends on quite un-Greek assumptions about the solemnity of religion, and is probably quite wrong.

The Hymns vary greatly in length. Thucydides (III.104) refers to the *Hymn to Apollo* as a *prooimion*, a 'prelude', which might indicate a mere preliminary to a more substantial piece. But the Hymn is 178 lines long if we confine ourselves to the Delian part, and 546 lines in all: the word *prooimion* taken in this sense seems much more appropriate to the shorter Hymns, some of which run to only a handful of lines. It is likely that by Thucydides' time the word could designate a complete and self-contained composition, whose relation to the 'prelude' in its strict sense was merely formal and historical. (For an example of the word's use where it has plainly lost the implication that it is no more than a preliminary, see **96** Aesch. *Sept.* 7–8.)

Hymns of the present type may have developed out of the simple practice of beginning a musical performance with an invocation of a god or gods. This practice goes back at least to Homer (**10** *Od.* VIII.499), but a special formalisation of it is ascribed in our sources to Terpander. Both the *prooimia* with which his performances began, and the *nomoi* or concert-songs that followed, were written like the Homeric Hymns in epic hexameters: they were pieces for a soloist accompanying himself on the *kithara* (**187** ps.-Plut. 1132c–1133c). Terpander's *prooimia* were sufficiently well known in their own right to preserve an independent identity in later antiquity: thus the *Suda* (s.v. *amphianaktizein*) says that the *prooimion* to Terpander's *Orthios nomos* began 'Sing to me, my mind, of the far-shooting lord.' (Cf. Aristoph. *Clouds* 595 with schol.) It is probable that the Homeric Hymns belong to a tradition of performance similar to that of Terpander and Archilochus. The longer pieces may be conceived either as greatly elaborated *prooimia* of Terpander's type, or as resulting from the abandonment of a division between the *prooimion* and the main composition. It is to be noted that the majority of the Hymns, whatever their length, end with a recapitulation of the address to a god, together with the formula 'I shall remember you, and another song too', suggesting that a further piece is to follow.

---

[1] For an explicit mention of the competition at which one of these hymns was performed see the second *Hymn to Aphrodite* 19–20.

In the early fifth century the elaborate hymns of Pindar and Bacchylides, with their various metres and rhythms, were certainly intended for choral performance, and the later, quasi-technical sense of the word *hymnos* had this implication. Proclus (320a 20) says that a *hymnos* in the strict sense was something sung by a stationary (not dancing) chorus, though this rule of usage was often broken. But the hexameters of the Homeric Hymns are unlikely to have lent themselves to choral interpretation: like most hexameter compositions, including the *prooimia* and *nomoi* of Terpander and Archilochus, the *hymnoi* of Hesiod (15 *W.D.* 650 ff) and the songs of the Homeric minstrels, they were designed as solo songs, to be accompanied by the *kithara*. It is possible, none the less, that they were sometimes enlivened by the mimetic dancing of a chorus (see e.g. 10 *Od.* VIII.262 ff and cf. n. 4 below: it is possible that this was the origin of the type of dancing known as the *hyporchēma*: see particularly 193 and 194 Ath. 628d, 631c.)

Hymn to Apollo

18   *Hymn to Apollo* 140–78

And you, far-shooting lord Apollo of the silver bow, walked sometimes on craggy Cynthus, and sometimes wandered among the islands and their people. You have many islands and wooded groves: all the peaks and high cliffs of the lofty mountains, and the rivers that flow to the sea, are dear to you. But you delight your heart, Phoebus, in Delos most of all, where the Ionians with their trailing robes come together, with their children and modest wives. They turn their minds to boxing and dancing and song, [150] and delight in them, whenever they set up their festival.[2] Anyone who saw them, when the Ionians were gathered together, would say that they were immortal and ageless for ever: for he would see the grace of them all, and would delight his spirit at the sight of the men and the finely girdled women, with their swift ships and their many possessions. And besides, there is that great marvel, whose fame will never die, the Delian maidens, servants of the far-shooter. These, when they have first sung a hymn to Apollo, and also to

---

2   *Agōn*, a 'gathering', but commonly meaning or implying a competition. The Delian festival of Apollo, and particularly the dances of the Delian maidens, were very famous in antiquity, but the competitions associated with the celebrations were apparently discontinued for some time. Thucydides (III.104) discusses this ancient festival. Much of his account is drawn directly from the present Hymn, some lines of which he quotes: he goes on to say that the Athenians purified the island (by removing all graves, and forbidding anyone to die or give birth there) in the winter of 426–5 B.C., and that subsequently they reinstated the competitions. 'Homer, then, gives this much evidence for the fact that in ancient times too there was a great gathering and a festival in Delos: later, the islanders and the Athenians continued to send choruses and offerings to the gods, but the competitions were mostly discontinued, owing to various difficulties, as it seems, until on the present occasion the Athenians held the competition, including a horse race, which there had not previously been.' On the dances of the Delian maidens see also 76 Eurip. *Heracles* 687 ff, and for some further details, particularly ones concerned with the Athenian connection, Callimachus, *Hymn to Delos* 275–326.

Leto and arrow-pouring Artemis,[3] [160] turn their thoughts to men and women of old, and sing a hymn of them, enchanting the tribes of men. They know how to imitate the voices of all people and their clattering:[4] everyone would say that their utterances were his own, so well is their beautiful song joined together.

But come now, may Apollo give his favour, and Artemis too; and farewell all you maidens. Remember me in time to come, when any of the men that live on the earth, some stranger who has met many hardships, comes here and asks you: 'Which do you think is the sweetest of the singers [170] that come here, maidens, and in whom do you most delight?' Answer him well, all of you, without dispute: 'He is a blind man, and he lives in rocky Chios; and all his songs are the best for ever.'[5] For my part, I shall carry your fame as far as I wander over the earth to the cities of men, in their good places: and they will believe me, since what I say is true. Nor will I ever cease from hymning far-shooting Apollo of the silver bow, whom beautiful-haired Leto bore.

> That ends the part of the Hymn which celebrates the association of Apollo with the island of Delos. The second part, which may be a separate poem, treats in a similar way his association with the Pythian shrine at Delphi.

19   *Hymn to Apollo 182–206*

Leto's glorious son goes to rocky Pytho, playing on his hollow *phorminx*, clothed in divine and scented garments. His *phorminx*, touched by the golden plectrum, gives a sweet ringing sound.[6] Thence he goes, swift as a thought, from earth to Olympus, to the house of Zeus, into the gathering of

---

[3]   Artemis, even more commonly than Apollo, was celebrated in maiden-dances: for an account of the Delphic version see *Hymn to Artemis* 11–20: cf. e.g. 75 Soph. *Trach.* 205 ff, 87 Eurip. *Troiades* 554–5.

[4]   Here some MSS read *bambaliastyn*, others *krembaliastyn*. The former word is thought to be associated with the chattering of teeth: the latter is plainly derived from *krembala*, 'clappers', 'castanets'. Even if the former reading is right, a noise like that of castanets may be indicated. Commentators who have found difficulty in identifying the relevance of castanets in the present context have interpreted the word as referring to the odd, 'chattering' pronunciation of foreigners. But an ingenious and probable hypothesis is suggested by Webster (*The Greek Chorus*, 55; *Greek Art and Literature*, 6–10): the 'voices' of all people are the dialects of the various races of the Greek-speaking world (there is no indication that genuine 'foreigners' ever had work performed at Greek festivals); and the *krembaliastys* of each is the locally grown rhythmic form, since rhythm is what *krembala* were used to emphasise. The poet is advertising the rhythmic and linguistic versatility of the Delian chorus, who might be asked to perform pieces from any of the literary and musical traditions of Ionia and the islands. If the chorus was involved in the performance of the present Hymn (which is not explicitly stated), it will have been as dancers of a mimetic *hyporchēma*, not as singers (see the introduction to the present chapter).

[5]   This passage is of course the origin of the tradition that Homer was a blind poet from Chios. Thucydides, for instance (III.104), assumes that this identification is correct, but it is most unlikely to be so.

[6]   *Kanachē*, typically the clashing sound of metal or other hard objects (hooves, *Od.* VI.82, teeth, *Il.* XIX.365); but also the sound of the *aulos* (e.g. Pindar, *Pyth.* 10.39).

the other gods. At once the thoughts of the immortals turn to song and the music of the *kithara*.[7] The Muses, answering all together with a beautiful voice,[8] [190] hymn the undying gifts of the gods and the sufferings of men, all that they receive from the immortal gods in their silly and helpless lives, where they can find no remedy for death, and no bulwark against old age. And the Graces with their lovely tresses, and the happy Seasons, and Harmonia[9] and Hebe, and Aphrodite, daughter of Zeus, dance with their hands holding one another's wrists.[10] Singing with them is one not ugly or small, but tall to look upon and enviable of form, Artemis, pourer of arrows, sister of Apollo. [200] Among them frolic Ares and the sharp-eyed killer of Argus, while Phoebus Apollo plays on the *kithara*, stepping with fine high steps. A radiance shines about him, the sparklings[11] of his feet and of his well-spun tunic. And golden-haired Leto and Zeus the counsellor delight their great hearts in watching their dear son at play among the immortal gods.

20   *Hymn to Apollo 513–23*

When they[12] had taken their fill of food and drink, they set out, led by the lord Apollo, son of Zeus, holding a *phorminx* in his hands and playing (*kitharizōn*) sweetly, stepping with fine high steps. The Cretans followed him to Pytho with stamping feet,[13] singing '*Iē paian*' like the Cretan paean-singers in whose breasts the Muse has placed honey-voiced song.[14] [520] With unwearied feet they came to the crest, and soon reached Parnassus and the lovely place where they were to live, honoured by many people. Apollo led them there, and showed them his sacred shrine and rich temple.

---

7   *Kitharis* seems here to have the sense 'music of the *kithara*', rather than naming the instrument itself. As usual in verse of this period, no distinction is made between *kithara* and *phorminx*. On both points see 9 *Od.* 1.155, n. 19.

8   'Answering', *ameibomenai*, cf. 8 *Il.* 1.604 with note. Here the suggestion that they are singing antiphonally is apparently negated by the words 'all together', and it is probably Apollo's *phorminx* that they 'answer'.

9   The divine personification of 'harmony' (in its most general, and not a specifically musical sense) was, appropriately, the daughter of Ares and Aphrodite (Hesiod, *Theog.* 933–7).

10   For this position of hands in the round dance (not a processional as in the excerpt from the Hesiodic *Shield* and at lines 513 ff below) cf. 7 *Il.* XVIII.594.

11   *Marmarygai*, 'flashings', perhaps here 'twinklings'. The reference is to a dancer's speed and agility, not to a special attribute of a god: the same expression is used of the feet of human dancers at 10 *Od.* VIII.265.

12   A company of Cretan sailors, whom Apollo had in effect kidnapped to become the keepers of his shrine at Pytho (Delphi).

13   The word *rhēssontes* refers to dancing, as at *Il.* XVIII.571, but its root sense is that of striking something hard (cf. Apoll. Rhod. 1.539). Apollo's 'fine, high steps' are also a dance movement, as in the previous passage, not merely a walking stride.

14   On the paean see introduction to *Iliad*. '*Iē paian*' means 'Hail, healer': cf. e.g. Aesch. *Ag.* 146, Soph. *O.T.* 154. For a myth of the origin of the cry see Callimachus, *Hymn to Apollo* 97–104. That the Cretans were known for their healing-songs is suggested by the remarks about Thaletas at 187 ps.-Plut. 1146b, cf. Paus. 1.14.4. For paeans as native to Crete, and attributed specifically to Thaletas (or 'Thales'), see Strabo X.4.16, cf. X.4.18: hesitantly attributed to Thaletas at 187 ps.-Plut. 1134d.

Hymn to Hermes

> This marvellous poem should be read as a whole, though the excerpts given
> here include everything in it that relates to music. It tells of the birth of
> Hermes, and how on the day of his birth he not only invented the tortoise-
> shell *lyra*, but also stole the cattle of Apollo with many crafty ruses and
> stratagems (inventing also, along the way, wickerwork sandals and the art
> of making fire). Apollo suspects him of the theft, and eventually persuades
> him to return the cattle; and his anger is soothed by the music which
> Hermes plays on his new invention. Apollo is so taken with the *lyra* that he
> accepts it from Hermes as a peace-offering, while Hermes becomes the
> keeper of Apollo's herds, and the two become firm friends. Later, we are
> briefly told, Hermes invented the herdsman's and shepherd's instrument,
> the *syrinx*, for his own use. For another, and comic, rendition of the story,
> see Sophocles' satyr-play, the *Ichneutai*.[15]

21   *Hymn to Hermes 1–61*

Muse, sing of Hermes, son of Zeus and Maia, ruler of Cyllene and Arcadia
with its many flocks, luck-bringing messenger of the gods, whom Maia bore,
Maia the beautiful-haired nymph who mingled in love-making with Zeus.
She was shy, and shunned the company of the blessed gods, living in a
deep-shadowed cave; and there the son of Cronos used to couple with the
beautiful-haired nymph at dead of night, while sweet sleep held white-armed
Hera fast, unseen by gods and mortal men. [10] But when great Zeus' plan
was fulfilled, and for her the tenth month was now fixed in the sky, she
brought her child to the light, and a remarkable thing was accomplished. For
then she bore a son of many wiles, a cunning deceiver, a thief, a cattle-driver,
a bringer of dreams, a spy in the night, a watcher at the gates, who would
soon show forth wonderful deeds among the immortal gods. He was born at
daybreak; at noon he played on the *lyra*;[16] and in the evening he stole the
cattle of far-shooting Apollo, on the fourth day of the month's first half, the
day that great Maia bore him.

[20]   When he had leaped from his mother's immortal limbs, he did not lie
for long, waiting in his sacred cradle, but jumped up, and sought out the
cattle of Apollo, passing out over the threshold of the lofty cave. But there he
found a tortoise, and won delight a thousandfold, for Hermes it was that
first made the tortoise a singer. The tortoise met him at the gateway of the
courtyard, browsing on the rich herbage in front of the dwelling, walking
with waddling feet. When the luck-bringing son of Zeus noticed it he
laughed, and said at once: [30] 'Already an omen of great luck for me! I do not

---

15   The play is translated in the Loeb *Greek Literary Papyri*, and as *The Searching Satyrs*
in *Two Satyr Plays*, tr. R. L. Green (Harmondsworth, 1957). The text is fragmentary,
and the reader should note that lines 440 ff in the Penguin edition are invented by the
translator to complete the play.

16   *Enkitharizen*: but as the sequel shows, the instrument is what we know as the *lyra*.
See 9 *Od.* 1.155, n. 19.

despise it. Hail, you with your lovely form, plucked at the dance, companion of the feast, appearing now most welcome! Where did you get that pretty plaything, that glittering shell that clothes you, a tortoise living in the mountains? I shall take you and carry you indoors: you will help me, and I shall not dishonour you, though you will profit me first. It is better to be at home: being out at the gates brings harm. Living, you shall be a charm against baneful witchcraft, but if you die, you could sing most beautifully.'

So he spoke: and lifting it in both hands [40] he went back into the dwelling, carrying his delightful toy. Then he up-ended it, and with a grey iron chisel he scooped out the life of the mountain tortoise. And as swiftly as thought pierces the heart of a man beset by flocking troubles, or as flashing glances whirl from the eyes, so glorious Hermes planned word and deed at once. He cut stalks of reed to measure and fixed them, fastening them by the ends through the back of the tortoise's shell.[17] Then he stretched oxhide over it by his skill, [50] and added arms, with a crossbar fixed across the two of them; and he stretched seven harmonious strings of sheep-gut.[18]

When he had made it, he picked up the lovely toy and tried it part by part with a plectrum. Under his hand it rang out awesomely. Then the god sang to it beautifully, trying out improvisations, like young men mocking each other with taunts at a feast.[19] He sang of Zeus, son of Cronos, and Maia of the pretty slippers, how they used to dally in the partnership of love, telling the whole tale of his own glorious begetting. [60] And he sang the praises of the handmaidens and the shining home of the nymph, and the tripods all about the house, and the abundant cauldrons.

17   The function of these reeds (*donakes*) was apparently to affix and support the oxhide membrane. They were inserted through holes in the tortoiseshell, in such a way as to lie horizontally across its opening. The membrane was stretched over them, and tied by them at its edges. Later they were replaced by devices made of horn: see Pollux iv.62, Hesych. s.v. *donax hypolyrios*, and cf. 139 Aristoph. *Frogs* 232–3. For other uses of the *donax* in musical instruments see notes to 27 Pindar, *Pyth.* 12.

18   'Harmonious': the word in the MSS is *symphōnous*, lit. 'concordant', but plainly no technical notion of concord is involved. One ancient source replaces this word with *thēluterōn*, giving the sense 'seven strings of gut from female sheep'. Strabo (xiii.618) records the tradition that the seven-stringed instrument was invented by Terpander, quoting as his evidence the lines 'We shall reject the four-voiced song, and sound new hymns on a seven-stringed *phorminx.*' This evidence can hardly be relied on, but there is more to the tradition than that. It was widely and persistently held that Terpander altered in some way the form of the 'scale' to which the strings were tuned, and that the number of strings involved was seven (180 ps.-Ar. *Probs.* xix.32, cf. 187 ps.-Plut. 1140f, 1141c). If Strabo's claim is accepted, the present Hymn must be considerably later than Terpander, since it assumes that a *lyra* will have seven strings.

19   The reference is probably to the practice whereby one guest at a dinner-party would sing a fragment of a song, and the next would complete it, or 'cap' it with something appropriate. On occasion this 'capping' might take the form of musical insult. See 134 Aristoph. *Wasps* 1218–48 with schol. to 1222 and 1239, Aristoph. *Lysistr.* 1236–8; and for a related practice cf. the song-contest at Theocr. *Idylls* 5.80 ff, esp. 116–23.

22   *Hymn to Hermes* 416–512

Apollo has now discovered that it was Hermes who stole his cattle.

But he easily softened the far-shooting son of glorious Leto just as he wished, mighty though Apollo was. Taking the *lyra* in his left hand he tested it part by part with a plectrum. Under his hand it [420] rang out awesomely. And Phoebus Apollo laughed with delight as the lovely clamour of the divine sound went through his heart, and sweet longing took hold of his spirit as he listened. Then the son of Maia, playing sweetly on the *lyra* (*lyrēi kitharizōn*), took courage, and stood on the left of Phoebus Apollo. Next, to the clear sound of his playing, he sang, in the manner of a prelude,[20] and the voice that followed was lovely.[21] He told of the immortal gods and the dark earth, how they first came to be and how each acquired his destined portion. Of all the gods he first honoured Memory with his song, Memory, [430] mother of the Muses; for the son of Maia was in her portion.[22] Next the splendid son of Zeus honoured the other gods in order of age, as each had been born, uttering everything in due order as he played the *lyra* on his arm. And an irresistible passion seized Apollo's spirit within his breast, and he spoke to Hermes these winged words.

'Killer of oxen, schemer, busy worker, comrade of the feast, this invention of yours is worth fifty cows. I think that we shall soon settle our dispute peacefully. But come now and tell me, clever son of Maia, [440] was this marvellous thing with you from your birth, or did one of the immortals, or a mortal man, give it to you as a noble gift, and teach you divine song? For this new-uttered sound that I hear is marvellous, and I say that no man, and none of the immortals who have their home on Olympus has ever learned it except you, you thief, son of Zeus and Maia. What is this skill? What is this music for unresolvable cares? What is this method?[23] Surely there are here to be taken three things, all together, joy and love and sweet sleep. [450] I too am a follower of the Olympian Muses, who care for dances and the bright path of singing, the flowering of song

---

20   *Amboladēn*, 'in the manner of an *anabolē*'. Homer uses the related verb at e.g. 9 *Od.* 1.155. An *anabolē* was originally a preliminary section of a piece, usually instrumental (e.g. 26 Pindar, *Pyth.* 1.4). Here the *anabolē* is vocal, and the song is evidently an extended, independent composition. Like *prooimion* (see introduction to *Homeric Hymns*), the word *anabolē* came to have such a reference, with a special additional implication. It indicated a relatively unstructured piece, particularly one without strophic responsion. Thus the *Suda* attributes the introduction of *anabolē* into dithyramb to Melanippides: cf. 136 Aristoph. *Birds* 1385 and the discussion of similar changes in 169 ps.-Ar. *Probs.* XIX.15.

21   'Followed', probably in the sense 'sang the same tune as' the *lyra*.

22   This means that Hermes, as a musician, was part of her sphere of patronage and influence. Memory was regularly treated as mother of the Muses: see e.g. Hesiod, *Theog.* 915–17. That poem is a paradigm of the type that Hermes now sings.

23   *Tribos*, lit. 'path'. The sense is 'How do you do it?' 'What is the technique?' Cf. Parmenides' *hodoi dizēsios*, 'roads of enquiry', which turn out to be *methods* of enquiry. (Frs. 2.2, 6.3, 7.2.)

and dance (*molpē*) and the lovely reverberation of *auloi*.[24] Yet never before did I care in my heart like this for any of those skilful feats that young men perform at their revels. I am astonished, son of Zeus, at the loveliness of your playing. But now, since you possess such splendid skill, little though you are, sit down, my lad, and take note of your elder's words. There will be glory among the immortal gods for you yourself and for your mother. I will tell you surely. [460] By this spear of cornel-wood, I promise that I shall make you a renowned and prosperous leader among the immortals: I shall give you fine gifts, and shall not deceive you, right to the end.'

Hermes answered him with clever words. 'You ask me subtle questions, Far-worker; but I do not grudge you your initiation in my art. You shall learn it today ... [474] You are free to learn whatever you desire. But since your spirit is so eager for you to play the *lyra* (*kitharizein*), sing and play it, and give your mind to revelry, taking this as a gift from me: and you, my friend, give me glory. Sing well, with this clear-voiced mistress in your arms, you who know how to utter things beautifully and in good order. [480] From now on bring it confidently to the flourishing feast, the lovely dance and the renown-loving revel,[25] a delight by night and by day. Whoever enquires of it cleverly, with skill and wisdom, to him it will teach with its voice all kinds of things pleasing to the mind, being played easily with gentle familiarities: for it rejects toilsome labour. But if anyone ignorantly questions it at first with violence, to him it will chatter mere airy nonsense. You are free to learn whatever you desire; [490] and I will give you this, glorious son of Zeus. For my part, Far-worker, I shall pasture the roaming cattle on pastures in the mountains and the horse-feeding plain; and the cows will mate with the bulls and bear abundant calves, male and female. Keen though you are for profit, you should not now be enraged with anger.'

With these words he held out the *lyra*, and Phoebus Apollo accepted it. Into Hermes' hands he put the shining whip that he had,[26] and gave him the office of keeper of cattle. Maia's son accepted it with delight. [500] Then the glorious son of Leto, far-working lord Apollo, took the *kitharis* in his left hand and tried it part by part with the plectrum. It rang out awesomely under his touch, and the god sang to it beautifully.

Then the two turned the cattle towards the sacred meadow, and themselves hurried back, those most handsome sons of Zeus, to snowy Olympus, delighting in the *phorminx*.[27] So Zeus the counsellor was glad, and united the pair in friendship. And Hermes loved the son of Leto always, as he does

---

24   This suggestion that the *aulos* was known in Greece before stringed instruments runs counter to the fact of the primacy of the *phorminx* in Homer, and contradicts the treatment of the *aulos* as a foreign usurper of the *lyra*'s proper position, found in many legends. See Plut. *De Cohib. Irae* 456b–d, Diod. Sic. III.59.2–5; cf. 187 ps.-Plut. 1131f, 1132d: but see also 1132e–1133a.

25   The epithet *philokydēs*, 'renown-loving', suggests once again the competitive aspect of much Greek music-making.

26   Reading *echōn*, with the MSS, not Martin's emendation *hekōn*.

27   *Phorminx* here, and *kitharis* above, are plainly used as straightforward synonyms for *lyra*.

even now, having given the lovely *kitharis* [510] as a token to the far-shooter who played it expertly, holding it on his arm. But for himself he then found out the skill of another clever art, and made the sound of the *syringes*,[2] which can be heard far off.

Hymn to Pan

23   *Hymn to Pan 14–26*

Then at evening he lifts his voice alone, as he come back from the hunt gently playing sweet music on his reeds [i.e., the *syrinx*]. In melodies he could not be surpassed even by the bird who among the leaves of flowery spring pours forth her lament, her honey-voiced song. With him then go the clear-singing mountain nymphs, [20] singing and dancing with swift feet by a dark-water spring. Echo sounds loud about the mountain top; and the god gliding hither and thither among the dancers, and then into the middle, leads the dance with swift feet. On his back he has a spotted lynx-skin; and he rejoices in the clear-toned singing, in a soft meadow where crocus and sweet-scented hyacinth bloom, mingling with the grass in close embrace.

[28]   The *syrinx* is usually associated with Pan (e.g. **23** *Hymn to Pan* 14 ff, **123** Eurip *Electra* 699 ff, **124** *Ion* 492 ff), who was Hermes' son. It was also usually thought to be an earlier invention than the *aulos*: e.g. Callimachus, *Hymn to Artemis* 242–5.

CHAPTER 4

From Archilochus to the late sixth century

The Homeric bards and the simple songs and dances described by Homer, Hesiod and their immediate successors seem far removed from the elaborate art music of the fifth century and the combined romanticism and intellectualism of the fourth. For the origins of the transformation we must look to the song-writers of the seventh and sixth centuries, or even a little earlier, if Archilochus belongs partly to the eighth. It was their innovations in metre and rhythm, in melodic elaboration and structure, in the use of instruments, and in their multiplication of music's social and cultural roles, that made the classical forms possible, though they should not of course be regarded merely as stepping-stones to higher things. They expressed, and in part created, a style of life, feeling and thought that differed in important ways from what preceded and followed.

Unfortunately, the work of the lyric writers and most of the elegists survives in a pitifully fragmentary form. Though musical references can be identified, little that remains is substantial enough on its own to be quoted independently here. Many of the most useful passages are put together and discussed in our two main later sources, ps.-Plutarch and Athenaeus, where further notes will be found. The present chapter attempts no more than a brief sketch of the context within which such passages are to be read: it contains only three additional excerpts from Greek authors (23(a), 24 and 25), two of them looking back from a much later period.

These years are best known as the golden age of Greek lyric. The expression 'lyric poetry' suggests a personal, private art, poems to be recited or sung without the paraphernalia of public performance. It is true that such private music is a feature of the sixth century, and many of the songs of Ibycus, Anacreon, Sappho and Alcaeus were designed for a small circle of friends, to be sung, normally by the poet himself, at symposia or other gatherings in their own homes. But music was still – as it continued to be – predominantly public, attached to religious and civic or even military ceremonials and practices, and to such semi-public occasions as weddings. Terpander, as we have already seen, was famous for his solo concert-pieces, accompanying himself on the *kithara* (kitharodic *nomoi*), and both he and Thaletas were credited with using such songs to promote public order in Sparta (187 ps.-Plut. 1146b–c, Plut. *Lyc.* 4, cf. 21). The kitharodic *nomos* enjoyed great popularity in this period, and was an important event at the competitive festivals: many of the lyric poets were *kitharōdoi*. (See particularly 187 ps.-Plut. 1132d–e, 1133b–d: cf. Proclus, *Chrest.* 320a, and e.g. Herodotus' story of Arion, 1.24. On the *nomos* as a genre see Ch. 15, Appendix A.)

More culturally significant, however, was choral song and dance, and here again the lyric poets played an important role. Alcman was especially well known for his maiden-songs, pieces performed (again in Sparta) by companies of singing and dancing girls. (The best preserved example is *P.M.G.* 1.) Arion was reputed to have been a prominent composer of dithyramb,[1] a circular choral dance and song associated with the cult of Dionysus, which came, at least later, to have an especially complex diction

---

[1] Hdt. 1.23. Since it was already known to Archilochus and was probably older, Arion cannot be supposed to have invented it. He may merely have introduced it into Corinth, or have done something to establish its canonical form. On this matter, and the changes in the dithyramb at the end of the sixth century, see notes to 29 Pindar, fr. 61.

and form. The reputation of Stesichorus rested largely on his choral works. Sappho wrote songs for girl-choruses which, like Alcman, she herself trained to dance and sing: and like many of the others she wrote wedding songs. At the end of this period, Lasus, Simonides, Bacchylides and Pindar were almost exclusively engaged in composing choral works for public performance. One of Sappho's songs, probably written for a wedding, describes the marriage of Hector and Andromache: the closing lines give a vivid impression of the music that such festivities would involve.

23(a)   Sappho, fr. 44.24–34

> The papyri are mutilated: words in square brackets are conjectural. I have omitted lines 28–9, which cannot be securely reconstructed.

The sweet-singing *aulos* and the [*kitharis?*] were mingled, and the noise of *krotala*, and maidens [clearly?] sang a pure song, and a wondrous sound echoed to the sky . . . And myrrh and cassia and frankincense were mingled, and the women, those that were older, whirled in the dance, and all the men cried out a high (*orthios*) and lovely song, calling on Paon [i.e. Apollo Paion] the far-shooter with the fine *lyra*, and hymned godlike Hector and Andromache.

We cannot be sure how far poets and musicians altered the form or the substance of the ceremonies for which their works were created. But from the purely musical point of view, the period shows astonishing creative and innovative vitality. The area of innovation that displays itself most clearly to us now is that of metre, with which was linked the rhythm of music and the dance. All the oldest poetry we have is based on the dactylic hexameter: Terpander and his contemporaries continued to work within its framework,[2] which also formed the metrical foundation of elegy. Other metres were certainly known from early times,[3] though before the eighth century they probably occurred only in unsophisticated folk music: what is certain is that in seventh- and sixth-century lyric we are faced with an amazing proliferation of metrical and rhythmic patterns, which in their turn served as models for the elaborate songs of fifth-century drama.

Later commentators also mention innovations of a melodic kind. Different forms or styles were attributed to the various composers under the geographical titles used by theorists to designate the *harmoniai* and *tonoi* that belong to the technical analyses of the fourth century and after (see Ch. 10, Appendix A). These labels are rarely used by the poets themselves before the end of the sixth century,[4] and we can now have only the most imperfect conception of what they meant by them, or to what genuine features of sixth-century music the commentators are drawing attention. It seems certain that distinct varieties of melodic idiom were involved, and no doubt they were drawn originally from different areas of the Greek world. Quite probably the differences between these idioms, like those between *harmoniai* as later conceived, were at least partly rooted in differences that were capable of being analysed as distinctions of scalar structure. But little reliance can be placed on the analyses of the fourth century for interpreting the terminology of the sixth: and we are left with only a handful of passages, mainly in ps.-Plutarch and Athenaeus, which seem to give

---

2   187 ps.-Plut. 1132b–c. But this is not necessarily incompatible with rhythmic innovation: cf. 1135b–c.
3   See *P.M.G.* 880 (a reconstruction of the Linus song), and cf. 18 *Hymn to Apollo* 162 with n. 4.
4   Examples are Alcman, *P.M.G.* 126, Stesichorus, *P.M.G.* 212 (Phrygian), Lasus, *P.M.G.* 702 (Aeolian).

good clues about what these early structures may have been. They will be discussed in their place, but many of the details must be left unsatisfactorily vague.

There is good reason of another sort, however, for taking seriously the compilers' belief that at least the foundations of the later scale-forms, the *harmoniai*, were laid down in this period. The lyricists seem to have been, by Greek standards, unusually receptive to innovations in the structure and character of their instruments. Hitherto, the only stringed instrument of which we hear is the Homeric *phorminx*, but quite early in the lyric era the standard range of Greek instruments is complete, and their canonical forms are largely established. The word *lyra* appears first in Archilochus (fr. 51.47 Diehl). What he meant by it we do not know, but the late seventh or early sixth century gives us, in **21–2** *Hymn to Hermes*, a detailed description of the tortoiseshell instrument that came to monopolise the name. In the seventh century the *kithara* proper makes its entry on the scene, as does the *barbitos*: the *barbitos* is said by Pindar to have been Terpander's invention,[5] while the *kithara* is claimed for the next generation after him (**187** ps.-Plut. 1133c).

The most important innovation here is not the diversification of instrumental type. It is the invention, ascribed to Terpander,[6] of an instrument with seven strings, and the subsequent treatment of this number as a fixed norm.[7] If the hint in the lines attributed by Strabo to Terpander is reliable,[8] earlier instruments had only four strings, and the new arrangement plainly had far greater melodic potential. But there is more to it than that. A four-stringed instrument, perhaps tuned to a pair of fourths separated by a whole tone, does little to fix a clear-cut form of scale. A seven-stringed instrument must do so, though later writers were in doubt as to exactly which notes Terpander's scale incorporated (see the references given in n. 6 above). More crucially, the use of an instrument tuned to a definite scale makes possible the beginnings of a systematic *variety* of scale forms. If the strings have to be tuned to a definite and relatively complete note-series (complete, that is, over an octave or perhaps a seventh)[9] in advance of a performance, the musician must be conscious of the form of scale he is using, and of the alterations needed to produce an alternative system. It was in this period, then, that it became possible, indeed essential, for practising musicians to become aware of the structural differences between the regional forms of melody, and so to establish in at least a rudimentary way the basis of the later *harmoniai*.[10]

Instruments of quite a different sort also began to appear. Sappho is credited with the invention or introduction of the *pēktis* (**196** Ath. 635e), perhaps purely on the strength of her line 'far sweeter-singing than the *pēktis*': but the *pēktis* is also said by Pindar to be a Lydian instrument known in the time of Terpander (**196** Ath. 635d). Anacreon is quoted (**196** Ath. 635c) as mentioning a twenty-stringed *magadis*: and

---

5   See **196** Ath. 635d. But Neanthes of Cyzicus (**188** Ath. 175e) attributed it to Anacreon.

6   E.g. Strabo XIII.2.4. But other issues seem to be involved here too: see e.g. **180** ps.-Ar. *Probs.* XIX.32 (cf. **176** *Probs.* XIX.25, and *Probs.* XIX.7, 44, 47), **187** ps.-Plut. 1140f.

7   Further increases in the number of strings were made in the fifth century: e.g. **187** ps.-Plut. 1141c, 1142a, Nicom. 274, Cleonides 202: and cf. the stories told about Phrynis and Timotheus, Plut. *Prof. Virt.* 13, *Inst. Lac.* 17, Paus. III.12.10, **196** Ath. 636e, cf. **187** ps.-Plut. 1144f.

8   'We shall reject the four-voiced song, and sound new hymns on a seven-stringed *phorminx*.' A tradition recorded by Diod. Sic. (1.10) says that the earliest *lyra* had only three strings. For the four-stringed *phorminx* in eighth-century art see Fig. 3.

9   Ps.-Ar. *Probs.* XIX.7, 47, cf. Nicom. 244.

10   The use of the regional labels becomes relatively commonplace in Pindar, e.g. *Pyth.* 2. 69–71, *Nem.* 3.79 (Aeolian); *Ol.* 1.17–18, *Ol.* 2.2–5, *Pyth.* 8.20 (Dorian); fr. 180 (Aeolian and Dorian); **30** fr. 125 (Ionian? and Locrian).

the same passage introduces a controversy as to whether *pēktis* and *magadis* were really the same instrument. Again, Ibycus is said to have introduced the *sambyke* (**188** Ath. 175d–e and *Suda* s.v. Ibycus). A good many other varieties of stringed instrument, the *trigōnos* and the *epigoneion*, for example, seem to have come into use among the Greeks during the sixth century. Some information about these instruments will be found in Athenaeus: for the present, two points are of particular interest. First, all of them, or almost all, are 'many-stringed' instruments, capable of producing complex melodic patterns. Secondly, their tone colour would have been quite different from that of the *kithara* and its relations, since unlike them they were always plucked with the fingers, not struck with a plectrum.[11] Their sound was more intimate, and it seems clear that in the Greek context they are to be associated with private music-making rather than public performance, in which they were hardly ever used. If the account that is usually accepted is right, another new dimension was introduced into music by the *magadis* (and perhaps reproduced by the *epigoneion*): it is thought to have had strings tuned in pairs, the two strings of each pair sounding an octave apart, and to have been used for playing a melody in both octaves simultaneously. Even if this view of the *magadis* is questionable, the sixth-century quotations on which it is partly based undoubtedly show a lively interest in the possibility of 'answering' a melody, or part of a melody, at a different pitch.[12]

During the period which saw these developments in the art of lyric, parallel changes were taking place in music for the *aulos*. We know, if anything, even less about them: our best source is ps.-Plutarch (see particularly **187** 1132c–1137a), and I shall not discuss his evidence in detail here. The *aulos* had, from the time of Archilochus, a special connection with elegiac poetry: that is, not necessarily songs of an 'elegiac' or mournful character (very few extant early instances are of that kind), but songs written in the metre of the elegiac couplet. If our remaining examples are representative, their character was generally either bracing and martial (as especially in the poems of Tyrtaeus), or convivial: the large collection of verses ascribed (not all reliably) to Theognis, for instance, like Athenaeus' collection of Attic *skolia* (694c ff), was probably put together in the fifth century as a symposiasts' song book.[13]

Since it is impossible simultaneously to sing and to play a wind instrument, singers of *aulōdia* in any form had to provide an accompanist. According to ps.-Plutarch, the earliest auletes of repute were all Phrygians, and we have other evidence to suggest that the art was for some time the preserve of foreigners (e.g. **192** Ath. 624b, quoting Alcman and Hipponax). As late as the end of the sixth century, perhaps the early fifth, the accompanying aulete in a public performance was officially of a lower standing than the singer or singers (**187** ps.-Plut. 1141c–d, **190** Ath. 621b, cf. **161** Ar. *Pol.* 1341a). But by then that situation was visibly anomalous. Both solo *aulos* playing and *aulōdia* had long extended their scope beyond war-songs and drinking parties: both, for example, were introduced into the Pythian games in 586 B.C. Both, in fact, if we can trust the traditions that ps.-Plutarch reports about Olympus and Clonas, had

---

[11] They are called generically *psaltika*, things pulled with the fingers, in contrast to *krousta* or *krouomena*, things struck. They may be broadly classified as belonging to the harp family, with certain possible or probable exceptions.

[12] See **196** Ath. 634c ff, especially 636b–c. For the verb *magadizein*, to 'magadise', used of choirs singing in octaves, see e.g. **172** and **183**, ps.-Ar. *Probs.* XIX.18, 39.

[13] For references in it to the reveller's use of the *aulos* see lines 239–43, 531–2 (mentioning also the *lyra*), 825–8, 939–44, 1041–2, 1063–8. An earlier reference, if it is genuine, is in Athenaeus' quotation from Archilochus at 447b.

eld substantial places in serious music-making from at least the early seventh entury. Certainly the *aulos* had a significant niche in the choral songs and dances of eligious celebration, particularly but not exclusively in the dithyramb. This form ook on a new lease of life, at least in Athens, during the late sixth century, where its stablishment was linked with the name of Lasus of Hermione, a musician famous or his improvements in auletic technique (**187** ps.-Plut. 1141c, cf. schol. to Pindar, *Ol.* 13.26). These two facts about him may be related. In the early fifth century, hough stringed instruments were more important to him, Pindar's choral works ertainly used the *aulos* on occasion (*Ol.* 3.8, 10.93–4, *Nem.* 3.29): some types of horal work, notably the *prosodion* ('processional'), seem to have been quite specifically the *aulos'* preserve (**187** ps.-Plut. 1132c, cf. Proclus, *Chrest.* 320a 18 ff).

Speculations about the structure of scale forms used by the early auletes are reproduced by ps.-Plutarch (**187** 1134f–1135b, 1137a–e). Although one of the features of he *aulos* to which later writers most often refer is its versatility in modulating between scale forms (e.g. **149** Plato, *Rep.* 399c–d), there is no reason to suppose that he scales themselves had a history that differed substantially from those used by performers on the *kithara*. What gave to the *aulos* an independent and specialised music of its own was rather the exploitation of its extensive capacity for dramatic and emotional expression. Its versatility of mood recommended it to symposiasts, and its range of tone colour and volume – far more various than that of any Greek stringed instrument – opened up striking possibilities for direct musical representation, 'mimesis'. The *Pythikos nomos* described by Pollux, which goes back to the sixth century, illustrates the point vividly, as does the account of the origin of the *aulos* and the *polykephalos nomos* given in **27** Pindar, *Pyth.* 12. The passage of Pollux, together with a related excerpt from Strabo, deserves full quotation.

24   Pollux, *Onomastikon* IV.84

The auletic *Pythikos nomos* has five parts, *peira, katakeleusmos, iambikon, spondeion* and *katachoreusis*. The *nomos* is a representation [*dēlōma*, lit. 'showing', 'display'] of the battle of Apollo against the serpent. In the *peira* ['test', 'trial'] he surveys the ground to see if it is suitable for the contest. In the *katakeleusmos* ['challenge'] he calls up the serpent, and in the *iambikon*[14] he fights: the *iambikon* also includes sounds[15] like those of the *salpinx* and gnashings like those of the serpent as it grinds its teeth after being pierced with arrows. The *spondeion*[16] represents (*dēloi*) the victory of the god; and in the *katachoreusis* ['dance of triumph'] the god performs a dance of victory.

25   Strabo, *Geography* IX.3.10

[At the Pythian games] to the *kitharōdoi* they added auletes and kitharists, who performed with no singing, and played a melody called the *Pythikos nomos*. It has five parts, *ankrousis, ampeira, katakeleusmos, iamboi* and

[14]   For the import of this name see Strabo's interpretation of *iamboi* in the next passage.
[15]   *Kroumata*, usually the sounds of a stringed instrument struck with a plectrum, but sometimes used more generally: this application to wind instruments is not unparalleled.
[16]   'Libation song', associated with spondaic rhythm. For an account of a very early auletic *spondeion* see **187** ps.-Plut. 1134f–1135b, 1137b–d.

daktyloi, syringes . . . The intention is to celebrate, through this melody, the contest of Apollo against the serpent, representing (*dēlōn*) the prelude with the *ankrousis*, the first onslaught of the contest with the *ampeira*, the contest itself with the *katakeleusmos*, the triumphal song (*epipaiōnismos*) over the victory with the *iamboi* and *daktyloi*, using rhythms of which the dactylic is suitable for hymns, the iambic for insults, as in the word *iambizein* ['insult' or 'satirise'], while with the *syringes* the players imitated the death of the monster as it expired with its final whistlings (*syrigmous*).[17]

It was only natural that with the development of tragedy and comedy in the fifth century, the dramatists retained the connection with the *aulos* that had characterised the predecessors of the drama: it was always the principal accompanying instrument and often the only one. But in the early years of the century, the ever-increasing dramatic expressiveness and technical virtuosity of its practitioners met outrage and hostility. The *aulos*, a mere 'menial', was seen as usurping the proper position of the singer,[18] and destroying the noble simplicity of traditional music (Pratinas quoted at 189 Ath. 617c–f). From here to the end of antiquity, the same complaint in one form or another is continually reviewed by aesthetic conservatives and morally concerned social theorists (most notably Plato). But for the very reasons that these worthies frowned on it, it became and remained much the most important instrument of popular entertainment; and it is notable that even as solid a citizen as Pindar singled out two of its supposedly most decadent features – its melodic versatility and its capacity for mimetic changes of tone colour – for special praise.[19]

It has usually been accepted that throughout the classical period the normal Greek practice was for the accompanying instrument to play in unison with the singer. It might play a prelude at the beginning, and might add short passages between vocal phrases: but otherwise it had no independent melody, and 'harmony' in the modern sense was unknown. This view scarcely does justice to the evidence, however: at the very least, three qualifications that are relevant to the lyric era should be noticed. First, we hear of something called *krousis hypo tēn ōdēn*, 'playing under the song', contrasted with *proschorda krouein*, which indicates playing in unison with the voice. Ps.-Plutarch attributes the invention of this practice to Archilochus:[20] it evidently involved playing different notes from those of the singer, but may sometimes

---

17 *Ankrousis* seems to mean simply 'striking up'; *ampeira* 'trial', 'attempt'; *katakeleusmos* 'summons' or 'challenge'. The name *syringes* is simply the plural form of *syrinx*, and probably refers here to the imitative effects produced by very high notes. On the *aulos* these effects may have been generated by the use of the device known as the 'syrinx of the aulos', which seems to have served the function of a 'speaker' hole: see 187 ps.-Plut. 1138b, Aristox. *El. Harm.* 21.1, Plut. *Non Posse Suav.* 1096b: on the *kithara*, perhaps by light stopping with the finger-nails to yield high harmonics, though this suggestion is speculative. See 196 Ath. 637f–638a with notes.

18 Not that of the *lyra* or *kithara*, as some commentators have asserted. Pratinas' diatribe shows no sign of being part of a controversy between proponents of wind instruments and those of strings: the issue concerns only the status of voice and *aulos* in musical forms where both were incontrovertibly at home.

19 See particularly 27 *Pyth.* 12, and cf. the use of the adjective *pamphōnos*, 'all-voiced', *Ol.* 7.11–12, *Isth.* 5.26–8.

20 187 1141a–b. 'Under' indicates subordination, not lower pitch. The text is unclear, and the intention may be to ascribe this innovation to Crexus in the late fifth century. The same passage attributes other novelties in musical practice to Archilochus: recitative (*parakatalogē*) with accompaniment, and the practice of speaking some

mply no more than reproducing the melody an octave higher, something that became very common (e.g. **167, 168, 170–2, 186** ps.-Ar. *Probs.* XIX.12, 14, 16–18, 49). But econdly, ps.-Plutarch also indicates (**187** 1137b–d) that certain notes of the scale in certain forms of music were used by musicians only in the accompaniment, to form both concords and discords. How they were employed we do not know, though it was plainly simultaneous with the melody without being part of it: sometimes, perhaps, they were drones, sometimes elements of decorations leading to a cadence. One fourth-century source speaks, as though it were a commonplace phenomenon, of instrumentalists playing different notes from the singer during the course of the song, but finishing either in unison with him or at the octave: here the octave evidently does not count as a 'different note'.[21] Again, we have no details of the practice, nor do we know how old it is. It may, however, be related to a third point, which is that the auletic techniques developed in the sixth century made possible the performance of an extensive repertoire of complex ornamental figures around the principal melody: in the fifth and fourth centuries these attained an astonishing intricacy, and were the butt of many a critic's tongue.[22] It seems clear that they flowed over also into the art of the *kithara*-player: attempts by kitharists to rival the new techniques of the *aulos* in other ways, particularly in the area of dramatic representation, go back at least to the late sixth century.[23] While it is true that at that date these developments still had a long way to go, it must be recognised that the instrumental techniques, as well as the melodic and rhythmic resources familiar to our next major writer, Pindar, were already a world away from those of the Homeric and Hesiodic traditions.

(iambic) lines to music, singing others. The latter practice, according to ps.-Plut., had a significant future in dithyramb and tragedy: the former was probably used in tragedy too, but little is known of it: see however **165** ps.-Ar. *Probs.* XIX.6, and cf. perhaps Arist. Quint. 6.4–5.

21 **183** ps.-Ar. *Probs.* XIX.39. See also the rather obscure remark at **187** ps.-Plut. 1138b, where he speaks of the 'conversations' (*dialektoi*, perhaps simply 'styles') of accompaniment among the ancient composers as being more complex than those of the moderns.

22 On fifth-century developments in auletic technique see e.g. **187** ps.-Plut. 1138b, **195** Ath. 631e, cf. 131b, Pollux IV.80, Plut. *Non Posse Suav.* 1096b. For criticisms of elaborate roulades and ornamentation in music of various kinds, Pherecrates quoted at **187** ps.-Plut. 1141e–1142b, Aristoph. *Clouds* 334 with schol., and see Ch. 7 below.

23 **196** Ath. 637f–638a, cf. **25** Strabo IX.3.10. For later developments see the Pherecrates fragment cited in n. 22, and cf. **158** Plato, *Laws* 812d–e.

CHAPTER 5

Pindar

Pindar belongs to the first half of the fifth century: he is roughly contemporary with Aeschylus. He is best known for his 'epinician' odes, songs sung in honour of victors at the games,[1] a considerable collection of which survives. The rest of his large output (all of which, so far as we know, was composed for public occasions) now exists only in fragments. The victory odes were designed for choral performances (see e.g. *Pyth.* 5.103–4, 10.6, *Isth.* 8.1–4), though that does not mean that all parts of them were sung by the whole choir. There were 'leaders' who sang solo parts (*Ol.* 6.87–92), and it seems clear that a substantial vocal role was assigned to the accompanist, in addition to his playing on what Pindar usually calls the *phorminx* (less often *lyra*: see **26** *Pyth.* 1.1 with n. 5). In at least some cases this performer was probably Pindar himself. His frequent references to himself as singer might be treated as merely conventional, and certainly he was not always present in person (e.g. *Pyth.* 2.67–8): but the pervasiveness of the convention, and the personal tone of e.g. *Ol.* 11, *Pyth.* 11, can leave little doubt that it had real substance. (See also particularly *Nem.* 4.13–16.) Sometimes the ode appears to be sung as a preliminary to a choral piece (*Nem.* 2.24–5, 3.3–5). The choruses, commonly of young men (e.g. *Pyth.* 5.103–4, *Nem.* 3.3–5, *Isth.* 8.1–4), undoubtedly danced as well as singing (e.g. **26** *Pyth.* 1. 1–4).

Some of the odes were performed at the ceremony in which the victor was crowned (e.g. *Ol.* 11), others later, at the victor's return to his home city (e.g. *Ol.* 10: *Ol.* 11 constitutes a promissory note for *Ol.* 10). *Pyth.* 2 was 'sent across the sea' to Syracuse (see lines 67–8, and cf. *Pyth.* 5.23–4, 10.55–6, 11.1–16). At the crowning itself, if no specially composed ode was ready, it was apparently the practice to perform an ancient victory song of Archilochus (*Ol.* 9.1–4 with schol.). The genre, in one form or another, is clearly therefore very old: Pindar himself traces it back as a formal institution for several generations (*Nem.* 4.80 ff).

All the odes, with the exception of **27** *Pyth.* 12 on the victory of an aulete, celebrate prowess of an athletic kind, and their subject matter is thus not specifically musical. But Pindar is an extremely self-conscious writer, and like others in a choral tradition stretching back to Alcman and beyond, he often refers to his own music and verse. The references are scattered through his work, and are usually too brief to merit individual quotation, so that an indication of some of their more important implications may usefully be given here.

They tell us rather little about the details of performing practice, aside from the points mentioned above: they reveal much more fully Pindar's attitude to music and to his role as a composer. Nevertheless, some facts about performance do emerge. Of its five main elements – words, rhythms, melody, dance and accompaniment – we have the words, and their metres allow us to form some conception of the rhythms, which were certainly intricate and elaborately varied. That in turn tells us something about the dance, but Pindar does not, like Alcman, describe the activities of his dancers as they take place. The melodies, of course, are wholly lost. (The melody

---

[1] The genre had attained a high level of sophistication by this date. Pindar is not its only distinguished exponent: the best known of the others are his near-contemporaries Bacchylides and Simonides.

alleged to have come from the beginning of *Pyth.* 1, and published by Kircher in 1650, is certainly a forgery.[2]) It is true that he mentions melodic styles or genres quite commonly, far more often than any of his predecessors, giving them geographical names of the kind later associated with the *harmoniai* and *tonoi:*[3] but we have no more notion of their real significance in his writing than in the poets of the previous century.

Of the instruments that accompanied the songs we know rather more. A very large number of references guarantees that a stringed instrument was usual, but *auloi* were sometimes used with it (*Ol.* 3.8, 7.11–12, 10.93–4, *Nem.* 9.8–9, *Isth.* 5.26–8), and perhaps occasionally without (*Nem.* 3.79). There is no mention of percussion in the performance of these pieces, but for its use in a different context, in the cult of the Mother Goddess, see *Isth.* 7.3–4 and **29** fr. 61.6–8.

Concerning Pindar's attitude to his art and to music generally, two points deserve special mention. First, in compositions dedicated to men's successes, it is natural to find expressions of the ancient theme that true glory is achieved only when deeds are immortalised in song. It is an idea to which Pindar often returns, and one might suspect him of giving it no more than the verbal allegiance that custom dictated, even of indulging in an opportunity to advertise the value of his wares (for he was a paid professional: *Pyth.* 11.41–2, cf. **28** *Isth.* 2.1–11). But Pindar treats the theme with a seriousness that gives us no good reason to doubt his sincerity (see particularly *Nem.* 7.12–16, *Ol.* 10.91–6); and though he is aware that the poet's skill may create for a man a reputation he does not deserve (*Nem.* 7.20–4), he insists that music and evil-doing are wholly alien to one another (**26** *Pyth.* 1.13 ff, 97–8, cf. *Pyth.* 2.14). He is writing in a tradition that still has its roots in hymns to the gods, and in singing the praises of men he is investing them with something of the same divinity. Hence his compositions acquire a significance transcending the immediate occasion of their performance.

Secondly, the many descriptive words and phrases that Pindar applies to his own music tell us something perhaps a little surprising about its mood and tone. Songs performed to honour an athletic victor and to glorify his native city might be expected to have simple, stirring tunes of a patriotic flavour, and to be characterised by the hearty swagger of pomp and circumstance, rather than by subtlety or charm. The delicate convolutions of his diction and his ideas, and the intricacy of his rhythms, should already make us suspicious of this assumption, and if what he says about his melodies is to be trusted, the truth is quite the opposite. Of his favourite epithets for his music, much the commonest are drawn from the intimate lyric tradition of Sappho and Alcaeus, and suggest sweetness, delicacy, and a soothing softness. His song is a draught of nectar, the gift of the Muses, the sweet fruit of his mind (*Ol.* 7.7–8): his *phorminx* is sweet-songed (ibid. 11–12), the *lyra* is sweet-speaking and the *aulos* sweet, giving delight (*Ol.* 10.93–4): his hymns are honey-voiced (*Ol.* 11.4–5), and the young men of the chorus are builders of honey-voiced revels (*Nem.* 3.4–5): his ode is 'honey mixed with white milk, whose mingled dew wreathes the cup' (ibid. 76–9). Music is soothing (*Pyth.* 1.5–14): Pindar wishes that his honey-voiced hymns could cast a magical spell (*Pyth.* 3.63–5): songs, daughters of the Muses, beguile the victor as they touch him, and fine words accompanied by the *phorminx* soothe him even better than a bath of warm water (*Nem.* 4.1–8). The victor's fame grows in gentle song (*Nem.* 9.49). Pindar is cultivating the garden of the Graces (*Ol.* 9.26–7). Many more instances could be cited.

Implications of subtlety and intricacy appear particularly with reference to the

---

[2]   See E. Pöhlmann, *Denkmaler altgriechischer Musik* 16.
[3]   Aeolian, *Pyth.* 2.69–71, *Nem.* 3.79, fr. 180; Dorian, *Ol.* 1.17–18, 2.5, *Pyth.* 8.20, fr. 180; Ionian (?) and Locrian, **30** fr. 125; Lydian, *Ol.* 14.17–18, *Nem.* 4.44–5. See also notes to **30** fr. 125.

accompaniment. The song is intricately accompanied (*Ol.* 4.2), the kitharist play
intricately (*Nem.* 4.14), the *phorminx* is subtle-skilled (*Pyth.* 4.296); and we may
connect with this idea the various uses of the metaphor of weaving: Athena wove
together the dirge of the Gorgons (*Pyth.* 12.7–8), and the sweet *phorminx* is told to
'weave out' a well-loved song (*Nem.* 4.44–5).[4] The other image that most commonly
recurs is that of music as a swift and truthful bearer of news. The chorus-leader is a
true messenger (*Ol.* 6.90); Pindar shoots the arrows of his song to distant places (*Ol.*
9.5–14), and its news travels faster than horse or ship (ibid. 23–6), penetrating even
to Hades (*Ol.* 14.20–1), unlike sculptures, which stay where they are put (*Nem.*
5.1–3). The arrow metaphor shifts in *Nem.* 6.28–9: he hits the mark with his words
as with a bow (cf. *Nem.* 9.55).

Any understanding of Pindar's conception of music and his practice of it must be
built up from the hundreds of brief references peppered about his work, and these
need to be read in their context. The excerpts given below are inadequate on their
own: they are simply examples of some of the more extended and significant passages
on the subject. I have included quotations from three fragments that do not belong to
victory odes. Pindar also wrote hymns, paeans, dithyrambs, processionals, maiden-
songs, *hyporchēmata*, encomia and laments: the quotations indicate special features
of some of these types, and raise one or two other general issues.

26   Pindar, *Pythian* 1.1–14, 92–100

The opening and the end of a long ode in honour of Hieron of Syracuse,
whose racing-chariot won the victory in 470 B.C. The fourth Ode of
Bacchylides celebrates the same victory.

Gold *phorminx*,[5] joint possession of Apollo and the violet-haired Muses, the
dance-step, leader of the revel, hears you, and the singers obey your signals[6]
when you are set quivering and create the beginnings of the chorus-leading
preludes.[7] You quench the spear-wielding thunderbolt of ever-flowing fire.

---

[4]   On the metaphor of weaving see note to 51 Eurip. *I.T.* 218–28.

[5]   As in earlier poetry, the use of this word does not imply any particular one of the
instruments of the *kithara* and *lyra* group. Pindar's instrument was certainly what
came to be called the *kithara*, though he himself does not use the word (*kitharis*
occurs once, in the sense 'the art of playing the *kithara*', *Pyth.* 5.65). In references to
his own music, his uses of the word *phorminx* outnumber those of the word *lyra* by
about four to one. With the conception of the *phorminx* as leader of the song and
dance, contrast *Ol.* 2.1.

[6]   *Samata* (= *sēmata*) are here probably 'signs' or 'signals' to begin, embodied in the
instrumental prelude, but having no special musical signification. The meaning 'unit
of time', sometimes given to the related word *sēmeion* in the context of theoretical
rhythmics, is not found except in late (and technical) Greek, e.g. Arist. Quint.
32.12 ff.

[7]   *Ambolē* (= *anabolē*), here 'beginning', and *prooimion*, here 'prelude', are virtually
identical in sense. An *anabolē* was normally an instrumental preliminary with no
fixed structure: hence when composers such as Melanippides began to produce dithyrambs not balanced and ordered metrically by strophe and antistrophe, they too were
referred to as *anabolai* (Ar. *Rhet.* 1409b, who goes on to quote Democritus of Chios
parodying Hesiod, *W.D.* 265: 'The man who does wrong to another does wrong to
himself, but worst of all to the doer is a long *anabolē*.') See also 22 *Hymn to Hermes*
426, 136 Aristoph. *Birds* 1385–6, 169 ps.-Ar. *Probs.* XIX.15, and cf. introductory
note to *Homeric Hymns*.

The eagle of Zeus sleeps upon his sceptre, with his swift wings drooping on both sides, lord of the birds; and you pour a dark mist on his bent head, a gentle closing of his eyes. As he sleeps he flexes his supple back, enthralled by your rushing motion. Even violent Ares, leaving aside the rough vigour of his spears, soothes his heart in slumber, and your shafts enchant the minds of the gods through the skill of Leto's son and the deep-girdled Muses.[8] But all things that Zeus has not loved are bewildered when they hear the cry of the Muses, either on the earth or on the irresistible sea . . .

[92]   Only the glory of a fame that follows behind mortals reveals their way of life, through story-tellers and singers. The generous virtues of Croesus do not fade, while pitiless-hearted Phalaris, who burned men in his brazen bull, is everywhere held down by words of hatred. No *phorminges* under the roof accept him, to be softly blended with the voices of boys. Good fortune is the first of prizes, and to be well spoken of is second. The man who wins both and holds them, has received the loftiest garland.[9]

27   Pindar, *Pythian* 12

> Written in honour of Midas of Acragas, winner of the auletic contest at Delphi in 490 and 486 B.C. The ode probably refers to the earlier occasion.

Lover of splendour, most beautiful of the cities of mortals, home of Persephone, you who live on the nobly built-upon hill above the banks of Acragas where the sheep graze, I ask you, queen, graciously to accept, with the kindliness of immortals and of men, this wreath from Pytho for glorious Midas: and accept him too, who has beaten Greece in the art which Pallas Athena discovered, when she wove together the deathly dirge of the fierce Gorgons, the dirge that she heard poured out in woeful grief from under the maidens' dreadful snaky heads, when Perseus killed one sister out of the three, bringing doom to sea-encircled Seriphos and to its people. He blinded the weird race of Phorcus: he made dreadful for Polydektes his wedding feast, his long enslavement of Perseus' mother, and the marriage-bed to which she was compelled, by pulling forth the head of fair-cheeked Medusa, he, Danae's son, begotten, we say, of a shower of gold that fell of its own will.

But when the maiden goddess had saved her dear friend from these toils, she made an every-voiced melody of *auloi*,[10] to imitate with instruments the

---

[8]   On the magical powers of music see *Pyth.* 3.51, 63–5, and for other references in fifth-century literature see Ch. 6, 110–20.

[9]   That the rewards of success are incomplete unless celebrated in song is a recurrent theme in Pindar: see e.g. *Ol.* 9.5–14, 10.91–3, *Pyth.* 3.112–15, *Nem.* 6.31, and especially *Nem.* 7.12–16. For an unusual slant on the matter, *Nem.* 7.20–4.

[10]   The word *pamphōnos*, 'every-voiced', is several times applied by Pindar to the *aulos* (*Ol.* 7.12, *Isth.* 5.27). Other authors commonly speak of it as e.g. *polyphthongos*, 'many-noted', to indicate the large number of notes it could produce (by cross-fingering, and by techniques of breath- and lip-control, as well as by the – later – increase in the number of finger-holes), by comparison with such instruments as the

clamorous wailing that burst from the ravening jaws of Euryale. The goddess discovered it: but when she had discovered it for mortal men to possess,
she named it the *nomos* of many heads,[11] that glorious suitor for contests to
stir the people,[12] coming through thin bronze and through the reeds that
grow by the city of the Graces with its lovely dancing-places, in the holy
place of the nymph of Cephisus, faithful witnesses to the dancers.[13] If there is
any success among men, it does not appear without labour. A god will end it,
perhaps even today, and what is fated cannot be escaped. But there will come
a time that will strike a blow unhoped for and beyond expectation, and will
give one thing, but not another.[14]

28   Pindar, *Isthmian* 2.1–11

> The beginning of an ode in honour of Xenocrates of Acragas, winner of the
> chariot race in about 470 B.C.

The men of old, Thrasyboulos, who stepped onto the chariot of the golden-
wreathed Muses together with the resplendent *phorminx*, shot lightly from
their bows their honey-voiced songs[15] for their loves – for anyone beautiful,
who had that sweetest ripeness that woos Aphrodite on her fine throne.
    The Muse was then not yet fond of profit,[16] and did not work for hire; nor
were the sweet, soft-voiced songs of honey-speaking Terpsichore for sale,

lyra and *kithara*. Cf. e.g. **149** Plato, *Rep.* 399c–d, where it is even called *polychor-*
dotatos, lit. 'of most numerous strings'. The same epithet is applied to it in a fragment ascribed doubtfully to Simonides (*P.M.G.* 947). The sense here is probably
similar. Alternatively it may refer to the instrument's emotional and representational
versatility. Wide variations in dramatic effect were associated with auletic *nomoi*,
like the one described here: see particularly **24** and **25**, the descriptions by Pollux
(IV.84) and Strabo (IX.3.10) of the *Pythikos nomos*.
11   On the Many-headed (*polykephalos*) *nomos*, see **187** ps.-Plut. 1133d–e. Other
auletic *nomoi* are mentioned in the same passage (1132b–1134d), which surveys the
ancient *nomoi* generally.
12   I.e., it is a competition-piece.
13   The reeds, *donakes*, are those used for the vibrating reed of the mouthpiece of the
aulos, and grew, so the scholiast tells us, near Orchomenos in Boeotia. There is a full,
if sometimes enigmatic, account of the way they were prepared and the reeds manu-
factured at **163** Theophrastus, *Hist. Plant.* IV.11. 'Cephisus' is here the name of a
river that flowed into Lake Cephisus or Copais, on whose western end Orchomenos
stood (cf. *Ol.* 14.1–4).
14   The scholiast relates a story, almost certainly apocryphal, to explain the reference of
the final lines. 'It is said that a strange accident happened to this aulete. While he was
competing, the reed was accidentally broken, and stuck to the roof of his mouth: but
he played on with nothing but the pipes, as though playing a *syrinx*. The hearers,
amazed and delighted, found the sound most pleasing: and that is how he came to
win.'
15   *Hymnoi*, 'hymns': commonly of music in praise of gods or heroes (see introduction to
Homeric Hymns): often of songs of almost any kind (see Ch. 6, **93–9**). In Pindar the
word usually retains its sense as meaning 'a song of praise', but the praise may be
directed at any person, human or divine.
16   The composer who first wrote for profit was said to be Simonides (Aristoph. *Peace*
695 ff). The schol. ad loc. says that it is to Simonides' mercenary character that
Pindar is referring here.

their faces silvered over. But now she tells us to take heed of the Argive's word that comes closest to truth itself: 'Money, money is man' he said, when he had lost possessions and friends alike.[17]

29   Pindar, fr. 61.1–21

> The opening of a dithyramb written for performance in Thebes. The main part of it, now lost, was apparently concerned with the exploits of Heracles.

In earlier times the song of the dithyrambs[18] crept along, stretched out like a rope,[19] and the 's' came out base-born from men's mouths,[20] but now new

[17] The Argive was Aristodemus, according to Alcaeus. Pindar seems to be apologising to his patron for charging him money: in *Pyth*. 11.41–4 he refers to the fact that he has to chop and change from one topic to another, and blames it on the constraints of working for hire. Note that the contrast in the first stanza is with love-songs, not with earlier victory odes: the suggestion seems to be that few poets now write personal lyric purely for their own satisfaction, and it is true that little seems to have been written after the end of the sixth century. The tradition of writing victory odes is traced back several generations at *Nem*. 4.88 ff. On other matters to do with musicians' pay see **187** ps.-Plut. 1141c–d, **189** Ath. 617b–f.

[18] The origins and nature of early dithyramb are much disputed. It is known to Archilochus (see **193** Ath. 628a–b), where it is already associated with Dionysus. Herodotus (1.23) speaks of Arion as having been 'the first of men that we know to have composed the dithyramb and named it and produced it in Corinth'. The exact sense of this is unclear: some scholars take Arion's innovation to have been the stationary, non-dancing chorus. Cf. schol. to Pindar *Ol*. 13.19, and discussion in Pickard-Cambridge, *Dithyramb, Tragedy and Comedy* (2nd ed.) 11 ff. (Ch. 1 of that book remains the best overall investigation of the subject.) At all events, we can be sure that the dithyramb was a circular chorus (e.g. line 3 of the present fr., Aristoph. *Clouds* 332 and schol., Ath. 181c), that it was sometimes, but perhaps not always, danced (e.g. **189** Pratinas ap. Ath. 617b, Pollux IV.104), that it generally had Dionysiac connections, though it also had an occasional and very special role in the cult of Apollo (Plut. *De E*. 9), and that it was accompanied by the *aulos* (Pratinas, loc. cit., cf. e.g. **187** ps.-Plut. 1141c, schol. to Aeschin. *In Timarch*. 10).

[19] The interpretation of this epithet (*schoinoteneios*) is uncertain. It cannot involve a contrast between a strophic and an unstructured form, since the unstructured type of dithyramb was apparently the invention of the rather later poet Melanippides (Ar. *Rhet*. 1409b). Taken with the rest of the passage, it seems most likely to indicate a plain and simple style, proceeding 'in a straight line' (the sense of *schoinotenēs* in Hdt. 1.189 and VII.23), by contrast with something more complex and verbally convoluted, which Pindar is advertising as his own. (By the time of Aristophanes, towards the end of the century, writers of dithyramb were proverbial for their obscure and over-decorated diction: e.g. **135** *Birds* 903 ff, **136** 1373 ff, and see Ch. 7 below.)

[20] The reference is evidently to the 'asigmatic' songs (songs not using the letter *san*, the Dorian word for *sigma*, 's'), which our authorities attribute to Pindar's teacher Lasus (Ath. 455c). Lasus was credited with the introduction of the dithyramb to musical competition in Athens (*Suda*, cf. schol. to Aristoph. *Birds* 1403), and with various innovations in dithyrambic music (**187** ps.-Plut. 1141b–c). Since the present piece does not avoid the 's', the sentence cannot mean 'People used to utter the base-born "s" in dithyrambs, but we do so no longer': it must mean 'People used to treat the "s" as base-born and therefore avoided it, but now we know better.' Since Lasus' objection to the 's' was that it was not sufficiently euphonious, Pindar may be understood as rejecting an over-sensitive refinement of diction.

gates have opened for our holy circles.[21] Cry out,[22] for you know what rites the gods too set up for Dionysus in their home, beside the thunderbolt of Zeus. The whirlings of *typana*[23] begin, beside the great and holy mother, and *krotala*[24] clatter, and the torch burns bright under the glowing pines; and the loud-sounding wails and frenzies and shouts of the river-nymphs arise amid the tumult of tossing necks. There the almighty thunderbolt, breathing fire, and Ares' spear are shaken, and the strong aegis of Athena resounds with the cries of ten thousand snakes. Artemis will come swiftly, alone, harnessing a wild company of lions for Dionysus, in Bacchic fervour; and he is charmed by the dancing herds of beasts. I have been chosen and set up by the Muse as a herald of wise verses for Greece, with its fine choruses, praying for the prosperity of chariot-riding Thebes . . .

30   Pindar, fr. 125

> The category of composition to which this sadly mutilated papyrus fragment belongs is uncertain. Little of it remains, but it is of interest both for what it says and implies about the so-called *harmoniai* in Pindar's time, and for its representation of the relationship between aulete and singer. I have followed the partial reconstruction given in Bowra's O.C.T., with the variants mentioned in my notes.

To rival the Ionian Muse,[25] a song and a *harmonia* for the *auloi* were devised by one of the Locrians who live by the white-crested hill of Zephyrion, a shining city beyond the Ausonian headland.[26] And he uttered aloud, like a

---

21   I.e., the dithyrambic choruses. The novelty which Pindar is claiming, to judge by the following lines, is an uninhibited and vigorously enthusiastic mode of expression, in contrast to the plain style, over-elegant diction, and perhaps absence of dancing in the dithyrambs of his predecessors. The opening of Pratinas fr. 1 (see n. 18 above) suggests that not only the new elaboration of *aulos*-playing credited to Lasus, but also the institution of dancing in the dithyramb was something to which objections might be made. Pindar is pointing out the inappropriateness of such staid and unenthusiastic performances in a rite connected with Dionysus: his theme is that we know what Dionysus is like, and that our celebrations of him should reflect that knowledge.

22   These two words are conjectural.

23   The *typanon* or *tympanon* was a tambourine-like drum. For its association with the Mother Goddess and with Dionysus see e.g. the Homeric *Hymn to the Mother of the Gods* 1–5, 63 and 65 Eurip. *Bacchae* 55–63, 151–67, 68 and 69 *Cycl.* 63–70, 203–5, 71 *Helen* 1338–52: cf. Fig. 18.

24   *Krotala* are clappers comparable to castanets (see Figs. 15 and 16): they have associations similar to those of the *tympanon*, e.g. 69 Eurip. *Cyclops* 203–5, 70 *Helen* 1308–14.

25   Of this first phrase, only the first three letters of 'Ionian' survive. I translate the remainder as conjecturally reconstructed by Schroeder: the sense is at least very probable.

26   The Locrian is Xenocritus: see schol. to *Ol.* 10.17, cf. 187 ps.-Plut. 1134c, e–f. That the Locrian *harmonia* had a definite 'character and feeling' (*ēthos* and *pathos*) was asserted on Heraclides' authority at 192 Ath. 625e, though what it was is not explained. The writer adds that it was used in the time of Simonides and Pindar, but subsequently went out of currency. The Ionian *harmonia*, with which it seems to be

clear-sounding chariot, a complete paean fit for Apollo and the Graces.[27] Hearing him playing his few notes,[28] and busying myself with my loquacious art, I am roused to rival his song, like a dolphin of the sea, moved by the lovely melody of *auloi* in the flood of the waveless ocean.[29]

31   Pindar, fr. 126.1–8

> Again, it is not certain to what class of composition this fragment belongs. Its subject matter suggests that it is a lament: it does something to show that the classification of compositions into sharply distinguished types was not just an invention of the scholars of Alexandria.

There are songs of paeans,[30] coming in their season, songs of the children of Leto of the golden distaff. There are also songs that long for the dithyramb,[31] out of the burgeoning ivy of Dionysus' wreaths. But in another song three goddesses put to rest the bodies of their sons.[32] One sings a dirge for clear-voiced Linus,[33] one in her newest hymns sings for Hymenaios [the god of marriage], whom Fate seized when he first lay touching another in wedlock, and one sings of Ialemos,[34] whose strength was shackled by a devouring illness.

contrasted here, is described by Heraclides (**192** Ath. 625b–c) as originally 'austere and hard, with a not ignoble weightiness': later, he goes on, it altered, becoming more luxurious in character. Plato (**149** *Rep.* 398e) speaks of an Ionian ('Iastian') *harmonia* which is called 'slack' (*chalara*), and associated with soft and voluptuous personalities. For other references in Pindar to regionally named melodic types see n. 3 above: on the technical differences between *harmoniai* see Ch. 10, Appendix A.

27   Punctuating after *armenon*. The word 'Graces' is missing from the text: 'Muses' would fit as well, as Diehl pointed out. The 'chariot' may be a reference to the chariot of the Muses, which the musician mounts (*Ol.* 9.121, *Isth.* 2.2, 8.62), but if so the metaphor is uncharacteristically expressed. It may be intended to evoke quite directly the sound made by the hole (called *syrinx*) in the nave of the wheel of a chariot, as it rotates: cf. e.g. Aesch. *Sept.* 205, *Suppl.* 181.
28   For the 'few notes' of early auletic, cf. **187** ps.-Plut. 1137b. Pindar is speaking of a time long before his own, since Xenocritus belongs to the seventh century (cf. ps.-Plut. 1134b–c).
29   On the dolphin's love of music see e.g. Eurip. *Electra* 432–7, *Helen* 1451–6, and cf. Herodotus' tale of Arion, 1.24.
30   On the paean see introductory note to *Iliad*.
31   The word 'dithyramb' is conjectural but probable.
32   The words 'goddesses' and 'of their sons' are conjectural. The three people mentioned in the next lines were all sons of Muses by Apollo.
33   On Linus and the Linus song see 7 *Iliad* xviii.570, with n. 12. 'Dirge' here translates *ailinon*.
34   The name of Ialemos, even more clearly than that of Linus, became synonymous with 'lament', e.g. **39** Aesch. *Suppl.* 115, Eurip. *Troiades* 1304, **44** *Phoen.* 1033. It is no doubt connected with the cry *Iē*, which, though most commonly a cry of joy (as in *Iē Paian*) can be an expression of grief, e.g. Aesch. *Persae* 1004, *Ag.* 1485.

CHAPTER 6

Fifth-century tragedy

This is not the place for a full account of the music of Greek drama. The subject is large, and detailed reconstruction depends heavily on analyses of metre and rhythm, inevitably relying on a close study of the Greek texts. In any case, such an account would be largely irrelevant in an introduction to the statements about music made by the tragedians themselves in their plays, since unlike Pindar they refer only rarely to their own music. (The main exception is in the instructions given from time to time by characters on the stage for the conduct of formal laments.) What their scattered remarks about music more fully depict is a range of attitudes to the art and its various forms as they existed in 'real life', or at least in the life that the action of the drama represented.

Two points about the plays themselves should however be briefly noted. First, the words of the tragedies are by no means all dialogue, spoken conversation advancing or deepening the action. Even some parts of the iambic dialogue were probably spoken to the accompaniment of the *aulos* (see **187** ps.-Plut. 1141a), and some anapaestic and lyric verses may have been delivered as a kind of recitative. But a large proportion of each play consists of formally constituted songs, accompanied by the *aulos* and choreographed for dance. The pace, rhythm and mood of the dance movements are extraordinarily varied, and at least in the earlier plays much of the effectiveness of a performance must have depended on its expressive choreography. The principal songs, or 'lyrics', were sung by the chorus, sometimes as a single choir, sometimes divided into semi-choruses, sometimes answering the solo phrases of their leader: but substantial solo odes and parts of odes were sung by principals in the drama, who also often sang antiphonally with the chorus. The main actors were professionals, but the members of the chorus were citizen-amateurs: a discussion of the constraints that this fact imposed is at **169** ps.-Ar. *Probs.* XIX.15. In early tragedy, song and dance constituted the bulk of the play. The origins of the drama lie in forms that were essentially choral song and dance,[1] and we are told, for example, that Phrynichus was primarily a contriver of dances (Ath. 22a, cf. Plut. *Quaest. Conv.* VIII.9.3, Aristoph. *Wasps* 1490) and a songwriter (**179** ps.-Ar. *Probs.* XIX.31, cf. Aristoph. *Birds* 748–52). The elements of dramatic action and spoken dialogue tended to increase as the century went on: more precisely, the proportion of lyric verses to spoken iambics reached its lowest level in certain of Sophocles' plays, and rose again in some of Euripides', but it never regained the predominance that it has in early Aeschylus. Even in the plays with the minimum of lyric, however, it forms a sizeable part of the whole: music still retains an important role.

Secondly, it is clear that the musical styles of the three chief tragedians differed markedly from one another, displaying a progression similar to that found in other areas of music during this period. Aeschylus is noted for his grave simplicity,[2] Sophocles (though our evidence here is thin) for his elegant and full-bodied sweetness,[3] and Euripides for his delicate fancy, dismissed as airy trifles by Aristophanes,[4] but much

---

[1] See e.g. Ar. *Poetics* 1449a, where the origin of tragedy is connected with the dithyramb. Cf. Diog. Laert. III.56, and the collection of passages assembled by Pickard-Cambridge, *D.T.C.* (2nd ed.) 69–72, dealing with the early tragedian Thespis.

[2] E.g. **187** ps.-Plut. 1137e, and note the comparisons drawn between Aeschylus and Euripides in the whole of the latter part of Aristoph. *Frogs* (758 ff).

[3] E.g. Aristoph. in Kock 581. See also n. 7 below.

[4] E.g. *Peace* 531–4, and again see *Frogs* 758 to the end.

admired in his own time and later (**188** Axionicus ap. Ath. 175b, Plut. *Nic.* 29, *Lys.* 15, cf. Dion. Hal. *De Comp. Verb.* XI). The metres of late Euripidean plays show clear signs of the loosening of formal structural restraints, introduced into other musical fields by composers such as Melanippides and Timotheus. The rhythms are now varied in a more lavish and less orderly way (e.g. *Orestes* 1369 ff, *I.A.* 1279 ff),[5] and the divisions between song and speech are less sharply marked. (See e.g. *Phoen.* 1485 ff, 1710 ff.) To what extent these innovations were associated, in the drama, with the new sorts of melodic intricacy credited to the writers of dithyramb and of kitharodic *nomoi* we do not know for certain: but Aristophanes' comments on Euripides and Agathon strongly suggest that simplicity was giving way to ornamentation and modulation in melodic as well as rhythmic composition.[6] Euripides is vigorously criticised for deriving the basis of his music from all kinds of unsuitable sources (**140** *Frogs* 1301–3: see also lines 849, 944, 1281–2). As to melodic type, *harmonia*, we know that a number of different forms were used, and that they were felt to be suited to different kinds of performer and different modes of action and emotion (e.g. **185** ps.-Ar. *Probs.* XIX.48). There are hints that Euripides tried out some unfamiliar practices here;[7] and one source (Plut. *Quaest. Conv.* III.1.1) attributes to Agathon the first use in tragedy of the 'chromatic genus'. If this is true, and if it means what it would have done in the hands of the technical writers,[8] it introduces into tragedy a quite new basis for melodic variation. Our fullest and most reliable commentator on the music of these dramatists, and of contemporary musicians working in other forms, is Aristophanes: for his views on the three great tragedians see particularly the *Frogs*.

Despite these changes, there is no purpose to be served by arranging in chronological order the remarks about music made by the characters that the tragedians put on the stage. In this respect the attitudes and assumptions of Aeschylean, Sophoclean and Euripidean figures differ more in emphasis than in substance, and I have thought it better to organise them by subject matter and theme. If they cast little light on the nature of their own performance, they are supremely revealing of many other aspects of Greek musical life. In the case of the one major exception, the ritual lament, I have included one passage (**41** Aesch. *Persae* 1038 ff) not for the musical descriptions that it offers, but as a fine example of the kind of activity to which many other passages refer.

(1) Lamentation

(a) The nightingale[9]

32   Aeschylus, *Supplices* 57–72

Chorus. If someone skilled in bird-lore is in the land nearby and hears my

---

5   Cf. Aristophanes' account of Agathon's methods of composition, **137** *Thesm.* 52–69.
6   On Agathon, especially **138** *Thesm.* 99 ff: on Euripides e.g. **140** *Frogs* 1314, cf. 1325–9.
7   The evidence is indirect, but Euripides was closely associated with the exponents of the 'new music', as Aristophanes' attitude makes plain: cf. also Satyrus, *Vit. Eur.* 39.22, Plut. *An Seni* 23. On Sophocles' 'Phrygian *melopoiia*' and 'dithyrambic style' see *Vit. Soph.* 23.
8   See n. 8 to **162** *Pap. Hib.* 2.5, n. 132 to **187** ps.-Plut. 1137e.
9   Procne, wife of Tereus, killed her son Itys in revenge for her husband's unfaithfulness. She was turned into a nightingale, he into a hawk (or, in some versions, a hoopoe). For an additional reference see **49** Aesch. *Ag.* 1140 ff. Other lamenting birds include the halcyon (Eurip. *I.T.* 1089–95) and the swan (Aesch. *Ag.* 1444–6, cf. Eurip. *Ion* 161–9, *I.T.* 1104). Cf. Plato, *Phaedo* 84e–85b.

lament, he will think he hears the voice of the sad wife of Tereus, the hawk-pursued nightingale, who, exiled from her fields and streams, mourns sadly for her accustomed haunts, and adds to her lament the fate of her child, killed by her kindred hand, struck by a cruel mother's rage. So I, continually lamenting in the Ionian way,[10] lacerate my tender sun-browned cheek and my heart, unused to tears.

33   Sophocles, *Electra* 147–9

Electra. But my mind is held fast by the moaning bird that laments 'Itys!', always 'Itys!', the grief-bewildered bird, messenger of Zeus.

34   Euripides, *Helen* 1107–16

Chorus. I call upon you who sit in the home of music among the leafy chambers of the trees, you, the melodious bird, best singer, tearful nightingale: come, trilling with quivering beak, to assist in my lament [see **42** *Helen* 178, n.37], as I sing the wearisome pains of Helen and the bloody pain of the Trojans under the Achaeans' spears.

35   Euripides, *Rhesus* 546–50

Chorus. I can hear something: by the river a nightingale sits, the bird that killed her child. She is at her music-making task, singing of her murderous marriage, with her many-stringed[11] voice.

36   Sophocles, *Ajax* 624–34

Chorus. Surely his mother, who lives with ancient days and white old age, when she hears of his mind-destroying sickness, will sing '*Ailinon, ailinon!*'[12] She will not sing the moan of the sorrowful bird, the nightingale,[13] but will wail shrill-stretched songs;[14] and there will fall

---

[10] Lit. 'in Ionian *nomoi*'. The word here probably does not refer to musical forms, but to the 'Eastern' manner of mourning, which the next lines describe: cf. **38** Aesch. *Choeph.* 424. It may be intended to suggest lamentation of the 'elegiac' rather than the frenzied type: cf. **36** Soph. *Ajax* 624 ff.

[11] *Polychordotatai*, that is, with a wide variety of notes. Though *polychordos* literally means 'many-stringed', it can be applied to any kind of instrument: **149** Plato (*Rep.* 399d) uses it of the *aulos*, Euripides of songs (**117** *Medea* 196).

[12] On the Linus song and the exclamation 'ailinon' see n. 12 to **7** *Il.* XVIII.570. For other occurrences in tragedy see Aesch. *Ag.* 121, 139, 159, Eurip. *Orestes* 1395–7 (cf. Hdt. II.79), *Heracles* 348–51 (on which see **189** Ath. 619c).

[13] This reflects a contrast between the quiet piteousness of one kind of mourning, and the vehement frenzy of another: the latter is described in the next group of passages.

[14] 'Wail', *thrēnēsei*: cf. the use of this word at lines 581–2 (**115**). 'Shrill-stretched', a literal rendering of *oxytonous*, reflecting the common link between tension, intensity, and high pitch.

the thudding of hands that beat the breast, and the tearing of grey hair.

(b) Frenzied and violent mourning

37 Aeschylus, *Persae* 935–40

Chorus [*addressing Xerxes*]. I give forth the ill-speaking cry that speaks to your home-coming, the wail, busy with evil, of a Mariandynian mourner,[15] a shriek of many tears.

38 Aeschylus, *Choephori* 423–8

Chorus. I struck with strokes like an Arian, in the style of a Cissian mourning-woman.[16] There were unceasing blows to see, much scattered blood, the stretching of hands one following another, upwards and downwards, and my wretched stricken head rang with the hammer-sound.

39 Aeschylus, *Supplices* 112–16

Chorus. I wail aloud and utter these sad sufferings, shrill, heavy,[17] raining tears – *iē, iē!* – champions of the *ialemos*:[18] while I live I adorn myself with groans.

40 Euripides, *Supplices* 71–8

Chorus. Another lament takes up the wailing and rivals it:[19] our attendants' hands echo aloud. Come, blows that accompany the song, come, partners in grief, in the dance that Hades respects, bloody your white nails

---

[15] Mariandynia is an area of Bithynia. The schol. ad loc. says that there were special *auloi* called 'Mariandynian' and quotes the anonymous line 'He pipes on Mariandynian reeds playing in the Iastian [*harmonia*].' (For another possible, but unlikely, association of an 'Ionian' *harmonia* with lamentation, see 32 Aesch. *Suppl.* 69.) Mourning rites were frequently described in terms of Oriental practices: see particularly the next passage quoted.

[16] Arian and Cissian are names for areas of Persia: see previous note. The word for a stroke or blow, *kommos*, gave its name to a form of antiphonal lament often found in tragedy (see 41–5). The 'outlandishness' of the practices described is reflected in the series of strange compound words present in the Greek: I have been unable to reproduce the effect in English.

[17] *Ligea* means 'shrill' or 'clear': *barea*, 'heavy', would normally mean 'deep-pitched' in a musical context. But lamentations, especially those of women, are always described as high-pitched. Here the word must mean 'heavy' in the sense 'burdensome', though no doubt the paradoxical conjunction of the two epithets is intentional.

[18] On the *ialemos* (here in the variant form *iēlemos*) see 31 Pindar, fr. 126, with n.34.

[19] A reference to the antiphonal form of lament exemplified in 41–5. Cf. also Aesch. *Suppl.* 1022–3.

on your cheeks, make your skin red. What belongs to the dead is beauty enough for the living.

(c) The antiphonal lament[20]

41   Aeschylus, *Persae* 1038–77

Xerxes. Drench suffering with tears: come homewards.[21]
Chorus. I groan and am drenched with tears.
X. Cry now an answering sound for me.[22]
C. An evil gift of evils to evils.
X. Shout, making your song together.[23]
C. *Otototototoi!*[24]
       This catastrophe is heavy –
       Oh! my grief for it is great.
X. Beat, beat[25] and groan for me.
C. *Aiai, aiai!*[26] Sorrow, sorrow![27]
X. Cry now an answering sound for me.
C. That is our task, my lord.
X. Lift high your voice[28] with wailing.
C. *Otototototoi!*
       I mingle in –
       Oh! – a black and groaning blow.

X. Beat your breasts and raise aloud the Mysian cry.[29]
C. Grievous, grievous![30]
X. Tear from your chin the white hairs . . .
C. Clutching tightly, groaning.

[20]   For an early description of this kind of lament see **3** *Il.* XXIV.719–76. Antiphonal singing is of course not restricted to chants of mourning, but has a special prominence in them.

[21]   A feature of this processional lament, which ends the play, is the series of instructions given by Xerxes, acting as leader, to the chorus. His words give us a guide to the choreography and musical structure of the passage: 'Come homeward' tells the chorus to begin the steps of the processional.

[22]   The chorus is instructed to sing antiphonally with Xerxes.

[23]   This countermands the order for antiphonal singing: the chorus is to sing together a brief, but independent lament.

[24]   In longer or shorter versions (*ototoi, otototototoi totoi*, etc.) a cry of grief, quite common in tragic lyric.

[25]   Lit. 'row' (as with oars).

[26]   Invariably a cry of amazement or sorrow.

[27]   The Greek *dua* functions as a cry of grief, an onomatopoeic sound, as well as a noun.

[28]   *Eporthiaze*, employing the *orthios* stem, as in the *Orthios nomos* of e.g. Aristoph. *Knights* 1279, Hdt. 1.24, 187 ps.-Plut. 1133f.

[29]   'Mysian' may mean no more than 'Persian', 'Eastern', cf. **37** *Persae* 935–40 and **38** *Choeph.* 423–8. But the Mysians were proverbial for effeminacy and feebleness (e.g. Plato, *Tht.* 209b): the suggestion may therefore be of a supine hopelessness. But Mysian dances at Soph. *Ajax* 699 are dances of joy.

[30]   Again, the Greek *ania* is an onomatopoeic exclamation as much as an adjective.

X. Shriek shrilly.

C. That I will do.

X. Rip with your fingers your flowing robes.

C. Grievous, grievous.

X. Pluck[31] your hair to lament the army . . .

C. Clutching tightly, groaning.

X. Drench your eyes.

C. Yes, I am moistened.

X. Cry now an answering sound to me.

C. *Oioi, oioi!*

X. Go wailing into the house.

C. *Iō, iō!*[32]

X. *Iōa!* throughout the town.

C. *Iōa!* Yes, yes!

X. Mourn, go on soft feet.

C. *Iō, iō!* The Persian land is hard to tread.

X. *Ēe, ēē!*[33] for those who died in the three-tiered ships. *Ēe, ēē!*

C. With harsh-crying groans I take you home.

42   Euripides, *Helen* 164–90

Helen. Stricken as I am with great griefs and troubles, what lament shall I find to rival them? Or to what music shall I turn, with tears or wailing or mourning? *Aiai!*

Come Sirens, youthful winged maidens, virgin daughters of earth, come to join my laments with the Libyan *lōtos* or the *syrinx* or the *phorminx*,[34] with tears to accompany my sorrowful[35] misfortunes.

---

31   *Psalle*: the verb is the one regularly used for plucking an instrument with the fingers, by contrast with the use of the plectrum.

32   Always a cry of suffering or a call for help.

33   Plainly here a sound of mourning: but elsewhere *ē*, or *ēē*, is sometimes used to attract a person's attention or to express disapproval (like the English 'hey'). Cf. Eurip. *Heracles* 906, Aristoph. *Frogs* 271, *Clouds* 105.

34   The word *lōtos* is used as the name of various plants. Here it is the tree *Celtis australis*, fully described in Theophrastus, *Hist. Plant.* IV.3.1–4. The use of its wood for the pipes of the *aulos* is mentioned at the end of the passage. The tree is said to be native to Libya and other parts of North Africa, and 'Libyan *lōtos*' in the present passage may mean no more than '*aulos* made from the wood of the Libyan *lōtos*-tree'. If, alternatively, the Libyan *aulos* was reckoned a distinct type of instrument, we do not know what its peculiarities were. (But for a conjecture see n. 109 below.) There was a tradition that the *aulos* was invented in Libya (and not, as was usually thought, in Phrygia): 189 Ath. 618c. The word *lōtos* is used by itself to mean *aulos* quite commonly by Euripides and later poets, but occurs in this sense in no earlier source. It seems probable that just as *phorminx*, here as often, names the class of instruments to which the *lyra* and the *kithara* belong, and not one specific type, so 'Libyan *lōtos*' means no more than *aulos*, taken quite generally. Note also that the list given here makes it plain that no one type of instrument was thought necessary for the accompaniment of a lament.

35   'Sorrowful', *ailinois*, derived from the '*ai linon*' of the Linus lament. Cf. 36 Soph. *Ajax* 624 ff, with note.

And may Persephone send griefs to answer griefs, songs to answer songs, choirs to sing with my wailings, all stained with blood, so that with my tears she may receive a paean for the dead,[36] to grace the halls of night.[37]

Chorus. On the twisted green grass by the dark blue water I was spreading clothes, purple with sea-dye, to dry upon shoots of reeds in the golden rays of the sun. There I heard the sound, when my mistress cried out pitifully, a lyre-less elegy,[38] moaning with groans – for whatever reason it may be – like a woodland nymph uttering a *nomos*[39] of flight in the mountains, with wails in the rocky hollows lamenting her coupling with Pan.

43   Euripides, *Supplices* 798–801

Adrastus. Mothers, cry out and utter the lament for the dead below the earth, responding when you hear my own laments.[40]

44   Euripides, *Phoenissae* 1033–9

Chorus. Homes were filled with groaning, *ialemoi* of mothers, *ialemoi* of maidens: one voice after another gave out its separate cry in turn,[41] throughout the city, a lamentable[42] cry, a lamentable song.

45   Euripides, *Troiades* 146–52

Hecabe. Like the mother of fledgling birds I shall lead[43] the cry, the song, not

---

[36] For uses of the word 'paean' see 100–9. Here it is a song to honour and to win the assistance of the dead.

[37] Throughout this strophe Helen has been speaking the language of antiphonal song. As leader of the lament, she seeks a respondent to sing in answer (just as she does at 34 line 1113). At the same time she uses this language to ask for a music that will be suited or proportionate to her grief: it will balance it in emotion and counterbalance its misery with its charm and delight, at least in the ears of the dead. The beauty of the ode, and the ideas it evokes, indicate a lament of the quieter of the two types contrasted at 36 Soph. *Ajax* 624–34: hence these too can be antiphonal.

[38] 'Lyre-less', *alyron*: see 51 Eurip. *I.T.* 143–7, and in general 46–60. 'Elegy': an *elegos* was originally a song accompanied by the *aulos*. Where it indicates a piece written in elegiac couplets it has no special connection with lamentation: but in non-technical Greek it commonly means 'lament', without reference to any particular metre or instrumental accompaniment. (Cf. e.g. Aristoph. *Birds* 218.) The phrase 'lyre-less elegy' recurs at *I.T.* 146. (For the connection with the *aulos* see e.g. 187 ps.-Plut. 1132d, Eust. ad *Il.* XXIV.720.)

[39] Here used with no implications beyond 'song', as a metaphor for 'cry'.

[40] This is an instruction for the beginning of an antiphonal lament, running from here to line 836.

[41] 'In turn', *diadochais*, a more complex form of antiphony. 'Gave out its cry', *epōtotyze*, 'cried "otototoi"': cf. 41 Aesch. *Persae* 1043.

[42] *Ieïeion*, a cry of 'ie, ie', as in the *ialemos* or *iēlemos*, 31 Pindar, fr.126.

[43] *Exarxō*: cf. e.g. 3 Hom. *Il.* XXIV. 747, 761. The *exarchos* is the leader to whose cries the rest respond, or in a dance the one who sets the beat, and whose movements the others follow (e.g. 7 Hom. *Il.* XVIII. 606). Cf. the expression *exarchos Bromios*, Eurip. *Bacch.* 140, and the use of the word *chorēgos* at *Helen* 1454.

the same as that which I used to lead, leaning on Priam's sceptre, with the loud-sounding beats of the foot that rules that dance, in honour of the Phrygian gods.[44]

(d) Sorrow as the negation of music

46   Aeschylus, *Eumenides* 952–5

Athena. It is clear that their work [the Erinyes'] among men is absolute and fixed, giving songs to some, to others a life darkened with tears.

47   Euripides, *Alcestis* 341–7

Admetus. Should I not weep, when I am losing so noble a wife as you? I shall put an end to the revellers and companies of drinking-companions, the garlands and the music which have filled my house. Never again shall I touch the *barbitos*[45] or lift my heart to cry out to the Libyan *aulos*:[46] for you have taken the joy out of my life.[47]

48   Aeschylus, *Agamemnon* 705–12

Chorus. [Divine anger has punished] those who blasphemously sang[48] the bride-honouring song, the *hymenaios*,[49] which it fell to the lot of

---

[44] The sharp division between lamentation and music as usually conceived is the subject of the next section. Cf. also *Troiades* 511–14: 'Sing for me, Muse, in tears, a funeral song, an unfamiliar hymn for Ilium', where 'funeral song' translates *ōidan epikēdeion*. According to Serv. ad Virg. *Ecl.* 5.14, the *epikēdeion* is a song sung before the burial, contrasted with *epitaphion*. There was an *aulos* called the *epikēdeios aulos*, played on such occasions (Plut. *Quaest. Conv.* 657a).

[45] The variant of the *lyra* most closely associated with revelry. It is thus appropriate here, though as usual in poetry, no particular stringed instrument may be intended.

[46] See **42** Eurip. *Helen* 171 with n. 34.

[47] With these sentiments compare Eurip. *Hippol.* 1135–6, a passage that has a musicological interest of its own: 'Unsleeping music, under the *antyx* of the strings, shall abandon his father's house.' *Antyx* is properly the rim or edge of anything curved. In Homer it commonly means the curved rail at the front of a chariot, and is later transferred to mean the chariot itself. The apparent sense here, 'bridge of an instrument' (for which the later, technical name is *magas*), is not attested elsewhere; but the basis of the usage is made clear by such passages as *Il.* v.262 and 322, where the horses' reins are described as being tied to the *antyx*, the chariot-rail. Here the strings of the *lyra* are passed over the bridge like reins across the rail: rail and bridge are of similar shape, upright and slightly curved. The Muse, or music, is 'under' the *antyx* in the sense of being reined or harnessed to it. (For this sense of *hypo*, 'under', cf. the Homeric expression 'yoking the horses to (*hypo*) the chariot', e.g. *Od.* iii.478.) The metaphor arises from its context: Hippolytus is a charioteer, and his feats in that activity have been mentioned three lines earlier.

[48] Lit. 'honoured'.

[49] On wedding songs see **77–81**.

Helen's kin by marriage to sing. The ancient city of Priam has un-learned one song and learned another, and loudly groans a hymn[50] of much lamenting.

49 Aeschylus, *Agamemnon* 1140–55

Chorus. You are crazed, and driven by the god, and you sing a lament for yourself, a *nomos* that is no *nomos*,[51] like some trilling nightingale, crying insatiably from her sorrowing heart 'Itys, Itys!' as she mourns her life overladen with troubles.

Cassandra. Iō, iō, the fate of the clear-voiced nightingale! For the gods cast feathers around her body, and gave her a sweet race to run,[52] without tears. But for me there remains the cutting of the two-edged spear.

Chorus. Whence came to you these rushing, god-driven, empty laments? You are beating out fearful things in song, in unutterable clamour and high-pitched *nomoi*.[53] Whence came to you the ill-speaking marks of the road of prophecy?

50 Euripides, *Troiades* 115–30

Hecabe. Oh, my head, my forehead, my ribs! How I long to twist and rock my back, my spine, like a boat, to either side in turn, to elegies of continual, miserable tears. Music,[54] ever the same, sounds dance-less[55] dooms for the unfortunate.

You ships with your prows, that came with swift oars across the purple sea from the sheltering harbours of Greece, to the hateful paean[56] of *auloi* and the voice of well-sounding *syringes*, in the bays of Troy you tied up the woven works of Egypt's skill.[57]

51 Euripides, *Iphigenia in Tauris* 143–7, 179–85, 218–28

Iphigenia. Women who serve me, I am wrapped in loud-lamenting lamenta-

---

[50] There is a slight but no doubt deliberate paradox here, given the normal associations of 'hymn' with songs of celebration and praise. Though it had long been used in a more general way (e.g. **15** Hesiod *W.D.* 662), it retained enough of this association to be used quite frequently by tragedians in non-celebratory contexts to generate this kind of paradoxical effect. See **93–9**, especially **99** Aesch. *Sept.* 866–70.

[51] The musical sense of the word *nomos* has close connections with its political meaning 'law' or 'custom', the basis of order (see e.g. **155** and **157** Plato, *Laws* 700b–c, 799e–800a, **178** ps.-Ar. *Probs.* XIX.28, **187** ps.-Plut. 1133c and Appendix A, Arist. Quint. 59.1 ff). Hence the implication here is 'song without order or bounds', an apt description of Cassandra's frenzied utterances.

[52] Lit. 'a sweet contest'. The nightingale's task is to sing like a competitor at the games.

[53] *Orthiois nomois*: see n. 28 above. But here it means no more than 'high-pitched songs'.

[54] Lit. 'the Muse'.

[55] *Achoreutous*, 'without choruses'. Cf. **58** Aesch. *Suppl.* 678–83.

[56] Cf. **99** Aesch. *Sept.* 866–70, and on the paean generally, **100–9**.

[57] That is, as the schol. explains, ropes made of plaited or twisted papyrus.

tions, in the lyre-less elegies of ill-sounding song (*aiai, aiai!*), in gloomy mourning.

Chorus. [179] I shall loudly sing songs that respond to you,[58] my lady, and the barbaric sound of Asiatic hymns,[59] the music that is sung in lamentations for the dead, the hymns that Hades sings, with no paeans.[60]

Iphigenia. [218] But now, a stranger by an inhospitable sea, I live in a grudging house: I have no husband, child, city or friend: I do not sing to Hera, as in Argos: I do not weave with my shuttle on the well-sounding loom[61] intricate pictures of Athenian Pallas and the Titans: but I encompass a bloody, unmusical[62] doom for strangers who cry out with a piteous voice and drop piteous tears.

(2) Evocations of evil

52   Aeschylus, *Agamemnon* 990–3

Chorus. But still my heart within me prompts itself to sing the Erinyes' dirge, the hymn without a *lyra*.[63]

53   Aeschylus, *Agamemnon* 1186–93

Cassandra. Never shall this house be abandoned by the chorus that utters

---

58   *Antipsalmos* is used here as an alternative to e.g. the *antiphōnos* of **43** Eurip. *Suppl.* 800, 'antiphonal', 'answering'. *Psallein* is to pluck an instrument with the fingers: hence *antipsalmos* is lit. 'plucked in answer'. The verb *antipsallein* occurs at Aristoph. *Birds* 218, in the phrase 'to pluck a *phorminx* in answer to elegies': there the sense seems to be 'accompany' rather than 'respond'. Cf. also **196** Ath. 635 b-d.
59   Cf. e.g. **37** Aesch. *Persae* 935–40, **38** *Choeph.* 423–8.
60   Here evidently in the sense 'songs of joy', as at e.g. **107** Aesch. *Ag.* 243–7.
61   Expressions linking music and weaving are common in Greek poetry: see note to **140** Aristoph. *Frogs* 1316. It is possible that the musical epithets given here to the loom and there to the shuttle do not refer directly to the sounds of weaving: the rattle of the bobbin-carrying shuttle as it is thrown across the warp cannot be intended. That sort of shuttle is a modern invention; and in any case the reference here, as commonly (e.g. lines 813–17 of this play), is to tapestry-weaving, which does not involve the vigorous passage of the shuttle right across the 'shed'. It seems more likely that the epithets are suggested partly by the visual similarity of the (upright) loom to a stringed instrument, and partly by the way in which the weaver creates intricate designs and pictures by passing his continuous thread across the warp, covering some warps and revealing others. Similarly the musician, with the continuous 'thread' of his melody, passes back and forth across the strings, sounding some and omitting others, and so building up the sonorous 'picture' constituting the whole piece.
62   *Dysphorminga*, 'hostile to the *phorminx*'. The text of the sentence is not entirely certain, but this word, and the general sense, are not in doubt.
63   As passages in the previous section used the negation or absence of instruments to indicate sorrow, so this one and others in the group use it as a symbol of something sinister or deadly.

together, but with no pleasing voice:[64] their words are evil; and drunk with human blood, and so grown bolder, this revelling rabble of kindred Erinyes stays in the house, hard to cast out.[65] They sit by the palace and chant their hymn, the origin of crime and doom: and each in turn[66] they spit, in fury at the man who soiled his brother's bed.

54   Aeschylus, *Choephori* 466–8

Chorus. O kindred grief and bloody blow of doom, hostile to music.[67]

55   Euripides, *Phoenissae* 1028–31

Chorus [addressing the Sphinx[68]*].* With lyre-less music and an accursed Erinys, you brought bloody troubles to my homeland.

56   Sophocles, *Oedipus Coloneus* 1220–3

Chorus. The deliverer comes at last to all alike, when the doom of Hades is revealed, without wedding song, without *lyra*, without dance, death at the end.

57   Sophocles, *Antigone* 810–16

Antigone. But Hades, everyone's bedfellow, leads me living to the shore of Acheron, with no share in wedding songs: no hymn will hymn me at my bridal, but it is Acheron's bride that I shall be.

58   Aeschylus, *Supplices* 678–83

Chorus. May no man-killing ruin come against this city and wreck it, giving

---

[64] The chorus (i.e. the Erinyes, the Furies) is *symphthongos* but not *euphōnos*. *Symphthongos*, lit. 'voicing together', is a rare word: its conjunction with 'not *euphōnos*' brings to mind the word *symphōnos*, again lit. 'voicing together', but regularly meaning 'concordant' and hence 'pleasant'. Aeschylus is aiming for the effect of a paradox – united or concerted sound which is yet not blended into a concordant whole.

[65] 'Rabble', *kōmos*, usually of merry-makers at a festival. We are perhaps intended to remember the carousing suitors in the *Odyssey*.

[66] An oblique reference to the more complex kind of antiphony, cf. **44** Eurip. *Phoen.* 1033–9. For another instance not concerned with lamentation, see **66** *Bacch.* 1056–7, cf. **85** *Heracles* 760 ff.

[67] *Paramousos*, 'contrary to *mousikē*', contrary to the ideals and practices of the Muses, or of civilised 'culture', Cf. **60** Eurip. *Phoen.* 785.

[68] The Sphinx is often spoken of as a 'singer': Soph. *O.T.* 36, 130, 391, 1199–1200, Eurip. *Phoen.* 49–50, 807, 1505–7, 1728–31.

arms to Ares the chorus-less, the lyre-less,[69] father of tears, and to the clamour of the people.

59   Sophocles, *Ajax* 1192–1206

Chorus. He should have passed into the great sky, or into Hades, the common home of all, that man who first taught the Greeks to join together in war with its horrible weapons. O troubles, fathers of troubles! It was he that ruined mankind. He brought me for my lot no joy of garlands or deep wine-cups, nor the sweet clamour of *auloi*,[70] that evil man, nor pleasing sleep in the night; and from love, from love he has barred me.

60   Euripides, *Phoenissae* 784–91

Chorus. Ares, bringer of toil, why are you surrounded by blood and death? Why are you in discord[71] with the festivals of Dionysus? You do not loose your hair among the garlands and fine dances of girls in the ripeness of youth, singing in accord with the breath of the *lōtos*[72] a song full of the graces that create the dance;[73] but with your men at arms you inspire the Argive army with desire for Theban blood, leading the chorus in a revelling dance accompanied by no *aulos*.[74]

(3) The music of Dionysiac and other cults

61   Sophocles, *Antigone* 963–5

Chorus. He tried to put an end to the god-inspired women and the Bacchic fire, and angered the *aulos*-loving Muses.[75]

---

[69] For Ares, god of war, no dancing and no playing on instruments is appropriate: it is the joylessness of war that is indicated. 'Lyre-less' here translates *akitharin*, 'without the *kithara*'. Ares has been described as *achoros*, 'chorusless', 'without dancing', earlier in the play (635: cf. **50** Eurip. *Troiades* 121, **56** Soph. O.C. 1223).

[70] 'Clamour', *otobos*, usually of a loud clattering sound, e.g. Aesch. *Sept.* 151, Soph. O.C. 1479: also of percussion instruments, *krotala*, Antim. *Eleg.* fr. 17.

[71] *Paramousos*, 'contrary to music': cf. **54** Aesch. *Choeph.* 467.

[72] On the word *lōtos* see **42** *Helen* 171 n. 34. 'In accord with' translates the preposition *kata*, 'according to', 'in agreement with'.

[73] *Choropoios*, 'making the dance', is a parallel formation to *melopoios*, with its noun *melopoiia*, regularly meaning 'melodic composition'. The sense may be comparable here, but *choropoios* in poetry sometimes means 'leader of the dance', e.g. Soph. *Ajax* 698. If it does so here, 'graces' should perhaps be 'Graces'.

[74] *Anaulotatos*, the superlative form of *anaulos*, 'with no *aulos*'. The force of the superlative is untranslatable.

[75] The chorus is singing of the king of the Edonians, who had sought to suppress the rites of Dionysus: cf. the plot of Eurip. *Bacch.*

62   Euripides, *Bacchae* 378–81

Chorus. His [Dionysus'] powers are these: to revel in dances, to laugh with the *aulos*, and to put an end to cares.

63   Euripides, *Bacchae* 55–63

Dionysus. Come, my mystic company of women, who have left Tmolus,[76] bulwark of Lydia, whom I have brought from foreign lands to be my companions and join my travels: lift up the *tympana*[77] native to your Phrygian city, inventions of Rhea the Mother Goddess and me: go round this royal house of Pentheus and strike up, so that all the city of Cadmus turns to look. And I shall go to the folds of Cithaeron, where my Bacchae are, to join in their dances.

64   Euripides, *Bacchae* 120–34

Chorus. O den of the Curetes and holy Cretan caves where Zeus was reared, the caverns where the Corybantes with their triple plumes discovered this ring covered in stretched hide![78] Mixed with the Bacchic, high-stretched, sweet-crying breath of Phrygian *auloi*[79] they placed it in the hand of Rhea the Mother Goddess, a beat for the wild cries of the Bacchae. From the Mother Goddess the crazy Satyrs acquired it, and fitted it to their dances at the three-yearly festivals in which Dionysus delights.

65   Euripides, *Bacchae* 151–67

Chorus. Among their wild shouts he[80] roars aloud 'Go, Bacchae! Go, Bacchae! In the glory of gold-streaming Tmolus sing Dionysus, to the

---

[76] A mountain near Sardis in Lydia, home of Dionysus: cf. **65** line 154.
[77] The *tympanon* was a small hand-drum. On its construction and legendary origin see **64** lines 120–34; cf. **71** *Helen* 1341–52.
[78] I.e. the *tympanon*.
[79] Not only were Dionysiac rites associated with Phrygia, but the invention of the *aulos* was commonly placed there too (cf. e.g. **187** ps.-Plut. 1132f). This may be enough to explain the occurrence of the expression 'Phrygian *aulos*' here and in comparable passages. But there was a special kind of *aulos* called 'Phrygian' (also known as the *elymos aulos*), of which we have descriptions at **188** Athenaeus 185a and Pollux IV.74. One of its pair of pipes was much longer than the other, and ended in a bell made of horn: possibly it sounded a drone, a suitable enough sound for Dionysiac music. Aelian (ap. *Porph. Comm.* 34.11–16), speaking apparently of Phrygian *auloi* generally, and not of this special type, says that their bore is much narrower and hence their sound is lower in pitch than that of Greek *auloi*: this agrees with Athenaeus loc.cit., but hardly with the epithet 'high-stretched' in the present passage.
[80] The leader or celebrant of the revels, the *exarchos Bromios* (line 140), representing the person of Dionysus. Cf. **67** *Cyclops* 37–40.

sound of deep-thundering *tympana*! Shout to celebrate the joy-shouting god in ringing Phrygian cries, while the sacred *lōtos*[81] with its lovely sound loudly utters its sacred playfulnesses in time with the tread of those who go to the mountain, to the mountain; and each of the Bacchae in delight, like a foal with its mother in the field, swings her swift-footed leg and leaps.

66   Euripides, *Bacchae* 1056–7

Messenger [describing the Bacchic women]. Some of them, like foals released from their decorated yokes, sounded a Bacchic song, answering each other in turn.[82]

67   Euripides, *Cyclops*[83] 37–40

Silenus [to the chorus of Satyrs]. The clatter of your Sikinnis-dance[84] is no longer what it was when you came to Althaia's house, a band of revelling comrades led[85] by Bacchus, swaggering to the songs of *barbitoi*.[86]

68   Euripides, *Cyclops* 63–70

Chorus of Satyrs. Here is no Dionysus, no dances, no Bacchae with their ivy-wands, no clamouring[87] of *tympana* by the flowing springs, no sparkling drops of wine. I am not in Nysa, singing with the Nymphs the Iacchus-song[88] to Aphrodite, whom I used to hunt with the white-footed Bacchae.

69   Euripides, *Cyclops* 203–5

Polyphemus [to the Satyrs]. Come on! Get working! What's all this? What's

---

[81] The *aulos*. See **42** *Helen* 171, n.34.

[82] A good example of antiphony not associated with lamentation.

[83] The *Cyclops* is not a tragedy but a satyr-play.

[84] A lively, noisy dance especially associated with satyr drama. It is a genus or type of dance rather than a single species: cf. Pollux IV.100. Various origins were suggested in antiquity: see Ath. 20e, **194** 630b, Lucian, *Salt.* 22, Dion. Hal. VII.72.

[85] Lit. 'revelling shield-followers of Bacchus', supporting him as an army supports its leader.

[86] The *barbitos* or *barbiton* is a common instrument of satyrs and of Bacchic revelry (and of carousing in general), and is often depicted as such in vase paintings of the period (e.g. Figs. 5 and 6). At line 444 the satyrs mention the 'Asian *kithara*', which may possibly be the same instrument: but **187** ps.-Plut. 1133c says that the 'Asian' *kithara* is the standard concert instrument whose form was established 'in the time of Cepion, pupil of Terpander'.

[87] *Alalagmoi*, usually of shouting: of the sound of the *aulos*, **71** Eurip. *Helen* 1352.

[88] Iacchus was a mystic title of Dionysus and (as here and at e.g. Hdt. VIII.65) a song in his honour. It is called a song to Aphrodite here only because the satyrs are represented as 'pursuing Aphrodite', love-making, with the women devotees of Dionysus.

this slacking? What's all this Bacchic roistering? There's no Dionysus here, no bronze *krotala*,[89] no clattering of *tympana*.

70   Euripides, *Helen* 1308–14

Chorus [describing the search for Persephone]. The Bacchic *krotala* sounded aloud with their piercing clamour, when the goddess yoked wild beasts to her chariot, to seek for her daughter, snatched out of the circling dance of maidens.[90]

71   Euripides, *Helen* 1338–52

Chorus. When the Mother Goddess had put a stop to feasting among the gods and the race of mortals, Zeus soothed her bitter anger, saying: 'Go, revered Graces, go to Demeter, who is enraged over her daughter, and sing joyfully[91] to end her sorrow. Go, Muses, too, with hymns and dances.'[92] Then first of the blessed immortals went Aphrodite, with the earth-born voice of cymbals,[93] and the finest *typana*[94] covered with stretched hide. And the goddess laughed, and accepted into her hands the deep-noised *aulos*,[95] delighting in the joyful sound.

72   Euripides, *Helen* 1358–65

Part of the same ode as the previous passage.

Chorus. There is great power in dappled fawnskin garments, in the shoot of ivy twisted upon the sacred fennel-stalk, in the quivering vibration of

---

89 *Krotala* are 'clappers', comparable to castanets, though larger, and held in the hand in a similar way, made of shell or wood or bronze (Eust. ad *Il.* XI.160). Like the *tympana* they were associated with the rites of Dionysus and of Cybele: cf. Homeric *Hymn to the Mother of the Gods* 3, and **70** *Helen* 1308. For their quite different link with the lascivious dancing of seductive women, see **140** Aristoph. *Frogs* 1305–6. They are apparently the same as the *krembala*: see **196** Ath. 636c-e.

90 The relation between the rites of Dionysus and those of the Mother Goddess has been suggested at **63** and **64** *Bacch.* 55–63, 120–34. The present passage and the next three are principally concerned with the cult of the latter, as celebrated in the Eleusinian Mysteries.

91 Lit. 'end her sorrow with an *alalē*', that is, a cry of '*alalaï*'. These words and their cognates signify any loud shout, war-cries in particular, and the cries of Bacchic revelry (e.g. *Bacch.* 593, 1133). The word translated 'joyful sound' at the end of this passage is another from the same stable, *alalagmos*: cf. *Cyclops* 55.

92 Lit. 'with hymns of [choral] dances': the singing and dancing are parts of the same activity, not separate items.

93 Lit. 'of bronze', and the reference might be to bronze *krotala* (see n. 89 above) rather than cymbals, *kymbala*.

94 A variant form of *tympana*.

95 The epithet 'deep-noised' suggests a reference to the specifically 'Phrygian' *aulos*. Cf. n. 79 above.

the *rhombos*,[96] circling through the air, in tossing hair, inspired by Dionysus, and in the night-long festivals of the goddess.

73   Euripides, *Ion* 1074–98

Chorus. We shall feel shame before the god of many hymns [Apollo] if, unsleeping, by night, he looks upon the torch that witnesses our ceremonies,[97] by the streams where there is fine dancing, when Zeus' starry heaven lifts up the dance, and the moon dances, and so do the fifty daughters of Nereus in the sea and in the ripples of the ever-flowing rivers, dancing to the gold-wreathed maiden and her holy mother [Persephone and Demeter]. There[98] the foundling of Apollo hopes to be king, and to seize the reward of others' labour.

See, you who make music and sing songs that resound with malice about women's lusts, their lawless, unholy couplings inspired by Aphrodite, see how much we women exceed in innocence the unrighteous furrows ploughed by men. Let the song recoil upon itself, and let the lecheries of men be the object of malicious-sounding music.[99]

74   Euripides, *Heraclidae* 777–83

Chorus [addressing Athena]. To you is given the honour of unceasing sacrifices, and the day of the waning moon is not forgotten, when the young men sing and the music of dancers is heard. And on the windy hill the joyful cries[100] of maidens ring out to the night-long beating of their feet.[101]

---

[96] A flat piece of wood with a cord attached to it, swung around vigorously and producing a whirring sound: a 'bull-roarer'. Cf. Archytas, fr. 1. It was used in cult, in magical practices, and as a child's toy. Theocr. *Idylls* 2.30 refers to a *rhombos* made of bronze.

[97] Lit. 'the twentieths', i.e. the twentieth day of the month Boedromion, which was the sixth day of the festival of the Eleusinian mysteries.

[98] At Athens, home of the Eleusinian mysteries. The chorus complains that Apollo is dishonouring their city by foisting on it, as its future king, a 'nobody' brought up in his temple. Hence Apollo will be an unwelcome and embarrassing witness of the Athenian women's sacred rites.

[99] This antistrophe tells us nothing about the music of cult, the subject of the present group of passages, but it has an independent interest. For its theme, with some similar language, see **97** Eurip. *Medea* 419–27.

[100] *Ololygmata.* The word and its various cognates (e.g. *ololygmos, ololygē*) are plainly onomatopoeic, and usually signify cries of joy or victory (e.g. **82** Aesch. *Ag.* 28, *Choeph.* 387, *Eum.* 1043, Eurip. *Medea* 1176), but sometimes loud cries of any kind (e.g. *Il.* VI.301, Thuc. II.4), and at **109** Aesch. *Sept.* 268 the sound of the paean that gives confidence before battle. Cf. the verb *anololyzein*, used of a magical incantation, **116** Eurip. *I.T.* 1337.

[101] The reference is to the Panathenaea, the principal Athenian festival, dedicated to celebration of the goddess Athena.

75   Sophocles, *Trachiniae* 205–21

Chorus. Let the house that will soon receive its husband ring with the *ololygmos*, with *alalagai* at the hearth.[102] Let the men join in a cry to Apollo of the fine quiver, our champion, and with them, maidens, raise the paean, and shout to his sister, Ortygian Artemis, huntress of the deer, bearer of two torches, and to the Nymphs, her neighbours.

I am uplifted: I shall not reject the *aulos*, oh king of my mind.[103] See, the ivy rouses me to frenzy – *euoi!* –[104] whirling the Bacchic company. *Iō, iō Paian!*[105]

76   Euripides, *Heracles* 674–96

Chorus. I shall not cease to mingle the Graces with the Muses, a most sweet conjunction. Let me not live without music: may I be always among the wreaths.[106] Even in old age a singer can still celebrate Memory, and I still sing the victory song of Heracles,[107] accompanied by Dionysus the wine-giver, or by the song of the seven-toned tortoiseshell[108] and the Libyan *aulos*.[109] I shall never put a stop to the Muses, who first set me dancing.

The Delian maidens,[110] whirling about the gateways in a lovely dance, sing a paean to the splendid son of Leto; and at your house I, like a swan, aged singer that I am, shall utter paeans from my grey-bearded mouth: for there is a good theme for my hymns, the son of Zeus.

(4) Weddings

77   Euripides, *Troiades* 325–40

Cassandra. Beat your foot! Raise up the leaping dance! *Euan, euoi*[111] for my father's happy fate! The dance is holy. Come now, Apollo, at whose

---

102   On the *ololygmos* see n. 100, on *alalagē* n. 87 and n. 91 above.

103   I.e., Dionysus, with whose revels the *aulos* and the ivy-wand are closely linked. He is invoked here as the bringer of joy.

104   A cry used only in the cult of Dionysus, one of whose titles was Euios.

105   That is, 'praise to the Healer', Paian being a title of Apollo, e.g. 20 *Hymn to Apollo* 517, 100 Eurip. *Ion* 125. The emotional celebrations of this passage have generated the unusual combination of elements from Apolline and Dionysiac cult.

106   Or 'may I always be wreathed'. There are three possible references: to the wreath given to a victor at the games, to that habitually worn by musicians at public performances, or to that worn as an accompaniment to merry-making generally (cf. 83 line 781).

107   'Victory song', *kallinikon*, cf. e.g. Pindar, *Ol.* 9.1–4, *Pyth.* 5.106–7.

108   I.e., the *lyra*, with its tortoiseshell sound-box (see 21 *Hymn to Hermes*). 'Seven-toned' or 'seven-stretched', *heptatonos*, is a variant for 'seven-stringed', 'seven-voiced', etc. *Tonos* means 'stretching', 'tension', and comes to have the sense 'pitch'.

109   See n. 34 to 42 Eurip. *Helen* 171. It is just possible that 'Libyan *aulos*' indicates the lighter-toned instrument that Aelian treats as properly 'Greek', in contrast to the deeper Phrygian instrument. See n. 79 above.

110   On the Delian choruses see 18 *Hymn to Apollo* 156 ff and Thuc. III.104.

111   See n. 104. Dionysiac and Apolline elements are again mingled here.

temple I serve, under the laurel. Hymen, O Hymenaie, Hymen![112]
Dance, mother, laugh aloud, whirl hither and thither, moving your
dear steps with my feet. Cry out the wedding song, Oh, with happy
songs, sing to the bride with joyous cries. Go, Phrygian lasses, finely
dressed, sing the husband destined for my marriage-bed.[113]

8   Euripides, *Heracles* 9–12

Amphitryon. Creon was the father of this woman, Megara, for whom all the
Thebans shouted aloud[114] with wedding songs to the sound of the
lōtos, when great Heracles brought her to my house.

79   Euripides, *Iphigenia in Tauris* 1123–51

Chorus. An Argive ship with fifty oars will take you home, my lady; and the
wax-bound reed[115] of Pan who lives on the mountains will whistle[116]
and call to the oars,[117] and Apollo the prophet, singing with the sound
of the seven-toned *lyra*, will take you safely to the shining land of the
Athenians. You will go with foaming oars and leave me here: the
fore-stays will spread out the sail of the swift-journeying ship above
the prow.

I wish I could go on the shining horses' journey where the sun's fire
travels: that I could fly with wings, and then fold them on my back in
the chambers of my own home: that I could stand in the dance-choruses
at noble weddings, as, when I was a girl, I whirled near my mother's
feet in the joyful bands of my young friends, entering the contests of
the Graces, the rivalry of our rich, soft hair, and shadowing my face
with scarves, intricately adorned, and with my flowing locks.

---

112   Technically an evocation of the god of marriage, and the traditional refrain to the
song sung by the bride's attendants, as they escorted her to the groom's house. See 7
Il. XVIII.490 ff. with n. 11.

113   Cassandra is dedicated to virginity, as the priestess of Apollo, but after the fall of
Troy she has been picked by Agamemnon as his prize. The passage comes from her
frenzied pastiche of a song of joy in prospect of her coming 'marriage'. It is of interest
for the instructions it gives, however ironically, for the conduct of the singing and
dancing of a bridal procession.

114   *Synēlalaxan*, shouted the *alalagmos* together.

115   See 121–8, and particularly note to 121 Aesch. *P.V.* 574. For the *syrinx* as a nautical
instrument cf. 50 Eurip. *Troiades* 127, and for other references to music in a marine
context, Eurip. *Electra* 432–7, *Helen* 1451–6.

116   *Syrizein*, the verb cognate with *syrinx*, is used of many whistling or hissing noises as
well as of the sound of the *syrinx* itself – of the sound made by the hole in the nave of a
wheel (commonly called *syrinx*), or by the prow of a ship moving through the waves,
or by the letter 's', etc.

117   On music to keep time with oars cf. 139 Aristoph. *Frogs* 202–68.

80   Euripides, *Iphigenia in Aulis* 435–9

Messenger. Come then, get ready the sacred baskets for these rites; garland your heads; and you, lord Menelaus, prepare the wedding. Let the *lōtos* cry out inside the tents, let feet be set beating! This dawn will be a blessed one for the maiden.

81   Euripides, *Iphigenia in Aulis* 1036–57

Chorus. What a joyous cry did the god of wedding songs set up with the Libyan *lōtos*, the *kithara* that loves the dance, and the reeds of the *syrinx*,[118] when the Muses with their lovely hair, beating their gold-sandalled feet upon the ground, came up Mount Pelion to the marriage of Peleus,[119] among the feasting of the gods, praising Thetis and the son of Aeacus with melodious voices all through the woods of Pelion on the mountains of the Centaurs. The son of Dardanus, Phrygian Ganymede, cherished delight of Zeus' bed, poured out the libation wine in the golden hollows of mixing-bowls; and over the white-shining sand the fifty daughters of Nereus whirled in their circling dance.[120]

(5) Miscellaneous celebrations

(a) Occasions of victory or success

82   Aeschylus, *Agamemnon* 22–31

Watchman. Welcome, beacon. You kindle daylight in night, and the setting up of many dances[121] in Argos, in thanks for this event.

Iou, iou![122] I call piercingly to Agamemnon's wife, that she must rise from her bed and lift up in the palace an *ololygmos* of good omen to this beacon: for the city of Troy is taken, as the fiery messenger makes plain; and I myself shall dance the prelude.[123]

83   Euripides, *Heracles* 781–93

Chorus. Put on a wreath, river Ismenus! Shining streets of the seven-gated city, dance! Come, Dirce with your lovely streams, come Nymphs,

---

[118] *Syringōn kalamoessan*, lit. 'reedy *syringes*', or '*syringes* made of reed (*kalamos*)'. The reeds used in the construction of the *syrinx* are more usually called *donakes* (cf. 121 Aesch. *P.V.* 574 with note), but *kalamoi* is not uncommon, e.g. 128 Eurip. *I.A.* 577.

[119] This occasion is briefly mentioned at *Il.* xxiv.62–3.

[120] The circling dances of the Nereids are mentioned again at e.g. Eurip. *I.T.* 421–9.

[121] *Choroi.* 'Setting up', *katastasis*, suggests the formal establishment of a ceremony, not merely spontaneous revelry: cf. e.g. Soph. *Electra* 280.

[122] A cry of joy, as here, or of sorrow: the usages are equally common.

[123] *Phroimion*, a contraction of *prooimion*: any kind of preliminary, but especially a 'prelude' in speech or music. See introduction to *Homeric Hymns*, 26 Pindar, *Pyth.* 1.4, and e.g. *Pyth.* 7.1–3, *Nem.* 2.1–3, Aesch. *Ag.* 829. For extended senses see Thuc. III.104, 96 Aesch. *Sept.* 8.

daughters of Asopus, leave your father's waters and come to join us in singing of the victorious struggle of Heracles. Wooded rock of Delphi, and homes of the Muses of Helicon, come to my city with a joyful shout.

84   Euripides, *Electra* 859–65, 873–9

Chorus. Set your step to the dance, Electra, leaping lightly with joy like a bounding fawn. Your brother has won a wreath greater than those given beside the streams of Alpheios.[124] Sing to my dancing the song of victory . . .[125]

[873]   Bring garlands for his head; and we shall tread a dance that the Muses love. Now our own former line of kings will rule this land again, having destroyed those who ruled it wrongfully. Let the cry of joy go up with the sound of the *aulos*.

85   Euripides, *Heracles* 760–7

Chorus [*divided here into two groups, or perhaps into a leader and a chorus, who chant antiphonally*[126]].
A. Old men, the wicked man is dead.
B. The house falls silent: let us turn to dancing.
A. Our loved ones, those we wished to win, have won.
All. Dances, dances and merry-making are now our task throughout the city of Thebes: for changes of tears, changes of fortune, have bred new songs.[127]

(b) Other celebrations, various types

86   Euripides, *Electra* 705–19[128]

Chorus. A herald stood on the stone steps and cried out 'Come, people of Mycenae, to the *agora*[129] to see the wonderful sight, this marvel that the happy king has got . . .'[130] Then golden braziers were placed around, and fire from the Argive altars gleamed throughout the city:

---

124   That is, the wreaths given to victors at the games at Olympia, through whose plain the river Alpheios flows. The text of this line is somewhat uncertain.
125   *Kallinikon ōidan*: cf. **76** *Heracles* 681 and note.
126   For some other references to antiphony unconnected with lamentation, see n. 66 above.
127   'New' is not in the text, but is suggested by Wilamowitz to fill out the metre. The suggestion that different types of circumstance are reflected in different kinds of music is commonplace enough, but may be understood as the principal foundation of philosophical theories of musical 'ethos'.
128   For the immediately preceding lines of this ode (699 ff) see **123**.
129   The place of common assembly.
130   Lines 711–12 are corrupt, and cannot be reliably interpreted.

and the *lotos*, servant of the Muses, gave out its beautiful voice, and lovely songs rose loud, celebrating[131] Thyestes' golden lamb.

87   Euripides, *Troiades* 542–55

Chorus [*describing the scene when the wooden horse was dragged into the city of Troy*]. When the dark of night came down over their cheerful toil, the Libyan *lotos* rang out, and Phrygian songs,[132] and maidens sang with a joyful cry to the beat of their high-stepping feet, while in the house the ever-glowing light of the fire dispelled the dark rays of night.[133]

I was at home, singing with companies of dancers to the mountain goddess, the virgin daughter of Zeus.

88   Sophocles, *Trachiniae* 640–3

Chorus. Soon will the beauteous-crying *aulos* return for you again, not uttering a hostile din, but a sound responding to the *lyra*,[134] of divine music.

(c) **Everyday merry-making**

89   Euripides, *Ion* 1177–8

Messenger. [After the meal, and when the guests' hands had been washed . . .] . . . the time came for *auloi* and for general drinking.[135]

90   Euripides, *Heraclidae* 892–3

Chorus. The dance is sweet to me, if the clear-sounding charm of the *lotos* is there.[136]

---

[131] The word *epilogoi* is quite obscure in this context. It may be connected with the sense of the verb *epilegein* in which it means to call something by its name.

[132] 'Phrygian' here only because Troy is in Phrygia.

[133] Translating in accordance with Heimsoeth's emendation, given in the app. crit. to the O.C.T.

[134] *Antilyron*, which should mean 'in place of', or 'in response to' the *lyra*: cf. e.g. the uses of *antiphōnos*, 'answering', and similar terms at **196** Ath. 635b–636c, with notes ad loc. The schol. offers 'in response to' or 'sounding like' the *lyra* as interpretations of the word here, without choosing between them.

[135] Though the occasion described here is a feast celebrating a special event, this sequence reflects the standard course of any dinner-party of the Classical period. Cf. e.g. **134** Aristoph. *Wasps* 1208 ff.

[136] The text of the end of the sentence is uncertain: perhaps 'is there at the feast'.

91   Euripides, *Rhesus* 360–5

Chorus. Will ancient Troy ever see again bands of merry lovers drinking toasts all day, with the plucking of strings[137] and tipsy contests for the capacious wine-cups?

92   Euripides, *Cyclops* 488–93

Chorus of Satyrs. Sh! He's drunk and singing – a most unpleasant racket. How clumsy and out of tune![138] He'll be sorry for it. He's coming out of the rocky cave: let's teach the untutored oaf how to sing.[139]

(6)   Uses of the terms 'hymn' and 'paean'

(a) Hymn

93   Euripides, *Ion* 881–6

Creousa. You who arouse the singing sound of the seven-voiced *kithara*, whose lifeless ox-horns[140] give forth the well-sounding hymns of the Muses,[141] I denounce you, son of Leto, to the rays of the sun.

94   Euripides, *Alcestis* 445–54

Chorus. Many minstrels will sing your praises to the seven-toned mountain tortoise[142] and in hymns without the *lyra*,[143] when the cycle of the Spartan Carneian festival[144] comes round, at the high season of the month when the moon is in the sky all night, and in the gleaming of rich

---

137   *Psalmos*, the plucking of strings with the fingers. The term came to have the sense 'song sung to the accompaniment of strings', 'psalm', only much later.

138   *Apōidos*, cognate with the verb *apaidein*: cf. **157** Plato, *Laws* 802e, ps.-Ar. *Probs.* XIX.26, 46.

139   Lit. 'instruct him in *kōmoi*', the songs of merry-making. The satyrs proceed to sing a song of love and drinking, which Polyphemus clumsily copies. Even at drinking-parties, singing was an expertise, with its own standards and practices: cf. e.g. **134** Aristoph. *Wasps* 1222 ff.

140   The *kithara*, properly so-called, was wooden throughout. The arms of the *lyra*, however, were often made of horn. The present passage may therefore refer to the *lyra*, or alternatively may be transferring a feature of the *lyra* to the *kithara*, on account of their roughly similar shape. But as with so many passages, the intention may be quite imprecise.

141   Hymns here are simply songs: no special kind is indicated.

142   Cf. **76** *Heracles* 683.

143   I.e., unaccompanied choral songs, here in honour of a dead person. For once, the epithet *alyros* seems to mean no more than it says: contrast e.g. **110** Aesch. *Eum.* 332, Eurip. *Heracles* 891.

144   The Carneia was the chief Spartan festival, associated with the harvest, and held in August. It included musical contests as well as military, athletic and agricultural activities. It was probably this festival that delayed the Spartan dispatch of help to Athens on the occasion of the battle of Marathon (Hdt. VI.102–3, 105–6).

Athens. Such is the music of songs that your death has bequeathed to singers.

95   Euripides, *Troiades* 1242–5

Hecabe. If a god were to turn things upside-down and bury this world below the earth, we should be forgotten, and would not be hymned in song, or provide a theme for musicians among men in time to come.[145]

96   Aeschylus, *Septem* 5–8

Eteocles. But if – may it not be so! – disaster falls, then I, one man alone, shall be much hymned[146] by the townsfolk in loud-roaring preludes[147] and wailings.

97   Euripides, *Medea* 419–27

Chorus. Honour for womankind is on its way: no longer will ill-shouting slander hold women in its power. The music of singers of times past will leave off its hymns[148] about women's faithlessness. Apollo, lord of songs, never placed the divine melody of the *lyra* as a gift in women's minds, or it would have resounded back[149] a hymn against the race of men.[150]

98   Aeschylus, *Persae* 619–27

Queen Atossa. But oh my friends, sing well-omened hymns over these libations to the dead, and call upon the spirit of Darius, while I convey to the gods below these honours that the earth will drink.
Chorus. Queen, revered by the Persians, send down libations to the halls beneath the earth, and we with hymns shall pray the guides of the dead to show kindness in the world below.[151]

---

[145]   The text is confused and uncertain: my translation gives no more than the general sense. The unspoken thought is 'It would be better so', an unusual twist to the idea that the dead live on in song and poetry. But 'hymned' here has the sense 'celebrated', even if the celebration is unwelcome.
[146]   Here the word is used, perhaps ironically, in the reverse of its usual sense: the 'hymn' is a chant of execration. Cf. the next passage.
[147]   *Phroimiois*, i.e. *prooimiois*: cf. 82 Aesch. *Ag.* 31. Here it is an independent song or hymn, not a preliminary to something else: cf. e.g. Thuc. III.104.
[148]   Again, songs directed against something, not celebrating it.
[149]   *Antachēse*, from *antēchein*: cf. 103 *Alcest.* 423.
[150]   For the thesis that songs standardly do no justice to women and gloss over the faults of men, see 73 *Ion* 1090–8.
[151]   Cf. Aesch. *Choeph.* 475.

99   Aeschylus, *Septem* 866–70

Chorus. But before you speak it is right for us to cry forth the ill-sounding hymn of the Erinys, and to sing the hateful paean of Hades.[152]

(b) Paean

100   Euripides, *Ion* 125–7

Ion. O Paian, O Paian!
      Happy, happy may you be
      O son of Leto.[153]

101   Euripides, *Heracles* 820–1

Chorus [at the sight of the goddess Iris, and Madness, who have appeared above the palace]. Lord Paian, turn away evils from me.[154]

102   Sophocles, *Oedipus Tyrannus* 4–5

Oedipus. The city is filled with burning incense, with paeans[155] and with lamentations, all together.

103   Euripides, *Alcestis* 422–4, 430–1

Admetus. Now I shall arrange her body's funeral rites. Come, remain here, and sing back[156] a paean to the god of the dead,[157] who makes no truce. . . . [430] And let there be no sound of *auloi* or of the *lyra* in the city until twelve months are fully past.

104   Aeschylus, *Choephori* 149–51

Electra. Upon such prayers I pour these libations; and you, my friends, must

---

152   Paeans, except where they are prayers for healing or deliverance, are songs of joy even more regularly than are hymns, though this is not invariable. For the present usage, see also **104** Aesch. *Choeph.* 151, **103** *Alcest.* 423–4. But 'ill-sounding hymn' and 'hateful paean' are certainly deliberate oxymorons.

153   Paian, 'Healer', is a regular title of Apollo. These lines form a refrain, repeated at 141–3.

154   Apollo is appealed to in his role as healer or deliverer. See introductory note to *Iliad*.

155   Again, prayers for healing or deliverance.

156   Cf. the use of the verb *antēchein* at **97** *Medea* 426.

157   A song in the god's honour, plainly not a prayer for deliverance, since this god 'makes no truce'.

play your part[158] by decking them with the flowers of wailing, uttering aloud a paean for the one that is dead.

105   Euripides, *Iphigenia in Aulis* 1466–9

Iphigenia [*on the preparations for her own sacrifice*]. I forbid the shedding of tears. Young women, sing a paean[159] of good omen over my fate to Artemis, daughter of Zeus, and let the Greeks keep silence.

106   Euripides, *Ion* 902–6

Creousa [*addressing Apollo*]. Alas! My son – and yours – is gone, a pitiable feast for the birds to snatch: yet you go on with your twanging, singing paeans to your *kithara*.[160]

107   Aeschylus, *Agamemnon* 243–7

Chorus. She [Iphigenia] often used to sing, in the well-furnished men's hall of her father's house; and pure-voiced, virginal, she lovingly graced the cheerful paean of her dear father's third libation.[161]

108   Aeschylus, *Persae* 388–95

Messenger [*describing the beginning of the battle of Salamis*]. First, the loud sound of well-omened singing rang out from the Greeks, and the echo cried back in answer, high-pitched,[162] from the island rock. Then fear entered all the Persians, bewildered in their minds; for the Greeks were singing this solemn paean[163] not as men on the point of flight,[164] but as

---

158   Lit. 'it is *nomos* for you'. The direct meaning is that of propriety according to custom, but the resonance of the musical sense should not be forgotten.
159   Here both a song of good cheer and a prayer for a remission of Artemis' enmity: the latter is to be achieved by Iphigenia's sacrifice.
160   Paeans in general are characteristic of Apollo, but the word here means no more than 'cheerful songs'.
161   That is, the song accompanying the third, and final, libation to the gods that preceded general carousal at a banquet.
162   *Orthios*. For the notion, perhaps suggested here, that an echo sounds higher than its original, see ps.-Ar. *Probs.* XI.6, XIX.11.
163   For the paean as a song to build up confidence before battle, see the next passage, and Eurip. *Phoen.* 1102–3.
164   The Persians had been misled into believing that the Greeks would try to retreat during the night.

setting themselves to battle with boldness and in good heart: and the *salpinx* with its cry inflamed their whole array.[165]

109 Aeschylus, *Septem* 267–70

Eteocles. Hear what I ask; then raise the paean of the holy *ololygmos*[166] of good fortune, the customary Greek practice of the cry over the sacrifice, encouraging our friends, undoing their fear of war.

(7) Music and magic

110 Aeschylus, *Eumenides* 306–11, 328–33

Chorus of Erinyes [to Orestes]. Hear this hymn with which we bind you [*the binding-song*[167] *begins*].
> Come then, let us link our chorus,[168]
> Since this has been decreed:
> We must show forth our hateful music [lit. 'Muse'],
> And tell how this company apportions
> The fates allotted to men . . .

> [328] This is the song over the victim,
> A frenzy, a mind-destroying madness,
> A hymn from the Erinyes
> That binds the mind, lyre-less,[169]
> Withering to mortals.[170]

111 Aeschylus, *Choephori* 1023–5

Orestes. I am defeated: my wits are out of control and drag me along; and

---

165 The *salpinx* is always an instrument of summons or command, not of music. For military uses see e.g. Aesch. *Sept.* 393–4, Eurip. *Phoen.* 1377–9, *Rhesus* 988–9: as a starting-signal at the games, Soph. *Electra* 711: other uses, Aesch. *Eum.* 566–9, cf. Soph. *Ajax* 17. It is commonly called 'Etruscan', e.g. Eurip. *Heraclid.* 830–1, and the passages from *Phoen.*, *Rhesus*, *Eum.* and *Ajax* just cited. It was normally made of bronze (Soph. *Electra* and *Ajax* loc. cit.): a rustic equivalent, called the *kochlos*, was simply a large spiral shell (Eurip. *I.T.* 301–3).
166 See n. 100.
167 Magical 'binding' by incantation was not confined to supernatural agents like the Furies: for an example of a wholly different kind see Theocr. *Idyll* 2, and cf. e.g. the summoning of Darius' ghost, *Persae* 628 ff. (cf. 118).
168 'Link', *hapsōmen*, 'fasten', 'tie'. The chorus presumably link hands and perform a circular dance round Orestes as they sing.
169 *Aphormiktos*, 'without a *phorminx*'. Since plainly no specific instrument is intended, I have translated 'lyre-less' for the sake of euphony. Cf. 46–60.
170 These lines form a refrain, repeated at 341–6. With the magical singing of the Erinyes may be compared that of such other supernatural beings as the Sirens (14 *Od.* XII.36 ff) and the Sphinx (see n. 68 above).

fear in my heart is ready to sing and dance at the promptings of malevolence.[171]

112   Euripides, *Heracles* 867–79, 892–9

> Madness is here personified: she will send Heracles into a frenzy in which he kills his own children.

Madness. See! He tosses his head as he leaves the starting-line, silently rolling his gorgon eyes. His breath is frenzied, like a terrible bull about to charge. He roars,[172] and calls upon the deadly fiends of Tartarus. I shall make you dance more yet! I shall pipe to you with terror![173] Iris, lift up your noble feet and go to Olympus, while I shall enter Heracles' house, unseen.

Chorus. Otototototoi! Lament! The flower of your city is cut down, the son of Zeus. Miserable Greece, you will cast out and destroy your benefactor, set dancing by the *aulos*-accompanied frenzies of Madness. . . .
[892]   The dance without *tympana* has begun,[174] not for the blood that is graced by Bacchic ivy wands, . . . nor for the pouring of Dionysus' libation of the grape. . . . It is a song of destruction that the *aulos* sings. The hound hunts the children: the dance of Madness in this house will not be unfulfilled.

113   Aeschylus, *Eumenides* 902

Chorus [*to Athena*]. What then do you urge me to sing upon this land?[175]

114   Aeschylus, *Agamemnon* 16–18

Watchman. When I set off to sing or hum, shredding in[176] that remedy, music that substitutes for sleep,[177] then I weep and groan for the troubles of this house.

---

[171]   'At the promptings of': the construction suggests 'to the [musical] accompaniment of', 'in response to the lead of'.

[172]   The text is in doubt, but the sense is not seriously affected.

[173]   *Kataulein* is to cast a spell on someone by means of *aulos* music: cf. **151** Plato, *Rep.* 411a, *Laws* 790e. 'With terror': in the same way as in the preceding passage, the construction suggests that terror is the instrument, metaphorically identified with the *aulos*.

[174]   Cf. **46–60**. The following sentences are interspersed with cries from within the house, which I have omitted.

[175]   Sing upon', *ephymnēsai*. The sense is 'What [beneficent] spell do you urge me to cast . . .?'

[176]   A metaphor from the preparation of drugs or magical potions: shredding a herb into the mixture.

[177]   *Antimolpon*, 'a song that is a substitute'. Cf. Eurip. *Medea* 1176, 'a scream, songsubstitute (*antimolpos*) for a cry of joy'.

115 Sophocles, *Ajax* 581–2

Ajax. It is useless for a clever doctor to wail[178] songs of healing over an ill that needs the knife.

116 Euripides, *Iphigenia in Tauris* 1336–8

Messenger [describing Iphigenia pretending to perform a human sacrifice]. After a while, to make us think she was carrying the business further, she cried aloud[179] and sang a magical incantation[180] of barbaric songs, as though she was washing away the blood.

117 Euripides, *Medea* 190–203

Chorus. You would make no mistake if you said that they were fools, not wise at all, those men of old who invented hymns[181] to go with festivities and banquets and dinners, sounds bringing delight to life; while no one found out how to put a stop, through music and songs with their many notes,[182] to mortals' miserable griefs, from which death and misfortune come to wreck our homes. And yet, for mortals to cure these things with songs would be a great benefit, whereas, if a dinner is good, why do they uselessly stretch out the cry?[183] Fullness after eating gives delight to mortals, just by itself.

118 Aeschylus, *Persae* 633–9, 686–8

Chorus. Does he hear me, the blessed, god-equalling king, as I give forth my clear, barbaric, intricately quivering, everlasting, ill-sounding utterances?
Ghost of Darius. [686] You lament, standing near my tomb, and mournfully call upon me, shrieking high with soul-compelling[184] wails.

---

178   *Thrēnein*, to mourn or lament. Since the doctor is not literally lamenting, the reference must be to the 'keening' sound of medical incantations (for the word, see line 632 of this play). The use of music in medicine was well known: cf. e.g. Pindar, *Pyth*. 3.51, 63–5, and for the use of *aulos* music in particular **192** Ath. 624a–b, referring to an account given by Theophrastus.

179   *Anōlolyxe*, related to *ololygmos* etc.: see n. 100.

180   *Katēide … mageuousa*. *Kataeidein* is to sing an incantation or spell (e.g. Hdt. VII.191): *mageuein* is to engage in magical practices of any kind.

181   Here in the word's most general sense, songs of any kind.

182   *Polychordois*, lit. 'with many strings', but applied by Euripides elsewhere (**35** *Rhesus* 549) to the voice of the nightingale, and by Plato (**149** *Rep*. 399d) to the *aulos*.

183   That is, if you are already satisfied by a good dinner, there is no point in singing as well. Music ought to be used – if only it could – to relieve suffering, not to add pleasure when we have enough of it already.

184   *Psychagōgois*, here in its literal sense 'soul-leading'. In philosophical Greek *psychagōgia* comes to mean 'influence on the soul' by means of persuasion etc., and later 'entertainment'. Music may be 'psychagogic' in any of these senses.

119   Euripides, *Iphigenia in Aulis* 1211–15

Iphigenia. Father, if I had the voice of Orpheus, to persuade by the magic of my singing,[185] so that the rocks would follow me and I could charm with my words whoever I wished, then that is what I would do. But shedding tears is the only skill I have, and I will shed them.[186]

120   Euripides, *Phoenissae* 822–4

Chorus. The gods came to the wedding of Harmonia:[187] the walls of Thebes rose up at the sound of the *phorminx*, and its towers at the command of Amphion's *lyra*.[188]

(8) The music of the *syrinx*[189]

121   Aeschylus, *Prometheus Vinctus* 574–5

Io. The wax-bonded, sounding reed[190] murmurs back a sleep-giving *nomos*.

122   Euripides, *Orestes* 145–8

Electra. Hush, my friend. Speak to me like the breath of the slender reed of a *syrinx*.[191]

---

[185]   The verb is *epaidein*, regularly used of singing magical incantations: a favourite word of Plato, e.g. *Phaedo* 114d, *Rep.* 608a, *Phaedrus* 267d, *Tht.* 157c, 158 *Laws* 812c. Its cognate noun, *epaoidē*, is used in this sense at Aesch. *P.V.* 173. Cf. also the use of *ephymnein* at 113 *Eum.* 902.

[186]   For other references in tragedy to the power of the music of Orpheus, see Aesch. *Ag.* 1630, Eurip. *Bacch.* 560–4, *Alcest.* 357–60.

[187]   See 19 *Hymn to Apollo* 195, n. 9.

[188]   Amphion was a legendary musician, son of Zeus and Antiope. This passage refers to the story that the stones brought to build Thebes fitted themselves together spontaneously, charmed by the sound of his *lyra*. For details of the tale, and other traditions about him, see Paus. II.6.4, IX.5.7–9, 187 ps.-Plut. 1131f, *Exc. ex Nicom.* 266 (Jan). The story was apparently told by Hesiod: Palaephatus 42.

[189]   The passages collected here display the *syrinx* primarily in its pastoral character, for which it is best known. But it was not restricted to that role: cf. e.g. 42 Eurip. *Helen* 171, 50 *Troiades* 127, *I.T.* 125–6. The earliest occurrence of the word, at *Il.* X.13, is not in a pastoral context. But the instrument never seems to have been used in serious 'art' music.

[190]   *Donax.* In addition to its use in the construction of the early *lyra* (21 *Hymn to Hermes* 47) and of the vibrating reed of the *aulos* (27 Pindar, *Pyth.* 12.25, with note), the *donax* was the reed used for the pipes of the *syrinx* (e.g. 23 *Hymn to Pan* 15), and the word sometimes simply means '*syrinx*', as in this passage. The pipes of the instrument were bonded together with wax. This fact gives the sense of *kēroplastos*, 'wax-bonded': equivalent words are *kērodetas* (79 Eurip. *I.T.* 1125) and *kērodetos* (Theocr. *Epigr.* 5.4, 188 Ath. 184a). Cf. Pollux IV.69, and Gow's notes to Theocr. *Idylls* 1.129. Wax had another function in the *syrinx*, that of determining the sounding lengths of the pipes, but that is clearly not what is indicated here (see 175 ps.-Ar. *Probs.* XIX.23).

[191]   That is, quietly: but its sound had a carrying quality, 126 Eurip. *Rhesus* 551–3, cf. 50 *Troiades* 127. 'Reed' is *donax*, as in the previous passage.

Chorus. See how quiet I make my voice's muted reed.[192]

123 Euripides, *Electra* 699–705

Chorus. A lamb under its tender mother, so the ancient tale still runs, was found in the mountains of Argos and taken by Pan, who breathes sweet-voiced music on his well-tuned reeds,[193] Pan, master of the wild: and its lovely fleece was golden.[194]

124 Euripides, *Ion* 492–502

Chorus. O haunts of Pan! O cliff that stands near the caverns of the Long Rocks, where the three daughters of Aglauros[195] tread dances with their feet on the grassy lawns before Athena's temple, to the quivering cries of the songs of the *syrinx*, when you, Pan, play it in your sunless caves!

125 Sophocles, *Philoctetes* 211–13

Chorus. The man is not far off, but in this place; but he does not carry with him the song of the *syrinx*, like a shepherd of the fields . . .

126 Euripides, *Rhesus* 551–3

Chorus. And now the flocks are grazing on Mount Ida: I can hear the sound of the *syrinx* resounding through the night.

127 Euripides, *Alcestis* 568–87

Chorus. House of Admetus, ever-generous to your many guests. In you Pythian Apollo, skilled with the *lyra*, was content to live, and did not disdain to be a herdsman there, piping[196] shepherds' wedding-tunes in the pastures on your sloping hillsides. Spotted lynxes pastured with him for delight at his melodies, and tawny companies of lions came

---

[192] *Hyporophon boan*, lit. 'a cry under a reed'. The adjective is unique to this passage. *Orophos* is a kind of reed used mainly in thatching houses, and hence the word sometimes means 'roof': it is not found in musical connections elsewhere. Hence it is possible that the phrase here means 'a cry under a roof', i.e. one closed in by the mouth, a whisper, rather than picking up Electra's allusion to quiet syrinx-playing. Perhaps the ambiguity is deliberate.

[193] 'Reeds' here are *kalamoi*, not *donakes*. See n. 198 below.

[194] The continuation of this passage (705–19) will be found at **86** above.

[195] Aglauros was the daughter of Cecrops. Her three daughters, after disobeying the commands of Athena, went mad and threw themselves to their deaths from the Acropolis. Here they are spirits, or ghosts.

[196] *Syrizōn*, evidently in the sense 'playing the *syrinx*', as shepherds do. In the latter part of the passage Apollo, more characteristically, sings to the *kithara*.

from the valley of Othrys: around your *kithara*, Phoebus Apollo, danced the dappled fawn, stepping with light ankles out from the lofty pine-woods, in joy at your cheerful song.

128   Euripides, *Iphigenia in Aulis* 573–8

Chorus. You came, Paris, to the place where you were reared, a herdsman among the shining white cattle of Mount Ida, piping foreign tunes on the *syrinx*, breathing imitations of Olympus[197] on the reeds of Phrygian *auloi*.[198]

---

[197] Olympus was a semi-legendary figure, treated as one of the founders of the auletic art. He is said to have been the pupil of Marsyas: Phrygia, where they and Marsyas' precursor Hyagnis came from, was the traditional home of the *aulos*. Our sources suggest that there were two ancient auletes called Olympus, the first a Phrygian, the second a Mysian, but the evidence is very unclear. What passed as the melodies of Olympus were still known in the fourth century, and were universally acclaimed as models and masterpieces. Our main source is **187** ps.-Plut.: see 1132f, 1133d-f, 1134e–1135b, 1136c, 1137a–d, 1143b–c.

[198] 'Reeds' here is *kalamoi*: the word usually refers to the pipes (not the vibrating reed) of the *aulos*. But it is also used sometimes in place of *donakes* for the pipes of the *syrinx* (e.g. **81** Eurip. *I.A.* 1038, **123** Eurip. *Electra* 702), and it is not clear which instrument Paris is playing here. Despite my translation, the noun *syrinx* does not occur in the previous clause: and since the verb used there, *syrizein*, may refer to any kind of whistling noise, it may be the allusion to the *syrinx* in the translation that is misleading. But herdsmen and shepherds traditionally played the *syrinx* (*syrizein* is used with precisely this in mind at **127** Eurip. *Alcest.* 576): and the last clause could, at a stretch, be translated 'breathing on your reeds imitations of Olympus' Phrygian *auloi*'. There is a further, less likely possibility. The word *aulos* is sometimes used to refer to the shepherd's 'single pipe', the 'single-caned *syrinx*' of **188** Ath. 184a, the '*aulos* without a *glōssa* [vibrating reed]' of Pollux II.100, 108. The word has this meaning at e.g. Theocr. *Idylls* 5.7, 6.42–6. The instrument was made of a single tube of straw or reed: it had finger-holes, and was sounded, like the 'many-reeded (*polykalamos*)' *syrinx*, by blowing across the hole at the upper end. But in order to construe the present passage as referring to it, we would have to explain away the fact that *auloi* are referred to in the plural, as they commonly are when the instrument is a double *aulos*.

The tunes are 'imitations of Olympus' just in the sense that they are the ones that Olympus played, or ones like them. Olympus played them on the *aulos* (see passages cited in the previous note), but Paris may not have done. They are 'foreign' because they are Phrygian, not Greek.

CHAPTER 7

The musical revolution of the later fifth century

It seems appropriate to interrupt the sequence of quotations at this point, as in Chapter 4, and to offer a brief summary of our main information about the musical developments of this turbulent period. Most of our substantial evidence comes from later sources, particularly ps.-Plutarch and Athenaeus. Together with other compilers and commentators, they have preserved fragments of the writings of the composers in question, and important passages of contemporary comment: apart from these, our most significant fifth-century witness is Aristophanes (see Chapter 8). Remarks in Plato, Aristotle, Aristoxenus and certain other writers of the fourth century can sometimes add to our knowledge, but it is often difficult to assign dates to the developments they mention.

Apart from the drama, the musical forms to which our sources pay most attention are the dithyramb and the kitharodic *nomos*. These types of composition are distinct, the latter being a solo concert-piece with *kithara*-accompaniment, the former – at least usually – a choral piece accompanied by the *aulos*, but the principal changes in musical style seem to have followed much the same course in both. The major composers of the period, notably Melanippides, Phrynis, Philoxenus and Timotheus, wrote works in both genres, though Cinesias and Telestes are known only for their dithyrambs. (There was no lack of minor composers, but few of them are now much more than names.)

Melanippides' dates are uncertain: he was writing somewhere between about 480 and 430. In a passage referring explicitly to his *kithara* music,[1] Pherecrates accuses him of being the first to set music on its degenerate path towards over-elaboration and complexity. He speaks of Melanippides' 'twelve strings', which made music 'slacker'.[2] Melanippides was especially notorious for his *anabolai*, 'preludes', long lyric passages without strophic response, with which he apparently replaced the strophe–antistrophe form, rather than merely prefacing the one with the other (Ar. *Rhet.* 1409b). The object, it appears, was an increase in dramatic realism:[3] the musical context was probably the dithyramb.[4] In his *Marsyas*, quoted at 189 Ath. 616e, we have his only surviving reference to music: 'Athena threw away the instruments [the *auloi*] from her holy hand and said: "Away, shameful distorters of the body. I do not give myself to ugliness."' Despite the comment in Athenaeus, this need not be taken to represent Melanippides' own attitude to the *aulos*: he was, after all, composing for it, and the story of Athena and the *auloi* was a traditional subject

---

[1]   The Pherecrates fragment is one of our most important documents, and one to which the present chapter will repeatedly refer. It is to be found at 187 ps.-Plut. 1141d–1142a. Lines 3–5 refer to Melanippides.

[2]   The word *chalaros*, 'slack', is sometimes used in musical contexts to mean 'relaxed', 'flabby', 'self-indulgent', e.g. 149 Plato, *Rep.* 398e. This sense is possible here, but 'flexible', i.e. readily moulded to different *harmoniai* and styles, is more likely.

[3]   169 ps.-Ar. *Probs.* XIX.15, though Melanippides is not mentioned there by name.

[4]   For which he was especially popular: Xen. *Mem.* 1.4.3, cf. *Suda* s.v. Melanippides (2). The *Problems* passage referred to in n. 3 above is explicitly concerned with the dithyramb. On *anabolai* in dithyrambs see also Aristoph. *Peace* 827 ff.

positively begging to be set by a composer with a specialist knowledge of auletic technique. The fact that Melanippides presented the story in its usual form, whereas Telestes (quoted in the same passage, 616f) chose to express his championship of the *aulos* by challenging the tradition directly, proves nothing about Melanippides' views. His reputation, despite the sneers of Pherecrates, was high, and lasted into late antiquity (Plut. *Non Posse Suav.* 13).

Phrynis is another of those attacked in the Pherecrates fragment. It may be read as attributing to him a new device for tuning the *kithara*, enabling him to 'get twelve *harmoniai* out of seven strings'. The interpretation is uncertain, but plainly points to a practice of modulation between different systems of tuning. He was famous for his *kampai*, 'bends' or 'twists',[5] which seem to be instrumental melodic turns, not necessarily purely ornamental, but involving, according to one authority, 'twists' from one *harmonia* to another (schol. to Aristoph. *Clouds* 334). They are also attributed to other composers of the period, especially Cinesias (ibid., and Pherecrates loc. cit.). Phrynis is said to have set out as a singer to the *aulos*, but was taught *kitharōdia* by Aristoclides (schol. to Aristoph. *Clouds* 970): his innovations were displayed in kitharodic *nomoi*, and it was for them that he was principally known (e.g. Ath. 638c, cf. Plut. *Prof. Virt.* 13). Ps.-Plutarch treats him as the first to introduce 'modulation' of *harmonia* and rhythm to this genre (**187** 1133b, cf. Proclus, *Chrest.* 320a): he is also one of those credited with the addition of extra strings to the *kithara* beyond the traditional seven (Proclus loc. cit.).

Cinesias is attacked in the Pherecrates fragment too, accused of 'exharmonic'[6] *kampai* in his strophes (or perhaps, between them[7]), and of composing dithyrambs in such a way that 'the right side looked like the left', as in a mirror. What exactly this notion of being the wrong way round was intended to express is unclear – possibly no more than the common contention that dithyramb writers in general, and Cinesias in particular, wrote nothing but airy gobbledegook.[8] Extant examples of contemporary dithyrambic diction tend to bear out this judgement. One cause of the phenomenon may have been the growing domination of the instrument and the music over the singer and the words: words were composed to fit musical ideas, rather than the other way about.[9] Aristophanes treats him as the paradigm case of the nonsensical and pretentious dithyrambist, and his hostility is sufficient evidence that Cinesias was prominent and popular. (See **136** *Birds* 1373 ff, with introductory note.) This is confirmed by Plato (*Gorgias* 501e), who speaks of him as one who devoted his efforts to writing what would please the public, rather than what would be instructive or edifying.

Philoxenus was probably a more substantial composer than Cinesias, once again specialising in dithyrambs. His name appears in the passage of ps.-Plutarch that quotes the Pherecrates fragment, but the text is in some doubt; and apart from the claim, attributed there to Aristophanes, that he introduced 'songs' (*melē*, possibly but not certainly solos) into the dithyramb, we cannot be sure that anything in the passage applies to him. He was born in Cythera, and was active in the last years of the

[5] Pherecrates loc. cit., cf. **132** Aristoph. *Clouds* 970–1. The word is close to being a technical term in these contexts, and may have been so used by the composers themselves.
[6] Fairly certainly in the sense 'going outside the prevailing *harmonia*', rather than just vaguely 'unmusical'.
[7] This interpretation is supported by the schol. to Aristoph. *Clouds* 334.
[8] Especially **136** Aristoph. *Birds* 1372 ff (where the schol. quotes the proverb 'you make even less sense than a dithyramb'), cf. *Peace* 827 ff.
[9] Plato remarks on this development and criticises it vehemently: e.g. **149** *Rep.* 399e, 400d, cf. **154** *Laws* 669b–670a.

fifth century and the beginning of the fourth: he spent a short but eventful period in Sicily at the court of Dionysius.[10] As to his music, the evidence is confusing. His name is commonly coupled with that of Timotheus (e.g. **187** ps.-Plut. 1142c, Polyb. IV.20.8, quoted at **192** Ath. 626b), in contexts that make it clear that he is considered a representative of the 'new music'. His dithyrambs are formally contrasted with Pindar's, as standard examples of the new and old styles (**187** ps.-Plut. 1142b–c). Yet Philodemus claims that while the 'characters displayed' in the two poets' dithyrambs are quite different, the 'style' (*tropos*) of their dithyrambs is the same (*De Mus.* 1 fr. 18.6 ff). It is not clear what we are to make of this, but Philodemus has a special axe to grind, and may perhaps be safely ignored. Again, Dionysius of Halicarnassus (*De Comp. Verb.* 131) places Philoxenus among those whose dithyrambs modulated between Dorian, Phrygian and Lydian, and who shifted between the enharmonic, chromatic and diatonic genera, while varying rhythms as they pleased. Earlier dithyramb, he tells us, was not like that: it was 'orderly'. Aristotle (**161** *Pol.* 1342b) says something rather different, that Phrygian is the natural *harmonia* for the dithyramb, and that one proof of this is the failure of Philoxenus' attempt to compose one in Dorian: the very nature of the dithyramb, Aristotle asserts, made him 'fall back' into the proper *harmonia* again, the Phrygian. The *Suda* says that he was called 'Ant', which may be a reminiscence of the 'ant-runs' attributed to Agathon by Aristophanes (**138** *Thesm.* 100) and to Timotheus by Pherecrates (**187** ps.-Plut. 1142a): these were probably quick, decorative figures, intricately meandering. Most of these comments seem to have been made with critical intent: a much more flattering judgement is made by his near-contemporary Antiphanes (quoted at Ath. 643d). Philoxenus, he says, is head and shoulders above other composers. He uses new words of his own (cf. schol. to Aristoph. *Clouds* 335): he blends his songs very well with modulations and 'colourings':[11] he knows what is truly musical, unlike composers now, who set to their miserable words 'ivy-wreathed, fountainy, flower-fluttering, wretched stuff, weaving in non-belonging melodies (*allotria melē*)'. (A typical purveyor of this 'ivy-wreathed, fountainy stuff' is caricatured by Aristophanes at **135** *Birds* 903 ff, cf. **136** *Birds* 1373 ff.) Some of the features of the 'modern' school are clearly mentioned here, though Philoxenus apparently avoided the airy silliness typical of some of its members, but the difficult phrase 'non-belonging melodies', of whose perpetration he is said to be innocent, may suggest a qualification to his modernism. If it means 'melodies in different and inappropriate *harmoniai*', then Philoxenus' departure from tradition in that area at least must have been modest. But it is possible that the sense is 'melodies that do not belong to the composer', 'other people's tunes', in which case Philoxenus is simply being acquitted of plagiarism.

Of all the new-wave composers, Timotheus of Miletus is the most important. Hence in the Pherecrates fragment he is treated as by far the worst of the dreadful moderns, the chief torturer of music. He was a defiantly self-conscious innovator; the following quotation sets out his principal boast.

129 Timotheus, fr. 20, *P.M.G.* 796, quoted at Ath. 122c–d

I do not sing the old songs, for my new ones are better. A young Zeus reigns, and it was in olden times that Cronos ruled: away with the ancient Muse!

[10] For the stories told about him there see Diod. Sic. XV.6, Lucian, *Adv. Indoct.* 15, schol. to Aristides 309d.

[11] *Chrōmata*: probably not a reference to the chromatic genus, but to 'colourings' of an emotional or dramatic kind. See e.g. **196** Ath. 638a, cf. **153** Plato, *Laws* 655a with n. 61.

But he was not an unthinking iconoclast. Our extensive fragment of his *Persae*[12] ends with the following lines.

130   Timotheus, fr. 15, *Persae*, *P.M.G.* 791, lines 202–40

But O uplifter of the new-made music of the golden *kithara*, Lord Paian, come as a helper to my hymns. For the noble, long-lived, great leader of Sparta, a people abounding with the flowers of youth, shakes me and flares up against me and drives me with the fire of blame, because I dishonour the older music with my new hymns.[13] But I bar no one, young or old or of my own age, from these hymns of mine. It is the ancient-music-wreckers that I keep off, outragers of songs, stretching out the shrieks of shrill and loud-voiced criers.[14] It was Orpheus, son of Calliope, with his intricate music, who first begot the tortoiseshell on Mount Pieria:[15] Terpander yoked music to the ten songs[16] – it was Aeolian Lesbos that bore this famous man, at Antissa. And now Timotheus with his eleven-struck metres and rhythms makes *kitharis* spring up anew,[17] opening the Muses' chambered treasury of many hymns. The city of Miletus, home of a twelve-walled people, first of the Achaeans, nurtured him. But far-shooting Pythian, may you come with prosperity to this holy city, sending to this untroubled people a peace that flourishes in good civic order.

What then did Timotheus' 'new music' amount to? The fragments provide adequate evidence of his association of different rhythms, of a strained and artificial diction, and of linguistic fancy embroidering ideas beyond the limits of sense. In 130, for instance, Timotheus uses the three numbers he mentions – ten, eleven and twelve – to suggest some kind of progression. But there is none there: the numbers are the merest ornament, and the suggestion of significance at which the sequence hints is a mirage. On the purely musical side, metres and rhythms apart,[18] two points are indicated. First, Timotheus seems not to object to old-fashioned music as such, but to its treatment by his contemporaries. Their performances debase a music of which in

---

[12] A kitharodic *nomos*, not a dithyramb: see Plut. *Philop.* 11.

[13] The story is told of Timotheus, as of Phrynis, that the Spartan authorities objected to his adding extra strings to the *kithara*'s traditional seven: Paus. III.12.10, 196 Ath. 636e, Plut. *Inst. Lac.* 17, where a similar tale is told also of the much older composer Terpander.

[14] *Kērykōn*, 'heralds', perhaps here 'town criers'.

[15] The text at this point is uncertain, and there is probably a short lacuna.

[16] That is, probably, the canon of kitharodic *nomoi* attributed to him at Pollux IV.65, cf. 187 ps.-Plut. 1132c–d. But these texts give no clear authority for the number ten: Pollux lists eight, though he mentions two others which, so he says, were sometimes wrongly included (they are in fact auletic *nomoi*), ps.-Plutarch seven. The *Suda* s.v. *Orthios nomos* gives the number seven.

[17] 'Eleven-struck', i.e. played on eleven strings. The use of eleven strings is credited to Timotheus at Paus. III.12.10, Nicomachus 274.5–6 (Jan), and the *Suda*, and probably by Pherecrates at the end of ps.-Plutarch's quotation, though there the text is uncertain. The word *kitharis* is a deliberate archaism. Of its two senses, '*kithara*' and 'the art of the *kithara*', the latter is the more likely here.

[18] His association of different metres in a single work is reflected in a remark of Hephaestion, *Poem.* 3, where he cites Timotheus' kitharodic *nomoi* as examples of 'relaxed' or 'free' verse, 'composed at random and without a definite metre'.

itself he voices no criticisms (beyond saying in **129** that his own songs are better), though we cannot tell whether he is objecting to anything more specific than a generalised insensitivity. On the subject of his own music, **130** contains only the reference to his 'eleven-struck' metres and rhythms. The addition of extra strings to the *kithara* was certainly intended to facilitate both the performance of intricate ornamental figures, and modulations between *harmoniai*, systems of tuning. Both of these are suggested by the Pherecrates fragment, which accuses him of 'pulling out winding exharmonic ant-paths' at an absurdly high pitch, and of filling the whole of music with *kampai*, like caterpillars in a cabbage.[19] However these accusations are precisely to be understood, it is again clear that the object of Timotheus' innovations was to produce music that was emotional, dramatic, highly coloured and ornately decorated, in contrast with the 'grave simplicity' of the past (cf. e.g. **187** ps.-Plut. 1135c–d). According to a well-known story, he was encouraged in his early efforts by Euripides, and from a position of initial unpopularity he came to be the leading figure in the music of his period.[20] His *nomoi* and those of Philoxenus survived to become schoolchildren's classics in Arcadia centuries later (Polyb. IV.20.8, quoted at **192** Ath. 626b).

Our authorities ascribe no specific innovations to Telestes, whose work spans the very end of the fifth century and the start of the fourth. But he was a prominent member of the new school of composers, and it is said that his dithyrambs, with those of Philoxenus, were among the works of literature taken by Alexander on his campaigns (Plut. *Alex.* 8). He is of interest principally for the handful of remarks about music that have survived in fragments of his poetry. They demonstrate an enthusiasm for the *aulos*, and they contrast its originally 'Lydian' melodies, native to Phrygia, with the Dorian music proper to mainland Greece. One also mentions the *magadis*, offering an interesting if enigmatic description of its operation.[21]

Given the new music's emphasis on emotional expression and decorative elaboration, it is not surprising that specialist performers on the *aulos* attained a particular eminence in this period. Thebes was especially noted for them: the most famous was Pronomus, who belongs to the fifth century, followed at the turn of the century by Antigenidas and a little later by Dorion: the 'schools' of the latter two became champions of rival styles.[22] We have little detailed information about their work, though it certainly followed, in general character, the innovations of the other composers we have been reviewing. (See e.g. **195** Ath. 631e.) One piece of evidence about Pronomus is particularly significant: he was, we are told, the first to play all the *harmoniai* on one pair of *auloi*, auletes having previously had a different pair for each. Pronomus' achievement involved technical modifications to the instrument's structure.[23]

---

19   On *kampai* see the discussion of Phrynis above. Pherecrates is punning on two words, *kampē* in its musical sense, and *kampē* meaning a caterpillar, which differ only in their accent, and not even that in the genitive plural form, used here.

20   For the story, Satyrus, *Vit. Eur.* fr. 39, Plut. *An Seni* 23. For his pre-eminence cf. e.g. Ar. *Metaph.* 993b.

21   The passages are all quoted by Athenaeus. See **189** 616f (passages from two poems) and **192** 625e on the *aulos*, **196** 637a on the *magadis*.

22   On the reputation of Pronomus see e.g. Paus. IX.12.5, cf. **188** Ath. 184d. On Antigenidas and Dorion, see especially **163** Theophrastus, *Hist. Plant.* IV.11.4–5, **187** ps.-Plut. 1138b.

23   **195** Ath. 631e, Paus. IX.12.4. Cf. also Pollux IV.80 on another Theban aulete: 'Up to that time the *aulos* had four holes: it was made many-holed by Diodorus the Theban, who opened sideways paths for the breath.' See also Theophrastus' remarks (cited in n. 22 above) on the way in which new techniques of *aulos* playing demanded changes in the process of preparing reeds.

It may be worth emphasising two substantial points that emerge from all this. One is that the period was characterised by a rapidly developing growth of complexity and variety in all aspects of musical composition – in melody, in rhythm and metre, in poetic diction – coupled with an abandonment both of repetitive formal structures and of rigid divisions between musical styles. These trends were of course an extension of tendencies already existing in the music of the sixth century and the early fifth: but they gathered momentum, as trends in the arts will, and elaboration and artifice outgrew their aesthetic roots.

Secondly, our accounts of the composers' handling of the *harmoniai* make it clear that now if not before, these are primarily conceived as being, or at least as demanding, different forms of scalar structure, associated with specific ways of tuning an instrument. Our authorities link the practice of shifting from one *harmonia* to another with the addition to instruments of devices for playing additional notes – new strings on the *kithara*, extra holes and means of opening and closing them on the *aulos*. If the scholiast's note on *Clouds* 334 is to be trusted, the *kampai* so beloved of these composers were melodic contrivances for getting from one *harmonia* to another, in short, phrases designed to prepare modulations. These claims are comprehensible only if the *harmoniai* were by now much more than vaguely conceived styles, with their own special emotional characters (though they were certainly that): a new *harmonia* demanded a new set of notes, to be found by retuning an instrument, by picking up a different one, or by using an instrument on which 'extra' notes, beyond those of the original *harmonia*, were already available.

It remains an open question just what the scales or patterns of tuning characterising the *harmoniai* of this period were, how they differed from one another, and whether they were related in any kind of 'system' such as those described by the theorists of the fourth century and later. For the present, two points are worth making: first, that the theorists were not working in a vacuum, and that at least some rough basis for their systems must have existed in the realm of practice; and secondly that it seems to be beyond reasonable doubt that the primary differences between the *harmoniai* lay in the interval structures of the scales they employed. Certainly the different structures were usually performed in practice at characteristically different levels of pitch, but pitch was a secondary factor, rather than one on which a formal analysis of *harmoniai* could be based. They were more like modes than like keys, though probably they corresponded exactly to neither. (On these matters see Ch. 10, Appendix A.)

CHAPTER 8

Aristophanes

The earliest musical and literary criticism comes in a form very different from the analytic prose of modern musicologists. Whether it appears in comic drama or in other kinds of public musical performance, it is in verse, designed to be spoken aloud or sung, and its methods are those of satire and abuse. Aristophanes is not its only exponent, or the first. Athenaeus' quotation (189 617b–f) from a *hyporchēma* of Pratinas[1] goes back to the early fifth century, and has many affinities with Aristophanic polemic. Closer still in style, and roughly contemporary in date, is the passage of a comedy by Pherecrates that ps.-Plutarch quotes at 187 1141d–1142a. The practice of commenting on other men's music in one's own compositions was evidently well established: further examples exist in poets as different as Pindar (e.g. 29 fr. 61 and *Isth.* 2.1–11) and Timotheus (130 *Persae* 216 ff). But we have far more of Aristophanes than of any comparable author, and his plays contain a variety of sustained attacks on what he sees as the corruption of the arts in his day. Their abusive vigour, their elements of knock-about farce, and their pervasive sexual innuendos should not be allowed to conceal the serious intentions underlying them, or blind us to the detailed information about music and musicians that they quite casually dispense. A number of less polemical passages also have features of musical interest. In general, Aristophanes' works are studded with brief but often illuminating references to musical matters, far too numerous to be collected here: we can only pick out a few plums. It should be emphasised that Aristophanes is far from being a disinterested observer. By instinct and conviction a conservative in aesthetic and social matters, Aristophanes was producing his plays during the last thirty years of the fifth century and the first decade of the fourth, and they are thus contemporary with the later works of Sophocles and Euripides, and with many of the innovative compositions discussed in the previous chapter. Of the latter and their burgeoning popularity he has little good to say; and though he deals rather more gently with Euripides, he too is tarred with the brush of modernism. Good music, in Aristophanes' book, is the allegedly simple and manly music of the early years of the fifth century, typified by the compositions of Aeschylus.

Clouds

This play was produced in 423 B.C., but later thoroughly revised. Its theme is the contrast between the straightforward, honest, upright manners and educational practices of the 'old days', and the disruptive, disrespectful and irreligious way of life now in fashion, whose sources are identified with the intellectually unscrupulous arguments and teachings of the sophists. In the first passage, Strepsiades has gone to learn from Socrates: he wants to be instructed in the 'unjust argument' which, he thinks, will enable him to outwit his creditors. Socrates, made here to represent an archetypal sophist, insists that he needs preliminary training in other matters first (cf. e.g.

---

[1] For other relevant quotations from Pratinas see 192 and 195, Ath. 624f–625a, 632f–633a.

Plato, *Prot.* 318d–319a), including questions to do with music. We know
little in detail about the forms of musical instruction and enquiry used by
the sophists. The most significant theorist among them was certainly
Damon,[2] of whose ideas the present passage may well be a parody, but there
is no doubt that others also dabbled in the field of music, to a greater or
lesser degree.[3] It is at any rate clear that what Aristophanes is currently
attacking is not a particular kind of music, but the pretensions of the new
'science' of musical analysis, together with its claims to form a significant
part of an accomplished citizen's education.

131   *Clouds* 635–67

Socrates. Tell me then, what do you want to learn first, that you haven't been
taught before? Well? About measures,[4] or words,[5] or rhythms?
Strepsiades. Oh – measures for me! [640] The barley-seller swindled me out of
two quarts only the other day.
Soc. That's not what I'm asking: I want to know which of the measures you
think is best, the triple measure or the quadruple measure.[6]
Str. Half a gallon's what I like!
Soc. Idiot! You're talking nonsense.
Str. What? Don't you agree that four measures make half a gallon?[7]
Soc. What an oaf! Quite unteachable! To hell with you! But maybe you could
learn something about rhythms.
Str. How will rhythms help me earn a crust?
Soc. [650] First, they'll teach you to behave properly in company, if you know
which rhythm is the martial sort[8] and which goes finger-wise.[9]
Str. Finger-wise? Hey! I know that!
Soc. Tell me then.

---

[2] Plato's references to him make this clear. See particularly *Laches* 180d, 197d, *Alc. I*
118c, **149** and **152** *Rep.* 400a–c, 424c, and among the other sources Isoc. xv.235,
Plut. *Peric.* 4. His importance is beyond doubt, but the details of his teaching and
researches are obscure and controversial. See Ch. 10, Appendix B.
[3] The most clear-cut example is the polymath Hippias. See especially Plato, *Prot.* 318e,
Hipp. Ma. 285c–d, *Hipp. Mi.* 368c–d.
[4] 'Measures', *metra*, here means 'metres', but Strepsiades takes it in its commonplace
sense, 'measures' of volume, length, etc.
[5] *Epē*, often referring specifically to poems in epic hexameters, but here simply to
words as they occur in poetry, poetic diction.
[6] Lit. 'the trimeter or the tetrameter', technical terms of metrical analysis, but again
given a down-to-earth interpretation by Strepsiades.
[7] The *hekteus* is eight *choinikes*, the *hēmihekteon* (here rendered as 'half a gallon', since
that is four pints) is four. The *hekteus* was in fact about two gallons.
[8] The 'enhoplian' rhythm is that of the war-dance: cf. Xen. *Anab.* v.1.11, **188**
Ath. 184f. According to Bacchius (316.7–8 Jan), the associated metre is
˘ –|˘ ˘|– ˘|˘ –: it has affinities with the anapaestic marching rhythms commonly
used for the entrance of the chorus in tragedy. On the rhythms mentioned here see
also **149** Plato, *Rep.* 400b, where the analysis offered is explicitly Damonian.
[9] Socrates means 'which is dactylic' (i.e. based on the foot – ˘ ˘): the term is derived
from the Greek *daktylos*, 'finger', and the more literal translation is needed for the
sake of the obscene by-play of the succeeding lines.

Str. Isn't it just this finger here? Though before, when I was a boy, I used *this* instead.

Soc. Bumbling nincompoop!

Str. But this isn't what I want to learn, you horrible little man!

Soc. What *do* you want then?

Str. That argument! That unjust argument!

Soc. But there are other things you have to learn before that, like which four-footed beasts are truly male.[10]

Str. [660] I know *them* all right, unless I'm going mad. There's ram, buck, bull, dog, fowl, . . .

Soc. See what's happened? You're giving the female fowl the same name as the male!

Str. How? Explain.

Soc. How? You say 'fowl' and 'fowl'.

Str. Hey! So I do! What should I call them now?

Soc. One 'fowl', the other 'fowless'.

Str. 'Fowless'? Oh, very good! . . .

The passage continues in similar vein, to line 692.

132 *Clouds* 961–72

An excerpt from a description of the old style of education: the speaker is the *Dikaios Logos*, 'Just Argument', personified.

Just Argument. I will tell you of the upbringing that was laid down in the old days, when I, the speaker of Justice, flourished, and moderation was in fashion.

First, children's voices had to be kept low, and not heard.

Secondly, they had to go in an orderly way along the roads to the kitharist's school — all the boys of the village together, stripped right down, even if it was snowing as thick as flour.

Next, he taught them to sing a song without knotting their legs

---

10 The passage that follows, only a part of which is included here, is usually thought to parody the linguistic researches of Protagoras and others. But it is offered as a *preliminary* to matters concerning 'words' (*logoi*, 'arguments'). We know from Plato (**149** and **152** *Rep.* 400a–c, 424c) and elsewhere that Damon gave analyses of the ethical character of different musical forms. It is likely that he based his account on supposed qualitative distinctions between the various notes, intervals, rhythms, and so on. One later source who mentions Damon, and who may have derived his theories from him, makes the male–female distinction fundamental to his account of these qualitative differences. (Arist. Quint, 66 ff: the reference to Damon, in an entirely appropriate context, is at 80.25–81.3. For more detail on these matters see Ch. 10, Appendix B. On the suitability of distinct rhythmic and harmonic structures to men and women see also **157** Plato, *Laws* 802e.) If Damon did so too, then he may also, like Protagoras, have had a theoretical interest in the 'proper' genders of things, with a view to recommending the 'proper' musical ways of representing them. (Cf. also his association with Prodicus, attested at *Laches* 197d.) In that case, the nonsense of the present passage may be as much Damonian as Protagorean.

together – something like 'Pallas the terrible sacker of cities', or 'The cry that rings out afar' – stretching out the melody[11] which their fathers had handed down. And if any of them fooled around with the tune or twisted any twirls[12] – the sort of knotted-up twists we get nowadays from Phrynis – he was soundly beaten for obliterating the true Muses.

> With this passage it is worth comparing a short excerpt from the *Knights* (produced in 424 B.C.), an attack on the politician Cleon, constantly the butt of Aristophanes' wit on account of his lowly origins and alleged vulgarity.

133   *Knights 985–95*

Chorus [singing]. This is something that amazes me too –
　　His piggish taste in music.
　　For the boys that went with him to school
　　Say he wouldn't tune his *lyra* to anything but Dorian:[13]
　　Any other *harmonia* he just refused to learn.
　　And then, they say, the *kithara* teacher
　　Got furious and told him to get out of there,
　　Asserting that the only *harmonia* the boy could take in
　　Was Bribery-style.[14]

Wasps

> The play appeared in 422 B.C. Its plot is unimportant here: in the present excerpt Bdelycleon is trying to persuade his father Philocleon to adopt 'society' manners. Here he describes the course of an imaginary dinner-party.

[11] *Enteinamenous*, 'keeping it tight': 'melody' translates *harmonia*. But the latter term may well have its technical sense 'scale structure' here, so that what they are doing is keeping the *harmonia* tight, not allowing it to relapse into a different one. See Ch. 7 n. 2.

[12] *Kampē*: see p. 94 above, and cf. Pherecrates at **187** ps.-Plut. 1141d–1142a.

[13] The Dorian *harmonia* was associated with manly and straight-forward music. In most contexts (e.g. **149** Plato, *Rep.* 399, **161** Ar. *Pol.* 1340b, 1342a–b) it is therefore highly valued. Here the point is that a restriction to nothing but the Dorian style indicates a lack of sensibility and proportion (cf. **151** *Rep.* 410a–412a, **154** *Laws* 666e–667a): it also prepares for the pun in the last line. Note the explicit association of a particular *harmonia* with a way of tuning an instrument: cf. Ch. 10, Appendix A.

[14] The Greek is *Dōrodokisti*, a pun on *Dōristi* ('Dorian'): the word recurs at *Knights* 403. The association between ability to play a stringed instrument and being a man of decent education is again brought out at *Wasps* 959, where 'he doesn't know how to play the *kithara*' (*kitharizein*, used of playing any of this family of instruments) means 'he's uneducated': cf. 989, where 'I don't know how to play the *kithara*' means 'I'm a plain man'.

134   Wasps 1208–50

Bdelycleon. Enough of that. Now lie down here, and learn how to comport
yourself when drinking in company.

Philocleon. [1210] All right: how do I lie down? Come on, tell me!

Bde. Do it *elegantly.*

Phi. Like this?

Bde. No! Not like that!

Phi. Then how?

Bde. Keep your knees straight, and subside with fluid athleticism among the
cushions. Next, make a complimentary remark about the table-ware;
look at the ceiling; admire the hall's tapestries. [*to an imaginary
servant*] Water for our hands! Bring in the tables! [*to Philocleon*] We
eat . . . we wash again . . . now the libation . . .

Phi. Heavens! Are we having a dream-feast?

Bde. The *aulos*-girl has blown.[15] Our fellow drinkers [1220] are Theorus,
Aeschines, Phanus, Cleon, and another one, a stranger, next to
Acestor's head. In that company you must cap the *skolia* with real
finesse.[16]

---

15   On the normal course of a dinner-party, and its music, see e.g. 89 Eurip. *Ion* 1177–8,
Plato, *Symp.* 174e–176e, and especially 141–4, 146–7 Xen. *Symp.* 1–3, 7, 9.

16   A guest would sing a little *skolion*, a drinking-song or catch, and the next guest would
try to complete it with his own. See also *Lysistr.* 1236–8, cf. 21 *Hymn to Hermes*
55–6. The word *skolion* means 'crooked', and the ancient authorities give various
accounts of its derivation, and of the practices associated with it. The schol. on Plato,
Gorgias 451e offers three explanations, supposedly referring to three different types
of *skolion*. According to the first, that of Dicaearchus, there would be sung after a
meal (a) a song by all the guests together, (b) songs by each guest in order round the
room, and (c) songs performed just by the musical experts present. These last were
called *skolia* because of the 'crooked' pathway round the room made by the sequence
of performances. See also Ath. 694a–c. On the second account, ascribed to
Aristoxenus and Phyllis, guests at weddings sat round a table and sang songs one
after another, while holding a sprig of myrtle. The name *skolion* was derived from the
crooked course of the myrtle twig, given an irregularly arranged room. Thirdly, we
are told that at public celebrations in the Athenian Prytaneion, *skolia* were sung in
praise of great men: Harmodius (see line 1225) is among those mentioned. These, it is
asserted, were called *skolia* by way of a figure of speech, that of 'saying the opposite
of what is meant', because they were easy, not complicated or 'crooked'. Again, the
scholiast says, the sprig of myrtle was passed round: those who were unmusical were
shown up when their turn came.
     See also Plut. *Quaest. Conv.* 1.1.5, schol. to Aristoph. *Clouds* 1364. The schol. on
the present passage (line 1222) refers to the custom by which a guest would sing a
piece – for instance one by Simonides or Stesichorus – up to a certain point, and then
hand the sprig to anyone whom he chose, who had to continue the song. Here the
word is derived from the difficulty, *dyskolia*, of taking over a piece in mid-course
without warning. The schol. to line 1239, however, distinguishes between singing or
reciting to the myrtle sprig, which everyone would do, and singing to the *lyra*, which
only accomplished guests would attempt: hence, as the *Gorgias* scholiast and
Plutarch say, the *lyra* followed a crooked course, and its songs were called *skolia*.
     No doubt all these customs had their place. The one referred to here, however, is
plainly that described by the schol. on 1222. For a selection of the songs that were
called *skolia* see Ath. 693f ff.

Phi. Really? I'll cap them – no Diacrian better.

Bde. I'll test you. Now – I'm Cleon, and I'll start the Harmodius song:[17] you cap it.

> [*sings*] 'There was never man born in Athens who . . .'

Phi. [*sings*] . . . was such a villainous thief as you!

Bde. So that's your game, is it? He'll bellow you to a pulp! He'll tell you he'll wreck you and ruin you [1230] and kick you out of the country!

Phi. Me? If he threatens me, by God I'll sing another:

> [*sings*] Hey there you,
>> You power-mad fool!
>> You'll tip up the city –
>> It's shaking already![18]

Bde. But what if Theorus, who's lying by Cleon's feet, takes him by the hand and sings

> [*sings*] 'Hear Admetus' words, my boy,
>> And learn to love good men . . .'[19]

[1240]   How will you find a *skolion* to cap that with?

Phi. Like a real musician!

> [*sings*] Never act the fox's way
>> And never be both sides' friend.

Bde. Next Sellus' son Aeschines takes over – what a clever, cultivated[20] fellow! He'll sing

> [*sings*] 'Money we had and muscle,
>> Cleitagoras and I,
>> And with the men of Thessaly . . .'

Phi. [*sings*] We boasted to the sky!

Bde. Well, you clearly know how to do this pretty well. [1250] Let's go to Philoctemon's for dinner.

---

[17]   Harmodius, with his friend Aristogeiton, plotted against the tyranny of Hippias son of Peisistratus, and his brother Hipparchus. They killed the latter, and were themselves killed (514 B.C.). They came to be revered as heroes and martyrs in the democratic cause. The Harmodius song was a popular *skolion*, mentioned for instance at *Acharn.* 978–80 and 1093. Athenaeus gives a version of it (695a–b): the line quoted in our present text, apparently the first line of the version Aristophanes knew, does not appear there. The joke, sustained through the remainder of the passage, is that Philocleon 'caps' the lines he is given, not with their proper sequel, but with something rude, invented for the occasion.

[18]   A parody of Alcaeus, fr. 141 (Lobel–Page), itself part of a piece probably sung as a *skolion*. Philocleon changes the word *maiomenos* to *mainomenos*, 'seeking power' to 'mad for power'.

[19]   The Admetus song was another familiar catch. According to the schol. on this passage, this was its beginning: it went on
>> Keep clear of cowards, knowing well
>> You'll get no joy from them.
See also Ath. 695c.

[20]   *Mousikos*: the description is no doubt ironical.

Birds

This play was produced in 414 B.C. At the opening of the first passage quoted, the new city in the sky, Cloudcuckoo Town, has been founded, but its founders are pestered by an unwelcome series of visitors intent on making a quick profit out of the occasion. There is a soothsayer, a surveyor, an official colony-inspector, and a seller of laws: but first there is a poet. His pose and language are even more airy and insubstantial than those of Agathon in *Thesmophoriazousae* (see 137 and 138), but his motives are entirely mercenary. The type is further illustrated in the person of Cinesias at 136 1373–1409: cf. *Peace* 828–31. Aristophanes seems to have associated it especially with composers of dithyrambs.

135   *Birds* 903–57

Peithetairus. Let us pray, and sacrifice to the feathered gods.
  Poet [enters singing]. Praise, Muse, in songs of thy hymns,
      Cloudcuckoo Town the blessed!
Peith. What on earth is this? Tell me who you are!
  Poet. I utter the song of honey-tongued lays,
    The busy servant of the Muses –
    [910] In Homer's words.
Peith. Then if you're a slave, why have you got long hair?
  Poet. No: but all we who teach
    Are busy servants of the Muses –
    In Homer's words.
Peith. No wonder your cloak is so busy, then.[21] Well, poet, what ill wind
  blows you here?
  Poet. I have made songs for your Cloudcuckoo Town,
    Many lovely circle-songs[22]
    And maiden-songs[23]
    And pieces like Simonides'.[24]
Peith. [920] When did you compose them? How long ago?
Poet. For long, so long, I have extolled this town!
Peith. What? Aren't I just making its tenth-day sacrifice? I've only this
  moment named the baby!
  Poet. But the word of the Muses is as fleet
    As are twinkling horses' feet!

[21] The comic application of the poet's adjective *otrēros*, 'busy', 'quick', 'active', to his cloak is a little mysterious. Some commentators suppose that it is here (uniquely) used as equivalent to *tetrēmenos*, 'full of holes': more probably, I think, the poet makes affected gestures with it, and hence it is 'busy' – he is Hamlet's Osric, that gesturing 'water-fly'.
[22] I.e. dithyrambs, sung by choruses in a circle round an altar.
[23] Songs for a chorus of dancing maidens. Such pieces were composed by Alcman, Pindar and Bacchylides, and many others: the maiden choruses of Sparta and of Delos were especially famous.
[24] The implication is unclear: Simonides wrote lyric poems and choruses of many types and for many occasions. But perhaps the reference is to Simonides' reputed obsession with monetary reward: see *Peace* 695 ff, cf. 28 Pindar, *Isth*. 2.6.

> 'Now, father, founder of Aetna,
> Namesake of the sacred rites',[25]
> Give to me what in your mind you wish
> [930] Kindly to give to me of yours.

Peith. This nuisance will give us trouble if we don't give him something to get rid of him. Hey you! You've got a jerkin as well as a tunic: take the jerkin off and give it to the clever poet. Here, have it! You certainly seem cold to me.[26]

> *Poet.* The beloved Muse accepts this gift
> Not unwillingly:
> But allow me to call to your mind
> A saying of Pindar . . .

Peith. [940] The man isn't going to leave us alone.

> *Poet.* 'Among the roaming Scythians
> Wanders Straton:
> He has no loom-swung garment:
> Inglorious goes' a jerkin with no tunic –
> 'Grasp what I mean.'[27]

Peith. I grasp that you want to take the tunic. Strip it off, you! We have to help the poet. Now take it and go.

> *Poet.* I go,
> And as I go I'll compose this for the city:
> [950] O golden-throned,
> Give praise to the quivery, shivery;
> To the much-sown, snow-covered plains I have come –
> *Alalai!*[28] [*exit*]

Cloudcuckoo Town has been founded, and applicants for citizenship are flocking in, begging to be equipped with wings. One of them is the dithyrambic poet Cinesias. None of the references to him in ancient literature are

---

25 These lines, continued at 941–5 below, are a garbled version of the opening of a *hyporchēma* by Pindar (fr. 94). The scholiast asserts that Pindar, like the poet here, was looking for a roundabout and poetical way of asking his patron for a present. The Pindaric lines are addressed to Hieron of Syracuse, founder of the city of Aetna: his name is identical with the word here translated 'rites'. Pindar is quoted by Aristophanes without irony at *Knights* 1329, but is not otherwise mentioned. We need find no hostility to him in the fact that the poet of the present passage takes his language, or something very like it, as his model.

26 This is a joke: to call a poet or any speaker 'cold' was a common form of abuse: it seems to have meant 'stiff', 'uninspiring'. Cf. **138** *Thesm.* 170, Plato, *Euthyd.* 284e, **157** *Laws* 802d.

27 Pindar's lines have 'waggon-carried house' for 'loom-swung garment'. The scholiast alleges that Pindar had persuaded Hieron to give him some mules, and was now asking for a chariot to go with them. 'A jerkin with no tunic' is of course no part of the quotation. The last line of all, according to the schol. on Pindar, *Pyth.* 2.127, was the first of the piece, preceding the lines given at 926–7 above.

28 The city is 'quivery' etc. because it is a city in the clouds. The word translated 'snow-covered' is used again at **136** line 1385 as an epithet of the airy *anabolai* of the dithyrambic poets. *Alalai* is a cry of joy: at *Birds* 1763 and *Lysistr.* 1291 it is coupled with the shout *iē paiōn*.

complimentary: see the discussion in the previous chapter. The main facts relevant to Aristophanes' portrayal of him are that he wrote dithyrambs, more richly endowed with imagery than with meaning, and directed, according to Plato, less to edification than to the gratification of popular tastes for 'pleasure'; that he trained choruses to sing and dance these works; that his music was full of the modulating turns that our sources call *kampai*; and that he was extremely thin. We hear also that he wrote a *pyrrichē* or 'war-dance' (*Frogs* 161), and that he was instrumental in abolishing the practice whereby choruses in comedy were trained and equipped at the expense of wealthy Athenian citizens: this may be why he is called 'chorus-killer' in a comedy by Strattis (schol. to *Frogs* 404). A passage from an oration by Lysias, quoted by Athenaeus (551a), accuses him and his associates of habitual impieties and anti-social practices. Aristophanes gives in addition a vigorous and unkind, but for our purposes less relevant lampoon on Cinesias at *Lysistr.* 845–979.

136   *Birds* 1373–1409

Cinesias [enters singing]. 'Up I fly on light wings to Olympus',[29]
          From one path of song to another I fly . . .
Peithetairus. Here's something that'll need a whole load of wings.
    Cin. [*singing*] With fearless mind and body
          Pursuing the path that is new.[30]
Peith. Welcome, lime-woody Cinesias![31] Why have you circled your circling club-foot here?[32]
    Cin. [*singing*] [1380] To become a bird is my desire,
          A clear-voiced nightingale.
Peith. Do stop singing and just tell me what you mean.
Cin. [*speaking*] I want you to give me wings, so I can fly up aloft and gather new wind-blown, snow-clad *anabolai* from the clouds.[33]
Peith. Can one gather *anabolai* from the clouds?
Cin. Oh yes! Our entire craft hangs on them. The glories of a dithyramb are all airy and misty and purple-glistening [1390] and whirled on feathers – listen and you'll understand at once.
Peith. Oh no I won't!
Cin. Oh yes you will!
    [*singing*] For you I'll traverse the whole air,
          A shadow of winged, walking-on-aether,

[29] A quotation from Anacreon (*P.M.G.* 378).
[30] Cinesias' claims to move from one 'path of song' to another, and to pursue novelty, reflect notorious aspects of the 'new music' discussed in Ch. 7.
[31] According to the schol., this means 'as light as lime-wood'. Athenaeus (551d) supposes that it means that Cinesias wore lime-wood stays or corsets to support his lanky body.
[32] 'Circling' refers to the circular dance of the dithyramb. 'Club-foot': presumably, as the scholiast says, Cinesias was lame. The style of the line seems to parody the poetical affectations of Cinesias' own verse.
[33] On *anabolai* see 26 Pindar, *Pyth.* 1.4 with note. For the epithet 'snow-clad' see 135 line 952, and for its ironical associations, line 935.

Slim-necked birds . . .

Peith. Hey!

Cin.   May I take the road to the sea,
And walk on the breaths of the winds . . .

Peith. By God! I'll stop your breath!

Cin.   Now taking a southerly way,
Now nearing the north with my body,
[1400] Ploughing the harbourless furrow of aether . . .
[*speaking*] What a clever trick you've played on me, old man! Charming![34]

Peith. Don't you like being whirled on feathers, then?

Cin. Is this what you do to the circular-chorus trainer, the one that the tribes are always fighting to get?[35]

Peith. Would you like to stay here, then, and train the tribe of Krekopis[36] for Leotrophides as a chorus of flying birds?

Cin. You're making fun of me, I can tell. But I won't stop, you know, till I've got my wings and wander through the air [*exit*].

Thesmophoriazousae

The date of the production of this comedy is uncertain, but was probably 410 B.C. The central character in the passages quoted is Agathon, a successful, fashionable, and aesthetically pretentious tragedian, best known to us as the host in Plato's *Symposium*. Here Agathon's servant has just emerged from his house: the other characters are the tragedian Euripides and his elderly relative Mnesilochus. The servant is as affected as his master, Mnesilochus even more vulgar than the translation has been able to suggest.

137   *Thesmophoriazousae 39–69*

Servant. Let all the people be silent, closing their mouths; for the holy company of Muses has come to visit, and is composing songs in my master's house. Let the aether hold back its breath and be windless, and let not the grey wave of the sea make a noise . . .

Mnesilochus. Gobble gobble!

Euripides. Sh! What are you saying?

Serv. Let the races of feathered ones take their rest, nor let the feet of the wood-wandering wild beasts be moved . . .

Mnes. Gobble gobble gobble!

---

[34] Peithetairus has been sticking feathers on him as he sings, and is now flapping him around the stage.

[35] Each 'tribe' or 'ward' of Athenian citizens organised its own chorus, and sought a professional trainer for it.

[36] If the MSS reading is correct, this seems to be a word-play on the name of the Athenian tribe Kerkopis and the name of a bird, *krēx*, the corn-crake.

Serv. For our leader, Agathon of the beautiful verses, is about to . . .

Mnes. [50] To have a screw? Surely not!

Serv. Who's that?

Mnes. The windless aether!

Serv. . . . to construct the framework of the hull of a drama. He is bending new curves for his verses: he is chiselling some bits, fixing some with song-glue, knocking up maxims, making periphrases, wax-moulding, rounding, casting . . .

Mnes. And whoring!

Serv. What kind of oaf is this, lurking under our back wall?

Mnes. The kind that'll stuff his prick up your back wall, [60] and your pretty-versey poet's too! And he'll screw it around! And he'll cast it in your mould!

Serv. My! What a rude fellow you must have been when you were young, old man!

Eur. Take no notice of him, my dear chap, but call Agathon out here to me as quickly as you can.

Serv. You needn't ask: he'll be coming out immediately, since he's starting to compose his songs. Now that it's winter, it isn't easy to bend the strophes into curves unless he brings them outside into the sun.[37]

138   *Thesmophoriazousae 95–174*

Eur. [*to Mnesilochus*] Be quiet!

Mnes. What is it?

Eur. Agathon is coming out.

[*By a manoeuvre of stage machinery, Agathon is revealed, dressed in fantastical and effeminate clothes, and surrounded by a luxuriant assortment of objects, detailed at 137 ff, below. He has been composing, and is preparing himself to run through his piece.*]

Mnes. Which one is he?

Eur. That one – there, in the machine.

Mnes. Then I must be blind: I can't see a man in there at all, only Cyrene.[38]

Eur. Be quiet! He's getting ready to sing.

[*Agathon does some preparatory humming.*]

Mnes. [100] Is it ant-paths that he's warbling, or what?[39]

Agathon [*singing, in the role of actor*]. Maidens, accept the torch sacred to

---

[37]   The image suggests rhythmic flexibility in particular, but the verb *katakamptein*, 'bend', may contain an allusion to the notorious melodic *kampai* as well.

[38]   A well-known courtesan.

[39]   This famous phrase seems to refer to the intricate running backwards and forwards of the notes of Agathon's composition: cf. the Pherecrates fragment at 187 ps.-Plut. 1141d–1142a, which refer to Timotheus' 'ant-hills' of notes, and to music being filled with wriggling caterpillars, like a cabbage. On the use of rapid ornamental flourishes and decorations of the melody, 158 Plato, *Laws* 812d–e: cf. n. 68 below.

the goddesses of the dead, and dance with the free cry of your fatherland.

[*in the role of chorus*] For which god is this revel? Tell me now: it is easy to persuade me to worship the gods.

[*as actor*] Come, Muse, and bless Phoebus who draws the golden bow, whose place is in the dells [110] of the land by the river Simois.

[*as chorus*] Hail, Phoebus, in beauteous songs, you who give the sacred prize in musical contests.

[*as actor*] Sing too of huntress Artemis, the maiden in the oak-bearing mountains.

[*as chorus*] I follow, praising her in song, blessing the holy child of Leto, virgin Artemis.

[*as actor*] [120] Sing too of Leto, and the playing of the Asian *kithara*,[40] with Phrygian-dancing feet to the well-rhythmed whirlings of the Graces.

[*as chorus*] I honour Leto the queen, and the *kitharis*, mother of hymns, with a splendid masculine cry, which makes light flash from divine eyes, because of our sudden song. Then praise Apollo the king with honour! Hail, blessed son of Leto!

Mnes. [130] What a sweet song, you goddesses of birth! So womanish, making such deep tongue-kisses! When I heard it the titillation penetrated to my very fundament! Young man, I want to ask you who you are, in Aeschylus' words from his *Lycourgia*: 'Whence come you, girlish lad? What is you country? What is this array?'[41] What reshuffling of life is this? Why is a *barbitos* chatting to a saffron robe?[42] Why a *lyra* with a hair-net? Why an oil-flask and a girdle? They just don't go together.[43] [140] What's a mirror doing with a sword? And what are you, my child? Are you a man? Then where's your prick, your cloak, your Laconian shoes? Or a woman? Then where are your breasts? What do you say? Why don't you speak? Then I'll guess what you are from your song, since you refuse to tell me.

Ag. Old man, old man, I hear your bitter spite but feel no pain. I wear the clothes that fit with my imagining; for a poet [150] should adopt the ways that suit the dramas that he must compose. Hence if women are the subject of his play, his body must share in their ways too.[44]

Mnes. [*to Euripides*] So did you screw astraddle, while you were composing Phaedra?[45]

---

40   No noun occurs in the Greek, but the *kithara* is plainly intended: see line 124, and cf. 187 ps.-Plut. 1133c.
41   From Aeschylus, *Edonians*, which formed part of the sequence of plays *Lycourgia*.
42   A woman's dress. The *barbitos* was primarily an instrument of masculine revelry.
43   The questions hint at the fashion for combining different and traditionally conflicting musical styles. See Ch. 7 and e.g. 155 Plato, *Laws* 700d–e.
44   This and its sequel parody an early, probably Damonian version of the thesis that the artist, or any performer of 'imitations', takes on the character of what he imitates. It is best known as a Platonic doctrine, e.g. *Rep.* 395c–e.
45   I.e., when writing the *Hippolytus*. Mnesilochus takes the notion of 'adopting the character of a woman' to what is – in Aristophanic terms – its logical conclusion.

Ag. But if he composes manly things, there must be manhood in his body. What we do not possess ourselves, imitation must hunt out.[46]

Mnes. [*to Euripides*] Then when you're writing about Satyrs, call me up, so I can rear myself behind you and join in.[47]

Ag. And what an unmusical thing it would be to see a poet [160] who was harsh and rough! Consider how Ibycus, Anacreon of Teios and Alcaeus, those who added seasoning to music,[48] wore ribbons round their heads and moved like *this*; and Phrynichus, whom you yourself have heard, was beautiful and beautifully dressed. That's why his plays were beautiful too,[49] for a man must make things like what his nature is.

Mnes. Then that's why Philocles, beast that he is, writes beastly stuff,[50] [170] and frigid Theognis' works are frigid.[51]

Ag. It has to be so. It's because I knew this that I've tended myself so carefully.

Mnes. Good God! How?

Eur. Do stop yapping! I was just like him when I was that age, when I first set out to be a poet.

Frogs

In 405 B.C., when *Frogs* was first staged, Aeschylus was dead long since, and Euripides and Sophocles had died the previous year. The play tells the story of Dionysus' journey to Hades to fetch Euripides back, since no worthwhile poet is now left in Athens. In the event, he finds that Euripides has ejected Aeschylus from the poetic throne of the underworld; and he is made to serve

---

[46] The innuendo, obviously enough, is that it is manliness that Agathon does not naturally possess, and must therefore sometimes try to mimic.

[47] The reference to satyrs does not point to any particular Euripidean play, but to the tragedians' practice of writing satyr-dramas as tail-pieces to sequences of tragedies. The *Cyclops* is the only example of Euripides' satyr-plays that we possess.

[48] Cited here as writers of graceful and voluptuous love-lyrics. Cf. e.g. Ath. 598b–c, 600d–e, 601b–c.

[49] Phrynichus was an important early writer of tragedy, an older contemporary of Aeschylus. Aristophanes' references to him here, at *Birds* 748–52, and at *Wasps* 220, have usually been taken by commentators as genuinely complimentary: the implied abuse of him put into Euripides' mouth at *Frogs* 910 would support this interpretation. The main impression we get from Aristophanes, particularly in the *Birds*, is of the sweetness of his lyrics: but it is not clear that this amounts to a whole-hearted commendation such as is given to Aeschylus in the *Frogs*. After all, if a criticism in the mouth of Euripides amounts to an Aristophanean compliment, the compliment put here into the mouth of Agathon must count as a bad mark. Perhaps, though beautiful and sweet, the compositions of Phrynichus did not have quite the solemnity and weight of those of Aeschylus (cf. **140** *Frogs* 1298–1300): and perhaps, if we are right to see a reference to Phrynichus in the Pratinas fragment at **189** Ath. 617e, he was thought to have conceded too much to the versatility and ornamentation of the new *aulos* music, forsaking the noble simplicity of traditional melodic lines.

[50] Philocles was a nephew of Aeschylus, noted for his acerbity: see *Wasps* 462.

[51] Not the lyric poet of that name, but a minor tragedian: Aristophanes regularly calls him 'cold' or 'frigid': the scholiast tells us that his nickname was 'Snow', and this was evidently a standing joke. See *Acharn.* 11, 170, cf. **135** *Birds* 935.

as judge in a contest between them, involving close comparisons of their poetic and musical styles.

Our first excerpt gives the famous chorus of frogs, singing in the Acherousian lake as Dionysus rows across in Charon's boat. They are the ghosts of frogs who had lived in the marshland of Athens near Dionysus' temple and the theatre: this conceit is reflected in their songs. In the rest of the play a different chorus is used, composed of initiates in the Eleusinian mysteries: their processional (lines 316–459, not quoted here) is a highly informative representation of the Eleusinian celebrations. The present passage begins with Charon, the infernal ferryman, trying to teach the foppish Dionysus to row.

139   *Frogs 202–68*

Charon. Stop mucking about! Brace your feet and pull hard!

Dionysus. How can I pull? I've never done it! I'm not a seaman or a Salaminian.

Char. You'll do it easily; and the moment you've dipped your oar in once, you'll hear the loveliest songs.

Dion. Who'll sing them?

Char. Frog-swans – amazing music!

Dion. Call out the time, then.

Char. Heave-ho, heave-ho.

> *Chorus of Frogs.* *Brekekekex ko-ax ko-ax,*
> [210] *Brekekekex ko-ax ko-ax.*
> Come, marshy children of the waters,
> Let us cry aloud our hymns
> *Aulos*-accompanied, our good-voiced song,
> (*Ko-ax, ko-ax*)
> The one that we screeched in the Marshes[52]
> To praise Zeus' son, Dionysus of Nysa,
> When the festival crowds, merry with boozing,
> Came to our sanctified home on the pot-feast day.[53]
> *Brekekekex ko-ax ko-ax.*

Dion. My arse is starting to hurt – oh *ko-ax, ko-ax*!

Frogs. *Brekekekex ko-ax ko-ax.*

Dion. I don't suppose you care.

Frogs. *Brekekekex ko-ax ko-ax.*

Dion. To hell with you and your *ko-ax*! '*Ko-ax*' is all you are!

> *Frogs.* True enough, nosey!
> For I am the darling of the Muses with lovely *lyrai*,
> [230] Of horn-footed Pan, playing games with the noise of his reeds;[54]

---

[52]   The *Limnae*, the area of Athens mentioned in the introductory note.
[53]   *Chytroi*: the reference is to the third day of the festival of the Anthesteria.
[54]   I.e. the *syrinx*: see next note.

And Apollo with his *phorminx* delights in me too
For the sake of the reed
That I grow in my marsh, in the water,
The reed that goes under the *lyra*.[55]
> *Brekekekex ko-ax ko-ax.*

Dion. Oh my blisters! My backside's been sweating for ages – any moment
it's going to bend over and shout '*Brekekekex ko-ax ko-ax*' itself. [240]
You song-obsessed lot, please stop![56]

Frogs. No no, we'll sing still louder,
If ever on sunlit days
We leapt through galingales and reeds
In the joy of the chant of our diving-songs,
Or else, to get out of the rain,
We sang a shimmering dance-chorus
Deep in the water,
To the gurgling babble of bubbles.[57]

Frogs and Dion. [250] *Brekekekex ko-ax ko-ax.*

Dion. I'll take your *brekekekex* myself, then![58]

Frogs. That's a terrible thing to do to us!

Dion. It'll be even more terrible for me if I row till I burst.

Frogs and Dion. Brekekekex ko-ax ko-ax.

Dion. Moan all you like: it doesn't bother me.

Frogs. Whatever you say, we'll go on yelling all day, [260] as loud as our
throats can stand.

Frogs and Dion. Brekekekex ko-ax ko-ax.

Dion. You're not going to win at this!

Frogs. You won't beat us, no way!

Dion. And you won't beat me either. Never! I'll yell all day if I have to. I'll go
on till I get on top of your *ko-ax*ing.

---

[55] The reeds played by Pan are *kalamoi*; those used in the construction of the *lyra* are
donakes. For their uses, and the word *hypolyrion* ('under the *lyra*'), see **21** *Hymn to
Hermes* 47, and **27** Pindar, *Pyth.* 12.25–7 with notes, Ch. 6 121–8 with notes 190,
198.

[56] The point, as the sequel shows, is that the singing of the frogs gives the rhythm by
which the rower times his stroke: Dionysus cannot rest on his oars unless they stop
their singing. It is a comic example of the genre of working songs, well known in
Greece. For another reference to rowing songs see Longus, *Daphn.* 3.21, and cf. e.g.
79 Eurip. *I.T.* 1123 ff. There is a list of working songs generally at **189** Ath.
618d–619c, and another at Pollux IV.53: cf. Longus op. cit. 4.38, 4.40, Callimachus,
Hecale 1.4a. 11–12, Aristoph. *Clouds* 1357–8, **140** *Frogs* 1296–7, *Acharn.* 554, Plut.
Sept. Sap. 14.

[57] The bubbles are treated as an instrumental accompaniment, as the construction of
the sentence shows.

[58] Dionysus decides that the only way to slow the pace is to take over the rowing song
himself. The frogs refuse to abandon their prerogatives, and the passage develops
into a singing (or shouting) competition. In general terms, it is a pastiche of a singing
contest: within the structure of the play it prefigures, in a brief and farcical manner,
the genuine music competition between Euripides and Aeschylus which is the climax
of the drama.

BREKEKEKEX KO-AX KO-AX!

[*silence*]

I knew I'd stop your *ko-ax*ing in the end.

It would be inappropriate to quote more than a small part of the contest between Aeschylus and Euripides. It is very long (905–1471), and much of it concerns matters other than music. The tragedians criticise, at length, each other' subject matter, diction, imagery and morals. At 1198 they turn to more technical issues, each ridiculing the other for the monotony of his metres and rhythms. First Aeschylus shows (1198–1247), of a series of Euripidean prologues, that in each of them, by the third line, there comes a point at which both metre and grammatical structure can be completed by the tag '*lēkythion apōlesen*' ('broke his jar of oil', metrically $^-|\smile\smile\smile|\smile\,^-|\smile\,^-$, a variant of the last three and a half feet of an iambic line). In return (1261–80) Euripides attacks Aeschylus' *melē* (choral songs), by exhibiting the way they invariably approximate in rhythm to the epic dactylic hexameter: and he goes on (1281–95) to do much the same with what he calls 'another collection of *melē* gathered from his kitharodic *nomoi*'. These too, as it turns out, are parts of choral odes; but while the first group was accompanied by an aulete off stage (1264 with schol.), in the second set Euripides follows each line he quotes with the noise *phlattothratto phlattothrat*: it is generally agreed that this is meant to represent the monotonous strumming of a *kithara*-player.

But there is a puzzle about the relation between the two sets, which needs brief discussion. Aristophanes cannot mean that the second group were really *kithara* songs when performed in Aeschylus' plays. Not only was the *aulos* universally the accompanying instrument of tragedy; it is also the case that two of the lines of the second group and one line from the first belong to the same strophe of the same ode of the *Agamemnon*. Some commentators have supposed that in calling them kitharodic *nomoi* Euripides meant only that he proposed to give them a *kithara* accompaniment here: but that is linguistically impossible. The point is, I suggest, merely contemptuous. Euripides is not distinguishing between the two sets, but dismissing the whole collection as nothing but *kithara* songs. That is, they have the rhythms and character of the epic hexameter, which was normally recited, or chanted to the accompaniment of a *kithara* or a similar stringed instrument: pieces based on the hexameter were transformed into *nomoi*, songs with genuine melody and a regular formal structure, at the hands of Terpander, according to 187 ps.-Plut. (1132c). What they did not have is the dramatic, mimetic character proper to tragedy, which is achieved through the versatility of the *aulos* and, so Euripides is arguing here, flexibility and diversity of rhythm and metre.

The passage continues as follows.

140   *Frogs* 1296–1318

Dionysus. What *is* this '*phlattothrat*'? Where did you get these rope-twisters' songs?[59] From Marathon, or where?

---

[59]   This may be a reference to a working song: see n. 56. But it is perhaps more probably an allusion to the drawn-out length of Aeschylus' lines, or to their straightforward simplicity: cf. 29 Pindar, fr. 61.1, with note.

eschylus. I brought them from the noble to the noble:[60] I did not wish [1300] to seem to pluck flowers in the same meadow of the Muses as did Phrynichus.[61] But this Euripides picks up his songs from any filthy source: from Meletus' drinking songs,[62] Carian *aulos* tunes,[63] dirges, dances, . . . I'll show you straight away. Bring in a *lyrion*![64] – no, we don't need a *lyra* to deal with *him*! Where's the girl that bangs the *ostraka*?[65] Come hither, Muse of Euripides, the right accompanist for singing songs like these! [*Enter a girl dressed as a prostitute, carrying ostraka.*]

)ion. Surely the Muse was never a whore? Never!

 Aesch.[66] 'Halcyons who chatter by the ever-flowing
  [1310] Waves of the sea,
  Moistening, bedewing the colour of your wings
  With watery drops . . .'[67]

  'You cohorts of spiders, who
  Under the roof, in the corners,
  We-e-e-e-eave with your fingers
  The weft from its reel, stretched on the loom . . .'[68]

---

[60] I.e., from Homer's epic to Athenian drama.

[61] See n. 49 above.

[62] *Skolia:* see **134** *Wasps* 1222 ff with note 16.

[63] Carian *aulēmata* and Carian songs were associated with lamentation (e.g. Pollux IV.75, Eust. ad *Il.* XXIV.720, **157** Plato, *Laws* 800e), but also with *aulos* tunes played by girls at drinking parties (Plato Comicus, fr. 69.12–13, Kock). The genre was probably languid, plaintive and emotional. For a similar *melange* of associations see Ch. 6 n. 29 on the word 'Mysian'. A general link between Caria and obscenity or degeneracy is suggested at Ath. 580d.

[64] Diminutive of *lyra*, but probably not here suggesting an instrument of any particular size.

[65] An *ostrakon* is a pottery vessel (or a piece of one), or an oyster shell. Here it is a percussion instrument like a castanet, made either from pottery or from shell: Didymus at **196** Ath. 636e interprets it in the latter sense. Percussion instruments were closely associated with mystery cults, and especially with women's rites: see e.g. **63–5,** Aristoph. *Lysistr.* 387–98, **196** Ath. 636c–e. The phrase 'singing to the *ostraka*' (by contrast with the *lyra* or the *aulos*) was proverbial for ugly music: Phryn. *Epit.* 79 (de Borries).

[66] Aeschylus now recites, to the accompaniment of *ostraka*, various disconnected quotations from Euripidean lyric. He seems to have several points of criticism in mind: the complexity and irregularity of the metres, the affected elaboration of imagery and diction, and – in one case – the distortion of words to suit melodic ornamentation. I have included only the first four of his six quotations. On the metrical issues involved see B. B. Rogers, *The Frogs of Aristophanes,* 2nd ed. (London 1919), xxxi–xxxiv.

[67] These lines, according to the scholiast, are from the *I.A.* They do not occur in our texts of this play, but it is notoriously incomplete and corrupt. The lines seem also to have a distant affinity with *Hippol.* 125–9.

[68] The source of this quotation is unknown. The schol. tells us that the repeated 'e–e–e' (in Greek *ei–ei–ei*, at the beginning of *eilissete*) is 'in imitation of the melodic composition (*melopoiia*)'. It is not therefore introduced to 'fill up' a metre or rhythm, but to represent the setting of a single long syllable to a cluster of shorter notes, forming an ornamental turn.

'. . . the cares of the minstrel shuttle . . .'[69]

'Where the *aulos*-loving dolphin leaps
By the dark blue prows . . .'[70]

Aeschylus goes on to parody Euripidean monody (1330–63), pointing particularly to his treatment of commonplace incidents in highly coloured and emotional language. Next, the verses of the two poets are assessed for 'weight' – literally weighed out on a weighing machine – a round won hand down by Aeschylus[71] (1368–1410): and a final round (1419–65) attempts to assess which of the two would prove the better adviser to Athens on political and moral matters. Dionysus has said (1419–21) that this point will decide the contest: whichever poet wins on that score will return with him to Athens. In the event, however, it is not clear that this or any other determinate consideration is the final criterion: Dionysus simply chooses 'the one that his soul desires' (1468, cf. 1475–8), and it is Aeschylus. Euripides is not even left with the poetical kingship of Hades: in his absence Aeschylus entrusts his throne to Sophocles (1515–23).

---

[69] This seems again to be a genuine quotation from Euripides, though not from an extant play (fr. 523). On metaphors to do with weaving, in a musical context, see e.g. 27 Pindar, *Pyth.* 12.8, *Nem.* 4.44, Soph. frs. 595, 890, and 51 Eurip. *I.T.* 221 with n. 61.

[70] Quoted from *Electra* 435–6. For the music-loving dolphin cf. e.g. 30 Pindar, fr. 125.

[71] On the light or trifling nature of Euripides' songs, as assessed by Aristophanes, cf. *Peace* 531–2, *Acharn.* 398–400.

CHAPTER 9

Xenophon

The astonishing public literary creativity of the fifth century is gradually replaced, around the beginning of the fourth, by a mood of more sober reflectiveness. Our best sources, correspondingly, are no longer the poet-composers themselves, but philosophers and scientists, bent on assessment, criticism, recommendation, analysis and formalisation. Their writings are not only more reflective but also in a sense more private, since they are of course not designed for performance before mass audiences: but it cannot be too strongly emphasised that their objective is still public and social, and that their overriding aim is to work out the proper place of the arts in the life of a man conceived as a citizen, not as a self-sufficient unit of individuality. Hence the context of the most significant of the philosophers' discussions of music is that of education for citizenhood. Before turning to the major writings of Plato and Aristotle, however, we must find a place for a little cameo from the pen of Plato's contemporary, the historian and essayist Xenophon.

Xenophon lived from about 430 to 355 B.C. Like Plato, he was in his youth an adherent of Socrates, and as Plato did, he wrote dialogues and other pieces to preserve and defend his teacher's memory. Unlike Plato, Xenophon was no great hand at abstract thought, and the Socrates he presents, though charismatic, enquiring, and morally upright, is a less impressive figure both ethically and intellectually than his Platonic counterpart. Xenophon's *Symposium*, from which the extracts below are taken, is then of much smaller philosophical significance than Plato's: but as a record of what went on at a dinner-party of the period in a wealthy Athenian's house, it is substantially more informative. For chronological reasons, if no others, the work should not be treated as a factual description of an actual historical occasion. It is fiction, but fiction of a kind that might plausibly be thought true; and the details are no doubt put together from Xenophon's experience of symposia of a similar sort. Of course the party described is in some ways untypical. The host is a very rich man, and the entertainment therefore more lavish than was common. Moreover, the entertainment is interrupted, modified, and sometimes silenced by the conversation of Socrates and his friends. But the work – the most charming and readily enjoyed of all Xenophon's writings – is still very useful for our purposes. I have included all the main passages concerned with the musical entertainment, and a brief excerpt referring to musical practices of a different kind.

Symposium

The first chapter explains that Callias[1] has invited Socrates and a number of others to dine at his house in Piraeus: it goes on to relate various events that occurred during the course of the meal. At the opening of Ch. 2 the meal itself is over.

---

[1] An extremely wealthy man, known for his patronage of sophists. His home in Athens is the setting of Plato's *Protagoras*.

141   *Symposium* 2.1–3

When the tables had been removed, and they had made a libation and sung a paean,[2] a man from Syracuse came in to provide entertainment,[3] with an excellent *aulos*-girl,[4] a girl dancer – one of those trained to perform spectacular displays[5] – and a boy in the flower of his youth who played the *lyra*[6] and danced most beautifully. The man earned his living by displaying all this as a spectacle. [2.2] When the *aulos*-girl had played for them and the boy had played the *lyra*, both of them apparently giving a most satisfactory amount of enjoyment, Socrates said: 'Really, Callias, you are entertaining us perfectly. You have not only given us a meal beyond criticism: you are providing us with the most delightful sights and sounds.'

[2.3]   Callias replied: 'How about someone bringing us some perfume too, then, so that we can revel in its fragrance?'

'Oh no,' said Socrates, . . .

142   *Symposium* 2.7–8

'But now let's go on with the entertainment we are being given,' said Socrates. 'I can see that the dancing-girl has taken her place, and someone is carrying in some hoops for her.'

[2.8]   Just then the other girl began to play for her on the *aulos*, and a man stood next to the dancing-girl and passed up the hoops to her, twelve of them in all. She took them, and as she danced she threw them spinning upwards, judging precisely how high she had to throw them in order to catch them in time with the rhythm. . . .

143   *Symposium* 2.11–23

Next a ring-shaped stand was brought in, bristling with upright sword-blades. The dancing-girl turned somersaults over them, in and out of the ring, so that the spectators were afraid she would hurt herself; but she completed the act confidently and safely. [2.12] Socrates called out to Antisthenes:[7] 'I can't believe that anyone watching this performance would

---

[2]   The libation and the paean are here tokens of thanksgiving, equivalent to a 'grace'. For the custom in this context see e.g. **134** Aristoph. *Wasps* 1217, **187** ps.-Plut. 1147a, cf. 1131c–d.

[3]   He is a professional impresario, mounting cabaret performances with his group of musicians, whom he himself apparently trains: cf. **143** 2.16.

[4]   The *aulētris* or *aulos* girl was the staple of all Greek after-dinner entertainment: she would usually dance as she played: cf. **145** 6.4.

[5]   I.e., she performed acrobatic dances, some of which are mentioned in the sequel. See e.g. Fig. 16.

[6]   The verb is *kitharizein*, capable of referring to performance on any instrument of this group; but the boy's *lyra* is mentioned at the beginning of **144** Ch. 3.

[7]   A friend of Socrates and a philosopher of some importance, often treated as the founder of Cynicism. He may have been the first to write Socratic dialogues.

ersist in denying that courage is something that can be taught, when this
irl, female though she is, throws herself so daringly on to the swords.'

2.13] 'Hadn't the Syracusan better exhibit this dancing-girl to the city,'
eplied Antisthenes, 'and say that if the Athenians pay him, he will make all
ne Athenians dare to charge upon the points of the spears?'

2.14] 'By God yes,' said Philippus,[8] 'I'd dearly love to see that rabble-rouser
eisander[9] learning to turn somersaults on to knives! As it is he refuses to
erve in the army at all because he can't look spears in the face.'

2.15] At this point the boy did a dance. 'Do you see,' said Socrates, 'how the
oy, beautiful though he is, looks even more beautiful with the dance figures
ɔ help him than when he is still?'[10]

2.16] 'You seem to be complimenting his dancing teacher,' said
Charmides.[11]

'Yes indeed,' said Socrates; 'and there's something else I've noticed too,
hat in his dancing no part of his body was idle, but his neck and his legs and
ɩis hands were exercised together, just the way one should dance if one is to
mprove the gracefulness of one's body. Speaking for myself,' he went on, 'I
hould be delighted if you would teach me the dance figures, my Syracusan
riend.'

'What will you use them for?' asked the man.

2.17] 'I shall dance, to be sure.'

At that everyone laughed. 'Are you laughing at me?' asked Socrates, with a
nost serious expression on his face. 'Is it at the notion that I want to improve
ny health with exercise, or at my enjoyment of eating and sleeping? Or is it
t the idea that – unlike long-distance runners, who build up their legs but
ʻmaciate their arms, or boxers, who build up their arms but emaciate their
egs – I have set my heart on exercises of a kind by which I can work hard
vith my whole body, and give it even proportions throughout? [2.18] Or are
ʻou laughing because I won't need to look for a training-partner or take my
:lothes off in a crowd at my advanced age, since a room that'll take seven
:ouches will be plenty for me to work up a sweat in, just as this room was for
he boy here a moment ago? And in bad weather I shall exercise indoors, and
n the shade when it's too hot. [2.19] Is that what you're laughing at, or is it
ɔecause my stomach is bigger than it ought to be, and I want to make it a
nore moderate size? Don't you know that a day or so ago Charmides here
:aught me dancing at dawn?'

'That I did,' said Charmides, 'and to begin with I was stupefied, and
ɪfraid that you'd gone crazy. But when you told me the same sort of thing

---

8   Described in this work as a 'comic' or 'joker': his jokes tend to fall rather flat.

9   For his reputed cowardice cf. Aristoph. *Birds* 1556 ff.

10 'Dance figures' here and elsewhere in this piece translates *schēmata*. It will become
     clear that they include all the postures and gestures of representational acting, as well
     as dancing in the more familiar sense: see particularly **147** 9.5–6.

11 A cousin of Plato: see Plato's dialogue named after him. He was a party to the brutal
     oligarchy of 404–3 B.C.

that you're saying now, I went off home myself and didn't dance, exactly since I've never learnt how, but I flapped my arms about. I knew how to do that.'

[2.20] 'Yes indeed,' said Philippus, 'and now your legs look so evenly matched with your arms that if you weighed your lower bits against the upper ones for the market inspectors they wouldn't fine you.'[12]

'Give me a call, Socrates,' said Callias, 'when you're going to learn to dance, so that I can be your partner and learn with you.'

[2.21] 'Well now,' said Philippus, 'let the girl play the *aulos* for me, so can dance too.' He stood up, and went through an imitation of the boy's and the girl's dances. [2.22] First, because people had expressed appreciation of the way the dance figures had made the boy look even more beautiful Philippus by contrast, as he moved each part of his body, presented it in an even more ludicrous guise than nature had given it. And because the girl had bent over backwards and imitated a hoop, Philippus tried to imitate a hoop by bending the same bits of himself over forwards. Finally, because they had praised the boy for exercising the whole of his body in the dance he told the *aulos*-girl to set a quicker rhythm, and let fly with his legs and hands and head all together. [2.23] When he was exhausted, he lay down again and said: 'There's a demonstration, my friends, that even my dances give good exercise. I'm thirsty, at any rate: get the boy to pour me a big cupful.'

'Certainly,' said Callias, 'and some for us too. We've all got a thirst from laughing at you.'

144   *Symposium* 3.1–2

After that, the boy tuned his *lyra* to the *aulos* and played and sang with it.[13] Everyone praised the performance, and Charmides added: 'It seems to me, my friends, just as Socrates said about the wine,[14] that this mixture of the youthful bloom of these young people with the notes of music puts cares to rest and awakens thoughts of love.'

[3.2] Then Socrates spoke again. 'These people, gentlemen,' he said, 'have proved themselves capable of delighting us. Yet I know that we suppose ourselves to be much better than they are. Won't it be shameful if we don't even try to edify or to entertain one another a bit, while we are together?'

---

[12] The reference is to market inspectors checking that the loaves or other produce at the bottom of a pile were the same size as what was displayed on top.

[13] The sense of *synērmosmenē* ('tuned to') may possibly be more general, indicating no more than that the *lyra* was now 'musically linked' with the *aulos*. But the sense given is more probable: the non-musical meaning of *synarmozein* is to make one thing fit or agree with another. For an unambiguous case of the sense given here see **151** Plato, *Rep.* 412a, cf. **189** Ath. 617e–618b.

[14] Socrates has said (2.24) that wine puts troubles to sleep and awakens gaiety.

145   *Symposium* 6.3–6

Socrates has been chaffing Hermogenes[15] for staying silent while the others talked. Hermogenes retorts that there has been no chance to get a word in.

'Callias', said Socrates, 'have you any way of helping a man who's being beaten in argument?'

'Yes I have', he replied. 'When the *aulos* sounds, we are all to be totally silent.'

'Do you want me to talk to you to the accompaniment of the *aulos*,' asked Hermogenes, 'like the actor Nicostratus who used to recite tetrameters with *aulos* accompaniment?'[16]

[6.4]   'Oh please do that, Hermogenes,' said Socrates. 'I imagine that just as a song is sweeter when sung to the *aulos*,[17] so your words might be sweetened somewhat by the notes, especially if you make gestures to fit your words, like the *aulos*-girl.'[18]

[6.5]   'So when Antisthenes here crushes someone in argument during the party,' said Callias, 'what shall the *aulos* tune be then?'

'For the one who is crushed,' said Antisthenes, 'a whistle[19] would be appropriate, I think.'

[6.6]   While they were talking like this the Syracusan realised that they were taking no notice of his show, but entertaining one another. So he said peevishly to Socrates . . .

146   *Symposium* 7.1–5

Some of the guests now urged Philippus to do a 'likeness',[20] while others begged him not to. In the middle of the uproar Socrates spoke again.

'Since all of us are keen to speak, isn't this the best time for us to sing together?' And he immediately struck up a song. [7.2] When he had sung it, a potter's wheel[21] was brought in for the dancing-girl: she was going to do a spectacular dance on it. At this Socrates said: 'My Syracusan friend, it looks as if I really am a thinker, as you say. At all events, I am now pondering on the

---

15   A follower of Socrates who has a prominent role in Plato's *Cratylus*.
16   Nothing is known of Nicostratus. The remarkable feature of his act was evidently that the verses accompanied by the *aulos* were spoken, not sung: cf. **187** ps.-Plut. 1141a–b. 'Tetrameter' generally refers to the trochaic tetrameter, a line consisting of four double feet, each of the form ‒ ˘ ‒ ˘.
17   Cf. e.g. **184** ps.-Ar. *Probs.* XIX.43.
18   The use of gesture by auletes to enliven a performance was not restricted to convivial occasions: cf. e.g. Paus. IX.12.5 on the great Theban aulete Pronomus.
19   *Syrigmos*, cognate with *syrinx*: any kind of whistling or hissing, as for instance that made by the Pythian serpent in its death-throes, imitated in the *Pythikos nomos* (**25** Strabo IX.3.10): here whistles or hisses of disapproval from the audience, cf. e.g. **155** Plato, *Laws* 700c.
20   Not 'to perform an imitation' or 'impersonation', but to declaim witty similes cleverly likening a person to something else, as the rather laboured repartee of 6.8–10 (not included here) shows.
21   This translates the Greek literally: presumably something larger is intended.

way this boy and girl of yours can have the easiest time, while we get the greatest pleasure from watching them. I'm sure that's what you want too. [7.3] Now it seems to me that somersaulting among knives is a representation of danger, something quite unsuitable for a drinking-party. Again, writing or reading while spinning round on a wheel[22] may be an astounding feat, but even there I can't think what pleasure it could give. Nor is it any more enjoyable to watch beautiful young people twisting their bodies round and imitating hoops than it is to watch them at rest. [7.4] As a matter of fact, there are always plenty of astonishing things to be found, if they are what you want. It's always possible to marvel at things that are right in front of us – for instance, why the lamp provides light as a result of having a bright flame, while a piece of bronze, bright though it is, makes no light, but contains and gives out the brightness of other things; or how the oil, which is liquid, feeds the flame, while water, because it is liquid, extinguishes the fire. Still, even this sort of thing doesn't give the same results as wine does. [7.5] But if these young people were to dance to the *aulos* some figures in which the Graces and the Seasons and the Nymphs were depicted,[23] I think that they would have a much easier time, and the party would be much more delightfully elegant.'

'You are absolutely right, Socrates,' said the Syracusan, 'and I'll put on a show that you'll all enjoy.'

> Chapter 8 contains a long discussion on the subject of love. In the final chapter of the work Xenophon, with some artistry, uses the entertainers' closing performance to illustrate and round off the topic with which the guests had been concerned.

147   *Symposium* 9.2–7

Just then a kind of seat was put down in the room, and the Syracusan came in. 'Gentlemen,' he said, 'Ariadne will enter the bedchamber which is hers and Dionysus': next Dionysus will come, after having a drink or two with the gods, and will go in to her: then they will have some fun together.'

[9.3]   At that Ariadne came in, first of all, decked out as a bride, and sat down on the seat. Then, while Dionysus was still off-stage, the bacchic rhythm[24] was played on the *aulos*. Here the spectators expressed admiration for the dance teacher, for as soon as Ariadne heard it she behaved in such a way that everyone could see she heard it with delight. She did not go to meet him or even stand up, but it was plain that she could scarcely keep still. [9.4] When Dionysus caught sight of her, he danced over to her with the vividest possible expressions of passion: then he sat on her knees, put his arms round

---

22   A curious form of entertainment, but the text is unambiguous. Perhaps the point was to show various commonplace activities being undertaken with equanimity by the dancer in the physically awkward circumstances described. See also **196** Ath. 635a.

23   Lit. 'are painted' or 'drawn'.

24   For the various metrical forms called *baccheios* see Arist. Quint. 36.6 ff: for their 'bacchic' or Dionysiac associations, indicated here, cf. ibid. 37.2–3.

her, and kissed her. She gave the impression of being shy, but still embraced him lovingly in return.

When the guests saw it, they all applauded and shouted for more. [9.5] Dionysus stood up, and helped Ariadne to her feet too; and here the audience were able to watch the dance figures that showed them kissing and embracing each other. When they saw that Dionysus was genuinely good-looking, and Ariadne in the bloom of her youth, and that they were not just pretending but really kissing with their mouths, they all went wild with excitement as they watched.[9.6] Then they heard Dionysus asking her if she loved him, and Ariadne assenting so convincingly that not only Dionysus but everyone present would have sworn that the boy and the girl really were in love with one another. It looked as if they had not rehearsed the dance figures, but were set free to do what they had long desired.

[9.7] When eventually the guests saw them locked in each other's arms and looking as if they were going off to bed, the bachelors swore they would get married, and the married men jumped on their horses and rode off to their wives, to do the same themselves. Socrates and the others who remained set out to walk with Callias to the home of Lycon and his son: and that was the end of the party.

CHAPTER 10

Plato

Plato, whose claim to be the greatest of the Greek philosophers could be disputed only by Aristotle, lived from about 428 to 347 B.C. His career as a writer and teacher belongs entirely to the fourth century, after the death of his master Socrates (399 B.C.). A large corpus of his published writings, possibly the whole of it, survives: all these works, with the exception of some letters, take the form of philosophical dialogues, in most of which Socrates is the principal speaker. While it is likely that the 'Socrates' of the earliest dialogues is intended to represent the person and teachings of the historical Socrates more or less faithfully, there is no doubt that the ideas argued out in the later works are those of Plato himself, and that 'Socrates', or whatever character is given the leading role, is to be understood, with certain qualifications, as the author's own mouthpiece. Of the passages quoted here, the first (148 from the *Ion*) belongs to the early 'Socratic' group: the others, though they were written over a considerable period of years, fall in this sense into the second category.

Allusions to music can be found throughout Plato's works. Some are casually historical: the majority are closely linked with the structure of his philosophical thought.[1] They fall, broadly speaking, into three groups. The first concerns the role of music in moral education, and includes, beside Plato's own recommendations, many illuminating references to the 'corrupt' music of the time. The second, which is closely connected with the work of contemporary Pythagoreans, deals with the abstract analysis of musical structures, and sets out a programme for harmonics as a mathematical science. The third provides the link between the two, relating mathematically specifiable harmonic structures to the constitution of the human soul, and to that of the universe at large. Of these three groups the first is represented in the present selection, while passages exemplifying the second and third will appear in Vol. 2. Though there is inevitably some overlapping between the groups, this classification reflects tolerably well Plato's own way of organising his material. So far as the first group is concerned, I have thought it best not to attempt to collect representative passages from the full range of Plato's works, but to concentrate on two major dialogues, the *Republic* (written in the middle period of his working life) and the *Laws* (his last piece of writing), in which matters to do with education and social ethics hold the centre of the stage.[2] The excerpts from these dialogues are prefaced by one short passage from the *Ion*.

---

[1] No general account of Plato's philosophy can be attempted here. On the other hand, his views about music can be understood only imperfectly if they are not placed within the framework of his wider interests, ideas and arguments. Hence the passages quoted here need to be read against the background of a wider study of his dialogues, or at least of a competent modern survey of Plato's thought. E. A. Havelock's *Preface to Plato* will be found particularly rewarding for present purposes.

[2] Other passages of particular interest in this context include *Charm.* 156d–157a, 159c, *Clitoph.* 407b–d, *Laches* 188d, cf. 193d–e, 200a, *Lysis* 209b, *Crito* 50d–e, *Prot.* 326a–b, 327a–c, 346c–e, *Gorgias* 501d–502c, *Phaedo* 35e–86d, 91c–95a, *Symp.* 187a–d, 215b–c, *Philebus* 55e–56c, *Tim.* 47c–e, 80a–b, 88c, 90c–d, in addition to the more technical discussions to be quoted in Vol. 2.

Ion

Ion is a *rhapsōdos*, a professional reciter of Homeric epic and an expert commentator on Homer's poetry. The main thrust of Socrates' argument in his conversation with him is that such people know nothing: they are divinely inspired mouthpieces for the Muses and the poets, but their inspiration carries with it no understanding. In the present passage Socrates uses this line of thought to explain why it is that while people who understand the arts can always discourse freely on any number of artists in their field, Ion can speak on no subject but Homer. But he also extends his thesis to cover poets and musicians, as well as *rhapsōdoi*: all are inspired, and none has knowledge. This attitude to music and poetry pervades Plato's dialogues, and underlies his treatment of them in *Republic*, *Phaedrus*, *Laws* and elsewhere.

Socrates has given examples from various fields to illustrate his claim that students of the arts typically have a grasp of them that covers their whole field. Their 'skill' (*technē*) is always generalisable beyond the works of any single practitioner. His last example is from music.

148   *Ion 533b–535a*

Socrates. Again, it seems to me, in the fields of *aulos* playing or *kithara*-playing or *kitharōdia* or *rhapsōdia*, you never met a man who is an expert at discussing Olympus or Thamyris or [533c] Orpheus or Phemius the *rhapsōdos* of Ithaca,[3] but who is at a loss about Ion of Ephesus, and is incapable of working out what is good and bad in his rhapsodic performances.

Ion. I can't deny what you say, Socrates: but as to myself, I am clearly aware of being amply equipped to speak best of all men about Homer – and everyone else agrees that I speak well – but not about the other poets. Can you see how to explain this?

Soc. I can, Ion, and I'll try to show you what I think the [d] situation is. This capacity you have for speaking well about Homer is not a skill,[4] as I was saying just now, but a divine power that moves you, like that in the stone that Euripides calls the Magnet, but most people call the Heraclean stone. This stone not only attracts iron rings, but also puts into the rings a power that enables them to act in the same way as the stone and attract other rings, [e] so that sometimes there is a long chain of rings and iron objects all fixed to one another: the power is transmitted to all of them from the original stone. In the same way the Muse inspires people herself, and through these inspired people a chain of others,

---

[3] On Olympus see **187** ps.-Plut. 1132f, 1133e ff, 1137a ff, cf. e.g. **161** Ar. *Pol.* 1340a9: on Thamyris see **187** ps.-Plut. 1132a–b, **5** *Il.* 11.594–600, Eurip. *Rhesus* 915–25, Plato, *Rep.* 620a. Orpheus is of course the well-known legendary singer, commonly treated as quasi-historical: cf. e.g. **187** ps.-Plut. 1132f, 1133f, 1134e. Phemius is the minstrel who sings for the suitors in the house of Odysseus, **9** *Od.* 1.150 ff, etc. He was not strictly speaking a *rhapsōdos*: see introductory note to Homer.

[4] *Technē*, a competence involving the application of knowledge.

filled with divine fervour, is linked together. All good writers of epic poetry utter all those beautiful poems of theirs not as a result of skill, but inspired and possessed. So too with good composers of songs:[5] just as the Corybantes[6] [534a] are out of their minds when they dance, so these composers are out of their minds when they compose those beautiful melodies. When they embark upon *harmonia*[7] and rhythm, they are in a state of Bacchic possession, just as the Bacchic women draw out milk and honey from the rivers when they are possessed, but not when they are in their right mind: the souls of the composers of songs achieve just the same thing, as they say themselves. For the poets tell us that they gather their melodies [b] from the honey-flowering springs in the gardens and vales of the Muses, and bring them to us like bees, and that they fly like bees too.[8] And what they say is true. For a poet is a light, winged, sacred thing,[9] and is incapable of composing until the god has entered him and his wits have left him, and his mind is in him no longer. Until he acquires this gift, no man can compose, or sing prophecies.[10] Because it is not through skill that they compose and say many fine things about [c] their subjects, as you do about Homer, but through a divine apportionment, each can compose well only about the subject towards which the Muse arouses him, one composing dithyrambs, another *encōmia*, another *hyporchēmata*, another epics, another iambics; and each of them is a poor hand at all the others. It is not through skill that they say these things but through a divine power, since if they understood through a skill how to speak well about one subject, they could also speak well about all the others. The god's purpose in taking their minds away when using [d] these prophets and divine seers as their servants, is that we who hear them may know that it is not these people, whose mind is not in them, who are saying these things that are of such value, but that the speaker is the god himself, and that he is addressing us through them. Very strong evidence for what I say is provided by Tynnichus of Chalcis, who never composed any poem that anyone would think worth remembering except the paean that everyone sings, perhaps the most beautiful of all songs, and incontrovertibly, as he says himself, [e] 'an invention of the Muses'. In

5   *Melopoioi*, the poet-composers of 'lyric' poetry. Their *melē*, songs, are contrasted with the *epē* of the epic poets, whose work, in this period at least, was normally spoken, not sung. In much of the sequel the words 'poet' and 'composer' are interchangeable.

6   The devotees of the goddess Cybele or Rhea, the mother goddess, noted for their wild dancing. Cf. e.g. Homeric *Hymn to the Mother of the Gods*, 70–2 Eurip. *Helen* 1308–14, 1338–65.

7   On the senses of '*harmonia*' see Appendix A.

8   Cf. e.g. Pindar, *Ol.* 7.7–8, 9.26–7, *Nem.* 3.76–9, *Isth.* 6.74: these conceits are of course common in poetry, as Plato suggests.

9   Cf. e.g. 136 Aristoph. *Birds* 1373 ff.

10 *Chrēsmōdein*, a verb commonly used for the utterances of oracles. Plato assimilates poets to the class of oracles and prophets because of the supposedly divine source of their creations.

this example, it seems to me, the god has shown us most vividly, so that we should be in no doubt, that these beautiful compositions are not human or the work of men, but divine and the work of gods, and that the poets are nothing but the god's interpreters, each possessed by whichever god it may be. It was to demonstrate this that the god deliberately sang the finest of melodies through the poorest of poets. [535a] Or do you think that what I am saying is untrue, Ion?

Ion. I agree with you completely. Your words touch my soul, Socrates, and I do believe that through a divine dispensation, good poets say these things as the gods' interpreters.

Soc. And don't you *rhapsōdoi* in your turn interpret what the poets say?

Ion. That is true too.

Soc. So you are interpreters of interpreters.

Ion. Absolutely.[11]

Republic

Socrates is discussing with his companions, Glaucon and Adeimantus, the nature of the best form of political organisation, and the means whereby it might be established. (The discussion has arisen out of an attempt to define justice, and to show that for an individual or a community to possess this virtue is necessarily in its best interests.) Such an organisation, Socrates has argued, requires organisers, and they must be properly suited to their task. Only sound education can produce such people; and the conversation therefore turns (376) to the proper form that a child's education should take, from its earliest years. It has two parts: physical education ('gymnastic'), and what we might call 'cultural' education, *mousikē*, primarily an exposure to poetry and to the music that is its vehicle. This division is adopted out of familiar Greek practice, where it corresponded to the need to train both the body and the soul: but it is Plato's quite surprising contention (410–12) that neither gymnastic nor the rhythmic aspect of music is ultimately to be understood as serving the well-being of the body. The true function of all education is the improvement of the soul and the harmonisation of its elements.

The discussion of *mousikē* begins with a long passage on the proper subject matter for poetry (377–92). Its details cannot be treated here, but its gist is simple. The stories that poetry tells are for the most part untrue, but they need be none the worse for that, so long as the beliefs they inculcate about the gods, about death, and about the satisfactions and miseries, virtues and vices of human life are salutary, encouraging attitudes that reflect moral truth. It follows, Plato argues, that stories displaying gods as wicked, violent, deceiving, immoral or frivolous, or as the authors of any kind of evil in the human world, must all be banned: so must descriptions of passionate mourning, and accounts of death that might undermine courage: so must depictions of legendary heroes, models for children to emulate, which portray them as having moral faults of any kind: so must all

---

[11] Plato would certainly extend this thesis to include every kind of performer who executes other people's compositions.

tales that exhibit the wicked prospering or virtue going unrewarded. In a single argument Plato has outlawed the bulk of Greek narrative and dramatic verse.

Having disposed of subject matter, Socrates turns to 'diction', *lexis*, the manner in which a poet presents his material (392c). He distinguishes two types, narration (*diēgēsis*) and imitation (*mimēsis*), the latter including not only the dramatic representation of characters on the stage, but also any direct speech embedded in a narrative medium, for instance in Homer. Drama is wholly imitative, while epic and related forms are a mixture: the best example of the poet speaking purely in his own person, Socrates interestingly suggests, is dithyramb (394c). It is then argued, on a general principle previously established (initially and broadly at 369–70, more specifically at 374), that the prospective guardians of the city should not be encouraged to indulge in 'imitation' of any sort. In the first place, nobody does two things as well as he does one. Tragedians do not write good comedies: no one can be a good *rhapsōdos* as well as a good actor: the same actor cannot even play well both comic and tragic roles (395a). Hence by practising activities foreign to the character they ought to have and becoming more skilled in these, the children will become less 'expert' in the forms of behaviour that they ought to display. Secondly, imitation leaves its mark on the character and behaviour of the imitator, and thus if they imitate anything, it must only be what is good and noble (395c–e).[12] We pick up the passage at this point: Socrates is the narrator.

149   *Republic* 397–401b

'Well then,' I said, 'the man who is not like this will go right through everything, and the more so the more despicable he is. He will think nothing unworthy of him, so that he will make great efforts, before large audiences, to imitate everything, as we were saying just now – thunder, and the noises of winds and hail and axles and pulleys, and the voices of *salpinges* and *auloi* and *syringes* and instruments of every kind, and even the sounds of dogs and sheep and birds [cf. **154** *Laws* 669b–670a]: [397b] and his diction will consist entirely of imitations by voice and gesture, or will include just a smattering of narration.'

'That is inevitable as well,' he said.

'Now those,' I said, 'are the two forms of diction I was speaking of.'

'They are,' he said.

'Isn't it true, then, that one of the two involves only slight changes,[13] and if

---

12   Plato ties the arts still more closely to *mimēsis*, 'imitation', in *Rep.* Bk x and elsewhere, and he uses this link as a basis for a purge of poetry and music even more radical than the one suggested here. See *Rep.* 595–608, **154** *Laws* 668a ff, 798c–d.

13   That is, in a direct sense, changes in characterisation. But it is assumed that different characters require for their representation different musical forms, both harmonic and rhythmic; and hence in these formal respects too, the approved kind of diction demands little change in the course of a composition, while the other kind demands much. Here and in similar passages Plato has a critical eye on the 'new' music of Timotheus and his like, in which rhythmic and melodic modulation was a prominent feature. Note that in rejecting it Plato was rejecting a 'modernism' that was by now some eighty or more years old.

one adds to the diction an appropriate *harmonia* [see Appendix A] and rhythm, it may be correctly uttered in virtually the same manner throughout – in one *harmonia*, that is, since the changes are slight, and in [c] a rhythm that is similarly uniform?'

'That is certainly so,' he said.

'What of the nature of the other? Doesn't it require the opposite – all the *harmoniai* and all the rhythms – if it in its turn is to be correctly uttered, since it involves multitudinous forms of change?'

'Very much so.'

'And don't all poets, and those who say anything, find themselves using one of these forms of diction or the other, or else one that they mingle together out of both?'

'They must,' he said.

[d] 'What shall we do, then?' I asked. 'Shall we admit all of them into our city, or just one or other of the unmixed types, or just the mixed?'

'If my opinion is to decide,' he said, 'it will be the unmixed imitator of the good man.'

'All the same, Adeimantus, the mixed type is undeniably pleasant, and the opposite kind to the one you choose is pleasantest to children and to their tutors,[14] and to the mass of the people.'

'Pleasantest it is, no doubt.'

'But perhaps you may say,' I went on, 'that it would not harmonise[15] with the [e] constitution of our city, where no one is a double or a multiple man, since each person does one thing.'

'No, it would not harmonise.'

'Isn't it therefore only in this kind of city that we shall find that the cobbler is a cobbler and not a ship's master on top of his shoe-making, the farmer a farmer and not a juryman on top of his farming, the soldier a soldier and not a businessman on top of his soldiering, and so on with all of them?'

'That is true,' he said.

[398a] 'It seems then that if there came to our city a man with the expertise to become anything whatever and to imitate all things, and if he brought with him his compositions and wanted to present them in public, we should do him homage as a sacred and marvellous and delightful person, but would say that there is no one like that in our city, and that the law allows none to enter; and we would send him off to another city, after pouring myrrh on his head and crowning him with wool,[16] while we ourselves would employ a more austere and less delightful poet [b] and story-teller for our own good, one who would imitate the diction of the good man, and utter his words in the ways which we laid down at the beginning, when we were setting out to educate the soldiers.'

14 *Paidagōgoi*: not 'teachers', but slaves whose task it was to escort and look after the children when they were out and about.

15 *Harmottein*, cognate with *harmonia*: 'fit with', 'be in tune with'.

16 As befits the celebrant of sacred rites.

'Yes,' he said, 'we would certainly do that, if it was up to us.'

'Well my friend,' I said, 'it looks as though we have completely dealt with the aspect of *mousikē* that is concerned with words and stories. For we have explained what is to be said and how it is to be said.'

'That's my opinion too,' he said.

[c] 'Then isn't the next task to deal with the matter of style in song and melody?'

'Evidently.'

'Well, wouldn't absolutely anyone be able to work out what we should say about the way these things ought to be, if we are to conform harmoniously[17] to what we have said previously?'

Glaucon laughed. 'In that case, Socrates,' he said, 'I must be no one: for at present I am quite unable to come to a conclusion about the sorts of things we should say – though I can make a guess.'

'At any rate,' I said, 'You can take this first step, and say [d] that song is put together out of three things, words, *harmonia*,[18] and rhythm.'

'Yes,' he said. 'I can say that, at least.'

'So far as its words are concerned, they surely don't differ from words that are not sung, in that they must be uttered in the same mould and in the same manner as we said just now.'

'True,' he said.

'And *harmonia* and rhythm must follow[19] the words.'

'Certainly.'

'But we said that in the words there was no need for mourning and lamenting.'[20]

'No.'

[e] 'Then which are the mournful *harmoniai*? Tell me: you know about music.'[21]

---

[17] *Symphōnein*, lit. 'to sound in concord with'.

[18] The word here has its wider musical sense 'organisation of pitches'. It is not therefore simply 'melody': Plato's usage points to the fact that the existence of melody depends on the prior existence of an organised scheme of pitches standing to one another in determinate relations, on the basis of whose relations the selection that generates a melody is made. 'Rhythm', correspondingly, means the element of rhythmic organisation that any composition must possess, an individual rhythm being the formal rhythmic structure underlying an individual piece or type of piece, its overall pattern of movement. This in its turn is variously instantiated in the particular rhythmic nuances of a particular piece, just as a *harmonia* may be instantiated in any of a number of melodies.

[19] This is a rule on which Plato insists: his insistence may indicate the frequency with which it was broken by modern composers. See particularly **149** 400d, 601a–b, **154** *Laws* 669d–e.

[20] On this point as it relates to music see also 605c ff.

[21] 'You are *mousikos*', here meaning 'knowledgeable about music', not 'cultured' or 'educated' generally, and not necessarily 'musical' or 'a musician' in the sense of being a good performer or even an enthusiastic listener. Cf. Aristox. *El. Harm* 31.20, 32.5–6.

'The Mixolydian,' he said, 'and the Syntonolydian, and some others of hat kind.'[22]

'Mustn't they be got rid of, then?' I said. 'They are useless even for women who are to be of good character, let alone men.'

'Certainly.'

'Again, drunkenness is a most unsuitable thing for our guardians, as are softness and idleness.'

'Of course.'

'Then which of the *harmoniai* are the soft and convivial ones?'

'The Iastian and some of the Lydian *harmoniai* are called "slack" chalarai),' he said.

399a] 'Will there be any use for these, then, my friend, among men who are warriors?'

'Not at all,' he said. 'But you seem to be left with just the Dorian and the Phrygian.'

'I'm no expert on the *harmoniai*,' I said,[23] 'but leave the one that would appropriately imitate the sounds and cadences[24] of a man who is brave in deeds of war and in acting under pressure of any kind, and who, if he is faced with wounds or [b] death or falls into any other catastrophe, confronts his fate in all these situations with self-discipline and steadfastness. Keep another, too, which will imitate those of a man engaged in peaceful activities, acting of his own will, not under pressure, when he is persuading someone of something or making a request, either to a god in prayer or to a man by teaching and advice, or when he is giving his attention to someone else making a request or giving instruction or exercising persuasion. The man will be one who acts in these circumstances in accordance with his intelligence, without excessive conceit, but behaving in all these matters with restraint and moderation, [c] and being content with the results. Leave us these two *harmoniai*, the one of compulsion, the other of free choice, which will most beautifully imitate the sounds of those in misfortune and those in good fortune, the self-restrained and the brave.'[25]

22 On these *harmoniai* and the others named below see Appendix A.
23 Lit. 'I do not know the *harmoniai*'. Whether or not this pose of ignorance (construed as applying to Plato, not Socrates) is false modesty, it at least shows that the capacity to distinguish them and to name the *harmoniai* associated with each character was a matter of specialist expertise, not common knowledge. No doubt a musical layman could recognise something of style and emotive association, and Aristophanes gives evidence enough that some of the names of the *harmoniai* were familiar and comprehensible. But beyond that, the matter is the province of specialists: cf. 154 and 157, *Laws* 668c–671a, 802b–e.
24 *Phthongoi* and *prosōdiai*. *Phthongoi*, in musical parlance, are notes, but may also be simply 'sounds' in a more general context. *Prosōdia* has various uses: the one relevant here indicates the movement of the voice up and down in pitch on different parts of spoken words or sentences, 'speech-melody'. See Aristox. *El. Harm.* 18.13–14.
25 A tangled sentence, and the text has been doubted. If we accept it as it stands (I believe that we should), the expressions 'of compulsion' and 'of free choice' (in each case literally 'a thing of . . .') qualify the two *harmoniai* respectively: between them they imitate the sounds of the self-restrained and the brave man, each of them both in good fortune and bad.

'But the ones you are asking me to leave,' he said, 'are none other than the ones I mentioned just now.'[26]

'In that case,' I said, 'we shall have no need of a multiplicity of strings or an assemblage of all the *harmoniai*[27] in our songs and melodies.'

'I think not,' he said.

'Then we shall not bring up craftsmen to make *trigōnoi* or *pēktides* or any of the instruments that [d] have many strings and all *harmoniai*.'[28]

'Apparently not.'

'Well, will you admit makers or players of the *aulos* into the city? Or isn't it the most numerous-noted of all,[29] and aren't the 'panharmonic' instruments themselves simply an imitation of the *aulos*?'[30]

'Obviously,' he said.

'Then you are left with the *lyra*,' I said, 'and the *kithara*,[31] as things useful in the city; and in the countryside the herdsmen might have some sort of *syrinx*.'

[26] I.e., Dorian and Phrygian. See Appendix A.
[27] 'Assemblage of all the *harmoniai*' translates *panharmoniou*, 'the panharmonic'. This has sometimes been thought to be the name of an instrument ('panharmonium') or a class of instruments, but that is quite improbable: see Adam's note on *panharmonia* at 399d, and cf. the occurrence of the word at 404d. The suggestion that it designates a style of composition allowing free movement between *harmoniai* in the manner of Timotheus and the rest is very plausible: alternatively, the reference may be entirely abstract, as my translation tries to suggest.
[28] On instruments with many strings shifts from one *harmonia* to another were obviously more feasible. The *trigōnos* or *trigōnon* was a triangular harp with strings of different lengths but equal tension: see 175 ps.-Ar. *Probs.* XIX.23, where it is called the *trigōnon psaltērion*. It was of foreign origin (Aristox. ap. 188 Ath. 182f). It is mentioned in some fifth-century writers (Eupolis ap. 188 Ath. 183f, where it is associated with the *tympanon*; 638e, where it is to accompany songs for adulterers to sing to their mistresses; Soph. ap. 188 Ath. 183e, where it is called Phrygian and linked with the 'Lydian *pēktis*'): so also Diogenes ap. 196 Ath. 636b. The *pēktis* was another foreign instrument, but well established in Greece: it is mentioned as early as Sappho (fr. 156) and may have been introduced well before (Pindar, fr. 110). Its main associations are to do with relaxed and convivial enjoyment. It was played (like the *trigōnos*) with the fingers, not with a plectrum (Aristox, ap. 196 Ath. 635b), and it may have been a variant of the *magadis*, on which see 196 Ath. 634c–637a. If that is correct, it would explain Sopater's description of it as *dichordos*, 'two-stringed' (188 Ath. 183b): this cannot be taken literally, in view of passages like the present one, but might mean 'with two courses of strings', a feature of the *magadis*, in which the courses were tuned an octave apart.
[29] Lit. 'with most numerous strings', a bold but perfectly comprehensible metaphor, by no means unparalleled. This and similar descriptions of the *aulos* are common even in the early fifth century, long before the modifications to the *aulos* attributed to Pronomus (195 Ath. 631e): e.g. 27 Pindar, *Pyth.* 12.19, Simonides, fr. 46. It seems likely that the phenomenon to which these early writers refer is the aulete's capacity for generating a wide variety of notes from only a few finger-holes, by means of techniques of breath- and lip-control.
[30] Cf. 161 Ar. *Pol.* 1341a17–b8, and 196 Ath. 637f–638a, with notes. The 'panharmonic' instruments are of course such things as the *trigōnoi* and *pēktides* referred to previously.
[31] Even the *kithara* is outlawed by Aristotle (161 *Pol.* 1341a19), but only as an instrument to be practised as part of a citizen's education. Its use is proper to professionals (for whom it was the usual stringed instrument, the *lyra* having little carrying power), and Aristotle does not prohibit its employment in public performances.

'Yes, that is what the argument suggests,' he said.

[e] 'After all,' I said, 'it's nothing new that we are doing, in judging Apollo and his instruments to be superior to Marsyas and his.'[32]

'No indeed,' he said, 'I don't think it is.'

'And look here,' I said. 'Without noticing it we have been repurifying the city which we said just now was growing over-luxurious.'

'Well, that was sensible of us,' he said.

'Come on then,' I said, 'and let us purify the rest. Following on from *harmoniai* we should next deal with rhythms, to ensure that we do not pursue intricately varied ones with every kind of movement,[33] but discover the rhythms that are those of an orderly and courageous life. When we have found them we must make the [400a] foot[34] and the melody follow the words proper to such a life, and not make the words follow the foot and the melody. It is your job to say which these rhythms are, as it was with the *harmoniai*.'

'But I can't tell you, I assure you,' he said. 'I have studied enough to say that there are just three kinds from which the movements are woven together, just as in notes there are four, from which come all the *harmoniai*:[35] but which kinds are imitations of which sort of life I cannot say.'

[32] For the story see Apollodorus 1.4.2: contrast the legend that the *aulos* was invented by Athena (e.g. 27 Pindar, *Pyth.* 12, 161 Ar. *Pol.* 1341b2 ff). Plato should not be understood as suggesting that it was normal for Greeks to reject the *aulos* in favour of the *kithara* or *lyra*, or to prefer the 'Apolline' to the 'Dionysiac', the Greek to the foriegn, or anything else of the kind. By saying that his proposal is 'nothing new' he means only that the story provides a precedent.

[33] 'Movement', *baseis*, lit. 'steps', 'goings'.

[34] That is, the rhythmic or metrical foot.

[35] The three kinds of rhythm are probably those adopted into Aristoxenean theory, and set out by Arist. Quint. at 33.29 ff. Each foot is divided into a 'rise' and a 'fall' (*anō* and *katō*, later *arsis* and *thesis*), and the kinds are classified according to the ratios of the durations of each. Some have *arsis* and *thesis* equal to one another, some in the ratio 3:2, some in the ratio 2:1. An interest in this aspect of rhythms is reflected in the ideas attributed to Damon at 400b.

The four 'kinds' that form the basis of the *harmoniai* pose a trickier problem. One would expect them to parallel in some way the rhythmic 'kinds', and the obvious candidates are then the ratios of the four fundamental intervals of Pythagorean analysis, 2:1 (octave), 3:2 (fifth), 4:3 (fourth), and 9:8 (tone): see e.g. Nicom. 252.17–253.3, quoting what purports to be a piece by Philolaus; *Sect. Can.* Prop. 12. This probably remains the best interpretation, but it is not without its difficulties, and many other suggestions have been made. Not the least of the difficulties lies in the fact that the manipulation of these ratios allows the construction of *harmoniai* only in the diatonic and chromatic genera, not the enharmonic, which, so Aristoxenus says, was the focus of all early harmonic theory (2.7 ff: see also *Sect. Can.* 17–18). This problem may be avoided by noting that Aristoxenus' 'harmonic theorists' do not include those in the Pythagorean tradition, to whom the system of ratios belonged: no trace of anything but diatonic occurs in Nicomachus' alleged quotation from Philolaus, and Plato, following that tradition, restricts himself to the diatonic in the scale constructed in the *Timaeus* (35b ff). He would still be ignoring a significant part of current Pythagorean practice, however, since Archytas (according to Ptol. *Harm.* 30.9 ff) gave analyses in all three genera, using a much richer variety of ratios than this passage would allow.

The best of the other suggestions known to me (versions of all of which are mentioned in Adam's note ad loc.) is that the four 'kinds' are the four notes of the

[b] 'Then on these points we shall take advice from Damon,' I said, [see Appendix B] 'and ask him which movements are suitable for illiberality, conceit, madness and other vices, and which rhythms we should keep and assign to their opposites. I think I have heard him – though I didn't quite follow – mentioning by name a "composite *enhoplios*", a "dactyl" and a "heroic", organising the rhythm in ways I don't understand, and making the rise and the fall equal as it moved to the short and the long:[36] and I think he named an "iambus", and called another a "trochaeus", and assigned them their long and [c] short elements.[37] And I believe that he criticised and applauded the tempo[38] of the foot of each of them as much as he did the rhythms themselves – or it may have been both together: I can't say. But as I said, let us turn these matters over to Damon, for it would take no little discussion to decide them. Or do you disagree?'

'Not I – not in the least,' he said.

'But do gracefulness and gracelessness[39] go with good and bad rhythm?' I said. 'That is something you can decide, isn't it?'

'Certainly they do.'

[d] 'But of good and bad rhythm, the one follows and is brought to resemble beautiful diction, the other the opposite; and the same goes for goodness and badness of *harmonia*,[40] if rhythm and *harmonia* really follow the words, as we said just now, and not the words them.'

tetrachord: but (a) it is not known how, if at all, a tetrachordal analysis was applied to the *harmoniai* at this date (cf. Aristox. *El. Harm.* 2.18–21), and (b) manipulation of the notes of a single tetrachord is insufficient to generate all the *harmoniai* that are required. For a further conjecture see Appendix B.

36   The 'composite *enhoplios*' is probably ˘ - ˘ ˘ - ˘ ˘ -, well known as a processional rhythm (see n. to 131 Aristoph. *Clouds* 652). To call a rhythm 'composite', according to Arist. Quint. 34.19 ff, is to say that it is made up of rhythmic elements of more than one genus or 'kind' (see n. 35 above). A 'composite foot' is merely one divisible into smaller feet, Arist. Quint. 33.19, but the composite *enhoplios* is not a foot.
  'Dactyl' is the name of a foot (- ˘ ˘): to make it the name of a rhythm we would have to emend to e.g. *daktylikon*, 'dactylic'. But Plato is not even pretending to be precise or systematic.
  'Heroic' can be the name of a foot (the dactyl), but is here probably the name of a rhythm, that exhibited by the dactylic hexameter of Homer and other epic. In such a rhythm the 'rise and fall' (see n. 35) are equal, a long syllable counting standardly as equivalent to two shorts. 'As it moved to the short and the long': this perhaps means 'whether an individual foot ended in a short (as in the dactyl, - ˘ ˘) or in a long (as in the spondee, - -, which frequently replaces one or more of the dactyls in an epic line). That the present passage constitutes a more or less routine pastiche of Damonian exegesis is suggested by its resemblance to 131 Aristoph. *Clouds* 651–2.
37   The iambus is ˘ -, the trochaeus or trochee - ˘.
38   'Tempo', *agōgē*. See Arist. Quint. 39.26–30, 40.1–3, 84.3–5.
39   *Euschēmosynē*, 'gracefulness', is a quite general term for beauty of shape or form: but note its relation to *schēma*, which as well as meaning 'shape' is the term regularly designating a 'figure' or 'posture' in the dance. See e.g. 143 Xen. *Symp.* 2.15 and passim, cf. 153 *Laws* 654e with n. 60.
40   *To euharmoston kai anharmoston*, lit. 'the well-tuned [or adjusted] and ill-tuned'. *Anharmostos* may mean 'contrary to the rules of music', musically wrong or inept (e.g. Aristox. *El. Harm.* 18.23, 52.24), differing from what is musically acceptable 'by the difference in the way its incomposite intervals are put together' (18.32–19.1).

'Certainly,' he said, 'it is they that must follow the words.'

'But what of the manner of diction,' I said, 'and the words themselves? Do they not follow the character of the soul?'

'Undoubtedly.'

'And the other things follow the diction?'

'Yes.'

'Then good diction and good *harmonia* (*euharmostia*) and gracefulness and good rhythm follow [e] good character, not the foolishness to which we give that name[41] by way of a euphemism, but the mind that is genuinely well and beautifully constituted in its character.'

'I entirely agree,' he said.

'Then mustn't these things be universally pursued by our young men, if they are to do the work proper to them?'

'They must.'

[401a] 'Now painting and all crafts of that kind are certainly full of them, as are weaving and embroidery and house-building and the making of all other artefacts, and so is the structure of our bodies and that of other living things: for in all of them there is gracefulness and its opposite. And gracelessness and bad rhythm and bad *harmonia* are sisters of bad speech and bad character, whereas their opposites are sisters and imitations of the opposite, of a self-restrained and good character.'

'Undoubtedly,' he said.

[b] 'Then we must give orders to our poets, and compel them to create in their poems only the image of good character, or else to make no poetry in our city . . .' [Cf. 605c–608b.]

150   *Republic* 401d–402a

'For these reasons, then, Glaucon,' I said, 'isn't training in *mousikē* of overriding importance, because rhythm and *harmonia*[42] penetrate most deeply into the recesses of the soul and take a powerful hold on it, bringing gracefulness and making a man graceful [401e] if he is correctly trained, but the opposite if he is not? Another reason is that the man who has been properly trained in these matters would perceive most sharply things that were defective, and badly crafted or badly grown, and his displeasure would be justified. He would praise and rejoice in fine things, and would receive them into his soul and be nourished by them, [402a] becoming fine and good: but he

Cf. n. 46 below. But Plato is evidently using it to mean 'morally bad', 'tuned to a morally unacceptable *harmonia*', not 'in breach of morally neutral musical laws'. We should not in any case take it for granted that Plato believed in the existence of such morally neutral laws: all standards relating to propriety, beauty and the like have, on his view, a single basis, and all carry moral weight (esp. *Rep.* 505a ff). See also the argument at *Phaedo* 93a–94b.

41   I.e., the name *euētheia*, lit. 'good character', but used euphemistically to mean 'stupidity', 'naivety'.

42   Here in its wider sense, 'patterns of order exhibited by movement and melody'. For the general thesis cf. 605c–606e, 153 *Laws* 656b, 659d ff, 157 802c–d.

would rightly condemn ugly things, and hate them even when he was young, before he was able to lay hold on reason. And when reason grew, the person trained in this way would embrace it with enthusiasm, recognising it as a familiar friend.'

'It seems to me,' he said, 'that the purposes of a training in *mousikē* are of just these kinds.'

> In 403 Socrates sets out to discuss the physical regimen that the young men must adopt. It too must be simple and austere: at 404d–e he compares a licentious way of life and a varied and luxurious diet to 'the type of musical composition and song that employs the entire range of *harmoniai* and all the rhythms', and which has already been outlawed. Variety in music, he goes on, breeds lack of self-restraint, and variety in physical life-style and diet breeds disease, while simplicity in music engenders moderation in the soul, and simplicity in gymnastic engenders health in the body. From here he naturally turns to consider the very modest roles that are to be allotted to the legal and medical professions in his ideal state. For the most part, the passage that follows is concerned with music only in so far as it is a part of *mousikē* more widely conceived. But the ideas expressed are important as guides to Plato's views in the narrower field as well.

151   *Republic* 410a–412b

'It is clear,' I said, 'that the young men will be extremely circumspect about incurring the need to go to law, since they practise that simple form of *mousikē* which, we have said, engenders moderation.'

'Certainly,' he said.

[410b]   'And surely the man trained in *mousikē* who follows the same footsteps in pursuing gymnastics can choose, if he wishes, never to require the doctor's attention except in extremities.'

'I agree.'

'Further, he will work at the labours of gymnastics with an eye to the improvement of the spirited part[43] of his nature rather than that of his strength, unlike other athletes who undertake dieting and exercises for the sake of making themselves strong.'

'Very true,' he said.

'Then the purpose of those who established education as the [c] combination of *mousikē* and gymnastics,' I said, 'was not, as some people think, Glaucon, to cultivate the body with one of them and the soul with the other.'

'Then what was it?' he asked.

'The chances are,' I said, 'that both of them were established principally for the sake of the soul.'

---

[43]   'Spirit' etc. here and throughout the sequel stand for the untranslatable *thymos* and its cognates. The reference is not to a 'spirit' in the sense of 'ghost' or 'soul', but to that element in us that is 'spirited', as a horse or a plucky sportsman may be described as 'having plenty of spirit'. It is the element, according to Plato, on which such traits as courage and self-confidence depend, as do also, on the morally negative side, excessive ferocity, harshness, rashness, pride and ambition.

'How so?'

'Aren't you aware,' I asked, 'of the mental disposition of those who are involved in gymnastics throughout their life, but have no contact with *mousikē*? Or that of those whose situation is the opposite?'

'What do you mean?' he asked.

[d] 'I mean ferociousness and hardness on the one side,' I said, 'and softness and gentleness on the other.'

'I know,' he said. 'Those who practise nothing but gymnastics turn out more ferocious than is proper, while those who practise nothing but *mousikē* become softer than is really good for them.'[44]

'Yes,' I said. 'It is the spirited element in man's nature that produces ferociousness. If it were correctly trained it would be courageous, but if it is intensified[45] more than it should be it becomes hard and recalcitrant, as is to be expected.'

'I agree,' he said.

[e] 'And then isn't it the philosophical nature that possesses gentleness? If it is too far relaxed it is softer than is right, but gentle and orderly if its training is good.'

'That's so.'

'We say, don't we, that the guardians must have both these elements in their nature?'

'They must.'

'And mustn't they be harmonised[46] with one another?'

'Of course.'

'And the soul of the man who is thus harmonised is temperate [411a] and brave?'

'Certainly,'

'But that of the man who is unharmonised is cowardly and uncouth.'

'Very much so.'

'Then whenever anyone lets music entrance his soul with its piping,[47] and lets it pour into his soul through his ears, as though through a funnel, the sweet and soft and mournful *harmoniai* that we were discussing just now [**149** 398e], and when he uses up the whole of his life humming, enraptured by song, then to begin with, if he has anything of the spirited element in him,

---

[44] This is of course an antique commonplace: e.g. *Il* III.54, XXIV.261, *Od.* VIII.246 ff, and in Plato also *Symp.* 179d.

[45] 'Intensified' here and 'relaxed' in Socrates' next speech (*epitathen, anethentos*) are metaphors from the tightening and slackening of the strings of an instrument, very commonly used in psychological contexts. Cf. e.g. 151 412a, Ar. *Pol.* 1290a 26–9. For the (non-Platonic) doctrine that the soul consists in a *harmonia* see Plato, *Phaedo* 85e ff.

[46] *Hērmosthai*, cognate with *harmonia*: 'be attuned'. 'Harmonised' and 'unharmonised' in the following sentences translate *hērmosmenos* (a participle of *hērmosthai*) and *anharmostos*. *Hērmosmenos*, especially in the form *to hērmosmenon*, lit. 'the attuned', is Aristoxenus' regular term for what is musically sound and proper, conforming to the laws of music, e.g. 4.12, 19.11. *Anharmostos* is used as its negative.

[47] *Kataulein*: see 112 Eurip. *Heracles* 871, Plato, *Laws* 790e.

this man will temper it like iron, and make useful [b] what was useless and hard. But if he persists in entrancing it without ceasing, he will eventually dissolve it and melt it away, till he pours away his spirit, and cuts, as it were, the sinews from his soul, and makes of it a "feeble warrior" [quoting *Iliad* XVII.588].'

'Quite true,' he said.

'And if to begin with,' I said, 'his natural character lacks spirit, this process will be quickly completed, But if it is spirited, then by weakening his spirit he will make it easily swayed, quickly inflamed [c] and extinguished by trifling matters. Such people become quick-tempered and quarrelsome instead of spirited, full of peevishness.'

'Absolutely.'

'Suppose, instead, that he works hard at gymnastics and revels in them greatly, but has nothing to do with *mousikē* and philosophy. Won't the first result be that he will have a healthy body, and will be filled with self-confidence and spirit, and will become braver than ever before?'

'Yes indeed.'

'But what if he does nothing else, and has no association of any kind with the Muse? [d] If there was anything in his soul that loved learning, then because it is given no taste of any learning or enquiry, doesn't it become weak and deaf and blind, since it is not awakened or fed, and its powers of perception are left unpurified?'[48]

'Yes,' he said.

'Then such a person, I suppose, comes to hate reasoning[49] and reject *mousikē*. He no longer uses words to persuade, but accomplishes everything, [e] like a wild beast, by violence and ferocity, and lives without rhythm or grace in ignorance and stupidity.'

'That expresses the facts precisely,' he said.

'I should say then that God seems to have given us two skills for the sake of these two elements in us, *mousikē* and gymnastics, that is, for the spirited and the philosophic parts, and not for the soul and the body, except as an unimportant by-product. Their task is [412a] to tune those two elements to one another by tightening and relaxing them[50] until the proper relation is reached.'

'That seems to be so,' he said.

'Then the man who can best blend gymnastics with *mousikē* and administer them, perfectly measured, to the soul, is the one whom we should most

---

[48]   Perception in the literal sense, as well as 'intellectual perception', is indicated here, as being indispensable to proper judgement in music. Plato is not exclusively rationalistic in these matters. See **154** and **158** *Laws* 670a ff, 812b–c, and cf. the views of Aristoxenus, especially 33.1 ff.

[49]   Cf. *Phaedo* 89d ff.

[50]   'Tune to' *synharmosthēton*. See **144** Xen. *Symp.* 3.1 and note. 'Tightening and relaxing', *epiteinomenō* and *aniemenō*, regularly used for the processes of raising and

correctly call the complete musician and the true expert in harmony,[51] much more than the man who can tune strings to one another.'

'Yes, Socrates,' he said, 'with good reason.'

'In our city, then, Glaucon, we shall constantly need the services of such an instructor, if the constitution is to be preserved.'

[b]　'Nothing could be needed more urgently.'

> In the latter part of Book III and the early sections of Book IV, a number of proposals have been made concerning the life-style of the city's rulers (whom Plato calls 'guardians') and the conditions of public and private life generally. Some of the suggestions are radical and surprising, and Adeimantus expresses some scepticism: the requirements are too difficult. Socrates' reply follows in the next excerpt: its theme is elaborated at length in the *Laws*.[52]

152　*Republic* 423d–425a

'The demands we are imposing on them, my dear Adeimantus,' I said, 'are neither numerous nor large, as some people might suppose. No, they are [423e] all trivial, just so long as the guardians preserve the one great thing – or rather not "great" so much as "sufficient".'

'What is that?' he asked.

'Their education and upbringing,' I said. 'If they are well educated and become men of moderation, they will easily understand all this and other things too, which we are now omitting – to do with the possession of wives and marriages and the begetting of children – and will see that in all this they must [424a] do everything they can to ensure that "friends' goods are common goods",[53] as the saying has it.'

'That would be entirely correct,' he said.

'Then if only our city can set off well,' I said, 'it will progress and grow like a circle.[54] If a worthy upbringing and education are maintained they produce good natures, and worthy natures in their turn, by taking hold of this kind of education, grow to be even better than before, both in their breeding qualities, [b] as with the other animals, and in all other respects too.'

'That seems likely,' he said.

'To put it briefly, then, those in charge of the city must devote themselves

---

　　lowering the pitches of strings: cf. n. 45. As Adam says in his note ad loc., the suggestion is that the spirited and philosophical elements are, as it were, the strings of the soul, the former tightened by gymnastic and relaxed by *mousikē*, the latter conversely. Both practices therefore affect both 'strings'.

[51]　*Euharmostotaton*: the word would more naturally be taken to mean 'best tuned' or 'adjusted' in his character, as at 413e. But here the emphasis is not so much on a man's character as on his skills. For the sense of *mousikōtaton* ('complete musician') cf. **149** 398e with n. 21.

[52]　Particularly **153, 156, 157**, 656d ff, 799a–b, 799e ff.

[53]　Lindsay's translation.

[54]　The simile is obscure and has been variously understood: perhaps the image suggested is that of the growth of the circular ripple caused when a stone is thrown into a pond.

to ensuring that this principle is not destroyed without their noticing it, and to guarding it above all else, the principle, I mean, that no innovations shall be made in gymnastics and music beyond what is laid down, but that what is laid down shall be preserved as closely as possible [cf. e.g. **156** *Laws* 799a–b]. When someone says that

> People praise more highly the song
> That is most newly come to minstrels' lips[55]

[c]   they should fear that people might easily suppose the poet to mean not just new songs, but a new style of song, and that they would applaud the latter. Such a thing should not be applauded, nor should the poet be so understood. People should beware of change to new forms of music, for they are risking change in the whole.[56] Styles of music are nowhere altered without change in the greatest laws of the city: so Damon says, and I concur.'

'You can count me in as another of those who concur,' said Adeimantus.

[d]   'It seems then,' I said, 'that it is here, in music, that the guardians must build their guard-house.'

'It is easy for this law-breaking to creep in undetected,' he said.

'Yes,' I replied. 'It is treated as a matter of mere amusement and as doing no harm.'

'That's because it does nothing,' he said, 'except to establish itself little by little, and quietly insinuate itself into characters and practices. From there it emerges enlarged, and enters men's dealings with one another, and from these dealings it moves [e] to attack laws and constitutions with the most wanton extravagance, Socrates, until in the end it overturns everything in both public and private life.'

'I see,' I said. 'Is all that really so?'

'I think so,' he said.

'Then as we were saying at the very beginning, mustn't our children be set, from the start, to more law-abiding amusements, since when amusements are lawless, children are so too, and it is impossible for law-abiding and honest [425a] men to grow up out of these?'

'Inevitably,' he said.

'Then surely when children make a good start with their amusements, and are equipped through *mousikē* with a law-abiding spirit, this spirit, the opposite of what you have described, will follow along with everything and augment it, and will set right anything in the city that was previously laid low.'

Laws

The Athenian Stranger, the principal speaker of the dialogue, has – like Socrates in the *Republic* – stressed the crucial importance of good educa-

---

[55]   A rough quotation or a variant version of **9** *Od.* 1.351–2. For the idea cf. Pindar, *Ol.* 9.48, and for the form of the idea that Plato rejects, *Ol.* 3.4.

[56]   I.e., in the whole constitution and fabric of the state. Cf. **155** *Laws* 700a–701b.

tion to the well-being of the state. Education consists, he tells us, in the development within each individual of appropriately oriented dispositions for feeling pleasure and pain, and of the right attitudes towards these feelings. In children the moral goodness that it creates cannot be based on knowledge, and even adults may never acquire knowledge of the relevant kind. Instead, the discipline that provides the foundation for the development of moral goodness, both in childhood and in adult life, is primarily to be found in music.

53 *Laws* 653c–660c

Athenian. .... Now these properly trained pleasures and pains, which are forms of education, are subject to slackening and destruction to a great extent during men's lives: but the gods, in pity [653d] for the race of men, born to toil, established for them as respites from their labours the festivals of thanksgiving to the gods; and they gave them the Muses, with their leader Apollo, so that they might be set right again, along with the nourishing that comes from joining in festivals with the gods. So we must consider whether the account that people sing[57] nowadays is true to nature or not. It says that virtually every young creature is incapable of keeping still with either its body or its voice, but [e] is always trying to move and make sounds, leaping and skipping as though dancing and sporting with pleasure, and uttering noises of every kind. Other creatures, it says, have no perception of order and disorder in movements, the names for which are rhythm and *harmonia*. But for us, to whom as we said the gods have been given [654a] as fellow-dancers, these same gods have given the capacity to perceive rhythm and *harmonia*, and to enjoy them, and through this capacity they move us and lead us in the dance, joining us to one another with songs and dances: and they have given 'choruses' their name by derivation from the *chara* ['joy'] that is natural to them.[58] Are we then to accept this, to begin with? Shall we assert that education comes first from the Muses and Apollo, or what?

Clinias. We shall.

Ath. Shall we then say that the uneducated man is without choric expertise, [b] while the educated man is to be reckoned adequately trained in the art of the chorus?

Clin. Certainly.

Ath. The choric art (*choreia*) as a whole consists of dance and song.

Clin. It must.

[57] *Hymneitai*, 'is hymned'.
[58] The derivation is of course wholly fanciful. In much of this passage the word translated 'dance' is *choros*, or one of its derivatives, indicating the combination of choral dance and song.

Ath. Then the man who is well educated would be able to sing and danc
well.[59]

Clin. So it seems.

Ath. Let us then consider what this expression means.

Clin. Which one?

Ath. We said 'he sings well and dances well'. [c] Should we or should we no
add 'if he sings and dances good things'?

Clin. We should.

Ath. What then if he believes what is really good to be good, and what i
really ugly to be ugly, and treats them accordingly? Will we say that i
is this sort of man that is better educated in the choric art and in music
or the one who can always adequately accommodate himself, with
body and voice, to what he supposes to be good, but enjoys what is no
good and fails to dislike what is bad? Or is it the man who is no
entirely able [d] to give a correct performance with his voice and hi
body, or to form the correct conceptions, but who is correct in hi
pleasures and pains, embracing all the things that are good and disap-
proving of all those that are not?

Clin. The difference in education that you mention is a large one, stranger.

Ath. Then if we understand what is good in song and dance, we can also
distinguish correctly the educated man and the uneducated. But if we
do not know that, we shall be unable to grasp whether there is any
safeguard for education, and where it is to be found. [e] Is that not so?

Clin. It is.

Ath. Then what we must next track down, like hunting dogs, is good posture,[60] good melody, good song, and good dancing. If all these things
run away and elude us, all the rest of our discourse about correct
education, whether Greek or foreign, will be futile.

Clin. Yes.

Ath. Well then, what should we say constitutes good posture or good
melody? Consider: when a courageous soul is caught up in troubles,
and [655a] a cowardly soul in ones that are equal and the same, are their
resulting postures and utterances alike?

Clin. How could they be, when even their colourings are different?

Ath. Well said, my friend. But in music there are postures and melodies, since

59   'Well', 'good', here and in the sequel, translate *kalos* etc., a word of wide associations
whose primary meaning is 'beautiful', 'fine'. Plato here reserves it, for the most part,
to indicate the condition of complete excellence in music, whatever that may turn out
to depend on. The other key word in the passage is 'correct', *orthos*, indicating
correspondence to a fixed standard. On its implications for music see especially **154**
667b ff.

60   *Schēma.* The root meaning is 'shape': it is also used to mean 'dance-figure', or 'position of the body in the dance', and that sense is in Plato's mind here. But he does not
restrict it to the context of the dance, and I have therefore used the more general
rendering 'posture' in these excerpts.
      It is quite likely that the sentence should read 'good posture and good melody in
song and dance', adopting Ritter's *kat'* for the MSS *kai*.

music is concerned with rhythm and *harmonia*, and hence one can speak correctly of 'well-rhythmed' or 'well harmonised' melody and posture; while one cannot correctly speak – in the metaphor chorus-trainers use – of melody or posture as 'well coloured'.[61] One can also speak correctly of the 'postures' and 'melodies' of the coward and the brave man [cf. **149** *Rep.* 399a ff], and it is [b] correct to call those of brave men 'good' and those of cowards 'ugly'. To forestall a lengthy discussion about all this, let us agree that all the postures and melodies belonging to goodness of soul or body – to virtue itself or any image of it – are good, while those belonging to badness are altogether the opposite.

Clin. What you assert is correct. Let us be on record now as answering that it is so.

Ath. Here is another point. Do we enjoy all kinds of choric performance [c] to the same extent as one another, or is that far from true?

Clin. Very far.

Ath. Then what do we say produces the variations[62] between us? Are the things that are good not the same in the case of each of us, or are they the same, but do not seem to be the same? No one is going to say that choric expressions of badness are better than those of goodness, or that he himself enjoys the postures of depravity while other people enjoy music [lit. 'a Muse'] of an opposite kind. Yet most people certainly say that musical [d] correctness consists in the power to provide pleasure for the soul. But that assertion is intolerable and cannot even be uttered without blasphemy. It is more likely that what leads us astray is this.

Clin. What?

Ath. Since what is involved in choric performance is imitations of characters, appearing in actions and eventualities of all kinds which each performer goes through by means of habits and imitations,[63] those people to whom the things said or sung or performed in any way are congenial (on the basis of their [e] nature or their habits or of both

---

61 Metaphorical references to 'colouring' in music seem to refer to expressive effects involving either 'tone-colour' or nuances of tuning. For the former sense see e.g. **196** Ath. 638a, 643d, Gaudentius 329, cf. Plato, *Rep.* 601b, **161** Ar. *Pol.* 1342a24. The latter sense gives rise to the title 'chromatic genus', used of the varied set of scale-forms described by Aristoxenus (particularly 50.25 ff): see also **154** *Laws* 669c. On metaphorical applications of colour terms to music see also Ar. *Top.* 106a–b, 107a.

  The Athenian affects to take Clinias' remark about people's different facial complexions partly as a reference to the 'colourings' of their utterances. His point seems to be that while 'well-rhythmed' etc. are terms that can be applied directly, without metaphor, both to music and (in a quasi-moral sense) to people, 'well-coloured' cannot. He is looking for ways in which music and people share identically the same attributes, and this is not the case where the term is attached to one member of the pair metaphorically.

62 Lit. 'makes us wander', with the suggestion of being led astray: I have used 'leads astray' as a translation of this word in the last sentence of the paragraph.

63 That is, by using his own ingrained habits (to represent characters like himself), or imitations of others where the character represented is foreign to his own. The idea is not Plato's invention: cf. e.g. **138** Aristoph. *Thesm.* 155–6.

together) enjoy them and praise them, and must call them good: bu
those to whose nature or disposition or habit they are contrary canno
enjoy or praise them, and must call them bad. As for those who ar
correct in their natural responses but the reverse in those due to habi
or correct in those due to habit but the reverse in their natural ones
[656a] the praises that these people speak are ones that oppose thei
pleasures. They say that all such things are pleasant but disgraceful
they are ashamed to make movements of these kinds with their bodie
in the presence of those whose judgement they trust; and they ar
ashamed to sing them in such a way as to suggest seriously that they ar
good, while nevertheless they enjoy them privately.

Clin. You are absolutely right.

Ath. Is any harm done to a person, then, by his enjoyment of the postures o
melodies of depravity, and do those who find enjoyment in the oppo
site kinds gain any benefit from it?

Clin. It seem likely.

Ath. [b] Isn't it not so much likely as inevitable that the case is the same a
that of a man whose time is spent among the depraved habits of bac
people, who does not detest them but accepts and enjoys them, and ye
criticises them in a playful sort of way, perceiving the wickednes
involved only as in a dream? Here it is inevitable that the man wil
become like whichever kind of thing he enjoys, even if he is ashamed tc
praise it. Yet what greater good or evil than this kind could we say
comes to us with such total inevitability?[64]

Clin. None, I would say.

Ath. [c] Do we suppose, then, that wherever laws are established, or will be ir
the future, concerning education and recreation in the sphere of music
artists will be allowed to teach whatever the composer himself like
best in the way of rhythm or melody or words in a composition – tc
teach them to the children of people whose laws are good, and to the
young men in the choruses, no matter what the result may turn out tc
be in the field of virtue and vice?

Clin. That has no sense to it, obviously.

Ath. [d] Yet at present this is just what is permitted in virtually every city
except in Egypt.

Clin. What sort of laws do you say they have concerning such matters ir
Egypt?

Ath. Even to hear them described is astonishing. Once, long ago, so it seems
they came to understand the argument that we have just been setting
out, according to which the young men in each city must become
practised in good postures and good melodies. These they prescribed
and they advertised which they are and what they are like in the

---

64   That is: 'What greater inescapable blessing or curse [what more influential law of
nature, as it were] is there than the fact that our characters inevitably become
assimilated to that of the kinds of thing we enjoy?'

temples: [e] it was forbidden, as it still is, for painters or any other portrayers of postures and representations to make innovations beyond these, or to think up anything outside the traditional material, in these areas or in *mousikē* in general. If you look you will find that what was written or depicted there ten thousand years ago – and I mean ten thousand literally, not as a figure of speech – is neither better [657a] nor worse than what is made nowadays, but is done with the same art.

Clin. What you say is amazing.

Ath. It is, you will admit, a supreme expression of the aims of the lawgiver and the statesman, though you could find other things there that are bad. But as concerns music, it is true and noteworthy that it was possible in these matters for a bold man to lay down lasting laws prescribing melodies that possess a natural correctness. To do this would be a task for a god, or a godlike man, just as in Egypt they say that the melodies that have [b] been preserved for this great period of time were the compositions of Isis. Thus, as I said, if one could somehow grasp the nature of correctness in melodies, one ought boldly to bring them under law and regulation. For pleasure and pain, in their constant pursuit of new music to indulge in, have little power to destroy a choric art that is sanctified, just by mocking its antiquity. In Egypt, at least, it does not seem to have been able to destroy it: quite the contrary.[65]

Clin. [c] That certainly seems to be so, to judge from what you said just now.

Ath. Do we then bodly state that correct procedure in music, and in recreation involving choric activity, is something like this: we enjoy ourselves when we think that we are flourishing, and we think that we are flourishing whenever we enjoy ourselves?[66] Isn't that so?

Clin. Yes.

Ath. And in such a condition, one of enjoyment, we cannot keep still?

Clin. That is so.

Ath. [d] Now isn't it true that those of us who are young are prepared to perform in choruses themselves, while those of us who are older think of ourselves as suitably occupied in watching them, enjoying their games and festivities? For our nimbleness has now left us, and it is our nostalgic longing for it that makes us set up contests for those who can best arouse us, in our memory, into youthfulness.

Clin. Quite true.

Ath. Should we then refrain from treating as entirely futile what most people say [e] about those engaged in festivities – that the one who gives us the most delight and enjoyment should be thought most skilful and judged

---

65   On Egypt see further **156** 799a.

66   This thesis does not by itself constitute the 'procedure' signalled at the beginning of the sentence: it merely introduces it. The procedure is described at length in the sequel.

the winner? For since we give ourselves up to recreation on these occasions, we should give the greatest honour, and the prize of victory, as I said just now, to the one who gives the most pleasure to the greatest number of people. [658a] Isn't this thesis correct, and wouldn't things be rightly done if they were done in this way?

Clin. Perhaps.

Ath. But we shouldn't judge something like this hastily, my friend. Let us divide it up and consider it in the following way. Suppose that someone were to set up a competition without characterising it at all, without specifying it as a competition in gymnastics or music or horse-racing, but assembling everyone in the city, offering prizes and announcing that anyone who wished could compete simply in giving pleasure, [b] and that the winner would be whoever gave most delight to the onlookers, no matter in what way — whoever came out best in doing just that to the greatest extent, and was adjudged to have been the most enjoyable of the competitors. What do we imagine would happen as the result of such an announcement?

Clin. In what respect do you mean?

Ath. Probably one person, like Homer, would put on a *rhapsōdia*, one a *kitharōdia*, one a tragedy, another a comedy: it wouldn't be surprising if someone even [c] thought he was most likely to win by putting on a puppet show. With all these and thousands of other competitors entering, do we have any way of saying who would deserve to win?

Clin. That's an absurd question. Who could give you an informed answer to that before he had listened to them, and heard each of the competitors for himself?

Ath. All right then: would you like me to give you the answer to this absurd question?

Clin. Go ahead.

Ath. Well, if little children do the judging, they will give the prize to the one who puts on a puppet show, won't they?

Clin. [d] Inevitably.

Ath. And if it is older children who do it, they will choose the one who presents a comedy. Educated women will choose a tragedy, as will adolescents and most of the mass of the people.

Clin. That's very likely.

Ath. But we old men would listen with most pleasure to a *rhapsōdos* giving a good performance of the *Iliad* or the *Odyssey*, or of one of Hesiod's works, and would say that he had won by a long way. So who would correctly be judged the winner? That's the next question, isn't it?

Clin. Yes.

Ath. [e] It's obvious that you and I will inevitably say that victory would correctly be given to those adjudged the winners by people of our own age. For it seems to us that our own character is far the best of those now to be found in all cities anywhere.

Clin. Certainly.

Ath. Even I agree with the majority to the extent of saying that music should be judged by the criterion of pleasure, but not just anyone's pleasure. I would say that the best music is probably that which delights the best people, those who are fully educated, and especially [659a] that which delights the one man who is outstanding in excellence and education. That is why we say that judges of these matters need to be good men, in that they need to possess moral wisdom of all kinds, but courage especially. A true judge should not take instruction from the audience and his own lack of education; nor should he knowingly perjure himself, under the influence of cowardice or timidity, and give his judgement insincerely, through the very mouth with which [b] he called upon the gods when he was setting out as an adjudicator. For the judge takes his seat, or properly should, as a teacher, not a pupil of the spectators, and as one who will stand up against those who offer the spectators pleasure in an unfitting or incorrect way. For under the ancient Hellenic laws it was not permitted to follow what is the present custom in Sicily and Italy, by which responsibility is given to the mass of spectators, and the winner is decided by show of hands: this practice has corrupted the composers themselves, [c] since by composing for the depraved pleasure of the judges they have made the spectators their own teachers, and it has corrupted the pleasures of the audience too. For they ought always to be listening to things that are better than their own characters, and so improve their standard of pleasure, whereas exactly the opposite happens to them as a result of what they do now. What then is the significance of everything that our discussion has covered? Is it perhaps this, do you think?

Clin. What?

Ath. It seems to me that this is the third or fourth time that the argument [d] has come round to the same place, to the thesis that education consists in drawing and leading children towards what the law says is correct, and is agreed to be correct in fact by the best and oldest, as a result of their experience. So in order that the child's soul should not become habituated to enjoying and disliking things in defiance of the law and those who obey the law, but should follow it, enjoying and disliking the same things as an old man does, [e] for these purposes there exist what we call 'songs'. These are really incantations[67] that work on their souls, seriously aimed at what we call 'concord' (*symphōnia*): but because the souls of the young cannot bear seriousness, they are called 'games' and 'songs', and practised as such, just as those whose business it is try to give to the sick, and to those who are physically weak, [660a]

---

[67] *Epōidai*, used especially of incantations sung over the sick, e.g. *Od.* XIX.457, Pindar, *Pyth.* 4.217, Plato, *Rep.* 426b. Cf. 119 Eurip. *I.A.* 1212 with n. 185.

wholesome nutriment in pleasant foods and drinks, and that consisting of unwholesome things in unpleasant ones, so that they may be correctly habituated to welcome the one and detest the other. In the same way the lawgiver who acts correctly will persuade the poet by fine words and flattery, and will compel him if he fails to persuade, to compose correctly in his rhythms the postures of men who are moderate and brave and in all respects good, and to compose their melodies in his *harmoniai*.

Clin. [b] Good heavens, my friend! Do you suppose this is what they do in other cities? So far as my experience goes, I know of nowhere that the things you mention are done, except in my own country [Crete] and in Sparta. Novelties are constantly being introduced in dancing and in all the rest of music, and these changes are not inspired by laws, but by unrestrained pleasures of one kind and another; and these pleasures are far from remaining the same and keeping their tendency constant, like [c] the things in Egypt you were describing, but never stay the same.

Ath. Well said, Clinias. But if you thought I was saying that the practices you mention are going on now, I expect I gave this mistaken impression by not saying clearly what was in my mind. Rather, I was saying what I wished to be the case in the field of music, but perhaps I expressed myself in such a way that you thought I was saying the other thing. Denouncing things that cannot be cured and are far gone in error is by no means enjoyable, but sometimes it has to be done.

> Given that music is to be used to inculcate salutary beliefs and attitudes in the young, and to reinforce them in the citizens generally, the discussion passes to the practical arrangements needed to ensure that this is done.

154   *Laws 664b–671a*

Ath. The next subject is one I must speak of myself. I say that all the choruses, of which there are three, must sing incantations over the souls of the children, while they are still young and tender, enunciating all the good things that we have gone through previously or may go through later; and let their overall gist be this: by saying that it is the gods' assertion that the most pleasant life is identical with that which is best, [664c] we shall simultaneously be saying what is most true and persuading those who have to be persuaded more readily than we could by speaking in any other way.

Clin. We must agree with what you say.

Ath. To begin with, then, it will be correct for the chorus of the Muses, which is composed of children, to enter first upon these themes, and to sing them with all its energy before the whole city; and secondly the chorus of those up to thirty years old will call Apollo Paian to witness that what is said is true, and will pray him to come to the young people [d] with grace and persuasion. Thirdly, those between the ages of thirty and sixty must also sing. Those who have passed this age, and who can no longer sustain a song, are left to be story-tellers, speaking with inspired voice about the same modes of behaviour.

Clin. Who exactly are the members of this third chorus that you speak of, stranger? We do not understand very clearly what you meant to say about them.

Ath. But most of our previous remarks were designed to introduce them.

Clin. [e] We still have not understood. Please try to put it more clearly.

Ath. We said, if you recall, at the beginning of our discussion, that the nature of all young things is fiery, and is therefore incapable of keeping still with either its body or its voice, but is continually calling out and leaping about in a disorderly way; and that while none of the other animals attains a perception of order in these two things, the nature of man alone does possess this. The name for [665a] order in movement is rhythm, and order of the voice, where high and low are mixed together at once, is given the name *harmonia*, while the combination of the two is called *choreia*. And we said that the gods, in pity for us, have given us Apollo and the Muses as companions in the chorus and chorus-leaders; and we mentioned a third as well, if you recall, Dionysus [**153** 653d ff].

Clin. How could we fail to recall?

Ath. Well, the chorus of Apollo and that of the Muses have been described, [b] so that the third and last chorus to be spoken of must be that of Dionysus.

Clin. What? You must explain. At first hearing a chorus of Dionysus composed of old men sounds exceedingly odd, if you really mean that men over thirty, even fifty and up to sixty, will sing and dance to him.[68]

Ath. What you say is quite true. Some argument is needed here, I think, to show that it would be reasonable for such a thing to happen.

Clin. Yes.

Ath. Are we agreed about the things we said before?

Clin. [c] Which ones?

Ath. That every adult and child, free and slave, female and male, and the city as a whole, must sing incantations to itself of the sorts we have described, without ceasing; and that these should be continually altered, providing variety of every kind, so that the singers have an insatiable appetite for the hymns, and enjoy them.[69]

---

[68] *Choreuein.* Clinias' surprise, and the elaborate proposals that follow, suggest that the music usually associated with Dionysus was still at this date orgiastic and unrestrained. Since the music of Dionysus goes together with the Phrygian *harmonia*, this militates against the suggestion that Plato's acceptance of this *harmonia* in the *Republic* (**149** 399b–c with Appendix A) reflected a change in historical practice towards a more stately and dignified form of song and dance. It seems rather that Plato saw in Dionysiac music a powerful force that could usefully be harnessed, if it could once be tamed.

[69] The recommendation of 'variety' is new: it is, of course, such variety as can be accommodated within the fixed norms.

Clin. We must certainly agree that these things should be done as you suggest.

Ath.[d] Then what place do we give to the best group of our citizens, the most trustworthy of those in the city by virtue of both age and wisdom, so that by singing the best things they may produce the greatest good? Or shall we be so thoughtless as to pass them by, those who have the highest capacity for the best and most beneficial songs?

Clin. To judge by what you are saying now, we cannot possibly pass them by.

Ath. Then how can the thing be fittingly done? Like this, do you think?

Clin. How?

Ath. As he becomes older, everyone loses the confidence to sing songs, [e] and enjoys it less; and when the necessity arises, he is the more diffident the older and more respectable he becomes. Isn't that so?

Clin. Yes.

Ath. Then standing up and singing in the theatre in front of people of every kind will make him even more bashful. And if such people were forced to train their voices and diet themselves thin, like choruses competing for a prize, they would find their singing altogether disagreeable and shaming, and would do it quite without enthusiasm.

Clin. [666a] Inevitably.

Ath. So how shall we encourage them to be enthusiastic about singing? Shall we legislate, first, that children up to the age of eighteen must not taste wine at all, teaching that it is wrong to add fire to fire in either the body or the soul, before they begin to set about their work, and guarding against the wild propensities of the young? Next we shall say that up to the age of thirty they may take wine in moderation, but that a young man [b] must completely avoid drunkenness and heavy drinking. When he reaches the age of forty and joins in the festivities of the communal meals, he may invoke all the gods, and may call upon Dionysus in particular to come to the older men's ceremonial and recreation, for which he gave people wine as a medicine that fights against the crustiness of old age, so that we may renew our youth, and the character of the soul, through forget-fulness of its troubles, may lose its hardness and become [c] softer and more malleable, like iron placed in the fire. Isn't it true that everyone whose disposition has been changed in this way will be more enthusias-tic and less diffident about singing songs or 'incantations', as we have often called them — not before a large audience, or one composed of people of a different sort, but before one of a moderate size, whose members are people of his own kind?

Clin. Very much so.

Ath. Then this procedure for inducing them to join in our singing [d] would not be altogether uncouth.

Clin. By no means.

Ath. What sort of music will the men sing? Presumably it must be of a kind that is appropriate to them?

Clin. Obviously.

Ath. Then what music would be appropriate to godlike men? The kind characteristic of choruses?

Clin. Well, stranger, neither we nor they could manage any kind of song except the one we have learned and become familiar with in choruses.[70]

Ath. That is not surprising, since the truth is that you have had no experience [e] of the best kind of song. For your constitution is that of an army rather than that of townsmen, and you keep your young men like a herd of colts all mustered together to crop grass in a pasture. None of you takes his own colt, and drags him protesting and complaining away from his fellows, and puts him privately under the charge of a horse-trainer, and educates him with stroking and soothing, giving him everything appropriate to an upbringing that will make him not only a good soldier, but a man [667a] who can organise a city and its townships, a man who, as we said at the beginning, is more of a warrior than the warriors of Tyrtaeus,[71] in that he values courage, both in individuals and in the city as a whole, as the fourth, not the first element in virtue.

Clin. You are belittling our lawgivers again in a sort of way, stranger.

Ath. If I am, it isn't intentional, my friend. But if you are willing, we must go where the argument carries us. If we have a music that is better than that of the choruses and [b] that of the public theatres, let us try to provide it for those who we said are ashamed of the latter, but who are eager to join in the kind that is best.

Clin. By all means.

Ath. First of all, then, mustn't it be true of everything that is accompanied by any kind of delightfulness that its most important aspect is either this delightfulness itself, or some sort of correctness, or, thirdly, its usefulness? For instance, food and drink and nourishment in general carry with them, I would say, the sort of delightfulness that we would call pleasure: [c] but their correctness and usefulness, what we regularly call the wholesomeness of the things that are offered us, this, I suggest, is really the correctest aspect of them.[72]

Clin. Certainly.

Ath. Learning, too, carries with it the sort of delightfulness that is pleasure, but what produces its correctness and usefulness, its goodness and excellence, is truth.

Clin. Yes.

Ath. What about the techniques of representation that produce likenesses? [d] Isn't it true that if they fulfil this objective,[73] the pleasure generated in

---

[70] Cf. **169** ps.-Ar. *Probs.* XIX.15.
[71] Tyrtaeus was the great poet of Spartan militarism (seventh century), possibly Athenian by birth, who wrote marching songs and elegiacs that were sung by the troops before battle. He is mentioned in the *Laws* at 629a: cf. e.g. Paus. IV.15.6, **194** Ath. 630e.
[72] There seems to be a confusion of expression here: I take Plato to mean that their correctness and usefulness are the most 'important' aspect of them (667b).
[73] I.e., that of accurately representing the original intended.

association with them, if there is any, should most properly be called delightfulness?

Clin. Yes.

Ath. But correctness in things of this kind, to put it quite generally, would be produced by equality of quantity and quality, rather than by pleasure.[74]

Clin. True.

Ath. Then the only thing that could be correctly judged by the criterion of pleasure is that which produces no usefulness or truth or likeness, [e] nor indeed any harm, but is created only for the sake of that which follows along with the others, delightfulness, which would best be given the name 'pleasure' when none of the others accompanies it.

Clin. You mean just the harmless kind of pleasure.

Ath. Yes; and I say that when this pleasure does no harm or good worth mentioning seriously, it is also play.

Clin. Quite true.

Ath. Then shouldn't we say, on the basis of this discussion, that the last criterion by which any imitation should be judged is pleasure and false opinion, and neither should any equality be so judged? [668a] For it is not because of someone's opinion, or because someone finds no pleasure in it, that an equal thing is equal or a proportionate one proportionate: it is because of what is true, first and foremost, and not at all because of anything else.

Clin. Absolutely.

Ath. Now don't we say that all music is representational and imitative?

Clin. Yes.

Ath. Then when someone says that music should be judged by the criterion of pleasure, what he says must be totally rejected, and music that gives pleasure, wherever it is to be found, is not to be pursued [b] as something of importance: such importance belongs only to the kind that bears a likeness to an imitation of what is good.[75]

Clin. Quite true.

Ath. Then those who are looking for the best kind of singing and music must look not for the kind that is pleasant but that which is correct: and as we have said, an imitation is correct if it is made like the object imitated, both in quantity and in quality.

Clin. Certainly.

---

74   That is, a thing is not to be accounted a good representation just on the grounds that it is pleasing to look at or hear, but only if its dimensions and qualities reflect those of the original. On the mathematical imprecision of musical representation see *Philebus* 55e–56a.

75   This probably means: suppose that *x* is a representation of what is good: then if a given piece of music is in that respect 'like' *x*, it is worth taking seriously. Alternatively it could indicate a three-tiered hierarchy, like the hierarchy of original and 'imitations' in *Rep.* 596 ff, involving an original that is good (in the *Republic*'s terms

Ath. Now this is a claim about music to which everyone would agree – that all its compositions consist of imitation [c] and representation.[76] Wouldn't everyone agree to that, composers, listeners and performers alike?

Clin. Emphatically.

Ath. Now I suppose that the man who is to make no mistakes about compositions must understand the nature of each one of their details. For if he does not understand its essence, what its intention is and of what it is really a reprsentation, he can hardly decide whether its intention is correctly or incorrectly fulfilled.

Clin. Hardly – no doubt about that.

Ath. [d] Would a person who does not understand what is correct ever be able to distinguish what is good and what is bad? I am not putting this entirely clearly: perhaps it would be more clearly expressed like this.

Clin. How?

Ath. Among things perceived by sight we obviously have thousands of things made as likenesses.

Clin. Yes.

Ath. Suppose, then, that someone didn't know what each of the bodies imitated in this manner is. Could he ever know which of the imitations was made correctly? I mean, for instance, whether it has the same number of elements as the body and [e] the proper arrangement of each group of parts, with the right kinds of part related in the appropriate order, and the colours and shapes as well, or is made in such a way that all these things are in confusion. Do you suppose that anyone could decide on these points if he had no idea what the creature represented was?

Clin. How could he?

Ath. Suppose next that we know that the thing painted or sculpted is a man, and that the artist's skill has given it all the parts, [669a] colours and shapes that belong to it. Must it follow that if someone knows this, he also knows at once whether it is beautiful [*kalon*: see n. 59], or in what respect it falls short of beauty?

Clin. If that were so, pretty well all of us would know which pictures[77] are beautiful.

Ath. Quite right. Isn't it the case, then, that in respect of each individual representation, whether in painting or music or any other field,

a 'form' or ideal), an imitation of it (e.g. some real man's character and actions), and thirdly a likeness of this imitation (the musical composition). Though this conception is certainly to be found in the *Republic*, the elaborate metaphysics lying behind it are not even hinted at in the present passage. Cf. also 669e.

76 It is not clear that this thesis was as universal as Plato suggests, even in intellectual circles: cf. the qualifications indicated in 169 and 185 ps.-Ar. *Probs.* XIX.15, 48.

77 *Zōia*, meaning originally 'animals', 'living things', but also 'pictures'. The latter seems indicated here.

anyone who is to judge intelligently must have the following three qualifications? Mustn't he know, first, what the original is, [b] secondly, whether the particular representation is made correctly, and thirdly, whether it is made well?[78]

Clin. So it would seem.

Ath. Then let us not avoid saying what it is that is so difficult about music; for since it is more highly esteemed[79] than other representations, it requires the most cautious treatment of them all. Anyone who made a mistake about it would be most seriously damaged, [c] by favourably embracing bad dispositions, and his error would be very difficult to detect, because human composers are much poorer composers than are the Muses themselves. For the Muses would never make so gross an error as to compose words suitable for men, and then give the melody a colouring[80] proper to women, to put together melody and postures of free men, and then fit to them rhythms proper to slaves and servile persons, or to start with rhythms and postures expressive of freedom, and to give them a melody or words of opposite character to the rhythms; nor would they ever put together in the same piece the sounds of wild beasts [d] and men and instruments, and noises of all sorts, as though in imitation of a single object. But human composers, weaving and jumbling all such things nonsensically together, would be laughed at by everyone who, as Orpheus puts it, 'has attained the full bloom of joyfulness'. For they can see all these things jumbled together: and further, the composers tear rhythm and posture away from melody, putting bare words into metres, [e] setting melody and rhythm without words, and using the *kithara* and the *aulos* without the voice,[81] a practice in which it is extremely difficult – since rhythm and *harmonia* occur with no words – to understand what is intended, and what worthwhile representation it is like.[82] It is essential that we accept the principle that all such practices are utterly inartistic, if they are so enamoured of speed and precision and animal noises that they use the music of the *aulos* and the *kithara* [670a] for purposes other than the accompaniment of dance and song: the use of either by itself is characteristic of uncultured and vulgar showmanship.[83]

So much for that: however, we are not considering how those who are over thirty, or have passed fifty, ought not to use the Muses, but how they ought. It seems to me that our discussion of these matters

---

78   The MSS add 'in its words, melodies and rhythms', and the phrase is retained in the O.C.T.: but it is probably an interpolation.

79   *Hymneitai*, 'is celebrated in song', but here wholly metaphorical: cf. 153 653d.

80   *Chrōma*, possibly here in the sense related to tuning: see n. 61, and cf. 157 802e.

81   *Psilēi*, lit. 'bare', regularly used of playing an instrumental solo: cf. e.g. 196 Ath. 637f.

82   On the sense cf. 668b with n. 75. Contrast the claims made at 177 ps.-Ar. *Probs.* XIX.27.

83   Plato perhaps has in mind 'showmanship' (*thaumatourgia*) of the sort exemplified in Xenophon's *Symposium*.

already indicates one conclusion, [b] that those of the fifty-year-olds who are fitted for singing ought to have a better training than the one offered by choral music. It is essential for them to have both acute perception and understanding84 of rhythms and *harmoniai*. How else could anyone understand correctness of melodies, the correctness of the Dorian *harmonia*, for instance – what it is suited for and what it is not – and of the rhythm which the composer has attached to it, correctly or incorrectly?85

Clin. In no other way, plainly.

Ath. At any rate it is ridiculous for the mass of the people to suppose that they have an adequate understanding of what is harmonically and rhythmically good86 and what is not – those of them who have been drilled in singing to an accompaniment87 and stepping in rhythm, [c] but do not grasp the fact that they do these things without understanding any of them. But every melody whose constituents are appropriate is correct, and any whose constituents are inappropriate is faulty.

Clin. Inevitably.

Ath. What then of the man who does not even know what its constituents are? Can he know whether any melody is correct, the issue we have been talking about?

Clin. What possible techniques could he use?

Ath. It appears, then, that we are now discovering once again that our singers, whom we are calling on and [d] compelling, in a sort of way, to sing of their own free will, must be educated up to the point where they can follow every element in the movements of the rhythms and the notes of the melodies. The object is to enable them, when they survey *harmoniai* and rhythms, to select things that are appropriate, and suitable for people of their age and character to sing, and so to sing them; and to enable them, through their singing, to have enjoyment of harmless pleasures then and there, and also to become [e] leaders of the younger men in appropriately embracing high standards of behaviour. If they were educated up to this level, they would have had a more thoroughly detailed training than that of the mass of the people, or indeed than that of the composers themselves. For though a composer must understand *harmonia* and rhythm, the third subject, whether a given representation is good or not, is one of which he need have no knowledge.88 But our singers must understand all these, so that

---

84 Cf. **151** *Rep.* 411d with n. 48.
85 Some editors have excluded the lines from 'the correctness of the Dorian' to the end of the sentence: but they are probably to be retained.
86 *Euharmostos* and *eurhythmos*: cf. **149** *Rep.* 400d with n. 40.
87 Some editors emend *auton* to *aulōi*, giving the sense 'those who have been drilled in singing to the *aulos*'.
88 Cf. **157** 801c, 802b–c, Aristox. *El. Harm.* 31.18 ff. Plato may mean to hint not only

they can pick out what is best and what is second-best, or else [671a] there will never be a singer of incantations who is capable of attracting the young to virtue.

> The Athenian has been describing the self-discipline and the respect for law and for their betters which characterised the citizens of Athens up to the time of the Persian wars. The libertarian excesses, as he sees them, of the subsequent democracy are quite a different matter: and he now proceeds to trace their origins, which he finds not in changes to do with political organisation directly, but in music. His respondent here is the Spartan Megillus.

155   *Laws* 700a–701b

Ath. Under the ancient laws, my friends, our common people were not masters of anything, but were in a sort of way voluntary slaves to the laws.

Megillus. What laws do you mean?

Ath. Those, first of all, to do with the music they had then, if we are to describe the growth of the excessively liberated life from its beginning. In those days our music was divided into [700b] various types and forms. One type of song consisted of prayers to the gods, the name given to these being 'hymns'. There was another type, the opposite of the first, which one might best call 'lamentations': another consisted of paeans, and there was another, invented, I think, by Dionysus, known as the 'dithyramb'. To another class of song they assigned the name '*nomoi*' itself,[89] adding the title 'kitharodic'. With these types and various others properly distinguished, it was not permitted to use one type of melody [c] for the purposes of another. The authority responsible for knowing them, for judging them, once known, and for penalising anyone who disobeyed, was not the whistling (*syrinx*) or the uneducated (*amousoi*) shouts of the mob, as it is now, or clappings that signal applause: instead, it was the rule for those in charge of education themselves to listen in silence to the end, while for the children and their attendants, and for the mass of the people generally, there was the discipline of the stick to keep order. [d] While these matters were organised like this, then, the mass of the citizens were content to be governed, and not to have the effrontery to adjudicate by their hubbub. But later, as time went on, there appeared as instigators of unmusical law-breaking composers who, though by nature skilled at composition, were ignorant of what is right and lawful in music. In a Bacchic frenzy, and enthralled beyond what is right by pleasure, they mixed

---

that such knowledge is unnecessary for composing music and poetry, but that poets and musicians are quite unlikely to have it: see the excerpt from *Ion* given above (**148**).

[89]   *Nomos*, outside a musical context, means 'law': cf. **157** 799e.

lamentations with hymns and paeans with dithyrambs, imitated *aulos* songs with their *kithara* songs, and put everything together with everything else, [e] thus unintentionally, through their stupidity, giving false witness against music, alleging that music possesses no standard of correctness, but is most correctly judged by the pleasure of the person who enjoys it, whether he is a better man or a worse. By creating compositions of these kinds and by choosing corresponding words, they inspired the masses with lawlessness towards music, and the effrontery to suppose that they were capable of judging it. As a result the audiences, which had been silent, [701a] became noisy, as if they understood what is good in music and what is not, and a musical aristocracy was displaced by a degenerate theatocracy.[90] Now no doubt it would have been no very terrible thing if a democracy of free men had arisen just in the field of music: but in fact, from a starting-point in music, everyone came to believe in their own wisdom about everything, and to reject the law, and liberty followed immediately.[91] Believing themselves knowledgeable, people became fearless, and fearlessness bred shamelessness. When boldness prevents one fearing [b] the opinion of a better man, that amounts to depraved shamelessness: it is caused by a liberty that is too self-confidently grasped.

> Returning to the subject of education, the Athenian has dealt with gymnastics, and now proposes to discuss once again the branch that 'relates to Apollo and the Muses'. He begins (797a) by emphasising the crucial importance of organising and prescribing a fixed set of the 'correct' games for children, from their earliest years: innovation, even here, is to be outlawed. Changes of any kind are perilous, and initiation in novel games creates children who are different from their fathers, and who will therefore seek new customs and standards. In particular, any changes that might have an effect on people's conceptions of human goodness and badness are most stringently to be avoided.

156   *Laws* 798d–799b

Ath. Well then, do we still have confidence in what we said before, when we said that everything to do with rhythms and with music as a whole consists in imitations of the behaviour of better and worse men? [See **154** 668b ff.] [798e] Or what do we think?

Clin. Our opinion has not changed, at any rate.

Ath. Do we say, then, that every possible technique should be used to prevent the children from wanting to try out other kinds of imitation in their

---

[90] I.e., rule by the spectators.

[91] 'Liberty' (*eleutheria*), though a high ideal of fifth-century democrats, was to Plato a deeply suspect notion. That everyone should have the freedom to judge and choose for himself was, in his view, nonsense, given that some people have much greater knowledge and understanding than others. Cf. e.g. *Rep.* 557 ff.

dances and songs, and to prevent anyone from tempting them with all sorts of pleasure?

Clin. You are quite right.

Ath. [799a] Then does any of us have a better technique for the purpose than that of the Egyptians? [See 153 656d ff.]

Clin. Which one do you mean?

Ath. That of dedicating all dancing and all melodies to religion. First, they[92] should determine the festivals, putting together for the year a list of which festivals should be held at which times, in honour of which individual gods, which children of the gods, and which demi-gods. Next, they should determine which song ought to be sung at each of the sacrifices to the gods, and what sort of dancing should adorn the various sacrifices. [b] These ordinances should first be made by certain persons; and then all the people should join in common sacrifice to dedicate them to the Fates and to all the other gods, consecrating each of the songs, with a libation, to the appropriate gods and other beings. If anyone brings forward other hymns or dances beyond these for any of the gods, the priests and priestesses, with the guardians of the laws, will be acting with both religious and legal propriety in excluding him; and the man who is excluded, if he does not accept his exclusion voluntarily, will be liable for the whole of his life to prosecution for impiety by anyone who wishes.

Clin. And rightly so.

157   *Laws* 799e–802e

Ath. We are saying, then, that the strange fact should be accepted that our songs have become *nomoi* ['laws'] for us, just as in ancient times people gave this name, so it appears, to songs sung to the *kithara*.[93] Hence they would probably [800a] not have disagreed with our present contention, which one of them perhaps dimly divined, as it were in a dream or a waking vision. At any rate, let that be our decree concerning this matter. And no one may make utterances or move in the dance in breach of the civic and sacred songs and the whole choric practice of the young, any more than he may break any other of the laws (*nomoi*). To the person who conforms no penalty is to attach, but as we said just now, the guardians of the laws [b] and the priestesses and priests are to punish anyone who disobeys. Are we to regard these points as established, for the purposes of our discussion?

Clin. Yes.

[92] I.e., those in charge of such matters in the proposed new city.
[93] We cannot be sure that this derivation of the musical sense from the political one is correct, but it was commonly held to be so in antiquity (cf. e.g. 187 ps.-Plut. 1133c and Ch. 15, Appendix A). Plato speaks as if kitharodic *nomoi* were the only kind: this is certainly not true (e.g. aulodic, 187 ps.-Plut. 1132d, auletic 1133d), but they were the first and most important, and the most commonly mentioned by ancient writers.

Ath. How then could one prescribe these things by law without laying oneself wide open to mockery? Let us investigate the following suggestion about them, that the safest procedure is as it were to cast moulds[94] of them in words; and I suggest that one such mould is something like this. Suppose that when a sacrifice is being held, and the sacred offerings have been burned, some person without official standing, a son, perhaps, or a brother, [c] were to stand beside the altars and the offerings and utter blasphemies of every descripton; would we not say that his utterances would fill his father and the rest of his family with despondency and forebodings of evil?

Clin. Certainly.

Ath. Yet in our countries this is what happens, one may just about say, in virtually all cities. For whenever an official makes a civic sacrifice, there arrives immediately not one chorus but a crowd of them: they do not stand [d] at a distance from the altars, but often close by, and they pour out every kind of blasphemy upon the sacred offerings, stretching[95] the souls of the listeners with their words, their rhythms, and their most mournful *harmoniai*: and whichever chorus causes the sacrificing city to weep most bitterly, then and there, carries off the prize of victory. Shall we not vote to reject this custom (*nomos*)? And if it is really necessary for the citizens to hear lamentations of this sort (not on holy days, but on days of ill omen), [e] then would it not be better for there to come some hired choruses of singers from abroad, just as it is hired mourners with their Carian music[96] who escort the bodies of the dead? That is the sort of procedure that would be appropriate for songs of this kind too; and the dress appropriate for funeral songs[97] would not be wreaths and gilded adornments, but just the opposite – to express the point in such a way that I may be done with it as quickly as possible. But I want to ask us just this question once again, whether we are content to lay this down as the first of the moulds in which our songs must be cast.

Clin. What is it?

Ath. That of well-omened utterance: must not the kind of song that we have [801a] be wholly well-omened in all respects? Or shall I ask no further questions, but lay it down that this is so?

Clin. Lay it down by all means: this law (*nomos*) is carried by a unanimous vote.

---

[94] *Ekmageia*, moulds in which an impression is made, and which may then be used to cast reproductions of the original.

[95] *Synteinontes*, a metaphor from increasing the tension on the string of an instrument. Cf. **151** *Rep.* 410d–e with n. 45.

[96] For the association of mourning rites with Eastern people see **37, 38, 41**. On Caria see **140** Aristoph. *Frogs* 1302 with n. 63.

[97] *Epikēdeioi ōdai*. According to Plut. *Quaest. Conv.* 657a there was a special type of *aulos*, the *epikēdeios aulos* associated with these funeral lamentations. Strictly, the *epikēdeion* was the song sung while the body was lying exposed to view.

Ath. What, then, after well-omened utterance, is to be the second law of music? Is it not that there should be prayers to the gods to whom we sacrifice on each and every occasion?

Clin. Certainly.

Ath. And the third law, I think, will be that the poets, knowing that prayers are requests made to the gods, must take thought most carefully [b] to avoid unintentionally asking for evil as though it were good; for I take it that if such a prayer were made, it would be a grotesque error.

Clin. Of course.

Ath. Were we not convinced earlier by the statement that wealth should not be enshrined in our city either in silver or in gold?

Clin. Yes indeed.

Ath. What then are we to say that this statement serves to exemplify? Isn't it the fact that poets as a class are not entirely [c] competent to understand properly what is good and what is not?[98] Surely then, when a poet incorporates this error in his composition of words or song – composing prayers that are not correct – he will be making our citizens pray for the opposite of what is good, in matters of the greatest importance. Are we then also to lay this down as one of the laws and models that relate to music?

Clin. What? Tell us more clearly.

Ath. That the poet shall compose nothing beyond what is deemed lawful and right [d] and fine and good by the city, and that he may not display his compositions to any private person until they have been displayed to those who are appointed as judges in these matters, and to the guardians of the laws, and have been approved by them. We have in fact appointed judges already, those whom we chose to be lawgivers in things musical, and the overseer of education. Well then, I ask my repeated question again: is this to stand as our third law and model and mould? What do you think?

Clin. Certainly: let it stand.

Ath. [e] Next after these it would be most correct for hymns and laudations of the gods, coupled with prayers, to be sung, and after the gods, the demigods and heroes would be given the prayers and praises that are appropriate to them all.

Clin. Certainly.

Ath. Then after this, the following law may be formulated without criticism, that it should be thought right for all citizens who have completed their lives after achieving noble and difficult deeds with either body or soul, and who have been obedient to the laws, to become the object of songs of praise.

Clin. Undoubtedly.

Ath. [802a] It is not safe, certainly, to honour those who are still living with

---

[98] Cf. 154 670e with n. 88. The statement 'exemplifies' the ignorance of the poets because it is not unknown for poems to contain prayers for wealth.

laudations and hymns, before each has run the full course of his life and made a noble end. However, let us give all these honours equally to both men and women who have conspicuously achieved goodness. The right way to organise the songs and dances is this. Among the musical works of the ancients there are many fine old compositions, and similarly dances for the body to perform, and no jealousy will be aroused by our selecting from these [b] what harmonises[99] fittingly with the constitution that is being established. Those chosen to assess these works and to make the selection should not be less than fifty years old; and whichever of the ancient compositions is adjudged adequate they are to select, while whatever is deficient or wholly inappropriate they must either discard completely or study more carefully and revise. They should get both poets and musicians to assist them,[100] making use of their talents for composition, but not placing any reliance [c] on their pleasures and desires, except in the case of a few such people. Thus by working through fully the intentions of the lawgiver, they will put together in closest correspondence to the sense of these intentions dancing, singing, and choric practices in general. Every disorganised musical activity becomes a thousand times better when it accepts organisation, even if no musical sweetness is added: all such activities alike give pleasure. For when someone passes his life from childhood up to the age of steadiness and sense among temperate and ordered music, [d] then when he hears the opposite kind he detests it, and calls it unfit for free men: but if he was brought up amid the sweet music that is generally popular, he says that the opposite kind to this is frigid[101] and unpleasing. Thus, as we said just now, neither is better than the other in respect of pleasantness and unpleasantness: the difference lies in the fact that the one kind always makes those brought up in it better, the other worse.

Clin. Well said.

Ath. It will also be essential for the lawgiver to distinguish [e] in outline what are suitable songs for men and women respectively, and he must match them appropriately to *harmoniai* and rhythms. For it would be dreadful for singing to be wrong in its entire *harmonia*, or rhythm in its entire rhythm, if he assigned *harmoniai* and rhythms that were quite unsuitable for the songs.[102] Hence it is necessary to lay down at least the outlines of these by law as well. We must assign to both kinds of song the rhythms and *harmoniai* that are essentially bound to them, and must clearly expound the character of those of the female type by

---

[99] *Harmotton*: cf. **149** *Rep.* 397e.
[100] 'Poets' would normally include composers, and *mousikoi andres* would most naturally mean 'people who are educated in music', rather than composers or musical performers: cf. **149** *Rep.* 398e with n. 21. But the remainder of the sentence suggests that Plato has no musical expertise in mind except that of the composer.
[101] Cf. **135** Aristoph. *Birds* 935 with n. 26.
[102] That is, specifically, for songs to be sung only by members of one sex or the other.

reference to that in which the nature of each type is distinct. Thus it must be said that magnificence and that which tends towards manliness is of masculine type, while that which leans rather towards orderliness and moderation is to be treated as more of a female kind in both law and theory.[103] That, then, is how this is to be organised.

> Education in gymnastics and *mousikē* is to be compulsory for all children, both boys and girls (804d–e): the proposition that the girls' education should be identical with the boys' is then defended (804e–806c). Returning to the details of the curriculum, which is now said to include reading and writing, the *lyra*, and mathematical calculation (809c), the Athenian suggests that reading and writing should occupy three years from the age of ten, and the *lyra* three years from the age of thirteen (810a). He sets out proposals about what the children should read (810e–812a), and then turns his attention to instruction in playing the *lyra*.

158   *Laws* 812b–e

Ath. After the writing teacher, mustn't we next speak to the *kithara* teacher?[104]

Clin. Yes.

Ath. Now I think we should recall what we said earlier [**154** 668c–671a], when we are assigning to the *kithara* teachers what is proper in their teaching and in the whole of the education that relates to these matters.

Clin. On what subject do you mean?

Ath. We said, I believe, that our sixty-year-old singers to Dionysus must have acquired good perception in respect of rhythms [812c] and the constitution of the *harmoniai*, so that when considering a representation in song, whether it is done well or badly – a representation in which the soul comes under the influence of the emotions – each of them shall be able to pick out the likenesses of both the good kind and the bad, and while rejecting the latter, shall bring the former before the public, and sing them to enchant the souls of the young, summoning each of them to pursue the acquisition of virtue in company with them, by means of these representations.

Clin. You are quite right.

Ath. [d] For these reasons, then, both the *kithara* teacher and his pupil must, for the sake of making the notes[105] distinct, use the notes of the *lyra* in such a way as to give out its sounds in unison with the sounds of the song.[106] As for the use of different notes and ornamentation on the

---

[103]   The distinction between types of music proper for men and for women, which chimes uneasily with Plato's remarks on the identical upbringing to be given to both sexes (804–6), may well be derived from Damon: see Appendix B.

[104]   *Kitharistēs*: but the instrument of instruction is in fact the *lyra* (812d), as was usual in Greek education: cf. Fig. 8.

[105]   Lit. 'strings' (*chordai*): 'notes' in 'notes of the *lyra*' in the next clause is *phthongoi*.

[106]   Lit. 'give out the utterances in unison (*proschorda*) with the utterances'.

lyra,[107] when the strings play one set of tunes and the composer of the melody another,[108] or when people perform a combination of small intervals with wide ones[109] or of speed with slowness[110] or of high pitch with low, [e] whether in concord or in octaves,[111] and similarly when they fit all kinds of elaboration of rhythms to the notes of the *lyra*, no such things should be taught to those who must assimilate quickly, in three years, that which is beneficial in music. For the opposites[112] disrupt one another and make learning difficult, whereas the young ought to learn everything as easily as possible, since the subjects that are prescribed for them are neither small nor few. So let our educator look after these matters in that way, so far as music is concerned. As for the melodies and the words themselves, we have already discussed all the types which the chorus-trainers ought to teach [**157** 800b], and we said that when they have been consecrated to religion, each kind being fitted to its appropriate festival, they would be of good service to the cities, providing them with enjoyment and good fortune [**157** 799a–b].

Appendix A: the *harmoniai*

Harmonia, outside musical contexts, means 'fitting together', 'adapting' or 'adjusting' one thing to another. The noun and its cognates have a number of important and

[107] *Heterophōnia* and *poikilia*, both probably referring to instrumental decoration of a melody.

[108] This indicates that the 'heterophonic' accompaniment was not part of the original composition, which was constituted by the melody alone: the 'embroidery' was the invention of the performer. But this seems not to have been the invariable rule, to judge by the common criticisms of composers of the 'new music', exemplified by the diatribe of Pherecrates ap. **187** ps.-Plut. 1141d ff.

[109] *Pyknotēs* and *manotēs*, lit. 'density' and 'open texture'. The adjective *pyknos* is commonly used for a 'narrow' or 'compressed' interval, *manos* or *araios* for a wider one (e.g. Aris. Quint. 11.21–3, cf. Plato, *Rep.* 531a): in Aristoxenus *to pyknon* comes to have a special technical sense (24.11, 48.27–49.2, and passim). Plato's meaning here seems to be that the singer sings a wide interval, while the accompanist fills in the gap with a sequence of small ones.

[110] Another aspect of ornamentation and 'filling in gaps': the melody moves, as it were, in crotchets, the accompaniment in semiquavers.

[111] I take this qualifying phrase only with the preceding six words. The practices described previously do not necessarily involve accompaniment at very different pitches from those of the melody, and certainly involved relations other then those of the octave and the minor concords (the fourth and the fifth). Here the reference is, I think, to an accompaniment that does not decorate, but strictly parallels the melody either at the octave above, or at a fourth or a fifth. For these practices, and for the use of the term *antiphōnon* ('corresponding note') to indicate the octave, see **170–172** ps.-Ar. *Probs.* XIX.16, 17, 18. There the author clearly denies that parallel singing was ever done at the fourth or the fifth: it was restricted to the octave. Possibly, then, Plato's reference is only to the use of an occasional note, not a complete parallel melody, at the interval of a minor concord. But the author of the *Problems* may be talking exclusively about the relation between two lines of singing, and not about instrumental accompaniment: **170** *Probs.* XIX.16 contains a hint that instrumentalists' practice was sometimes different. For other indications about non-unison accompaniment see esp. **183** *Probs.* XIX.39, and **187** ps.-Plut. 1137b–d, which purports to refer to music of a much earlier era.

[112] I.e. those such as speed and slowness listed above.

overlapping musical uses, of which the primary one is probably that which designates the adjustment or tuning of the notes of an instrument. What is created by tuning is a 'fitting together' of notes, a structure of relations that can be used to form the basis of melodies. In Plato, *harmonia* conceived generally is the melodic counterpart to rhythm: it is the scheme of order that distinguishes the notes used in a piece of music from a mere collection of pitches. 'The name for order in movement is "rhythm", and order of voice, when high and low are mixed together, is given the name "*harmonia*"' (**154** *Laws* 665a).

Since there was not just one, but several different patterns of pitches and intervals that might legitimately form the basis of a melody, the Greek authors, including Plato in the *Republic* and elsewhere, speak of *harmoniai* in the plural, and remark on the special characters and emotions associated with each. It is these that are given the names 'Dorian', 'Phrygian', and so on in the present period, though it should be noticed that several of the same names were later taken over by the Aristoxenian system of *tonoi* (roughly 'keys'), which came to replace the *harmoniai* in most of their functions, at least in the writings of the harmonic theorists. Each *tonos* had the same pattern of intervals: they differed from one another, as modern keys do, only in respect of pitch. But it seems quite clear that the *harmoniai* of the late fifth and early fourth centuries (whatever may have been true of their ancestors, to which the poets of the sixth and early fifth centuries enigmatically refer) were distinguished from one another primarily by being constituted out of different sequences of intervals. There is quite good evidence, admittedly, from several periods, that each *harmonia* was in practice associated with a particular range of pitch, some being thought of as 'high', others as 'low' (e.g. **192** Pratinas ap. Ath. 624f, cf. Lasus, quoted immediately before, at 624e; Heraclides ap. Ath. 625d; **161** Ar. *Pol.* 1342b20 ff; **187** ps.-Plut. 1136c); and this fact no doubt helped to give them the different perceived characters to which our sources refer. But the earliest technical analyses about which we have any information pay small attention to this phenomenon, and specify the *harmoniai* almost exclusively by the different interval-structures that they exhibited. (See especially Arist. Quint. 15.10–20, 18.5–19.10, Aristox. *El. Harm.* 2.22–5, cf. Cleonides 197.4–199.3, Bacch. 303.5–27, 308.17–309.12.) It is true that the more systematic of these sources put the *harmoniai* together in a way that embodies a scheme of pitch-relations; but this, it seems clear, was not in order to represent faithfully the characters they displayed in performance, or to indicate appropriate ways of modulating from one to another (Aristox. *El. Harm.* 7.28–34, cf. 37.8–38.17). It was rather for the sake of theoretical tidiness and ease of diagrammatic representation (*El. Harm.* 7.22–5). Aristides Quintilianus even cites two ways of relating them, the first setting them at different pitches, the other combining them within a single range of pitch, and he treats the two representations as entirely equivalent (15.10–20). There are adequate grounds for believing, nevertheless, that when the theorists placed the *harmoniai* at different pitches within their overall system, the facts about the relative pitches at which they were traditionally performed were taken, on the whole, as at least a rough guide.

At a date probably not far from that of the *Republic*, theorists were engaged on the project of organising the structures of the existing *harmoniai* into the framework of a single, co-ordinated system. It is this system that most of the later sources record, and we do not know precisely how artificial it was, how carefully or how cavalierly it treated the facts of real performance. Nor do we know whether the system, in this form, was familiar to Plato. So far as the relative pitches of the *harmoniai* are concerned, if the relations embodied in the system were, as I have suggested, fairly independent of practical usage, the question will be of little importance: in so far as is remarks about them relate to pitch, Plato will undoubtedly have been thinking of the pitches of melodies in performance, not of those suggested by a theorist's diagrammatic representation of scales. But the development of a system depends also on the existence of similarities or analogies between the structures of the different *harmoniai*, and the question whether these similarities existed in practice, or were foisted on disparate traditional structures by tidy-minded theorists, is of real musical significance.

We are not completely without information on this matter. Aristides Quintilianus is unique among our sources in that he not only set out the tidy system of *harmoniai* put together by theorists in the earlier part of the fourth century, but also describes a less systematically organised set of scales which he alleges to be the *harmoniai* of Plato's *Republic*. If what he says about these were reliable, it would be of the greatest value. The issue is controversial, and cannot be fully pursued here (see especially Winnington-Ingram, *Mode in Ancient Greek Music*: Aristides' scales are discussed on pp. 22–30, and the book as a whole remains the most judicious modern assessment of questions relating to the *harmoniai*). I am inclined, however, to treat his evidence with cautious respect, on the hypothesis that it is derived fairly directly from Aristoxenus' account of the work of his own predecessors. (This is more fully argued in Barker, *Classical Quarterly* 32 no. 1, 1982.) Some necessary qualifications to this position will be introduced below, but I shall ignore them for the present.

In what follows, I have set out the substance of what Aristides says. The lists give the structures first of the allegedly Platonic *harmoniai*, and secondly of the systematised series: the latter may be found in a number of other Aristoxenian sources as well, notably Cleonides and Bacchius in the passages cited above, and it is probably referred to at Aristox. *El. Harm.* 36.30–1. I have expressed the first group in Aristides' own terms, that is, as sequences of intervals. He describes the second differently, by reference to the named note in the system from which each *harmonia* begins: for the sake of easy comparison I have converted this description into terms comparable to those used in the first. The 'systematic' description given by Aristides apparently presupposes the diatonic genus: I have expressed it in an enharmonic version because (a) the members of the 'unsystematic' group are more nearly enharmonic than they are anything else, and (b) Aristoxenus tells us (*El. Harm.* 2.7 ff) that his predecessors worked in this genus and no other.

(1) Arist. Quint. 18.5 ff (structures attributed to the *harmoniai* of Plato's *Republic*).

Lydian: q,d,t,q,q,d,q (complete octave).
Dorian: t,q,q,d,t,q,q,d (octave plus tone).
Phrygian: t,q,q,d,t,q,q,t (complete octave).
Iastian: q,q,d,$\frac{1}{2}$,t (octave less a tone).
Mixolydian: q,q,t,t,q,q,tritone (complete octave).
Syntonon Lydian: q,q,d,$\frac{1}{2}$ (octave less two tones).

(2) Arist. Quint. 15.10 ff (structures in the systematically organised series).

Mixolydian: q,q,d,q,q,d,t.
Lydian: q,d,q,q,d,t,q.
Phrygian: d,q,q,d,t,q,q.
Dorian: q,q,d,t,q,q,d.
Hypolydian: q,d,t,q,q,d,q.
Hypophrygian: d,t,q,q,d,q,q.
Hypodorian: t,q,q,d,q,q,d.

The systematic character of the second set is clear. The *harmoniai* are displayed as cyclic rearrangements of a single basic interval series covering an octave. The series may be represented, in Aristoxenian terms, as composed of two tetrachords, each of the form q,q,d, together with a tone that Aristoxenus conceives as disjoining the two tetrachords. The interval-structure of any *harmonia* can be converted into that of its successor simply by removing the interval at the bottom of its series and replacing it at the top. Thus, for instance, the Dorian series is generated by removing the ditone from the bottom of the Phrygian *harmonia* and adding a ditone at the top. The sequence of *harmoniai* is cyclic: that is, if we were to continue the process by performing the same operation on the last *harmonia*, the Hypodorian, we should have returned to the structure of the first, the Mixolydian.

Let us now adopt the assumption that this method of organisation was used, as far as possible, to co-ordinate the facts of actual performance, that the structures of the individual *harmoniai* were not invented out of thin air, and that the data of practice were modified and standardised only to the degree necessary to create a cyclic system. The question may then be asked whether the scales of Aristides' 'disorganised' collection may reasonably be construed as representing the *harmoniai* of actual practice, on which the theorists conducted their systematising operations. If the cap fits tolerably well, we shall have less reason to be sceptical about Aristides' contention that these *harmoniai* were a reality in Plato's day, and that it is to them that the *Republic* refers.

The first *harmoniai* mentioned in the *Republic* are the Mixolydian and the Syntonolydian (**149** 398e). The relation between Aristides' two versions of Mixolydian seems clear: the version of **15.11** has 'regularised' the other by combining pairs of tones into ditones in two places. (For a related controversy about the structure of Mixolydian see **187** ps.-Plut. 1136d.) The name 'Syntonolydian' does not appear in Aristides' cyclical system, nor in its equivalents in the other authorities, but since its 'Hypolydian' corresponds exactly to the 'Lydian' of 18.10, and since its 'Lydian' is placed adjacent to the Mixolydian, it is fair to conjecture that its 'Lydian' is intended as the counterpart of the 'Syntonolydian' of the other passage. And in fact this Syntonolydian corresponds moderately closely to the 'tidied up' Lydian, taken only in the upper part of its range.

Both Mixolydian and Syntonolydian are associated with high pitch: among the formal analyses this is made explicit at Bacch. 303.7. While this may reflect a fact about performing practice, in the theoretical context it means only that any given named note, specified by its position in the fixed cycle of intervals (as, for instance, *mesē* is specified as the note below the disjunctive tone), stands at a higher point in the series of notes constituting Mixolydian than it does in any other *harmonia*. If we imagine, for theoretical purposes, that an instrument tuned to various *harmoniai* successively was always tuned within the same range of pitch, then *mesē* (or any other named note) in Mixolydian would be a higher pitch than it is elsewhere. Correspondingly, a tune written in Mixolydian and using a given set of named notes would be at a higher pitch than a tune using the same named notes written in another *harmonia*. Syntonolydian may be high (or 'tense', as its name indicates) not only in this sense and in its correspondence to only the upper segment of the regularised Lydian, but also in the sense that its highest interval is 'stretched' by an extra quarter-tone beyond what the theorists' formulations would lead us to expect. (Cf. the *syntonōteros spondeiasmos* of **187** ps.-Plut. 1135a–b.)

The next pair of *harmoniai* mentioned by Plato are the Iastian and the Lydian *harmoniai* that are called 'slack' (*chalarai*, 398e). Aristides gives an Iastian at 18.18, but not at 15.10 ff (nor does the name appear in the parallel analyses of Cleonides and Bacchius). This Iastian is the least tractable of all the *harmoniai* in Aristides' putatively older list: it bears no clearly discernible relation to anything in the cyclic system. Ionian *harmoniai* are discussed by Heraclides ap. **192** Ath. 624c ff, especially 625b–c: he asserts that an older, well-disciplined style was superseded among the Ionians by a more voluptuous variety, and it is presumably the latter that Plato had in mind. The former is commonly equated with the Hypophrygian of the cyclic system, but this gives no clue to the nature of the 'slack' type. It may be conjectured that the 'slack' Iastian came to be treated as 'foreign' to an anomalous degree, and was dropped from the theorists' repertoire. The 'slack' Lydian is more straightforward: it is presumably to be identified with the 'Lydian' of 18.10, and this is the same as the 'Hypolydian' of 15.13.

Plato's language, in his reference to these 'slack' *harmoniai*, strongly suggests the existence of a network of rather similar *harmoniai* (e.g. those generically described as Lydian in the phrase 'some of the Lydian *harmoniai*'), whose interrelations and differences may have been only rather imprecisely conceived. Heraclides' remarks on the three *harmoniai* that he treats as fundamental, and particularly on the Ionian, appear to have the same implication. There were thus more or less co-ordinated 'families' of *harmoniai*, grouped together under headings such as 'Lydian', etc. Since there are 'Lydians' in both the high-pitched and the 'slack' category, the resemblances between members of such a family cannot have been directly to do with pitch, and are more likely to have been structural. (This they certainly were in the cyclic system, where, for instance, both Hypodorian and Dorian are composed of a fourth, q,q,d, and a fifth, t,q,q,d: in Dorian the fourth is below the fifth, in Hypodorian above it. The same kind of relation holds between Phrygian and Hypophrygian, Lydian and Hypolydian.) At the same time, there were groupings related to 'character' (as where Plato speaks of Mixolydian, Syntonolydian, and 'others of that kind'), in whose identification matters of pitch were probably a good deal more relevant. But the question of what counts as a distinct *harmonia* and what as a mere variant becomes an issue only in the context of a rigid theoretical formalisation, of which Plato's discussion is innocent.

Finally, at 399a, Plato introduces his favoured *harmoniai*, Dorian and Phrygian. Aristides' two versions of Dorian are identical, except for the extra tone at the bottom of the form given at 18.13. The Phrygian of 18.16 is also obviously close to a regular type of structure: it can be converted into its 'cyclic' equivalent by shifting the highest tone an octave down, and amalgamating the two adjacent tones that result. Dorian is generally taken to be the primary Greek *harmonia*, the norm to which all others must be related, not only in the context of moral theory but in abstract harmonics too. All the analyses of the classical theorists, except on the rare occasions when they say otherwise, apply to a Dorian structure. It was the centrality of this form that allowed Aristoxenus to replace, for theoretical purposes, the system of *harmoniai* with a system of *tonoi* ('keys'), every one of which displayed the Dorian pattern of intervals.

It has proved possible, in all cases but one, to see how Aristides' 'ancient scales' might have been adapted to the formal requirements of the systematisers. This correspondence gives some support to the conjecture that Aristides' material was derived from a source not too far from Plato in date, perhaps a harmonic theorist whose work was discussed in Aristoxenus' book *On the Opinions of the Harmonikoi* (*El. Harm.* 2.26–30, 6.14–19). In that case, there is some reason to believe that they represent structures that are at least moderately close to what Plato had in mind. But even in this tentative form, the conclusion needs qualification. It should not be construed as asserting that Plato consciously conceived the *harmoniai* in terms of analyses of this sort: it is quite unlikely that he did. He had a profound contempt for harmonic scientists of the 'empiricist' school involved (*Rep.* 531a–b); and in so far as his conceptions here were guided by theoretical considerations of any kind, they were probably not even those of the Pythagoreans, to whom he later gives some carefully qualified approval (*Rep.* 531b–c), but those of Damon. It is arguable that a Damonian analysis would have been based on principles of a wholly different sort (see Appendix B).

On the 'moral' dimension of the *harmoniai* Plato may best be left to speak for himself. But a few brief remarks are in order. His account of the character of the *harmoniai* he rejects seems to have been largely uncontroversial, though of course his rejection of them, and his reasons for such rejection, were very far from it. As to those he accepts, the association of Dorian with manliness and courage is routine among Greek writings on the subject. (See e.g. Plato, *Laches* 188d, *Ep.* VII.336c, Heraclides ap. **192** Ath. 624d, **187** ps.-Plut. 1136d–1137a, cf. Ar. *Pol.* 1290a19 ff, **161** 1340b4, 1342a29 ff.)

There is a notorious difficulty, however, concerning Plato's characterisation of the Phrygian. Plato wishes to link it with moderation and self-restraint, and the voluntary behaviour of good men and women (perhaps particularly women, **157** *Laws* 802e) in everyday life. But the majority of our other sources make it the *harmonia* of frenzied inspiration, associating it especially with the cults of Dionysus and Cybele, and the music of the *aulos*. Aristotle, for instance, criticises this part of the *Republic* on precisely those grounds (**161** *Pol.* 1342a32 ff, cf. 1340b4–5): see also e.g. **63–5** Eurip. *Bacch.* 55–63, 120–34, 151–67, Telestes ap. **192** Ath. 626a. Two kinds of conjecture have been made to explain Plato's position. According to the first, he has deliberately ignored the facts of current practice, preferring to base his view on the close similarity in structure (and perhaps pitch) between the Phrygian *harmonia* and the Dorian: rationally considered, the two ought to have close links, even if the perversions of modern performance disguise the fact. According to the second, by Plato's time the cult of Dionysus, where the Phrygian *harmonia* was most at home, no longer involved ecstatic and frenzied rites, at least in Athens: it had become dignified and solemn. The only fault that Plato would have found in its music was its use of the *aulos*, and this is banned in the succeeding argument. (For a summary of these rival explanations and a survey of the evidence, see Anderson, *Ethos and Education* 107–9.) While the second suggestion has a good deal of historical backing, it would be odd, if the matter were so simple, that Aristotle and the other ancient commentators failed so completely to understand it; and I think it likely that the scheme of justification that Plato had in mind was of a more abstract and theoretical order. See also **154** *Laws* 665b with n. 68.

The main passages on the *harmoniai* in the remainder of this volume are: **161** Ar. *Pol.* 1341b ff, **185** ps.-Ar. *Probs.* XIX.48, **187** ps.-Plut. 1136c–1137a (cf. also 1135b with n. 89, 1137e with n. 130, 1140f with n. 177, 1141b with n. 187, 1143b–c), **192** Ath. 624c–626a.

Appendix B: Damon

The impressive but shadowy figure of Damon stands behind much of Plato's theorising about the moral effects of music. If his works had survived they would be among our most valuable sources, but we are in fact left with the slightest of fragments. Damon belongs to the later fifth century: he is to be included among the Sophists, and was an associate of Pericles. Plato mentions him with respect on a number of occasions, and there is probably nothing ironical about the *Republic*'s suggestion that he is the expert to be consulted on the details of its musical proposals.

rom Plato, with a cautious admixture of later sources, we can put together a rough
utline of some of his views. First, and fundamentally, music has moral power and
ignificance: change in musical forms breeds changes in social and political struc-
ures. (This at least is well attested: apart from Plato, especially **152** *Rep.* 424c, see
*hilodemus 1.13, Kemke pp. 7 and 55, iv.33.37–34.5, Kemke pp. 104–5, and **193**
Ath. 628c. Plato depicts the idea historically at **155** *Laws* 700a–701b.) Secondly, this
ower is connected with the fact that different kinds of music, categorised according
o their particular *harmoniai* and their particular varieties of rhythm, are capable of
epresenting different qualities of character, virtues and vices. (This is mainly an
nference from Plato's treatment: for an earlier version, possibly connected with
)amon, see **138** Aristoph. *Thesm.* 146 ff, and see also Arist. Quint. 80.25–9.)
Thirdly, music is the product of a special kind of movement in the soul (**193** Ath.
28c with n. 135): this makes the close relation between character and musical style
nore comprehensible, since the nature of a particular soul determines that of the
novements it will create, and those with which it will feel an affinity when they are
eard. Finally, *harmoniai* and rhythms may be analysed in such a way as to reveal not
)nly their own structures, but also the elements in them on which their affinities with
lifferent types of character depend. (This is an inference from **149** *Rep.* 400a–c.)

The nature of the relation involved at this point in Damonian theory is, however,
|uite obscure. There is no evidence to connect Damon with quantitative harmonic
nalyses of a Pythagorean or any other kind, and hence no grounds for supposing that
e associated types of character with *harmoniai* specified as quantitatively analysed
tructures. Very probably, like Aristides Quintilianus long after him (whose theory
)f musical ethics has often been thought of as derived from Damon's), he linked
noral character not with measured sizes of interval or numerical ratios between notes,
)ut with supposed qualitative distinctions between the notes themselves. Aristides
)ffers an account of the characters of notes based on the male–female dichotomy,
generating notes of four kinds, each kind of note being exemplified in each
tetrachord. (See 79.3 ff, especially 15–25.) *Harmoniai* of different character were to
)e produced by shifting the positions of intermediate notes in the tetrachord towards
the 'male' or the 'female' end, or by omitting some entirely. Aristides asserts directly
that among the '*harmoniai* handed down by Damon' there are some in which 'female'
movable notes predominate, others in which 'male' ones do, and some in which one
type or the other is left out (80.29–81.2). Cf. also **131** Aristoph. *Clouds* 659 with n.
10, **157** Plato, *Laws* 802e.

If Damon's theory is to be construed along these lines, it gives us yet another
possible way of understanding the reference to the four 'kinds' that form the basis of
the *harmoniai* (**149** 400a). It is to be expected that the implied analysis is Damonian,
and in this case it may, as I have suggested, be qualitative rather than quantitative.
Aristides' account gives notes of four qualities (male, female, and two 'combined'
types, one predominantly female, the other predominantly male), and it would be
possible to conceive the different *harmoniai* as constructions built out of notes that
had been selected on the basis of these qualifications. The moral character of a
harmonia would then be the direct result of the 'maleness', 'femaleness', or 'inter-
mediacy' of its predominant ingredients. The interpetation remains distressingly
vague; but once it is granted that Aristides' analysis is really Damonian in conception, it would be surprising if it had no bearing at all on the issue of the four 'kinds'.

CHAPTER II

Aristotle

We possess an extensive collection of Aristotle's works. They contain a closely reasoned and in many respects systematic study of the world in a multitude of its aspects, so impressive that it formed for centuries the basis of all educated Europeans' conceptions of the universe and man's place within it. Yet it is not presented as a fully worked-out system: in a sense it is not 'presented' at all, since the writings we have were designed not for publication, but as materials around which Aristotle conducted his teaching and research in the Lyceum. Almost everything that he deliberately prepared for publication is lost. The existing works show all the marks of a lecturer's notes, used and reused from time to time, being full of partially incorporated revisions, amendments, new queries, new points of view, new modes of presentation, second thoughts of every description. Further, his arguments are set out as enquiries, not, for the most part, as evidence marshalled in a straightforward way to a conclusion. We are shown different ways of looking at a subject, different kinds of consideration bearing on it, often with contrary implications, and in many cases with no complete resolution of the issues involved. Aristotle's 'system' is much more a system of investigative methods and of concepts within which the answers will form themselves, than a fixed and determinate set of substantive doctrines.

By comparison with Plato, Aristotle is catholic in what he will count as evidence bearing on a problem. Pure reason is not the sole key to truth. Hence he does not pursue the path constructed, from an origin in Plato, by later Platonists and Pythagoreans, which attempts to deduce facts about music, the human soul, and the universe at large from propositions in pure mathematics. His contributions to the scientific study of musical phenomena are rooted in the evidence of the senses, carefully interpreted within his general conceptual framework, and occupy the fields of physical acoustics, the physiology of voice production, and the physiology and psychology of hearing. They have little to do with abstract theories of means and ratios. Some of his work in these areas, and that of his colleagues and successors, appears in Vol. 2.

Little of his views about musical aesthetics has survived: the early chapters of the *Poetics* contain a few remarks suggestive of more to come, but the work is incomplete, and there is not much with a direct bearing on music in what remains. The educational and social aspects of the subject, however, are studied in a substantial – though again incomplete – passage at the end of the *Politics*: it forms a fitting accompaniment to the discussions of Plato's *Republic* and *Laws*. Aristotle treats it as a fundamental mistake to conceive ethics and political theory as abstract sciences, in which truths may be demonstrated by reasoning from first principles, as in geometry. Here the data are human experiences in all their confusion and variety, expressed in common opinions, in desires and tastes, in laws and customs, as well as in the meditations of previous philosophers. The philosopher's task is to sift and organise this evidence, to display as clearly as possible the tensions inherent in it, and, if he can, to defuse them, by showing how opposed views may be reinterpreted and related harmoniously as different parts or aspects of a common aspiration to human excellence and happiness. He will thus help others to tread a path through the prevailing babble of social advice and exhortation towards a more coherent and satisfying life. He will not stand upon a pinnacle of metaphysical doctrine and cast down rationally excogitated commandments to expectant and dutiful disciples.

From this arise two central features of Aristotle's treatment of music in the *Politics*. One is its lack of dogmatism. He considers different views and sets them in relation to one another, rejecting them only if he can point to their basis in plain misunderstandings or mistakes of fact. He tries to show the grounds for others' opinions, and hence to mark out the proper scope of their application, rather than accepting or rejecting them outright. The second is its willingness to embrace, in the role appropriate to it, anything that people have found valuable and good. Instead of Plato's uncompromising dismissal of any form of music not conducive to moral education, Aristotle seeks to find for the convivial *harmoniai*, for the exciting instruments, for professional methods of training and performance, and so on, their proper place within the life of a well adjusted society. Plato is important in other ways, but so far as the musical atmosphere of his own day is concerned, his value as a source derives mainly from his descriptions of the practices he attacks. The positive proposals that he develops bear no resemblance at all, as he himself makes clear, to any state of affairs that has ever really existed. With Aristotle the case is different. He does not give much in the way of direct historical description, polemical or otherwise, and his references to common opinions are not always easy to interpret. But though he is concerned to recommend and not merely to describe, it is the data of real practice and the views of ordinary educated Greeks that form his point of departure. The pragmatism of this approach leaves the reality of the music of his time much closer to the surface than does Plato's pursuit of a radically fresh start.

Aristotle was born at Stagira in 384 B.C. He came to Athens in 367, and studied there with Plato for the next twenty years. On Plato's death he left Athens, and continued to live a life of teaching and research first at Assos in the Troad, and later at Mytilene. For a brief period he was tutor to the young Alexander of Macedon. In 335 he returned to Athens and founded the school of philosophy known as the Peripatos or Lyceum: he left Athens again in 323, and died in Chalcis in the following year.

Politics

159   *Politics* 1337b23–36

There are four things, broadly speaking, which it is usual to teach children: writing, gymnastics, music, and fourthly, in some cases, painting. Writing and painting are taught as being useful for the purposes of life in many ways, and gymnastics as conducive to courage. About music, however, one might be in some doubt. Most people nowadays engage in it for the pleasure it gives: but it was originally prescribed as part of education because nature itself demands, as we have often said, that we should not only go about our work in the correct way, but should also be able to occupy our leisure well. This one principle is at the root of everything,[1] and we should discuss it once again. Now if both things are necessary, but leisure is to be preferred to labour and is more to be pursued as an end, we must try to discover the way

---

[1]   See 1333a30 ff.

in which our leisure ought to be occupied. It should not be occupied in play since it would follow that play is the object of our lives.

160   *Politics* 1338a9–37

It is clear, then, that there are certain things one must learn and be trained in with a view to the conduct of leisure,[2] and that these objects of training and instruction exist for their own sake, while the things in which one is trained and instructed with a view to work are there as a matter of necessity and to serve other ends. Hence people in earlier times prescribed music as part of education not as being a necessity, since it is no such thing, nor as being practically useful, in the way that writing is useful in business, in the management of the household, in learning, and in many affairs of state, or as painting, too, seems to be useful for improving our capacity to assess craftsmen's work. Nor was it prescribed, like gymnastics, for the sake of health and strength, since we never see either of these arising from music. Only the conduct of our leisure is left; and they themselves make it plain that it was for this purpose that they introduced it, since they included it in the way of life (*diagōgē*) that they thought proper to free men. That is why Homer said 'It is a good thing to call to the sumptuous feast',[3] and of some other people he says 'They called the singer to delight them all [a rough quotation of *Od.* XVII.385]'. Elsewhere Odysseus says that the best part of one's life is when people are enjoying themselves, 'And banqueters, sitting in order in the house, listen to a singer [*Od.* IX.7–8].'

It is plain, then, that there is a kind of education which should be given to our sons not because it is practically useful or necessary, but because it is liberal and good.[4] Whether there is one such kind or several, and what they are and how they should be taught, will be discussed later. For now, we have advanced along the road far enough to say that we have the witness of the ancients to support us, drawn from the subjects of education that they laid down, since music makes the point clear.

161   *Politics* 1339a11–1342b34

Concerning music we raised some questions earlier in our discussion, and it will now be a good thing if we pick them up again and develop them further

---

2   'Conduct', *diagōgē*, Aristotle's word here and in the sequel for the activities of life that are not forced on us by the demands of making a living, etc., but which constitute our voluntarily adopted 'way of life'. It is not simply 'amusement' or 'entertainment', being more serious and substantial than either. It is the life of the mind, the body and the emotions which, in the ideal case, constitutes 'living well', and for the sake of which other tasks are undertaken. I can find no adequate English equivalent: 'recreation' is sometimes suitable, but I have usually preferred the more general 'way of life': I have signalled some of the word's main occurrences as they appear in the text.
3   The line is corrupt, and no version of it occurs in our texts of the *Iliad* and *Odyssey*.
4   'Liberal', *eleutherion*, 'befitting a free man'. 'Good', *kalēn*, 'beautiful', 'noble'.

so that they may provide the keynote[5] for what anyone else may say in giving an account of the subject. For it is not easy to identify precisely the power that music has, nor the reasons why one ought to engage in it. Is it for the sake of play and relaxation, like sleep and drinking? These things are not seriously worth while in themselves, but they are enjoyable, and 'put an end to care', as Euripides says [62 *Bacch.* 381]: and this is a reason why people recommend music, and use all these things – sleep, drinking and music – in the same way, sometimes adding dancing to the list as well. Or should we rather think that music is conducive in some degree to virtue, on the grounds that just as gymnastics produce modifications of the body, so music has the power to modify the character, and to habituate people in correct forms of enjoyment? Or does it contribute to our way of living (*diagōgē*) and increase our wisdom, since this must be mentioned as the third of the things that people say of it? Well, it is obvious that young people should not be educated for the sake of play, since no one plays as he learns: learning is accompanied by hard labour.[6] Again, it is inappropriate to equip children of that age with a complete way of life (*diagōgē*), since nothing that is incomplete is fit for its final objective. But it might be thought, perhaps, that the efforts of youth are undertaken for the sake of the amusement that they will enjoy when they have achieved complete manhood. Yet if the matter stands like that, why should they need to learn themselves, instead of behaving like the kings of the Medes and Persians, and getting both their pleasure and their instruction from the performances of others? After all, it is inevitable that those who have trained themselves fully in the techniques of this profession will perform better than those who have studied it only for the length of time demanded by education. If it is incumbent on them to work at things like this, they ought also to train themselves in the craft of cookery: but that is absurd. The same problem arises if music has the power to improve character: [1339b] why should they learn it themselves, instead of becoming able to enjoy it and judge it correctly by listening to others, as the Spartans do? They do not learn music, but are able nevertheless, so they say, to judge correctly which melodies are good and which are not. The same argument applies also if music is to be used to promote the happy life (*diagōgē*) of free men. Why should they learn it, instead of luxuriating in the performances of others? We may also consider here the assumptions we make about the gods, for the poets never describe Zeus as singing or playing the *kithara*: rather, we say that such practitioners are vulgar artisans,[7] and that what they do is not for real men, unless they are drunk or joking.

---

5 *Endosimon.* The word sometimes means 'serving as an introduction' or 'prelude', but more commonly refers to that which gives the pitch to singers at the start of a piece. Cf. Ar. *Rhet.* 1414b24, *De Mundo* 399a19: for a metaphor similar to the present one see *Rhet.* 1415a7.

6 Contrast 161 1340b15–16, 154 Plato, *Laws* 659e–660a.

7 *Banausous.* The word carries implications both of vulgarity as contrasted with culture, education and nobility, and also of being a hired practitioner, a person who

Perhaps we should put off an investigation of these issues till later. The first question to be asked is whether music should or should not be made a part of education, and which of the three powers that we have been puzzling about belongs to it, that of instruction, amusement, or promoting the conduct of life. It is plausible to suggest that it is prescribed for all these purposes, and it does appear to have all these powers. Amusement exists for the sake of relaxation, and relaxation must necessarily be pleasant, since it is a kind of medicine for the pain that labour brings; and it is generally admitted that the conduct of one's life ought to afford not only nobility but pleasure as well, since happiness comes from the combination of both. We all say that music is one of the pleasantest things, whether it is purely instrumental[8] or accompanied by song: as Musaeus says, 'song is the sweetest thing to men'. That is why people very reasonably bring music into their social gatherings and recreations (*diagōgai*), on the grounds that it can bring joy. There are thus these reasons for supposing that young people ought to be educated in it; for all harmless pleasures are well adapted to promoting not only the final end of life, but relaxation as well. Since it happens only rarely that men are in possession of the final end, while they often take relaxation and engage in amusements without any objective beyond the resulting pleasure, it follows that it is useful to take recreation in the pleasures that music gives.

There are people who make amusements their ultimate goal. It may be true that the ultimate end includes some pleasure, but not just any kind; and in seeking the one kind they are accepting the other as though it was the first, since it has some resemblance to the final objective of our actions. For the final objective is not chosen for the sake of anything to come in the future, and pleasures of these kinds exist on account not of things that are to come, but of things in the past, such as labours and pain. This may fairly be supposed to be the reason why they look for happiness in pleasures like these: and we may suppose that people participate in music not for this reason alone, but also because it is obviously a valuable aid to relaxation. But we should enquire further whether, [1340a] while this is true, the nature of music is more honourable than the uses mentioned would suggest, and we ought not only to gain from it the common sort of pleasure, which everyone has the capacity to perceive (since music dispenses pleasure of a natural kind, so that the use of it is beloved by all ages and characters), but ought also to see whether it has a tendency to improve the character and the soul. We would have proof of that, if we are caused by music to acquire specific qualities in our characters. And indeed we do acquire specific qualities, as is shown by many things, and especially by the melodies of

---

does something not for the sake of its own value but for financial reward: cf. 161 1341b10 ff. Aristotle's remark is no doubt a true representation of the opinion of most people of his class, but has a bizarre ring in the context, given the nature of the activities traditionally ascribed to Apollo and the Muses.

8   *Psilē*, lit. 'bare', the term regularly used for the music of an instrument used by itself, not as an accompaniment to the voice.

Olympus:[9] for it is generally agreed that they inspire our souls with ecstasy, and ecstasy is a qualification of the character of the soul. Again, when people listen to imitations, their feelings are always changed in sympathy with them, even when they are not accompanied by rhythms and melodies.[10]

Since music is one of the things that are pleasant, and virtue is to do with enjoying, loving and hating things correctly, it is clear that we should not learn or habituate ourselves to anything so much as judging correctly and enjoying fine characters and noble deeds. There exist in rhythms and melodies likenesses, most closely approximating to the realities, of anger and mildness, of courage and moderation and their opposites, and of all other dispositions, as the facts make clear; for our souls are altered when we hear such things. Habituation in feeling pain and pleasure in likenesses is close to being affected in the same way by the realities themselves: for instance, if someone enjoys the sight of an image of something because of its appearance and for no other reason, he must also find pleasure in the sight of the actual object whose image he is looking at.

Now the fact is that among the objects of the other senses – those of touch and taste for example – there are no likenesses of character, and they scarcely exist among the objects of sight.[11] Dance figures belong to this category, no doubt, but only to a small degree, and not everyone shares equally in this sort of perception: besides, these things – figures and colours associated with characters – are not likenesses of character, but rather signs, serving as marks to distinguish the emotions. For all that, to the extent that there is better and worse in respect of the sight of these things, young people ought not to look at the products of Pauson, but rather those of Polygnotus and any painter or sculptor there may be whose work has moral significance. But melodies themselves do contain imitations of character. This is perfectly clear, for the *harmoniai*[12] have quite distinct natures from one another, so that those who hear them are differently affected and do not respond in the same way to each. To some, such as the one called Mixolydian, they respond with more grief [1340b] and anxiety,[13] to others, such as the relaxed *harmoniai*,[14] with

9 On Olympus see **187** ps.-Plut. 1132f, 1133e ff, 1137a ff, and Ch. 15 Appendix B: cf. Plato, *Symp.* 215c.
10 Or, with Susemihl's emendation, 'even when there are no words, owing to the rhythms and melodies themselves'. If the emendation is accepted, Aristotle is attributing imitative character to wordless instrumental music: see the next paragraph, and cf. **177** ps.-Ar. *Probs.* XIX.27: contrast **154** Plato, *Laws* 669e. The emendation is made the more probable by the reference to Olympus above, since his reputation was that of a composer for solo *aulos*, as is made clear by ps.-Plutarch and especially at Plato, *Symp.* loc. cit. On the whole issue see Anderson, *Ethos and Education*, Appendix B.
11 See **177** ps.-Ar. *Probs.* XIX.27, and cf. 29.
12 With Aristotle's discussions of the *harmoniai* cf. **149** Plato, *Rep.* 397a ff, and Ch. 10, Appendix A.
13 *Synestēkotos mallon*, lit. 'more compacted' or 'more contracted'. Some translators suppose it to mean 'restrained' here: for the sense suggested in my version cf. the uses of the cognate noun *systasis* at e.g. Thuc. VII.71, Eurip. *Hippol.* 983. On the Mixolydian cf. **149** Plato, *Rep.* 398e, **187** ps.-Plut. 1136d.
14 Aristotle probably has in mind the 'slack' (*chalarai*) *harmoniai* of **149** *Rep.* 398e.

more mellowness of mind, and to one other with a special degree of modera
tion and firmness, Dorian being apparently the only one of the *harmoniai* t
have this effect, while Phrygian creates ecstatic excitement.[15] These point
have been well expressed by those who have thought deeply about this kin
of education; for they cull the evidence for what they say from the fact
themselves. With rhythms the situation is the same. Some of them have
character that produces stability, others one that produces movement, an
of the latter some have movements of a more degenerate sort, while other
have ones fitting for free men. From all this it is clear that music is capable o
creating a particular quality of character in the soul, and if it can do that, it i
plain that it should be made use of, and that the young should be educated i
it. Instruction in music is particularly well fitted to people's nature at thi
age, since young people, because of their youth, do not willingly put up wit
anything unpleasant, and music is naturally among the things that giv
delight. There also seems to be a close relation of some sort between the sou
and *harmoniai* and rhythms, which is why many wise men say either that th
soul is a *harmonia*, or that it contains one.[16]

We must now discuss the question that was raised earlier, whether th
young ought to learn music by singing and playing instruments themselves
or not. It is perfectly clear that if a man takes part in an activity himself, he i
in a much better position to acquire the relevant qualities: it is impossible o
at least difficult for those who have not taken part in activities to becom
adequate judges of them. At the same time children must have some way o
occupying themselves, and Archytas' rattle[17] seems an excellent invention: i
is given to children to use, to prevent them breaking things around the house
since young creatures cannot keep still. This device is well suited to infants
and the rattle[18] for bigger children is education. Considerations of this sor
show that music should be taught in such a way that the pupils take part i
its practice. It is not difficult to distinguish what is suitable and what i
unsuitable to their age, and to resolve the problems advanced by those who
say that this pursuit is low and vulgar. In the first place, the object of their
participation in practice should be the development of judgement, so tha
people ought to engage in practice when they are young: when they are older
they should abstain from it, while having the capacity to judge what is good
and to enjoy things correctly, as a result of what they learned when they were
young. As to the accusation that some people make, that music turns people
into vulgar artisans, this is not hard to refute if we consider the degree to

---

[15] Cf. 1342a–b below. On the contrast with Plato's view (**149** *Rep.* 399a–c) see Ch. 10,
Appendix A.

[16] The latter class includes Plato. For the former see e.g. Plato, *Phaedo* 85e ff, Ar. *De An.*
407b28 ff.

[17] The Pythagorean philosopher, mathematician and musical theorist Archytas of
Tarentum was well known for his love of children (Aelian, *V.H.* XII.15 = DK 47.A8):
as well as the rattle mentioned here he is said to have invented a mechanical dove that
flew (Gell. X.12.8 = DK 47.A10a).

[18] I.e. the device best suited for keeping them harmlessly occupied.

which those who are being educated towards civic excellence ought to engage in musical practice, [1341a] which kinds of melody and rhythm they ought to take part in, and also which instruments their instruction ought to employ, since it seems that this too makes a difference. The refutation of the accusation lies in these issues, for there is nothing to prevent certain kinds of music from having the results that are alleged. It is plain, then, that people's learning of music ought not to impede the activities they will engage in later in life, nor ought it to make the body uncultivated [*banauson*: cf. n. 7] and unfit for the affairs of war and politics – for the learning of them now, and the practice of them later.

The right approach to learning would be achieved if the students learned neither the techniques required for professional contests,[19] nor the spectacular and very difficult practices which have now been adopted in the contests and have moved from the contests into education, but learned things of this sort[20] only to the extent needed to enable them to enjoy good melodies and rhythms, and not merely music of the kind that is universally enjoyed, even by some of the animals and by the common run of slaves and children. These considerations also make it clear what instruments should be used. *Auloi* should not be introduced into education, and neither should any other instrument proper to professional experts (*technikon organon*), the *kithara*, for instance, and others of that sort, but only those of them that will make people good students of musical or any other sort of instruction. Again, the *aulos* is not a moral instrument but rather one that excites the emotions,[21] so that it should be used in the kinds of circumstances where the spectacle offers more potential for *katharsis* than for learning.[22] Let us add

---

[19]   Lit. 'neither what contributes to technically skilled contests . . .' (*tous agōnas tous technikous*).

[20]   Omitting Immisch's addition of *mē*, 'not', adopted by the O.C.T., and giving the sense 'learnt things not of this sort . . .' I take it that the reference of 'things of this sort' is fairly vague, 'things to do with music', not specifically to the professional techniques that have been mentioned.

[21]   I.e., it is an instrument that should not be used to habituate our character to the pattern of behaviour it represents, since that pattern is undesirable as a fixed disposition. Its music is suitable only for occasional use, for the purpose of arousing emotion and generating *katharsis*. Because habituation to its music is dangerous, a citizen should not learn to play it: his exposure to it should come only from listening to performances by hired professionals, with whose morals and way of life Aristotle is not concerned. See next note, and cf. 1314b ff.

[22]   Aristotle's conception of emotional *katharsis*, 'purification' or 'purgation', well known from his (tantalisingly sketchy) treatment in the *Poetics*, is always sharply distinguished from that of (moral) learning. The latter proceeds by habituation, towards an assimilation by the individual of the form of character represented in the music or poetry. The former acts instantaneously at the time of hearing, not cumulatively over the course of a person's development: the music or drama that is witnessed stimulates in us certain intense emotions, which are rapidly exhausted. Rather than habituating us to feeling these dangerous emotions, occasional exposure to such music 'works them off' in a harmless context, and allows us to pursue our ordinary activities with our head of emotional steam released. The principal 'circumstances'

that the *aulos* prevents the player from using words; and this is another fact about it that militates against education. Hence our forefathers did well to forbid its use to young people and free men, though to begin with they had used it themselves. As their affluence brought them greater leisure and increased their aspirations towards virtue, and as their opinion of themselves increased as a result of their deeds (in earlier times as well as after the Persian wars), so they set themselves to learning of all sorts, making no settled distinctions, but rather enquiring.[23] For this reason they introduced *aulos*-playing as a subject for study. In Sparta there was a chorus-leader[24] who played to the chorus on the *aulos* himself, and in Athens it was so widespread that probably the majority of free men engaged in it, as is demonstrated by the tablet dedicated by Thrasippus when he was *chorēgos* for Ecphantides.[25] Their experience later caused them to reject it, when they were better able to judge what is conducive to virtue and what is not. Similarly, they rejected many of the instruments used by the ancients, such as *pēktides* and *barbitoi*, and those that promote the pleasure of people who hear their executants, such as *heptagōna* and *trigōna* and *sambykai*, [1341b] together with all those that demand great manual expertise.[26] The fable told by the ancients about the *auloi* also has a sound rational basis: they say that Athena

where such release is appropriate are those of the performance of tragic drama. See also n. 31. Aristotle's remarks here are a good example of his refusal to reject outright anything that is enjoyed or valued, seeking rather to find its appropriate place. Much that is useless or pernicious in formal education has a worthwhile role elsewhere.

[23] That is, they did not insist in advance that this was good and that was bad, but set out to discover which was which without preconceived distinctions. Hence they initially allowed (by way of experiment, as it were) things that were later prohibited in the light of experience.

[24] This is probably the meaning of *chorēgos* here: cf. e.g. **154** Plato, *Laws* 665a. At Athens it regularly indicated the person who put up money for the training and presentation of a chorus, but we have no evidence that this latter usage existed in Sparta. In any case, the point here is that he was a citizen, not a hired professional. As the form of words indicates, Aristotle is thinking of some one occasion, not a regular practice.

[25] An early writer of comedies. Perhaps Thrasippus' tablet named a number of citizens who played the *aulos*, or conceivably it suggested that members of his chorus were required to perform on the instrument in the course of the production of some play.

[26] This list of instruments partly corresponds to the class indicated by Plato at **149** *Rep.* 399c–d. Of those not mentioned there, the *heptagōnon* (not otherwise known) may be assumed, from its name, to have had seven sides, and was probably a kind of harp, like the *trigōnon*. Our sources describe the *sambykē* as an instrument with a boat-shaped body and a string-holder rising from it at an angle: it was said to be similar in shape to the siege-engine of the same name. It may have been a harp of a type common in Egypt and the Middle East, but the diagnosis is uncertain. See **188** Ath. 175d–e, **196** 634a and 637b; Arist. Quint. 85.10–12. The word *barbitos* usually designates a version of the *lyra*, and if it does so here it is not one of the many-stringed foreign instruments that fall under Plato's ban. But the name seems to have had other possible uses: see **188** Ath. 175e with n. 19. However, the *lyra*-like *barbitos* was almost exclusively associated with Dionysiac revelry, and would not therefore have appeared conducive to moral education. Certainly it was not an instrument on which the young received instruction in the classical period. For an example of an instrument whose use was abandoned because of the technical difficulties it presented, see the passage of Artemon quoted at **196** Ath. 637b ff, on the *tripous* of Pythagoras of Zacynthus.

invented the *auloi* and then threw them away. It makes a good story to say that the goddess did this because she was put out by the way it distorted her face; but it is more likely to have been because training in *aulos*-playing contributes nothing to the intelligence, knowledge and skill being things that we attribute to Athena.[27]

We reject, then, a technical education in instruments and in performance on them. By 'technical' education we mean that which equips people for competitive performances. The player does not pursue it to improve his own virtue, but to promote the pleasure of the listeners – a depraved pleasure, at that – and for this reason we reckon the task to be appropriate not to free men, but to menials. Its practitioners acquire the character of vulgar artisans, since the target that they set themselves to reach is a bad one. It is commonplace for a depraved audience to cause changes in music, so that they mould both the characters of the technical experts who dance atten-dance on them, and their bodies, because of the movements involved.[28]

We must turn, then, to consider the *harmoniai* and the rhythms. We must ask whether all the *harmoniai* and all the rhythms should be used,[29] or whether a division should be made, and next whether the same division should be prescribed for the people who work at education, or whether they need a different one. Thirdly,[30] we see that music consists in melodic compo-sition and rhythms, and we must neither forget the educative power that each of them has, nor neglect to ask whether music with good melody or music with good rhythm is to be preferred. Now since I believe that many excellent things have been said about these matters both by some contem-porary musical experts and by those philosophers who have been well acquainted with education in music, I shall hand over to them the people who wish to pursue a precise account of every detail, and deal with the issues only in general terms for the present, stating no more than their outlines.

We accept the division of melodies that various philosophers make, classifying some as moral, some as invigorating, and some as inspirational.[31]

---

[27] The tale was well known: some scholars have seen a genuine musical controversy in certain of its appearances in the fifth century. See the lines from Melanippides and Telestes quoted at **189** Ath. 616e–f. For a quite different account of the relation between Athena and the *aulos* see **27** Pindar, *Pyth.* 12.

[28] For the general thesis cf. **153** Plato, *Laws* 659b–c. On the movements with which professional instrumentalists accompanied their performance see e.g. **145** Xen. *Symp.* 6.4, cf. Paus. IX.12.5–6.

[29] Omitting *kai pros paideian* ('and with respect to education') in line 20. The distinc-tions required in education are mentioned in the next clause, where it is explicitly asked whether they should be the same as the ones needed here. Aristotle seems to be asking first whether any *harmoniai* or rhythms should be rejected altogether, and secondly whether the answer to that question is sufficient to tell us what is proper for education, or whether further distinctions are needed.

[30] Reading *tina heteron, triton de*, with Susemihl.

[31] It will not do to equate these with representations of character, action and emotion respectively. There is nothing in Aristotle to suggest that an 'emotional' melody, for instance, is not a representation of an emotional character. The point is that only the first type represents the character of a good man, and hence it is only here that the

They set out also the type of *harmonia* that is appropriate to each of them, a different one for each type of melody. But we say that music should be used to give benefits of several sorts, not just one: it should aim at both education and *katharsis* (I shall not now enlarge on what I mean by *katharsis*, but I shall explain it more clearly later, in my work on Poetics[32]), and thirdly at amusement for the sake of relaxation and relief from tension. [1342a] It is clear, then, that all the *harmoniai* should be used, but not all of them in the same way. The most moral ones should be used for education, while the most invigorating and inspirational ones should be used when we listen to other people performing. For a passion that strongly affects certain souls occurs in all, varying only in that it may be greater or less: this is the case, for instance, with pity and fear, and with inspired ecstasy too. Some people are capable of being entirely possessed by this last disturbance, but we observe that when these people make use of melodies that greatly excite the soul, out of the resources of sacred melody, they are put right again, just as if they had been given medication and purgation (*katharsis*). This must also happen to those who are particularly prone to pity or fear or emotion of any kind, and to others to the extent to which such things affect them: *katharsis* and alleviation come to all, and pleasure with them. In the same way invigorating melodies also provide harmless delight for people; and this is why we should allow the contestants who perform the music of the theatre to employ *harmoniai* and melodies of these sorts.

Since there are two kinds of spectator, the one a free and educated man, the other vulgar (this group consists of artisans and hired menials and others of that kind), we should provide contests and spectacles for the relaxation of the latter sort too. Now their souls are as it were bent away from the character nature gave them: and in the same way there exist deviant *harmoniai* and melodies, those that are tense[33] and artificially coloured.[34] Each man is given pleasure by what fits his nature, and this is why contestants should be given licence to use this category of music when dealing with that sort of spectator. But for education, as we have said, we must use those melodies that are moral [cf. n. 31 above], and *harmoniai* of

character represented is relevant to its proper use. The 'moral' kind is to be used in education for the purpose of character-formation, and neither of the others is. They may only be heard, not performed by citizens, to avoid the development of undesirable habits. The invigorating kind, used like this, gives harmless pleasure, Aristotle says (1342a15–16). The third type arouses passionate feelings, and allows us to purge our soul of emotions in harmless ways (see n. 22). That the emotional *harmoniai* can affect the character if we become habituated to them is indicated by Aristotle's rejection of Phrygian for the purposes of education, not because it has no moral effect, but because it has the wrong one (1342a28 ff).

32   The reference is probably to a part of the *Poetics* that is now lost: in what we have there are relevant passages at 1449b26–8 and 1452b30 ff.

33   *Ta syntona*, especially associated with emotional lamentation. See particularly **149** Plato, *Rep.* 398e and 1340a42–b2 above, cf. e.g. **36** Soph. *Ajax* 624–34.

34   *Parakechrōsmena*: see **153** Plato, *Laws* 655a with n. 61.

he same sort. The Dorian is of this kind, as we said earlier;[35] and we should
ccept any other *harmonia* that is recommended to us by those who are
·articipants in the pursuit of philosophy and in musical education. But the
Socrates' of Plato's *Republic* [149 399a–c] is wrong to retain just the
·hrygian along with the Dorian, especially since among the instruments, the
·ulos is one that he rejects [149 399d]. [1342b] Among the *harmoniai* the
·hrygian has the same power as does the *aulos* among instruments: both
·nduce ecstasy and emotion. For all Bacchic revelry and all dancing[36] of that
·ort is done to the *auloi* more than to any other instrument, and these things
·lso find what is appropriate to them in Phrygian melodies, out of all the
·armoniai [see Ch. 10, Appendix A]. Composition itself makes clear how the
·lithyramb is by common consent a Phrygian form. People who work in this
·ield of study bring many examples to prove it, including that of Philo-
·enus,[37] who when he tried to compose his *Mysians* in the Dorian was unable
·o, but fell back again into the appropriate *harmonia*, Phrygian, compelled
·y nature itself. As to Dorian, everyone agrees that it is most steadfast and
·nost manly in character. Again, since we approve of the mean between
·extremes and say that it should be pursued, and since the Dorian has this
·ature in relation to the other *harmoniai*,[38] it is clear that Dorian melodies
·hould be taught most of all to the young.

   There are two things to keep our eye on, what is possible and what is
·itting: everyone should set his hand to things that are possible and things
·hat are fitting. These things are determined in relation to age: for instance it
·s difficult for those who have been enfeebled by time to sing the tense
·*harmoniai*: nature indicates for them the *harmoniai* that are relaxed.[39] For
·this reason some musical experts quite fairly find fault with Socrates for
·excluding the relaxed *harmoniai* from education, not because he supposed
·them to be intoxicating, and to have a power like that of drinking (since
·drinking is more inclined to make a man riotous), but because he thought
·them enfeebled.[40] For the sake, then, of a later stage of their lives, that of old
·men, people should practise *harmoniai* and melodies of these kinds too, and
·also any other such *harmonia* there may be that is suitable for children's time
·of life because of its capacity to contain both elegance and educativeness

---

[35] Aristotle is perhaps thinking of 1340b3–4: see also 1342b12 ff.
[36] *Kinēsis*, lit. 'movement'.
[37] See p. 95 above. Editors have emended the text to give the title of the piece as it
   stands in the translation: on both title and structure see 187 ps.-Plut. 1142f with
   n. 216.
[38] In the cycle of the formalised system of *harmoniai*, Dorian is in the middle, and is
   therefore of mean pitch. See Ch. 10, Appendix A.
[39] *Aneimenas:* the context here suggests lower absolute pitch, with no special implications about relaxed or 'slack' character. See 149 *Rep.* 397b, 398e.
[40] 149 *Rep.* 398e, where the implications of Socrates' reference to drunkenness are not
   made entirely clear.

together, something that seems to apply to the Lydian *harmonia* more than
to any other.[41] It is clear, then, that there are these three limits to be imposed
upon education: moderation, possibility, and propriety.

[41] Aristotle is arguing that while Dorian is proper for children because it educates them
for manhood, we must consider their needs at other times of life too. 'Relaxed'
harmoniai should be practised in childhood so that we can use them when we are old:
and Lydian exemplifies another kind of *harmonia*, one required to fill the needs of
childhood itself. Plato rejects all the varieties of Lydian that he mentions (**149** *Rep.*
398e). Heraclides treats both it and the Phrygian as forms of the Ionian, and as
essentially non-Greek (**192** Ath. 624c, 625e ff). It was generally thought of as
charming, plaintive and convivial, e.g. Telestes ap. **192** Ath. 626a, high-pitched and
suited to lamentation, **187** ps.-Plut. 1136c. High pitch may be reflected in the present
passage, which seems to suggest that it is peculiarly well suited to the treble voice.

The Hibeh Papyrus on music[1]

The date of this short fragment is uncertain. The papyrus itself belongs to the middle of the third century B.C., but it has been argued that its contents are at least a hundred years older. The case for the early dating is briefly as follows. First, its style has been identified as (with qualifications) Isocratean, but belonging to an early phase in the development of that style: this would place it around 390 B.C. (see W. Crönert, 'Die Hibehrede über die Musik', *Hermes* 44 (1909)). Secondly, the suggestion (col. 2 lines 4–5) that the enharmonic genus was generally used in tragedy is said to place it before Aristoxenus, in whose time this genus was approaching extinction (*El. Harm.* 23.4–23, cf. Plut. *Quaest. Conv.* VII.8.1). Thirdly, Anderson has argued (*Ethos and Education* 149–50, 188–9) that col. 2 line 13 refers to the wooden benches for spectators in the theatre at Athens, which were replaced with stone in the middle of the fourth century.

Of these arguments the first must be regarded as not proven, and the third is described by Anderson himself as 'tentative': it can be no more (see n. 12). The second looks more substantial. But Aristoxenus does not say that the enharmonic was disused in his time. What he claims is that 'nowadays', when people try to play in the enharmonic, they get its intervals wrong, and approximate to a form of the chromatic. That is, there still remained a practice of playing in what was *called* 'the enharmonic', but in fact, by Aristoxenus' strict standards, it was corrupt and inaccurate. It should also be noted that if the fragment was written before Aristoxenus, and is to be understood as referring to the genera, enharmonic, chromatic and diatonic, it is the only pre-Aristoxenian source we have that does so (see n. 8). A date in the fourth century, even the early fourth century, remains possible, but I do not think it has been established. (See also n. 12.)

The piece is an extract from a speech: we know nothing of the circumstances of its delivery. It contains a three-pronged attack on music critics of the day. In the first place they direct their criticisms to practical music-making, in which they claim no special expertise: their remarks are therefore based on mere ignorance. Secondly, the theoretical matters in which they affect to be experts are a tissue of fabrications. These 'theories' turn out to be ones concerned with musical *ēthos*, associating specific types of music with specific effects on the human character, in a way made familiar by Plato and Aristotle, and ultimately derived from Damon. No particular theory of *ēthos* seems to be under attack: the author rejects the notion of musical *ēthos* in general. Thirdly, the persons attacked claim to be experts also in the science of harmonics, but their attempts at analysis are haphazard and unsystematic, besides reflecting an inaccurate grasp of the real data of performance.

It is the second aspect of the polemic that has received most scholarly attention (see Anderson 147 ff, with his notes), understandably in view of the fact that we possess no comparable attack on theories of musical *ēthos* dating from anything like so early a period. But the other aspects should not be ignored. Aristoxenus tells us something about the harmonic analyses offered by his contemporaries and predecessors: together with a few remarks of Plato (especially *Rep.* 531a–b), the papyrus gives some

---

[1] Grenfell and Hunt, *The Hibeh Papyri* Vol. 1 (London, 1906) no. 13.

tenuous but significant information about the practical activities on which at least some theorists' researches were based.

162   Hibeh Papyrus 1.13, col. 1.1–col. 2.15

It has often occurred to me to be surprised, men [of Greece],[2] at the way certain people construct demonstrations not belonging to [their own areas of expertise], without your noticing. For they say that they are 'harmonicists';[3] and they pick out [various songs] [1.5] and judge them against one another, condemning some, quite at random, and unsystematically extolling others.[4] Again, they say that it is not their business to think about instrumentalists and singers:[5] these matters, they say, they leave to others, while their own special province is the [1.10] theoretical branch. Yet they actually display an immoderate enthusiasm for the things they leave to others, while improvising haphazardly in the areas where they say their strength lies.

They also say that some melodies make people self-disciplined, others prudent, others just, [1.15] others brave, and others cowardly,[6] not understanding that the chromatic cannot make cowards nor the enharmonic make brave men of those who employ it. For who does not know [2.1] that the Aetolians and Dolopes and all those at Thermopylae,[7] though they employ diatonic music, are braver than singers in tragedy, who have [always] been accustomed to singing in the enharmonic?[8] Hence [2.5] the chromatic does not make people cowardly, nor does the enharmonic make them brave.

---

[2]   Conjectural restorations of doubtful words, where they affect the sense, are placed in square brackets.

[3]   *Harmonikoi*, students of *harmonikē*: it is Aristoxenus' word for his predecessors in the field of 'harmonic' analysis.

[4]   The sense is that their judgements are based on no discernible principle: this need of course mean no more than that the present author could detect none. But see also n. 12.

[5]   Or perhaps '. . . that one ought not to consider them instrumentalists or singers' (Anderson). The word 'instrumentalists' translates *psaltas*, lit. 'players of plucked stringed instruments' (e.g. the *psaltērion*, col. 2.14). But the intention, on either interpretation of the sentence, seems quite general. Cf. n. 12.

[6]   The claim that certain types of music make people just is not Plato's, but is ascribed to Damon. See Philodemus 1.13 with III.77 (pp. 7 and 55, Kemke), and IV.24.9–35 (pp. 92–3, Kemke).

[7]   The word is partly conjectural. If correct, it perhaps means 'those who come together [for festivals involving music] at Thermopylae'.

[8]   If the references to chromatic (*chrōma*), enharmonic (*harmonia*) and diatonic (*diatonos mousikē*) are construed as allusions to a supposed ethos belonging to each of the genera, they echo nothing in Plato or Aristotle: we find distinctions between genera made first in Aristoxenus. The distinct characters of the three are clearly set out only by late authors, e.g. Theon Smyrn. 54–6 (Hiller), Arist. Quint. 92.19–30, cf. 16.10–18, *Anon. Bell.* 26; but cf. also Aristox. *El. Harm.* 19.23–29, 187 ps.-Plut. 1142d. The word 'genus', however, does not occur in the present passage, and it is possible that the author has something vaguer in mind. *Chrōma*, 'coloured' or 'shaded' music (see e.g. **196** Ath. 638a, and cf. **187** ps.-Plut. 1137e with n. 132), seems not to be distinguished here from *diatonos mousikē*: it may be distinguished from *harmonia* only as a form of music that 'colours' and varies its interval structure is

These people have the effrontery to waste [their entire life] on strings.[9] They play on strings [much worse than real instrumentalists], they sing much worse than real singers, and in their critical comparisons they do everything worse than any orator one might come across.[10]

[2.10] As to what is called 'harmonics',[11] with which they say they have a special familiarity, they have nothing articulate to say, but are carried away with enthusiasm: and they beat the rhythm all wrong, on the wooden bench where they sit, [simultaneously] with the sounds of the *psaltērion*.[12]

[2.15] They do not even hesitate to state openly that some melodies will have a feature [peculiarly characteristic] of laurel, others of ivy . . .[13]

---

distinguished from one that is rigidly fixed. (Cf. also 187 ps.-Plut. 1145c–d, though the point at issue there is quite different.) This latter will no doubt in either case actually *be* a music that fits the enharmonic structure, the only kind that had been given a fixed analysis by Aristoxenus' predecessors (*El. Harm.* 2.7 ff).

[9] I.e., on experiments with string-tuning. Cf. Plato, *Rep.* 531a–b.

[10] That is, anyone trained in the skills of rhetoric, designed to equip a man to 'speak well' on any topic whatever. See e.g. Plato, *Gorgias* 453a, 456a ff.

[11] Apparently conceived here, in a general way, as the theoretical analysis of musical structures.

[12] *Psaltērion* means 'instrument plucked with the fingers' (not played with a plectrum), and normally designates a member of the harp family. But the author has used the verb *psallein* and the noun *psaltēs* to refer apparently quite generally to string playing and string players (col. 1.7, col. 2.7 and probably 8), and *psaltērion*, correspondingly, may mean simply 'stringed instrument'.

Anderson (p. 188) is right in construing the word *sanidion* ('wooden bench') as a reference to the seats of the audience, not to a wooden part of the performer's instrument or a wooden foot-board used by the performer to mark the rhythm. But his connection of the benches with the Athenian theatre of Dionysus (see introductory note) is wholly speculative.

The overall implication of the paragraph is that their alleged expertise in theoretical analysis does not help them to get even the rhythms right when faced with an actual performance. The author's attack on the harmonicists' pretensions, apart from the issue of musical ethos, amounts to this: first, they have no general principles providing a systematic basis for their analyses and comparisons, which as a result are random and haphazard; and secondly, they have an inadequate grasp on the audible data of performance. These contentions exactly match Aristoxenus' main criticisms of his predecessors, though he expresses them a good deal more clearly (see particularly *El. Harm.* 2.25–3.4, 6.13–19, 32.29–31). It seems extremely likely that the present author is drawing on Aristoxenus: if so, the case for an earlier dating dissolves.

[13] Laurel was associated with Apollo, ivy with Dionysus. The classification reflects a difference between a more sober and restrained style and a music that is emotional and ecstatic, the former being primarily that of the *kithara*, the latter that of the *aulos*.

Two more lines of text exist, badly mutilated. In the first, some scholars have seen a (scathing) reference to the notion of musical *mimēsis*, 'imitation', fundamental in Plato's discussions of music. The second seems to end with the phrase 'satyrs dancing to the *aulos* (?)'. Nothing substantial can reliably be made of either line.

CHAPTER 13

Theophrastus

Theophrastus, a pupil first of Plato, later of Aristotle, and Aristotle's successor as head of the Lyceum, researched and wrote on a wide variety of topics. His interest in theoretical aspects of music is exhibited in an extract preserved by Porphyry (*Comm.* 61.22 ff), and said to come from the second book of his *On Music* (the passage is quoted in Vol. 2). One of the works that have come down to us more or less complete is his *Historia Plantarum*, a substantial 'flora' of Greece and some other parts of the Mediterranean area. He commonly adds to his descriptions of the plants an account of their uses. In the present passage he describes both the natural history of the plant from which the vibrating reeds of *auloi* were made, and the process of their manufacture. The excerpt is part of a study of the flora of Lake Copais or Cephisos in Boeotia, on which the town of Orchomenos stood: cf. 27 Pindar, *Pyth.* 12.27.

163   Theophrastus, *Historia Plantarum* IV.11.1–7

Of the reed they say there are two kinds, the auletic reed and the other:[1] for this other kind, they say, is a single type, though its plants differ from one another in being strong and thick or thin and weak. . . .
[2]   Concerning the auletic reed, it is not true, as some people say, that it grows only once in nine years, this being the principle of order to which it conforms:[2] generally speaking, it grows whenever the lake has filled up. Because in former times people supposed that this happened for the most part every nine years, they ascribed this period of growth to the reed as well, taking what was merely accidental to be a principle of order. [3] It grows whenever there has been a spell of rain, and the water stays in the lake for at least two years; and it is better if the water stays longer. People recall that this happened, in recent years, most notably at the time of the battle of Chaeronea [338 B.C.]. Before that, they told me, the lake was deep for several years, and at a later date, when there was a severe plague, the lake filled but the water did not stay in it: the winter rain failed, and the reed did not grow. They say, and they seem to be right, that when the lake is deep the reed increases its length, and if it stands during the following year it becomes mature: the matured reed becomes suitable for the *zeugos*,[3] and that around

---

[1]   The word for 'reed' in this passage is always *kalamos*, not *donax*. On these words, and on the commonest uses of reeds in musical instruments, see 121–8 with notes 190, 198. 'Auletic reed', i.e. that used in the manufacture of *auloi*.

[2]   They believe, that is, that the nine-year cycle of growth is natural to the plant, and not a merely 'accidental' result of a periodicity in the weather.

[3]   Lit. 'yoke', commonly used of any two things regarded as a pair. In the *aulos* it is the 'double reed' that vibrates between the player's lips, as in the modern oboe. On the suggestion of some scholars that parts of this passage refer to the 'single reed', as in the clarinet, see n. 10.

186

which the water does not remain is suitable for the *bombyx*.[4] That then, they say, is the way it grows.

[4]   It is said to differ from other reeds, broadly speaking, by the luxuriance of its growth, being better filled and more fleshy, and in general female in its appearance. Its leaf, furthermore, is flatter and whiter, and its flower-head is smaller than that of other reeds, and some of them, which they call 'eunuch-reeds', have no flower-head at all. From these, they say, come the best *zeugē*, though few of them come out right in the making.

Before the time of Antigenidas, when they played the *aulos* without elaboration,[5] the right time for cutting the reed, so they say, was in the month Boedromion, at the time of the rising of Arcturus [about September]. Though reed cut in this way became usable only after a good many years and required a lot of preliminary playing,[6] the opening between the tongues closed up well, which was useful for the purposes of projection.[7] [5] But

---

[4]   Some authorities suppose that the *bombyx* here is a 'cap', on the assumption that the *aulos* sometimes had a reed-cap like the crumhorns, rauschpfeifen, schryari etc. of the Renaissance. I know of no good evidence for this. The word has a variety of meanings, generally related to depth of pitch: the *bombyx* note of the *aulos* at Ar. *Metaph.* 1093b is its lowest note. Hence the *bombyx aulos* is a deep-toned version of the instrument, e.g. Pollux IV.82. In his list of parts of the *aulos* at IV.70, Pollux includes *bombykes*: this has been taken to refer either to the supposed 'cap', or to the rings or collars that were used on more elaborate instruments to cover some of the finger-holes (cf. Arcadius 186, Barker). But it is more probable that Pollux means 'pipes', i.e. the main body of each member of a pair of *auloi*, since otherwise these will be missing from the list of parts; and that is likely to be the sense here. The same sense is plainly intended by Aesch. ap. Strabo x.3.16. (These pipes were made from a variety of materials, Pollux IV.71, including reed: note that when Pollux tells us in IV.70 that the pipes of the 'Etruscan *aulos*', an organ or bagpipe, are made of bronze, the word he uses for 'pipe' is *kalamos*, 'reed'. For other references to *auloi* whose body was made of reed see e.g. Pindar, *Nem.* 5.38, 188 Ath. 176c–e.)

[5]   On Antigenidas (late fifth to mid-fourth century) see 187 ps.-Plut. 1138b with n. 138. 'Without elaboration', *aplastōs*: there are further references to *plasis* and to playing *meta plasmatos* in section 5. *Plasis* is 'moulding' or 'forming': it seems here to refer to a sophisticated elaboration of melodic shapes, presumably involving decorative 'turns' (*kampai*). Playing *aplastōs* is then playing in a plain style, without elaborate ornamentation.
    We are told (section 5, below) that the salient feature of the more modern *zeugē* was their maintenance of a wide opening between the 'tongues'. Theophrastus' other remarks in the paragraph suggest that they may have been more flexible than their predecessors. A wide opening will give greater volume in the lower register. Combined with flexibility, it also gives more opportunity for effects depending on control of the reed by the lips and breath, allowing easier access to the upper register, and admitting a variety of pitch-changes without changes in finger-position. (See esp. Ar. *De Aud.* 804a = Porph. *Comm.* 75.30–1.) The player then has the use of notes above and intermediate between those theoretically determined by fingering, and can even perform controlled 'slides' between adjacent notes. Little of this would have been possible with the tightly closed, inflexible reeds of the previous era. (On another technique giving access to the higher harmonics see 187 ps.-Plut. 1138a.)

[6]   *Prokataulēsis*, 'preparatory playing'. The word might refer either to a craftsman's process for 'breaking in' a new *zeugos* to make it playable, or, more probably, to the performer's wetting and softening of the reed before each occasion of its use, as is normal with modern reeds.

[7]   The 'tongues' are the two elements of the double reed. The expression *pros tēn diaktērian*, which I have translated 'for the purposes of projection', is thoroughly

when they changed to an elaborate style of playing,[8] the time for cutting
the reed was altered too; and nowadays they cut it in Skirophorion and
Hekatombaion, at the time of the solstice or a little earlier [the latter part
of June]. They say that it becomes usable in three years, and needs
preliminary playing for only a short time, and that the tongues maintain
wide openings, which is essential for performers who play in the elaborate
style.[9] These then, they say, are the proper times for cutting the reed used
for the *zeugos*.

[6]   The manufacture is done like this. When they have gathered the reeds
they place them in the open air for the winter, still in their skin. In the
spring they clean them down and rub them thoroughly, and then lay them
in the sun. Later, during the summer, they cut them into the sections that
lie between the knots, and again lay them in the sun for some time. On each
such section they leave the knot nearest the growing-point:[10] the length of
the sections is no less than two palms' breadth.

Now the best of the sections for making *zeugē*, they say, are those in the
middle of the total length of the reed. The sections nearer the growing-
points make very soft *zeugē*, and those nearer the root very hard ones. [7]
Tongues made from the same section sound in consonance with one
another, while others do not:[11] the one from nearer the root goes on the

obscure. It has been emended to '. . . *diaktorian*', and translated 'for the purpose of
accompaniment', presumably with a view to the sense of the noun *diaktoros*,
'minister', 'servant'. Other emendations have been suggested. I have assumed a connection with the verb *diagein*, 'to carry through', taking the reference to be to the
penetrating quality of a sound produced by a stiff, tightly closed reed.

8   'An elaborate style of playing', *plasis*: see n. 5.
9   'Maintain wide openings': this seems to be the sense of *kataspasmata ischein*, by
contrast with 'closed up well' above. The verb *kataspaein* means 'to pull down':
kataspasmata are therefore 'pullings down', meaning, I take it, the pulling of the
'tongues' away from one another to form an opening. 'In the elaborate style', *meta
plasmatos*: see n. 5. .
10   That is, at the upper end, furthest from the root. Some scholars have been misled by
this statement, I think, into supposing that what is described here is the 'single' or
'beating' reed, like that of the clarinet, since that requires a tube with a closed end.
But this cannot be right. Theophrastus continues to use the word *zeugos*, which must
refer to something representable as a 'pair' (see n. 3). More importantly, he explains
(section 7) that several mouthpieces are made from the same internodal section, and
the knot could close only one. Nothing in the passage is inconsistent with the thesis
that the double reed, in two different versions, is the subject of discussion
throughout. The knot left at the upper end of each section of reed cannot be a part of
the finished product since, again, it could have been part of only one of the mouthpieces made from that section. Perhaps it was left there at this stage of the process to
help the reed keep its shape: it would certainly have served to indicate which end of
each section had originally been uppermost, information needed to distinguish a
'right-hand' from a 'left-hand' mouthpiece according to the procedure mentioned in
section 7.
11   *Symphōnein*, not, presumably, in the technical sense 'sound a concord' (the interval
of the fourth or the fifth, for instance), but either 'sound well together' or perhaps
'sound simultaneously', cf. e.g. Plato, *Rep.* 617b, 177 ps.-Ar. *Probs.* XIX.27. (It is
indeed difficult to make two reeds of very different texture 'speak' between one's lips
at precisely the same moment.) For the use of *symphōnein* in reference to the
members of a pair of *auloi* see 187 ps.-Plut. 1144e.

left, and that from nearer the growing-point on the right.[12] When the section is divided, the mouth of each of the two tongues is made at the end towards the place where the reed was cut.[13] If the tongues are made in any other way, they do not sound properly in consonance. That, then, is the way they are made.

[12]   I.e., they form the mouthpieces, respectively, of the left-hand and right-hand members of a pair of *auloi*. The 'tongues' must be ones from higher and lower parts of a single internodal section, forming a pair that 'sound in consonance': they are not ones from near the bottom and the top of the whole reed, and hence no conclusions can safely be drawn about their relative hardness and softness and the resulting character of sound.

[13]   This might mean 'towards the place where the reed was *originally* cut', i.e. at the lower end: more probably the reference is to the cut just mentioned, that is made between the two parts of an internodal section. The opening into which the aulete blows is made, in each of the two mouthpieces, at the place where they previously met, and their vibrating ends will thus be as nearly as possible identical in size and texture.

CHAPTER 14

The Aristotelian *Problems*

These sets of 'problems' are not by Aristotle. They comprise a collection of questions on a wide variety of topics, together with suggested answers. Their repetitions, alternative answers, and quite frequent conflicts of doctrine indicate that they are the work of a number of hands, and the collection was probably put together over a considerable period. The general trend of its ideas is in most cases broadly Aristotelian: it may have been a sort of manual of research hints, gradually accumulated and put together by students in the Lyceum.

Book XIX contains problems concerning music: together with Book XI (problems to do with the physics of sound and the physiology of voice-production) it is an important source for aspects of both theory and practice. Some of the questions it raises, and all the relevant passages of Book XI, relate directly to harmonic or acoustic theory: these are reserved for Vol. 2. Of the ones concerned with the more practical aspects of music and with musical ethos, some again demand a familiarity with detailed points of theory. Here I have attempted only brief explanations, and referred the reader to the relevant parts of the second volume.

Many of the 'solutions' offered are confused, weak, or simply silly. They are often of value none the less for the small items of information that they dispense in passing. In several cases it is the question, rather than the answer, that conveys the most useful data (e.g. **167** XIX.12, 'Why does the lower of the notes always take the melody?'). Their obvious intellectual inadequacies, and the fact that they are not arranged in any coherent order, make difficulties for the reader: for the translator there is the additional hazard of a seriously corrupted text, which cannot always be confidently restored. The collection is a jumble of odds and ends, some broken beyond repair, but one that is well worth sifting.

Ps.-Aristotle, *Problems* Book XIX (selections)

164   *Problems* XIX.5

Why do people listen with more pleasure to people singing songs that they happen to know already than to songs that they do not know? Is it because it is more obvious when the singer hits his target, as it were, if they know the piece being sung?[1] Or is it because contemplation is more enjoyable than learning?[2] The reason for that is that the latter is the acquisition of knowledge, while the former is its use and recognition. And again, what is familiar is more enjoyable than what is not.[3]

---

[1]   Cf. **166** *Probs.* XIX.9. The author apparently assumes that enjoyment consists, at least in part, in perceiving a performance as correct.

[2]   With Bonitz's emendations. Cf. Ar. *Nic. Eth.* 117a–b, *Metaph.* 1074b–1075a.

[3]   The same question, with a similar explanation, appears at *Probs.* XIX.40. Contrast **9** *Od.* 1.351–2, with note ad loc.

165   *Problems* XIX.6

Why is *parakataloge* in songs tragic?[4] Is it because of contrast?[5] For contrast is emotionally affecting in extremities of calamity or grief, while uniformity has a less mournful effect.

166   *Problems* XIX.9

Why do we listen with more enjoyment to a solo song if it is sung to the accompaniment of an *aulos* or a *lyra*?[6] Yet in both cases they sing the same tune with unison accompaniment.[7] For if there is more of the same thing, it ought to be more enjoyable when accompanied by many auletes. Is it because it is more obvious when the singer hits his target, if he signs to an *aulos* or a *lyra*? Singing to the accompaniment of many auletes or many *lyrai* is not more enjoyable, because it obscures the song.

167   *Problems* XIX.12

Why does the lower of the notes always take the melody?[8] For if one omits *paramese* when one ought to have played it with *mese*, the melody is there none the less: but if one omits *mese* when both should have been played, it is not.[9] Is it because what is low is large,[10] and hence powerful? What is small is included in what is large: and in division[11] there are two *netai* in *hypate*.

---

[4]   *Parakataloge* is something between melodic singing and speech: 'recitative'. See **187** ps.-Plut. 1141a: there its invention is ascribed to Archilochus.

[5]   I.e., contrast with the properly melodic parts of the song.

[6]   As the sequel shows, this means 'to a single *aulos* or *lyra* rather than an ensemble of several'. But in **184** *Probs.* XIX.43 exactly the same form of words means 'to an *aulos* rather than to a *lyra*', and that sense is a much more natural interpretation of the Greek. Very probably the question that originally began *Probs.* XIX.9 has been mistakenly replaced with that belonging to *Probs.* XIX.43.

[7]   *Proschorda*: see e.g. **158** Plato, *Laws* 812d, **187** ps.-Plut. 1141d.

[8]   See also **186** *Probs.* XIX.49. In the expression *krousis hypo tēn ōdēn*, 'playing under the song', used for non-unison accompaniment at e.g. **183** *Probs.* XIX 39, **187** ps.-Plut. 1141 b, 'under' indicates subordination, not lower pitch.

[9]   The text here is corrupt and obscure: I have translated the emended version of Monro. But because of the textual confusion, no conclusions about the details of performing practice can reliably be based on this sentence. *Paramese* is a tone above *mese*.

[10] The Greek word for 'low', here as usually, is *bary*, lit. 'heavy'. Passages (particularly from *Probs.* XI) exploiting the theoretical consequences of this metaphor will be reviewed in Vol. 2.

[11] That is, when intervals are constructed by proportional division of a single string. See particularly *Sect. Can.* 19–20, and cf. **175** *Probs.* XIX.23. *Nētē* is an octave above *hypatē*: if a *hypatē* string is divided by a bridge at the half-way point, each half sounds *nētē*.

168   *Problems* XIX.14

Why is it that the octave remains hidden and seems to be in unison, as in the *phoenikion* and in the human voice?[12] For the notes at the higher pitches are not in unison,[13] but are analogous[14] to one another at the octave. Is it because the analogy makes them seem as if they were the same note? Analogy, in the case of notes, is equality, and equality belongs to a single thing. People are deceived in the same way by *syringes*.[15]

169   *Problems* XIX.15

Why were *nomoi* not composed antistrophically, while other songs, those for choruses, were?[16] Is it because *nomoi* were pieces for competitors,[17] and since they were able to perform imitatively and to sustain lengthy exertions, their song became long and multiform? Like the words, then, the melodies followed the imitation in being continually varied.[18] There was even greater

[12]   The *phoenikion* is said to be an instrument of Phoenician origin, similar to the *magadis* in having its strings tuned in pairs an octave apart, as the present passage implies: see **196** Ath. 636b, 637b. Herodotus (IV.192) says it had 'arms' made of horn, suggesting a structure similar to that of the *lyra*. According to Semus of Delos (ap. Ath. 637b) they were originally made from the Delian date-palm called the *phoenix*: but this account, and the associated derivation of the name, are probably to be laid at the door of a misplaced patriotism. On the *magadis* see **196** Ath. 634c ff, especially 636c. 'In the human voice' probably refers to the effect of two voices singing in octaves (cf. **172** *Probs.* XIX.18), though possibly to a voice together with an instrumental accompaniment in the higher octave.

[13]   With the lower ones: the higher notes are the accompaniment (**167**).

[14]   *Ana logon* may mean 'in a ratio' or 'proportion': the clause might be translated 'stand to one another in the ratio of an octave'. (For the use of ratios by the writers of the *Problems* for the purpose of expressing intervals see e.g. **175** and **183** *Probs.* XIX.23 and 39.) But the point of the explanation seems to be that notes in one octave are analogous in melodic function to the equivalent notes in another octave, and ratio theory seems irrelevant here. Cf. **171** *Probs.* XIX.17. For an important discussion of melodic function, see Aristox. *El. Harm.* 47.8–50.14, cf. 40.4 ff, though he does not mention the 'analogies' of the octave. A discussion of the octave relation with a bearing on the present passage is at Ptol. *Harm.* 58.21–59.12.

[15]   This is believable enough. The Pan-pipe *syrinx*, like the modern recorder, produces relatively 'pure' tones, sounds with few overtones or harmonics. If the note C, for instance, is played on such an instrument, the hearer will readily identify it as a C; but he may find it very hard to decide whether it is e.g. 'middle C' or the C an octave higher. Overtones or harmonics, lacking in such sounds, seem to be required as perceptual clues if we are to locate the range of pitch to which the sound belongs.

[16]   On *nomoi* see **187** ps.-Plut., Appendix A. Antistrophic composition involved the repetition of rhythmic (and probably melodic) patterns: a strophe would be followed by an antistrophe whose structure was identical. The form is normal in Pindar and in the choruses of tragic drama. A freer rhythmic form, without strophic responsion, may have characterised the solo *nomos* from an early period: it was introduced, notoriously, into the dithyramb by Melanippides (see Ch. 7), where non-responding pieces became known as *anabolai*. It should be noted that the latter part of the sentence does not mean 'other choric songs', as Hett's translation has it: that is not the sense of the Greek, and it suggests, falsely, that *nomoi* could be something other than solo pieces.

[17]   Implying 'trained professionals': cf. **161** Ar. *Pol.* 1341a–b.

[18]   Cf. e.g. **149** Plato, *Rep.* 397a ff, **155** *Laws* 700d–e, Pherecrates ap. **187** ps.-Plut. 1141d ff.

need for imitation in melody than in words. That is why the dithyrambs, when they became imitative, no longer had antistrophes as they did before.[19] The reason is that in old times free men performed in the choruses themselves, and it was hard for a large group of people to sing in the competitive manner:[20] hence they sang songs within a single *harmonia*.[21] For it is easier for one person to execute many modulations[22] than for many, and easier for a competitive artist than for those who maintain the character.[23] That is why they composed simpler melodies for them. Antistrophic composition is simple: there is just one rhythm, based on a single unit of measurement.[24] The same reason explains why the songs of performers on the stage are not antistrophic, but those of the chorus are.[25] For the actor is a competitive artist and an imitator, while the chorus does less imitating.[26]

170   *Problems* XIX.16

Why is correspondence more pleasant than concord?[27] Is it because the existence of concord is then more obvious than when one sings to the

[19]   On developments in the dithyramb early in the fifth century see **29** Pindar, fr. 61. But the reference here must be to the innovations introduced by Melanippides: see n. 16.
[20]   Cf. **154** Plato, *Laws* 666d–e, 670b–c.
[21]   *Enharmonia melē.* The expression could mean 'songs in the enharmonic genus', but that seems scarcely to the point (unless, perhaps, restriction to the enharmonic is taken in a sense contrasting with 'coloured' music, as suggested at n. 8 to **162**, the Hibeh Musical Papyrus). I take 'enharmonic' here to be the antithesis of 'exharmonic' at e.g. Pherecr. ap. **187** ps.-Plut. 1141e: 'exharmonic' there seems to mean 'modulating outside the prevailing *harmonia*'. This conjecture is supported by the next sentence.
[22]   *Metabolai*, 'changes', perhaps indicating variations of mood and feeling, without technical implications. But *metabolē* is the musicologists' term of art for modulation of rhythm, genus, *harmonia*, or *tonos*. In any case, variations in character and effect were normally taken to be generated in accordance with changes in structural elements of these kinds, e.g. **149** Plato, *Rep.* 397b–c, 398d ff.
[23]   'Maintain', *phylattousin*; perhaps more directly 'guard', 'watch over'. The contrast is between the versatile professional who is required to represent the changing emotions and attitudes of a person involved in action, and the chorus, who are required to maintain a steadiness of character representing the 'proper' attitude to events. The subject under discussion is still apparently the dithyramb, or more generally any musical component of religious ceremonial involving both solo song and chorus: the special issues involved in the drama have not yet been raised. Hence the chorus must preserve the ethos appropriate to upright citizens. On the imitative versatility of the professional see e.g. **149** Plato, *Rep.* 397a–b, 398a; cf. **154**, **155**, *Laws* 669b–700a: for the contrast with the steadiness proper to citizens, **149** *Rep.* 399a–e, **156**, **157** *Laws* 799a–800b, and many other passages.
[24]   Lit., 'there is one rhythm, and it is measured by one thing': that is, the rhythmic pattern is repeated from stanza to stanza, and the pulse determining the tempo (*agōgē*, see **149** Plato, *Rep.* 400c) is constant.
[25]   Here the writer has turned to the music of the drama. Those 'on the stage' are the actors performing solo roles, as distinct from the chorus.
[26]   On the contrast between the music of actors and chorus see also **185** *Probs.* XIX.48.
[27]   'Correspondence', *to antiphōnon*. In the *Problems* the expression almost always refers to the octave, but it seems not to *mean* 'octave'. It means rather 'sounding a corresponding note', that is, one melodically equivalent to the original (cf. **168** *Probs.* XIX.14 with n. 14). As the next *Prob.* argues, this correspondence is in fact

accompaniment of a concord?[28] For one of the notes must be in unison, so that two notes played against one voice obscure the other note.[29]

171   *Problems* XIX.17

Why do people not sing in correspondence at the fifth?[30] Is it because the concordant note is not the same in this consonance,[31] as it is in the octave? For there the low note has an analogous role in the low range to the high note in the high range:[32] it is, as it were, simultaneously the same and different. But notes a fifth or a fourth apart do not stand in this relation, so that the sound of the correspondence does not clearly show itself, since it is not the same.[33]

172   *Problems* XIX.18

Why do people sing only the concord of the octave?[34] For they magadise[35] in this concord, but no other. Is it because it alone is constituted out of corresponding notes, and in corresponding notes, whichever of them one sings, the

achieved only at the octave, but the form of the question given there shows that it at least makes sense to ask why singing in fifths is not singing 'antiphonally'. Similarly *Probs.* XIX.13 asks why the lower note of an octave is *antiphōnon* to the upper. Here, then, the question is why singing to an accompaniment of equivalent or 'corresponding' notes, which will in fact be in octaves, is more pleasant than singing to a non-corresponding though concordant accompaniment. See also **157** Plato, *Laws* 802a with n. 111.

[28] The expression is confused. It appears that the first occurrence of the word 'concord' (*to symphōnein*) in this sentence includes the concord of the octave, while the second (*symphōnia*) excludes it. Perhaps the sense of the first occurrence is general and metaphorical, 'agreement'.

[29] The assumption is that the voice is accompanied at each step by two notes, one in unison with it, the other at an octave or at a fourth or a fifth above. In the latter case (but by implication not the former; cf. *Probs.* XIX.7 12, 13) the doubling of the lower note obscures the sound of the higher.

[30] On *antiphōna*, 'in correspondence', see n. 27. Here the question is about choruses singing at two pitches (cf. **172** *Probs.* XIX.18), not the accompaniment of a voice by an instrument.

[31] Not the same, that is, as the other note of the pair.

[32] On 'analogous' see n. 14: the pitch is different, the melodic function the same.

[33] The thesis seems to be that in movement from e.g. *hypatē* to *parhypatē*, paralleled at the fifth above by movement from *paramesē* to *tritē* (as movement from E to F is paralleled by movement from B to C), the movement of the higher notes is not 'analogous' to that of the lower. This can only mean 'not analogous in melodic function' (see references to Aristox. and Ptol. in n. 14). The higher notes do not clearly display themselves as singing the same melody, since they fall into a functionally distinct section of the *harmonia* or scale.

[34] This question, like the previous one, is principally concerned with singing in two parts by choruses, rather than with instrumental accompaniment, which certainly could use relations other than the octave (see e.g. **183** *Probs.* XIX.39, **158** Plato, *Laws* 812d–e, **187** ps.-Plut. 1137c–d). However, the reference to the *aulos* shows that instruments are also in the writer's mind: they also accompany the voice only at the octave on those occasions when they merely play the same melody as the voice at a different pitch. They do not play in parallel with the voice at the fourth or the fifth.

[35] The verb indicates singing in parallel octaves: cf. **183** *Probs.* XIX.39. It is derived from the noun *magadis*, the name of an instrument strung in such a way that the same tune could be played on it in two octaves simultaneously. For references see n. 12.

effect is the same?[36] For the one of them contains in some way the sounds of both,[37] so that when one of them is sung in this concord the concord is sung, and when people sing both, or when one is sung and the other played on the *aulos*, it is as if they both sing one note. Hence that note alone is sung,[38] since things in correspondence have the sound of a single note.

173   *Problems* XIX.20

Why is it that if after tuning the other strings one shifts *mesē* and then plays the instrument, the sound is painful and seems ill-adjusted not only when one plays the note belonging to *mesē*, but also in the rest of the melody, while if one shifts *lichanos* or any other note, the difference is apparent only when one plays that note?[39] Or is this only to be expected? All good tunes make frequent use of *mesē*: all good composers have continual recourse to this note, and soon revert to it when they leave it, but do not revert in the same way to any other note. Just as, if certain conjunctive words such as *te* and *kai*[40] are removed, what is said is no longer Greek, while the removal of other words causes no offence (since some words must be used frequently if anything is to be said, but others need not), so *mesē* is, as it were, a conjunction between notes, especially in good music, because its sound is involved most frequently.[41]

174   *Problems* XIX.22

Why is it that many people singing together maintain the rhythm better than a few? Is it because they concentrate more on the one man who is their leader,

---

[36] Lit., 'if one sings either of the two, one does the same thing'. Cf. n. 33.
[37] Cf. *Probs.* XIX.7, 12, 13: the lower is 'larger', and 'contains' the higher.
[38] Or 'is the melody'.
[39] The note *mesē* was certainly in some sense fundamental in Greek melodies, but its exact function is unknown. It has often been compared with our 'tonic', but the comparison must be used with great caution. The extant fragments of Greek music show that there was, for instance, no fixed convention of using *mesē* as the final note of a melody. We should certainly not allow talk of a 'tonic' to make us assume, without further evidence, that Greek music involved a system of modes or of keys corresponding at all closely to modern ones. It seems clear that when tuning an instrument a performer would tune *mesē* first, and adjust the others to it (see **181** *Probs.* XIX.36), and that a melody was felt somehow to revolve around that degree of the scale. Beyond this, few safe inferences can be made.
[40] Both are conjunctions meaning 'and'.
[41] This last 'because' clause plainly does not explain the alleged fact previously stated: it merely offers some evidence for it. The comparison between *mesē* and grammatical conjunctions has drawn withering criticism from some modern commentators; and if *mesē* was anything at all like a tonic, the comparison certainly seems fairly inept. But the author need not be trying to tell us everything about the melodic function of this note, and his overall thesis is by no means absurd, if it is that *mesē* serves to bring the other notes of the melody together into a coherent structure. Melody, like language, has a structure, and our grasp on the structure of a melody depends on our perception of the relation of its other notes to *mesē*: hence *mesē* must be frequently restated.

and begin more slowly,[42] so that they easily hit upon the same instant? For error is more common in what is swift.[43]

175   *Problems* XIX.23

Why is *nētē* double *hypatē*?[44] Is it, first of all, because when the string is plucked at half its length and as a whole, the notes form the concord of an octave? The case is similar in *syringes*,[45] for the sound through the hole in the middle of the *syrinx* forms the concord of an octave with that through the whole *syrinx*. Again, in *auloi* the octave is formed by doubling the distance, and that is how those who bore *auloi* form it: the fifth, similarly, is formed by the ratio 3 : 2. Again, those who tune *syringes* mould the wax into the very end of the *hypatē* reed, but fill the *nētē* reed up as far as half-way:[46] and similarly they form the fifth by the ratio 3 : 2 and the fourth by the ratio 4 : 3.

That seems to be the nub of the matter. No doubt the analogy with conjunctive particles in grammar breaks down: they are not 'focal' in the same way, but then nothing in grammar is. The writer has resorted to a weak analogy to express his meaning, but an adequate meaning is nevertheless there to be detected. See also **181** *Probs.* XIX.36.

[42] It is not clear what the author has in mind – perhaps the notion that a large body is stirred into motion more slowly than a small one. Choral conductors will be familiar with the phenomenon of 'inertia' in a large group of singers: mass perception of the beat seems to 'begin more slowly' than does the perception of people who are consciously singing as individuals. Whether the writer's conclusion is sound is another matter.

[43] A similar explanation is offered in *Probs.* XIX.45, where it is added that members of a small group are more likely to 'compete' against one another, and so to ignore the leader.

[44] The theory of ratios underlying this passage (originated by the Pythagoreans and used by both Plato and Aristotle) is most carefully worked out in the Euclidean *Sectio Canonis*. A good deal of its background, real and imagined, is described in Nicom. 242.20 ff. In the present passage, as most commonly (but not in the *Sectio*, for its own special reasons), the larger number is assigned to the higher note: hence the author is thinking in terms of the greater 'velocities', or possibly vibration rates (see **183** *Probs.* XIX.39) attached to higher notes, rather than the lengths of strings or pipes: indeed, he seems to be trying to 'explain' the former by reference to the latter.

[45] Here the word must refer to the body of an instrument with finger-holes, not the Pan-pipe *syrinx*, which had none. Nor is it the *aulos*, since that, like the Pan-pipe, is separately discussed below. It is presumably, then, the so-called *monokalamos syrinx*, sometimes known as the *aglōttos aulos* (for the 'single-reeeded' *syrinx* see **188** Ath. 184a, for the 'tongueless' *aulos* Pollux II.100, 108). It had no vibrating reed mouthpiece (*glōtta*), and was a simple pipe with finger-holes, sounded (like the Pan-pipe) by blowing across the open top end. It is probably the pastoral instrument referred to at e.g. Theocr. *Idylls* 5.7: cf. Pollux IV.77.

[46] Here it is the Pan-pipe *syrinx* that is intended. In its usual Greek form, the pipes of this instrument were of equal length, fixed together with wax to form a rectangular shape (hence the epithet 'wax-bound', found at e.g. **188** Ath. 184a, Theocr. *Epigr.* 5.4, cf. **127** Aesch. *P.V.* 574, Theocr. *Idylls* 8.18–19). The different pitches were created, as described here, by filling up different proportions of the lower part of each pipe with wax. The usual number of pipes seems to have been seven, but we have references to instruments with five (Pollux VIII.72) and nine (Theocr. *Idylls* 8.18). The more familiar 'wing-shaped' *syrinx*, described at Pollux IV.69 and normal in Roman times, seems to have been a later invention.

Again, in triangular *psaltēria*[47] where the tension is equal, the concord of an octave is produced when the length of one string is double, that of the other half.[48]

176   *Problems* XIX.25

Why is *mesē* so called in the *harmoniai*, given that there is no mean of eight? Is it because in the old days the *harmoniai* were heptachords, and seven has a mean?[49]

177   *Problems* XIX.27

Why is it that what is heard, alone among perceptibles, has moral character?[50] For even if there is a melody without words, it has moral character none the less,[51] but neither colour nor smell nor flavour have it. Is it because it alone has movement, though not the movement that the sound stirs up in us, since that kind of movement exists in the other perceptibles too (thus colour moves the vision)?[52] But we perceive the movement that follows upon a sound of this kind.[53] This movement has likeness[54] both in rhythms and in the ordering of high and low notes, though not in their mixture: a concord has no moral character.[55] This character does not exist in any other perceptibles. But the

47 Commonly called simply *trigōnoi*, 'triangles', as at **149** Plato, *Rep.* 399c. This was a variety of harp, plucked with the fingers, not played with a plectrum (this is the general implication of the word *psaltērion*). Its other major difference from instruments of the *lyra* family is indicated here: on the latter the lengths of the strings were equal, and pitch-differences depended on their thickness and tension, while on harp-like instruments generally the shape of the framework admitted gradations of string length.
48 For the sense in which the author's remarks might count as an answer to the original question, cf. e.g. *Probs.* XI.6, 13, 62.
49 The word *mesē* means 'middle [string]'. On the ancient heptachords see **180** *Probs.* XIX.32.
50 Cf. **161** Ar. *Pol.* 1340a–b.
51 Contrast **154** Plato, *Laws* 669e, though it is to be noted that Plato stops short of denying this claim outright.
52 That is, sound does not differ from other perceptibles in that it moves the organ of sense: all perception takes place through such movements in us.
53 The sentence is awkward: The general meaning might be that whereas other perceptibles do not need to move in order to be perceived, the cause of sound is an external movement, and sound itself is a movement of the air, which we perceive when it reaches our ear. Cf. e.g. Archytas ap. Porph. *Comm.* 56.11 ff = DK 47. B1, *Sect. Can.* 149.3 ff (Jan), Ar. ap. Porph. *Comm.* 67.24 ff = *De Aud.* 800a, *De An.* 420a. But the sequel suggests an alternative which is probably to be preferred. The movement is not that involved in the production of a single note, but the 'movement' of the voice or instrumental sound from note to note in a melody. This melodic 'movement' is often discussed in theoretical writings: see particularly Aristox. *El. Harm.* 3.5 ff.
54 I.e., likeness to moral character.
55 'Concord' (*symphōnia*) may here have its etymologically basic meaning 'sounding together', referring to the coincidence of any two notes. Moral character is represented by movement from note to note, not by notes played simultaneously. The doctrine may have arisen in the context of a polemic against heterophonic forms of accompaniment (cf. **158** Plato, *Laws* 812c–d): different notes played with the melody obscure the ethos without adding to it.

movements themselves are related to action, and actions are indications of character.[56]

178   *Problems* XIX.28

Why are the *nomoi* that people sing called by that name? Is it because before they learned writing they sang their laws,[57] so as not to forget them, as is the custom even now among the Agathyrsi? And they therefore gave to the first of their later songs the same name that they gave to their first songs.[58]

179   *Problems* XIX.31

Why were Phrynichus and his school song-writers first and foremost?[59] Is it because in those days there were many times more songs than spoken lines in tragedies?[60]

180   *Problems* XIX.32

Why is the *dia pasōn* so called, instead of being called *di' oktō* to correspond with the number, like the *dia tettarōn* and the *dia pente*?[61] Is it because in old times there were seven strings? Then Terpander took away *tritē* and added *nētē*,[62] and that is why it was called *dia pasōn* and not *di' oktō*, since there were seven strings.

---

[56]   The gist of this argument is repeated in *Probs.* XIX.29.
[57]   Greek *nomoi*. Cf. **157** Plato, *Laws* 799e ff.
[58]   The text of the last sentence is in doubt. Possibly the first occurrence of 'first' means 'most important'. On musical *nomoi* and the origin of the term's musical use see Ch. 15, Appendix A.
[59]   On Phrynichus' reputation as a composer of charming and elegant songs see Aristoph. *Birds* 749–51, **140** *Frogs* 1299–1300.
[60]   'Spoken lines', *metra*. The earliest plays of Aeschylus are still primarily 'lyric' dramas, song and dance taking precedence over spoken dialogue.
[61]   *Dia pasōn*, 'through all [the strings]' is the normal term for 'octave'. *Di'oktō* means 'through eight', *dia tettarōn* 'through four' (the interval of a fourth), and *dia pente* 'through five' (the interval of a fifth).
[62]   On Terpander's contributions to music in general see **187** ps.-Plut. 1132c ff. Particularly relevant to the present context are 1140f and 1141c. The tradition that 'in the old days' stringed instruments always had seven strings is well attested elsewhere: see especially **21** the Homeric *Hymn to Hermes* 51, and cf. **176** *Probs.* XIX.25. The sense here, as at **187** ps.-Plut. 1140f and probably *Probs.* XIX.7 (where, however, the text is in serious disrepair), is that Terpander did not alter the number of strings on his instrument, but altered their organisation. The simplest hypothesis is that the earlier note series is thought of as comprising two conjunct tetrachords, e.g. E,F,G,A,B^b,C,D, the common note of the two being *mesē* (A). This, of course, does not span an octave: Terpander 'took away *tritē*' (i.e. *tritē synēmmenōn*, B^b) and 'added *nētē*' (*nētē diezeugmenōn*, E), creating a *harmonia*, a system of tuning, that spanned an octave. The later addition of an eighth string permitted the completion of the upper tetrachord with the note *paramesē* (B), generating the familiar octave system of two tetrachords disjoined by the interval of a tone. See also *Probs.* XIX.47.

181   *Problems* XIX.36

Why is it that if *mesē* is shifted, the sound of the other strings is also spoiled, while if *mesē* is left still and one of the others is moved, only the sound of the one that was moved is spoiled?[63] Is it because for all the other strings, being attuned is standing in a certain relation to *mesē*, and the position of each is already determined by it? Thus when the cause of their attunement, and that which holds them together,[64] is removed, it[65] no longer seems to be the same. But when one string is out of tune while *mesē* stays still, it is to be expected that only what corresponds to that string fails, since in the other strings the attunement persists.

182   *Problems* XIX.38

Why does everyone enjoy rhythm and melody and the whole class of concords?[66] Is it because we naturally enjoy all natural movements? An indication of this is that children enjoy these things from the moment they are born.[67] We enjoy different styles[68] of melody because of their moral character, but rhythm because it is characterised by a recognisable and orderly number, and moves us in an orderly way.[69] Orderly movement is in its nature more closely akin to us than disorderly, and so is more natural. An indication of this is that if we exert ourselves and eat and drink in an orderly way we

For the possible association of the earlier conjunct system with the 'Aeolian' *harmonia* see **187** ps.-Plut. n. 177. Compare the account of Pythagoras' 'invention' of an octave structure by the addition of an eighth string, Nicom. 244.14 ff, and for a different allegedly ancient heptachord structure spanning an octave, 252.19 ff.

63 For the sense of the question, and some suggestions relating to its solution, see **173** *Probs.* XIX.20 with notes.

64 *To synechon.* The expression may indicate only a generalised notion of coherence. Alternatively it may be related to the technical concept of 'continuity', *to syneches*, which consists in the relations between notes forming a legitimate scalar series. See Aristox. *El. Harm.* 27.15–29.1, 52.33–53.32, 58.14–60.16, and many of the theorems in his Bk 3. In that case the author will be saying that being a legitimate scalar series consists in being a set of notes that stand in a correct and complete series of relations to *mesē*, rather than e.g. being a set of notes each standing in the correct relation to its predecessor.

65 I.e., the position of each note.

66 The explanation offered falls into two parts, one dealing with rhythm and melody, the other with concord. Both emphasise the element of orderliness in these phenomena.

67 Cf. e.g. **153** and **154** Plato, *Laws* 653d–e, 664e–665a.

68 'Styles', *tropoi*. Some authors use the term, on occasion, as an equivalent for *harmonia*, in the sense 'scale-structure' (e.g. Arist. Quint. 8.20, 13.9–10, etc.), but its meaning is usually broader. A 'style' of melody may be determined by any combination of scale-structure, pitch, and melodic shape. The sentence seems to reflect the common view, articulated by Plato, that people enjoy music that 'imitates' the character that they themselves possess. See e.g. **153** and **157** *Laws* 655d–656a, 802c–d, cf. Arist. Quint. 80.10–22.

69 Rhythms were classified by the ancient theorists in terms of 'number', specifically the numerical ratio holding between the two parts of the metrical foot, or other rhythmic unit. Thus for instance the dactyl (- | ˘ ˘) is in 'equal' ratio, 1 : 1, the iambus (˘ | -) in 'duple' ratio, 1 : 2. See Arist. Quint. 33.29 ff, cf. **183** *Probs.* XIX.39.

preserve and improve our nature and our strength, whereas by proceeding in a disordered way we destroy and disrupt it: for diseases are movements of an unnatural ordering of the body. But we enjoy concord because it is a blend of opposites that stand in a ratio to each other.[70] Ratio is a form of order, which, as we have shown, is naturally pleasant. Anything that is blended is pleasanter than what is unmixed, especially if the ratio, being something capable of being perceived, has the power of the two extremes in equal balance.[71]

183   *Problems* XIX.39

Why is correspondence[72] pleasanter than unison? Is it because correspondence is concordance at the octave? Correspondence arises when young children combine with men, whose pitches differ as do *nētē* and *hypatē*. Now every concord is pleasanter than a simple sound (we have explained why already[73]), and the octave is the pleasantest of the concords, while the sound of a unison is simple. People magadise[74] in the concord of the octave, because just as in metres the feet exhibit the ratio of equal to equal or two to one or some other,[75] so the notes in a concord have a ratio of movement to one another.[76] In the case of the other concords the endings of one note or the other are incomplete, finishing at the half-way point.[77] For this reason they are not equal in power; and since they are unequal, a difference is present to our perception, just as there is in choruses when some people sing louder

---

[70] Cf. Ar. *De Sensu* 448a. Greek theorists typically emphasise the 'blending' of the two notes in a concord, to form a whole in which neither is heard independently.
[71] Cf. Ar. *De An.* 424a, 426a–b, *De Sensu* 447a.
[72] Reading *antiphōnon* (see 170 *Probs.* XIX.16, n. 27) for the MSS *symphōnon*, 'concord': the reply to the question is wholly concerned with the relation of the octave.
[73] In 182 *Probs.* XIX.38. Concord adds a form of order to mere pitched sound.
[74] See 172 *Probs.* XIX.18 with n. 35. The first part of the present passage refers only to choral singing: instrumental accompaniment is discussed separately in the second half.
[75] See n. 69. The ratios of the unison and the concords are the same as those of the principal genera of rhythm.
[76] On the theory of pitch ratios generally see n. 44. The sequel to this sentence presupposes the theory that pitch varies not with the velocity of a sound's transmission (as Archytas, Plato, Aristotle and most of the Peripatetics believed), but with the rapidity of the impacts made on the air by a vibrating string or column of air. This more sophisticated view is adopted also in the Introduction to the *Sect. Can.*, and is hinted at in *Probs.* XIX.42 and by Theophrastus ap. Porph. *Comm.* 63.19–28: cf. Aristotle ap. *Comm.* 75.14–27 (= *De aud.* 803b–804a), Heraclides ap. *Comm.* 31–2.
[77] 'The other concords', i.e. those other than the octave. In the concord of a fifth, for instance, the ratio between the notes is 3 : 2. This means, according to the present theory, that the higher-pitched string strikes the air three times while the lower-pitched string strikes it twice. Since the third pulse of the higher string will occur later than the second pulse of the lower, the latter will be 'complete' before the former. (The expression 'at the half-way point' seems to be intended quite vaguely, 'part-way through its duration', or else to be offered just as an example.) The theory presupposes, most interestingly, that a note is not complete as a note, is not that definite pitch, until a certain number of pulses have occurred.

than others at the end.[78] Now it happens that *hypatē* has the same ending of the periodic movements in its notes: for the second blow on the air made by *nētē* is *hypatē*.[79] Since they finish at the same time, though their effect is not the same, the function they perform is one and common to them both,[80] as in the case of people who play an accompaniment under a song.[81] Though elsewhere these people do not play the same notes as the melody,[82] still, if they finish on the same note, the pleasure they give with the ending is greater than the pain they give with the differences before the ending, because the common note, that arising from the octave, comes most pleasingly after differences.[83] Magadising arises from opposed sounds; and that is why they magadise in the octave.[84]

184   *Problems* XIX.43

Why is it that we listen with more enjoyment to a solo song if someone is singing to the *aulos* than if he is singing to the *lyra*?[85] Is it because anything mixed with what is more pleasant thereby becomes still more pleasant? The *aulos* is pleasanter than the *lyra*, so that a song mixed with the *aulos* would be pleasanter than mixed with the *lyra*, since what has been mixed is pleasanter than what is unmixed, so long as one grasps a perception of both elements simultaneously.[86] Wine is pleasanter than

---

78   'Difference', *diaphora*: the sense is simply that one seems stronger to our hearing. The reference of the last clause is probably to choral 'magadising', singing in two parts at the interval of an octave. What creates the 'difference' is in this case mere loudness, since the peculiarity relating to the 'completions' of notes in a concord does not apply in the case of the octave (see the next sentence).

79   *Hypatē* has the same 'ending' as *nētē*, since *nētē* is an octave (ratio 2 : 1) above *hypatē*, so that *hypatē*-pulses coincide with every alternate *nētē*-pulse. Thus every instance of the sound of *hypatē* is complete at the same moment as some instance of the sound of *nētē*, and conversely. (It is assumed that *nētē* is not complete until the string has struck the air twice: see n. 77.)

80   On the common function of notes an octave apart see 168, 170–2, *Probs.* XIX.14, 16, 17, 18.

81   *Hypo tēn ōdēn*: see note 8 above. The expression cannot refer here to playing in octaves with the tune, since the 'different notes' of the *hypo tēn ōdēn* accompaniment are contrasted below with the 'common note' effect of the final octave consonance. The accompaniment in question is therefore 'heterophonic': cf. 158 Plato, *Laws* 812c–d.

82   They are not *prosaulountes*, lit. 'playing the *aulos* in unison [with the voice]'.

83   Reading *tōi ek diaphorōn to koinon, to ek tou dia pasōn, hēdiston ginesthai*.

84   The last sentence seems to belong to a different explanation: its treatment of notes an octave apart as 'opposed' is foreign to the tenor of what precedes it (cf. Ar. *De Sensu* 448a). The underlying sense is that 'blends' or 'mixtures' are pleasanter than simple sounds: cf. 182 *Probs.* XIX.38.

85   Cf. the question that begins 166 *Probs.* XIX.9, with n. 6.

86   Parts of two explanations seem to be conflated here. The first argues that the mingling of a vocal line with a pleasanter accompaniment gives a pleasanter result, and that the *aulos* is pleasanter than the *lyra*. The second, expanded in the sequel, claims that two elements that blend more completely give a pleasanter result than elements that blend inadequately; and *aulos* and voice blend better than *lyra* and voice. The

oxymel[87] because things mixed by nature are more mingled with one another than are things mixed by us. Wine is a mixture of sharp and sweet flavour, as the so-called 'wine-pomegranates' show. Thus the song and the *aulos* mingle with one another because of their similarity, since both arise through the breath; while the note of the *lyra*, either because it does not arise through the breath or because it is less perceptible than the sound of *auloi*, is less capable of mixing with the voice. Because it creates a distinction in the perception,[88] it pleases us less, as has been said in the case of flavours. Again, the *aulos* conceals many of the mistakes in the song, through the similarity of its own sound, whereas the notes of the *lyra*, being bare[89] and less capable of mixing with the voice, being perceived on their own and actually existing on their own, make a mistake in the song stand out clearly, acting as it were as yardsticks for them.[90] When there are many mistakes in the song, inevitably the common result of the two elements is worse.

185   *Problems* XIX.48

Why do choruses in tragedy sing neither in Hypodorian nor in Hypo-phrygian?[91] Is it because these *harmoniai* have melody to the smallest extent, and melody is most necessary to a chorus?[92] Hypophrygian has an

---

division between the two explanations comes at the (quite inappropriate) word 'since'. The qualification that the two elements must be perceived simultaneously does not mean that each must be grasped independently, in its own character, at one and the same time: quite the reverse. Being perceived simultaneously involves being perceived as a blend in which the independent elements are submerged. See Ar. *De Sensu* 447b–448a.

[87]   A mixture of wine and vinegar.

[88]   I.e., because we perceive the sounds of *lyra* and voice as distinct unblended elements.

[89]   *Psiloi*. The word is commonly used of instrumental music unaccompanied by the voice. Here the voice accompanies it, but is isolated from it by its incapacity to mix.

[90]   'Yardsticks', *kanones*, 'measuring-rods'. (The title of the Euclidean *Sectio Canonis* means 'division of a measuring-rod', in that case one used to mark off intervals along a length of string.) Here the precisely pin-pointed notes of the *lyra* act as 'measures' or 'standards' against which the accuracy of the singer's notes can be assessed.

[91]   On the structure and associations of these *harmoniai* see 187 ps.-Plut. 1137a, n. 121. They are again said to be used by actors but not by choruses in tragedy in *Probs.* XIX.30, where the author explains that this is because they are 'imitative', and because they 'do not have (perhaps 'admit') an antistrophe' (this seems to be the sense). Why these *harmoniai* should not lend themselves to strophic treatment is unclear. Possibly it has something to do with the claim of the present passage, that they 'have melody to the smallest extent'. If, as is likely, strophe and antistrophe were sung to the same melody as well as with the same rhythm, then the lack of melodic opportunities offered by these *harmoniai* would make them unattractive in strophic form. For the association of this form with choruses see 169 *Probs.* XIX.15.

[92]   If the *harmoniai* are conceived wholly as scale-structures, it is hard to make sense of the claim that these ones have little melodic potential. The idea suggests a scale of

nvigorating character,[93] which is why in the *Geryonē* the episodes of marching out and of putting on armour are composed in this *harmonia*, while the Hypodorian is magnificent and stately, and hence is the most suited of the *harmoniai* to *kitharōdia*. Both of these are unfitting for a chorus, but more appropriate to those on the stage.[94] For the latter are imitators of heroes; and in the old days only the leaders were heroes, while the mass of the people were mere humans, and it is to these that the chorus belongs. Hence a mournful and quiet character and melody is suited to them, since these are human. The other *harmoniai* have these features,[95] but Phrygian has them to the smallest extent, since it is inspirational and Bacchic.[96] Under the influence of this *harmonia*, then, we are affected in a particular way; and the weak are more prone to being affected than the strong, so that this *harmonia* too is suited to a chorus. Under that of Hypodorian and Hypophrygian, however, we respond with action,[97] something that is not appropriate to a chorus. For the chorus is an inactive attendant: all that it offers is good will towards those in whose company it is.

186   *Problems* XIX.49

Why is it that of notes composing a concord the quality of the lower note is softer?[98] Is it because melody is in its own nature soft and still, becoming rough and stimulating[99] only through mixture with rhythm? Since the low

---

limited range, but we know nothing of 'defective' versions of Hypodorian and Hypophrygian, comparable to the other scales set out at Arist. Quint. 18.5 ff. Both *harmoniai*, however, are associated with low pitch, and it may be this feature that renders them melodically unmanageable.

[93] *Praktikon*, conducive to action: the point is elaborated below. Cf. **161** Ar. *Pol.* 1341b–1342a.

[94] I.e., to the principal actors: cf. **169** *Probs.* XIX.15.

[95] Here the Latin translation of Theodore Gaza (a Greek scholar of the fifteenth century, who seems to have had access to manuscripts additional to those that now survive) adds 'but the Mixolydian undoubtedly displays them most markedly': these words have somehow dropped out of our Greek texts. On the use of Mixolydian in tragedy see **187** ps.-Plut. 1136c with n. 110.

[96] See **161** Ar. *Pol.* 1342a–b, and Ch. 10, Appendix A: cf.p. 63 n. 7.

[97] This is an expansion of the Greek, which merely means 'we act', contrasting it with 'we are affected'.

[98] *Malakōteron*, 'softer' in the sense 'gentler', 'milder', not necessarily 'quieter'.

[99] Here and in the next sentence 'stimulating' translates *kinētikon*, 'conducive to movement'. Contrast Philodemus 71.47–8, reporting the Stoic view that he will attack: 'melody is by nature *kinētikon*'. The sentence reflects the usual Greek convention that where melody and accompaniment had different notes, the melody had the lower part: cf. **167** *Probs.* XIX.12.

note is soft and still, while the high note is stimulating, it follows that when two notes have the same melody, the lower note will be softer in the same melody, since we have agreed that melody in itself is soft.[100]

[100]   The argument is weak and confused: it contains hints of the following line of reasoning. Melody is 'naturally soft': melody 'naturally' takes the lower part. Hence of any pair of notes played simultaneously, the lower is to be construed as having the melody: hence it must be naturally softer. Possibly the ideas were taken from what was originally an answer to the quite different *Probs.* xix.12 (167): the lower note takes the melody because (a) lower notes are naturally softer, and (b) melody as such, abstracted from rhythm, is 'naturally soft and still'. The thesis that melody is soft, rhythm stimulating and active, is reflected in the identification of melody with female, rhythm with male, reported at Arist. Quint. 40.20–5, 77.5–16. In either form the discussion carries the interesting implication that non-unison accompaniment above the melodic line is thought of as primarily a rhythmic phenomenon. The discords and resolutions introduced by the higher notes (see e.g. 183 *Probs.* xix.39, 187 ps.-Plut. 1137b–c), as well as the decoration of slow-moving melody with quick instrumental note-clusters (158 Plato, *Laws* 812c–d), are there to create and emphasise rhythmical tensions and relaxations, not to provide additional melodic interest. This attitude may help to explain the theorists' exhaustive division of musical form and structure into the rhythmic and the melodic, and their failure to give separate consideration to simultaneous 'harmony', or to interrelations between simultaneous melodies.

CHAPTER 15

The Plutarchian treatise *On Music*

Most scholars agree that this work is not by Plutarch, though there is no good reason for assigning it a date very far from his (first to second centuries A.D.). It is an example of what had become a common and largely a fossilised genre, that is, a report of 'table talk' among witty or learned men, assembled to eat, drink, and entertain themselves. The author makes little attempt to breathe life into this fiction: the form is the merest convention, a pale ghost of the symposia depicted by Plato and Xenophon, and serves only to provide a vehicle for the exposition of material better suited to a straight-forward essay.

The importance of the treatise lies in its lack of originality. It sets out to discuss the history of Greek music and certain aspects of musical theory, and does so to a great extent through quotations and paraphrases of much earlier sources, notably Glaucus of Rhegium, Plato, Aristotle, Aristoxenus and Heraclides. Thus the bulk of its material comes from writers of the fourth century B.C., and some from the fifth; and though the compiler is often clumsy in his ways of putting the sources together, he seems on the whole to have reported them faithfully. Most of the works which he drew upon are now lost, and his compilation is packed with information that would otherwise have been lost with them.

In dealing with so rich and complex a work any commentator must balance pre-cariously on the shoulders of his predecessors. Lasserre's edition contains, in addi-tion to rather speculative essays on a number of topics to do with Greek music, a useful analysis of the structure of the work, and an account of the interrelations of its sources. On these matters I have nothing to add. My own commentary is heavily indebted to his, and still more to the older edition of Weil and Reinach, whose exhaustive study is an invaluable aid on points of detail. I have not usually followed them, however, in their cavalier emendations and reorganisations of the text.

187   *De Musica*

1. [1131b] The wife of Phocion the Good used to say that his exploits as a general were her adornment.[1] For myself, I consider my teacher's enthusiasm for rational enquiry to be an adornment not for myself alone, but for every-one in his circle. We know, after all, that a general's most glorious successes only produce safety from immediate dangers for a few soldiers or a single city or at best a single nation, [c] and do nothing to improve the character of the soldiers or the citizens, or those who belong to the nation; whereas we find that education, which is the essence of happiness and the cause of good counsel, is of value not only to a household or a city or a nation, but to the whole race of mankind. Thus the degree to which the benefit derived from education is greater than that derived from any military achievements indicates the degree of serious attention that the discussion of education deserves.

---

[1]   There is a *Life of Phocion* by Plutarch. For his wife's remark see 750d.

2. On the second day of the Saturnalia[2] the excellent Onesicrates had invited to his feast men who were experts in music: they were Soterichus of Alexandria, and Lysias, one of those who enjoyed a pension from Onesicrates. When the usual ceremonies were completed, [d] Onesicrates said: 'A drinking-party like this, my friends, is not the time to investigate the causal basis of the human voice,[3] since that is an enquiry which demands a more sober period of leisure. However, since the best authorities on writing define sound[4] as "air which has been struck, and which is perceptible to hearing",[5] and since, as it happens, we were yesterday enquiring into the art of writing, conceived as that art which enables us to reproduce vocal sounds in letters and to preserve them for our recollection, let us consider which of the sciences concerned with vocal sound comes after this one, in second place.

'In my opinion it is music; for it is a pious act, and one of the highest importance for mankind, to sing hymns to the gods who have given articulate voice to mankind alone. This is indicated by Homer, when he says, [e] "All day long the Achaeans sought to appease the god with song, singing a beautiful paean, chanting to far-shooting Apollo: and he heard, and rejoiced in his mind."[6] So come now, you devotees of music, and recount to our companions who it was that first employed music, what advances in it time has discovered, and who has achieved fame, among those who have undertaken the science of music: and tell us also how many purposes, and what kinds of purpose, the practice of music serves.'[7] That was what our teacher said.

3. [f] 'The question you raise, noble Onesicrates,' replied Lysias, 'is one which many have sought to answer. Most of the Platonists and the best of the

---

[2]   In Greek, *Kronia*, the festival of Kronos, celebrated from ancient times at various times of year in different cities. By this period it seems to have been absorbed into the Saturnalia, the major Roman winter festival, beginning on 17 December, to which the Greek word then came to refer.

[3]   As studied in such works as Ar. *De An.*, *De Sensu*, ps.-Ar. *Probs.* XI, and many other Peripatetic writings.

[4]   *Phōnē*, lit. 'voice', and often reserved for the human voice (see e.g. Ar. *De An.* 420b), but here sound of any sort: cf. Aristox. *El. Harm.* 14.3–4.

[5]   This (Stoic) definition is found in such grammarians as Mar. Vict. VI.4.13 (Keil), Donatus 367.5 (Keil): cf. Diog. Laert. VII.55, Diog. Bab. fr. 17 (von Arnim). It can be traced back to the investigations of Archytas and Plato in the fourth century (Porph. *Comm.* 56.11 ff, Plato, *Tim.* 67b), through the researches of the Peripatetics (e.g. Ar. *De An.* 420b, *De Audib.* ap. Porph. *Comm.* 67.24 ff, ps.-Ar. *Probs.* XI.6, 14, etc., XIX.35a, 37, cf. Heraclides ap. Porph. *Comm.* 30.2 ff), and into both the Pythagorean (e.g. Nicom 242.20 ff) and Aristoxenian (e.g. Arist. Quint. 5.20 ff) traditions of harmonic science: a version is adopted by Ptolemy (*Harm.* 3.2).

[6]   1 *Il.* 1.472–4. This paean is not, of course, merely a hymn in celebration of a god: it is a prayer for release from plague.

[7]   The division of the subject suggested here corresponds roughly to the course of the dissertations that follow. The earliest musicians are discussed at 1131f–1136b, innovations at 1136b–1138c and 1140f–1142c, harmonic science at 1138c–1140b, the uses of music, particularly in education, at 1140b–f and 1142c–1146d: but the topics have a bearing on one another, and inevitably overlap.

Peripatetics felt it important to write both about ancient music and about music's degeneration in their own times;[8] and all the most cultivated experts in the sciences of grammar and harmonics have also given it a great deal of attention.[9] Consequently there are many discordant views among those who have written on the subject.

'Heraclides[10] in his *Collection of Musicians*[11] says that the original inventor of singing to the *kithara* and of poetry to be sung to the *kithara* was Amphion, son of Zeus and Antiope:[12] [1132a] it was his father, obviously, who taught him. The evidence for this is in the inscription preserved at Sicyon,[13] which Heraclides relies on for his list of the priestesses at Argos, and of the poets and musicians.

'About the same time, Heraclides says, Linus of Euboea was composing dirges, Anthes of Anthedon in Boeotia was composing hymns, and Pieros of Pieria his poems about the Muses, while Philammon of Delphi recounted in songs the wanderings of Leto and the birth of Artemis and Apollo, and was the first to establish choruses at the temple of Delphi.[14] Thamyris, a Thracian by birth, sang more melodiously [b] and with a more beautiful voice than anyone else in those days, which led him to compete, so the poets say, in a contest against the Muses. He is also said to have composed a piece on the war of the Titans against the gods. There was also in those ancient times the musician Demodocus of Corcyra, who composed pieces on the sack of Troy

---

8   Among the 'Platonists' the author no doubt has in mind Plato himself and Heraclides, and perhaps later Platonising 'Pythagoreans' of the kind exemplified by Nicomachus. The 'best' of the Peripatetics will include Aristotle, Theophrastus and Aristoxenus, together with a number of later authors. Aristoxenus and Heraclides are certainly major sources for this work.

9   *Harmonikoi*. The term might refer to any specialist writers on musical theory, but probably indicates specifically those recognised by Aristoxenus as his predecessors, and named in this way by him. Their testimony will have come to our author partly through Aristox. himself (perhaps in the work mentioned at *El. Harm.* 2.25 ff, 6.15 ff), partly through Heraclides who may have relied in turn on the account given by Glaucus of Rhegium (see 1132e).

10   Heraclides was a pupil of Plato and later of Aristotle. He wrote on many subjects: Athenaeus (192 624c) mentions and quotes from a work *On Music*.

11   Or perhaps 'of facts about music'.

12   Cf. Plin. *Nat. Hist.* VII.204. Amphion is wholly legendary: tracing music (and other arts) to a divine source is commonplace in Greek thought (cf. e.g. 1135f, out of many hundreds of examples), but perhaps especially characteristic of the religiously minded Heraclides.

13   Jacoby III.B550, p. 536. The inscription seems to have been a list of poet-composers and musicians, dated by reference to the tenure of priestesses at Argos. It may have been set up in one of the Sicyonian temples. Similar lists existed naming victors in athletics at the games: this one may have listed victors in the musical contests.

14   On Linus see 7 *Il.* XVIII.570 and note. Nothing is recorded elsewhere of a musician called Anthes. 'Pieros' is a name invented by some late authors for the father of the Muses, whose common title *Pierides* means 'from Pieria', the place of their sacred mountain Helicon, but which could be taken to mean 'daughters of Pieros'. We have little information about Philammon, treated as an archetypal *kitharōdos*, beyond what is mentioned here: see also 1133a, cf. Pherecydes, fr. 120 (Jacoby). All these people are entirely mythical, and are grouped together as children of the gods, belonging to the very earliest times.

and the marriage of Aphrodite and Hephaistos; while Phemius of Ithaca composed one on the return of Agamemnon and his company from Troy.[15] 'The diction in the poems of the people I have mentioned was [c] not rhythmically undisciplined[16] or lacking in metre, but resembled that of Stesichorus and the ancient composers of song, who composed hexameter poems and set them to music.[17] Heraclides says also that Terpander, a composer of kitharodic *nomoi*, set his own hexameter verses and those of Homer to music appropriate to each *nomos*, and sang them in competitions; and he tells us that Terpander was the first to give names to the kitharodic *nomoi*.[18] Clonas, like Terpander, the first to construct aulodic *nomoi* and processionals, was a composer of elegiacs and hexameters.[19] Polymnestus of Colophon, who lived later than Clonas, employed the same poetic forms.[20]

[15]   On Thamyris see 5 *Il.* II.594–600. The basis for the remarks about Demodocus is in the songs given to him at 10 *Od.* VIII.72 ff, 266 ff, 499 ff: Phemius' song is the one mentioned at 9 *Od.* I.325–7. This group of musicians is conceived as a 'second generation', immediate precursors of Homer. Though the type they represent is historically real, the individuals are of course as mythical as the members of the first group.

[16]   *Lelymenē*, 'released', 'free'. The comparison intended is with composers who were modern in the time of the original source, i.e. Timotheus and his successors. The principal feature of their 'free' diction was its lack of a constant metre, a metrical unit (whether a foot, a line or a strophe) regularly repeated. Cf. Hephaestion, *Poem.* 3, and see Ch. 7 above.

[17]   As noted in Ch. 4, while the basis of the early elegiac tradition was certainly the *epē*, epic hexameters, of Homer and others, the metrical exemplars for the lyric poets (*melopoiioi*, here 'composers of song') were probably found in folk song, and were not of the dactylic hexameter type. Their metres, nevertheless, were regular rather than 'free'.

[18]   Terpander (seventh century: see 196 Ath. 635d–e) is a figure of heroic stature in early musical history, but he does belong genuinely to history, however misty, rather than mere legend. We cannot be sure how many of the innovations credited to him are really his. He was born in Lesbos (e.g. Ath. loc. cit., 130 Timotheus, *Persae* 237 ff), but spent most of his life in Sparta, where he was afterwards treated as the greatest of all musicians (e.g. *Suda* under the heading *meta Lesbion ōdon*, cf. 1134b and 1146b below). The reference to his hexameters and those of Homer seems to mean that he was the first to set such works to genuine melodies, by contrast with the chants of the Homeric minstrels and the recitations of the *rhapsōdoi*. (Cf. Proclus, *Chrest.* 45.) But it seems clear that not all Terpander's poetry was in hexameters, if we may judge from the names given to his kitharodic *nomoi* (1132d) and from the ascription to him of new metrical forms at 1140f. Among the other musical achievements linked with his name are the invention of the *barbitos* (Pindar ap. Ath. loc. cit.) and alterations to the form of the scale (180 ps.-Ar. *Probs.* XIX.32, cf. 7,25,44,47, ps.-Plut. 1140f). On the basis of a (possibly genuine) quotation from his work given at Strabo XIII.2.4 and Cleonides 202.11–12, he is said by many ancient writers to have increased the number of strings on the *kithara* from four to the seven that became canonical. Here his importance is to do with the establishment of the genre known as the kitharodic *nomos*: see Appendix A.

[19]   The sentence is a little confused. It is probably intended to mean that Clonas stood to *aulōdia* as did Terpander to *kitharōdia*, not that Terpander as well as Clonas composed elegiacs, which seem never to have been a kitharodic form. *Prosodia* are processional songs sung to the *aulos* (Proclus, *Chrest.* 10): there is nothing to support Lasserre's suggestion that they are here simply aulodic 'preludes', comparable to the kitharodic *prooimia* credited to Terpander at 1132d. Of Clonas nothing substantial is known beyond what is said here and at 1133a.

[20]   Our information on Polymnestus is scanty. He was mentioned by Alcman and Pindar

4. [d] 'The *nomoi* used by these people,[21] noble Onesicrates, were the following, which are aulodic: *Apothetos, Elegoi, Kōmarchios, Schoiniōn, Kēdeios, Trimelēs*. Later the ones called *Polymnastia* were also invented.[22] The *nomoi* belonging to *kitharōdia* were established rather earlier, in the time of Terpander, and it was Terpander who first gave names to the kitharōdic *nomoi*, calling them Boeotian and Aeolian, *Trochaios* and *Oxys*, *Kēpiōn* and *Terpandreios*, and finally *Tetraoidios*.[23] Terpander also composed kitharodic preludes in hexameters.[24] [e] Timotheus provides evidence of the fact that the ancient kitharodic *nomoi* were composed in hexameters: he sang his earliest *nomoi* in hexameters, while mixing into them the diction of the dithyramb, thus ensuring that he would not be in obvious and immediate breach of the rules of ancient music.[25]

'Terpander seems to have been an outstanding practitioner of the art of singing to the *kithara*: it is recorded[26] that he won the Pythian contest four times in succession. The period at which he lived belongs to remotest antiquity: thus Glaucus of Italy,[27] in a book about the ancient poets and musicians, indicates that he was earlier than Archilochus, since he says that Terpander followed immediately [f] after the first composers of songs sung to the *aulos*.[28]

5. 'Alexander,[29] in his *Collection of Information about Phrygia*, said that Olympus was the first to introduce instrumental music[30] to the Greeks,

21 (1133a below): for further reports see 1134d, 1135c, 1141b, Paus. 1.14.4. In the comic poets 'Polymnestian songs' are indecent and lascivious (Aristoph. *Knights* 1287, cf. Cratinus, fr. 305 Kock), but it is not clear whether the implication attaches to the present Polymnestus or to a later poet of the same name. See also the next note.

21 'These people' might be Terpander and Clonas, despite the fact that the first list given is of aulodic *nomoi*, not applicable to Terpander. The author goes on to mention Terpander's *nomoi* immediately afterwards, and the remark that the 'so-called *Polymnastia*' came later has been thought to rule out the possibility that 'these people' are Clonas and Polymnestus. But the author might mean: these are the *nomoi* of Clonas and Polymnestus, and the 'so-called *Polymnastia*' (i.e., the indecent songs mentioned in n. 20 above) are really a later invention, nothing to do with this Polymnestus. See also 1133a.

22 On the *nomoi* listed here see Appendix A: on *Polymnastia* see the previous note.

23 For the significance of these names and an assessment of their authenticity see Appendix A.

24 'Preludes', *prooimia*: see introduction to the Homeric Hymns.

25 On Timotheus and the dithyramb see Ch. 7. His kitharodic *nomos* called *Persae* provides examples of hexameters side by side with other forms of rhythm, though that is a stage more advanced than what the present author describes. It is notable, as W. and R. justly remark, that the source had to argue for his conclusion from the indirect evidence of Timotheus: clearly no instances of Terpander's *nomoi* survived in his day.

26 *Anagegraptai*: the verb suggests an inscription of the type mentioned at 1132a above: it is probably the same as the one referred to in similar terms at 1134a, and evidently comprised a list of Pythian victors.

27 A historian of the later fifth century, the primary source for substantial portions of the present work.

28 *Aulōdian*: possibly we should emend to *aulētikēn*, 'music for solo *aulos*': see n. 30.

29 Alexander Polyhistor, a historian of the first century B.C.

30 *Kroumata*, plural of *krouma*, lit. 'strokes', 'blows'. Its original musical application is

though the Idaean Dactyls did so too,[31] and that Hyagnis was the first to play the *aulos*, followed by his son Marsyas and then by Olympus.[32] Terpander, he says,[33] modelled his work on the hexameters of Homer and the melodies of Orpheus;[34] whereas Orpheus appears not to have copied anybody, since he had no predecessors except the poets who composed songs sung to the *aulos*, and Orpheus' work is not like theirs in any respect. [1133a] Clonas, the composer of *nomoi* sung to the *aulos*, who lived a little later than Terpander,[35] was a Tegean according to the Arcadians, a Theban according to the

to the striking of a string with a plectrum, and hence designates music for *kithara* and similar instruments. W. and R., taking it in this sense, suppose that the whole quotation from Alexander is misplaced, and insert it in 1131f. But in late sources (and Alexander is substantially later than most of the authorities cited in this work) the word is used of the sounds of instruments generally, including those of *auloi* (see e.g. Plut. *Quaest. Conv.* 638c, Pollux iv.83, cf. 84). The alternative implication, which W. and R. accept, that Olympus is being credited with the introduction of music for stringed instruments, contradicts the major tradition that he, like Hyagnis and Marsyas, was an aulete only. The fragments of evidence adduced by W. and R. to connect them with the *kithara* are very tenuous.

Lasserre translates *kroumata* as 'les airs d'accompagnement à la flute'; but this is inadmissible. Though the word can be used of accompaniment, it never simply *means* 'accompaniment', always 'instrumental sound'. Then if the author intends his quotation from Alexander as an amplification of the reference to the *aulos* in the previous sentence, we should probably there read *auletikēn* in place of *aulōdian*. Olympus was known both as an exponent of solo *auletikē* (1133d ff) and as a composer of *aulōdia* (1134f ff with 1137b–d): but if the previous treatment of Clonas as the pioneer of *aulōdia* (1132c) is to be maintained here, Olympus must be treated for present purposes as a composer of *auletikē* only, and the case for emendation is further strengthened.

31   The Dactyls of Ida were a legendary race, said to have looked after the infant Zeus. Their relevance here is obscure, but the general sense must be: Olympus introduced instrumental music to Greece, though the Idaean Dactyls were admittedly responsible for introducing some such music, presumably music of other instruments. Conceivably they are supposed to have introduced an instrumental application of the rhythm with which their name is linked (cf. Clem. Alex. *Strom.* 1.15.73), a rhythm associated primarily with songs sung to the *kithara*, as in Terpander's *kitharōdia* (1132c). But no other authority links them with this instrument.

32   Hyagnis and Marsyas belong even more clearly to the mythological pre-history of music than does Olympus. Their main significance here is their common origin in Phrygia, by almost universal tradition the ancestral home of the *aulos*. By classical times the human Marsyas had been transformed into a satyr, and had become the prototype aulete (see esp. Plato, *Symp.* 215b–c). Hyagnis was his father, and was credited with the invention both of the *aulos* and of the Phrygian *harmonia* which was its special preserve. (See e.g. 1133f, *Marm. Par.* 10, *Anon. Bell.* 28, 192 Ath. 624b, *Anth. Pal.* ix.340, cf. 161 Ar. *Pol.* 1342b.) For the familiar story of Marsyas and Athena see also Plut. *De Cohib. Irae* 456b–d, and for his contest with Apollo, Diod. Sic. iii.59.2–5. More of Alexander's account of him is preserved in ps.-Plut. *De Fluviis* 10. Olympus was commonly said to be his pupil, e.g. 1133e, Plato, *Symp.* 215c.

33   The clumsy interpolation of the quotation from Alexander comprises only the previous sentence. Here we return to Terpander, and the source is Glaucus, as before.

34   Though Orpheus was, according to the legends, a Thracian, he became so clearly the 'patron saint' of the art of the *kithara* as to be almost an honorary Greek. He was said to have been taught by Apollo, and hence, as the present passage goes on to say, he had no human precursors in the art. The sense is therefore that Terpander based his melodies on the primary source, nearest to the divine.

35   If the author means that Clonas originated *aulōdia*, as W. and R. assume, we must

Boeotians. Archilochus is said to have lived after both Terpander and Clonas. Some other writers say that Ardalus of Troizene[36] preceded Clonas in composing music for singing to the *aulos*, and also that there was a poet called Polymnestus, son of Meles of Colophon, who composed Polymnestian *nomoi*.[37] Of Clonas the authorities record that he composed the *Apothetos* and *Schoiniōn nomoi*.[38] Polymnestus [b] is mentioned by two poets who composed songs, Pindar[39] and Alcman. It is also said that some of the *nomoi* sung to the *kithara* which were used by Terpander were constructed by Philammon of Delphi in ancient times.[40]

6. 'In general, the style of singing to the *kithara* employed by Terpander continued in a quite simple form down to the time of Phrynis.[41] In the old days *kithara* songs were not allowed to be performed as they are now,[42] or to include modulations of *harmoniai* and rhythms, since in each *nomos* the pitch which belonged to it was maintained throughout. This is why these pieces were given their name: [c] they were called "*nomoi*" because deviation from the form of pitching established for each type was not permitted.[43] After dedicating themselves to the gods in any way they wished, performers proceeded at once to the poetry of Homer or other authors, as is clear from the preludes[44] of Terpander. The *kithara* first acquired its shape in the time of Cepion,[45] the disciple of Terpander, and it was called the "Asiatic" *kithara* because it was used by the *kitharōdoi* of Lesbos, who live close to Asia. [d] The last of them, it is said, was Periclitus, a native of Lesbos, who won the contest for singing to the *kithara* in the Carneia at Sparta;[46] and on his death the continuous tradition among the Lesbians of singing to the *kithara* came to an end.[47] Some people wrongly suppose that Hipponax lived at the same

read *aulētikōn* for *aulōdikōn*, ('*nomoi* for the *aulos*' instead of '*nomoi* sung to the *aulos*') at the end of 1132f, since Clonas is later than Terpander and hence later than Orpheus. But that implication need not be intended.

36 A very obscure figure: cf. Paus. II.31.3, Plin. *Nat. Hist.* VII.204.
37 See 1132c–d with notes.
38 Cf. 1132d and Appendix A.
39 Pindar, fr. 178, quoted at Strabo XIV.1.29.
40 See 1132a: cf. *Suda* s.v. Terpandros.
41 I.e., for some 200 years. On Phrynis see Ch. 7. Much of the argument of this section is reproduced, with elaborations, at Proclus, *Chrest.* 45–52.
42 That is, in the time of ps.-Plutarch's source, here probably Heraclides (fourth century).
43 This explanation of the name *nomos* is discussed in Appendix A.
44 *Prooimia*: cf. 1132d. The structure suggested is clearly reflected in the formulae of the Homeric Hymns, which commonly proceed from the invocation of a god to the promise of 'another song'.
45 On Cepion see Appendix A. The author is evidently referring to the fully developed concert *kithara*. For a parallel account of the appellation 'Asiatic' cf. Douris, fr. 81 (Jacoby). 'Asiatic *kithara*' occurs in some fifth-century texts (e.g. Eurip. *Cyclops* 443), but it seems likely that it is intended there to designate the *barbitos*.
46 As did Terpander before him in the first such contest, 196 Ath. 635e. Nothing more of Periclitus is known.
47 On the early supremacy of the Lesbian *kitharōdoi* cf. Ar. fr. 545 (Rose), and Hesych. under the heading *meta Lesbion ōdon*.

time as Terpander, but it is clear that even Periclitus is earlier than Hipponax.[48]

7. 'Now that we have given an account of the ancient *nomoi* sung to the *aulos* and those sung to the *kithara* as well, we shall move on to consider separately the *nomoi* for solo *auloi*.[49] It is said that the Olympus whom I mentioned above, an aulete from Phrygia, originated the so-called "Many-headed" *nomos* for the *aulos*, dedicated to Apollo. This Olympus [e] is also said to have been a descendant of the first Olympus, the pupil of Marsyas, who had himself composed *nomoi* in honour of the gods.[50] The original Olympus was a favourite of Marsyas, and learnt from him the art of playing the *aulos*; and it was he who introduced into Greece the musical[51] *nomoi* which the Greeks now use at the festivals of the gods. Other people say that the Many-headed *nomos* was an invention of Crates,[52] a pupil of Olympus: but Pratinas[53] asserts that this *nomos* was invented by the younger Olympus.

'The so-called *Harmatios nomos* is said to have been invented by the first Olympus, the pupil of Marsyas. [f] Some people say that Marsyas' name was actually Masses, while others deny this and say that it was Marsyas: and they say that he was the son of Hyagnis, the original inventor of the art of playing the *aulos*.[54] The fact that the *Harmatios nomos* was the invention of Olympus may be learned from Glaucus' book about the ancient poets, which

---

48   The *Marmor Parium* dates Hipponax to the mid-sixth century: other sources have other guesses, but we have no substantial information about him.

49   *Aulētikoi nomoi*. On the *nomoi* mentioned in the sequel see Appendix A.

50   The issue is confused on two counts. First, the Olympus 'mentioned above' ought to be the first Olympus (1132f), but the second is plainly intended. Ps.-Plut. is evidently quoting unskilfully from his source. Secondly, the introduction of two musicians, both called Olympus, is guaranteed to create difficulties. Both the *Suda* and Clem. Alex. (*Strom.* 1.16) distinguish the two; but the clue to the issue is probably provided by the present passage. At the end of the paragraph the attribution of the *Poly-kephalos nomos* (see 27 Pindar, *Pyth.* 12) to a second Olympus is said to be based on the authority of Pratinas. Pratinas, however, is known to have been hostile to the growing domination of music by the *aulos* (see the fragment quoted at 189 Ath. 617c–f), and it seems likely that in ascribing one of its most spectacular set pieces to a mere descendant of the great Olympus, he was simply attempting to puncture its mystique. It is fair to guess that the reduplication of Olympuses in the later sources is derived solely from Pratinas' calculated piece of invention. (For a more detailed conjecture to the same general effect, see Lasserre p. 45.)

51   *Harmonikous*, possibly in the sense 'enharmonic', or rather 'proto-enharmonic', with reference to the early form (attributed to Olympus at 1134f) which lacked the quarter-tone intervals of the later variety. Olympus is explicitly said not to have used the latter form (1135b). If this interpretation is correct, it is of interest in suggesting that these 'primitive' forms were still in use in the time of the source ('. . . which the Greeks now use . . .'): this in turn adds authority to the analysis of Olympus' scale-structures at 1134 ff and 1137b–d, and an air of authenticity to references such as that at 161 Ar. *Pol.* 1340a. Olympus himself may be largely legendary, but it is possible that melodies retaining a genuinely ancient structure were preserved under his name down to the fourth century.

52   Nothing further is known of him.

53   Of Philius, but working in Athens in the early fifth century. See n. 50 above.

54   On Hyagnis and Marsyas see n. 32 above.

also informs us that Stesichorus of Himera took as his model not Orpheus or Terpander or Archilochus or Thaletas, but Olympus, since Stesichorus used the *Harmatios nomos* and the dactylic species of rhythm, which some people say is derived from the *Orthios nomos*.[55] Other people say that this *nomos* was invented by the Mysians, since there were some Mysian auletes in antiquity.[56]

8. 'Another ancient *nomos* is the one called [1134a] *Cradias*, which according to Hipponax was performed on the *aulos* by Mimnermus[57] (for singers to the *aulos* originally performed elegiacs set to music, as is made clear by the inscription dealing with the musical contest at the festival of the Panathenaea).[58]

'There was also Sacadas of Argos, who composed songs[59] and elegiac poems set to music. He was also a fine aulete, and it is recorded that he won the Pythian contest three times.[60] He is mentioned by Pindar.[61] In the time of Polymnestus and Sacadas there were three *tonoi*, Dorian, Phrygian and Lydian:[62] and it is said that Sacadas [b] composed a strophe in each of them, and taught the chorus to sing the first in the Dorian *tonos*, the second in the Phrygian, and the third in the Lydian: this *nomos* is said to have been called

[55] These *nomoi* and the allusion to Stesichorus are discussed in Appendix A. On Thaletas see 1134b–e, 1135c, 1146c.

[56] The *Suda* and Clem. Alex. (*Strom.* 1.16) call the older of the supposed pair of Olympuses a Mysian.

[57] For the ritual context of the *Cradias nomos* and an explanation of the reference to Mimnermus see Appendix A.

[58] If, as the context indicates (as does the description by Hesychius cited in Appendix A), the *Cradias nomos* was auletic, not aulodic, this parenthesis is puzzling, speaking as it does of singing to the *aulos*. (W. and R. make the difficulty the occasion for another of their textual transpositions.) Probably ps.-Plutarch is again excerpting unskilfully, linking two sentences related to Mimnermus in his source with a pseudo-explanatory 'for'. (Mimnermus is known as a writer of elegiacs.) For the early connection between elegiac verse and the *aulos* see esp. Paus. x.7.5. The wording of the last clause suggests that the inscription mentioned is the one recording Pericles' re-establishment of musical contests at the Panathenaea (Plut. *Peric.* 13, cf. Ar. *Ath. Pol.* 60.1), rather than a list of victors, as at 1132a.

[59] *Melē*, i.e. pieces of what we now call 'lyric'.

[60] *Aulētēs*, 'aulete', is Wyttenbach's conjecture for the MSS *poiētēs*, 'poet' or 'composer'. The emendation is likely for two reasons: first, because Sacadas' credentials as a poet have already been mentioned, and the word 'also' should introduce something new; and secondly because it was on his ability as an aulete that Sacadas' fame rested. Pausanias (x.7.4–5) says explicitly that he won his Pythian victories as an aulete, dating the occasions to 582, 578 and 574 B.C., and tells us also of a statue of Sacadas with his *auloi* at Helicon (IX.30.2). Pollux (IV.78, cf.84) and Pausanias (II.22.9) attribute to him the auletic *Pythikos nomos*.
    'It is recorded', again *anagegraptai*, as at 1132e: see n. 26 above.

[61] See Paus. IX.30.2 = Pindar, fr. 282.

[62] *Tonos* here has the sense of *harmonia*, 'system of tuning', as usually in the present author. The thesis that the ancient composers knew only these three systems seems to belong to an Aristoxenian tradition (see e.g. **196** Ath. 635e, 637d, Ptol. *Harm.* 56.4–6, Porph. *Comm.* 171.4–5, Bacch. 303.3–4), and contrasts with the doctrine of Heraclides that the *harmoniai* reduce to Dorian, Aeolian and Iastian (**192** Ath. 624c). On the *harmoniai* generally see Chap. 10, Appendix A.

Trimelēs because of the modulation.[63] But in the document at Sicyon concerning the poets,[64] Clonas is recorded as being the inventor of the *Trimelēs nomos*.

9. 'Musical institutions were first established at Sparta at the instigation of Terpander.[65] Thaletas of Gortyn, Xenodamus of Cythera, Xenocritus of Locri, Polymnestus of Colophon and Sacadas of Argos [c] are said to have been the prime movers in its second phase of organisation:[66] it is said to have been at their instigation that the festival of the Gymnopaidiai at Sparta was instituted, as well as those of the Apodeixeis in Arcadia and the ones called the Endymatia at Argos.[67] The poets in the circle of Thaletas, Xenodamus and Xenocritus composed paeans,[68] those associated with Polymnestus composed the so-called "orthians",[69] and those associated with Sacadas elegiacs.[70] Other people such as Pratinas say that Xenodamus composed *hyporchēmata* and not paeans, and a song by Xenodamus himself is preserved, which is plainly a *hyporchēma*.[71] [d] Pindar also used this form of

---

[63]   *Trimelēs*, 'three-melodied', is Burette's conjecture for the MSS *trimerēs*, 'in three parts', but the MSS have *trimelēs* at 1132d above. The emendation is probably right: it makes this *nomos* parallel with the kitharodic *tetraōidios*, 'four-songed', of 1132d, and gives a basis for the explanation of its form that is given here. The explanation is certainly mistaken (see Appendix A), as is the association of the piece with a chorus, since *nomoi* were always solos. If this is the same *nomos* as the *trimelēs* of 1132d, it is an *aulōdia*.

[64]   See 1132a and n. 13.

[65]   In the seventh and early sixth centuries, Sparta seems to have been the musical 'capital' of Greece, its prestige resting on the two great festivals of the Carnea and the Gymnopaideia. Sources cited at 196 Ath. 635e say that the Carnea was instituted between 676 and 673 B.C., and that Terpander won a victory on the first occasion it was held. The second 'organisation' (*katastasis*, cf. 157 Plato, *Laws* 802a) of music, associated here with Thaletas and others (cf. Ath. 678c), relates perhaps to the institution of musical contests at the Gymnopaideia in the late seventh century, rather than to the inauguration of the festival itself, which was probably substantially earlier. On the 'two periods' of ancient music, both contrasted with the music of his own time, cf. Aristox. *El. Harm.* 23.3–16.

[66]   The Cretan Thaletas (or Thales) is said to have been associated with Lycurgus in the establishment of sound legal order in Sparta (Plut. *Lyc.* 4). He was a composer of songs sung to the *lyra*: he was taken to be the inventor of the 'taut' rhythms characteristic of Crete, and of the Cretan tradition of paeans (Strabo x.48, cf. Porph. *Vit. Pythag.* 32, and 1134d–e below). He was reputed to have put an end by musical means to a 'plague' at Sparta (1146c, Paus. 1.14.4), though whether 'plague' refers to a real medical epidemic or is a metaphor for a condition of unhealthy political unrest is not clear. Of Xenodamus and Xenocritus little is known beyond what is said here and at 1134e–f. On Polymnestus see 1132c–d, 1133a–b, 1134d, 1135c, 1141b: on Sacadas see 1134a with n. 60, 1135c.

[67]   *Apodeixeis*, 'showings', 'exhibitions'; *Endymatia*, 'apparellings'. Nothing is known of either festival.

[68]   On paeans see introductory note to *Iliad*.

[69]   Presumably in the sense 'pieces characterised by high pitch', connected with the music of the *aulos* by the reference to Olympus at 1133f. See Appendix A.

[70]   Cf. 1134a.

[71]   *Hyporchēmata* were choric songs, distinguished from paeans by the imitative dances (*orchēmata*) that formed an essential ingredient of them. Some authors made Thaletas the inventor of this form: Pratinas, Pindar and Bacchylides are known to

composition; and it is clear from his poems that there is a difference between *hyporchēmata* and paeans, since he wrote pieces of both kinds.[72]

10. 'Polymnestus also composed *nomoi* to be sung to the *aulos*.[73] Whether or not he used the *Orthios nomos* in composing his melodies, as the *harmonikoi* claim, we cannot say for certain, since the ancient writers said nothing about the matter.[74] It is equally uncertain whether Thaletas of Crete was a composer of paeans. Glaucus says that Thaletas lived later than Archilochus, and that he imitated Archilochus' songs, though extending them to a greater length; and he says that Thaletas incorporated paeonic and cretic [e] rhythms in his compositions. These, he claims, had not been used by Archilochus, nor indeed by Orpheus or Terpander: it is from the *aulos* music of Olympus that Thaletas is said to have developed them, and thus to have acquired his reputation as an excellent composer.[75] As to Xenocritus, a native of Locri in Italy, it is uncertain whether he was a composer of paeans: it is said that he composed on heroic subjects [f] involving actions, which is why some people call his pieces dithyrambs.[76] According to Glaucus, Thaletas lived earlier than Xenocritus.

11. 'Olympus, so Aristoxenus says, is identified by the musical experts as the inventor of the enharmonic genus – all music before his time was dia-

[72] have composed *hyporchēmata*, and Xenodamus reappears in this connection at Ath. 15d. It seems clear that the category was fairly broad, since the dances for which *hyporchēmata* were written might be of any of a number of kinds (see e.g. schol. to Pindar, *Pyth.* 2.127). They were simply choral songs composed with the choreography of the dance particularly in mind (cf. 193 Ath. 628d). Fragments of both genres survive, but in themselves they give little clue to the distinctions that the present author has in mind.

[73] See nn. 20 and 21 above.

[74] On the *Orthios nomos* see Appendix A. The *harmonikoi* are probably those so called in Aristoxenus (see n. 9 above). The 'ancient writers' with whom they are contrasted are the lyric poets of the sixth century.

[75] Archilochus' songs were designed for singing to the *kithara*. The sense of the present passage seems to be that Thaletas, composing for the same kind of performances as Archilochus, extended and elaborated his structures, using new rhythms drawn from the repertoire of the *aulos*. Cretan music was primarily based on stringed instruments (e.g. 1140c, cf. 193 Ath. 627d), and there are no good grounds for supposing that Thaletas actually composed for the *aulos*. That his reputation was strictly that of a composer of *kitharōdia* is strongly suggested by 1133f. Note that Archilochus himself is credited with significant rhythmic innovations, including combinations involving paions (‿‿‑‿ or ‑‿‿‿) and cretics (‑‿‑), 1140f–1141a. The notion that Thaletas invented cretic rhythms (Ephorus ap. Strabo x.4.17) is probably due merely to his general reputation as the pioneer of Cretan music.

[76] Paeans seem to be distinguished from dithyrambs here by their subject matter, rather than their form or the occasion of their use. This account of the dithyramb, as comprising tales of heroic deeds, is unparalleled. But it is likely enough that this very flexible genre, well known in the fifth century for the fantastic musical and poetic excesses of its exponents, sometimes involved narratives of dramatic action, while the paean remained a hymn of praise and supplication. Plato describes the dithyramb as the best example of a style where the poet speaks only in his own character, without *mimēsis* (*Rep.* 394c): in its context this indicates an association between the dithyramb and the use of direct narrative.

tonic or chromatic.[77] They suggest that its invention occurred in something like the following way.[78] Olympus was working within the diatonic genus, and bringing the melody frequently to diatonic *parhypatē*, sometimes from *paramesē* and sometimes from *mesē*, while omitting the diatonic *lichanos*,[79] and he was struck by the beauty of the character of this procedure. His admiration for the *systēma* [1135a] constructed out of these proportions led him to adopt it, and to create in this *systēma* compositions in the Dorian *tonos*.[80] Now this *systēma* involved none of the features peculiar either to the diatonic or the chromatic, nor indeed those peculiar to the enharmonic.[81] Nevertheless, these were the features of his first enharmonic pieces, since our authorities consider the first of these pieces to be the *spondeion*, in which none of the divisions exhibits its special peculiarities.[82] (This holds unless one adopts the hypothesis, based on an inspection of the higher *spondeiasmos*, that the *spondeion* itself is diatonic.[83] But any such conjecture would be plainly false and in breach of the laws of melody, false because the interval involved is smaller by a diesis[84] than the tone next to the predominant note,[85]

[77] Aristox. discusses the genera at length in the *El. Harm.* (see particularly 21.31 ff, 46.19 ff). Briefly, they are based on an analysis of each form of the scale into a series of tetrachords, whose outer notes are 'fixed', remaining the same in each genus. The inner notes are movable, and different locations of these notes within the boundaries of the fourth create different genera of scale. The three genera are called enharmonic, chromatic and diatonic: the latter two possess variants, called 'shades' (*chroai*), which need not concern us here. Tetrachords in the enharmonic series have the form quarter-tone, quarter-tone, ditone; in the most important version of the chromatic they have the form semitone, semitone, tone-and-a-half; and in the most important diatonic the form semitone, tone, tone. For Aristoxenus' account of the order in which the genera came into use in Greek music, see *El. Harm.* 19.17–29.

[78] For an analysis of the structures involved in the following discussion, and at 1137b–d, see Appendix B.

[79] If we equate *mesē* with the note A, diatonic *parhypatē* is F, *paramesē* is B, diatonic *lichanos* is G. The sequel shows that *hypatē*, E, was also included.

[80] *Tonos* is probably to be understood here in its Aristoxenian sense, roughly 'key', designating primarily a range of pitch, rather than (as usually in ps.-Plut.) being equivalent to the older '*harmonia*'. The Dorian *tonos* in the Aristoxenian system is rather below middling pitch (see e.g. Arist. Quint. 20.9 ff). For the possibility that *harmoniai* in the sense 'scale structures' are intended, see n. 89 below.

[81] Here the special features of the diatonic are its sequence of two tones, of the chromatic its sequence of two semitones, of the enharmonic its sequence of two quarter-tones. (See n. 77 above.) The *spondeion* sequence semitone, ditone, might in theory be construed as an imperfect version of a tetrachord in any of the genera, depending on where the 'missing' note is inserted. But Aristoxenus thinks of the incomposite ditone as especially characteristic of the *spondeion* (1134f–1135a), and elsewhere he treats the true mark of the enharmonic as being its jump of an incomposite ditone (e.g. *El. Harm.* 22.24–23.23). This is why the *spondeion* scale is described as an ancestral version of the enharmonic, despite the apparent ambiguity of its structure.

[82] *Spondeion* means 'of libations', indicating the context of the usage of the compositions described. 'Divisions': i.e., the internal divisions of the tetrachord that distinguish the different genera.

[83] The general sense of this parenthesis is outlined in Appendix B.

[84] A quarter-tone, in Aristoxenus' usage.

[85] *Hēgemōn*, lit. 'leader', but the modern connotations of 'leading note' are inapposite. The note in question is *mesē* (see ps.-Ar. *Probs.* XIX.3, cf. Ar. *Metaph.* 1018b 24–9).

and in breach of the laws of melody because [b] to suppose that the specific nature of the higher *spondeiasmos* lies in the character of the interval of a tone involves the consequence that two ditones occur successively, one incomposite, the other composite.)[86] For the enharmonic *pyknon* used nowadays in the middle tetrachord is apparently not present in the music of this composer.[87] This can readily be understood by anyone who listens to the *aulos* being played in the ancient style, where the semitone in the middle tetrachord is also meant to be incomposite.[88]

'This, then, was the character of the first enharmonic melodies. Later the semitone was divided both in Lydian and in Phrygian compositions.[89] It is apparent that Olympus extended the resources of music by introducing something which previously did not exist, and was unknown to his pre-

On its 'predominance' see 173 and 181 *Probs.* XIX.20 and 36. The tone 'next' to it lies above it: in Aristoxenus' analyses of standard scale-forms it is the disjunctive tone separating two tetrachords. The size of this interval in effect defines the notion 'interval of a tone', since two tetrachords separated by the disjunctive tone span an octave, a fourth plus a fifth makes an octave, and the 'tone' is defined as the interval by which the fifth exceeds the fourth (e.g. *El. Harm.* 21.21–2, 45.34–46.1).

86   In the sequence as we have conventionally formulated it, the lower (incomposite) ditone is F–A, the higher A–C#, which is 'composite' because of the interposition of B. See Appendix B.

87   *Pyknon*, lit. 'compressed', 'dense', is a technical term in Aristoxenus. It names the composite interval bounded by the lowest and third-lowest notes of a tetrachord, in those genera where the interval in question is smaller than the residue of the tetrachord. (See *El. Harm.* 24.11–14, 50.15–19.) Thus in an enharmonic tetrachord (of the form q,q,d), the pair of quarter-tones comprise a *pyknon*. In the diatonic there is no *pyknon*, since the two lower intervals combined are greater than the remainder of the tetrachord (or, in one version of the genus, equal to it). See *El. Harm.* 25.6–9, 51.19–21. Here Aristoxenus means simply that the semitone E–F was not divided into quarter-tones in Olympus' music.

88   'Also', i.e. the semitone as well as the ditone is incomposite. Alternatively the expression may mean 'the semitone *even* in the middle tetrachord', suggesting that everyone will in any case grant that the semitone 'in the upper tetrachord', i.e., that between B and C, is undivided in these auletes' performances. ('Middle' tetrachord here indicates the span of a fourth below *mesē*, A, 'upper' tetrachord the span of a fourth upwards from *paramesē*, B.) That the semitone in the middle (but not the upper) tetrachord was sometimes divided in pieces related to the *spondeion* is indicated at 1137b–c.

89   The sense is not that the semitone was never divided in Dorian pieces (see e.g. Arist. Quint. 18.13–15), but perhaps that the compositions characteristic of Olympus were all either Lydian or Phrygian. The suggestion is that there once existed structures without quarter-tones from which the developed enharmonic Lydian and Phrygian arose. 'Lydian' and 'Phrygian' are not attached here to any noun such as *harmonia* or *tonos*. Their use is quasi-colloquial, and their sense is more likely to be reflected in the empirical analyses of Aristoxenus' predecessors than in his own novel system of *tonoi*. These analyses, as reported at Arist. Quint. 18.5 ff, make them more like *harmoniai*, scale-structures, than like Aristoxenian *tonoi*, 'keys'.
Aristides' account gives a *syntonon Lydion* whose structure is q,q,d,tone-and-a-half, and a Phrygian whose structure is t,q,q,d,t,q,q,t. Both plainly have as their core the sequence q,q,d, which can be derived from an ancestral series without quarter-tones, s,d. This series is characteristic of the *spondeion*, as described above (s,d,t,s, or in its *syntonōteron* variant s,d,t,three-quarters-of-a-tone), and we may treat Aristoxenus as suggesting that both the Lydian and the Phrygian of the later *harmoniai* were elaborations of the core that the *spondeion* contained. We need not suppose that the *spondeion* itself existed in different versions called 'Lydian' and 'Phrygian'.

decessors, and that he was the founder of the noble style of music that is specifically Greek.

12. 'We also possess an account[90] of rhythms: [c] several additional genera and species of rhythm were discovered, as were new genera and species of melodic and rhythmic composition. The earliest innovations, those of Terpander,[91] introduced a certain nobility of style into music. After Terpander's style had been adopted, Polymnestus employed a new one, though he maintained its elevated character, as did Thaletas and Sacadas. They also made innovations in rhythmic composition, but without stepping outside the elevated manner.[92] There is also an element of originality in Alcman and Stesichorus, but it still involves no retreat from the noble manner.[93] Crexus, Timotheus and Philoxenus,[94] however, and other poets of the same period, displayed more vulgarity and a passion for novelty, and pursued the style nowadays called "popular" [d] or "profiteering".[95] The result was that music limited to a few strings,[96] and simple and dignified in character, went quite out of fashion.

[90]   The 'account' contained in this short passage is almost devoid of content. The author merely rehearses a list of names associated in his source with rhythmic innovations, without saying anything about their nature. The list can be interpreted, to some degree, in the light of passages in this work and elsewhere: see notes on individual names. It is curious that Archilochus is not mentioned, since he figures prominently as a rhythmic innovator at 1140f–1141a.

[91]   At 1140f Terpander is credited with the introduction of the 'orthian' foot and the *sēmantos trochaios*. (See Arist. Quint. 36.3–6. Both belong to the iambic 'genus', in which the ratio of one part of the foot to the other is 2:1. The orthian has an arsis of four units of time and a thesis of eight, while the *sēmantos trochaios* has the same elements, but with the order of thesis and arsis reversed.)

[92]   Melodic but not rhythmic innovations are ascribed to Polymnestus at 1141b. At 1134c he is said to have composed 'orthian' pieces, but the references is probably to their high pitch, rather than to metre or rhythm (see Appendix A). To Thaletas is attributed (1134d–e) the introduction of paions and cretics (see n. 75), while Sacadas is said to have set elegiacs to music (1134a and c), though without any implication that he invented this style of composition.

[93]   Many different metres are described by ancient writers as 'Alcmanic' or 'Stesichorean'. A list is given in the Loeb edition of ps.-Plut. ad loc., and on Stesichorus cf. Dion. Hal. *De Comp. Verb.* 19.

[94]   The characteristic of the rhythms of these composers to which our sources most frequently refer is their flexibility, involving the juxtaposition of lines of different metrical and rhythmic types. Cf. 1132b and n. 16 above.

[95]   *Thematikon*, referring, according to Pollux III.153, to contests in which the prize was money, rather than the traditional crown of leaves. 'Popular', *philanthrōpon*, i.e., designed to please the crowd. In an anecdote told in Themistius, *Or.* 364c, Aristoxenus is described as having chosen to pursue artistic excellence (*technē*) rather than popularity (*philanthrōpia*). Lasserre reads (with most MSS) *ekdiōxantes*, 'driving out', for *diōxantes*, 'pursuing': he interprets *philanthrōpon* as meaning 'fit to be loved by people', and *thematikon* as meaning 'conforming to rules', 'traditional' or 'basic'. In that case, the *philanthrōpon* and the *thematikon* are what Timotheus and the rest drove into disuse, not what they sought to promote. Either interpretation is possible, though the former has more solid foundations: in any case the contrast is one already made familiar by Plato, e.g. 155 *Laws* 700a–e.

[96]   *Oligochordian*, 'fewness of strings', is Burette's emendation for the MSS *oligo-*

13. 'Now that I have described as best I can the earliest music and its first inventors, and have mentioned the people who added to its resources over the years with additional inventions, I shall bring my speech to an end and hand the subject over to my friend Soterichus, an enthusiast not only for music but also for the entire contents of a liberal education. I myself have been trained mostly in the performing side of music.' With these words Lysias finished his speech.

14. [e] Soterichus followed him; and the sense of his speech was as follows. 'The discussion you have asked us to undertake, noble Onesicrates, concerns an exalted and important activity, and one that is particularly pleasing to the gods. I applaud our teacher Lysias for his understanding, and also for the memory he has displayed in dealing with the inventors [f] of the earliest music and those who have written about such things. I shall remind you, however, that the account he gave us relied only on written evidence. But tradition has taught me that the inventor of the good things that belong to music was not a man: he was Apollo, the god adorned with every excellence. Thus the *aulos* is not, as some people suppose, the invention of Marsyas or Olympus or Hyagnis,[97] only the *kithara* being that of Apollo: in fact the god is the inventor of both arts, that of the *aulos* as well as that of the *kithara*. Evidence of this is provided by the choruses and sacrifices which used to be brought before the god to the accompaniment of *auloi*, as various people record, [1136a] including Alcaeus in one of his hymns.[98] Again, the statue of Apollo erected at Delos has in its right hand a bow, and in its left the Graces, each with a musical instrument. One plays the *lyra*, one the *auloi*, while the one in the middle holds a *syrinx* to her lips. That this is not a story I have invented myself is shown by the account of Anticlides, and by what Istrus says about the subject in his *Manifestations*: and the statue is so old that it is

---

choreian, 'fewness of dances'. The latter might conceivably refer to rhythmic simplicity, though it would be an awkward (and unique) coinage: in any case, there is no suggestion here that the older composers used few rhythms (quite the contrary: cf. 1138b–c), only that they used them in an orderly and dignified manner. *Oligochordia*, by contrast with *polychordia* (cf. e.g. 149 Plato, *Rep.* 399c–d), is often cited as a feature of ancient music (e.g. 1137a). The word is capable of referring both to the existence of 'gapped' scales, like that of the *spondeion*, and to the ancients' refusal to adopt 'many-noted' or 'many-stringed' instruments to facilitate harmonic modulation, as Timotheus and his school did (see e.g. the passage from Pherecrates quoted at 1141d ff).

97 Cf. 1132f, 1133f, and e.g. 188 Ath. 184a, *Anth. Pal.* 9.340, *Suda* s.v. Olympos.
98 Fr. 307. The *aulos* was certainly not excluded from celebrations of Apollo in the sixth century, as the existence of the auletic *Pythikos nomos* (24 Pollux IV.84) vividly testifies. Though the *aulos* was subject to attack by conservatives from at least the early fifth century (see 189 Pratinas ap. Ath. 617c–f), and the story of the contest between Marsyas and Apollo is no doubt old, the systematic confrontation between the *kithara* of Apollo, symbolising what was rational and purely 'Greek', and the *aulos* of Marsyas and Dionysus, symbolising the foreign, emotional and irrational, is a Hellenistic fancy, presumably based on Plato (esp. 149 *Rep.* 399e, cf. 161 Ar. *Pol.* 1341a–b).

said to have been made by the Meropes in time of Heracles.[99] It is also an aulete who comes with the boy who brings the laurel from Tempe to Delphi;[100] and it is said that the sacred offerings of the Hyperboreans [b] were brought to Delos in ancient times to the sound of *auloi*, *syringes* and *kitharai*.[101] Other people, such as Alcman, that outstanding composer of songs,[102] say that the god himself played the *aulos*, while Corinna goes so far as to say that Apollo was taught to play the *aulos* by Athena.[103] Thus music is in all respects a noble thing, and the invention of the gods.

15. 'In ancient times people treated music in accordance with its proper status, just as they treated all their other activities. Nowadays musicians have rejected its more dignified aspects, and in place of that manly and inspired music, beloved of the gods, they bring into the theatres a music of effeminate twitterings.[104] Thus Plato expresses his disapproval [c] of this kind of music in the third book of the *Republic*, where he rejects the Lydian *harmonia* on the grounds that it is high-pitched and suitable for lamentations.[105] It is said, indeed, that the first composition in this *harmonia* was a lament: Aristoxenus, in the first book of his work *On Music*, says that Olympus was the first to use Lydian, when he played a lament for the Python on the *aulos*.[106] Some people say that it was Melanippides[107] who originated

---

99 The statue is said by Pausanias (IX.35.3) to have been the work of Angelion and Tectaeus (probably late sixth century: see Paus. II.32.5, Plin. *Nat. Hist.* XXXVI.9). Coins of the second century, and a number of texts, represent the statue as holding the bow in its left hand and the Graces in its right, which is more probable. Anticleides belongs to the late fourth century, Istrus to the third.

100 The reference is to the ceremony called the Steptērion, representing the return of Apollo to Delphi from Tempe, where he had been purified after killing the Python (the feat celebrated in the *Pythikos nomos*). See Plut. *Quaest Gr.* 12, Aelian, *V. H.* III.1: the aulete is not mentioned in any other source.

101 On the Hyperboreans' offerings at Delos see Hdt.IV.33 ff. The musical accompaniment is not mentioned elsewhere, but the life of the Hyperboreans (an idealised northern race living in perfect happiness and peace) is evoked by their singing and dancing to the sound of *lyrai* and *auloi* at Pindar, *Pyth.* 10.37–40.

102 *Melōn poiētēs*, i.e., a composer of what has come to be called 'lyric'.

103 Contrast the familiar story told by Melanippides ap. 189 Ath. 616e, and the 'rejoinder' by Telestes, 616f.

104 Cf. 155 Plato, *Laws* 700a–e, Aristox. ap. 195 Ath. 632a–b.

105 149 *Rep.* 398d–e. Plato does not say directly that Lydian is a high-pitched *harmonia*, but is speaking of a so-called *syntonolydisti*, 'high' or 'tense' Lydian, in contrast to the 'slacker' forms mentioned at the end of 398e. Cf. also 161 Ar. *Pol.* 1342b with n. 41 ad loc. On the *harmoniai* mentioned here and in the sequel see also Ch. 10, Appendix A.

106 Cf. perhaps Aristoph. *Knights* 8–9: 'Come here now, so that we may sob a *nomos* by Olympus for *auloi* played together.' ('For *auloi* played together' translates *xynaulian*, lit. 'conjunction of *auloi*' (and so used at e.g. Pollux IV.83), but capable of referring to any music for more than one performer, e.g. Plato, *Laws* 765b. In the *Knights* it probably means music for *auloi* specifically, since the characters do not go on to sing a song, but to imitate instrumental noises, '*mu mu*, *mu mu*', etc., line 10. For a portrayal of a duet between two auletes see e.g. the vase illustrated at Besseler *et al.*, Pl. 43, dated around 460 B.C.) Note the relation between the subject matter of Olympus' lament and that of the auletic *Pythikos nomos* (Pollux IV.84).

107 The suggestion is obscure. It cannot coherently attribute the first use of the Lydian *harmonia* to the Melanippides mentioned in e.g. the quotation from Pherecrates at

this kind of melody, while Pindar in his *Paeans* says that the Lydian *harmonia* was introduced at the wedding of Niobe;[108] and others again, as Dionysius Iambus relates, say that it was first used by Torebus.[109]

16. 'The Mixolydian *harmonia* is also emotional, and appropriate for tragedies.[110] Aristoxenus says that [d] it was Sappho who originally invented the Mixolydian, and that the composers of tragedies learned it from her. That is, they adopted this *harmonia* and linked it with the Dorian, since the latter expresses magnificence and dignity, and the former emotion; and tragedy is a blend of both.[111] The *harmonikoi* in their historical works say that the aulete Pythoclides invented it,[112] and also that Lamprocles the Athenian, realising that the disjunction in this *harmonia* is not where almost everyone supposed it to be, but at the top of its range, gave it the form of the series from *paramesē* to *hypatē hypatōn*.[113] [e] It is also said that the relaxed

113 1141d, since he belongs to the mid-fifth century, and references to the Lydian go back much earlier. (Even Pindar, mentioned in the next clause, is earlier than Melanippides.) Unless an earlier composer of the same name is meant, the source may have intended to ascribe to him not the Lydian *harmonia* but the lament for the Python with which Olympus has just been credited. That would amount to an attack on its claims to respectable antiquity: cf. n. 50 above.

108   Cf. Paus. IX.5.7, Heraclides ap. 192 Ath. 625e.
109   Dionysius Iambus was a scholar of the third century B.C. Torebus the Lydian is probably legendary: he was credited by Boethius with the addition of a fifth string to the *lyra* (*De Mus.* 1.20), and with songs called *Torrhēbia melē* by Nic. Dam. (fr. 15, Jacoby).
110   On the character of the Mixolydian and its use in tragedy see e.g. 161 Ar. *Pol.* 1340b, 185 ps.-Ar. *Probs.* XIX.48 (with the addition to the text given in Th. Gaza's Latin translation: see n. 95 ad loc.), Plut. *De Rect. Rat. Aud.* 15, though the anecdote told there might suggest that the use of Mixolydian in tragedy was unusual, at least until Euripides.
111   Dorian is well known for its representation of manliness and associated virtues, e.g. 149 Plato, *Rep.* 399a–c, Heraclides ap. 192 Ath. 624d. Dorian and Mixolydian, in the analyses offered by the technical writers, also have close structural affinities, as W. and R. remark: see n. 113 below.
112   Since the principal source here is Aristoxenus, the *harmonikoi* are presumably his empirically-minded predecessors of the late fifth and early fourth centuries, as regularly in his writings. Pythoclides of Ceos was one of Pericles' teachers (Plato, *Alc. I*, 118c, Plut. *Peric.* 4), and Plato remarks that he was properly speaking a philosopher, as it were disguising himself as a musician (*Prot.* 316e). He is to be dated in the mid-fifth century, and can therefore hardly be supposed to have 'invented' or introduced the Mixolydian. More probably he was a rival claimant to the reform or reinterpretation of this *harmonia* that is credited here to Lamprocles.
113   Little is known of Lamprocles. He composed a hymn to Athena (schol. to Aristoph. *Clouds* 967) and dithyrambs (Ath. 491c), and probably belongs to the early fifth century. The (downwards) series 'from *paramesē* to *hypatē hypatōn*' is in the enharmonic genus (reversing the series to read upwards) q,q,d,q,q,d,t; and this is the form in which most technical writers record the Mixolydian (e.g. Arist. Quint. 15.11–12, Cleonides 197.4–7). In his account of the 'ancient scales', Arist. Quint. gives the form q,q,t,t,q,q,tritone (18.20–23). The insight attributed to Lamprocles is apparently that the irregularities of this structure can be resolved by construing it as a sequence of two tetrachords in conjunction, with an additional 'disjunctive' tone at the top. This involves inserting an extra note (*mesē*) into the originally incomposite tritone. The present text suggests an earlier analysis that may have understood the series as consisting of two groups, q,q,t and q,q,tritone, disjoined by a tone. The Lydian cited at Arist. Quint. 18.10–13 is q,d,t,q,q,d,q. Here the disjunction clearly falls between

Lydian, which is the antithesis of Mixolydian and close to Ionian, was invited by the Athenian Damon.[114]

17. 'Since one of these *harmoniai* is mournful and the other dissipated, it was only to be expected that Plato would reject them, and select Dorian as being appropriate for warlike and temperate men.[115] [f] This was most certainly not, as Aristoxenus claims in the second book of his work *On Music*, because Plato was ignorant of the fact that the other two *harmoniai* can also be of use to a well-ordered state.[116] Plato had studied musical science most carefully, and had been taught by Dracon of Athens and Metellus of Acragas.[117] The reason he preferred Dorian was rather, as I said before, because of its high degree of dignified nobility. He was well aware that many Dorian maiden-songs had been composed by Alcman, and by Pindar, Simonides, and Bacchylides as well, and so too had *prosodia*[118] and paeans: he knew that even laments had been set to music in the Dorian style in tragedy, as well as some love-songs.[119] [1137a] But he was satisfied to confine himself to compositions to Ares and Athena, and *spondeia*, since these are capable of putting strength into the soul of a temperate man.[120] Nor was he

q,d and q,q,d,q, and the early account of Mixolydian could have been based on an analogy with this division. So far as its structure is concerned, the regularised Mixolydian of Cleonides and the rest is in effect a conjunct scale of Dorian form, completing the octave with an additional tone at the top (cf. n. 111 above).

114   On Damon see **149** Plato, *Rep.* 400b and Ch. 10, Appendix B. If, as is likely, the 'relaxed' Lydian is the same as what became known as Hypolydian, its invention is attributed to the much older musician Polymnestus at 1141b. The contrast between Mixolydian and the 'relaxed' (*epaneimenē*) Lydian is evidently the same as that between Mixolydian and the 'slack' (*chalarai*) versions of Lydian made by Plato at **149** *Rep.* 398e. The same passage also links the 'slack' Lydian *harmoniai* with the Iastian (i.e. Ionian): cf. Pratinas' reference to the 'relaxed' (*aneimenē*) Iastian Muse, **192** Ath. 624f. The sentence here is probably based directly on an interpretation of *Rep.* 398e: the 'antithesis' is one of character (and probably pitch), and cannot be understood in terms of a contrast of scale-structures.

115   **149** *Rep.* 398d–399c. It is notable that the present author, writing in Plato's defence, makes no reference to his controversial treatment of Phrygian in the same passage (see **161** Ar. *Pol.* 1342a 32 ff).

116   As argued at **161** Ar. *Pol.* 1342a 1 ff.

117   Dracon is said to have been a pupil of Damon (Olympiod. *Vit. Plat.* 2). The name Metellus (a Roman form) is probably corrupt: we might read Megillus or Megyllus, but nothing of the persons involved is known.

118   'Processionals': cf. 1132c.

119   On the use of Dorian in tragedy see 1136d. Posidonius (ap. **196** Ath. 635c–d) says that Anacreon, a poet best known for his love-songs, mentioned and employed Dorian, as well as Phrygian and Lydian.

120   Since *spondeia* are treated in the present work as pieces for the *aulos*, and since the *nomoi* of Ares (1141b) and Athena (1143b–c, Pollux IV.77) are also auletic, W. and R. find this sentence difficult. Plato rejects the *aulos* altogether (**149** *Rep.* 399d), and sharply criticises purely instrumental music of any sort (**154** *Laws* 669e). But the author does not speak of specific *nomoi* known by these names: probably by 'compositions to Ares' he means no more than 'warlike music', and by 'compositions to Athena' he is indicating music that expresses wisdom and restraint (**149** *Rep.* 399a–c). An appropriate context for *spondeia*, in the general sense 'songs accompanying a libation [to the gods]', is suggested at **156** *Laws* 799b.

ignorant of the Lydian and Ionian *harmoniai*, since he knew that tragedy employed that kind of composition.[121]

18. 'None of the ancient composers who used only a few of the *harmoniai* did so through lack of familiarity with the rest. It was not ignorance that caused the narrowness of the range and the fewness of the notes[122] that they used, nor was it through ignorance that the associates of Olympus and Terpander and those who followed [b] the style they had chosen rejected multiplicity of notes and complexification.[123] The compositions of Olympus and Terpander and of all those who use the same style give evidence of this. Though they involve three notes only,[124] and are simple, they are so much better than those that are complex and use many notes that no one can imitate the style of Olympus, and all those who use many notes and many *tropoi*[125] are inferior to him.

19. 'It is clear that it was not through ignorance that the ancient musicians refrained from using *tritē* in the *spondeiazōn tropos*,[126] since they employ it

---

121   It is possible, as W. and R. suggest, that this 'Ionian' is not the 'slack' form of **149** *Rep.* 398e, but what Heraclides (ap. **192** Ath. 625b–c) describes as an earlier Ionian *harmonia*, 'austere, hard and serious' in character: it is, he says, well suited for tragedy. It may be identical with what was later called Hypophrygian (whose structure, according to the technical writers, was d,t,q,q,d,q,q in enharmonic, t,t,s,t,t,s,t in diatonic, e.g. Arist. Quint 15.14): the Hypophrygian is said to be invigorating in character and to be used in the songs of the tragic actors, but not by the chorus (**185** ps.-Ar. *Probs.* XIX.48, cf. 30).
    Lydian is not known to have been much used in tragedy (but cf. the association of its 'higher' form with Mixolydian at **149** *Rep.* 398e: Mixolydian does belong to tragedy, 1136c–d). W. and R. suggest that we should read 'Aeolian', which is described by Heraclides as showy, weighty, conceited, elevated and bold, and as identical with the later Hypodorian (**192** Ath. 624e–625a). The theorists give Hypodorian the structure t,q,q,d,q,q,d (enharmonic), t,s,t,t,s,t,t (diatonic): e.g. Arist. Quint. 15.15. Like Hypophrygian it is set in the lower range of pitch. Ps.-Ar. *Probs.* XIX.30 and 48 say that it too was used by actors but not by choruses: the latter (**185**) describes it as magnificent and stable, and therefore the best suited of all the *harmoniai* to *kitharōdia*.

122   *Oligochordia*: cf. 1135d.

123   *Poikilia*. The passage reflects Plato's comments at e.g. **149** *Rep.* 399c–d and **158** *Laws* 812d–e, rejecting the 'modernism' outlined in Ch. 7 above.

124   This probably means 'only three notes in each tetrachord'. The *spondeion* scale, to which the remark presumably refers, contained at least five notes (E,F,A,B,C or E,F,A,B,C+: see Appendix B). The author is recalling the analysis of that scale as avoiding the division of the semitone E–F into quarter-tones (1135b), so that its lower fourth (E,F,A) lacked one of the notes of the developed enharmonic tetrachord (E,E+,F,A). The discussion of the *spondeiazōn tropos* (1137b–d) refers to the omission of *tritē* (B+) in the upper part of the range: taken in conjunction with Terpander's alleged 'omission' of *tritē* and addition of *nētē*, the higher E (**180** ps.-Ar. *Probs.* XIX.32), which may reflect a memory of the same structure, we may conceive a three-note system in the upper fourth also, B,C,E.

125   The Greek uses the adjective *polytropos*, 'of many *tropoi*', that is, 'modulating between different melodic styles of *harmoniai*'.

126   On the details of this account of the *spondeiazōn tropos* see Appendix B.

in the accompaniment.[127] They could not have employed it to make a concord with *parhypatē* if they had not been familiar with its use; and it was
plainly the [c] nobility of character generated in the *spondeiakos tropos* by
the removal of *tritē* which led their perception to make the melody pass over
it to *paranētē*.

'The same may be said of *nētē*, which they also used in the accompaniment
as a discord with *paranētē* and a concord with *mesē*: but in the melody it
seemed to them unsuited to the *spondeiakos tropos*.

'It was not only these notes that they employed in this way, but *nētē
synēmmenōn* as well. In the [d] accompaniment they treated it as discordant
with *paranētē*, *paramesē* and *lichanos*, whereas any of them would have been
ashamed at the character which it created if he used it in the melody. That
Olympus and his followers were not unfamiliar with it is proved by their
Phrygian pieces, since they used it not only in the accompaniment but in the
melody as well, in their *Mētrōa* and other Phrygian compositions.[128]

'The case of the tetrachord *hypatōn* is also clear. It was not through
ignorance that they refrained from using this tetrachord in Dorian compositions, since they used it in the other *tonoi*,[129] and were therefore plainly
acquainted with it. It was with a view to preserving the proper character that
they avoided this tetrachord [e] in the Dorian, out of respect for the nobility
of that *tonos*.[130]

---

[127]   *Krousis*, which can mean simply 'instrumental music'; but the discussion shows
clearly that an accompaniment to a melody is intended. Cf. the usage at 1141a–b.

[128]   Olympus' auletic *Mētrōa*, pieces in honour of the mother of the gods, are mentioned
again at 1141b. *Mētrōa* were always compositions for *aulos*, and like the cult of the
goddess itself, were generally associated with Phrygia (e.g. Paus. x.30.9: on the
Phrygian music of the cult in general, Homeric *Hymn to the Mother of the Gods*
1–5). One source, exceptionally, links *Mētrōa* with Libya and the Libyan *aulos*
(Douris ap. 189 Ath. 618b–c).

[129]   Here equivalent to *harmonia*: see next note.

[130]   It seems likely that the 'avoidance' of notes in the tetrachord *hypatōn* in Dorian
compositions is to be explained in a different way from the one the author suggests.
The Dorian *harmonia* (structure q,q,d,t,q,q,d in enharmonic, s,t,t,t,s,t,t in diatonic)
is normally thought of as comprising the notes of the octave between *hypatē mesōn*
and *nētē diezeugmenōn*, which correspond to this structure. This octave is formed
from two tetrachords, the tetrachord *mesōn* (between *hypatē mesōn* and *mesē*), and
the tetrachord *diezeugmenōn* (between *paramesē* and *nētē diezeugmenōn*), lower E to
A, and B to higher E, in modern notation. The tetrachord *hypatōn* comprises a fourth
added in conjunction below *Hypatē mesōn* (i.e., from the lower E down to lower B):
in Dorian melodies covering an octave or less, these notes would not be needed. Other
harmoniai, at least in the versions set out by the theorists (e.g. Arist. Quint. 15.10 ff),
have structures corresponding to the same note-series beginning from a different
point. Thus Mixolydian, for instance (q,q,d,q,q,d,t, or in diatonic s,t,t,s,t,t,t) corresponds to the series beginning on *hypatē hypatōn*, the B below the bottom of the
Dorian octave. A performer tuning an instrument to this series would therefore
incorporate, at the lower end of his scale, the intervals belonging to the tetrachord
hypatōn. The notes were named according to their position in the series, considered
as a complete structure, not according to their absolute pitch. Since the effective
range of a (stringed) instrument was roughly the same in any form of tuning, a
note-series beginning from a lower named note in the complete system would effectively transpose that note upwards in pitch: this is at least one reason why *harmoniai*

20. 'Something similar applies to the composers of tragedy. To this day tragedy has never used the chromatic genus with its specific structure,[131] whereas the *kithara*, which is many generations older than tragedy, has used it from the start.[132] It is obvious that the chromatic genus is older than the enharmonic. (When we speak of one as "older", we must do so with respect to its discovery and employment by mankind: for so far as the nature of the genera themselves is concerned, none is older than another.)[133] Thus anyone who said that Aeschylus or Phrynichus refrained from using [f] the chromatic out of ignorance would surely be talking nonsense. One might just as well say that Pancrates knew nothing of the chromatic genus, since on the whole he avoided it; but in a few pieces he did use it.[134] Hence it is clear that he avoided it not from ignorance but from choice: as he says himself, indeed, he sought to emulate the style of Pindar and Simonides, and in general what people nowadays call archaic.

such as Mixolydian, beginning from 'lower' notes, were in fact treated as 'higher'. (The note *mesē*, for instance, defined as the note below the disjunctive tone, is the fourth note from the bottom of the Dorian structure, but rises to be next to the top in Mixolydian.) The 'higher' *harmoniai* which incorporate notes in the tetrachord *hypatōn* are Mixolydian, Lydian (the 'high', *syntonos* Lydian of 149 *Rep*. 398e), and Phrygian (Arist. Quint. 15.11–13, Cleonides 197.4–13, etc.).

[131] Plutarch says (*Quaest. Conv.* III.1.1) that Agathon (late fifth century) was the first to use the chromatic genus in tragedy: no other such instance is recorded. 'With its specific structure': the MSS have *kai tōi rhythmōi*, lit. 'and its rhythm', which I retain, translating *rhythmos* in its older and wider sense 'arrangement', 'condition', 'structure'. In a musical context, admittedly, it would naturally be taken in the sense 'rhythm', but this special sense seems not to occur before the last years of the fifth century, and the old sense continued in use (cf. the verb *rhythmizein* used in the old way in the quotation from Aristotle at 1139b). The present source (Aristoxenus) may be quoting an older authority: perhaps he wrote e.g. *tōi legomenōi rhythmōi*, 'the so-called *rhythmos*'. Lasserre takes it in the straightforward sense 'rhythm', but has to emend the text to make it comprehensible by adding the word *poikilōi*, 'varied'. W. and R. treat the reference to *rhythmos* as a misplaced marginal note, and excise it.

[132] We have no clear evidence to confirm this remark. The *chrōmata euchroa* of Lysander the kitharist (Philochorus ap. 196 Ath. 638a), to which the editors refer, are certainly to be understood otherwise (see note ad loc.). However, it seems likely that what the theorists call the 'chromatic genus' was not originally a clear-cut system of tuning, or set of such systems, as enharmonic and diatonic perhaps were. *Chrōma* ('colour') in semi-colloquial musical parlance indicates a shading, colouring or nuance, used for special expressive effect: Lysander's *chrōmata* were probably of this sort. The word came to have the more specific sense 'expressive shadings involving subtle alterations of the normal scalar intervals'. In Aristoxenus any variant of a standard genus of scale is called a *chroa* ('shade', 'colour'), and the so-called chromatic genus admitted more such *chroai* than did any other. Possibly Lysander was already using shadings of this sort: it is very probable that they were involved in the elaborate *kitharōdia* of Timotheus and his school. (On the popularity of the chromatic genus in the fourth century see Aristox. *El. Harm.* 23.9–22.) References by later authors to the 'chromatic genus' in fifth-century or earlier music should then be construed as indicating deviations from normal scalar intervals, not any one fixed system. The main forms of the 'chromatic genus' are unlikely to have been systematically analysed before Aristoxenus (see *El. Harm.* 50–52).

[133] See *El. Harm.* 19.20–29.

[134] Pancrates is unknown: he was presumably a fourth-century composer who devoted himself to writing in the 'ancient' style.

21. 'The same can be said of Tyrtaeus of Mantinea, Andreas of Corinth, Thrasyllus of Phlius,[135] and many others. We know that all of them chose to reject the chromatic genus, modulation, the use of many notes, and many other things [1138a] that were available in rhythms and *harmoniai*, in modes of diction, in composition and in performance. Telephanes of Megara,[136] for example, was so strongly opposed to the *syrinx* of the *aulos* that he forbade the makers of *auloi* to build it into the instruments, and it was primarily for that reason that he refused to perform at the Pythian games.[137] In general, if we treated the fact that someone did not use a given procedure as evidence that he was ignorant of it, we should be unwittingly condemning many even of our contemporaries, the school of Dorion for instance, [b] for not using the style of Antigenidas, which they despise, the school of Antigenidas for the same reason, since they reject the style of Dorion,[138] and the singers to the

[135] Of these musicians too, nothing is known, but like Pancrates they must have been archaising composers of the fourth century, deliberately avoiding the modern practices of the post-Timothean school, listed below.

[136] A well-known aulete of the fourth century: see e.g. Demosth. 21.17, Paus. 1.44.6, *Anth. Pal.* VII.159.

[137] No ancient writer gives a deliberate explanation of the expression 'the *syrinx* of the *aulos*'. *Syrinx* here patently does not refer to the Pan-pipe, and must have a sense related to its general meaning 'whistle'. Most commentators now accept the hypothesis of A. A. Howard ('The *aulos* or *tibia*', *Harvard Studies* 4, Boston 1893), to the effect that it was a small hole near the upper end of the *aulos* that could be opened (probably by sliding a ring) to facilitate the production of higher harmonics. Passages cited in support of this interpretation include Ar. *De Audib.* 804a (= Porph. *Comm.* 75.28 ff), Aristox. *El. Harm.* 21.1–5, Plut. *Non Posse Suav.* 1096a: for a summary see Macran (1902) 243–4, Düring, *Ptol. und Porph.*, 172–3. For a kind of kitharistic analogue to this technique see **196** Ath. 638a with Xen. *Anab.* VII.3.32–3 and **25** Strabo IX.3.10–11. The connection of the *syrinx* of the *aulos* with the Pythian games suggests a link with the highly dramatic *Pythikos nomos*, and no doubt one of the objects of extending the instrument's range was an increase in dramatic expression. Pollux (IV.81) represents the *Pythikos aulos*, the instrument used in the *Pythikos nomos*, as being of moderately low pitch: cf. Arist. Quint. 85.5–7. The *syrinx* would take such an instrument out of its characteristically 'masculine' range altogether, a shift that could obviously be exploited for representational or emotive effect. (Note also that one of the movements of the *Pythikos nomos* in the version recorded by Strabo is called *syringes*: this portrayed the sounds of the death-throes of the Python, and may give a further clue to the contexts in which these high harmonics were used.) We are to understand, then, that Telephanes rejected the highly coloured and expressive tradition of *aulos*-playing associated with the Pythian games, in favour of a more archaic style. The manipulation of sound as a means of dramatic representation is contrasted with an emphasis on the virtues of simple and shapely melody.

[138] Dorion was an aulete and composer of the mid- to late fourth century, patronised by Philip of Macedon: the special features of his style are unknown, but may have involved a certain over-refinement. (See Ath. 337b–338b, 435b.) Antigenidas of Thebes lived some forty years earlier (e.g. Ath. 131b, *Suda* s.v., cf. **195** Ath. 631f). He is mentioned by Theophrastus (**163** *Hist. Plant.* IV.11.4) as one of those who first played the *aulos* 'in the elaborate style', which demanded a flexible vibrating reed with a relatively wide opening (see notes ad loc.): he is not, as W. and R. assert, named as the inventor of this style. We have insufficient evidence to trace the contrast between Antigenidas and Dorion further: Lasserre is merely speculating when he associates Antigenidas with low-pitched compositions and Dorion with high-pitched ones.

kithara who reject the style of Timotheus, and have virtually abandoned it in favour of patchwork pieces and the compositions of Polyeidus.[139]

'Again, if you study the subject of complexity correctly and from a proper familiarity with it, and compare the older compositions with those of today, you will find that complexity was practised in the old days too. The forms of rhythmic composition used by ancient composers were more complex, since they had a great respect for rythmic complexity, and their patterns of instrumental idiom were also more complicated:[140] for nowadays people's interest [c] is in the melody, whereas in the past they concentrated on the rhythm.[141]

'As to fragmented melodies,[142] it is obvious that the ancient composers avoided them not through ignorance but from choice. This is not surprising. There are, after all, many other activities in life which are not unknown to those who refrain from them, but are ones which these people find uncongenial, and which they refuse to use because of their unsuitability for certain purposes.

22. 'I have shown that it was not through ignorance or lack of familiarity with them that Plato rejected the other styles, but because they were unsuitable for the kind of state he discusses. I shall go on to prove that he was an expert in harmonic theory.[143] In his account of the origin of the soul in the

139 Little is known of Polyeidus. He composed dithyrambs (Diod. Sic. xiv.46), and practised *kitharōdia*, a genre in which one of his pupils defeated the ageing Timotheus (Ath. 352b). He may possibly be the Polyeidus named by Aristotle as author of a tragedy (*Poetics* 1455a6, b10). 'Patchwork pieces', *kattymata*: the word refers literally to a patch of leather stitched onto the sole of a shoe. Its musical meaning is uncertain, but might be something like 'medleys', by contrast with structurally more organised pieces. On Timotheus see Ch. 7: the implication is that some of his innovatory techniques had been abandoned by Aristoxenus' time, at least by the popular *kattymata* composers.

140 'Patterns of . . . idiom', *dialektoi*. The word can mean 'discourse', 'conversation', and might suggest 'interplay' between accompaniment and voice: cf. 1144e. It can also have the sense 'language', 'dialect', and might here simply refer to musical idiom or style: cf. Ar. *De An.* 420b8. The statement that 'ancient' instrumental idiom was (rhythmically) more complicated is surprising, if it is the 'ancients' of Pindar's time and earlier who are being compared with 'moderns' of Timotheus' school. Pindar's rhythms are certainly not simple, but Timotheus' rhythmic shifts and changes were notorious, as was his elaborate instrumental ornamentation. Conceivably Timotheus is being treated as 'ancient' by contrast with the music of the late fourth century, as in the previous paragraph, but the appellation would be most unusual: and it is certainly not his school that is said to avoid 'fragmented' melodies in the next sentence. Perhaps the contrast is between Pindar and his contemporaries on the one hand and music in Aristoxenus' day on the other, the elaborate compositions of the period from Phrynis to Timotheus being at present disregarded.

141 Cf. Dion. Hal. *De Comp. Verb.* 19, where the contrast is between Stesichorus and Pindar as 'ancients' and the dithyrambists (presumably Cinesias and his like) as 'moderns'.

142 'Fragmented', *keklasmenos*, seems to refer to tunes of elaborate melodic structure, 'broken up' by modulations from one *harmonia* to another. Cf. Plut. *Pyth. Orac.* 6.

143 *Empeiros harmonias*, an expression that might indicate knowledge and skill in music under any of its aspects, but must here be equivalent to *harmonikos*, a 'harmonic scientist', as the sequel shows.

Timaeus he displays [d] his interest in mathematics and music in the following words: "And after that he filled up the double and triple intervals, cutting off pieces from his material and placing them within the intervals, so that there were two means in each interval."[144] This preamble depends on a familiarity with harmonics, as I shall now show. There are three primary means which are the basis of all the others: they are the arithmetic, the harmonic and that which is found geometrically. One of these means is greater than one term and less than the other by the same number, one by the same ratio, one neither by a ratio nor by a number.[145] Thus Plato, wishing to give a harmonic description of the *harmonia* of the four elements in the soul, [e] and of the cause of the concord generated between things that are unlike, exhibited in each interval two means belonging to the soul, corresponding to "musical" proportion: for in the musical concord of an octave there are two mean intervals,[146] whose proportionalities I shall now explain.[147] The octave is in duple ratio: this ratio can be constituted, to give a numerical example,

---

[144]   Plato, *Tim.* 35c–36a. 'From his material', lit. 'from there': the pieces are taken from a compound that has previously been mingled, *Tim.* 35a–b. The passage from which this excerpt comes was of enormous influence in the later mystical-mathematical tradition of 'Pythagorean' harmonic theory: cf. e.g. Nicom. 250.4 ff, Arist. Quint. 125.29 ff. See notes to the *Timaeus* and these later authors ad loc. for detailed points of interpretation (Vol. 2).

[145]   If B is the arithmetic mean between A and C, then $B-A = C-B$. Geometric proportion, though listed third, is described second: here the ratio of B to A is the same as the ratio of C to B, i.e. $B:A = C:B$. In harmonic proportion the part of the first term by which the mean exceeds it is the same as the part of the third term by which it exceeds the mean, i.e., if $B = A + (A/n)$, then $C = B + (C/n)$. The direct formula is $(1/A) - (1/B) = (1/B) - (1/C)$. It is understandable that the present author, plainly no mathematician, is content with a vague negative description.

[146]   The expression 'mean intervals' is inexact. Two means are involved, but each represents a note, not an interval. The number of intervals generated within the octave is three: see next note.

[147]   Plato's division of the soul-material involves segmentation on the basis of two number-series, 1, 2, 4, 8, and 1, 3, 9, 27. The present author ignores the second series, and treats the rest of Plato's account as a description of the insertion of means between each pair of numbers in the first. Taken on its own, the first corresponds to a sequence of three octaves, the octave being represented in Pythagorean harmonics by the ratio 2:1. The insertion of means divides each octave at the remaining boundaries of its two constituent tetrachords, a fourth above the lowest note (= a fifth below the highest), and a fourth below the highest (= a fifth above the lowest). (The interval of a fifth corresponds to the ratio 3:2, that of the fourth to the ratio 4:3. The mathematics involved are set out in detail in the Euclidean *Sect. Can.*: see Vol. 2.)
      The division makes no further explicit mention of the means listed previously. But the 'musical' proportion on which it is based (so called also by Nicomachus and Iamblichus) is in fact a form of proportion generated by combining the arithmetic and the harmonic. That is, it involves two means, one of each kind; and it is this proportion that represents the octave together with its primary intermediate notes. Thus if, as in the present text, we take 6 and 12 as the extremes of the octave, the intermediate points are 8 (harmonic mean) and 9 (arithmetic mean). 12:9 = 8:6 = 4:3, the ratio of a fourth. 12:8 = 9:6 = 3:2, the ratio of a fifth. 9:8 is the ratio of a tone, the 'disjunctive' tone between the tetrachords. We may then identify the numbers with notes in the system (in the central octave). 6 corresponds to *hypatē mesōn*, 8 to *mesē*, 9 to *paramesē*, 12 to *nētē diezeugmenōn*. In their conventional modern equivalents, 6 is the lower E, 8 is A, 9 is B, 12 is the upper E.

[f] by 6 and 12, and it is the interval from *hypatē mesōn* to *nētē diezeug-menōn*. Given that the numbers are 6 and 12, the number 6 belongs to *hypatē mesōn* and the number 12 to *nētē diezeugmenōn*. The remaining task is to find the numbers falling between these, so that one stands in epitritic ratio, the other in hemiolic.[148] These are 8 and 9, since 8 stands in epitritic ratio to 6 and 9 in hemiolic. This describes one of the extreme terms: the other, which is 12, stands in epitritic ratio to 9 and in hemiolic ratio to 8. [1139a] Since these numbers lie between 6 and 12, and since the interval of an octave is made up of the fourth and the fifth, it is clear that the number 8 will belong to *mesē* and the number 9 to *paramesē*. Given all this, the ratio of *hypatē* to *mesē* will be the same as that of *paramesē* to *nētē diezeugmenōn*; for from *hypatē mesōn* to *mesē* is a fourth, and from *paramesē* to *nētē diezeugmenōn* is the same. The same proportions [b] will be found to hold between the numbers as well: as 6 is to 8 so is 9 to 12, and as 6 is to 9 so is 8 to 12. 8 is in epitritic ratio to 6, as is 12 to 9, and 9 is in hemiolic ratio to 6, as is 12 to 8. What we have said is enough to show Plato's enthusiasm for mathematical studies and his familiarity with them.[149]

23. 'That *harmonia*[150] is something solemn, divine and great is asserted by Aristotle, the pupil of Plato, in the following words. "*Harmonia* is heavenly, and its nature is divine, beautiful and marvellous. It is fourfold in its natural capacities, and thus has two means, the arithmetic and the harmonic,[151] and its parts and magnitudes and excesses exhibit themselves in conformity with number and with equality of measure;[152] for melodies acquire their struc-ture[153] within two tetrachords."[154] [c] Those are Aristotle's words.

[148] 'Epitritic': i.e. the ratio 4:3. 'Hemiolic', i.e. the ratio 3:2. The existence of such one-word expressions for ratios of these kinds in Greek is given important theoretical significance in the introductory passage of the *Sect. Can.*

[149] The author is obviously impressed by these fairly elementary calculations. He is not as mathematically sophisticated as e.g. Nicomachus or the writer of the *Sectio* (let alone Ptolemy), but enthusiasm for the mathematical side of harmonics was not always allied to mathematical competence: there are, for instance, some desperately muddled passages in the third book of Arist. Quint.

[150] *Harmonia* in this passage has a double significance: it functions simultaneously as a general term for the phenomenon of music, conceived as consisting in orderly melodic relationships, and as the old Pythagorean name for the octave, the musical relation whose analysis reveals all the other relations on which melody is built. For the old use see Nicom. 252.4 ff: the junction of the two is well exemplified in the quotation from Aristotle that follows.

[151] The sense of these terms is explained in n. 147 above.

[152] The 'parts' are probably the four fundamental notes, represented by the numbers 6,8,9,12. (Some commentators take them to be the intervals of a tone, a fourth, a fifth and an octave. Cf. the rather similar difficulty at 149 Plato, *Rep.* 400a.) The 'mag-nitudes', to judge by Aristoxenian usage, are the intervals between the fundamental notes. The 'excesses' they embody are the numerical differences between the terms that represent the intervals' bounding notes. Thus the interval 12:9 has an excess of 3, which is equal 'in conformity with number' to the excess in the interval 9:6. The interval 12:8 has an excess of 4, displaying 'equality of measure', i.e. of proportion, with the excess in the interval 8:6 (since $4 = \frac{12}{3}$ and $2 = \frac{6}{3}$).

[153] *Rhythmizetai*, lit. 'are rhythmed'. See 1137e and n. 131.

[154] *Eudemus* fr. 47 (Rose) = *On Philosophy* fr. 25 (Ross).

'He said that its body[155] is made up of dissimilar parts, which nevertheless are in concord with one another, and also that its means are concordant in correspondence with numerical ratio.[156] Thus the highest note is attuned to the lowest in duple ratio, and yields the concord of an octave. It has, as we said earlier, a highest note of 12 units and a lowest of 6, and its *paramesē*, which forms a concord in hemiolic ratio with *hypatē*, has 9 units: *mesē*, we said, contains 8 units. And it turns out that the most fundamental intervals of music are constituted out of these – the fourth, which corresponds to epitritic ratio, [d] the fifth, which corresponds to hemiolic, and the octave, which corresponds to duple. The occurrence of the ratio 9 : 8 is also justified, since it is the ratio of the tone. Further, the amounts by which the parts of the *harmonia* exceed and are exceeded by the means are the same, both arithmetically and in terms of geometrical operations, as the amounts by which the means exceed and are exceeded by the parts.[157] Thus Aristotle ascribes the following properties to the means. *Nētē* exceeds *mesē* by a third part of itself, [e] and *hypatē* is exceeded by *mesē* in the same way:[158] hence these excesses are relational, since the terms exceed and are exceeded by the same parts.[159] (Thus the extremes exceed and are exceeded by *mesē* and *paramesē* in the same ratios, the epitritic and the hemiolic.)[160] That, then, constitutes an excess of the harmonic kind. By contrast the excesses belonging to *nētē* and to the arithmetical mean exhibit differences that are equal.[161] (The case

155   The 'body' of *harmonia* is sound, on which ratios are imposed as form. Aristotle no doubt has in mind the *Timaeus'* account of the body and soul of the universe.
156   *Kata ton arithmētikon logon*, which ought to mean 'in arithmetic ratio', as at 1138d. But this makes no sense as applied to the two means, which are in any case not concordant with one another. Either the text must be emended, or the sense is here more general, indicating simply that the ratios of the means (with the extremes) are expressible as ratios of whole numbers.
157   With W. and R.'s transposition of the words *mesotētōn* and *mesōn*. The MSS reading would mean 'the amounts by which the parts of the *harmonia* exceed and are exceeded by one another are the same . . . as the amounts by which the means exceed and are exceeded by one another'. If, as the following sentences suggest, the 'parts' here are the 6-unit note and the 12-unit note, and the 'means' the notes corresponding to 8 and 9, the MSS reading cannot stand.
158   *Nētē* corresponds to 12, *mesē* to 8, *hypatē* to 6. 8 is the harmonic mean, exceeding 6 by a third of 6 and less than 12 by a third of 12. The MSS have *paramesē* (i.e., 9) for the second occurrence of *mesē* in this sentence, a copyist having been misled, perhaps, by the irrelevant fact that 12 exceeds 9 by a third of 9. See also n. 160 below.
159   An abbreviated definition of harmonic proportion. The excesses are said to be 'relational', in the Aristotelian category of the *pros ti*, because they are to be understood through their relations to extremes, not through their own character as magnitudes.
160   *Nētē* exceeds *mesē*, and *paramesē* exceeds *hypatē* in hemiolic ratio (3 : 2), while *nētē* exceeds *paramesē*, and *mesē* exceeds *hypatē* in epitritic ratio (4 : 3). But this parenthesis is probably an interpolation by the same hand that wrote *paramesē* for *mesē* above (see n. 158), since *paramesē* has no place in a discussion of harmonic means (see the next sentence).
161   The text is certainly corrupt. The MSS read 'exhibit differences in an equal part (*isōi merei*)', which could only mean 'constituting an equal part of themselves', and would lead back to another discussion of harmonic proportion. If the sense of my translation is correct, we should perhaps substitute *plēthei* ('numerousness', 'quantity') for *merei*: but the correct reading may be lost beyond recall. The arithmetic mean corresponds to the note *paramesē* and the number 9.

of the excess of *paramesē* over *hypatē* is the same, [f] since *paramesē* exceeds *mesē* in the ratio 9:8, and again *nētē* is double *hypatē*, *paramesē* is in hemiolic ratio with *hypatē*, and *mesē* is tuned in epitritic ratio with *hypatē*.)[162] This, then, is the natural constitution of *harmonia* in respect of both parts and numbers, according to Aristotle too.[163]

24. 'At the most fundamental level of nature, *harmonia* and all its parts are constituted out of the natural principles of the unlimited, the limiting, and the even–odd.[164] The *harmonia* as a whole is even, since it has four terms: whereas its parts and ratios are even and odd and even–odd. [1140a] Its *nētē* is of 12 units and is even, its *paramesē* is of 9 and is odd, its *mesē* is of 8 and is even, and its *hypatē* is of 6 and is even–odd. Since *harmonia* and its parts are naturally related to one another in this way through their excesses and ratios, it is concordant with itself as a whole and with its parts.

25. 'Further, of the senses which are introduced into bodies through *harmonia*,[165] sight and hearing, which are heavenly and divine and are aided by God in giving sense-perception to men, [b] reveal *harmonia* with the assistance of sound and light.[166] The others, which are subservient to them in their

162   This parenthesis seems to be ps.-Plutarch's attempt to fill out the doctrine of the previous sentence, which is quoted from his source. The source has said that 'the excesses belonging to *nētē* and to the arithmetical mean (*paramesē*)' have 'equal differences': this means, I think, that the excess of *nētē* (12) over *paramesē* (9) is equal to the excess of *paramesē* over *hypatē* (6). The present sentence is a clumsy attempt to derive the latter fact from other propositions.

163   'Parts and numbers' refers to the relations between the elements of the octave in terms of (a) fractions of the extremes and (b) numerical equalities. 'Aristotle too', i.e., as well as Plato.

164   Here the source moves into an account which is purely Pythagorean, and no part of Platonic or Aristotelian metaphysics. The limiting and the unlimited are primary factors in Pythagorean cosmology (e.g. Ar. *Metaph.* 986a, 987a): here, however, the terms are used as synonyms for their special manifestations as odd ('limiting') and even ('unlimited') numbers (e.g. Ar. *Metaph.* 985b, *Phys.* 203a). An 'even–odd' number is one that is even, but which yields an odd number when divided by 2. The vague numerology that follows is quite uncharacteristic of Plato or Aristotle. It can readily be developed into absurdities of the kind sharply criticised by Aristotle in the last book of the *Metaph.*, and well exemplified in parts of Arist. Quint. Bk III.

165   *Harmonia* in this paragraph has roughly the sense 'proportion'. The doctrines expressed here are obscure, and their source is uncertain. The references to God have suggested to commentators Aristotle's (early) doctrine that the heavenly bodies have sight and hearing but no other senses: see *Eudemus* fr. 48 (Rose) = *On Philosophy* fr. 24 (Ross): but the parallel can hardly be pressed. It is just possible that the source is Aristoxenus: cf. fr. 73 (Wehrli), Philodemus 54.15 ff (Kemke). The doctrine that the use of the senses involves a proportionality between the organ and the object perceived is Aristotelian enough (e.g. *De An.* 4242a, 429a–b), but it seems most likely that ps.-Plutarch's source is a later compiler or commentator.

166   The general doctrine is apparently that (mathematical) *harmonia* is a feature of the universe as a whole and all its elements, and is manifested to us through different perceptual ranges. The fundamental proportionalities remain the same, whether they appear through objects of sight, of hearing, or of anything else. The notion attracted Pythagorising writers of later antiquity, but its roots are in Aristotle too: cf. *De Sensu* 448a.

role as senses, are also constituted in conformity with *harmonia*. For they achieve none of their results without the help of *harmonia*, and while they are inferior to sight and hearing they are not divorced from them. Sight and hearing occur in our bodies together with the presence of God and on the foundation of reason, and their nature is great and noble.[167]

26. 'These points make it clear that it was entirely reasonable for the Greeks of ancient times to be concerned most of all with musical education. They believed that they ought to mould and structure the souls of the young through music towards gracefulness and decorum, evidently on the grounds that music is of value [c] in dealing with all circumstances and for every action that is seriously undertaken, and especially in facing the dangers of wars. In the face of these dangers some, like the Spartans, used *auloi*: among the Spartans the tune called "The Melody of Castor" was played on the *auloi* when they advanced in good order to fight the enemy.[168] Others approached their opponents to the sound of the *lyra*: it is recorded, for instance, that the Cretans employed this practice over a long period, when going out to meet the dangers of war.[169] Others even in our own time continue to use the *salpinx*.[170] The Argives used to play the *aulos* at the wrestling match in the festival they called the Sthenaia: they say that this festival was originally founded in honour of Danaus, [d] but was later dedicated to Zeus Sthenios. What is more, it is customary even nowadays for the *aulos* to be played when the pentathlon is going on.[171] The music, admittedly, is neither cultivated nor in the ancient style: it is not of the kind that was current among the men of those times, like the music composed by Hierax for this contest,[172] a piece called the *Endromē*.[173] Nevertheless, the *aulos* is played, even if the music is feeble and uncultivated.

[167]   Cf. Plato, *Tim.* 47b–e, Ptol. *Harm.* 93–4.
[168]   Pollux (IV.78) says that the Melody of Castor was one used by the Spartans in battle, and describes its rhythm as *embatērios*, i.e. anapaestic. (The Spartan soldiers are said to have intoned an *embatērios* paean, meaning the paean accompanying an 'advance' against the enemy, Plut. *Lyc.* 22.) By the time of Pindar the expression 'melody of Castor' could be used for any kind of song or dance-tune appropriate to warriors (*Pyth.* 2.69, *Isth.* 1.15). The Spartans' use of the *aulos* in military contexts is mentioned in many sources, e.g. Thuc. V.70, Plut. *Lyc.* 21, 193 Ath. 627d.
[169]   Cf. 193 Ath. 627d: but Ephorus twice asserts that the Cretans used the *aulos* for this purpose as well as the *lyra* (ap. Strabo X.4.20 and Polyb. IV.20.6).
[170]   The *salpinx* is mentioned in the *Iliad* (XVIII.219, cf. XXI.388), and appears frequently as a military instrument in literature of all periods. Its origin was allegedly Etruscan (e.g. Pollux IV.85): hence its common designation in poetry as 'the Etruscan *salpinx*' (e.g. Aesch. *Eum.* 568, Eurip. *Phoen.* 1378). Arist. Quint. remarks on its continuing use in the Roman army, 62.6–19.
[171]   Cf. Paus. V.7.10, VI.14.10.
[172]   Hierax is probably legendary (the name means 'hawk', 'falcon'). Pollux (IV.79), mentioning a *nomos Hierakios*, says that he was a pupil and favourite of Olympus, who died young. Pollux also refers to a *Hierakion melos* (IV.78), which he says was played on the *auloi* at the festival of the Anthesphoria ('flower-carrying') dedicated to Hera at Argos.
[173]   The word means 'running in', or 'charge'. Very probably it refers to the run-up in the long jump, one of the components of the ancient pentathlon. The practice of

27. 'In still more ancient times, it is said, the Greeks knew nothing of the music of the theatre, and devoted all their skill to honouring the gods and educating the young. Among the people of those days no [e] theatres had been built at all: music still had its home in the temples, in which they used it to give honour to the divine and to praise good men.[174] This is not surprising, it is argued, since it was from *"theos"* that the word *"theatron"* was later derived, as was *"theōrein"* at a much earlier period.[175] But in our own times the corrupt kind of music has made such headway that no one ever mentions the educational sort [f] or even understands it, and everyone who practises music has joined forces with the music of the theatre.[176]

28. ' "My friend," someone might say, "are you suggesting that the men of old times made no discoveries and innovations at all?" I agree that fresh discoveries were made, but they were discoveries that conformed with dignity and propriety. Thus students of such matters have ascribed to Terpander the introduction of the Dorian *nētē*,[177] which had not been used in the melody by his predecessors. He is also said to have invented the entire Mixolydian *tonos*,[178] and the variety of Orthian melody that goes with the Orthian foot, and in addition to the Orthian foot the semantic trochee as well.[179] According to Pindar, Terpander was also the originator of the

---

engaging first-rate auletes to accompany this event is attested at Paus.VI.14.10. A number of vase paintings depict an aulete in full festal dress playing for long-jumpers (e.g. Boardman, *A.R.F.V.* Pl. 286, early fifth century): for depictions of the *aulos* used as accompaniment to other athletic events see Besseler *et al.*, Pls. 53–4.

[174] This passage may be a distant echo of Aristoxenus ap. 195 Ath. 632a–b, and more remotely of 155 Plato, *Laws* 700a–701b.

[175] *Theos*, 'god'; *theatron*, 'theatre'; *theōrein*, 'to look at'. These etymologies, though popular in the ancient sources, are plainly mistaken.

[176] This returns to the theme of the passages mentioned in n. 174 above.

[177] Terpander's scale had seven notes (see n. 18 above). Fourth-century sources (e.g. ps.-Ar. *Probs.* XIX.47) mention ancient seven-note scales spanning less than an octave, formed from two conjunct tetrachords (e.g., in diatonic, E,F,G,A,Bb,C,D). Terpander, however, is associated (180 *Probs.* XIX.32) with the 'removal' of *trite* (Bb) and the 'addition of *nētē*' (i.e., *nētē diezeugmenōn*, the higher E), which is here called 'Dorian *nētē*'. Eight-stringed instruments filled in the gap between A and C with the note *paramesē* (B), forming the characteristic Dorian scale of two tetrachords, each following the pattern semitone, tone, tone (in diatonic), disjoined by a tone. If *nētē diezeugmenōn* can be called 'Dorian *nētē*', it is a fair inference that *nētē synēmmenōn* (D in the conjunct scale quoted above) might be called *nētē* with some other regional designation. W. and R. conjecture that the scale formed by two conjunct tetrachords was the one originally called 'Aeolian': Aeolian was later identified (by Heraclides ap. 192 Ath. 624e–625a) with Hypodorian, whose scale structure as analysed by the theorists can be generated from the conjunct series above by the addition of an extra tone at the bottom.

[178] See 1136d with n. 113. The Mixolydian structure can be generated from the conjunct series by the addition of an extra tone at the top.

[179] On the melodic sense of *orthios* see Appendix A. For its metrical or rhythmic application see Arist. Quint. 36.3–4: the semantic trochee is described in the same passage. The former seems to have had the shape of a very slow iambus, the latter of a very slow trochee (four units of time followed by eight, and the converse): Aristides remarks on the solemnity of these rhythms (83.4–6). The *orthioi rhythmoi* of 194 Ath. 631b appear to be quite different.

melodies called *skolia*.[180] Again, Archilochus devised an additional pattern of rhythmic composition, the one that consists of trimeters:[181] he also introduced [1141a] combinations of rhythms of different genera,[182] and *parakatalogē*,[183] and the instrumental accompaniment that goes with these. He is also reputed to have been the first to use epodes, tetrameters, the cretic, the prosodiac and the augmentation of the heroic rhythm, and according to some people the elegiac too, as well as the combination of iambic rhythm with the *paeōn epibatos* and that of the augmented heroic rhythm with the prosodiac and the cretic.[184] People also say that Archilochus introduced the practice of having some iambics spoken with instrumental accompaniment and others sung, and that the tragic poets employed this procedure later, [b] as did Crexus, who adopted the practice and introduced it into the dithyramb.[185] Further, people think that it was Archilochus who invented the

180 I.e. 'drinking songs'.

181 That is, the iambic trimeter. Iambic verse probably had its origins in popular tradition, but was worked into a sophisticated form by Archilochus. On his metrical innovations generally (real or supposed) see Mar. Vict. VI.141 (Keil).

182 Rhythms in a single genus are those in which the ratio of arsis to thesis is the same. The standardly recognised genera have ratios of 1:1 (e.g. the dactyl), 2:1 (e.g. the iambus and the trochee), and 3:2 (e.g. the paeon). See Arist. Quint. 33.29 ff. But rhythms of the 3:2 type are said not to have been used by Archilochus (1134e).

183 *Parakatalogē* is mentioned without explanation at **165** ps.-Ar. *Probs.* XIX.6, where its 'tragic' effect is noted. It seems to be a form of accompanied recitative, somewhere between speech and song: cf. the 'intermediate' type of vocal movement mentioned at Arist. Quint. 6.3–5. The *Problem* describes it as occurring 'in songs', that is, in solo odes in the drama, and puts its emotional effect down to 'contrast', presumably the contrast between the melodic style of the song proper and the non-melodic 'chanting' of *parakatalogē*. See also n. 185 below.

184 An epode (the word occurs here, uniquely, in the neuter form *epōdon*) is often the final section of a choral passage in drama, following strophe and antistrophe. This sense is unlikely here. It also commonly means a 'refrain', returning at regular intervals in a poem: probably this is intended. (W. and R. suggest that it means a poem in two-line units, the second shorter than the first.) 'Tetrameters': trochaic tetrameters are common in the fragments of Archilochus. 'Cretic' sometimes means the foot - ⏑ -, sometimes the ditrochee - ⏑ - ⏑. The former is related to the paeon, and is probably not meant (cf. 1134e). The ditrochee occurs in the 'ithyphallic' metre, found in Archilochus' fragments. A variety of units are called 'prosodiac' (processional'): in several versions (e.g. at Arist. Quint. 37.19–23) it is related to an anapaestic rhythm, and that is probably intended here. The 'augmented heroic' must be the so-called 'Archilochean', a metre consisting of four dactylic feet followed by three trochees. Elegiacs: the author has previously claimed (1132c) that Clonas, who is said to be earlier than Archilochus (1133a) used this form. *Paeōn epibatos*: according to Arist. Quint., this is composed of long thesis, long arsis, two long theses, long arsis: he describes its emotional effect at 82.29–83.2. But it is uncertain what the term means in this passage.

185 The practice described is probably related to *parakatalogē*, if not identical with it. Phillis of Delos ap. **196** Ath. 636b says that the instruments to whose accompaniment iambics were sung were called *iambykai* (MSS *iamboi*), while those to which people 'chanted' or 'declaimed' poetry (*parelogizanto*) were called *klepsiamboi*. Pollux (IV.59) merely mentions these as stringed instruments: Hesychius adds no further information. It is possible that the names do not indicate distinct instrumental types, but mean only 'the [stringed] instrument used for the purpose indicated'. Crexus is mentioned earlier at 1135c. In tragedy most iambic lines (which constituted the dialogue) were spoken without accompaniment: it is not likely that the practices

accompaniment under the melody, the older composers having all used accompaniment in unison with the voice.[186]

29. 'The *tonos* now called Hypolydian[187] is ascribed to Polymnestus, and people say that he made much greater use than before of *eklysis* and *ekbolē*.[188] And the famous Olympus himself, who is credited with being the founder of Greek music and the music of the *nomoi*, is said to have invented both the enharmonic genus[189] and certain rhythms – the prosodiac, in which the *nomos* of Ares is composed, and the choreus, which is much used in the *Mētrōa*.[190] Some people think that Olympus also invented the baccheius.[191] The ancient melodies all demonstrate that this is so.

[c] 'Lasos of Hermione, by altering the rhythms for the movement of the dithyramb, and by pursuing the example of the multiplicity of notes belonging to the *aulos* (and so making use of more notes, widely scattered about), transformed the music that existed before him.[192]

---

described here occurred in dialogue: more probably they were used, like *parakatalogē*, to give dramatic variation to solo odes.

[186] On 'accompaniment under the melody', *krousis hypo tēn ōdēn*, see 183 ps.-Ar. *Probs.* XIX.39 and cf. 167 *Probs.* XIX.12: also e.g. Plut. *Quaest. Conv.* IX.9. As in *Probs.* XIX.39, the present reference is probably not to accompaniment at the octave (e.g. 168, 169, 172 *Probs.* XIX.14, 16, 18), but to the sort of heterophony described by Plato (158 *Laws* 812d–e) and hinted at above (1137b–d).

[187] Perhaps the *harmonia* called 'slack Lydian', *chalara Lydisti*, at 149 Plato, *Rep.* 398e. According to Arist. Quint. (18.10–13), this had the form q,d,t,q,q,d,q, which is the enharmonic equivalent of Cleonides' (diatonic) Hypolydian, t,t,t,s,t,t,s. We have previously been told, however, that the 'relaxed' (*epaneimenē*) Lydian, which was presumably the same as the 'slack', was invented by Damon in the fifth century (1136e), whereas Polymnestus seems to belong to the early sixth. The issue cannot be resolved with certainty.

[188] *Eklysis* is described by Arist. Quint. as an incomposite downwards interval of three quarter-tones, *ekbolē* as an incomposite upwards interval of five quarter-tones. The descriptions are associated with that of *spondeiasmos* (on which see 1135a–b and Appendix B), which he says is an upwards interval of three quarter-tones (28.4–6). See also Bacch. 300.17–20, 301.20–302.6: he adds the information that *eklysis* and *ekbolē* occur only in the enharmonic genus. All three are melodic movements, identified in part by their upwards or downwards direction, and are not therefore simply scalar intervals such as appear in Aristoxenus' analyses of genera and 'shades'. More probably they are conceived as 'stretchings' of normal intervals (the semitone and the tone) used for special melodic effect. Thus Aristides calls them not 'intervals' but 'qualifications' or 'modifications' of intervals (*pathē tōn diastēmatōn*, 28.6–7).

[189] See 1134f ff. and Appendix B.

[190] On the *nomos* of Ares cf. 1137a and Appendix A: on the *Mētrōa* see 1137d. For the prosodiac see n. 184 above: its anapaestic character makes it suited to martial music (cf. e.g. Xen. *Anab.* VI.1.11, schol. to Aristoph. *Clouds* 651). The choreus ('dancing' rhythm) may be the trochee - ˇ or the tribrach ˇ ˇ ˇ.

[191] 'Baccheius', from another dance rhythm, as its 'Bacchic' name implies (cf. 147 Xen. *Symp.* 9.3), is the name given to a wide variety of feet, e.g. - - ˇ or ˇ - - or ˇ - - ˇ or ˇ - - ˇ. Another possibility is - ˇ ˇ -, usually called the choriamb: this interpretation is preferred by W. and R.

[192] On Lasus, a most notable composer of the late sixth century, and the first important writer on musical theory, see Ch. 4. As a composer and practitioner he was especially famous for his introduction of the dithyramb on a regular basis to the festivals of Athens. 'Movement', *agōgē*, normally 'tempo'. Precisely what the innovation was is

30. 'In the same way the later composer Melanippides did not remain within the kind of music that had preceded him, and neither did Philoxenus or Timotheus.[193] Thus the notes of the *lyra*, of which there had been seven as far back as Terpander of Antissa, were scattered about and increased in number by Timotheus. There was also a change from simplicity to greater complexity in the music of the *aulos*. In the old days, up to the time of Melanippides, the composer of dithyrambs, the auletes were generally [d] paid by the poets, which shows that poetry took pride of place, and the auletes were subordinate to their instructors:[194] but later this custom too was abandoned, which led the comic poet Pherecrates[195] to put Music on the stage in the guise of a woman, her whole body displaying signs of ill-treatment. He then makes Justice ask what caused this outrage, and Poetry[196] answers: "I'll tell you willingly: the story will be a pleasure for me to tell and for you to hear. Melanippides[197] started my troubles. [e] He was the first of them: he grabbed me and pulled me down, and loosened me up with his twelve strings.[198] For all that, he was a good enough man to me compared with the troubles I have now.[199] That damned Cinesias of Attica has done me so much damage with the 'exharmonic' twists he makes inside the strophes,

    unclear: almost certainly not the abandonment of strophic form, which occurred later (see on Melanippides, Ch. 7). For changes in the character of the dithyramb at this period see **29** Pindar, fr. 61 and notes ad loc.
    'Multiplicity of notes' was notoriously a feature of the *aulos* (e.g. **149** Plato, *Rep.* 399d, cf. e.g. Pindar, *Ol.* 7.11–12, **27** *Pyth.* 12.19–21): Plato and others relate it to the instrument's capacity to modulate easily from one *harmonia* to another (whether by having many finger-holes, or through control by lips and breath). Something of the kind is probably intended here, though it is primarily a feature of fifth-century music: the verb translated 'scattered about' is used in the next paragraph of Timotheus' treatment of notes. It might mean either 'disconnected', referring to 'unrelated' notes belonging to different *harmoniai*, or simply 'widely spread', indicating an increased range.

[193] On these composers' innovations see Ch. 7 and notes on the quotation from Pherecrates below.

[194] Cf. **189** Ath. 617b–c, with the passage of Pratinas quoted there. The same section of Athenaeus contains Melanippides' well-known treatment of the story of Athena and the *aulos*, together with Telestes' supposed 'reply' (616e–617b).

[195] Approximately contemporary with Aristophanes, and a celebrated practitioner of the genre. The passage quoted is from his *Cheiron* (see *Exc. ex Nicom.* 274).

[196] So the MSS, but we should probably read 'Music'.

[197] If there really were two composers of this name (*Suda*), this no doubt refers to the second, active from about the middle of the fifth century.

[198] 'Pulled me down' (*anēke*): the verb is often used to indicate reducing the tension of strings in order to lower the pitch. 'Loosened me up' (*chalarōteran epoiēse*), lit. 'made me more *chalaros*': the adjective is the same as that used in such coinages as Plato's *chalara Lydisti* (**149** *Rep.* 398e). It carries the suggestion of luxuriousness, lack of discipline. We know nothing of a *kithara* with twelve strings: authors who attribute the addition of extra strings to this or that composer generally stop at eleven (attributed to Timotheus at *Exc. ex Nicom.* 274 and the *Suda*): but twelve are mentioned again below in connection with Timotheus. It seems clear that the scholars had a generalised tradition to the effect that the number of strings was varied and increased during the fifth century, but the details of their accounts are hopelessly inconsistent.

[199] There is a gap in the metre here: a few words of the Pherecrates passage have been lost.

that in the composition [t]   of his dithyrambs you'd mistake the right-hand side for the left, like a reflection in a shield.[200] But still, I could put up with him. Then Phrynis shoved in his own peculiar 'pine cone', bending and twisting me into a total wreck – twelve ways of tuning he had in his penta-chords.[201] All the same, even he was bearable: he went wrong, but he made up for it later.[202] But Timotheus is another matter. My dear, he's buried me in a hole and scraped me all away – it's awful!" [*Justice asks*] "Who is this Timotheus?" [*Poetry replies*] "He's a red-head from Miletus. [1142a]   The things he did to me were worse than all the others put together, with those perverted ant-crawlings he went in for. And when he found me out for a walk by myself, he untied me and undid me with his twelve strings."[203]

'(The comic poet Aristophanes also mentions Philoxenus, and says that he introduced melodies of these kinds into cyclic choruses.)[204] Music speaks the

200   On Cinesias see Ch. 7 and 136 Aristoph. *Birds* 1373 ff: other references are given in the introduction to that passage. 'Exharmonic twists': we are told that 'twists' (*kampai*) were instrumental turns introducing modulations (schol. to Aristoph. *Clouds* 332), hence 'exharmonic', 'outside the *harmonia*'. *Kampai* are ascribed to many composers of the period. The sense of *strophai* here is uncertain. Its literal sense is 'turns', but it commonly has the sense of its English transliteration 'strophes'. If the latter is meant here (but see next note) Cinesias may be being accused of using *kampai* even within his strophes, not just between them (cf. schol. to Aristoph. loc. cit.). But *en tais strophais* might mean 'between the strophes', rather than 'in' them. The sense in which one would mistake right for left in the 'composition' (*poiēsis*) of his dithy-rambs may relate to their pretentious and nonsensical words: but the sentence seems to derive the phenomenon from the purely musical *kampai* of the preceding clause. In that case Pherecrates is perhaps suggesting that the frequent modulations make his music structurally unintelligible – you might as well play it backwards.
201   On Phrynis see Ch. 7. The 'pine-cone' (*strobilos*) has been thought to be a device for retuning strings in the course of a performance. This is possible; but there is some authority for supposing it to be a chaotically structured form of composition (Plato Comicus, fr. 254 Kock). Plutarch (*Prof. Virt.* 13, *Agid.* 10) attributes to Phrynis an instrument with nine strings. If this is right, Lasserre is probably correct in treating 'pentachords' as analogous to the common use of 'tetrachords': the *kithara* was tuned to a sequence of two conjunct pentachords. (Cf. Ion of Chios ap. Cleonides 202.14–17.) For a conjecture about the 'twelve ways of tuning' see Lasserre ad loc. 'Bending and twisting', *kamptōn* and *strephōn*. The former is from the verb related to *kampē*, the latter from that related to *strophē*, which strengthens the case for under-standing *strophai* in the lines about Cinesias as (melodic) twists, rather than strophes in the English sense.
202   Suggesting a change of heart later in life. Nothing is known of this.
203   On Timotheus see Ch. 7. 'Perverted ant-crawlings' (*ektrapelous myrmēkias*): cf. *myrmēkos atrapous* (of Agathon's music) at 138 Aristoph. *Thesm.* 100, Aelian, *N.A.* VI.43. The reference seems to be to crooked or tortuous melodic pathways, rather than to very small intervals. 'By myself': this presumably refers to music for instru-ments without the voice. 'Untied' (*apelyse*) and 'undid' (*anelyse*): both words indicate undressing, in conformity with the comic innuendoes of the passage as a whole. It is a plausible guess that the first refers principally to the breakdown of rhythmic structure (cf. the use of *apolelymena* at Hephaestion, *Poem.* 3.3, Arist. Quint. 52.12–14), the second to the disruption of melodic forms by frequent modulation. On the 'twelve strings' see n. 198 above.
204   Perhaps this sentence, which I have treated as a parenthesis, should come after the next lines attributed to Music: those latter lines are probably a continuation (after a gap) of Pherecrates' description of Timotheus' compositions. The words translated 'of these kinds' are conjectural. Without them the sense might be that Philoxenus

following words: "... exharmonic high-pitched blasphemous warbles – he filled me up with wrigglings like a cabbage."[205]

'Other comic poets have also put on display the absurdity of [b]   later music-mincers.[206]

31. 'It is made clear by Aristoxenus that correct or distorted practice has its source in training and teaching. Thus it happened in his own time, he says, that when Telesias of Thebes[207] was young he was brought up on the best sort of music: among the highly reputable composers whose music he learned were Pindar, Dionysius of Thebes, Lamprus[208] and Pratinas, and the other lyric composers who produced good instrumental pieces. He also performed [c]   excellently on the *aulos*, and made a thorough study of all the other elements of a complete education. But when he had passed the prime of his life he was so completely seduced by the complicated sort of theatrical music that he came to despise the fine compositions on which he had been brought up, and learned very carefully those of Philoxenus and Timotheus, particularly the most complicated of their pieces, and the ones with the maximum amount of innovation. When he then set out to compose melodies, and tried his hand at both styles – that of Pindar and that of Philoxenus – he could achieve no success at all in Philoxenus' manner.[209] And the reason lay in the excellent training he had from his childhood.

32. 'Thus anyone who aims at beauty and discrimination in his treatment of music [d]   should model himself on the ancient style: in addition he should round it off with the other branches of learning, and take philosophy as his principal teacher,[210] since philosophy is able to assess the correct amounts in which things are appropriate and useful to music.

introduced solo songs into the 'cyclic chorus', i.e. the dithyramb, but such a remark would hardly fit the context. W. and R., assuming that the reference is to Aristoph. *Plutus* 293–4, insert the words 'of sheep and goats' to characterise 'melodies': an intriguing suggestion (cf. **149** Plato, *Rep.* 397a–b), but again hardly apposite in the context. On Philoxenus see Ch. 7.

205   It seems most likely that the subject is still Timotheus (see previous note). 'High-pitched', *hyperbolaious*: technically, 'belonging to the tetrachord *hyperbolaiōn*', the highest tetrachord of the system, rising to the note an octave above *mesē*. 'Warblings' (*niglarous*): the sense is uncertain. Both the schol. to Aristoph. *Acharn.* 554 and Photius s.v. *niglareuōn* treat it as a style of instrumental accompaniment. 'Wrigglings', a pun: in the genitive plural both the spelling and the accentuation of the word meaning 'twist' or 'modulation' and of the word meaning 'caterpillar' are the same (*kampōn*).

206   The word suggests chopping something up into small pieces: possibly small melodic intervals, but more probably a general reference to the disorganised 'hash' that modern composers have made of music.

207   Nothing further is known of him.

208   Dionysius gets a brief mention at Corn. Nep. *Vit. Epam.* 2. Lamprus is described by Plato (*Menex.* 236a) as a distinguished teacher of music: the same name, but not certainly the same person, appears at Ath. 20f, 44d, Phryn. Com. fr. 69 (Kock). Some scholars identify him with Lamprocles (see 1136d, Ath. 491c).

209   For the contrast between the dithyrambs of Pindar and Philoxenus cf. Philodemus Bk I, fr. 18.6, discussed on p. 95 above.

210   From here to 1144e the source (Aristoxenus) has modelled his discussion on Plato's

'Music as a whole has three divisions at the most general level. These are he diatonic, chromatic and enharmonic genera; and anyone who is setting ut on the study of music must understand the form of composition which nakes use of each of them, and he must be familiar with the kinds of erformance through which the resulting compositions are expressed.[211]

'It should first be understood that all learning in the field of music [e] is imply habituation, so long as there is not added to it a grasp of the reasons vhy each of the items that are taught is an essential part of what the student nust learn.[212] Secondly, we must realise that up to the present this sort of raining and learning has never been supplemented with a thorough enumeration of the *tropoi*:[213] on the contrary, most people learn whatever the eacher or the pupil happens to enjoy, while people who understand the natter criticise this unsystematic approach, as the Spartans did in the old lays, and so did the Mantineans and Pellenians. They used to pick out just ne *tropos*, or a very small number, which they believed [f] to be suited to the roper formation of character, and practised that sort of music alone.

33. 'This will become clear[214] if we enquire concerning each of the sciences n question what its field of study is. Thus Harmonics, for instance, is the cience of the genera of melodic order, of intervals, *systēmata*, notes, *tonoi* nd modulations between *systēmata*, and it is unable to advance beyond this oint.[215] Hence we cannot seek to discover through Harmonics whether the omposer – in the *Mysians*, for example – has made an appropriate choice in

211   proposals concerning rhetoric in *Phaedrus* 268a–274b. For detailed references see notes to the Loeb edition ad loc.

211   The central importance assigned here to the divisions of the tetrachord that mark the three genera may seem exaggerated, but the emphasis is to some degree reflected in Aristoxenus' *El. Harm.*, where the analyses of the genera and their variants occupy a considerable fraction of the work. Their differences of character are treated in ways suggesting that it is on them, rather than on the old *harmoniai* (which he abandons) or the *tonoi* (which represent only differences of pitch, 'keys'), that any theory of moral ethos in music must be built. Cf. also the apparent references to generic (rather than 'harmonic') ethos in the Hibeh Papyrus.

212   Cf. the contrasts made by Aristox. at e.g. *El. Harm.* 5.9–29, and e.g. **154** Plato, *Laws* 670b–e.

213   *Tropos* can hardly be a vague term, 'style', here, in view of the recommendation that the *tropoi* be thoroughly enumerated. But equally, it cannot mean simply *harmonia*, in the old sense: these had been enumerated in a systematic though 'unargued' way before Aristoxenus (*El. Harm.* 6.19 ff), and in any case they play no part in Aristoxenian theory. To interpret it as meaning *tonos*, with references only to pitch, 'key', gives an Aristoxenian sense (*El. Harm.* 37.8 ff), but Aristoxenus' concern in the present passage is evidently wider than that. Perhaps it means 'technically specifiable melodic genre', without prejudice as to the proper terms of the analysis of any such genre, and without presupposing that all will be analysed within a single framework.

214   Unless this passage is misplaced (as Westphal supposed), 'this' must be the need for grasping 'reasons', in addition to simple enumeration of elements (1142e), or, more generally, the need for musical learning to be guided and supplemented by philosophy (1142d).

215   For the general sentiment see Aristox. *El. Harm.* 1.23–2.7, 31.17–32.9. The list of the parts of Harmonics corresponds to that given at *El. Harm.* 35.1–38.27, except that the latter includes *melopoiia*, 'melodic composition' as its final element.

using the Hypodorian *tonos* at the beginning, Dorian at the end, and Hypo phrygian and Phrygian in the middle.[216] The science of Harmonics does not extend to such matters, and requires supplementation from many sources [1143a] since it has no understanding of the nature of appropriateness. Thus neither the chromatic nor the enharmonic genus carries with it the whole nature of what it is to be appropriate, through which the moral character of a musical composition is revealed: this is the task of the practitioner of the art.[217] It is clear that the sound of a *systēma* is different from that of a composition constructed within that *systēma*, and the study of the latter is not within the scope of the science of Harmonics.[218]

'The same may be said of rhythms, since no rhythm carries in itself the nature of what constitutes the appropriate in all its aspects: [b] for we invariably speak of "the appropriate" with an eye to moral character.

'Our view is that the cause of moral character is a particular kind of combination or mixture or both.[219] In the work of Olympus, for instance, the enharmonic genus was set in the Phrygian *tonos* and mixed with the *paiōn epibatos*, and it was this that generated the character of the beginning of the *nomos* of Athena:[220] for the enharmonic genus of Olympus[221] is

Melopoiia seems, however, to be excluded from harmonics at 2.1 ff. The apparent inconsistency probably reflects the fact that while the imaginatively constructive aspect of composing is no part of the subject matter of Harmonics (see 1143a), there are nevertheless features of compositions that extend beyond the scope of the present list, and which are capable of being theoretically described and classified. Thus one may analyse types of melodic phrase according to their shape and direction, one may distinguish continuous sequences from gapped sequences and repetitions of the same pitch, and so on. See especially Arist. Quint. 28.8 ff: the issue is briefly reopened at 1142f–1143a below. The list reappears, with minor variations, in many later theorists. *Systēmata*, lit. 'puttings together' (of intervals), means roughly 'scales.' 'Modulations between *systēmata*' must refer to modulations of *harmonia*, and *tono* are 'keys' distinguished only by pitch, as usually in Aristoxenus and his school.

216   *Mysians* (*Mysois, Musois*) is Bergk's conjecture for the *mousois, mousikois, mousais* of various MSS. If it is correct, it will refer to the same piece as is ascribed to Philoxenus at 161 Ar. *Pol.* 1342b, though there again the text is in doubt, and *Mysous* is an emendation for the MSS *mythous*. Aristotle seems to imply that the beginning of the composition (a dithyramb) was in the Dorian *harmonia*, the remainder, or at least the next section, in the Phrygian.

217   Contrast 154 Plato, *Laws* 670e.

218   See n. 215 above.

219   'Combination' (*synthesis*) and 'mixture' (*mixis*) are evidently not intended as synonyms, but they have no clear technical senses. In the next sentence a rhythm is 'mixed' with a melodic structure, which suggests a blending of two simultaneous but theoretically distinct elements. *Synthesis* might therefore indicate the putting together of a temporal sequence of elements, to form a larger structure. Alternatively, following the clue in the word *tethen*, 'set', in the next sentence (from the verb cognate with the '*thesis*' element in *synthesis*), *synthesis* might be the blending of two abstractly different aspects of the same element. Pitch and scale structure are in this sense 'aspects' of an actual melody; rhythmical structure and tempo (*agōgē*) are 'aspects' of a rhythm as actually performed.

220   On Olympus and the enharmonic genus see 1134 ff. *Tonos* here means 'key' and refers to pitch; but cf. 1137d. On the *paiōn epibatos* see n. 184 above. The *nomos* of Athena is probably identical with the *Polykephalos* ('many-headed') *nomos*: see 1133d and Appendix A, with 27 Pindar, *Pyth.* 12.

221   These words may well be an interpolation. Elsewhere the expression refers to melodic

constructed from these elements with the addition of the actual composition of the melody and the rhythm, and subtle modulations of the rhythm, but of nothing else, so that it becomes trochaic rather than paeonic.[222] But if the enharmonic genus and the Phrygian *tonos* are preserved, and with them the whole of the *systēma*, it is possible nevertheless for there to occur a considerable alteration [c] in moral character: for instance, the so-called *harmonia*[223] in the *nomos* of Athena is very different in character from the opening section. Thus it is evidently when judgement is allied to experience of music that a man will be a discriminating musical expert. A man who knows the Dorian, but without understanding how to judge where its use is appropriate, will not know what it is that he is producing: he will not even maintain its moral character. It is in fact an open question about Dorian compositions themselves whether the science of Harmonics is capable of distinguishing between them as some people think, or not.[224]

'The same is true of the whole science of rhythm. [d] The man who knows the *paeōn* will not understand where it is appropriate to use it just through his grasp of the *paeōn*'s structure. And it is an open question about paeonic compositions whether the science of Rhythmics can distinguish between them, as some people say, or whether its scope does not extend as far as that.[225]

'Two kinds of knowledge at least are thus necessary for anyone who is to distinguish the appropriate and the inappropriate. First, he must know the moral character which the construction seeks to produce, and secondly he must know the elements from which the construction is put together.[226] Our

       structure only. The sentence that follows is probably to be construed as a further description of the *nomos* of Athena.

[222] The main structural feature of paeonic rhythms in general is the divisibility of their feet into parts related in the ratio 3:2. Trochaic rhythms are in the ratio 2:1. Whatever the precise nature of the metrical forms intended here, the character of the 'modulation' must have been determined by the shift from 3:2 to 2:1. 'But of nothing else': i.e., no melodic modulations were involved.

[223] Probably the main section of the piece, but nothing is known of the word's significance here.

[224] One may 'know the Dorian', i.e., be able to grasp and identify its formal structure, without knowing when or how to use it (cf. 154 Plato, *Laws* 670e, Aristox. *El. Harm.* 31.17 ff). In the last sentence 'Dorian' is simply an example: the 'question' seems to relate to the issue whether composition (*melopoiia*) is or is not part of Harmonics. See n. 215 above. It seems not to be an 'open question' for Aristoxenus whether the proper usage of a given structure is a matter for harmonic theory: it is not. (On this point see 1144c ff.) What is doubtful is whether the (apparently quite undeveloped) study of compositional forms suggested at e.g. Arist. Quint. 28.8 ff is capable of producing an adequate classification of the melodic types that fall under a given structure. The unstated alternative is that moral and aesthetic judgements, or others not derivable from such an analysis, might be indispensable in any worthwhile classification. A good classification will perhaps begin from, and give analyses of, standardly recognised genres such as e.g. the paean, the dithyramb, the lament, the libation-song. The question is whether the salient differences between them can be captured by technical and formal distinctions of a kind proper to Harmonics.

[225] Arist. Quint. (32.10) makes *rhythmopoiia*, rhythmic composition, the final part of the science of rhythmics. The issue is exactly the same as that concerning harmonics.

[226] Cf. 154 Plato, *Laws* 670a ff.

remarks have thus been sufficient to show that neither Harmonics nor Rhythmics nor [e] any of the other sciences which are treated as dealing with a single element of the subject is capable on its own both of understanding moral character and of judging the other elements.

34. 'While these are the three genera into which melodic order is divided, and these are equal in the range of their *systēmata*, in the functions of their notes, and in those of their tetrachords, people in ancient times only studied one: for our predecessors gave theoretical consideration to neither the chromatic nor the diatonic, but only to the enharmonic, and even in this only to a *systēma* of one magnitude, the one called the "octave".[227] They disagreed about its shading, but were virtually [f] unanimous about there being only one "*harmonia*".[228] Thus a person whose knowledge had only reached this point could not have an overall grasp of matters related to the science of Harmonics: such a grasp belongs rather to the man who pursues both the sciences dealing with particular elements and the whole, unified body of music, together with the mixtures and combinations of the elements.[229] Anyone who is only a "harmonicist"[230] is in a way circumscribed.

'Speaking generally, then, perception and reason must run along together in their judgement of the elements of music. There must be no rushing ahead, [1144a] as there is when perceptions are precipitate and impetuous, and no lagging behind, as there is when perceptions are slow and hard to arouse. In some cases of perception there is even a combination of both, where the same perceptions both lag behind and rush ahead, because of some unevenness in their natural composition. These things must be got rid of if perception is to run along together with the intelligence.[231]

---

[227] The three genera, according to Aristoxenus, differed only in the intervals internal to their tetrachords. The names of the notes, including the 'movable' inner notes of the tetrachord, remained the same (though generic adjectives were sometimes added). The matter is well discussed at Aristox. *El. Harm.* 47.8 ff. On his predecessors' restriction to the analysis of enharmonic octave scales see *El. Harm.* 2.8–25.

[228] 'Shading', *chroa*, the exact nuance of interval that it incorporated. For disputes or doubts about the precise size of the intervals of the enharmonic, and Aristoxenus' own method of resolving the difficulty, see *El. Harm.* 22.26–23.23, 26.10–28, and cf. 49.10–15 with its context. 'Only one *harmonia*': this reflects Aristoxenus' pun at *El. Harm.* 2.8 ff, where he says that his precursors were well and truly *harmonikoi* because they studied only 'the *harmonia*'. There *harmonia* has its quite common sense 'enharmonic scale', and in particular 'enharmonic octave scale': the usage here is the same. (For the Pythagorean use of *harmonia* to refer to the octave see e.g. Nicom. 252.5–6.)

[229] See 1143b and n. 219 above.

[230] Another punning usage. A man who is only a student of harmonics is cut off from an understanding of the aspects of music mentioned at 1143b–e: one who has a grasp only of the enharmonic octave structure is ignorant of the other genera.

[231] On the roles of reason and perception in harmonics see *El. Harm.* 32.10–34.34, 38.27–39.3: cf. n. 239 below. I take it that perception may 'simultaneously lag behind and rush ahead' in the sense that it may have an uneven grasp of the various objects simultaneously presented to it, which are listed in the next paragraph.

35. 'Three minimal items must always fall on the hearing simultaneously, the note, the duration, and the syllable or letter.[232] From the progression of the notes we come to grasp the melodic structure, from that of the durations we grasp the rhythm, [b] and from that of the letters or syllables we grasp the words. Since all these progressions go on together we have to direct the attention of our perceptions to all of them at once. Yet it is also clear that if perception were not able to separate out each of the things we have mentioned, it would be impossible to follow them individually and to attend to the defects and the virtues of each. The first task is to gain an understanding of continuity, since the presence of continuity is necessary for the exercise of our critical faculty.[233] Good and bad do not lie in specific isolated notes or durations or letters, but in continuous sequences of them, since good and bad are varieties of mixture created by [c] practical composition out of incomposite elements. So much for the question of how we follow music.

36. 'The next thing to notice is that being a musical expert is not enough to equip one for the activity of critical assessment.[234] One cannot become a complete musician and critic just on the basis of what we treat as the departments of music as a whole – from familiarity with instruments, for example, and with singing, and from training in the exercise of perception (by which I mean the training directed towards a grasp of melodic structure and of rhythm), from the sciences of Rhythmics and Harmonics, [d] from the theory of instrumental accompaniment and the theory of diction, and from whatever other disciplines there may be.[235]

'We must try to gain a thorough understanding of the reasons why one cannot become a good critic on the basis of these alone. The first point is that some of the things which are objects of our judgement are ends in themselves, while others are not. An individual composition is such an end – a piece which is sung, for instance, or one played on the *aulos* or one played on the *kithara* – and so is the performance of any of these – the playing on the *aulos*, the singing, and all other such things. What are not such ends are the things that conduce to those we have mentioned, and the things that occur for their sake. The elements which go to make up a performance are of this kind. [e] A second point arises from composition, of which just the same things are true.

'When we hear an aulete playing we can judge whether the *auloi* are concordant or not, and whether their interplay is clear or unclear.[236] Each of these factors is an element in auletic performance, but neither is an end:

---

232   The 'letter' here is of course the elementary unit of speech as heard, not as written.
233   On musical 'continuity' (here *synecheia*, elsewhere sometimes *to hexēs*) see Aristox. *El. Harm.* 27.15–28.31, 52.35–53.32.
234   On the whole issue discussed here cf. 1143b ff.
235   This list of musical disciplines is obviously informal. Cf. the systematic classification at Arist. Quint. 6.8 ff.
236   The *auloi* are presumably the two members of a pair played together. 'Interplay', *dialektos*: see 1138b with n. 140.

rather, each is something done for the sake of the end. Over and above these matters and all others like them, judgement will be passed on the moral character of the performance, to decide whether the performer's interpretation is appropriate to the composition that was entrusted to him, and which he was seeking to execute and interpret. The same applies to the emotions expressed in compositions through the art which is proper to composers.[237]

37. [f] 'In ancient times, then, since their prime concern was with character, people valued above all the dignity and simplicity which was a feature of ancient music. Thus the Argives are said to have once laid down a penalty for breaches in the rules of music, and to have imposed a fine on the first man who tried to use more than the seven strings normally current among them, and who attempted to modulate into Mixolydian.[238]

'The worthy Pythagoras rejected the practice of judging music by means of perception, saying that its excellence was to be grasped by the mind.[239] Hence he used not to judge it on the basis of hearing, but on that of the *harmonia*[240] of proportions. [1145a] He also thought that it was enough to let the study of music come to an end with the octave.[241]

38. 'Nowadays, however, people have completely rejected the finest of the genera, the one most appreciated in ancient times because of its noble dignity, so that most people do not have even a casual understanding of enhar-

---

237   That is, composition is to be judged for its faithfulness, 'appropriateness', to the characters and emotions it is seeking to express. On the peculiar difficulty of this judgement in certain special cases see 154 Plato, *Laws* 669d–e.

238   Comparable stories are often told elsewhere about the magistrates at Sparta, e.g. Plut. *Inst. Lac.* 17, *Agid.* 10, Paus. III.12.10, 196 Ath. 636e–f. The verb *paramixolydiazein* occurs nowhere else. On the assumption that the preferred *harmonia* was the Dorian, the sense given in the translation must be approximately right (rather than 'modulate out of Mixolydian', or perhaps 'alter the form of the Mixolydian'). If the seven strings were tuned to two conjunct tetrachords of Dorian form – each q,q,d (enharmonic) or s,t,t (diatonic) – the Mixolydian octave structure could be formed simply by the addition of an eighth string at the top, a tone above the seventh (see 1136d with n. 113).

239   On this basic methodological division between 'Pythagorean' and 'Aristoxenian' theorists see e.g. Aristox. *El. Harm.* 32.18 ff, and most fully Ptol. *Harm.* 11.1 ff, 19.16 ff, Ptolemais and Didymus ap. Porph. *Comm.* 25.1 ff, cf. Theophrastus ap. Porph. *Comm.* 62.22–63.3. An outline of the theoretical stances taken by pre-Aristoxenian researchers is at Plato, *Rep.* 530e–531d. As these passages show, the issue was in fact much more complex than the crude opposition between perception and reason would suggest.

240   I.e., the 'fitting together' of notes according to their mathematically proper ratios. For the principles on which this 'fitting together' was based see Ptol. *Harm.* 11.1 ff, and cf. the procedures exemplified in the Euclidean *Sect. Can.*

241   Cf. the Pythagorean usage of *harmonia* = 'octave' (e.g. Nicom. 252.5–6). All the essential mathematical relations in a scale could be represented within the range of an octave of abstract pitch. What could not be so represented was the setting of such octave-scales in different keys, *tonoi*, to explicate the process of modulation between them; but this Aristoxenian procedure, involving a two-octave system, was relevant only for theorists with an interest in practical music, and not for the mathematical and cosmological 'Pythagorean' school.

1onic intervals. They are so idle and so mentally easy-going as to believe
hat the enharmonic diesis generates no impression at all that can be detected
y the senses, and they therefore eliminate it from singing and say that
•eople who have any views about it, or who have made use of this genus, are
•ehaving nonsensically.[242] [b] They think that the strongest proof of the
ruth of what they say lies first of all in the feebleness of their own percep-
ion, as though everything that escaped them must therefore be utterly non-
xistent and useless, and secondly in the fact that this magnitude cannot be
letermined by means of concords, as can the semitone and the tone and the
•ther intervals of that kind.[243] They have not realised that on this basis the
hird, fifth, and seventh magnitudes[244] would also be rejected (the first of
vhich contains three dieses, the second five and the third seven), and in
eneral that all [c] the intervals which turn out to be odd-numbered would be
lismissed as useless, on the grounds that none of them can be determined by
neans of concords. These would be all the ones that are odd-numbered
nultiples of the smallest diesis. From this it would follow that none of the
livisions of the tetrachord can be used except ones which employ nothing
•ut even-numbered intervals, that is, the divisions of the sharp diatonic and
he tonic chromatic.[245]

39. 'Saying and thinking this sort of thing not only brings people into
onflict with the evidence of perception but also involves them in incon-

[242] On attempts to identify the smallest detectable interval see Plato, *Rep.* 531a. In
Aristotle this interval is assumed to be the (enharmonic) *diesis*, the quarter-tone (e.g.
Metaph. 1016b 20–2): in Aristoxenus the *diesis* is the smallest interval that can
actually appear in music, though not the smallest that may be referred to in theoretical analysis (e.g. *El. Harm.* 14.18–25, 25.11–25). On the corruption and near-
extinction of the enharmonic genus in Aristoxenus' day see *El. Harm.* 23.4–22: but
note that there, and usually in that work, he treats as its central (and disputed)
feature not its use of quarter-tones, but its use of the ditone as an incomposite scalar
interval. For its abandonment in later antiquity see Dion. Hal. *De Comp. Verb.* 11,
Theon Smyrn. 55–6 (Hiller). Arist. Quint. says that it is the province of experts
alone: other people find it 'impossible' (16.13–18). His remarks are clearly based on
the same passage of Aristoxenus as is the present text.

[243] The process of finding an interval by means of concords is exemplified at *El. Harm.*
55.3 ff: cf. *Sect. Can.* Prop. 17. Though used by these authors as a tool of theory, it
probably reflects the practice of performers in tuning an instrument. Thus to tune
strings to a diatonic Dorian scale E–E', the performer, beginning from A (*mesē*), can
generate the entire series by steps of a fourth or a fifth, for instance: A to E, A to E'; E
(or E') to B; A to D to G to C to F. Intervals such as the tone A–B or the ditone F–A are
then said to have been found by means of concords. But no intervals smaller than the
semitone can be constructed in this way, any more than can the others mentioned in
the next sentence. This fact, despite what Aristoxenus says here, is a genuine difficulty
for his method: it is quite unclear how the performer is to construct or the theorist to
identify intervals of these sorts.

[244] Counting the enharmonic *diesis* as the first magnitude, the semitone (containing two
dieses) as the second, and so on. The intervals mentioned were all in practical use,
according to Aristoxenus: see next note.

[245] I.e., s,t,t and s,s,$\frac{1}{2}$. The other 'divisions' that Aristoxenus recognises are q,q,d (enhar-
monic), $\frac{1}{3},\frac{1}{3},\frac{11}{6}$ (soft chromatic), $\frac{3}{8},\frac{3}{8},\frac{7}{4}$ (hemiolic chromatic), s,$\frac{3}{4},\frac{5}{4}$ (soft diatonic): see *El.
Harm.* 50.19 ff. Here there are plainly various other intervals, as well as the odd-
numbered multiples of the *diesis*, which cannot be found by means of concords.

sistency, since it turns out that these very people are especially given to th
use of divisions of tetrachords [d] in which most of the intervals are eithe
odd-numbered or irrational.[246] They are always slackening the *lichanoi* an
paranētai,[247] and have even flattened some of the fixed notes,[248] flattenin
along with them, by an irrational interval, the *tritai* and *paranētai*;[249] an
what they imagine to be somehow the most meritorious treatment o
systēmata is the one in which most of the intervals are irrational, where no
only the notes that are naturally movable, but even some of the fixed note
are flattened, as anyone capable of perceiving such things can clearl
detect.[250]

40. 'Homer, that splendid poet, taught us the uses of music that ar
appropriate for a man. [e] Thus to show that music is of value in man
situations, his poem describes Achilles digesting his anger with the help o
music which he had learned from the wise Cheiron: "They found hin
beguiling his heart with the clear-sounding *phorminx*. It was beautiful an(
skilfully decorated, and the crossbar on it was silver: he had chosen it fron
the spoils when he sacked the city of Eëtion. With it he was giving delight t(
his heart, and singing the famous deeds of men."[251]

'"Notice," Homer is saying, "how music should be used, since it wa
suitable for Achilles, son of the most upright Peleus, to sing of the glories o
men and the deeds of demigods." [f] Homer has also shown us the occasio
which accords with its use, revealing it as a valuable and pleasant exercis(
for a man not actively occupied. Achilles was a man of war and action, but h
was taking no part in the perils of war because of his anger with Agamem

---

[246] 'Rational' and 'irrational' in Aristoxenus do not have their usual mathematical sense
An interval is 'rational' only if two conditions are both fulfilled. (i) It must be a
interval capable of being sung as part of a melody; and (ii) it must be recognisabl(
either directly by educated sense-perception, as a concord is recognised, *or* as th(
difference between two concords (the tone), *or*, thirdly, as commensurable with on(
of these, so long as the common measure is an actual melodic interval. Thus e.g. $\frac{1}{7}$ of a
tone is not rational, because its 'common measure' with the tone is $\frac{1}{7}$ of a tone, whic
is not a melodic interval. (This explanation is paraphrased from Macran pp. 237–40
q.v. for further details and the ancient evidence.)

[247] The upper of the movable notes inside the tetrachords below and above *mese* respec
tively. Such 'slackening' could generate e.g. the soft diatonic from the sharp, bu
Aristoxenus may have no particular alterations in mind. The movable notes hav(
definite ranges of movement, but are not determined to any fixed selection of pitche
within their range (*El. Harm.* 26.9–27).

[248] If this involves altering the interval between the bounding notes of a give
tetrachord, as it apparently must, no known Greek theory would treat it a
legitimate.

[249] The movable notes in the tetrachord above *mese*: but very probably we should rea(
'*tritai* and *parhypatai*', these being the lower movable notes in the tetrachords abov(
and below *mese* respectively.

[250] No very precise sense can be extracted from the remarks that begin with the allusio
to the flattening of fixed notes. Aristoxenus is attacking what he believed to be a
improper distortion of basic intervals. His target may be a fashionable flexibility i
that regard, rather than any specific system of tuning.

[251] *Il.* IX.186–9.

non: hence Homer thought it suitable for the hero to sharpen his spirit with the noblest songs, so that he should be prepared to go out into battle, as he was soon to do; and this is plainly what he was doing as he recounted deeds of long ago.

'That is what the ancient music was like, [1146a] and what it was useful for. Thus we hear of Heracles, Achilles, and many others making use of music, and their teacher, according to tradition, was the wise Cheiron, who gave instruction not only in music but in justice and in medicine as well.

41. 'Speaking quite generally, no person of intelligence would put the blame on the sciences if someone misused them through his own behaviour: the responsibility would be laid on the defects of the agent.[252] If someone has worked hard at the educational aspect of music, and receives suitable training in childhood, [b] he will applaud and accept what is fine and criticise its opposite in music and in everything else as well: he will not contaminate himself with any ignoble action, and through the great advantages he has reaped by means of music, he will become a substantial benefit to himself and to his city: he will have no truck with discordant deeds or words, and will maintain always and in all circumstances what is suitable, moderate and orderly.[253]

42. 'We could find many pieces of evidence to show that the cities with the best laws and customs have been careful to cultivate music of the noble kind. One might cite Terpander, who resolved the civil war that broke out at one time in Sparta,[254] [c] and Thaletas the Cretan, of whom it is said that he went to Sparta as the result of a pronouncement by the Delphic oracle, and cured the people there by means of music, releasing Sparta, as Pratinas says, from the grip of the plague.[255] Homer also says that the plague which beset the Greeks was brought to an end through music: he says "And all day long the young Achaeans sought to please the god with song and dance, singing a beautiful paean, celebrating far-working Apollo in song; and he heard it and was delighted in his heart."[256]

'I have used these lines to put the finishing touches on my speech about music, noble teacher, since it was through them that you expressed the power of music to us earlier.[257] For it is true that its first and [d] noblest task is to give grateful thanks to the gods, and the task that comes next, in second

---

[252]   Cf. Plato, *Euthyd.* 306d–307c, *Gorgias* 456d–e.
[253]   A thoroughly Platonic peroration: cf. especially 150 *Rep.* 401e–403a, 413e, 153 *Laws* 659c–660a.
[254]   There seem to be no early sources for this legend, but it is recorded at e.g. Philodemus 18.31–35, 85.49–86.19. Perhaps it originated in the idea that he put an end to *musical* chaos at Sparta.
[255]   Cf. Philodemus 85.33–39, 86.16–19, and e.g. Plut. *Lyc.* 4, Paus. 1.14.4. See n. 66 above.
[256]   *Il.* 1.472–4.
[257]   1131e above.

place, is to make for the soul a *systēma* that is purifying, melodious and harmonically well adjusted.'[258]

After saying that, Soterichus added: 'My noble teacher, there you have my drinking-party speech about music.'

43. Soterichus was admired for his speech: he had indeed made clear his enthusiasm for music through both his facial expressions and his voice.

'Apart from everything else,' said my teacher, 'I approve of one feature in particular of what each of you has done, the fact that each of you has kept to the role appropriate to him. Lysias has given us a banquet of the things that it is proper for a practising *kitharōdos* to know, and of nothing else: [e] whereas Soterichus has treated us lavishly with his teaching about matters related to the value of music and to its theoretical side, as well as to its power and its use. But there is one thing that they have left for me to say – deliberately, I imagine, since I shall not accuse them of cowardice by suggesting that they were ashamed to bring music down to the level of the dinner-party. If music is useful anywhere, it is so when we are drinking, as the noble Homer says in the passage [f] where he speaks of "singing and dancing, the ornaments of a feast".[259]

'No one should imagine that in saying this Homer meant that music is of value only as an aid to pleasure: there is a deeper thought hidden in his words. It was to give service and assistance of the highest importance that he brought in music on occasions like this, at banquets, I mean, and at gatherings, in those ancient times. The truth is that music was introduced because it is able to counteract and mollify the inflammatory power of wine, as your own beloved Aristoxenus says somewhere: he said that music was introduced because while it is of the nature of wine to send reeling [1147a] the bodies and minds of those who indulge in it to the full, music, through its own order and proportion, calms them and leads them into the contrary condition. It is as a guard against this contingency that Homer says that they used music in the old days.[260]

44. 'And yet, my friends, we have left out the most important point, and the one that especially displays music as something of the most serious significance: for it was said by the schools of Pythagoras, Archytas and Plato, as well as by the other philosophers of ancient times, that the motion of that which is, and the movement of the stars, come about and have their constitution through the influence of music: everything, they say, was constructed by

---

258   *Systēma*, in its musical sense (roughly 'scale'), is a metaphor for the overall 'constitution' of the soul: cf. Ptol. *Harm.* 97.34. 'Harmonically well-adjusted': for this use of *enharmonios* cf. Plut. *De Defect. Orac.* 36. It may be related to the directly musical usage of the phrase *enharmonia melē* at 169 ps.-Ar. *Probs.* XIX.15: see also 193 Ath. 628a.
259   *Od.* I.152.
260   For a comparable treatment of Homer's evidence see 193 Ath. 627e ff, cf. 180b ff.

God on the basis of *harmonia*.[261] But it would be inappropriate to undertake an elaborate discussion of this topic now. It is most important, and most characteristic of music, to give everything its proper measure.'

So saying he chanted the paean;[262] and after pouring libations to Cronos, to all the gods, his children, and to the Muses, he sent his guests on their way.

Appendix A: the *nomoi*

The sources on which ps.-Plutarch relies trace the origins of the musical genre called the '*nomos*' back to the seventh century. Outside a musical context, *nomos* means 'custom' or 'law': why certain types of musical composition were given the name is a matter of some uncertainty. (For a characteristic Greek account see 178 ps.-Ar. *Probs.* XIX.28: some other suggestions will be considered below.) There is no doubt, however, that most Greeks of the fifth century and later believed that the musical use of the word was in some way connected with a strict adherence to rules or 'laws', governing the musical forms by which, in earlier times, these pieces had been characterised, and which had divided them up into a number of carefully distinguished types (e.g. 155 and 157 Plato, *Laws* 700b–c, 799e–800a). Whatever the correct derivation of the term's musical usage, it is therefore proper to begin from the hypothesis that in the sixth century and perhaps even the seventh, something corresponding to these rules and distinctions genuinely existed. The credentials of the hypothesis will be examined shortly.

Nomoi were always solo pieces. (Lasserre, pp. 24–5, claims that the *Orthios nomos* was intoned by a chorus, but the passages he cites do nothing to confirm his assertion.) We hear of them most frequently as items performed at competitive festivals (e.g. 1132e, 27 Pindar, *Pyth.* 12.23–4, 25 Strabo IX.3.10), though this was not their only and perhaps not their original context. They were grouped into four major classes, kitharodic (songs accompanied by the singer on a *kithara*), kitharistic (instrumental solos for *kithara*), aulodic (songs accompanied by the *aulos*), and auletic (instrumental solos for *aulos*). Each class is divided up in our sources into a number of distinct types. Each of these is given a special name, and each is thought of as conforming to its own fixed pattern in respect of subject matter, the number and interrelations of its sections or 'movements', its tuning-scheme (*harmonia*), and its rhythm. (See particularly 1133b–c: cf. the *Suda*'s description of the kitharodic *nomos* as 'a style of song with a prescribed *harmonia* and a determinate rhythm'.) For each competitive or religious occasion, our authorities imply, the type of composition to be performed was laid down not only by class (kitharodic, auletic, etc.), but also by type within that class (see e.g. 1143b–c on the *nomos* of Athena, 24 Pollux IV.84 on the auletic *Pythikos nomos*, 25 Strabo IX.3.10 on a kitharistic version of the

---

[261] 'Musical fitting together', with special reference to the Pythagorean *harmonia* of the octave. The allusion is not only to the '*harmonia* of the spheres', conceived as an ordering of the heavenly bodies (e.g. Nicom. 241.1–242.18: all such accounts have as their ancestor Plato, *Rep.* 616b–617c): it suggests also the wider application of harmonic analysis to the orderings of nature in general. For two elaborate examples of this sort, entirely different in scope and approach, see Ptol. *Harm.* Bk III and Arist. Quint. Bk III, both of which find a starting-point, in effect, at Plato, *Tim.* 35b–36d. Aristides' (intellectually third-rate) version is infected with ideas from a number of other sources, including the species of mindless numerology referred to at Ar. *Metaph.* 1093a–b.

[262] For the paean in this context, roughly a 'grace after dinner', often accompanied by a libation, cf. e.g. 141 Xen. *Symp.* 2.1, Ath. 149c.

same type). The question whether or not we can reconstruct the nature of the *nomos* turns on our ability to interpret the names of the types that the (generally quite late) sources record, and to assess such explanations as they give.

Reputedly the most ancient and certainly the most respected class of *nomos* was the kitharodic (treated e.g. by 155 Plato, *Laws* 700b, as the only class worth mentioning). A number of writers name Terpander as the originator of an authorised canon of kitharodic types. However, the supposition that there existed any such canon as early as the seventh century is to be viewed with suspicion: the lists of types we are given do not inspire confidence: and the musical implications of the names listed are often obscure. It seems probable that the tradition on which our sources rely goes back to the fifth century: the historian Glaucus of Rhegium was certainly one of its originators. More or less systematic classification is characteristic of the authors of the fifth-century 'enlightenment', but not of their precursors, and we must ask what kind of material was likely to have been available for them to work on. Some poems and some melodies from the past survived, but the allegedly rule-bound practices of the earlier period did not. That some sort of norms, now obsolete, had been enforced or spontaneously adopted might have been inferred from remarks made by poets transitional between the old and the new, such as Pindar and Pratinas (e.g. 29 and 30 Pindar, frs. 61 and 125, Pratinas ap. 189 Ath. 617c–f), from the apparently systematic simplicity of surviving examples of the ancient music (e.g. 1137a–1138a, 1143b), and from the plain fact that the structurally and harmonically 'free' forms of contemporary composers, beginning with Phrynis, were still felt to be audacious novelties. The word *nomos* itself, however, does not come into common use as a musical term until the fifth century. Alcman refers once to the *nomoi* of the birds (fr. 40), but this is an isolated example, and even here *nomoi* may not mean 'songs' but 'customs', 'habits'. (The imposing structure that Lasserre, pp. 22–3, 26, builds on this tiny fragment has no foundation.) This fact is striking. It suggests that in formulating their lists of *nomoi* and explicating the sense of the term, the historians and classifiers were not reconstructing their predecessors' usage, but using a piece of modern terminology[263] as a convenient and apt label for ancient compositions supposed, on other grounds, to have been subject to strict rules. It is quite unsafe to conjecture that lists of nomic types existed before the fifth century, since there are no grounds for believing that the word *nomos* or any equivalent title was in use as a means of isolating one special category of composition. But if there were no ancient lists described by their authors as tables of *nomoi*, we must ask where the lists that the classifiers offer us could have come from.

The question cannot be answered without an inspection of the individual names that figure on the lists. But it will be helpful to begin by outlining, as a heuristic aid, the most sceptical position that could reasonably be taken. On this view, the classifiers began from a tradition that certain musical genres, to which they annexed the name *nomos*, had been determinate and rule-bound from the time of Terpander. They then proceeded to extract from the surviving poems of Terpander, and his contemporaries and successors, hints about the musical styles in which each piece

263   *Nomos*, in a musical sense, is used by Pindar, Aeschylus, Sophocles, and other fifth-century writers. In the great majority of its occurrences it means no more than 'melody', and certainly is not usually intended to designate solo pieces of a technically specialised sort. See e.g. Pindar, *Nem.* 5.25, 49 Aesch. *Ag.* 1153, *Sept.* 954. The basis of this common literary usage is obscure, though it may indeed be rooted in a notion of different 'customary' or 'familiar' kinds of song. But that is a long way from the precisely delineated conception imported by the later writers. The poets provided the word, with its general ambience: it was the music historians who took it over and converted it into a technical term.

was sung. Such hints might take the form of descriptive adjectives (e.g. 'high-pitched'), implications about the occasion for which the piece was designed (contained in e.g. an invocation of a particular god), references to regional or racial melodic styles (Aeolian, Dorian, and the like), the metres in which the poems were written, and so on. Needless to say, these would provide no proper basis for a rigid classification of types. It remains to be seen how well this sceptical hypothesis fares in the face of the individual names on the lists transmitted by ps.-Plutarch and others.

The list of Terpander's kitharodic *nomoi* given at 1132d matches fairly well the one at Pollux IV.65. Probably both authors are using the same source. Both of them mention a Boeotian and an Aeolian *nomos*, a *Terpandreios* and a *Cēpiōn*. Pollux gives explanations for the names, not all of which are seriously credible. The first two, he says, are named for the races to which Terpander himself belonged. This plainly incorporates late speculations about Terpander's birthplace: more probably the names were originally intended to designate types of melody or rhythm characteristic of different branches of the Greek people. But here our sceptical hypothesis is very plausible. It is all too likely that the names, in the sources from which the earliest classifiers retrieved them, were not meant to indicate nomic categories as later conceived. We may guess that they were drawn from quite casual mentions in the verse of Terpander or other poets, like the references to an 'Aeolian Muse', a 'Lydian melody', and so on, that sometimes appear in later lyric. These cannot usually be taken to refer to anything more than the melodic style of the particular song in which they occur. *Terpandreios* is self-explanatory, if unhelpful: *Cēpiōn*, so Pollux says, was named after a disciple and favourite of Terpander (mentioned also at ps.-Plut. 1133c). But the 'disciple' may be a mere commentator's invention to explain a reference (perhaps using the adjective *kēpaios*, 'to do with a *kēpos*, a garden') that was no longer adequately understood.

The rest of ps.-Plutarch's list comprises *Trochaios* and *Oxys*, cited as a pair, and *Tetraoidios*. Pollux has *Orthios* and *Trochaios* as one pair, *Oxys* and *Tetraoidios* as another. It is likely that *Orthios* (also named as an auletic *nomos* at 1133f, and perhaps as aulodic at 1134c–d) has dropped out of our texts of ps.-Plutarch.

Now Pollux, and presumably the common source, explain the name *Orthios*, like *Trochaios*, as being derived from the title of a rhythm, 'orthian'. The derivation is possible, since *orthios* can be the name of a metrical foot (e.g. Arist. Quint. 36.29): if it is correct, both *Orthios* and *Trochaios* may be names reflecting a scholar's analysis of the metres of existing poems. But elsewhere in musical contexts the word is almost always a classification by pitch, not rhythm, indicating a high-pitched piece (**49** Aesch. *Ag.* 1153, ps.-Ar. *Probs.* XIX.37, cf. e.g. Soph. *Antig.* 1206, Eurip. *Troiades* 1266, Aristoph. *Acharn.* 16, *Knights* 1279, Hdt. 1.24. But some of these may refer to the auletic *Orthios nomos*: see below). In these cases *orthios* is almost a synonym for *oxys*.

Oxys and *Tetraoidios* (lit. 'four-songed') are named, according to Pollux, from their *tropos*, that is, in older terms, from the *harmonia* or melodic structure associated with each. But while *Oxys* might have designated a high *harmonia* (cf. Appendix to Plato), it is most unlikely that *Tetraoidios* could have referred to a piece in four distinct *harmoniai*. Such 'harmonic' modulations were a new feature of music in the later fifth century (see Ch. 7). Ps.-Plutarch's explanation of the name *Trimelēs* ('three-melodied') for an aulodic *nomos* (1134a–b) is similarly suspect. If there was a *Tetraoidios nomos*, it was probably a piece that was simply divided into four sections, by contrast with what Pollux treats as the Terpandrean norm of seven.[264]

---

[264] IV.66. We do not know how old Pollux's authority for the seven sections is, and his list of them is not very informative. The sections are said to be *archa* (beginning),

But it is equally likely that the name comes from a commentator's speculations about the word *tetragērys*, 'four-voiced', which appears in a fragment of Terpander's verse quoted by Strabo (XIII. 2.4) and Cleonides (202.11–12): there, however, Terpander advertises himself as abandoning the 'four-voiced song' in favour of 'new hymns on a seven-strung *phorminx*', and 'four' evidently refers to the number of strings on the earlier instrument, not to the four 'movements' of a composition. In the confusion of our over-imaginative sources, it is possible that even the alleged seven sections of the canonical Terpandrean *nomos* owe their origin to the same text.

The names *Orthios*, *Trochaios* and *Tetraoidios* may well go back in the tradition about Terpander to the fifth century. *Oxys*, I suggest, was originally a synonym for *Orthios*. Pollux, or his source, will then have done some tidying up, explaining *Orthios* as a rhythmic category and *Tetraoidios* as a 'harmonic' one in order to complete a set of four neat pairs. But as I have indicated, the fifth-century tradition itself is already thoroughly suspect.

The evidential difficulties noted above apply equally, with a few exceptions, to the names given by our sources to *nomoi* in the other main classes: I shall not rehearse them all in detail. The names in the list of aulodic *nomoi* credited to Clonas and Polymnestus (1132d) may be roughly interpreted as follows. *Apothetos* means 'secret', 'hidden'. Lasserre's connection of it with the *apothetai* at Sparta, the place where malformed infants were exposed (Plut. *Lyc.* 16) is wholly speculative: one can imagine the term being taken from a poet's boast 'I shall reveal a new song, hidden until now', or the like. *Elegoi* may be named for the rhythm of the elegiac, or for the sense of *elegos* that means 'lament'. *Kōmarchios* means 'of the leader of the revel', the word *kōmos* having often, but by no means always, a Dionysiac association. Again, though the adjective is not known to have been used in this way, a poet might have referred to his song as a *kōmarchios ōdos* with no serious intent to classify (cf. e.g. Pindar, *Nem.* 3.5). *Schoiniōn* might mean 'rope-like', and could be connected with Pindar's use of *schoinoteneion* in 29 fr. 61.1 (see note ad loc.): alternatively it might have been taken from the name of a bird (Ar. *Hist. An.* 610a8) which may be a sort of wagtail. It suggests, in either case, no obvious category of classification.

Kēdeios is Lasserre's emendation for the MSS *Kēpion te kai Deios*, which is corrupt. It means 'of funerals'. (The copyist's eye evidently slipped from the first two letters of *Kēdeios* to those of *Kēpiōn* (*Cēpiōn*) in the list of kitharodic *nomoi* that follows: *Kēpiōn* certainly belongs there: cf. 1133c and Pollux IV.65.) *Trimelēs*, 'three-melodied', is plainly a description of a piece comprising a sequence of three sections, though as I said above, the author's account of its structure at 1134a–b is unlikely to be correct. Two additional facts may be recorded about *nomoi* of this class. First, Pollux (IV.79), attributing the *Apothetos* and *Schoiniōn* to Clonas, calls them auletic, not aulodic *nomoi*: but this may be a mere slip: cf. 1133a. Secondly, the name *Orthios*, which elsewhere characterises both kitharodic (Pollux IV.65) and auletic (1133f) *nomoi*, is attached to pieces by Polymnestus at 1134c, without the noun *nomos*: at 1135d it is said to be doubtful whether he used the *Orthios nomos* in his aulodic *nomoi*. In view of these remarks, and of the various uses of the adjective *orthios* elsewhere which we have already noticed, it seems probable that pieces of this characteristically high-pitched sort existed in a wide variety of musical genres.

Concerning auletic *nomoi* ps.-Plutarch says rather little. The Phrygian Olympus, who held much the same heroic status among auletes as did Terpander among kithar-

> *metarcha* (after the beginning), *katatropa* (perhaps 'turning round'), *metakatatropa* (after the *katatropa*), *omphalos* (lit. 'navel', i.e. 'centre'), *sphragis* (lit. 'seal', suggesting completion, finishing off), and *epilogos* (used elsewhere to mean 'peroration' in rhetoric, or the 'epilogue' or final section of a play).

odes (see esp. 1141b), is said to have invented the *Polykephalos* ('many-headed') *nomos* in honour of Apollo (1133d, but see also 1133e). The scholiasts identify this, plausibly enough, with the 'many-headed' *nomos* of 27 Pindar, *Pyth*. 12, though it is odd that the divinity honoured by it should be Apollo rather than Athena. They also give rival explanations of its title: either the 'heads' are musical sections, or they are the heads of the Gorgons' snaky locks, or they are the individual members of the chorus who sang the piece to *aulos* accompaniment. The last explanation at least is impossible, if this was an auletic *nomos*, and very improbable anyway, since there are no good grounds for believing that what our sources categorise as *nomoi* were ever anything but solos. No doubt, like the sixth-century *Pythikos nomos* (which was certainly auletic and dedicated to Apollo, 24 Pollux IV.84), the *Polykephalos nomos* exploited the capacity of the aulos for dramatic imitation. Ps.-Plutarch also attributes to Olympus the *Harmatios* ('Chariot') *nomos* (1133e, but see also 1133f). The ancient scholiasts and etymologists present a bewildering selection of possible explanations for this title, from which we can conclude only that they did not know what it meant. (See *Et. Magn.* 145.25–47, schol. to Eurip. *Orestes* 1384: in the *Orestes*, if the text is sound, *harmateion melos* indicates a passionate lament.) We are told that Stesichorus 'made use of' the *Harmatios nomos*, in imitation of Olympus (1133f), which suggests that its identifiable features were transferable to a different musical medium, since Stesichorus is not known as a composer of solos for *aulos*.

The same sentence connects the *Orthios nomos* with the use of a dactylic rhythm: hence here at least the name has no connection with the orthian unit of metre. The context makes it likely that this too is intended as a reference to an auletic *nomos*, and this is confirmed by Pollux (IV.71) and the schol. to Aristoph. *Acharn.* 16. ('The *Orthios* is an auletic *nomos*, so called because it is vigorous (*eutonos*, lit. 'well-stretched', 'well-strung') and involves *anatasis*, tension.') The *nomos* called *Cradias* ('of the fig-branch', 1134a) was 'played on the *aulos* over the human scapegoats as they were taken out, whipped with fig-branches and leaves' (Hesych. s.v. *Cradiēs nomos*). The ritual was part of the festival of the Thargelia. Ps.-Plutarch says that the *nomos* was played by Mimnermus (better known to us as a poet, but originally an aulete, Strabo XIV.1.28, Hermesianax ap. Ath. 598a): this does not mean that he 'invented' it. Other auletic *nomoi* credited to Olympus are the *nomos* of Ares (1141b), said to be in prosodiac rhythm, and the *nomos* of Athena (1143b–c). Of the latter we learn that its introduction (*anapeira*, cf. 25 Strabo IX.3.10) was of a very different character from its 'so-called *harmonia*', a word that seems here to have referred to the melody of its principal section. But it is implied that the formal basis (represented as enharmonic genus, Phrygian *tonos*, and a rhythm that subtly shifts from paeonic to trochaic) remained constant throughout. The change in 'character' was brought about by the composer's skill in putting the formal materials together.

Of kitharistic *nomoi* we hear nothing in the present work, and elsewhere little of any significance apart from the report of 25 Strabo IX.3.10. Pollux lists three such *nomoi*, those of Zeus, of Athena, and of Apollo, but gives no further information. The passage on solo *kithara*-playing at 196 Ath. 637f–638a may also be noted, though the term *nomos* does not occur in it.

This survey of the names assigned to *nomoi* is inevitably incomplete, but includes all the most important ones. It is possible that various other names attached to types of composition in authors like ps.-Plutarch were meant to be thought of as names of *nomoi*, even though the writer does not say so. Examples might be the *Mētrōa* of 1137d and even the *spondeion* of 1135a ff. But on the basis of the material we have set out, it may now be possible to draw some tentative conclusions.

It seems clear that some of the names on the lists were included even though they were not fully understood: the *Harmatios* and the *Cēpiōn* are likely cases. Here it may well be that the original reference was to pieces performed as parts of religious rituals already obsolete in the fifth century, and the account we are given of the *Cradias nomos* confirms that a location in ritual provided the historians with one means of classification (though the 'facts' about even this example come from a late source). But there are no adequate grounds for Lasserre's view (23 ff, particularly 26) that their religious niches established the basis for a whole archaic system of nomic types. He argues that the word *nomos*, 'custom', was originally attached to types of composition belonging to specific 'customary' religious rites. He supposes that the *nomoi* of the great competitive festivals were a secondary development, linked to the pieces initially called *nomoi* only by tenuous connections of melodic or rhythmic form, and that the fourth-century understanding of the word *nomos* as indicating a fixed set of musical rules was entirely mistaken. His explanation presupposes that the competition pieces of the sixth century were constructed in conscious imitation of forms existing in ritual, and that the name *nomos*, already current as a designation of the latter, was deliberately adopted for the former at the same time. This supposition ignores the virtual absence of the word *nomos* in its musical usage in pre-fifth-century texts, and the general and untechnical nature of its senses in literature of the earlier fifth century itself. If neither the competitive composers, nor the earlier musicians of ritual, nor again the immediate literary successors of these groups had a special word used to bring together the music of ritual and that of the contests, we no longer have any reason to believe that they saw a special connection between them. As our sceptical hypothesis suggested, the connection will have been made, along with others, by later fifth-century classifiers, who seized upon designations of all sorts – from cult, from melodic style, from pitch, from rhythm, and so on – to form the basis of their chaotic typology. It will also have been they who adopted the quite unspecialised term *nomos*, and gave it the technical sense that their systematisations demanded.

One may sympathise with Lasserre's contention that what the classifiers call 'nomic' forms exercised on music, in the pre-classical period, an influence scarcely less strong than that of Homer on literature. Ps.-Plutarch certainly tries to convey that impression. But the claim must be interpreted with caution, and severely qualified. In the first place, if the generic title *nomos* is the invention of fifth-century theorists, designed to cover a wide variety of earlier forms of musical solo, it becomes extremely rash to talk of *nomoi* in the earlier period as a co-ordinated category of music with a coherent and comprehensible 'influence'. The pieces attached to certain rituals may have developed into important musical forms (as for example, in a different musical area, did the dithyramb): they may have influenced the styles and structures that developed in the sixth-century competitions. Certainly some of these, in their turn, became major musical classics. We can agree that solo musical performance developed in important ways in the seventh and sixth centuries, without conceding that there was one special category of such music, the *nomos*, that was outstandingly significant. Whatever the truth about this, however, it is obvious that Lasserre's estimate of the importance of the *nomos* is in any case exaggerated. It ignores those aspects of the elegiac, iambic and lyric traditions that have nothing to do with either ritual or competition, and it ignores, more importantly, the entire field of choral dance and song, around which the musical life of Greece most crucially revolved. There is no evidence that the music of these genres was influenced by the development of the so-called *nomoi* any more strongly than the *nomoi* were influenced by it.

Returning, finally, to the sense of the term *nomos*, we may conclude that the interpretation given by Plato, and later by ps.-Plutarch and others, was not al-together wide of the mark. It was axiomatic in the later fifth century and afterwards that earlier music fell into determinate types, each regulated by precise rules, and that the degeneracy of 'modern' music consisted largely in its ignoring the rules and the demarcations between types. At a general level, this supposition may well have been correct. The requirements of religious cult tend to impose bounds on innovation in the associated music; and there is solid evidence that in at least some cases (e.g. the *Pythikos* and *Polykephalos nomoi*) even the competition pieces were delimited by rules governing structure and subject matter. Restriction of subject is natural in festivals devoted, in theory, to particular individuals or events in religious myth, and restrictions on form make excellent sense in the context of a competition. The description of the *Pythikos nomos* in Pollux and Strabo may be perfectly authentic. Some of the categories transmitted to us are somewhat vague (e.g. the *Orthios*), and many – perhaps most – represent hopeful interpretations of unsystematic poetical allusions, rather than a deliberate archaic scheme of classification. Nevertheless, the contrast between a rule-bound earlier music and a freer approach in later times may, in general terms, be allowed to stand.

We should not then hunt for the original sense of the word *nomos* as a term of classification among the practices of the seventh century, but among the historical assumptions of the fifth. It is a scholar's term of art, and it means what our sources say it does: a type of solo composition governed by strict rules. What the rules were, and what forms of composition corresponded to them, the historians for the most part did not know, and neither do we.

Appendix B: the *spondeion* and the *spondeiazōn tropos*

Two passages, 1134f ff and 1137b–d, give rather obscure and roundabout descriptions of scalar structures credited to the Phrygian musician Olympus. I shall attempt here to outline what I take to be their likeliest interpretation: see also the classic paper on the subject by Winnington-Ingram (*Classical Quarterly* 22 (1928)).

The first part of the earlier passage is straightforward. Olympus is said to have made his melody move from *paramesē* and *mesē* to diatonic *parhypatē*, omitting *lichanos*. *Paramesē* is a tone above *mesē*, and diatonic *parhypatē* is two tones below *mesē* (the 'omitted' *lichanos* being a tone below *mesē*). Reading from the top, this gives a series of three notes separated by a tone and a ditone: adopting the convention equating *mesē* with the modern note A, we have the sequence B,A,F, conceived as a framework for falling melodic figures.

1135a gives an additional note at the bottom. We are told that the semitone 'in the middle tetrachord' (i.e., in the musical space comprising a fourth below *mesē*) was incomposite, not divided into quarter-tones as in the developed form of the enhar-monic genus. In the developed enharmonic, the quarter-tones lie below the ditone, completing a tetrachord. Hence there is a semitone to be added below F, giving the note E.

The sequence E,F,A,B seems to be the core, but not the whole of the scale: it has an upwards continuation. 1135a–b contains a difficult discussion of what it calls the *syntonōteros spondeiasmos*, the 'tenser' or 'higher' *spondeiasmos*. While *spondeias-mos*, taken on its own, might mean simply 'interval characteristic of *spondeia* [lib-ation-pieces]', we are told by Aristides Quintilianus (28.4–5) that the word indicates an upwards melodic shift through the incomposite interval of three-quarters of a tone. Undoubtedly *syntonōteros spondeiasmos* refers to that interval here too, since at the end of 1135a it is said to be less than a tone by a diesis (quarter-tone). The word *syntonōteros* does not, I think, mean 'in the higher part of the scale', but indicates a 'tenser' interval, with an (abnormally) raised upper bounding note. Nevertheless, the subsequent discussion makes it clear that the interval did in fact occur in the upper part of the series, following the tone immediately above the ditone, since we are told that a (faulty) interpretation of the *spondeiasmos* as a whole tone will generate a sequence of two ditones, one incomposite, the other composite. The notes of this faulty series must be F,A,B,C# (1135b). The correct series, taken as a complete structure, will then be E,F,A,B,C+.

I suspect that *spondeiasmos* did not originally mean 'upwards shift of ¾ tone', but merely 'interval characteristic of *spondeia*'. To judge by 1134f and 1135b, that interval must have been the incomposite semitone below the ditone, exemplified by the interval between E and F. It was this interval that distinguished the *spondeion* from the only other Greek scale-form involving an incomposite ditone, the developed enharmonic. The *syntonōteros spondeiasmos*, I suggest, is a version of the *spondeiasmos* that 'stretches' it upwards by an additional quarter-tone; and Aristides, misunderstanding the passage of Aristoxenus quoted in the present text, treats the word *spondeiasmos* as itself referring to the ¾-tone interval of the *syntonōteros* form.

Unless Aristoxenus' discussion is wholly misleading, however, the 'stretched' interval must have occurred only at the top of the series, not also in the equivalent position in the fourth below *mesē*. The series is E,F,A,B,C+, not E,F+,A,B,C+, since the latter form, in the faulty version criticised at 1135b, would become E,F#,A,B,C#, which does not contain the sequence of ditones that Aristoxenus rejects.[265]

If the present interpretation is on the right lines, the adjective *syntonōteros*, 'tenser', indicates a comparison with a less tense *spondeiasmos*. I have argued that this would involve a semitone in place of the ¾-tone interval; and we have grounds, therefore, for assuming the existence of a form of the *spondeion* scale which makes this replacement. The scales of the *spondeion* attributed to Olympus are then these: a 'normal' version proceeding E,F,A,B,C, and a 'stretched' version E,F,A,B,C+. Olympus' melodies in this genre were apparently constructed out of these notes and no others. (Cf. 1137b, and also Pollux IV.80, which says that early *auloi* had only four finger-holes. The limitation is not surprising, since if the thumb is used only to support the instrument, only four fingers remain to cover the holes. Such an instrument would have five natural notes, as do the scales of Olympus, 'natural' notes being those that can be produced without special techniques of lip- and breath-control. For the later development of these see 163 Theophrastus, *Hist. Plant.* IV.11.4–5.)

The second passage (1137b–d) describes something called the *spondeiazōn* (or *spondeiakos*) *tropos*, roughly the 'libation style'. Its scale-form is not identical with that of the *spondeion*, but there are close affinities: it is perhaps a rather later development. Further, while the *spondeion* seems to have been a form for solo *aulos*, an 'auletic' style, the later passage introduces references to 'accompaniment', indicating that the *spondeiazōn tropos* was a style used in accompanied song. The

---

265   The principle on which these criticisms are based seems to be substantially more stringent than the version employed in the *El. Harm.* There two consecutive ditones are outlawed (63.34–64.11), but the reasoning behind the ban, which is admittedly complex and obscure, appears to apply only to the case where both ditones are incomposite. It is at least not obvious that it can properly be brought to bear where a composite ditone succeeds an incomposite one, as in the present case. Two composite ditones succeed one another in a form of the scale which Aristoxenus treats as perfectly normal and legitimate, the disjunct chromatic series s,s,½,t,s,s,½, e.g. E,F,Gb, A,B,C,Db,E. Here there are ditones between F and A and between A and Db.

aulos becomes the accompanying instrument, so that the genre is to be classed as 'aulodic'.

As regards the scale on which the vocal melody was built, it seems to differ from the *spondeion* in only one way, by including *parhypatē* (which must here mean enharmonic *parhypatē*, E+: see 1137b). This form of scale therefore 'divides the semitone' in the way characteristic of the developed enharmonic, a division not yet made in the *spondeion*. In the upper register the notes *nētē* (the higher E), *nētē synēmmenōn* (D), and (enharmonic) *tritē* (B+) are explicitly said to be avoided. Hence the vocal scale is E,E+,F,A,B,C, no mention being made of a 'stretched' version that replaces C with C+. (For a quite similar structure, though one that includes the note *nētē*, the higher E, see the heptachordal scale ascribed to Terpander at 180 ps.-Ar. *Probs.* XIX.32.)

The accompaniment in the *spondeiazōn tropos*, we are told, uses all three of the notes that the melody is said to avoid, and we may fairly assume that it also uses the ones that the melody includes. The complete series is therefore E,E+,F,A,B,B+,C,D,E. (In terms of Aristoxenean theory, the upper part of this would have to be interpreted as a combination of two forms, one having the tetrachord B,B+,C,E disjoined from the lower tetrachord in the regular way by the interval of a tone. The other contains the notes A,B,D, which are to be construed as an imperfect version of the enharmonic tetrachord A,A+,B,D, in conjunction with the lower tetrachord. The missing note, *tritē synēmmenon* (A+), is the one that 'divides the semitone'.)

This passage, together with 158 Plato, *Laws* 812d–e and some hints in 170–172, 183 ps.-Ar. *Probs.* XIX.16, 17, 18 and 39, contains almost the whole of our information about heterophonic accompaniment in Greek music. Few detailed conclusions can be drawn. *Tritē* (B+), we are told, was used to make a concord with *parhypatē* (E+), *nētē* (higher E) to form a discord with *paranētē* (C) and a concord with *mesē* (A), and *nētē synēmmenōn* (D) to form a discord with *paranētē* (C), *paramesē* (B), and *lichanos* (F). How these relations were used in the practical business of composition we do not know: 183 ps.-Ar. *Probs.* XIX.39 may be the best general guide.

It is impossible to be sure how good Aristoxenus' evidence was for the existence and antiquity of these forms, but we have seen that an earlier passage (1133e) indicates that 'enharmonic *nomoi*', attributed to Olympus, were still in practical use in his time (cf. also Plato, *Symp.* 215c, and 161 Ar. *Pol.* 1340a). If the present analyses of the *spondeion* and the *spondeiazōn tropos* refer to these 'enharmonic' forms, as seems very likely, they are based on the facts of experience, not on speculation alone. It is quite improbable, however, that the practices of accompanists in the fourth century, even when accompanying ancient melodies, preserved the practices of the original composers. (The composer was normally treated as the source only of the melody, not the accompaniment as well: 158 Plato, *Laws* 812d.) The present author feels it necessary to confirm Olympus' knowledge of *nētē synēmmenōn* by reference to other classes of his melodies (1137d), as well as the accompaniments of the *spondeiazōn tropos*. The notes used in the latter may therefore have had their source in modern 'harmonisations', and should not be treated as reliable evidence for styles of accompaniment before the later fifth century.

CHAPTER 16

Athenaeus

Athenaeus was born in Egypt about 160 A.D. Little is known of his life, but for present purposes the fact is unimportant. His mammoth work, the fifteen-book *Deipnosophistae* ('Experts at dining') is another example of the genre of 'table talk', presenting an encyclopaedic assortment of facts and opinions related to the art of convivial eating and drinking. Many of the remarks put into the mouths of his learned conversationalists are drawn from much older sources, often quoted verbatim: even more plainly than in the case of ps.-Plutarch, it is this feature of the work that gives it its value.

By comparison with the *Deipnosophistae* the ps.-Plutarchian essay is a masterpiece of elegant organisation. Athenaeus' treatise is an enormous scrapbook, linking its undigested morsels of quotation and summary with tenuous fragments of free association, mentioning topics only to drop them again and pick them up afresh hundreds of pages later. Information on music appears casually here and there throughout the work, but certain passages, especially in Books IV and XIV, constitute more extended displays of learning on the subject: it is from them that the extracts below are taken. At first sight they themselves appear to present their material in no sort of order; but though they are studded with items that might have looked better elsewhere, it is in fact possible to trace certain major preoccupations, and to mark the divisions between them. Athenaeus cares nothing for connections between topics, but once a subject has been raised he will often pursue it for some time, though with generous allowances for digression.

The whole of 188 (Book IV, 174a–185a), together with the first part of 189 (Book XIV, 616e–618c), can be thought of as an extended essay on wind instruments, particularly the *aulos*. 196 (633f–638a) constitutes a comparable treatise on stringed instruments, particularly those of the more exotic varieties. There is no doubt that these passages on instruments are the most valuable items, musically speaking, that Athenaeus has transmitted: much of his information is unique. But the intervening sections have their interest too. They include a short discussion of folk songs (189 618d–620a), a dissertation on types of popular musical entertainment (189–91, 620a–622d), and a more general essay on the psychological and educative powers of music, on the characteristics of the *harmoniai*, and on the nobility and dignity of Greek music and dance in its golden age (192–5, 623e–632a). Other topics are touched on by the way, and this scheme of organisation is far from being rigidly adhered to, but it may help to guide the reader through the *disiecta membra* of Athenaeus' exposition.

As a stylist, Athenaeus is nearly non-existent. His method is to introduce a topic, sometimes by raising a question or stating a controversial view, and to discuss it by the simple expedient of juxtaposing series upon series of opinions or remarks quoted from previous authors. His library was large, and his enthusiasm for research and compilation was omnivorous and indefatigable. Some of his sources are well-known literary figures, particularly the poets of the sixth century, the period in which Athenaeus displays the most persistent interest. Others are scholars of the Hellenistic age, many of them now quite obscure. Over a hundred such authors are cited in the passages included in this volume alone, and rather than allowing them to proliferate among the footnotes, I have collected their names together in an appendix, where brief indications of their dates and the general nature of their works will be found.

Athenaeus, *Deipnosophistae*

188   *Deipnosophistae* 174a–185a

While a good deal of talk of this sort was still going on, the sound of a *hydraulis*[1] was heard from the neighbours' house, very sweet and delightful, so that it attracted the attention of us all and [174b] entranced us by its melodiousness. Ulpianus glanced at the musician Alcides. 'Do you hear that fine and beautiful sound,[2] you most musical of men,' he asked, 'which has beguiled us all with its music and captured our attention? It's not like the *monaulos*[3] so common among you Alexandrians, which gives its hearers pain, rather than any musical delight.' 'All the same,' replied Alcides, 'this instrument, the *hydraulis*, whether you class it among the stringed instruments or the wind instruments, is the invention of one of my countrymen, an Alexandrian. He was a barber by trade, and his name was Ctesibius.[4]

[1]   That is, the 'water-organ', an organ in which the air pressure was supplied hydraulically. For an account of its construction see n. 9 below. It is usually treated as an Alexandrian invention, as here, and there is no reason to doubt that a technically sophisticated version was first constructed and described by the Alexandrian Ctesibius. The general principle of the organ seems, however, to have been quite widely known. Pollux (IV.70) gives both the hydraulic organ and the 'smaller kind, blown by bellows' (perhaps a sort of bagpipe) the name 'Tyrrhenian *aulos*', suggesting an Etruscan origin. Small organ-like instruments, quite closely related to the Pan-pipe *syrinx*, and blown by a bellows pumped with the foot, were known in the Middle East: see Sachs, *Hist. Mus. Instr.* p. 143 and Plate VIII(c).

[2]   Reading *euphōnias* with the MSS: Kaibel emends to *symphōnias*, lit. 'concord'.

[3]   *Monaulos* ('single *aulos*') is usually taken to refer to the ordinary *aulos* played singly, instead of as one of a pair. In that case it is not a distinct instrument, only a familiar one performed in an unusual way. But there are difficulties in this interpretation. First, it is hard to see how the instrument could be described as painful to listen to without implying criticism of *aulos* music in general, which seems not to be intended. Secondly, the *monaulos* is treated as a distinct invention, attributed by the Egyptians to Osiris (175e below): Pollux (IV.75) also calls it an Egyptian invention, saying that it was used particularly at weddings (cf. Anaxandrides at 176a below). Neither source suggests that this means that the Egyptians invented the *aulos*. Thirdly, Alcides in the present speech treats as two quite separate projects an excursus on the *monaulos* (175e–176e), and a demonstration that the Alexandrians *also* know a great deal about *auloi* (176e–182e). If it is not an ordinary *aulos* used singly, it is probably the so-called *monokalamos syrinx* or *aglōttos aulos*, a simple tube of reed with finger-holes, sounded by blowing across the end (see 184a below and 175 ps.-Ar. *Probs.* XIX.23). This view is to some extent supported by the identification of the *monaulos* with a *kalamos* (reed) at 176a, and of the *monaulos* player with the *kalamaulēs* or *kalamaulētēs* at 176c–d, as also by the probable attribution of its use to the infant Pan at 175f. In the Greek world this instrument was generally confined to the rustic music of shepherds etc. (e.g. Theocr. *Idylls* 5.5–7, 6.42–6), which would explain the urbane Ulpianus' contempt for it. Cf. also n. 20 below.

[4]   This is the same Ctesibius to whom Vitruvius attributes a wide range of mechanical and hydraulic devices: see particularly IX.8.2 ff, X.7.1 ff: he is said to have written

Aristocles recounts [c] this in his *On Choruses*, in some such words as these. '"People ask whether the *hydraulis* belongs among the wind instruments or the stringed instruments.[5] Aristoxenus does not know it,[6] but it is said that Plato gave a slight clue to its construction by making a chronometer for use at night rather like a *hydraulis*, something like a very big water-clock.[7] And the *hydraulis* [d] does indeed seem to be a sort of water-clock. Hence it should not be thought of as a stringed and plucked instrument,[8] but one might perhaps call it a wind instrument, since it is blown into by the agency of the water. For the pipes are turned downwards into the water, and the water is stirred up vigorously by a lad; and the pipes are blown into through tubes that penetrate right through the instrument, and produce a pleasant sound.[9] The instrument looks like a circular altar, and they say that it was invented by Ctesibius, a barber who lived there in Aspendia in the time of Ptolemy Euergetes II: they say that he [e] became very famous, and that he also taught his wife, Thais."

'Tryphon, in Book III of his *On Terminology* (the essay is concerned with *auloi* and instruments), says that a description of the *hydraulis* was written by Ctesibius the engineer: I am not sure whether he has got the name wrong.

'commentaries' on such things (X.7.4). According to Vitruvius (IX.8.2) he was the son of a barber, which explains his designation here and at 174d: Tryphon (below, 174e) more fairly calls him an 'engineer'. He is to be dated around the middle of the third century B.C.

5   The question seems an absurd one. Perhaps Aristocles does not mean that there is a serious musicological controversy over the matter, only that when people who are unfamiliar with the instrument hear it, they are initially at a loss to understand the means by which its sound is produced. Alternatively, the question might be an echo of a scholarly dispute, based on a scientific distinction between 'breath' (*pneuma*) and 'air' (*aēr*). (For a characteristic expression of the distinction in a musical context see e.g. ps.-Ar. *Probs.* XI.19: many comparable instances exist.) The organ is not properly speaking an *empneuston organon* (here translated 'wind instrument' but literally 'breathed-into instrument'), since it does not use an impact of *pneuma* to set the air in motion. On the other hand there seem to be no grounds, however perverse, for calling it an *entaton organon* (here 'stringed instrument', but literally 'stretched').

6   The point is that we should not therefore treat his comparison of wind instruments with stringed instruments (174e below) as incorporating an authoritative judgement on the *hydraulis*.

7   The term rendered '*hydraulis*' here and immediately below is *hydraulikon* (*organon*), 'the hydraulic instrument'. Plato's water-clock was perhaps a simpler ancestor of the one designed by Ctesibius, and described at Vitruvius IX.8.4 ff. It was 'for use at night' (Vitruvius says that Ctesibius' was used in the winter) simply because the time cannot then be told from the sun.

8   *Kathapton*, 'touched', must here have the sense 'plucked' (whether with the fingers or with a plectrum), and 'stringed' and 'plucked' go together to describe the same instrument. It has sometimes been translated 'percussion', giving the meaning 'neither a stringed nor a percussion instrument'; but when the phrase recurs below (174e) this translation gives a most improbable sense.

9   Either Aristocles has not understood the construction, or he has made very little effort to explain it. The essentials of Vitruvius' account (X.8) are these. A funnel-shaped air-container, open at top and bottom, is placed neck upwards on blocks in a water-vessel. Air is transmitted by hand-pumps into the neck of the air-container: a valve prevents its escape back to the pumps. This air displaces some or all of the water in the air-container, and creates air pressure in the wind-chest with which its neck

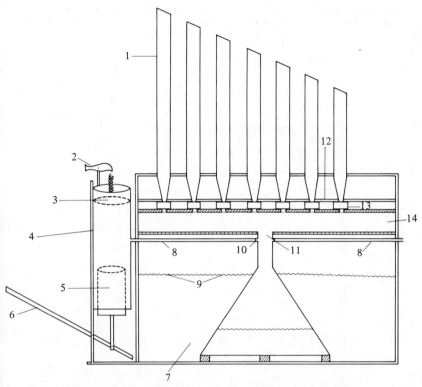

20 *Hydraulis*, front view: 1 pipes; 2 pivoted 'dolphin'; 3 valve; 4 cylinder; 5 piston; 6 pump handle; 7 water-container; 8 air-pipe; 9 water level; 10 valve; 11 pipe to wind-chest; 12 top board; 13 sliders linked to keys; 14 wind-chest.

Aristoxenus, however, judges instruments that are stringed and plucked [*kathapta:* see n. 8 above] to be better than wind instruments, saying that wind instruments are too easy; for many people – shepherds, for instance – play *auloi*[10] and *syringes* without having been taught. [f] That, Ulpianus, is the sum of what I have to tell you about the *hydraulis*.

> communicates. Above the wind-chest stand the pipes: a system of sliders releases air into whichever pipe is required to sound, the sliders themselves being moved from a keyboard by means of metal springs. In some instruments there were several ranks of pipes, each with its own wind-chest, the tubes to the chests from the air-container being opened and closed by taps. See also Figs. 20 and 21.
>
> Aristocles' remark that the water is 'stirred up vigorously by a lad' seems to reflect a misunderstanding of the function of the pumps; and his language further suggests, misleadingly, that the pipes were actually immersed in the water.
>
> 10 The word *aulos* in pastoral contexts usually refers to the *aglōttos aulos* (see n. 3 above: the Theocritus passages cited there are examples of this usage). Aristoxenus' judgement on wind instruments seems perverse as applied to the *aulos* of concert performers, whose use was a matter of considerable technical expertise.

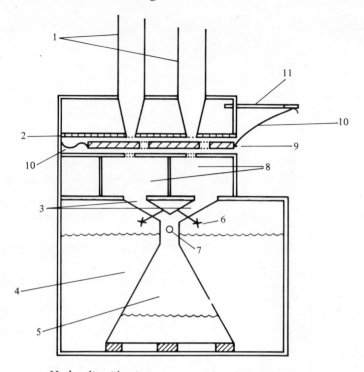

21   *Hydraulis*, side view. 1 two ranks of pipes; 2 top board; 3 pipes to wind-chest; 4 water-container; 5 air-container; 6 tap; 7 air-pipe to pump (not shown); 8 wind-chests; 9 slider; 10 iron spring; 11 key.

'Further, the Phoenicians, as Xenophon says,[11] used to use *auloi* called "*gingras*-pipes", a hand's span in length, which sounded high-pitched and mournful. The Carians used them too, in their laments (unless it is Caria that was being called "Phoenicia", a usage that can be found in Corinna and Bacchylides). The *auloi* are called *gingroi* by the Phoenicians, by derivation from the laments for Adonis, [175a] since you Phoenicians call Adonis "Gingras", as Democlides records.[12] *Gingras auloi* are mentioned by Antiphanes in *The Doctor*, Menander in *The Carian Woman* and Amphis in *Dithyrambus:* Amphis speaks as follows.
A. But what I like is the *gingras*, a very clever thing.
B. What's the *gingras*?

11   The authority is probably not Xenophon but a poetic source, to judge by the use of the form *gingrainoisi*. Various ways of emending the name have been suggested.
12   The same associations with high pitch, Carian laments, a Phoenician origin, and the Phoenician version of an Adonis cult are made by Pollux (IV.76), probably relying on the same source. Carian *aulēmata* are mentioned also by Aristophanes (140 *Frogs* 1303), and Carian mourning songs at e.g. 157 Plato, *Laws* 800e. Cf. also the title of Menander's play at 175a below, which probably refers to professional Carian mourners.

A. A new invention of mine. I haven't yet put it on show in the theatre, but it's already all the rage [b] at Athenian drinking-parties.
B. Why don't you bring it out in public?
A. Because I'm waiting for a tribe that's really keen for victory to draw the lot for it, since I know it'll heave up everything, like a trident, with the applause it gets.[13]

'And Axionicus in his *Euripides-Lover*: "Both of them are so sick with love for Euripides' songs that all others seem to them to be *gingras* melodies and a thoroughly bad thing."

'How much better, wisest Ulpianus, [c] is this *hydraulis* than the so-called *nablas*,[14] which Sopater the parodist in the play called *The Gates* says is also an invention of the Phoenicians. This is what he says: "Nor has the throaty-sounding beat of the Sidonian *nablas* been unstrung." And in *Mystacus' Servant* he says: "The *nablas* is not harmonious in the articulation of its lines: lifeless lotus-wood is fixed in its ribs, [d] and gives out a breathing music. No one ever woke to cry in joy at this melodious chorus of pleasure."[15] Philemon in *The Adulterer* has:
A. We ought to have an *aulos*-girl, Parmenon, or a *nablas*.
Parm. But what's a *nablas*?
A. Don't you know, you lunatic?
Parm. Not in the least.
A. What are you saying? You don't know the *nablas*? Then you don't know anything good – not even a *sambykē*-girl?[16]

---

[13] If the *gingras* is merely a small *aulos*, the point of the discussion is simply to compare the inventions of the Phoenicians unfavourably with those of the Alexandrians: this is also the theme of the passage on the *nablas*, 175c below. But Amphis' suggestion that the *gingras* is a surprising new invention might lead one to suppose that it is something more out of the ordinary (though we cannot rely on this conclusion, since we do not know the dramatic context of the excerpt). At the end of 175b the *hydraulis* is mentioned again, as if the subject had never been dropped. It seems at least possible that the *gingras* was in some way related to instruments of the organ family, being perhaps a small bellows-blown device like those mentioned in n. 1 above.
  The reference to lots is connected with the practice of drawing lots for the tribe to which a naturalised citizen was to be attached.

[14] The *nablas* is the Hebrew *nevel*, probably a harp held with the body upright, and the stick that held the strings horizontal. See Sachs, *Hist. Mus. Instr.* 115–17, and cf. the type represented in Fig. 11. It is compared with the *hydraulis*, to the latter's advantage, partly as a move in the friendly controversy between the Alexandrian Alcides and the Phoenician Ulpianus, partly in an attempt to undermine the contention ascribed to Aristoxenus at 174e above.

[15] The text of this quotation, especially the last sentence, is seriously in doubt. 'Harmonious' translates *eumelēs*, lit. 'well-melodied', here apparently a punning metaphor for 'beautifully shaped'. The import of the quotation is obscure, but I suggest that it is intended to juxtapose the visual ugliness of the instrument with the beauty of its 'breathing' music, not to suggest that the sound is also ugly. 'Breathing' makes an obvious contrast with 'lifeless', but in conjunction with the epithet 'throaty-sounding' in the previous quotation, it seems likely to be meant as a description of the instrument's tone-quality. The 'lifeless lotus-wood fixed in its ribs' must be the string-holder: cf. n. 14.

[16] *Sambykistria*. In a description of a Macedonian banquet at 129a, Athenaeus (quoting

'The instrument called the *trigōnon*[17] is said by Juba in the fourth book of his *History of the Theatre* to be an invention of the Syrians, like the so-called *lyrophoenix* [and the] *sambykē*.[18] But Neanthes of Cyzicus [e] says in Book I of his *Annals* that this instrument was the invention of Ibycus, the poet of Rhegium, just as the *barbitos* was that of Anacreon.[19]

'But since you disparage us Alexandrians as unmusical, and constantly mention the *monaulos* as endemic amongst us, listen to what I can tell you off the cuff about it now. In the essay I mentioned just now, Juba says that the Egyptians call the *monaulos* an invention of Osiris, as they do also the *plagiaulos* known as the *phōtinx*.[20] (I shall put on record a distinguished

the fourth- to third-century historian Hippolochus) mentions Rhodian *sambykis-triai*, who put on a lascivious performance together with the more usual *aulos*-girls, *aulētrides*. On the *sambykē* see 196 633f–634b.

[17] A triangular harp, sometimes called the *trigōnon psaltērion*. See e.g. 149 Plato, *Rep.* 399c, 175 ps.-Ar. *Probs.* XIX.23.

[18] Some words have dropped out of the text between *lyrophoinika* and *sambykēn*. On the *lyrophoenix*, often simply *phoenix* or *phoenikion*, see 168 ps.-Ar. *Probs.* XIX.14 and 196 Ath. 637a–b.

[19] The word *barbitos* here, as sometimes elsewhere (e.g. 196 635d, where its invention is attributed to Terpander, Plut. *Mor.* 827a, Theocr. *Idylls* 16.45), may perhaps not refer to the *lyra*-like instrument normally associated with the name. The context here suggests an instrument of the harp type, and Theocritus explicitly calls it 'many-stringed', an epithet usually reserved for harp-like instruments of foreign origin. To judge by representations on vase paintings, the *lyra*-like *barbitos* had no more strings than any other such instrument. A wide variety of names (including *barbiton*, *barmos*, *baromos*, *barymiton*) are treated in some of our sources as equivalent to *barbitos* (e.g. 196 Ath. 636c, Pollux IV.59): the terminological variety may conceal a confusion of instrumental types. Note that at 182f below the *baromos* and the *barbitos* are apparently thought of as distinct. The present link between the *barbitos* and the lyric poets does not count either way: Sappho's name, for instance, is some-times linked with the *pēktis*, an instrument of the harp family (196 635e: cf. also n. 21 below), while vase paintings commonly show her (and other lyricists such as Alcaeus) holding *barbitoi* of the sort related to the *lyra* (e.g. Boardman, *A.B.F.V.* Pl. 311, *A.R.F.V.* Pl. 261).

[20] *Plagiaulos* means 'transverse *aulos*', that is, a pipe played in a position similar to that of the modern flute. (See Apuleius, *Met.* XI.9.6.) Our sources agree that such instru-ments originated in Egypt or elsewhere in N. Africa (cf. Pollux IV.74). There are, however, no certain traces of a true transverse flute in the artistic and archaeological evidence from the Greek world, though there is one probable example from Etruria (second century B.C.: see Sachs, *Hist. Mus. Instr.* p. 142 and Pl. VIII(a)). Scholars are divided as to whether the *plagiaulos* or *phōtinx* was a true flute or an *aulos* with a laterally inserted reed. Our literary evidence is limited, but on the whole suggests the conclusion that a flute is intended. (The reference to 'lateral tongues', *glōssai plagiai*, at Ar. *De Audib.* 801b = Porph. *Comm.* 71.13, is probably to be interpreted in a wholly different sense.) First, for what it is worth, the present group of passages seems to treat it as distinct from the *aulos*, but links it with the *monaulos*, which may have been a flute blown across the open end (see n. 3 above). Secondly, it is sometimes found in pastoral contexts, where reed-less instruments were usual (Theocr. *Idylls* 20.29, Bion, fr. 7); and Bion clearly differentiates it from the *aulos*, attributing its invention to Pan (which hints at a connection with the *syrinx*), that of the *aulos* to Athena. Thirdly, a passage of Nicomachus (*Ench.* 243.10 ff) divides instruments into three groups: (i) *auloi*, *syringes*, *salpinges*, *hydrauloi*; (ii) stringed instruments of the *kithara* and *lyra* type; and (iii) monochords, *trigōnoi*, and '*plagiauloi* along with *phōtinges*'. In the first group, he argues, the production of lower notes involves greater power (because longer air-columns have to be moved): in the second, higher

authority [f] who mentions this instrument too.) The *phōtinx*, certainly, is native to our country, but the *monaulos* is mentioned by Sophocles in his *Thamyras*, as follows: "Gone are the plucked melodies of *pēktides*, and the *lyrai* and *monauloi* which we once enjoyed . . ."[21] Araros says, in *The Birth of Pan*: "He snatched up the *monaulos* and leapt at once, as lightly as you could imagine." [176a] Anaxandrides says, in *The Treasure*: "Picking up a *monaulos* I played the wedding tune", and in *The Cup-Bearer*:

A. Where have you put the *monaulos*, you Syrian?

B. *Monaulos*? What's that?

A. The reed.[22]

Sopater, in *Bacchis*, says: "And he sounded the melody of the *monaulos*."

'Protagorides of Cyzicus, in the second book of his *On the Festivals at Daphne*, says: "He set his hand to every [b] instrument, one after another, *krotala*, *tympanon*, *pandouron*,[23] and hums the sweetest *harmoniai* on the sweet *monaulos*." The Stoic philosopher Posidonius, in the third book of his

notes do so (because the strings, which are of equal length to the lower-pitched ones, are at greater tension). The third group are 'intermediate': he does not explain precisely why. In the case of monochords and *trigōnoi* it must be because their higher notes, like those of the *aulos* but unlike those of the *lyra*, are produced from shorter lengths, and yet they are stringed instruments. By parallel reasoning, higher notes in *plagiauloi* must, like those in *lyrai* but unlike those in *auloi*, involve greater force, even though they are wind instruments. This suggests a technique of overblowing, familiar in instruments of the flute family. At the least, the generic difference indicated here between *plagiauloi* and *auloi* proper seems a good deal more radical than that between instruments differing only in the angle at which their reeds are inserted.

21 It seems clear that the *pēktis* was an instrument of the harp family: it had many strings (149 Plato, *Rep.* 399d), and was played without a plectrum (Aristoxenus at 196 Ath. 635b): it seems to have been high-pitched (Pindar at 196 635d, cf. 635b), and could be described as Lydian (Sophocles at 196 635c, cf. 635d). Some writers identified it with the *magadis* (195 635b and e, cf. 183b below with n. 43), while others denied this identification (196 636a–b). Its use in Greece certainly goes back to the sixth century (e.g. 196 635e), but the controversies recorded at 635b ff show that the instrument, or at any rate an instrument known under this name, was obsolete by the later fourth century.

22 *Kalamos*, referring here to the reed from which on small and simple instruments the main pipe was sometimes made. See 163 Theophrastus, *Hist. Plant.* IV.11.3, and cf. 176d below. But for a conjecture about the implications of the word *kalamos* in this context see n. 3 above.

23 The *pandouron* (more commonly *pandoura*) was a necked instrument similar to the lute or guitar, the only one of its kind known in Greece, and mentioned only rarely. Pollux (IV.60) attributes its invention to the Assyrians, and calls it *trichordon*, 'three-stringed': other references to an instrument called a *trichordon* may therefore indicate the *pandoura* (e.g. 183b below). More details are given at 183f–184a (and for the best modern discussion see Higgins and Winnington-Ingram, *J.H.S.* 85 (1965)). Nicomachus (*Ench.* 243.14–15) says that the name *phandoura* was also used for the monochord: this was not usually an instrument of music so much as a device for use in scientific harmonics. Nicomachus, however, plainly implies that it was familiar to people other than harmonic scientists, and a trace of a genuinely musical monochord may exist at Pollux IV.60, where it is said to be an Arabian invention. Photius (427.26) uses the diminutive form *pandourion* for what he describes as 'a Lydian instrument, plucked without a plectrum'.

Histories, where he is describing the war of the Apameans against the Larisaeans, writes as follows: "They picked up daggers and bayonets covered in rust and dirt: they put on hats and visors, which gave shade but did not prevent their throats from breathing: they dragged along donkeys laden [c] with wine and food of all sorts, among which were packed *phōtingia* and *monaulia*, instruments of revelry, not of war."[24] And I know too that Amerias of Macedon in his *Dialects* says that the *monaulos* is called "*tityrinos*".[25]

'Here then, noble Ulpianus, you have someone who mentions the *phōtinx*.[26] The fact that the *monaulos* was what is now called the *kalamaulēs*[27] is clearly indicated by Hedylus in his *Epigrams*: this is what he says. "Under this mound lives Theon the *monaulos*, the sweet aulete, the delight of mimes on the stage. [d] When blind with old age he had a son, Scirpalus, whom he called 'Scirpalus son of Clever-Hand' as a baby, when he sang of his birth: he had this name to indicate the expertise of his hands. He played on the *aulos* the drunken frivolities of the Muses that Glauce sang, or the song of Battalos who loves to drink unmixed wine, or the songs of Kotalos or Pakalos.[28] But now say to Theon the *kalamaulētēs*, 'Farewell, Theon.'" Further, just as they now call those who play on the reed-pipe[29] *kalamaulai*, so too, [e] according to Amerias of Macedon in his *Dialects*, they call *rhappaulai* those who play on the *rhappa*, which is a reed.

'I would like you to realise, most noble Ulpianus, that there is no record of any people more musical than the Alexandrians: and I am not talking only about singing to the *kithara*, with which the most outright layman, even if he is illiterate, is so familiar that he can immediately point out the mistakes that happen in striking the instrument. On the contrary, they are highly musical in respect of *auloi* too, [f] not only those called "maiden-pipes" and "child-pipes", but also the man-pipes, which are called "complete" and "extra-

---

24   *Phōtingia* and *monaulia* are diminutive forms, but such locutions do not always imply small size: cf. e.g. the use of *lyrion* at 140 Aristoph. *Frogs* 1304.

25   *Tityrinos* may be related to the Doric or Sicilian form *tityros* for *satyros* (schol. to Theocr. *Idylls* 3.2), and if so might indicate an instrument of Dionysiac revelry. Alternatively and more probably the sense of *tityros* with which it is connected is that indicating a male goat (ibid.), reflected in the common shepherd's name Tityros, and the instrument is a pastoral one. See also 182d below.

26   As promised at 175e. The preceding sentence, interrupting the two references to the *phōtinx*, may be misplaced.

27   'Reed-piper': cf. *kalamaulētēs* in the quotation from Hedylus below. *Monaulos* here also refers to the player, not the instrument, again as in Hedylus' lines.

28   Glauce was a popular singer, perhaps the same as the singer of that name mentioned at Theocr. *Idylls* 4.31. 'Battalos' seems to mean 'The Stammerer', and the piece no doubt used musical 'stammering' as a comic effect. 'Kotalos' may be related to *kotilos*, 'twittering', used e.g. of swallows: the sense of 'Pakalos' is unknown. All were titles of well-known songs, and probably all were imitative in character. Their general context is the popular 'music-hall' style of entertainment, including mimes, for which Alexandria was notorious.

29   Lit. 'play the *aulos* on the reed' (*kalamos*), that is, on an instrument whose main pipe was made of reed.

omplete", as well as the *kitharistērioi* and the dactylic.[30] The *elymoi auloi*, vhich Sophocles mentions in the *Niobe* and the *Tympanistai*, are none other, o we are told, than the Phrygian *auloi*, another kind that the Alexandrians <now well.[31] They are also familiar with those that are two-holed, those that ɪre middle-sized, and those called "under-bored".[32] [177a] Callias, in the ᵓedetai, also mentions *elymoi auloi*. Juba says that they are an invention of he Phrygians, and that they are called "staff-pipes", in accordance with heir similar thickness.[33] Cratinas the Younger says in the *Theramenes* that he Cypriots use them.

[30]   The first four types on this list are clearly classified by pitch. At 196 634e–f, a classification into *parthenioi* (maiden-pipes), *paidikoi* (child-pipes), *kitharistērioi*, *teleioi* (complete) and *hyperteleioi* (extra-complete) is attributed to Aristoxenus: the present list presumably echoes the same source. Aristotle (*Hist. An.* 581b) confirms that *parthenioi auloi* were higher-pitched than *paidikoi*: at *El. Harm.* 20.32–4 Aristoxenus says that *parthenioi* and *hyperteleioi* were separated by a distance of three octaves. Whether or not the *kitharistērioi auloi* belong to this classification by pitch is unclear. Pollux (iv.81) tells us that they were called by this name because they accompanied the *kithara*; and he adds (iv.83) that there were *nomoi kitharistērioi*, pieces for *kithara* without the voice, called *iamboi* and *pariambides* (cf. 183c below, and 196 636b), which were accompanied by *auloi*. Cf. also 189 618a, 196 634e with n. 169, and Hesych. s.v. *magadeis*. Pollux also says (iv.81) that *parthenioi auloi* accompanied the choral songs of maidens, *paidikoi* those of boys, *hyperteleioi* those of men, while *teleioi*, also called *Pythikoi*, were used for the 'chorusless' *Pythikon aulēma*, i.e., the auletic solos typified by the *Pythikos nomos*, and also to accompany paeans. (On *paidikoi* see 182c below.)
   It is uncertain whether 'dactylic' refers to the metre of the pieces with which these *auloi* were especially connected, or simply to their thickness ('finger-*auloi*': cf. 177a below on 'staff-pipes'). The evidence about them is thin and confused. Pollux (iv.82) says 'Dactylic *auloi* are those used for *hyporchēmata*: but other people say that these are varieties not of *auloi* but of melodies.' In general, the descriptive terms applied by our sources to allegedly different forms of a given type of instrument cannot all be fitted into a single, orderly scheme of classification: for a luxuriant assortment of designations see Pollux iv.74–7.

[31]   Pollux iv.74: 'The *elymos aulos* is made of box-wood, and was invented by the Phrygians. It has an upwards-curved horn on one of the *auloi*, and it plays to the Phrygian goddess.' (The association between a deep-toned *aulos* and the ecstatic rites of Cybele and Dionysus is common: cf. e.g. 64 and 65, Eurip. *Bacch.* 120–34, 156, 71 *Helen* 1338–52. The title of Sophocles' *Tympanistai*, a play that is said here to include a mention of the *elymos aulos*, certainly refers to the devotees of the Phrygian Mother Goddess. Cf. 63 Eurip. *Bacch.* 59, Hdt. iv.76, Aristoph. *Lysistr.* 388.) Hesychius s.v. *enkeraulēs* adds that it was to the left-hand pipe that the horn was attached: note that in vase paintings etc., when the two *auloi* of a pair are represented as unequal in length, it is generally the left-hand pipe that is the longer: cf. 163 Theophrastus, *Hist. Plant.* iv.11.7. The *elymos* is evidently the same as the *aulos* called 'Phrygian' at 185a below, which is deep in pitch, and has attached to it a horn 'analogous to the bell of the *salpinx*'. Aelian (Porph. *Comm.* 34.11–16) says that the bore of Phrygian *auloi* was narrower than that of Greek ones, with the consequence that Phrygian *auloi* sounded at a lower pitch for their length than did their Greek counterparts. See also the remark attributed to Juba at 177a below, and cf. Theophr. ap. Porph. *Comm.* 64.8, Ar. *De Audib.* 804a = Porph. *Comm.* 76.8–10.

[32]   *Hypotrētoi*, 'bored from underneath'. Possibly these are *auloi* with a thumb-hole, which the simpler Greek *auloi* lacked. But some contrast may be intended with the kind that Pollux calls *paratrētoi*, 'sideways-bored', described by him as high in pitch and sounding sluggish or dull (*nōthes*), suitable for laments.

[33]   'Staff-pipes' translates *skytaleias*: the *skytalē* is any kind of staff or cudgel, but particularly the kind on which the Spartans rolled their secret dispatches.

'We also know the *auloi* called "half-holed", of which Anacreon says "Who has turned his heart towards lovely youth, and dances to the delicate half-holed *auloi*?" These *auloi* are smaller than the "complete" ones.[34] [182b] Aeschylus, at any rate, says in the *Ixion*, by way of a metaphor: [c] "The half-holed[35] is quickly swallowed up by the big." These are the same as the ones called "child-pipes", unsuitable for competitions, and used in merry-making. That is why Anacreon calls them "delicate". I am acquainted with other kinds of *auloi* too, the tragic, the lysiodic and the *kitharistērioi*,[36] which Ephorus mentions in his *Discoveries*, as does Euphranor the Pythagorean in his *On Auloi*, and Alexis as well, [d] in his *On Auloi*. The reed *aulos* is called "*tityrinos*" [see 176c above] by the Dorians who live in Italy, as Artemidorus the follower of Aristophanes records in Book II of his *Dorian Dialect*: "What is called the *magadis* is an *aulos*";[37] and again "The one called *magadis* displays simultaneously a high and a low note, as Anaxandrides says in his *Drill-Sergeant*: 'With the *magadis* I shall chatter to you small and great at once.'"

'The ones called "lotus-*auloi*" are those that the Alexandrians [e] call *phōtinges*. They are made of what is called "lotus", a wood that occurs in Libya.[38] According to Juba the *aulos* that is made from the legs of a fawn is an invention of the Thebans.[39] Tryphon says that the ones called "ivory *auloi*" were bored by the Phoenicians.

'I realise that the *magadis* is also a stringed instrument like the *kithara*, *lyra* and *barbiton*. Euphorion, the epic poet, says in his *On the Isthmian Games*: "The people now described as performers on the *nablas*, the *pandoura* and the *sambykē* are not using any new [f] sort of instrument: for the

---

[34]   'Half-holed' (*hēmiopoi*) seems to mean 'with half the usual number of holes' (cf. *diopoi*, 'two-holed', 176f above): but no source gives a clear interpretation of the word.
       At this point the MSS continue with the text numbered 177a–182b, which is plainly out of place here, and belongs between 187b and c. All editors agree in transposing.

[35]   The MSS add 'and the smaller', which is probably an explanatory marginal note. I follow Bethe in deleting it.

[36]   All these terms classify by reference to the type of composition accompanied. On *kitharistērioi* see 176f above: on the style of performance called *lysiōdia* see 189 620e, and cf. 211b, 252e.

[37]   This quotation was presumably preceded by an attribution: it is quoted again at 196 634e, and ascribed to the lexicographer Tryphon. The quotation from Anaxandrides reappears in the same passage (presumably Tryphon quoted it), which occurs in the context of a long discussion of the instrument (or instruments) called the *magadis* (196 634c–637a).

[38]   In some classical poetry, notably Euripides (e.g. 42 *Helen* 171) the term *lōtos* is used to designate an aulos of the familiar type, not the transverse *phōtinx*. (On the *phōtinx* see 175e above with n. 20.) Pollux (IV.74) agrees with the present passage in calling the transverse pipe Libyan, and in saying that it is made of lotus wood.

[39]   Pollux (IV.75) also ascribes this instrument to the Thebans. He adds that it is called the *thēreios aulos* ('wild-beast' *aulos*), and that its external appearance is that of bronze: it was perhaps covered with a thin sheet of metal, or stained to resemble it. Bones of other creatures were also used to make *auloi*: the Scythians, for instance, according to Pollux (IV.76), used those of birds.

baromos and the *barbitos*, which Sappho and Anacreon mention, and the *magadis* and the *trigōna* and the *sambykai* are ancient. In Mitylene, at any rate, one of the Muses was depicted by Lesbothemis holding a *sambykē*."[40] Aristoxenus describes as "alien instruments" the *phoenix*, the *pēktis*, the *magadis*, the *sambykē*, the *trigōnon*, the *klepsiambos*, the *skindapsos*, and what is called the *enneachordon*.[41] Plato says in Book III of the *Republic* [**149** 399c]: " 'In that case,' I said, 'we shall have no need of a multiplicity of strings or an assemblage of all the *harmoniai* in our songs and melodies.' 'I think not,' he said. [183a] 'Then as to *trigōnoi* and *pēktides* and all the instruments that have many strings and all the *harmoniai* . . .' "

'The *skindapsos* is a four-stringed instrument, as the parody writer Matron says in these lines: "But they did not hang it from the peg where there was strung up the four-stringed *skindapsos* of the woman without a distaff." Theopompus, the Colophonian writer of epic, mentions it too in the poem entitled *Harmation*: "Brandishing in his hands a great *lyra*-like *skindapsos*, [b] wrought of osier from a thriving willow tree." And Anaxilas in *The Lyra-Maker*: "I have made *barbitoi*, *trichordoi*,[42] *pēktides*, *kitharai*, *lyrai* and *skindapsoi*."

'Sopater the parody writer, in the piece called *Mystacus' Servant*, says that the *pēktis* is two-stringed: here are his words: "The two-stringed *pēktis*, exulting in a foreign Muse, [c] has somehow been set in your hand."[43] *Pariambides* are mentioned by Epicharmus in his *Periallus*: "Semele dances, and a clever musician pipes for them *periambides* to the *kithara*: and she is delighted as she hears the close-packed clatterings."[44]

---

40 *Magadis*: see **196** 634c–637a. *Barbiton*: see n. 19 above. *Nablas*: 175c with n. 14 above. *Pandoura*: n. 23 above and 183f–184a below. *Sambykē*: **196** 633f–634b. *Trigōnon*: 175e with n. 17 above.

41 *Phoenix*: see **168** ps.-Ar. *Probs.* XIX.14 and **196** Ath. 637a–b. *Pēktis*: see n. 21 above. *Klepsiambos*: see **196** 636b. Of the *skindapsos* little is known beyond what is said at 183a–b below: Hesychius says that the '*kindapsos*' is an instrument like the *kithara*, which agrees fairly well with Theopompus' epithet '*lyra*-like' in our passage. In non-musical usage the word means 'nonsense', or is sometimes the equivalent of the English 'a what's-its-name'. Both the *skindapsos* and the *enneachordon* (of which all we know is what its name tells us, that it had nine strings) are said to have become obsolete by the second century (**196** 636f).

42 The *trichordos* ('three-stringed') is probably the *pandoura*: see n. 23 above.

43 The *pēktis* is almost always associated with the 'many-stringed' instruments of the harp family (see n. 21 above): hence this description is puzzling. On the strength of its identification by some authors with the *magadis* (**196** 635b and e), it has been conjectured that the epithet means 'double-stringed', that is, having strings tuned in pairs an octave apart, as the *magadis* perhaps had. But the matter is quite uncertain; and it is of course possible that the word '*pēktis*', like many other terms used to designate instruments, had a variety of different applications.

44 *Pariambides* are not instruments, but as the quotation suggests, they are pieces of music in which the *aulos* accompanied the *kithara*. Their description by Pollux (IV.81) as *nomoi kitharistērioi* (cf. n. 30 above) shows that the *kithara* was conceived as the main instrument, the *aulos* as accompanist. Photius s.v. *pariambides* describes them as *kitharōdikoi nomoi*, implying that the *aulos* accompanied a musician who sang while playing the *kithara*.

'The *psaltērion*, according to Juba, was filled up with strings by Alexandros of Cythera:[45] when he was old he lived in Ephesus, and he dedicated this invention, as the cleverest product of his skill, in the temple of Artemis. Juba also mentions the *lyrophoenix* and [d] the *epigoneion*, which has now been remodelled into an upright *psaltērion*, but retains the name of its inventor. Epigonus was an Ambraciot by birth, a Sicyonian by adoption: he was an expert musician, and plucked the strings by hand without a plectrum.[46]

'With all the instruments I have mentioned, then, as well as *auloi*, the Alexandrians are familiar and accomplished, and I will give you a demonstration with any of them on which you would like me to be tested, though there are many more expert musicians than I [e] in my country. My fellow countryman Alexandros, who died recently, gave a public performance on the instrument called the *trigōnos*, and made all the Romans so music-mad that most of them can repeat the tunes he played. Sophocles mentions this *trigōnos* too, in his *Mysians*: "The Phrygian *trigōnos* sounds aloud, and in answer the accompanying strings of the Lydian *pēktis* sing."[47] He mentions it in his *Thamyris* as well. So does Aristophanes in the *Daitaleis* [f] and Theopompus in the *Penelope*. In the *Dyers* Eupolis says: "Who finely plays the *tympanon* and plucks *trigōnoi*."[48]

'The instrument called the *pandoura* is mentioned by Euphorion, as I have said, and by Protagorides in Book II of his *On the Festivals at Daphne*. The

---

[45]   That is, it became a 'many-stringed' instrument. The name *psaltērion* simply means 'instrument that is plucked' (without a plectrum), and is often the generic term for instruments of the harp family in general, though sometimes it seems to designate a particular type (e.g. Pollux IV.59). The relations between the various special forms was in any case a matter of dispute in Hellenistic times (see e.g. **196** 635c–636c). It is suggested at **196** 635c that harp-like instruments with many strings were unknown in Greece until after the time of Anacreon. This is unlikely: but if Alexandros of Cythera is close in date to Epigonus, mentioned just below, we have a hint of some new attention being paid to these devices towards the end of the sixth century: see next note.

[46]   On the *lyrophoenix* see n. 18 above. The *epigoneion* was a many-stringed instrument (according to Pollux IV.59 it had forty strings). The present text indicates that it was not originally 'upright': it was therefore presumably held flat, perhaps across the knees of the seated player (which gives an alternative explanation for its name, from the preposition *epi*, 'on', and *gony*, 'knee'). Sachs (*Hist. Mus. Instr.* 137) conjectures that it was a form of zither, an instrument whose strings lay across a flat sound-board.

    Epigonus (sixth century) is known as an influential musician with a following or 'school' of his own. He seems to have been one of the earliest musical theorists, as well as a practical performer (Aristox. *El. Harm.* 3.23–4). His 'school' is mentioned at **196** 637f as having been the first to adopt the colourful style of string-playing called *enaulos kitharisis* (see n. 205 below), and he is associated with others of the period who created innovations in styles of performance on the *kithara*. These innovations (described at **196** 637f–638a) may have been linked with a growing interest in the possibilities of many-stringed instruments, and led naturally to the addition of extra strings to the *kithara* itself, for which composers in the fifth century are well known.

[47]   See **196** 635c, where the lines are quoted again: there the context gives some help with the notion of 'answering' that is involved.

[48]   The text of this quotation is uncertain.

Pythagoras who wrote about the Red Sea says that the Troglodytes [184a] make the *pandoura* from the mangrove that grows in the sea.

'Horns and *salpinges*[49] are inventions of the Etruscans. Metrodorus of Chios in his *Trojan History* says that Marsyas invented the *syrinx* and played it at Celaenae, whereas his predecessors had played a *syrinx* with one reed only. Euphorion the epic poet, in his *On Song-Writers*, says that Hermes invented the single-reeded *syrinx* (though some say, he tells us, that it was Seuthes and Rhonaces the Maedi), that Silenus invented the many-reeded *syrinx*, and Marsyas the wax-bound kind.[50]

'All this comes to you, [b] word-hunter Ulpianus, from us Alexandrians, the people dedicated to the *monauloi*. You do not realise that Menecles, who wrote the *History of Barca*, and Andron of Alexandria in his *Chronicles*, say that the Alexandrians were the educators of all Greeks and foreigners at a time when the institution of a rounded education[51] was in decline because of the continual upheavals that took place in the period of the successors of Alexander. Education as a whole began to look up again, then, in the time of [c] the seventh Ptolemy to rule Egypt, the one aptly named "Evil-doer" by the Alexandrians. For he murdered many of the Alexandrians, and sent more than a few into exile, filling the islands and cities with men who had grown up with his brother – men of letters, philosophers, geometers, musicians, painters, trainers, doctors, and many other skilled persons. Their poverty drove them to teach what they knew, and many distinguished men were instructed by them.

[d] 'But in the old days music was a matter of concern to all the Greeks: hence there was great enthusiasm even for the art of the *aulos* [cf. e.g. 161 Ar. *Pol.* 1341a–b]. Chamaeleon of Heraclea, at any rate, says that all the Spartans and Thebans learned to play the *aulos*, as did the people of Heraclea in Pontus in his own time, and the most eminent of the Athenians as well, Callias the son of Hipponicus and Critias the son of Callaeschrus. Douris, in his work on Euripides and Sophocles, says that Alcibiades learnt *aulos*-playing not just from any common teacher, but from Pronomus, a man who achieved the highest reputation.[52] Aristoxenus says that [e] Epaminondas of

49 Horns, *kerata*, were simple trumpet-like instruments made from the horns of animals. Their acoustic properties are discussed by Aristotle, *De Audib.* 802a–b = Porph. *Comm.* 71.32 ff. Like the *salpinx*, they were used as instruments of summons in war, at the games, and so on, not to make music. A hint of an exception in the case of the *salpinx* is suggested by Aristotle, ibid. 803a = Porph. *Comm.* 74.4–6: 'that is why everyone, when engaging in revelry, relaxes the tension of the breath in the *salpinx*, so as to make the sound as gentle as possible.'

50 On the two kinds of *syrinx*, many-reeded and single-reeded, and for the sense of 'wax-bound' (*kērodetos*), see especially 175 ps.-Ar. *Probs.* xix.23 with notes, and cf. also 174b with n. 3 above.

51 'Rounded education' translates *enkyklios paideia*, a common semi-technical expression for the system of general education proper to a citizen, distinguished from professional training.

52 Pronomus of Thebes was a noted fifth-century aulete: Pausanias (ix.12.5) tells of the erection of a statue in his honour, and adds a comment on the expressiveness of his facial and bodily movements, which seem to have been much admired. (Such move-

Thebes too learnt to play the *aulos* from Olympiodorus and Orthagoras. Many of the Pythagoreans also cultivated the art of the *aulos*, Euphranor, for example, and Archytas and Philolaus, and a good many others.[53] Euphranor even left a treatise on *auloi*. And Aristophanes in the *Daitaleis* displays clearly the enthusiasm that the subject attracted when he says: "When practice on *auloi* and *lyrai* has worn me out, you tell me to dig?" [f] And Phrynichus in the *Ephialtes*: "Surely you never taught this man to play the *kithara* and the *aulos*?" Epicharmus in the *Muses* says that even Athena played the *enhoplios*[54] on the *auloi* for the Dioscuri.

'Ion, in his *Phoenix* or *Caeneus*, calls the *aulos* a cock, in these words: [185a] "An *aulos*-cock cried out a Lydian hymn." And in his *Phrouroi* he calls the cock an Idaean *syrinx*, as follows: "The *syrinx*, an Idaean cock, rushes forward."[55] The same Ion says, in his *Second Phoenix*, "Playing a loud, deep-pitched *aulos* in running rhythm", referring in this way to the Phrygian kind. For it is deep in pitch; and they therefore fit to it a horn, analogous to the bell of a *salpinx*.'[56]

189 *Deipnosophistae* 616e–620f

There were often many entertainments, of various different sorts, and since a great many things were said about them I shall leave out the speakers' names and simply record the substance.

---

ments are of course to be distinguished from the involuntary facial distortions that a good aulete was supposed to avoid, Pollux IV.68–9, cf. 189 616e–617a.) He was associated with the development of techniques of *aulos*-playing and construction that greatly increased their melodic versatility (cf. 195 631e). He is depicted in performance on the famous 'Pronomus Vase', reproduced in e.g. Besseler *et al.* Pl. 35, Charbonneaux, Pl. 314. The Theban school of auletes, to which the musicians mentioned in the next sentence also belong, was the foremost in Greece during the later fifth century and much of the fourth: cf. 163 Theophrastus, *Hist. Plant.* IV.11.4, 187 ps.-Plut. 1138a–b, Plin. *Nat. Hist.* XVI.170, and Pollux IV.80, which mentions a certain Diodorus of Thebes, who 'made the *aulos* many-holed, making lateral pathways for the breath'.

53 For a vehemently contrary view in the Pythagorean tradition see Arist. Quint. 91.27–92.3.

54 *Enhoplios* means 'armed', 'under arms', hence 'martial'. In musical references it appears with the nouns *nomos*, *melos*, and most commonly *rhythmos*, as at e.g. Xen. *Anab.* VI.1.11, 131 Aristoph. *Clouds* 651, 149 Plato, *Rep.* 400b (see n. 36 to this last passage for the structure of the rhythm). Dio Chrys. (11.61) says that *enhoplios orchēsis* was native to Crete: Arist. Quint. (63.15–18) associates dancing *enhoplia*, evidently meaning no more than 'war-dances', with the savage Thracians and Celts. *Enhoplia melē* are attributed to the Spartans at 194 630f. The present reference to the Dioscuri (Castor and Pollux) brings to mind the Spartan 'Melody of Castor' mentioned at 187 ps.-Plut. 1140c: see note ad loc.

55 Retaining the MSS *prothei*. The quotation might possibly mean, as the introductory sentence suggests, 'The cock, the Idaean *syrinx*, rushes forward.'

56 The reference is to what is elsewhere sometimes called the *elymos aulos*: see n. 31 above.

On the subject of *auloi*, then, someone said that Melanippides had ridiculed *aulos*-playing splendidly in his *Marsyas*, when he said of Athena: 'Athena threw the instruments from her holy hand and said "Away, shameful things, defilers of my body! [616f] I do not give myself to ugliness."'[57] Someone else responded by saying 'But Telestes of Selinus hit back at Melanippides in his *Argo*: speaking of Athena he said: "When the clever goddess had picked up the clever instrument in the mountain thickets, I cannot believe in my mind that she, divine Athena, frightened by the ugliness unpleasant to the eye, threw it away again from her hands to be a glory for Marsyas, that handclapping[58] creature born of a nymph. [617a] Why would sharp passion for love-inducing beauty have worried her, to whom Clotho had allotted virginity, marriageless and childless?" (He means that she would not have sought to avoid ugliness in her appearance because of her virginity.) He goes on: "But this is an empty story, unfit for choruses,[59] told by empty-talking minstrels, which has flown to Greece, an envious insult to a clever art among men." Afterwards he extols the art of the *aulos*, saying: "Which the uplifted breath of the noble goddess, with the swiftness of her quivering-winged hands, passed on to Dionysus to be his best helper." [b] In the *Asclepius*, too, Telestes ornately expressed the use of the *auloi* in these words: "Or the Phrygian king of beauteous-breathing, holy *auloi*, who first fitted together the quivering Lydian *nomos*, rival to the Dorian Muse, intertwining a well-winged breeze on his reeds with the voice of his breath."[60]

'But Pratinas of Phlius, when auletes and dancers who performed for hire took over the dance-floors,[61] took offence at the way the auletes failed to play accompaniments for the choruses, [c] as had been traditional, but the choruses, instead, sang accompaniments to the auletes. Pratinas showed his anger against the people who did this in the following *hyporchēma*.

'"What is this hubbub? What are these dances? What loud-clattering arrogance has come upon the Dionysian altar? [d] Mine, mine is Bromios: it is I who must cry aloud, I who must make a clatter[62] as I run across the

---

57 On Melanippides and Telestes, and the controversy that these extracts supposedly reflect, see pp. 93–4 above, and cf. 161 Ar. *Pol.* 1341b. On the facial distortions to which auletes were prone, cf. Pollux IV.68–9 and e.g. Charbonneaux, Pl. 348. Playing the *aulos* involved considerable stress on the facial muscles, which is why auletes commonly wore the strap called the *phorbeia*, to support their cheeks.

58 *Cheiroktypoi*: Meineke conjectures *choroktypoi*, 'beating [stamping] in the chorus', i.e. 'dancing'.

59 *Achoreutos*, perhaps in the sense 'an insult to music'. Cf. the tragedians' use of negations of musical terms, exemplified in 46–60.

60 The text of both quotations is uncertain. Their complex and pretentious diction is typical of late fifth-century dithyramb. The 'Phrygian king' is probably Olympus: cf. 187 ps.-Plut. 1136c, which also discusses the character of the Lydian *harmonia*. On the *aulos* in the cult of Dionysus see e.g. 61–5, cf. 161 Ar. *Pol.* 1342b.

61 The date is the early fifth century. Cf. 187 ps.-Plut. 1141c–d.

62 *Patagein*, perhaps a reference to the association between the cult of Dionysus and the use of percussion instruments. 'Bromios' is a title of Dionysus.

mountains with the Naiads, uttering like a swan a dapple-feathered melody. It is song that the Muse made queen. Let the *aulos* dance after it, since it is a servant: it should be content to be commander only in the revel and the fist-fights of young drunks [e] quarrelling at the door.[63] Batter the one that has a mottled toad's breath![64] Burn that spittle-wasting reed with its deep-chattering mouth and its step that wrecks tune and rhythm, a menial whose body is formed with a drill. [f] Look and see! This is the tossing of right hand and foot that is yours, dithyramb-triumphing, ivy-wreathed lord! Listen to my Dorian dance and song.''[65]

On the subject of the conjunction of *auloi* with *lyra*, since their *synaulia* by itself had often enchanted us,[66] Ephippus in *Goods for Sale* says: [618a] 'After all, my boy, music on *auloi* and *lyra* combines in our frivolities. For when a man tunes his style to fit those who are with him, then it is that the greatest delight is found.'[67] What *synaulia* involves is made clear by Semus of Delos in Book v of his *Delian History*. He writes as follows: 'Since most people do not know what *synaulia* is, I must explain. It was a sort of contest in concord, a correspondence of *aulos* and rhythm, without a singer adding words.'[68] [b] Antiphanes in *The Aulete*, with urbane wit, makes its character clear when he says:

A. Tell me, what sort of thing is that *synaulia* he was going on about?[69]
B. They understand it by continually having learned it from one another.[70]

So take the *auloi*, you and this girl, and go through whatever you like to

63 For the *aulos* in just this sort of context see Plato, *Symp.* 212c.
64 'Toad's' translates *phryneou*, which has been interpreted as a sneer at the tragedian Phrynichus. But we know nothing of Phrynichus that would connect him with the auletic excesses criticised here.
65 The contrast is certainly with Phrygian music, the special province of the *aulos* and of the ecstatic rituals of Dionysus. Pratinas seems to be appealing to a statelier, more solemn dithyrambic tradition: in this he appears to be in accord with Lasus of Hermione, and on the opposite side of the fence to Pindar, who is in this respect a 'progressive'. See 29 Pindar, fr. 61.
66 *Synaulia* is properly the combined music of several *auloi* played together: Pollux (iv.83) says that such music was performed at Athens during the Panathenaia. (Cf. the depiction of a duo of auletes in Besseler *et al.* Pl. 44.) But it may also refer to any 'concerted' music for instruments without the voice, e.g. Plato, *Laws* 765b. If, as seems likely, this clause is part of the quotation from Ephippus, it is a clear case where the word's reference is not to *auloi* only. See also the quotation from Semus below, and for related practices cf. nn. 30 and 44 above.
67 'Tunes his style', *synarmosēi . . . ton tropon*: a pun on the tuning of one instrument to accord with another. Cf. 144 Xen. *Symp.* 3.1, which is also another instance of the conjunction of *aulos* and *lyra*.
68 The singular *aulou* strongly suggests that this is not concerned with the conjunction of several *auloi*. Lucian (*Salt.* 16) refers to dancing to the *aulos* and *lyra* together on the island of Delos, and one might suspect that the expression 'of rhythm' (*rhyth-mou*) has somehow replaced 'of the *lyra*' (*lyras*) in the present text. But perhaps the *aulos* is treated as providing melody, the *lyra* as providing rhythm: cf. 184 and 186 ps.-Ar. *Probs.* xix.43 and 49, with notes.
69 *Eide*, lit. 'he was singing'.
70 The text is corrupt and the sense obscure. I take it to mean: 'People know how to do it by continually paying attention to what their partner has played, and taking their cue from that.'

play: she will take over the sequel from you. Where the parts combine, and where they separate again, give nods together without concealment, to indicate each bit.[71]

'The poets call the *aulos* "Libyan",'[72] says Douris in the second book of his work *On Agathocles*, [c] 'because it seems that Seirites was the first discoverer of the art of the *aulos*. He was a Libyan, one of the Nomadoi, and it was also he that first played the *Mētrōa* on the *aulos*.'[73]

'The following,' says Tryphon in the second book of his *Terminology*, 'are the names of types of piece for *auloi*: *kōmos*, *boukolismos*, *gingras*, *tetrakōmos*, *epiphallos*, *choreios*, *kallinikos*, *polemikon*, *hēdykōmos*, *sikinnotyrbē*, *thyrokopikon* (which is the same as *krousithyron*), *knismos*, *mothōn*.[74] All of these were played on the *aulos* in combination with dancing.'

[71] Lit. 'When there is something common, and when again [there is something] separate, [let there be] joint nods, not *problēmata*, by which each set of things is indicated.' (*Problēmata* are 'things put forward', sometimes in the sense 'puzzles', 'problems', which might be the meaning here: but I take it to mean 'things put forward as means of concealment', as in the word's use to indicate an excuse or defence.)
The kind of performance described here is plainly different from those mentioned by Ephippus and Semus above. It seems to have affinities with the practice of 'capping' lines sung by another guest at a drinking party, as at e.g. **134** Aristoph. *Wasps* 1224 ff.

[72] The epithet is quite common, despite the pervasiveness of the contrary tradition that the *aulos* originated in Asia Minor. See particularly **42** Eurip. *Helen* 171 with note ad loc. Pollux (IV.74) calls the transverse pipe Libyan (see nn. 20 and 38 above): but it may be more to the point here that he also attributes to the Libyan 'tent-dwellers' (nomads, as the present passage says) what he calls the *hippophorbos aulos*, the *aulos* used when herding horses at pasture. 'It is made of laurel with the bark stripped off: when the pith has been extracted it makes a high-pitched sound, which carries to the horses because of its high pitch' (IV.74).

[73] The *Mētrōa* are songs sung in honour of the Mother Goddess. Most traditions treat her cult as Asiatic, and associate *Mētrōa* with the Phrygian *aulos*: see particularly **192** 626a, **187** ps.-Plut. 1137d, 1141b.

[74] The names refer to types of song-and-dance with which the *aulos* was associated. Many, like the songs listed in the next paragraph from Tryphon, are evidently of folk origin. A *kōmos* is a revel, often Dionysiac, commonly involving processional merry-making to musical accompaniment: comic and improper songs were sung. *Boukolismos* means 'cattle-tending', 'pastoral', cf. 619b below: but *boukolos* and cognate words sometimes refer to the worship of a deity in the form of a bull, including Dionysus (Aristoph. *Wasps* 10). *Gingras*, as well as being the name of a wind instrument, is the Phoenician name for Adonis (**188** 174f–175a). *Tetrakōmos* means 'four-*kōmos*'. *Epiphallos* means 'to [or 'on'] the phallos', 'phallic': cf. the practices recorded at **191** 622b–c. *Choreios* means 'of the chorus'. *Kallinikos* means 'splendidly victorious', a traditional epithet of an athletic victor, found several times in Pindar, and dating as far back as Archilochus (fr. 119, cf. Pindar, *Ol.* 9.1–4 with schol.). *Polemikon* is 'of war': *hēdykōmos* is 'sweet-*kōmos*'. *Sikinnotyrbē*: the *sikinnis* was a dance performed by satyrs in the satyr drama (**194** 630b, cf. **67** Eurip. *Cyclops* 37, Lucian, *Salt.* 22); *tyrbē* means 'riot', 'confusion', and is used of Dionysiac dancing at Paus. II.24.6. *Thyrokopikon* and *krousithyron* both mean 'knock at the door': the verb *thyrokopein* can mean 'break down a door', and may be linked with drunkenness (Aristoph. *Wasps* 1254, cf. 617d above): LSJ, however, interpret *krousithyron* as meaning 'serenade'. *Knismos* means 'itching' or 'tickling'. *Mothōn* was the word used in Sparta for a Helot boy fostered in a Spartan home: in Athens it meant 'impudent person', 'upstart', and was also the name of a vulgar dance (Aristoph. *Knights* 697, Pollux IV.101, where it is especially linked with sailors).

[d]   Tryphon also lists the following terms attached to song. '*Himaios*, the one called the song of the mill, which they sang at the grinding: perhaps derived from *himalis*. Among the Dorians *himalis* means what is got back, the measures of wheat-flour left over.[75] The song of the loom-workers is called *ailinos*,[76] as Epicharmus relates in his *Atalantai*. The song of the wool-workers is called *ioulos*.' But Semus of Delos in his book *On Paeans* says: 'The handfuls of barley on their own they call *amalai*, but when they are collected together and a single sheaf is made out of many they called them *ouloi* or *iouloi*. And they sometimes call [e] Demeter "Chloe", sometimes "Ioulō". From Demeter's inventions they take the names *ouloi* and *iouloi*, and give them not only to the fruits, but also to the hymns to the goddess.' (These are *Dēmētrouloi* and *Kalliouloi*, and there is the line 'Send out a great sheaf, a sheaf, send out a sheaf.' But others say that this is a wool-workers' song.)[77]

The songs of nurses are called *katabaukalēseis* ['lullabies']. There was also a song for the *Eōrai*, devoted to Erigone, which they call 'The Song of the Wanderer'. Thus Aristotle says in his *Constitution of Colophon*: 'Theodorus himself later died a violent death. [f] He is said to have been a dissipated person, as is made clear by his poetry: for even now the women sing his songs at the *Eōrai*.'[78]

[619a]   The reapers' song is called *Lityersēs*.[79] There was also a song of the hired labourers who went to work in the fields, as Teleclides says in the *Amphictyons*, others sung by bath-attendants, according to Crates in *Daring Deeds*, and another by women winnowing, according to Aristophanes in the *Thesmophoriazousae*[80] and Nicochares in *Heracles the Chorus-Leader*. For people who led out the flocks there was what is called the *boukoliasmos*.[81] [b]

---

[75]   Cf. the Mytilenean mill-song recorded at Plut. *Sept. Sap.* 157d–e.
[76]   The word is the same as the name of the laments for Linus (see e.g. 7 Hom. *Il.* XVIII. 570, 31 Pindar, fr. 126, with notes, and cf. 619c below). *Linon* can mean flax or flaxen thread, and Linus may have been identified with this plant in his role as a symbol of the fertility, death and regeneration of the vegetable world.
[77]   The whole passage reflects a scholarly uncertainty about the application of the words *oulos* and *ioulos*. *Oulos*, as an adjective, is often applied to fleeces, in the sense 'woolly'. *Ioulos* commonly means 'sheaf of corn'. But various authorities give *oulos* as a synonym for this sense of *ioulos*, and both words seem to refer originally to anything fuzzy or bushy. The words *Dēmētrouloi* ('Demeter's sheaves') and *kalliouloi* ('fine sheaves') are evidently names of songs. In the line quoted, which seems to be the refrain of a working song, the words translated 'sheaf' are *oulos* twice and *ioulos* once.
[78]   The Festival of the Swings at Athens, in appeasment of the curse laid upon the maidens of Attica by Erigone, who hanged herself. See Hesych. s.v. *Alētis*, cf. Pollux IV.55, Nonnus, *Dion.* 47.34 ff. The word *eōra*, 'swing' (more commonly *aiōra*), may also mean 'noose', Soph. *O.T.* 1264.
[79]   On Lityerses see Ath. 415b. For the reapers' song named after him see also Theocr. *Idylls* 10.41 ff.
[80]   Not the extant *Thesmophoriazousae*: Aristophanes wrote a second play with the same name, which has not survived.
[81]   'Cattle-tending': cf. *boukolismos* at 618c above.

It was the Sicilian herdsman Diomus who first invented this kind: Epicharmus mentions him in *The Halcyon* and in *Odysseus Shipwrecked*. The song
sung at deaths and in mourning is called *olophyrmos*. The songs called *iouloi*
are proper to Demeter and Persephone. The song to Apollo is called *philhēlios*,[82] as Telesilla bears witness, and those to Artemis are called *oup-
ingoi*.[83] At Athens even the laws of Charondas used to be sung over the
wine,[84] as Hermippus says in the sixth book of his *Lawgivers*.

Aristophanes in his *Attic Dialect* says: '*Himaios*, a millers' song:
hymenaios, a song at weddings: [c] *ialemos*, a song in times of grief. But *linos*
and *ailinos* are sung not only in times of grief, but also "at the cheerful song
and dance", as Euripides puts it.'[85]

Clearchus, in the first book of his *Love Stories*, says that there is a song
called *nomios* ['pastoral'] which comes from Eriphanis. He writes as
follows. 'Eriphanis was a song-composer who fell in love with Menalcas
when he was hunting, and hunted him, in pursuit of her desires. In her
walkings and wanderings she passed through all the mountain copses,
making a mere legend of the famous travels of Io, so that not only the people
most oustanding for their harshness, [d] but even the cruellest of wild beasts
wept in sympathy with her affliction, when they perceived her passionate
hopes. So she composed a song, and when she had composed it she wandered
in the wilderness, so they say, crying aloud and singing what is called the
nomion, in which are the words "The oaks are high, Menalcas."'

Aristoxenus, in Book IV of his *On Music*, says: 'In the old days the women
sang a song called *Calycē*. It was Stesichorus' composition, in which a girl
named Calyce, who loved the young Euathlus, prays modestly to Aphrodite
that she may be married to him. [e] When the young man rejected her, she
threw herself from a cliff. This misfortune happened at Leucas. The poet has
represented the maiden's character as chaste: she is not willing to come
together with the young man on just any terms, but prays that she may
become Euathlus' lawful wife, if she can, but if that is impossible, that she
may be set free from life.' In his *Summary Notes* Aristoxenus says: 'Iphiclus
rejected Harpalyce, who loved him. She died; and girls have a song-
competition devoted to her, which is called *Harpalycē*.'

[f]   In the first book of his *On Heracleia*, Nymphis, while discussing the
Mariandynians, says: 'In the same way one may take note of some of the
songs they sing at a festival native to their country, in which they invoke one

---

[82]   Apollo is the sun god, and *philhēlios* means 'sun-lover'.
[83]   Callimachus, *Hymn to Artemis* 204 gives 'Oupis' as a name of Artemis. Songs called
       oupingoi are mentioned in this connection at Pollux 1.38 and Didymus in the schol. to
       Apoll. Rhod. 1.972, where they are said to have been sung at Troezen.
[84]   This claim is not made elsewhere for Athens: cf. 178 ps.-Ar. *Probs*. XIX.28, where it
       would have been apposite. According to Martianus Capella IX.926 the practice was
       common in Greek cities, but in general the evidence for it is thin.
[85]   Cf. n. 76 above. The Euripidean reference is to *Heracles* 348–51.

of the men of olden times, addressing him as Bormus. They say that he was the son of [620a] an eminent and wealthy man, and that in beauty and in the full bloom of his perfection he far surpassed all others. When he was in charge of work on his own property, and wanted to give the reapers some water to drink, he went to fetch water and disappeared. The folk of the countryside searched for him, singing a lament and an invocation of his name, and they all continue to perform it to this day. The person that the Egyptians call Maneros is similar.'[86]

There was no lack of *rhapsōdoi* at our drinking-parties, either. [b] For Larensius delighted in Homer's poems as no single other person ever did, so that he made Casander, once ruler of Macedonia, seem negligible. About the latter Carystius says in his *Historical Notes* that he loved Homer so much that he had most of the epics on the tip of his tongue, and wrote out the *Iliad* and the *Odyssey* with his own hand. The fact that *rhapsōdoi* were called *Homēristai* is recorded by Aristocles in his *On Choruses*, though the people called *Homēristai* nowadays were first introduced into the theatres by Demetrius of Phalerum. [c] Chamaeleon, in his *On Stesichorus*, says that not only used the works of Homer to be sung,[87] but so did those of Hesiod and Archilochus, and those of Mimnermus and Phocylides as well. Clearchus in the first book of his *Enigmas* says: 'Simonides of Zacynthus used to sit on a seat in the theatres and recite as *rhapsōdos* the poems of Archilochus.' Lysanias, in the first book of his *Iambic Poets*, says that the *rhapsōdos* Mnasion used to perform[88] some of Simonides' iambic pieces in the public shows. [d] Cleomenes the *rhapsōdos* recited Empedocles' *Purifications* at Olympia, according to Dicaearchus in *The Olympic Festival*. Jason, in the third book of his *Alexander's Divine Honours*, says that the comedy-singer Hegesias performed the works of Hesiod,[89] and Hermophantus those of Homer, in the great theatre at Alexandria.

There were also continually presented to us the people called *hilarōdoi*, whom some people nowadays call *simōdoi*, as Aristocles says in the first book of his *On Choruses*, because Simus of Magnesia was more accomplished than all other composers of *hilarōdia*.[90] [e] Aristocles in his *On Music*

---

[86] The name Bormus may perhaps be related to Dionysus' title 'Bromios'. For the story cf. the tale of Hylas in Theocr. *Idylls* 13. Maneros is identified with Linus by Herodotus (II.79), and by many later authorities. Herodotus says that equivalent stories and songs occurred in many countries: no doubt that of Bormus was one such. On Mariandynian laments cf. 37 Aesch. *Persae* 937.

[87] By contrast with the spoken recitations of the *rhapsōdoi*. Cf. 187 ps.-Plut. 1132c, 1133c.

[88] *Hypokrinesthai*, suggesting acting as well as recitation: the same word is used of Hegesias below.

[89] The MSS have Herodotus' name for Hesiod's, which can scarcely be right. The conjecture is Valckenaer's: others have been suggested.

[90] The discussion of *hilarōdoi* and related kinds of performance runs from here to 622d. For most of them the present passage is our best authority. Some of the types of performance mentioned are certainly very old, and have their origin in religious folk-rituals to do with fertility: see the discussions in Pickard-Cambridge, *D.T.C.*

mentions the following as well: '*Magōdos*: he is the same as the *lysiōdos*.' But Aristoxenus says that a man who acts both male and female characters is called a *magōdos*, while a man who acts female characters in a man's clothes is called a *lysiōdos*. They sing the same songs, however, and everything else about them is alike.[91] The *Iōnicologos* performs the so-called 'Ionic' songs of Sotades and his predecessors, Alexander of Aetolia, Pyretus of Miletus, Alexas, and other poets of that sort. [f] He is also called a *kinaidologos*.[92]

190   *Deipnosophistae* 621b–d

The performer called the *hilarōdos* is more respectable than poets like these, for he does not make lewd gestures. He dresses in a man's white costume and wears a golden crown, and in the old days he wore sandals, according to Aristocles, but nowadays he wears boots. The person who plays the stringed instrument[93] for him may be male or female, as may the accompanist for the *aulōdos*. The *hilarōdos* and the *aulōdos* are allowed to wear a crown, [621c] but the string-player and the aulete are not. The performer called the *mag-ōdos* has *tympana* and *kymbala* ['cymbals'], and all his clothes are women's: he makes lewd gestures and commits every sort of impropriety, sometimes acting the characters of women and adulterers and pimps, sometimes that of a drunk man going to a revel to meet his lover. Aristoxenus says that *hilar-ōdia*, which is solemn, is derived from tragedy, while *magōdia* is derived from comedy. [d] But though the *magōdoi* often took their situations from comedy, they acted them out with plot and organisation of their own devising. *Magōdia* got its name from its performance of as it were 'magical' verses, and its exhibition of powers belonging to magic potions.[94]

191   *Deipnosophistae* 622a–d

Semus of Delos in his *On Paeans* says: [622b] 'The so-called *autokabdaloi* ["improvisers"] went through their utterances standing, wreathed with ivy.'

Ch. 3 Sect. 2, Webster, *G.A.L.* Ch. 3. But it appears that by the Hellenistic period they were all treated as forms of popular entertainment, related to the mime, and perhaps roughly analogous to 'music hall': cf. Dio Chrys. *Or.* 32. *Hilarōdia* means 'joy song': the nature of the genre is explained at **190** 621b. Most MSS have 'Sēmus' for 'Simus', and some have *sēmōdoi* for *simōdoi*: but the term may refer to satyrs, sometimes called *simoi*, 'snub-nosed'.

[91]   On *lysiōdia* cf. 211b, 252e. According to Eust. ad *Od.* xxiii.134, the lysiodist had a male mask. The *lysiōdikos aulos* is mentioned at **188** 182c: *magōdia* is further discussed at **190** 621c–d.

[92]   The Ionians were notorious for licentiousness. Sotades, a tale about whom is given in 620f–621b, omitted here, was a notorious Alexandrian writer of scurrilous mimes and satires, noted for his outrageous obscenity. *Kinaidologos* means 'sodomy-talker'.

[93]   *Psallei*, suggesting an instrument plucked with the fingers, not struck with a plectrum.

[94]   *Pharmaka*, 'drugs'. The reference might conceivably be to their power of holding an audience 'spell-bound', but more probably derives from the origins of the genre in more or less magical forms of ritual, now wholly obscure.

Later they got the name '*iamboi*', as did their poems.[95] The people called
ithyphalloi,' he says, 'have a mask representing drunk men, and wear
wreaths, and have multicoloured cuffs: they wear white-striped tunics and
are wrapped around with a Tarentine apron, covering them down to the
ankles. They come through the doorway in silence, and then, when they have
reached the middle of the dancing-floor they turn to the audience and declaim: [c] "Stand back! Stand back! Make a wide way for the god! For the
god, erect and swollen, desires to go through your midst!" But the *phallo-
phoroi*,' he says, 'carry no mask, but tie round their heads a hat made of
thyme and holly, and put on top of this a wreath, bushy with violets and ivy.
They wrap cloaks around themselves and enter, some by the side entrance
and some by the centre doors, stepping in rhythm and declaiming: "Bacchus,
to you we sing this music of praise, pouring a simple rhythm to a varied
melody: [d] it is new, most virginal, used not at all in songs there have been
before: the hymn we are beginning is undiluted."[96] Then they used to run
forward and make fun of anyone they picked on, and carried on their performance standing still. But the phallus-carrier walked straight on, covered
in soot.'

192   *Deipnosophistae* 623d–626d

> Amoebus, a *kitharōdos*, has arrived at the party, and has been engaged in
> audible repartee with the cook outside the dining-room.

His words were greeted with loud applause, and everyone with one accord
shouted for him to come in. In he came, and when he had had a drink he took
up his *kithara* and delighted us so much that we were all astonished at his
swift and skilful playing, and at the tunefulness of his voice. To me, indeed,
he seems no less a performer than the Amoebus of old times, who settled in
Athens, according to Aristeas in his book *On Kitharōdoi*, and lived near the
theatre, and whenever he came out to sing was paid an Attic talent a day.[97]
[623e]   These were the things that some people said about music: others said
other things in our daily discussions, but all of them spoke in praise of this
amusement. Now Masurius is an excellent and clever man on every subject
(for he is second to none as an expositor of laws: he devotes himself unceas-
ingly to music, and even plays instruments), and this is what he said.
'The comic poet Eupolis, my friends, says "Music is a deep and
complicated thing"; and it is always offering new discoveries for those who
can grasp them. [f] That is why Anaxilas says in his *Hyacinthus*: "Music, like
Libya, by the gods, gives birth to some new creature every year." According

---

[95]   Probably reflecting the sense of *iambizein* 'to abuse' or 'to satirise'.
[96]   This seems to mean 'not weakened by having been spread thin over many past
performances': alternatively, perhaps, 'not plagiarised'.
[97]   Amoebus belongs to the third century: he is mentioned by Plutarch *De Virt. Mor.*
443a as a contemporary of the Stoic philosopher Zeno of Citium.

to the *Kitharōdos* of Theophilus, "Music is a great and secure treasure, good people, for all men of learning and education." For it is a fact that it educates characters, and calms people of turbulent disposition[98] and those whose thoughts are wayward. Thus Cleinias the Pythagorean, [624a] as Chamaeleon of Pontus relates, a man outstanding in his manner of life and character, used always to take up his *lyra* and play on it whenever he was vexed by anger. When people asked him why, he would say "I am calming myself." Homer's Achilles, too, calmed himself with the *kithara*,[99] the only thing that Homer allows him from the spoils seized from Eëtion, and which had the power to subdue his fieriness. In the *Iliad* he is the only one who uses music in this way; but Theophrastus in his *On Inspiration* recorded that music even cures diseases, [b] saying that sufferers from sciatica were permanently freed from it if someone played the *aulos*[100] over the place in the Phrygian *harmonia*. It was the Phrygians who first invented this *harmonia* and performed in it. That is why even among the Greeks auletes have Phrygian names, suitable for slaves. Examples are Sambas, Adon and Telos, mentioned by Alcman, and Cion, Codalos and Babys, mentioned by Hipponax: from Babys is derived the saying "Babys' *aulos*-playing gets worse", said of those whose playing on the *aulos* is always deteriorating. Aristoxenus ascribes its invention to Hyagnis the Phrygian.[101]

[c] 'But Heraclides of Pontus, in the third book of his *On Music*,[102] says that Phrygian should not even be called a *harmonia*, and no more should Lydian. There are, he says, three *harmoniai*, since there are three races of Greeks: Dorians, Aeolians and Ionians. There is no little difference between the characters of these races. The Spartans preserve more completely than the other Dorians the ways of their forefathers, and the Thessalians (it being they who laid for the Aeolians the foundation of their race) have [d] always practised virtually the same way of life: but of the Ionians the great majority have altered, because they adapted themselves to whichever foreigners were ruling them at the time. Thus they called the pattern of melody[103] that the

---

98   *Thymoeideis*: the reference is to what is known in Plato's classification as the 'spirited' part of the human personality (e.g. *Rep.* 440 ff).

99   4 *Il.* IX.185 ff. Homer, of course, calls the instrument a *phorminx*.

100   'Played the *aulos*' represents *kataulein*, a word with magical connotations: cf. 112 Eurip. *Heracles* 871, 151 Plato, *Rep.* 411a, *Laws* 790e. A comparable formation is *kataidein*, 'to sing magical incantations', e.g. 116 Eurip. *I.T.* 1337. The medical efficacy of the *aulos* was apparently reported as a common belief by Theophrastus, not as something to which he himself subscribed (see Gell. IV.13).

101   On the Phrygian origins of the art of the *aulos* see e.g. 187 ps.-Plut. 1132f, 1133d–f.

102   For an illuminating discussion of this difficult passage see Winnington-Ingram, *Mode in Ancient Greek Music* 13–14, 18–20, 60. It remains uncertain how far Heraclides' account is based on genuine musical knowledge, and how far it is shaped by a chauvinistic determination to exclude anything that was not thoroughly Greek. On the *harmoniai* see Ch. 10, Appendix A.

103   'Pattern' represents *agōgē*, more literally 'course'. The *harmoniai* are treated as theoretical abstractions from melodic sequences occurring in actual tunes characteristic of this or that race, rather than as scalar structures consciously adopted by the musicians themselves to form a predetermined framework for their melodies.

Dorians used the Dorian *harmonia*, and they called the one that the Aeolians sang the Aeolian *harmonia*; and Iastian was their name for the third *harmonia*, which they heard the Ionians sing.

'The Dorian *harmonia* displays manliness and dignity, and is neither languid nor cheerful, but stern and intense, and neither elaborate [e] nor various in style. The character of the Aeolians contains arrogance and weightiness, even boastfulness: these traits conform to their practice of horse-rearing, and the way they receive strangers. Their character is not given to wickedness, however, but is lofty and bold. That is why their love of drinking, their erotic proclivities, and the general relaxation of their way of life are quite in keeping with them; and it is also why they have the character of what is called the Hypodorian *harmonia*. For it is this one, so Heraclides says, that they used to call Aeolian, as Lasus of Hermione does in his *Hymn to Demeter of Hermione*. These are his words: "I sing Demeter, and Kore wife of great Hades, [f] raising a sweet-crying hymn in the deep-resounding Aeolian *harmonia*." Everyone sings this to a Hypodorian melody.[104] Hence, since the melody is Hypodorian, it is only natural for Lasus to say that the *harmonia* is Aeolian. Pratinas, too, says somewhere: "Do not pursue the tense, nor the relaxed Iastian Muse, but take the middle field and Aeolise in your melody."[105] And in the sequel he says, more straightforwardly: [625a] "The Aeolian *harmonia* is the song that suits everyone who is boisterous."

'In earlier times, then, as I said, they called this *harmonia* Aeolian, but later Hypodorian, believing, so some people say, that in *auloi* it was set at a lower pitch than the Dorian *harmonia*.[106] But it is my opinion that they noticed the weightiness and the sham nobility in the character of this *harmonia*, and thought of it not as Dorian, but as resembling Dorian in some way. Hence they called it Hypodorian, just as we speak of what resembles white as "whitish", and what is not sweet but nearly so as "sweetish". In the same way they also called what is not quite Dorian "Hypodorian".[107]

[b]   'Next let us investigate the character of the Milesians, the one that the Ionians obscurely display.[108] With their fine, fit bodies they have a swag-

---

[104]   The text has been doubted, but unnecessarily. The construction is: 'everyone sings these things Hypodorian as to their melody', the expression 'sings them Hypodorian' being comparable to 'sings them loud'. On the Hypodorian *harmonia* see **187** ps.-Plut. 1137a n. 121.

[105]   'Tense' could be taken, like 'relaxed', with 'Iastian', indicating the existence of both a *syntonos* and an *aneimenē* version of the Ionian *harmonia* (cf. Plato's *syntonos* and *chalara* versions of Lydian, **149** *Rep.* 398e, and on the distinct characters of different kinds of Ionian 625b–c below). Alternatively, the 'tense' Muse is the Dorian: certainly Heraclides wishes to understand it so.

[106]   One of the root meanings of *hypo* is 'under', 'below'. With this rather obscure reference to *auloi* compare Aristoxenus' use of the phrase 'Hypophrygian *aulos*' at *El. Harm.* 37.25.

[107]   The words translated 'whitish' and 'sweetish' are *hypoleukon* (*leukos* = white) and *hypoglyky* (*glykys* = sweet).

[108]   Lit. 'allow to show through', i.e., through an overlay of borrowed characteristics of other sorts (see 624d above). Heraclides treats the Milesians as the only remaining representatives of the ancestral Ionian character.

gering air, and are full of spirit: they are hard to placate, quarrelsome, giving nothing to kindliness or good cheer, and they display unfriendliness and hardness in their characters. Hence the Iastian type of *harmonia* is neither fresh nor cheerful, but severe and hard, with a not ignoble weightiness; and for that reason this *harmonia* suits tragedy well.[109] [c] But the character of the present-day Ionians is more self-indulgent, and the character of the *harmonia* is greatly changed.[110] They say that Pythermus of Teos composed drinking songs in this latter type of *harmonia*, and that because the composer was Ionian the *harmonia* was called Iastian. It is this Pythermus whom Ananius or Hipponax mentions in the *Iambics* . . .:[111] and elsewhere, as follows: "Pythermus says of gold that everything else is nothing." And Pythermus' own words are these: "Well, everything else is nothing, beside gold." On the evidence of this saying, then, it is quite plausible that Pythermus, coming as he did from those parts, composed the course[112] of his [d] melodies to harmonise with the character of the Ionians. Thus I take it that his *harmonia* was not the Iastian, but some strangely adapted pattern of *harmonia*.[113]

'One should therefore think poorly of those who are incapable of perceiving differences corresponding to kinds, but who focus on the height and depth of notes,[114] and posit a Hypermixolydian *harmonia*, and yet another above that. In fact I do not accept that even the Hyperphrygian has a special character of its own. And yet some people claim to have discovered another new *harmonia*, [e] a Hypophrygian.[115] But a *harmonia* must have a definite

---

109   It is conjectured that this old form of Ionian survived as the Hypophrygian *harmonia*, for whose character and role in tragedy see 185 ps.-Ar. *Probs*. XIX.48.
110   Hence, one must assume, Plato's attitude to this *harmonia* at 149 *Rep*. 398e.
111   The quotation is missing from the MSS.
112   *Agōgē*: cf. 624d above with n. 103.
113   Lit. 'some strange variation [or 'style', *tropos*] of a shape (*schēma*) of a *harmonia*'. The implication seems to be that the structure of intervals (*schēma*) that went to make up Pythermus' *harmonia* was an eccentric distortion of a more traditional form, presumably the ancient Ionian ('Iastian').
114   As a Platonist, Heraclides may have in mind Plato's injunctions to beware of arbitrary and unreal distinctions, and to divide things up only according to their genuine, 'natural' differentiations (e.g. *Phaedrus* 265e ff). But the comment is also strongly reminiscent of Aristoxenus, who insists that musical distinctions are not to be made on the basis of quantitative differences as such, but only in the places that correspond to perceptible differences of kind (*El. Harm*. 47.8–50.14).
115   The names Hypermixolydian, Hyperphrygian, Hypophrygian, belong to the Aristoxenian and post-Aristoxenian systems of *tonoi* ('keys'). Hypermixolydian is the highest of Aristoxenus' scheme of 13 *tonoi*, Hyperphrygian being the same *tonos* in the later system of 15. (Hence the remark about Hyperphrygian merely echoes the sense of the preceding comment.) The third *tonos* mentioned is described as 'Hypophrygian', but not as *the* Hypophrygian: this description probably means that it is of a Hypophrygian kind, and indicates the highest of the two later additions to Aristoxenus' set, called Hyperlydian, which is the Hypophrygian key repeated an octave higher. The substance of the present criticisms seems to lie in the fact that all three of the scales mentioned are effectively identical with other *tonoi* already in the system, merely raising them by an octave. Cf. Ptol. *Harm*. 58.21 ff. But the criticism

kind of character or emotion, as Locrian has:[116] this was used in the past by some of those who lived in the times of Simonides and Pindar, but later fell out of favour again.

'There are then these three *harmoniai*, as we said at the beginning, just as there are three races.[117] The Phrygian and Lydian *harmoniai* are foreign in origin, and were learnt by the Greeks from the Phrygians and Lydians who came down with Pelops [f] into the Peloponnese. Lydians came with him because Sipylus[118] was in Lydia, and Phrygians not because they share a border with Lydia, but because Tantalus was their king too. Everywhere in the Peloponnese, but especially in Sparta, you can see great mounds, which they call the tombs of the Phrygians who came with Pelops. It was from these people, then, that the Greeks learnt those *harmoniai*. That is why Telestes of Selinus says: [626a] "The first who sang a Phrygian *nomos* to the mountain mother, among the *auloi* beside the mixing-bowls of the Greeks, were the companions of Pelops: and they struck up a Lydian hymn with the shrill-sounding plucking of *pēktides*."[119]

'"It should not be accepted," says Polybius of Megalopolis [Polyb. IV. 20.5–21.9], "that music, as Ephorus asserts, was brought into use among men as a device for deception and cheating: [b] nor should it be thought merely fortuitous that the Cretans and Spartans of ancient times introduced the *aulos* and rhythm into warfare in place of the *salpinx*,[120] or that the earliest Arcadians adopted music into every aspect of their social organisation, to the extent that it was compulsory not only for children but for young men up to thirty years old to make it their constant companion, while being exceedingly strict in all other areas of their way of life. It is a fact that only among the Arcadians does the law require children, from their infancy, to become practised in singing the hymns and paeans with which each group of them celebrates their native heroes and gods, in conformity with the customs

is quite different from the tenor of Heraclides' previous remarks about *harmoniai*, and relates to a distinct form of harmonic analysis (that based on *tonoi*, 'keys', not *harmoniai* in the old sense 'structures of intervals'). It is likely that the present passage is inserted by Athenaeus from a different source.

116   Locrian seems to be the same as what Heraclides calls Aeolian and other writers Hypodorian (cf. Cleonides 198.10–13, Bacch. 309.7–9): the shift of terminology suggests that this sentence too is not from Heraclides.

117   That is, three races of Greeks: see 624c above. This reference back probably does not mark a return to the evidence of Heraclides, but introduces Athenaeus' own summing up.

118   His native city, ruled by his father Tantalus, mentioned below.

119   'Shrill-sounding': the Lydian *harmonia* was generally characterised as high in pitch. It is what Plato (149 *Rep.* 398e) calls *Syntonolydisti*: cf. 161 Ar. *Pol.* 1342b. See also 196 635c–e, which again links the Lydian *harmonia* with the high-pitched instrument called the *pēktis*. With this account of the sources of the songs to the Mother Goddess contrast that of Douris at 189 618c.

120   The Spartans marched and drilled to the *aulos*, in 'rhythm': the *salpinx* was not used to play tunes, and its calls set no rhythm.

of their forefathers.[121] After these, they learn the *nomoi* of Timotheus and Philoxenus,[122] and dance them[123] each year in the theatres [c] to the accompaniment of the auletes of Dionysus,[124] the boys in the children's contests, the young men in the men's. And throughout their whole life they make entertainments for themselves in their common gatherings not so much by employing performers brought in to be listened to, as through their own performances, requiring each other to sing in turn. In other fields of learning it is no disgrace to admit that one does not know something, but they treat refusal to sing as disgraceful. They practise *embatēria*[125] in an orderly drill, with the *aulos*; and they work hard at dances and exhibit them in the theatres each year, as a matter of communal concern and public expense.[126] [d] The ancients established these customs for them, not for the sake of luxury and excess, but because they perceived the toughness of each man's life and the sternness of their characters, which comes to them from the cold and dismal conditions which generally prevail in their country: for all men naturally grow into conformity with their environment . . .""'

193   *Deipnosophistae* 627d–629c

'This[127] is why the Spartans, the bravest of men, march to war to the *auloi*, the Cretans to the *lyra*, and the Lydians to *syringes* and *auloi*, as Herodotus relates.[128] Many foreign peoples conduct negotiations to *auloi* and the *kithara*, to soften their opponents' hearts. In Book LXVI of his *Histories* Theopompus says: [627e] "The Getae conduct negotiations holding *kitharai* and playing them." Hence it seems clear that Homer was being faithful to the old Greek way of life when he said: ". . . and the *phorminx*, which the

---

121   Polybius seems to treat the Arcadians as instantiating the ideals expressed by Plato, particularly in the *Laws*.
122   The daring and iconoclastic innovators of the fifth century have thus become the children's classics of the second, even in the most conservative of Greek societies.
123   The text of Polybius adds '*pollēi philotimiāi*', 'with a great passion for victory' (in the musical competition).
124   This has no specifically Dionysiac implications. Professional actors and musicians in the fourth century and later were called '*technitai* of Dionysus' (*technitai* meaning 'craftsmen', 'artists'), and were organised into 'guilds' (*synodoi*). A good short survey of the subject, with references, is in Michaelides, *Encyclopedia* 321–3.
125   *Embatēria* (sc. *melē*) are marching songs, also called *enhoplia* (194 630f, cf. 188 184f with n. 54), accompanied by the *aulos*. (Pollux v.82 says that the *embatērios aulos* was used to accompany *prosodia*, processionals, not necessarily of a military character.) Cf. 187 ps.-Plut. 1140c on the *Kastoreion melos*.
126   This last remark could have been made about any Greek city in the classical period: the Arcadians, in their remote area of the country, preserved customs that had become obsolete elsewhere.
127   That is, because rhythmical music inspires courage and good character: cf. 192 626a–b.
128   On the Cretans see e.g. 187 ps.-Plut. 1140c. Herodotus mentions the practices of the Lydians at 1.17.

gods made a companion to the feast",[129] implying that the art of music is useful also to people indulging in good cheer. This was the established custom, it appears, first so that those who were intent on getting drunk and filling themselves with food might have music as a cure for intemperate excess and disorder, and secondly because it softens boorishness. For it strips away gloom [f] and creates geniality and the cheerfulness that suits a free man, which is why Homer introduces the gods engaged in music, in the early part of the *Iliad*. For after their controversy over Achilles they went on to listen "to the most beautiful *phorminx*, which Apollo held, and the Muses, who sang, answering with a beautiful voice" [*Il.* 1.603–4]. For this was certain to put an end to their squabbling and quarrels, as I was saying. Most people, then, seem to introduce this science to social gatherings to promote good conduct and well-being: but the ancients also [628a] included in their customs and laws the injunction that everyone at feasts should sing hymns to the gods, so that with their aid our nobility and temperateness might be preserved. For if the songs are harmonious[130] and words concerning the gods are added to them, they add dignity to everyone's manners.

'Philochorus says that the men of old, when they poured libations, did not always sing dithyrambs:[131] when they pour libations they sing to Dionysus with wine and drunkenness, but to Apollo in calm and good order. Thus Archilochus says: "I know how to lead[132] the dithyramb, [b] the beautiful song of lord Dionysus, while my wits are thunder-struck with wine"; and Epicharmus in the *Philoctetes* says: "There is no dithyramb when you drink water."

'It is clear, then, from what has been said, that music did not originally find a place at feasts for the sake of superficial and vulgar pleasure, as some people think. But the Spartans, if they used to learn the art of music, say nothing about it: it is accepted among them, however, that they are capable of judging this art very well,[133] and they say that they have saved it from ruin three times.[134]

---

[129] The line as it occurs here is close to *Od.* XVII.270–1, slightly confused with *Od.* VIII.99.

[130] The adjective is *enharmonios*: obviously not 'enharmonic' here, perhaps simply 'fitting'. Gulick compares *enharmonia melē* at **169** ps.-Ar. *Probs.* XIX.15, but the sense there seems to be different again.

[131] Apparently here in a quite untechnical sense, meaning 'enthusiastic' songs of a Dionysiac character.

[132] *Exarxai* from *exarchein*, cognate with the noun *exarchos*. See 3 Hom. *Il.* XXIV.721 with note.

[133] This reflects **161** Ar. *Pol.* 1339b, where it is made clear that what the Spartans do not learn is the skill of performing music themselves. The proposition relates to Aristotle's own times: it is agreed, as the earlier part of this sentence implies, that in a more ancient period the Spartans did perform music, rather than relying on incoming professionals (**161** Ar. *Pol.* 1341b, cf. **188** Ath. 184d).

[134] The reference is uncertain. We have in **187** ps.-Plut. 1134b–c an account of two 'establishments' of musical order at Sparta, the first under the guidance of Terpander, the second associated with the names of Thaletas and others. Cf. also 1146b–c. But

'Music also contributes [c] to the exercise and sharpness of the intelligence: hence it is employed by every race of the Greeks, and of the foreigners who are known to us. It is well said by the school of Damon the Athenian that songs and dances are the inevitable result of a certain kind of motion in the soul: those souls that are beautiful and characteristic of free men create songs and dances of the same kind, while the opposite sort create the opposite.[135] This also explains the remark of Cleisthenes, tyrant of Sicyon,[136] a witty one, giving evidence of his educated intelligence. [d] They say that he saw one of his daughter's suitors (it was Hippoclides the Athenian) dancing in a vulgar manner, and said that he had "danced away his marriage", presumably believing that the man's soul was of the same sort too. For in both dancing and walking, elegance and orderliness are beautiful, while disorder and vulgarity are ugly.[137] This is why composers originally composed dances for free men, and used the dance figures only as expressions

we know nothing of any third 'establishment'. It is possible that the allusion is to the tales of various occasions on which composers were prevented by the Spartan authorities from using instruments with more strings than the traditional norm. The three incidents might be those connected with Terpander (Plut. *Inst. Lac.* 17), Phrynis (Plut. *Prof. Virt.* 13), and Timotheus (e.g. Paus. III.12.10, **196** Ath. 636e): this suggestion is Casaubon's.

[135] On Damon see Ch. 10, Appendix B. The connection between music and the motions of the soul is picked up and elaborated by Theophrastus (Porph. *Comm.* 61.22–4, 65.13–15) as well as by later Platonists. The last sentence might be construed with subject and object reversed: beautiful music creates beautiful souls. Both ideas are in the Damonian tradition: cf. Arist. Quint. 80.25–9. The music that a soul learns to enjoy determines its character, and its character determines what music it will create and enjoy.

[136] The story is told by Herodotus: the setting is the early sixth century. Suitors had come from all over Greece to seek the hand of Cleisthenes' daugher. They stayed in his palace for a year, during which Hippoclides emerged as the oustanding candidate. On the day when Cleisthenes was to declare his choice he gave a great banquet. The next part of the tale is worth quoting in full for the sake of its musical references.
193(a)   Herodotus, *Histories* VI.129
When they had finished dinner, the suitors competed before the company in music and in speaking. As the drinking went on, Hippoclides, who was proving much superior to the others, told the aulete to play an *emmeleia* [the tune of a serious dance proper to tragedy: see **194** Ath. 630e, cf. e.g. Plato, *Laws* 816b], and when the aulete complied, he danced to it. As far as he was concerned, his dancing was delightful, but Cleisthenes, who was watching, began to have misgivings about the whole affair. After a pause, Hippoclides called for a table to be brought in: when it was brought he first danced some Laconian figures [*schēmation* is a diminutive or contemptuous form of *schēma*] on it and then some Attic ones, and thirdly he stood on his head on the table and waved his legs about [the verb is *cheironomein*: cf. **143** Xen. *Symp.* 2.19]. While he was doing the first and second dances, Cleisthenes, though by now he detested the thought of having Hippoclides as his son-in-law, because of his dancing and shameless behaviour, nevertheless restrained himself, wanting to avoid an outburst against him: but when he saw him waving his legs about he could no longer hold himself back. 'Son of Tisander,' he said, 'you have danced away your marriage.' 'Hippoclides doesn't care', responded Hippoclides. [The remark became proverbial.]

[137] The terms 'beautiful' (*kalon*) and 'ugly' (*aischron*) contain also the moral implications 'noble', 'fine', and 'base', 'bad'. They combine these senses in most Greek authors, notably in Plato.

of the things being sung about, consistently maintaining their nobility and manliness: and that explains why such things were called *hyporchēmata*.[138] [e] But if anyone arranged the composition of his dance-figures in a way that went beyond due measure, or if when he came to his songs he said things that failed to agree with the dance, he was reckoned a fraud. Thus Aristophanes – or Plato – spoke as follows in *The Luggage*, according to Chamaeleon: "So if someone danced well, it used to be a fine spectacle. But nowadays there's no action: they just stand still as if they were paralysed, and howl." For the style of dancing used in the choruses was elegant and stately in the past, as though it was copied from the movements of men at arms. [f] That is why Socrates in his poetry[139] says that those who perform choral dancing most beautifully are the best in matters of war. These are his words: "Those who most beautifully honour the gods with choral dances are best in war." For the art of choral dancing was almost like parading under arms, and was an exhibition not only of the other aspects of good discipline, but also of the cultivation of physique.

[629a] 'Amphion of Thespiae, in the second book of his *On the Temple of the Muses on Helicon*, says that boys' dances are held, with great enthusiasm, on Helicon, and quotes this ancient inscription: "I did both things: I danced, and I taught the men at the Muses' temple.[140] The aulete was Anacus of Phialia. I am Bacchiadas of Sicyon; and this is an excellent prize, dedicated to the goddesses at Sicyon."

'A good remark was made by the aulete Caphisias,[141] when one of his pupils set [b] off to make a big noise on the *aulos* and devoted himself to practising that: Caphisias gave him a thump, and said that excellence does not lie in bigness, but bigness in excellence. The statues made by craftsmen of the past are also relics of the old style of dancing, which is the reason why the postures of their arms were composed with greater care. For here too they sought beautiful movements, suitable for free men, encompassing bigness in excellence:[142] from there[143] they transferred the gestures into their choral

---

138   Because the *orchēmata*, dances, were subordinate to (*hypo*) the theme of the poetry. *Hyporchēmata* were dances in which the performers sang as they danced (e.g. **194** 631c), normally accompanied by a stringed instrument, and especially associated with ceremonies to do with Apollo (Lucian, *Salt.* 16). But the *aulos* was also used (the 'dactylic' type, according to Pollux IV.82: see n. 30 above). The term *hyporchēma* seems to have been in practice fairly unspecific: any choral dance with song might be so designated.
139   This must apparently refer to the poems written by Socrates in prison: see Plato, *Phaedo* 60c–d.
140   That is, he was both the trainer and a member of the men's chorus sent by his city to compete in the festival of the Muses.
141   A musician in the retinue of Alexander the Great: see 538f.
142   'Bigness' in the sense 'significance' or 'impressiveness'. In Caphisias' remark above, there is a play on the ambiguity between 'big' meaning 'large', in music 'loud', and meaning 'impressive'.
143   That is, apparently, from the statues. This would imply that the ancient statues are 'relics' of ancient dancing in the sense that the gestures of the dance were derived from them, not the other way round.

dances, and from the dances into the wrestling schools. Further, [c] through their music and the cultivation of their bodies they acquired courage, and they exercised with song to train themselves in movements under arms. This was the origin of the movements of what are called the *pyrrhichai*,[144] and the whole of that style of dancing.'

194   *Deipnosophistae* 630b–631c

'The satyr dance, as Aristocles says in the first book of his *On Choruses*, is called *sikinnis*, and the satyrs are called *sikinnistai*. [See **189** 618c with n. 74.] Some people say that its inventor was a foreigner called Sicinnus, while others assert that Sicinnus was a Cretan by nationality. The Cretans are noted dancers, as Aristoxenus says. But Scamon, in the first book of his *On Inventions*, says that the dance is called *sikinnis* from the verb *seiesthai* ["to be shaken"], and that the first [630c] to dance the *sikinnis* was Thersippus. The movement of the feet was invented before that of the hands. For in the old days people exercised their feet more, in athletic contests and in hunting. The Cretans are enthusiasts for hunting, and so are swift-footed. There are some who say that "*sikinnis*" is an invented name, derived from *kinēsis* ["movement"], since the dance that the satyrs perform is very fast: for this kind of dance is without variation,[145] and so does not even slow down. In the old days all satyric composition consisted of choruses, as did also the tragedy of that period: hence it had no actors.

'There are three kinds of dancing in stage composition, tragic, comic and satyric; and [d] similarly there are three in lyric composition,[146] the *pyrrhichē*, the *gymnopaidikē* and the *hyporchēmatikē*. The *pyrrhichē* is similar to the satyric, since the main feature of both is speed. The *pyrrhichē* is plainly a war dance, since boys dance it under arms. Speed is essential in war for pursuing, and also to enable the vanquished "to flee and not [e] to linger, nor to be ashamed at being cowards".[147] The *gymnopaidikē* is comparable to the tragic dance called *emmeleia*:[148] weightiness and solemnity may be observed in each. The *hyporchēmatikē* is akin to the comic dance called the *kordax*:[149] both are frivolous.

---

144   The commonest and most important class of war-dance: see **194** 630e ff.
  I have omitted parts of the next passage, in which Athenaeus catalogues many forms of dance, retaining only the sections dealing with *pyrrhichai*, *hyporchēmata*, and dances in the drama.
145   *Pathos*, which I understand in the sense 'modification', 'qualification': alternatively, 'feeling', 'emotional content'. Some editors emend to *ēthos* '[moral] character'.
146   *Lyrikē poiēsis*, properly of compositions to be sung to the *lyra*. But the types of dance mentioned all seem to have been accompanied, at least sometimes, by the *aulos*. The significant contrast here is simply that between dramatic and non-dramatic.
147   A version of part of the oracle given to Croesus, Hdt. 1.55; cf. Plato, *Rep.* 566c.
148   On the *gymnopaidikē* see 631b below. *Emmeleia* is mentioned at 629d, and as a dance in tragedy at 20e, Plato, *Laws* 816b, schol. to Aristoph. *Clouds* 540: cf. Aristoph. *Wasps* 1530. At **193**(a) Hdt. VI.129 it is the tune for a dance.
149   The *kordax* was a frivolous and indecent dance-form characteristic of comedy. Cf. 631d, Pollux IV.99, *Suda* s.v. *kordakizein*.

'Aristoxenus says that the *pyrrhichē* took its name from Pyrrhichus, a Spartan by race, and that Pyrrhichus is a Spartan name to this day.[150] The warlike nature of the dance makes clear the fact that it is a Spartan invention. [f] For the Spartans are a warlike people, and their sons engage in the marching songs that are called *embatēria*. [Cf. 192 626c with n. 125.] When they are at war the Spartans themselves recite the poems of Tyrtaeus as they move forward in time with the rhythm. Philochorus says that when the Spartans had conquered the Messenians through the generalship of Tyrtaeus, they made it a custom on their campaigns, after they had eaten their meal and sung the paean,[151] to sing, one man at a time, a piece by Tyrtaeus. The commander was to be the judge, and to give meat as a prize to the winner. [631a] The *pyrrhichē* no longer survives among the other Greeks, and wars became extinct simultaneously with its disappearance. Only among the Spartans does it persist as an exercise of preparation for war: everyone in Sparta learns to master the *pyrrhichē* from the age of five years. The *pyrrhichē* familiar to us seems to be a Dionysiac genre, more civilised than the old type. The dancers have *thyrsoi*[152] instead of spears, and throw fennel-stalks at one another: [b] they carry torches, and dance the story of Dionysus and India, or the tale of Pentheus.[153] The most beautiful melodies and the orthian rhythms[154] are to be thought of as belonging to the *pyrrhichē*.

'The *gymnopaidikē* is similar to the one called *anapalē* in the old days.[155] All the boys dance it naked, performing various rhythmic movements and various figures with their arms in a gentle manner, and thus depict scenes from the wrestling school and the *pankration*, moving their feet in rhythm. Variants of it are the *Oschophorikoi*[156] and the Bacchic, so that this kind of

---

150   I.e., in the time of Aristoxenus. According to Pollux IV.99 (cf. Strabo X.3.8) Pyrrhichus was a Cretan. But it is likely that the person of that name was merely an invention designed to explain the title of the dance, whose real etymology is unknown.

151   The song of thanksgiving after a meal. Cf. 187 ps.-Plut. 1147a.

152   The *thyrsos* was the rod or wand carried by devotees of Dionysus. Typically it was twined with ivy and vine shoots, and topped with a pine cone.

153   I.e., the story told in Euripides' *Bacchae*.

154   See 187 ps.-Plut. 1140f with n. 179. But the slow and solemn 'orthian' of that passage is impossible in the context of the *pyrrhichē*. Perhaps the word *rhythmous* is corrupt, and the sense intended involves *orthios* in its melodic connotation, meaning 'high-pitched'.

155   *Gymnopaidikē* means '[dance] of naked boys', and was connected especially with the Spartan festival called the Gymnopaideia. The precise sense of *anapalē* is uncertain, but perhaps 'wrestling', as the next sentence suggests (the *pankration* was a sort of all-in wrestling event): or there may be a connection with the verb *anapallein*, 'swing to and fro', used of dancing at Aristoph. *Frogs* 1358, and elsewhere having a suggestion of urgency and speed.

156   *Oschophoria* ('carrying of bunches of grapes') was part of a festival of Athena at Athens: *oschophorika melē*, according to Proclus, *Chrest.* 28, were songs sung while two youths, dressed as women, led the procession carrying bunches of grapes.

dance too [c] is dedicated to Dionysus. Aristoxenus says that the men of old
used first to exercise themselves in the *gymnopaidikē*, and would then go on
into the *pyrrhichē* before entering the theatre. The *pyrrhichē* is also called
cheironomia.[157]

'The *hyporchēmatikē* is that in which the chorus sings as it dances. Thus
Bacchylides says: "Not a task for sitting down or for delay", and Pindar
says: "A troop of Spartan maidens". In Pindar's version it is danced by
Spartan men, and the *hyporchēmatikē* is a type of dancing for both men and
women.'

195   *Deipnosophistae* 631e–632c

'In the old days a noble beauty[158] was carefully preserved in music, and every
aspect kept to the orderliness proper to it, in conformity with the principles
of the art. That is why there were special *auloi* for each *harmonia*, and in the
competitions each aulete had *auloi* to suit each of the *harmoniai*. It was
Pronomus of Thebes who first played all the *harmoniai* on the same *auloi*.
[See 188 184d with n. 52.] But nowadays people approach music in a random
and unprincipled way. [631f] Long ago, being a favourite of the crowd was a
sign of a bad musician: thus when Asopodorus of Phlius was waiting off-
stage one day, and loud applause broke out for one of the auletes, he said:
"What's this? Something quite dreadful must have been going on!", meaning
that the aulete could not have won popular favour in any other way. (I realise
that some people have told this story with Antigenidas as the speaker.) Yet
performers nowadays make [632a] popularity with the spectators the goal of
their art.[159] That is why Aristoxenus, in his *Drinking-Party Miscellanies*,
says: "We are behaving like the people of Posidonia who live on the
Tyrrhenian Gulf. What happened to them was that though they were originally Greeks, they became foreigners through and through, and turned into
Etruscans or Romans: they changed their language and all their practices,
but to this day they will celebrate one festival characteristic of Greeks, in
which they come together and remember [b] those ancient words and
customs: they bewail and weep over them to one another, and then depart. In
the same way," he says, "now that the theatres have been utterly barbarised,
and this vulgar[160] music has advanced into the extremity of corruption, we
too, few as we are, come together by ourselves and remember what music
used to be like." That is what Aristoxenus says.

'For this reason it is my opinion too that one should devote philosophical

---

[157]   Lit. 'moving of hands [or arms]', 'gesticulation', sometimes 'shadow-boxing'. Cf.
143 Xen. *Symp.* 2.19, **193**(a) Hdt. VI.129.
[158]   *To kalon*, the very common and untranslatable expression representing beauty,
nobility, moral excellence.
[159]   These complaints echo closely those of Plato at **155** *Laws* 700a–701b.
[160]   *Pandēmos*: cf. Plato, *Symp.* 180e, 181a.

study to music. Thus Pythagoras of Samos, a philosopher of outstanding renown, is just one of many notable for having set themselves to music as no mere pastime: [c] indeed, he explains the whole being of the universe as held together by music.¹⁶¹ In general, it is to music that the ancient wisdom of the Greeks seems to have been most especially devoted. This is why they judged Apollo among the gods and Orpheus among the demigods to be both most musical and most wise: and they called all those who practised this art *sophistai*, as in Aeschylus' verse: "So then the *sophistēs*, clumsily mis-striking his tortoiseshell . . ."'¹⁶²

196   *Deipnosophistae* 633e–638a

'I still have many other things to say about music, but I can hear the reverberation¹⁶³ of *auloi*, and will end my long discourse by quoting the lines from Philetaerus' *Philaulos*: "Zeus, it's very good to die to the accompaniment of *auloi*. [633f] Only those who do so are allowed to make love in Hades. People of filthy habits who know nothing of music carry water to the leaky jar."'

After this, people were asking about the *sambykē*; and Masurius said that it is a high-pitched musical instrument, and that Euphorion the epic poet talked about it in his *On the Isthmian Games*: Euphorion says that the Parthians and [634a] the Troglodytes use it, and that it has four strings, stating that Pythagoras records this in his book *On the Red Sea*.¹⁶⁴ *Sambykē* is also the name of one of the types of siege-engine, whose shape and construction are explained by Biton in his *For Attalus: on Instruments*.¹⁶⁵ Andreas of Panormus, in the thirty-third book of his *Description of Sicily, City by City*, says that it was brought up against the enemy's walls from two

---

161   The clearest general picture of Pythagoras' views as conceived in later antiquity is that set out in Nicomachus' *Encheiridion*.

162   The text is uncertain, but if the version given is anything like correct, it is an oddly chosen quotation. *Sophia*, translated 'wisdom' above, can designate expertise or skill of any kind, and *sophistēs* did not originally have the special sense 'sophist' that it acquired in the late fifth century, and especially in Plato. It meant merely 'expert', 'practitioner of a skill'.

163   *Bombos*, suggesting a low-pitched buzzing sound, as of the Phrygian type of *aulos*.

164   The *sambykē* is usually treated as one of the 'many-stringed' instruments of the harp family, with which the sequel is largely concerned. Cf. 188 182e–f, and 635a below: but note also the suggestion (635c below) that 'many-stringed' instruments were a late development, and cf. Telestes on the *magadis* at 637a below. The Pythagoras mentioned here is said to have given an account of the three-stringed *pandoura* (188 183f). Possibly he spoke also of a four-stringed version, and somewhere in the sequence of authorities the name *sambykē* was mistakenly attached to it: but an argument in support of the identification of the *sambykē* with an instrument of the *pandoura* type is offered by Landels in *J.H.S.* 86 (1966). See also n. 166 below. On the instrument's high pitch cf. Arist. Quint. 85.10–12.

165   Perhaps rather '*On Mechanical Devices*': *organa* may be instruments, tools or contrivances of a musical or a non-musical kind.

ships, and was called the *sambykē* because when it is raised, its overall shape becomes that of a ship and a ladder, [b] and the shape of the *sambykē* is rather like it. Moschus says, in the first book of his *Mechanics*, that the contrivance is Roman, and that the form of it was invented by Heraclides of Tarentum. In the eighth book of his *Histories* Polybius says: 'When Marcellus at the siege of Syracuse was baffled by the constructions of Archimedes, he said that Archimedes had ladled water out of the sea with his ships, and that the *sambykai* had been thrashed and thrown out in disgrace, as if from a drinking-party.'[166]

After this Aemilianus said: 'Now, Masurius, my friend, [c] I am a music-lover myself; and it often occurs to me to consider the question of the instrument called the *magadis*, and to wonder whether it is a type of *aulos* or a type of *kithara*.[167] For Anacreon, that sweetest of poets, says somewhere: "I hold the *magadis* and pluck on twenty strings, Leucaspis, while you are in the prime of youth." But Ion of Chios in *Omphale* seems to be speaking of *auloi* when he says: "And may the Lydian *magadis-aulos* lead the cry." In explicating this iambic line Aristarchus the grammarian, whom Panaetius, the philosopher of Rhodes, [d] called "The Diviner" because of his facility in divining the meaning of poems, says that the *magadis* is a species of *aulos*, though Aristoxenus did not say so in his *On Auletes*, nor in his *On Auloi and Instruments*, and neither did Archestratus (who also wrote two books *On Auletes*): Pyrrhander in his *On Auletes* did not say so either, and nor did Phillis of Delos (who also wrote an *On Auletes*, as did Euphranor). Tryphon, in the second book of his *Terminology*, says this: "The so-called *magadis* is

---

166   Polyb. VIII.5–6. On the common assumption that the *sambykē* was a species of harp, the present passage would seem to mean that it had a boat-shaped body, held horizontally, with the stick holding the strings rising out of it 'like a ladder'. Sachs (*Hist. Mus. Instr.* 83–4) identifies it with the Babylonian *sabka*, mentioned in the (second-century) Book of Daniel, Ch. 3, in connection with the (sixth-century) court of Nebuchadnezzar. For criticisms of Sachs, and some alternative suggestions based on a detailed study of the comparison with the siege-engine, see Landels in *J.H.S.* 86 (1966). The central difficulty for Sachs' suggestion is that no instrument of the sort he describes appears on any Greek paintings or sculpture of the period. In all known Greek harps, the body, which is supposed to correspond to the boat, was held in a more or less vertical position. But possibly the casual military nickname given to the siege-engine simply ignored this fact about the position in which a performer held the instrument: several well-known types of harp would look approximately right if they were turned over, e.g. when placed on a table or hung on a peg on the wall. Note also that Aelian (Porph. *Comm.* 34.29) seems to identify the *sambykē* straightforwardly with the triangular harp, *trigōnos*.
      The last clause of the present paragraph, punning on the two senses of *sambykē*, might suggest that to perform on a *sambykē* at a drinking-party was to invite abuse: but this is misleading: cf. 188 175d with n. 16. The 'drinking-party' image begins with the reference to ladling water (like wine from a bowl): Archimedes' contrivances lifted Marcellus' ships out of the sea.
167   *Aulos* and *kithara* are used here very generally: the question is just whether the *magadis* is a wind instrument or a stringed instrument. The passage that follows (down to 637a) picks up and discusses this problem, which has already been hinted at in 188 182d–e. It contains, in a chaotic and often confusing form, most of what we know about the *magadis*.

an aulos";[168] [e] and again: "The *magadis* gives out a high and a low note at the same time, as Anaxandrides says in his *Drill-Sergeant*: 'On the *magadis* I will chatter to you something small and great at once.'"[169] No one but you, my noble Masurius, will be able to resolve this difficulty for me.'

'Didymus the grammarian,' said Masurius, 'in his *Arguments against Ion*, understands by "*magadis*" the *aulos kitharistērios*, Aemilianus my friend. He says that this instrument is mentioned by Aristoxenus in the first book of his *On the Boring of Auloi*, [f] where he says that there are five classes of *auloi*, namely maiden-pipes, child-pipes, *kitharistērioi*, complete and extra-complete [on all these see 188 176f with n. 30]. Alternatively, the conjunction "and" must be missing from Ion's line, so that it speaks of "the *magadis* and the *aulos*", the *aulos* being the one played to accompany the *magadis*.[170] For the *magadis* is a plucked instrument, as Anacreon says, and is an invention of the Lydians.[171] That is why Ion calls Lydian girls "pluckers of strings" in his *Omphale*, in these words: "Come now, Lydian girls, pluckers of strings, singers of hymns established of old, lull the guest to sleep."[172] [635a] And the comic poet Theophilus in his *Neoptolemus* calls plucking on the *magadis* "magadising", in these lines: "It's a wretched thing for a son and a father and a mother to sit on a wheel and magadise. None of us will sing the same tune."[173]

168   This is repeated from 188 182d, as is the quotation from Anaxandrides below. The present group of words may not be intended as a sentence, and might mean simply: 'the *aulos* called "*magadis*"'.

169   There is nothing in the quotation to confirm that it refers to *auloi* rather than to a stringed instrument. If the context, here and at 188 182d, is right in suggesting that it does, the *auloi* may have formed a pair of unequal length, capable of sounding high and low pitches simultaneously. It is generally agreed that the stringed *magadis* was a harp-like instrument with strings tuned in pairs an octave apart, though the evidence for this view, mostly contained in the present passage, falls well short of proving it. The verb *magadizein*, however, used of choirs, always refers to singing a tune in octaves (e.g. 172 and 183 ps.-Ar. *Probs.* XIX.18 and 39: cf. 635a below). But it is possible that even in these cases the connection with the instrument's name has to do with the rather general phenomenon of one sound 'answering' another, whether at the octave or not, and might suggest that the *magadis* was an instrument used most commonly to answer another one, not an instrument that itself gave out both notes together. See particularly 635b–c below, with n. 175. In this case Didymus' suggestion below that the kind of *aulos* called the *magadis* was the *aulos kitharistērios* (see 188 176f with n. 30) would make good sense.

170   On the interpretation of Didymus, *magadis* is the name of a kind of *aulos*, while on the alternative view it is not. In either case the *aulos* mentioned by Ion is not understood to have some special property, such as that of playing in octaves, but is treated as being one used to accompany a stringed instrument, this being the special role of the *aulos kitharistērios*.

171   The Thracians, according to Pollux IV.61: cf. 636f below.

172   'Pluckers of strings' translates *psaltriai*, indicating performers playing without a plectrum, as in the *psaltērion* (harp). Similarly 'plucked instrument' (*psaltikon*) above might be paraphrased 'instrument of the harp family'.

173   I suggest that 'magadise' here refers to singing in octaves (see n. 169 above), not to playing the *magadis*, as Masurius' introductory comment implies. It has been supposed that 'sitting on a wheel' is to be construed as some form of torture: but the literal sense may be the right one, and the reference may be to the rather curious variety of entertainment mentioned at 146 Xen. *Symp.* 7.2–3.

'Euphorion, in his *On the Isthmian Games*, says that the *magadis* is an ancient instrument, but that at a more recent period its conformation was altered and its name was changed to *sambykē*. It was commonest, he says, in Mitylene, to the extent that Lesbothemis, [b] a sculptor of ancient times, even made a statue representing one of the Muses holding it [see 188 182f]. Menaechmus, in his *On Experts in the Arts*, says that the *pēktis* (which according to him is the same as the *magadis*)[174] was invented by Sappho. Aristoxenus says that the *magadis* and the *pēktis* can be played without a plectrum, by plucking. He claims that this is stated by Pindar in his *skolion* addressed to Hieron, where he describes the *magadis* as "a plucking that sounds in answer", because the two kinds of instrument together, in octaves, [c] produce the concerted melody of men and boys.[175] And Phrynichus in the *Phoenissae* said: "singing answering melodies to the plucking of strings".[176] Sophocles in the Mysians says: "Often the Phrygian *trigōnos* sounds, and the concord of the Lydian *pēktis* sings to it in answer."[177]

'Some people are puzzled as to how it is, the *magadis* being what it was in Anacreon's time (for they say that instruments with many strings appeared later),[178] that Anacreon mentions it in the following terms: "I hold the *magadis* and pluck on twenty strings, Leucaspis." Now Posidonius says that Anacreon mentions three kinds of melody, [d] Phrygian, Dorian and Lydian, since these alone were employed by him.[179] Each of these is rendered on seven strings, so that it is natural for him to say that he plucks on twenty strings, taking away the one and making a round number.[180] But Posidonius does not

---

174 The controversy over this point, which runs through the following passage, indicates that at least by the third century the precise connotations of the words *pēktis* and *magadis*, as used by the poets of the sixth century, were no longer clearly understood. On the *pēktis* see n. 21 above.

175 The quotation from Pindar is continued at 635d below. There the 'answering' instrument is named as the *pēktis*: Masurius accepts Menaechmus' identification of *pēktis* with *magadis*, reasserted and ascribed to Aristoxenus at 635e. The contrary view is aired at 636a–c. The notion of 'sounding in answer' recurs several times in connection with these instruments in the present passage (*antiphthongon* here, *antispasta* in the quotations from Phrynichus and Sophocles below, cf. *antizygois holkois* quoted from Diogenes at 636b). None of these cases can be construed as referring to the instrument's answering *itself* at the octave, as the *magadis* is usually thought to have done: it is always in answer to something else. But the words *antiphthongon* etc. probably carry the implication 'at the octave', like *antiphōnos* in 170–2 and 183, ps.-Ar. *Probs.* XIX.16–18, 39. It seems clear that the high-pitched *pēktis* was commonly used together with an instrument, or a voice, sounding an octave lower.

176 This quotation seems to be related to the context only by its reference to 'answering', in connection with an unspecified plucked instrument.

177 The usual associations of 'Lydian' and 'Phrygian' indicate that the *trigōnos* is the lower instrument of the two. 'Concord', *synchordia*, implies no more than 'strings sounding together'.

178 The thesis is quite improbable: but see 188 183c with notes 45–6, and cf. 633f above.

179 For these as the only three *harmoniai* in the time of Polymnestus and Sacadas (somewhat earlier than Anacreon) see 187 ps.-Plut. 1134a.

180 Posidonius' suggestion is that Anacreon is referring not to twenty strings present simultaneously on a single instrument, but to his use of twenty (or twenty-one)

realise that the *magadis* is an ancient instrument, even though Pindar says plainly that Terpander invented the *barbitos*[181] to sound in answer to the *pēktis* used by the Lydians: "Which long ago Terpander of Lesbos first invented, [e] when he heard at the feasts of the Lydians the plucking that sounds in answer from the lofty *pēktis*." Now the *pēktis* and the *magadis* are the same instrument, as Aristoxenus says, and so does Menaechmus of Sicyon in his *On Experts in the Arts*. Menaechmus also says that Sappho, who is older than Anacreon, was the first to use the *pēktis*. But the fact that Terpander was earlier than Anacreon[182] is clear from the following considerations. Terpander was the first of all the victors at the Carneia,[183] as Hellanicus records in both the verse and the prose versions of his *Carneian Victors*. The Carneia was established [f] in the twenty-sixth Olympiad [i.e., between 676 and 672 B.C.], as Sosibius says in his *Chronology*. But in his *On Kitharōdoi*, which is the fifth book of his work *On the Poets*, Hieronymus says that Terpander lived in the time of Lycurgus the lawgiver; and all historians unanimously agree that it was Lycurgus, together with Iphitus of Elis, who organised the first numbered instance of the Olympic Games.[184] Moreover Euphorion, in his *On the Isthmian Games*, says that the many-stringed instruments differed from one another only in their names,[185] and that their use is of great antiquity.

[636a] 'Diogenes the tragedian, on the other hand, thinks that the *pēktis* is different from the *magadis*. In his *Semele* he speaks as follows: "And yet I hear that the turban-wearing women of Asiatic Cybele, children of the rich Phrygians, making a loud sound with *tympana* and *rhomboi* and the booming of bronze-clashing cymbals in both their hands . . . [celebrate]'[186]

---

different strings, in the sense 'different notes', overall, when playing stringed instruments in general. This must certainly be wrong: the quotation cannot support the intepretation, and in any case the three melodic forms, no matter how they were conceived in Anacreon's time, can scarcely have demanded twenty-one *different* notes.

181 According to Neanthes of Cyzicus at 188 175e, it was invented by Anacreon. On the type of instrument in question see n. 19 ad loc.; but quite possibly it is the *lyra*-like *barbitos* usually given this name, whose large size gave it the low pitch that the present passage implies.

182 The implication is that Menaechmus is wrong, since Pindar associates Terpander with the *pēktis*, and Terpander predates Sappho. But Pindar only attributes to Terpander an acquaintance with the *pēktis*, not its use, nor even its introduction from Lydia into Greece.

183 The most important of the Spartan festivals. Cf. 187 ps.-Plut. 1133d, 1134b–c.

184 This would place Terpander about 100 years earlier than Sosibius' estimate, almost certainly too early. (The real dates of Lycurgus, a historical figure who attained legendary status, are not known.) But contradictory though his evidence may be, Masurius is certainly right to locate Terpander substantially before Anacreon.

185 This is plainly untrue, though the differences in type are hard to establish. It suggests only that the Alexandrian scholars had no clear understanding of the terminology used in the sixth century.

186 There is a gap of at least a line in the quotation here, which must have contained a verb: the sense 'celebrate' is likely enough. On the *rhombos* see 72 Eurip. *Helen* 1362 with note.

the skilful singer and doctor of the gods. And I hear that Lydian and Bactrian maidens, who live beside the river Halys, worship Artemis, goddess of Tmolus, in the laurel-shaded grove, [b] twanging the *magadis* with the pluckings of *trigōnoi* and with counterbalancing pullings[187] of *pēktides*, where the *aulos*, welcomed as a guest, agrees in friendship with the choruses, in Persian style." Phillis of Delos, in the second book of his *On Music*, also says that the *pēktis* is different from the *magadis*, in these words: "*Phoinikes, pēktides, magadides, sambykai, iambykai, trigōna, klepsiamboi, skindapsoi, enneachorda.*[188] Those to which they sang iambics," he says, "they called *iambykai*: those to which they intoned poetry [c] they called *klepsiamboi*.[189] They called *magadides* those to which they sang in octaves, with the parts given to the singers tuned to equal intervals.[190] There were other instruments too, besides these: the *barbitos* or *barmos*,[191] for example, and several more, provided both stringed instruments and resonators."[192]

'There were indeed certain other instruments apart from those that are blown into and those that are divided up by strings, namely those that merely produce a noise, *krembala* for instance.[193] Dicaearchus speaks about them in his *History of Greece*, saying that certain instruments were once excessively popular with women for the accompaniment of dancing and singing, [d] such that when they were played with the fingers they made a high, clear sound. This, he says, is demonstrated in the song to Artemis that begins: "Artemis, my mind inspires me to weave for you a lovely hymn drawn from the gods . . . with gold-shining *krembala*, bronze-cheeked, in

---

187 This clumsy phrase represents the Greek *antizygois holkois* more or less literally. It would be possible to translate: 'with pluckings of *trigōnoi* and *pēktides*, twanging the *magadis* with counterbalancing pullings'. But if the 'counterbalanced' instruments are to be understood, like 'answering' instruments, as playing an octave apart, the quotation from Sophocles at 635c above indicates that *trigōnoi* stand in this relation to *pēktides*: the two are unlikely to play in unison and be 'answered' by a third instrument. Just possibly *magadis* here is not the name of an instrument at all, and *krekousas magadin* simply means 'playing in octaves': cf. 638a below with n. 206.

188 The list is quoted from Aristoxenus: see 188 182f and n. 41.

189 *Iambykai* and *klepsiamboi* are mentioned by the ancient lexicographers without much substantial information. It appears that the names refer not to specialised forms of instrument, but to familiar instruments in specialised uses. An *iambos* is often a satirical or abusive song: for a more specific use see Semus of Delos quoted at 191 622b. *Klepsiambos* seems to mean 'thieving *iambos*': the sense is obscure. Hesychius says that *klepsiamboi* were 'certain melodies of Alcman'. See also 636f below.

190 Once again, there is no suggestion here that the *magadis* itself played in octaves: it is treated as the instrument characteristically used to accompany singing in octaves, just as *iambykē* and *klepsiambos* are distinguished only by their use, not their structure or musical capabilities.

191 On this instrument (or instruments) see n. 19 above.

192 *Enēcha*, probably referring to percussion instruments (see the sequel), not to wind instruments, as L.S.J. have it.

193 Generally understood as equivalent to *krotala*, clappers or castanets. But see next note.

their hands."[194] Hermippus in his *Gods* calls playing on them *krembalizein*, in these lines: "Knocking limpets off the rocks, they krembalise."[195] [e] And Didymus says that some people hit shells or bits of pot together to make a rhythmical sound for the dancers, instead of using a *lyra*, as Aristophanes says in the *Frogs* [140 1304–7].

'Artemon, in the first book of his *On the Guild of Dionysus*, says that Timotheus of Miletus is thought by most authorities to have used a *systēma* with a greater number of strings, on the *magadis*.[196] Hence he was examined by a Spartan tribunal, accused of undermining the ancient music, and when someone was on the point of cutting off his extra strings, [f] he gestured to a statuette of Apollo that they had, which was holding a *lyra* whose strings were equal in number to his own arrangement; and he was acquitted.

'Douris, in his *On Tragedy*, says that the *magadis* was named after Magdios, a native of Thrace [contrast 634f above]. Apollodorus, in his *Response to the Letter of Aristocles*, says: "The *magadis* is what we now call the *psaltērion*, while what was called the *klepsiambos*, like the *trigōnos* and the *elymos* and the *enneachordon*, have come to be used much less commonly." [637a] Alcman says: "to put aside the *magadis*", and Sophocles in *Thamyras*: "well-made *lyrai* and *magadides*, and all the Greeks' sweet-tuned instruments that are made of carved wood". In the dithyramb *Hymenaeus*, Telestes says that it has five strings, in these words: "Each man sent out a different clamour as he roused the horn-sounded *magadis*, rapidly turning his hand to and fro in its race round the course, among the five-staffed jointing of the strings."[197]

194   Though *krembala* is usually an alternative term for *krotala* (as probably in the next quotation), the passages cited here suggest something rather different. The 'high, clear sound' (*ligyron psophon*) atrributed to them by Dicaearchus hints at an instrument with a more ringing, metallic timbre, possibly the sistrum, which was well known in Egypt. On the other hand the description of *krembala* in the song to Artemis would best fit the cymbals.
195   Gulick translates: 'They knock the very limpets off the rocks when they rattle their crembala.' But the sense may be rather that they knock limpets off the rocks and use them as *krembala*: see the next sentence.
196   Versions of the story are told elsewhere (e.g. Plut. *Inst. Lac.* 17, Paus. III.12.10), without any suggestion that Timotheus' instrument differed in structure from the familiar *kithara*, except in the number of its strings. The words *tēi magadi* in the present text may be interpolated. Alternatively, and quite probably, they should be taken in apposition with *systēmati*, in which case *magadis* is not here the name of an instrument, but a way of designating a special sort of arrangement of pitches on the strings of the *kithara*. Perhaps Timotheus' extra strings were so tuned as to make it possible for him to play phrases that 'answered' other ones an octave above.
197   The elaborate dithyrambic diction creates several problems. *Keratophōnos*, 'horn-sounded', might mean 'horn-voiced', describing the timbre of the instrument. Gulick suggests that it means 'struck by a plectrum', citing Plato, *Laws* 795a for the fact that plectra were sometimes made of horn. But the *magadis* is usually treated as an instrument plucked without a plectrum: cf. especially 635b above. The final phrase is certainly most readily understood as attributing five strings to the *magadis*, but it is usually a many-stringed instrument (with 20 strings according to the quotation from Anacreon at 634c). It seems clear that the names of 'foreign' instruments were not always consistently used: cf. 634a above on the *sambykē*, and perhaps 188 183b on the *pēktis*.

'I know of another instrument too, used by the kings of the Thracians at their banquets, as Nicomedes says in his *On Orpheus*. [b] It is the *phoinix*, which Ephorus, and Scamon in his *On Inventions*, say was invented by the Phoenicians, and so received this name. But Semus of Delos, in the first book of his *History of Delos*, says that it is because its arms were made from the Delian phoenix tree.[198] And he claims that the *sambykē* was first used by the Sibyl, of whom . . .[199] Scamon, who was mentioned above: but he says that it was named after Sambyx, the man who invented it.

'On the subject of what is called the *tripous* (which was also a musical instrument), the Artemon whom we mentioned previously [636e] writes as follows. "Thus people are not even sure, in the case of many instruments, [c] whether or not they ever really existed: the *tripous* of Pythagoras of Zacynthos[200] is a case in point. It flourished only briefly; and because it was thought a laborious thing for the hands to work, or for whatever other reason, it quickly became extinct and most people entirely forgot it. It resembled the Delphic tripod, from which it got its name, and it could be played as a triple *kithara*. Its legs were set on a base that could be turned easily, [d] like the pedestals made for revolving stools, and Pythagoras stretched strings over the three separate spaces that lay between leg and leg. At the top of each space he fitted an arm, and attached string-holders below them, and he made a decoration on the upper part which joined the cauldron[201] to the sound-boxes fixed beside it. This gave it an elegant appearance, and also added a fuller sound. He assigned the three *harmoniai*, Dorian, Phrygian and Lydian, one to each space. He himself would then sit on a seat, roughly the same as the *tripous* in the proportions of its construction: [e] he would pass his left hand through to strike,[202] while preparing to use the plectrum with the other: with his foot he would turn round the base, which was easily rotated, to correspond to whichever of the *harmoniai* he chose first: then he would play on, striking a different side, and then another. The ready movement of the base, propelled by his foot, brought the *systēmata* so swiftly under his hand, and he had practised the manual control of it to so high a degree of dexterity, that if one did not actually see what was happening, but judged by hearing alone, one would think that one was

---

198   That is, a palm tree. But see 168 ps.-Ar. *Probs.* XIX.14 with note.
199   Some words are missing from the MSS here.
200   This Pythagoras probably belongs to the middle of the fifth century. He was also a theoretician: see Aristox. *El. Harm.* 36.33. He is to be distinguished both from the famous philosopher of that name, and from the geographer mentioned at 188 183f and 634a above.
201   This refers to the bowl on the top of the Delphic tripod, and in the instrument acted as an additional sound-box, common to all three parts. Sound-boxes and string-holders were at the top, the narrowest part: hence, as the shape would suggest, the three *kitharai* are to be envisaged as upside-down.
202   *Pros tēn epibolēn*, probably referring to the kitharist's use of the left hand both to pluck the strings and to damp those not intended to sound under the stroke of the plectrum. *Epibolēn* is echoed by *epiballōn*, 'striking', below.

hearing three *kitharai*, [ɾ] all differently tuned. This instrument was greatly admired, but after Pythagoras' lifetime it quickly fell into disuse.''[203]

'Playing the *kithara* by itself,[204] according to Menaechmus, was first introduced by Aristonicus of Argos, a contemporary of Archilochus who had gone to live in Corcyra. Philochorus, however, in the third book of his *Attic History*, says: "Lysander, the kitharist of Sicyon, was the first to alter the character of *psilokitharistikē*, stretching the strings at great tension and giving bulk to the sound, and giving an *aulos*-like performance on the *kithara*, of the kind that the school of Epigonus were the first to employ.[205] [638a] He overthrew the thin style usual among solo kitharists, and was the first to play the *kithara* with colourful shadings, playing *iamboi* and the *magadis* – the *syrigmos*, as it is called.[206] Of all performers up to his time, only he made alterations to the instrument, and when he had improved his skill he was the first to set a chorus about him." Dion of Chios, Menaechmus says, was the first to play the *spondeion* of Dionysus on the *kithara*.[207] And Timomachus in his *History of Cyprus* says that Stesander of Samos greatly improved the art, and was the first to perform the battle scenes from Homer as a *kitharōdos* at Delphi, beginning with the *Odyssey*.'[208]

[203] We have no further independent information about this instrument.
[204] *Psilē kitharisis*, referring especially to performance on the instrument without singing (see **154** Plato, *Laws* 669e). Cf. *psilokitharistikē*, below.
[205] The date of these developments is the second half of the sixth century. According to Paus. x.7.7 the *psilē kitharistikē* (an expression equivalent to the *psilē kitharisis* and *psilokitharistikē* of the present text) was first performed at the Pythian games in 558 B.C. '*Aulos*-like perfomrance on the *kithara*' represents *enaulos kitharisis*, an obscure expression supposed by some commentators to mean '*aulos*-like sound on the *kithara*', which is wholly improbable, and by others to mean 'playing the *kithara* with *aulos* accompaniment', which does not seem to fit the context. On the basis of the information given in the sequel I conjecture that it means 'playing the *kithara* in the manner of the *aulos*', in the sense 'playing with the colourful and dramatic expressiveness characteristic of the *aulos*': this is argued more fully in Barker, *C.Q.* 32 (1982) (ii).
[206] 'Colourful shadings', *chrōmata euchroa*: probably not a reference to the chromatic genus of scale, but to 'tone-colouring', though this may have involved nuances of interval that varied standard practice. *Iamboi, magadis* and *syrigmos* have been understood as the names of instruments, but only *magadis* is a very plausible candidate. I take them to refer to special 'effects', usually connected with the dramatic representations of the auletic *Pythikos nomos* (**24** Pollux IV.84), of which a kitharistic version also existed (**25** Strabo IX.3.10). Cf. the occurrences of the terms *iamboi, syringes, syrigmoi* in their descriptions. *Syrigmon* in our passage seems to be in apposition with *magadin*: this term seems to be capable of bearing the sense 'high harmonic', derived presumably from the practice of accompanying a tune at the upper octave, associated with the noun *magadis* and the verb *magadizein*. The evidence is discussed in the paper cited at n. 205: in addition to the information relating to the *magadis* at 634c ff above, see especially Xen. *Anab.* VII.3.32–3.
[207] *Spondeia* (libation melodies) were normally played on the *aulos*: hence this too indicates the way in which string players were attempting to emulate the accomplishments of the *aulos*.
[208] The introduction of *kitharōdia*, including songs based on the words of Homer, goes back to a much earlier period than the developments discussed in the present passage. (See especially **187** ps.-Plut. 1132c–e, cf. 1133b–c). If Stesander belongs to the sixth century, his innovation must have been his representation of battle scenes, indicating again a new emphasis on the dramatic.

Appendix: Athenaeus' sources

The following is a list of the authors whom Athenaeus mentions as sources for his quotations and summaries. Each name is followed, in parentheses, by references to the author's native city, the nature of his works, and his date, where these are known. I then give references to the passages in Athenaeus where the authors are mentioned, including the title of the work cited, in the cases where Athenaeus gives it. Where he names no title, the fact is signalled by the abbreviation 'n.t.'

Aeschylus (Athens: tragedian, early to middle of fifth century). *Ixion* 182b, n.t. 632c.
Alcman (Sparta: lyric poet, seventh century). N.t. 624b, 637a.
Alexis (poet of Middle Comedy, fourth century). *On Auloi* 182c (this attribution is probably wrong).
Amerias (Macedon: grammarian, probably late third century). *Dialects* 176c, 176e.
Amphion (Thespiae: date unknown). *On the Temple of the Muses on Helicon* 629a.
Amphis (comic dramatist, fourth century). *Dithyrambos* 175a.
Anacreon (Teos: lyric poet, sixth century). N.t. 177a, 182c, 634c, 634f, 635c.
Ananius (iambic poet, sixth century). *Iambics* 625c.
Anaxandrides (Rhodes: comic dramatist, fourth century). *The Treasure* 176a, *Drill-Sergeant* 182d, 634e.
Anaxilas (comic dramatist, fourth century). *Lyra-Maker* 183b, *Hyacinthus* 623f.
Andreas (Panormus: historian, date unknown). *Description of Sicily, City by City* 634a.
Andron (Alexandria: historian, second century). *Chronicles* 184b.
Antiphanes (comic dramatist, fourth century). *The Doctor* 175a, *The Aulete* 618b.
Apollodorus (Athens: grammarian, second century). *Response to the Letter of Aristocles* 636f.
Araros (son of Aristophanes, Athens: comic dramatist, fourth century). *Birth of Pan* 175f.
Archestratus (musicologist). *On Auletes* 634d.
Archilochus (Paros: iambic and lyric poet, probably seventh century). N.t. 628a.
Aristarchus (grammarian, second century). N.t. 634c.
Aristeas (? grammarian, ? third century). *On Kitharōdoi* 623d.
Aristocles (scholar, late second century). *On Choruses* 174b–c, 620b, 620d, 630b, *On Music* 620e, (621b).
Aristophanes (Athens: comic dramatist, fifth century). *Daitaleis* 183f, 184e, second *Thesmophoriazousae* 619a, *The Luggage* (ascription doubtful) 628e, *Frogs* 636e.
Aristophanes (Byzantium: scholar, third to second century). *Attic Dialect* 619b.
Aristotle (Stagira: philosopher, fourth century). *Constitution of Colophon* 618e.
Aristoxenus (Tarentum: musical theorist and philosopher, fourth century). *On Music* 619d, *Summary Notes* 619e, *Drinking-Party Miscellanies* 632a, *On Auletes* 634d, *On Auloi and Instruments* 634d, *On the Boring of Auloi* 634e, n.t. 174e, 182f, 184e, 620e, 621c, 624b, 635b, 635e, 638b.
Artemidorus (Tarsus: scholar, early first century). *Dorian Dialect* 182d.
Artemon (Cassandreia: historian and grammarian, probably third century). *On the Guild of Dionysus* 636e, 637b.
Axionicus (comic dramatist, fourth century). *Euripides-Lover* 175b.
Bacchylides (Ceos: lyric poet, early fifth century). N.t. 174f, 631c.
Biton (probably a writer on mechanics, second century). *For Attalus: on Instruments* 634a.
Callias (Athens: comic dramatist, fifth century). *Pedetai* 177a.

Carystius (Pergamum: historian, second century). *Historical Notes* 620b.
Chamaeleon (Heraclea: scholar, fourth to third century). *Protrepticus* 184d, *On Stesichorus* 620c, n.t. 624a, 628e.
Clearchus (Soli: philosopher and essayist, fourth to third century). *Love Stories* 619c, *Enigmas* 620c.
Corinna (Tanagra: lyric poetess, late sixth century). N.t. 174f.
Crates (comic dramatist, fifth century). *Daring Deeds* 619a.
Cratinas the Younger (comic dramatist, fourth century). *Theramenes* 177a.
Damon (Athens: musical theorist, fifth century). N.t. 628c.
Democlides (scholar, date unknown). N.t. 175a.
Dicaearchus (historian and geographer, fourth to third century). *The Olympic Festival* 620d, *History of Greece* 636c.
Didymus (Alexandria: grammarian and prolific scholar, first century). *Arguments against Ion* 634e, n.t. 636e.
Diogenes (Sinope: tragedian, fourth century). *Semele* 636a.
Douris (Samos: historian, third century). *On Euripides and Sophocles* 184d, *On Agathocles* 618b, *On Tragedy* 636f.
Ephippus (comic dramatist, fourth century). *Goods for Sale* 618a.
Ephorus (Cyme: historian, fourth century). *Discoveries* 182c, n.t. 637b.
Epicharmus (Megara in Sicily: comic poet, fifth century). *Periallus* 183c, *Muses* 184f, *Atalantai* 618d, *The Halcyon* 619b, *Odysseus Shipwrecked* 619b, *Philoctetes* 628b.
Euphorion (Chalcis: epic poet and historian, librarian at Antioch, third century). *On the Isthmian Games* 182e, 183f, 633f, 635a, 635f, *On Song-writers* 184a.
Euphranor (Pythagorean musicologist, probably fourth century). *On Auloi* 182c, 184e, *On Auletes* 634d.
Eupolis (comic dramatist, fifth century). *Dyers* 183f, n.t. 623e.
Euripides (Athens: tragedian, fifth century). *Heracles* 619c.
Hedylus (probably Samos: poet, third century). *Epigrams* 176c.
Hellanicus (Mytilene: historian, fifth century). *Carneian Victors* 635e.
Heraclides (Heraclea in Pontus: philosopher, fourth century). *On Music* 624c ff.
Hermippus (comic dramatist, fifth century). *Lawgivers* 619b, *Gods* 636d.
Herodotus (Halicarnassus: historian, fifth century). *Histories* 627d, (628c).
Hieronymus (Rhodes: philosopher and historian, third century). *On the Poets*, Bk v = *On Kitharōdoi*, 635f.
Hipponax (Ephesus: iambic poet, sixth century). N.t. 624b, *Iambics* 625c.
Ion (Chios: tragedian and lyric poet, fifth century). *Phoenix* or *Caeneus* 184f, *Phrouroi* 185a, *Second Phoenix* 185a, *Omphale* 634c, 634f.
Jason (Nysa: historian, first century). *Alexander's Divine Honours* 620d.
Juba (king of Mauretania, grammarian and historian: first century B.C. to first century A.D.). *History of the Theatre* 175d, 175e, n.t. 177a, 182e, 183c.
Lasus (Hermione: lyric poet, late sixth century). *Hymn to Demeter of Hermione* 624e.
Lysanias (grammarian: fourth to third century). *Iambic Poets* 620c.
Matron (Pitane: parodist, fourth to third century). N.t. 183a.
Melanippides (Melos: dithyrambist, fifth century). *Marsyas* 616e.
Menaechmus (historian, third century). *On Experts in the Arts* 635b, 635e, n.t. 637f, 638a.
Menander (Athens: comic dramatist, fourth to third century). *Carian Women* 175a.
Menecles (Barca: historian, probably third century). *History of Barca* 184b.
Metrodorus (Chios or Scepsis: grammarian and historian, second to first century). *Trojan History* 184a.

Moschus (otherwise unknown). *Mechanics* 634b.
Neanthes (Cyzicus: historian, third century). *Annals* 175e.
Nicochares (comic dramatist, fourth century). *Heracles the Chorus-Leader* 619a.
Nicomedes (otherwise unknown). *On Orpheus* 637a.
Nymphis (Heracleia: historian, third century). *On Heracleia* 619f.
Panaetius (Rhodes: philosopher, second century). N.t. 634d.
Philemon (comic dramatist, fourth to third century). *The Adulterer* 175d.
Philetaerus (comic dramatist, fourth century). *Philaulos* 633e.
Phillis (Delos: writer on music: date uncertain). *On Auletes* 634d, *On Music* 636b.
Philochorus (historian, fourth to third century). *Attic History* 637f, n.t. 628a.
Phrynichus (Athens: tragedian, sixth to fifth century). *Phoenissae* 635c.
Phrynichus (comic dramatist, late fifth century). *Ephialtes* 184f.
Pindar (Thebes: lyric poet, fifth century). *Skolion to Hieron* 635b, 635d, n.t. 631c.
Plato (comic dramatist, late fifth century). *The Luggage* (ascription doubtful) 628e.
Plato (Athens: philosopher, fifth to fourth century). *Republic* 182f.
Polybius (Megalopolis: historian, second century). *Histories* 626a, 634b.
Posidonius (Apameia: philosopher, historian, polymath, second century) *Histories* 176b, 635c.
Pratinas (Phlius: tragedian and lyric poet, sixth to fifth century). A *hyporchēma* 617c, n.t. 624f.
Protagorides (Cyzicus: historian, second century). *On the Festivals at Daphne* 176a, 183f.
Pyrrhander (otherwise unknown). *On Auletes* 634d.
Pythagoras (geographer, fourth to third century). *On the Red Sea* 183f, 634a.
Sappho (Lesbos: lyric poetess, sixth century). N.t. 182f, cf. 635b, 635e.
Scamon (Mitylene: historian, date uncertain). *On Inventions* 630b, 637b.
Semus (Delos: historian, third century). *Delian History* 618a, 637b, *On Paeans* 618d, 622a.
Socrates (Athens: philosopher, fifth century). His poems 628f.
Sopater (Paphos: comic dramatist, fourth to third century). *The Gates* 175c, *Mystacus' Servant* 175c, 183b, *Bacchis* 176a.
Sophocles (Athens: tragedian, fifth century). *Thamyras* 175f, 637a, *Niobe* 176f, *Tympanistai* 176f, *Mysians* 183e, 635c.
Sosibius (historian, third century). *Chronology* 635f.
Stesichorus (Himera: lyric poet, seventh to sixth century). N.t. 619d.
Teleclides (comic dramatist, fifth century). *Amphictyons* 619a.
Telesilla (Argos: lyric poetess, sixth to fifth century). N.t. 619b.
Telestes (Selinus: dithyrambist and lyric poet, fifth to fourth century). *Argo* 616f, *Asclepius* 617b, *Hymenaeus* 637a, n.t. 626a.
Theophilus (comic dramatist, fourth century). *Kitharodos* 623f, *Neoptolemus* 635a.
Theophrastus (Eresus: philosopher and scholar, fourth to third century). *On Inspiration* 624a.
Theopompus (comic dramatist, fifth century). *Penelope* 183f.
Theopompus (Chios: historian, third century). *Histories* 627e.
Theopompus (Colophon: epic poet, probably third century). *Harmation* 183a.
Timomachus (probably fourth century). *History of Cyprus* 638a.
Tryphon (grammarian: first century B.C. to first century A.D.). *Terminology* 174e, (182d), 182e, 618c, 634d.
Xenophon (Athens: historian and essayist, fifth to fourth century). N.t. (ascription doubtful) 174f.

Bibliography of works by modern authors

This is far from being a complete bibliography. It ventures hardly at all into the more technical areas covered in Vol. 2. It includes all the books and articles mentioned in the notes, and a selection of others which I have found particularly helpful: I have restricted the latter to works written in English. For fuller bibliographies see three of the works cited below: Anderson's *Ethos and Education*, Lippman's *Musical Thought in Ancient Greece*, and Winnington-Ingram's 'Ancient Greek Music 1932–1957'. *The New Grove* ed. Sadie, in addition to its own well-researched summaries of information, offers useful bibliographies under each of the relevant headings (see especially the heading 'Greece, Ancient'). I have not duplicated here the titles mentioned in the list of texts and abbreviations given above.

Adam, J. ed. *The Republic of Plato*, 2 vols., Cambridge 1929.
Anderson, W. D. 'The Importance of Damonian Theory in Plato's Thought', *Transactions of the American Philological Association* 86 (1955), 88.
   Ethos and Education in Greek Music, Cambridge, Mass. 1966.
Apel, W. 'The Early History of the Organ', *Speculum* 23 (1948), 191.
Baldry, H. C. *The Greek Tragic Theatre*, London 1971.
Barclay, W. *Educational Ideals in the Ancient World*, London 1959.
Barker, A. D. 'Aristides Quintilianus and Constructions in Early Music Theory', *Classical Quarterly* 32 (1982), 184.
   'The Innovations of Lysander the Kitharist', *Classical Quarterly* 32 (1982), 266.
Beazley, J. D. *The Berlin Painter*, Berlin 1930, revised ed. Mainz 1974.
Beck, F. A. G. *Greek Education 450–350 B.C.*, London 1964.
Besseler, H. and Schneider, M., eds. *Musikgeschichte in Bildern*, Vol. 11.4, *Griechenland* ed. M. Wegner, Leipzig 1963.
Boardman, J. *Athenian Black Figure Vases*, London 1974.
   Athenian Red Figure Vases, the Archaic Period, London 1975.
Bowra, C. M. 'Xenophanes on Songs at Feasts', in *Problems in Greek Poetry*, Oxford 1953.
   'A Love Duet', *American Journal of Philology* 79 (1958), 376.
   Greek Lyric Poetry from Alcman to Simonides, 2nd ed., Oxford 1961.
   'Arion and the Dolphin', *Museum Helveticum* 20 (1963), 121. (This and 'A Love Duet' are included in his *On Greek Margins*, Oxford 1970.)
Burn, A. R. *The Lyric Age of Greece*, London 1960.
Campbell, D. A. 'Flutes and Elegiac Couplets', *Journal of Hellenic Studies* 84 (1964), 63.
Charbonneaux, J., Martin, R. and Villard, F. *Classical Greek Art 480–330 B.C.*, London 1972.
Clements, E. 'The Interpretation of Greek Music', *Journal of Hellenic Studies* 42 (1922), 133.
Dale, A. M. *The Lyric Metres of Greek Drama*, Cambridge 1948.
Dodds, E. R. *The Greeks and the Irrational*, Berkeley 1956.

Dover, K. J. *Aristophanic Comedy*, London 1972.
Düring, I. *Ptolemaios und Porphyrios über die Musik*, Göteborg 1934.
'Studies in Musical Terminology in Fifth-Century Literature', *Eranos* 43 (1945) 176.
'Greek Music: its Fundamental Features and its Significance', *Journal of World History* 3 (1956), 302.
Else, G. F. '"Imitation" in the Fifth Century', *Classical Philology* 53 (1958), 73.
Finley, J. H., Jr. *Pindar and Aeschylus*, Cambridge, Mass. 1955.
Finley, M. I. *The World of Odysseus*, 2nd ed., London 1977.
Galpin, F. W. *A Textbook of European Musical Instruments*, London 1937.
Georgiades, T. *Greek Music, Verse and Dance*, New York 1956.
Gombosi, O. 'Key, Mode, Species', *Journal of the American Musicological Society* 4 (1951), 20.
Gow, A. S. F. *Theocritus*, 2 vols., Cambridge 1952.
Harap, L. 'Some Hellenic Ideas on Music and Character', *Musical Quarterly* 24 (1938), 153.
Harriott, R. *Poetry and Criticism before Plato*, London 1969.
Hammond, N. G. L. *A History of Greece to 322 B.C.*, 2nd ed., Oxford 1967.
Havelock, E. A. *Preface to Plato*, Cambridge, Mass. 1963.
Henderson, I. 'The Growth of the Greek *harmoniai*', *Classical Quarterly* 36 (1942), 94.
'The Growth of Ancient Greek Music', *Music Review* 4 (1943), 4.
'Ancient Greek Music', in *The New Oxford History of Music* ed. E. Wellesz, Vol 1, London 1957.
Higgins, R. A. and Winnington-Ingram, R. P. 'Lute-Players in Greek Art', *Journal of Hellenic Studies* 85 (1965), 62.
Howard, A. A. 'The *Aulos* or *Tibia*', *Harvard Studies in Classical Philology* 4 (1893), 1.
Landels, J. G. 'The Brauron Aulos', *Annual of the British School at Athens* 58 (1963), 116.
'Shipshape and Sambuca-Fashion', *Journal of Hellenic Studies* 86 (1966), 69.
Lawler, L. B. *The Dance in Ancient Greece*, London 1964.
The Dance of the Ancient Greek Theatre, Iowa 1964.
Lever, K. *The Art of Greek Comedy*, London 1956.
Lippman, E. A. *Musical Thought in Ancient Greece*, New York and London 1964.
MacGillivray, J. A. 'The Cylindrical Reed Pipe: its Classification and Scope', in *Music, Libraries and Instruments*, London 1961.
Macran, H. S. *The Harmonics of Aristoxenus*, Oxford 1902.
Michaelides, S. *The Music of Ancient Greece: an Encyclopaedia*, London 1978.
Monro, D. B. *The Modes of Ancient Greek Music*, Oxford 1894.
Morrow, G. R. *Plato's Cretan City*, Princeton 1960.
Mountford, J. F. 'The Musical Scales of Plato's *Republic*', *Classical Quarterly* 17 (1923), 125.
Norwood, G. *Pindar*, Berkeley and Los Angeles 1945.
Pickard-Cambridge, A. W. *Dithyramb, Tragedy and Comedy*, Oxford 1927, 2nd ed. revised by T. B. L. Webster, Oxford 1962.
The Dramatic Festivals of Athens, Oxford 1955.
Pöhlmann, E. *Denkmäler altgriechischer Musik*, Nuremburg 1970.
Raven, D. S. *Greek Metre*, London 1962.
Reese, G. *Music in the Middle Ages*, New York 1940.
Rimmer, J., *Ancient Musical Instruments of Western Asia in the British Museum*, London 1969.

Sachs, C. *The History of Musical Instruments*, New York 1940.
 The Rise of Music in the Ancient World, New York 1943.
Sadie, S., ed. *The New Grove*, London 1980.
Schlesinger, K. *The Greek Aulos*, London 1939.
Sedgwick, W. B. 'A Note on the Performance of Greek Vocal Music', *Classica et Mediaevalia* 11 (1950), 222.
Shirlaw, M. 'The Music and Tone-Systems of Ancient Greece', *Music and Letters* 32 (1951), 131.
Webster, T. B. L. *Greek Art and Literature, 700–530 B.C.*, London 1959.
 The Tragedies of Euripides, London 1967.
 An Introduction to Sophocles, 2nd ed., London 1969.
 Greek Theatre Production, 2nd ed., London 1970.
 The Greek Chorus, London 1970.
Wilkinson, L. P. 'Philodemus on Ethos in Music', *Classical Quarterly* 32 (1938), 174.
Winnington-Ingram, R. P. 'The Spondeion Scale', *Classical Quarterly* 22 (1928), 83.
 Mode in Ancient Greek Music, Cambridge 1936.
 Euripides and Dionysus, Cambridge 1936.
 'The Pentatonic Tuning of the Greek Lyre: a Theory Examined', *Classical Quarterly* 6 (1956), 169.
 'Ancient Greek Music 1932–1957', *Lustrum* 3 (1958), 6–57, 259–60.

Index

The index includes entries for the names of instruments, musical genres, and the like, the technical terms transliterated from the Greek, a selection of topics of musical interest, and proper names: but to avoid inordinate length I have not given references to authors where they are merely cited in the notes as sources of information, unless the identity of the source is of special importance. As an aid to the use of the index, I have added to many of the entries a brief indication of the profession or role of the person referred to (historian, aulete, etc.), or the general sense of the term given in the heading.

skolion (drinking song): by Alcaeus, 104 n. 18; Athenaeus' collection of, 50, 103 n. 16, 104 n. 17; capping lines in, 43 n. 19, 103–4; forms and practices of, 103 n. 16; in Ionian *harmonia*, 283; by Simonides, 104 n. 18; as source for Euripides' music, 115; by Stesichorus, 103 n. 16; by Terpander, 233–4; by Theognis, 50

'Snow' (nickname of Theognis the tragedian), 111 n. 51

social consequences of musical change, 140, 145, 156–7, 158, 169, 247, *cf.* 284–6

Socrates: in Aristophanes, 99–101; in Plato, 124–40, 181; poems of, 288; in Xenophon, 117–23

Sopater (comic poet), 263, 265, 269

sophists, 99–101, 168

Sophocles (tragedian): quoted, 64, 72–3, 78, 82, 85, 89, 91 references elsewhere: Aristophanes on, 116; character of his music, 62, 63 n. 7; death of, 111; on *elymos aulos*, 267; on *lyra* and *magadis*, 298; on *pēktis* and *trigōnos*, 270, 295

Sosibius (historian), 296

Sotades (writer of mime), 279

Soterichus (musicologist, speaker in ps.-Plutarch), 206, 219–48

soul: affinities with music, 127–63 passim, 176, 248; constitution of, 124, 136 n. 43, 176, 228–9, 281 n. 98; effects of music and gymnastics on, 136–9, 232; general relation of music to, 127, 134–6, 137–8, 159, 162, 169, 287; *see also* character

sound, definition of, 206

Sparta: *apothetai* at, 252; *aulos* at, 178, 232, 271, 284, 285; Carneia at, 83, 211; conservatism of, 96, 148, 239, 244 n. 238, 281, 298; dances at, 290–1; Gymnopaideia at, 214; martial music of, 232, 272 n. 54, 284, 285, 290; music and civic order at, 47, 247; music judged but not practised at, 173, 286; music and plague at, 247; music saved from ruin at, 286; musical institutions established at, 214, 286 n. 134; musical understanding commended, 239; Terpander at, 47, 208 n. 18, 214, 247, 286 n. 134; Thaletas at, 47, 214, 247; Timotheus at, 96, 286 n. 134, 298;

Tyrtaeus at, 151 n. 71, 290

speaker-hole, see *aulos*, construction of (*syrinx* of)

Sphinx, 72

spondeiakos, see spondeiazōn tropos

spondeiasmos (abnormal interval), 166, 216–17, 235 n. 188, 255–6

spondeiazōn tropos (in early *aulos*-music), 223–4, 255–7

spondeion (libation music): of Dion of Chios, 300; of Olympus, 216–17, 218 n. 96, 223 n. 124, 253, 255–7; in Plato, 222; in *Pythikos nomos*, 51

Stesander (*kitharōdos*), 300

Stesichorus (poet): Calyce song of, 277; choral works of, 48; and *Harmatios nomos*, 213, 253; hexameter pieces of, 208, *cf.* 213; on Phrygian music, 48 n. 4; rhythms of, 213, 218, *cf.* 208; *skolia* of, 103 n. 16

Strabo (geographer): quoted, 51–2; on paeans, 41 n. 14; on Terpander, 43 n. 18, 49

stringed and wind instruments compared, 201–2, 261, 264 n. 20

strings of instruments: experts on, 185; materials and means of attachment, 4, 14, 30, 43; multiplicity of, *see polychordia*; number, on *lyra, kithara*, etc., 4, 43, 49, 78, 79, 83, 94, 96–7, 98, 208 n. 18, 218, 221 n. 109, 236–7, 244, 252, 286 n. 134, 298, on *magadis*, 293, 295, 298, on *sambykē*, 292, on *skindapsos*, 269; ratios of lengths, 196, *see also* ratio; tuning, 49, 139, 196, 199, *see also harmonia*, tuning

strobilos (invention of Phrynis), 237 n. 201

strophic response, 44 n. 20, 56 n. 7, 59 n. 19, 93, 193, 202 n. 91

swan, 63 n. 9, 78

symphōnia ('concord'), *symphōnein*, 43 n. 18, 72 n. 64, 130 n. 17, 147, 188 n. 11, *see also* concord

symposium (dinner-party, drinking-party): *aulos* at, 15, 51, 69, 82, 103, 118, 120, 121, 122, 262–3; music in general at, 69, 82, 83 n. 139, 118–23, 248–9; songs at, 43 n. 19, 47, 86 n. 121, 103–4, 120, 121, *see also skolion*; stringed instruments at, 45, 69, 83, 118, 120, 263 n. 16, 293 n. 166; *see also* feast